Modern Social Theory

An Introduction

Edited by

Austin Harrington

OXFORD

UNIVERSITY PRESS

OXFORD

UNIVERSITY PRESS

Great Clarendon Street, Oxford OX2 6DP

Oxford University Press is a department of the University of Oxford.
It furthers the University's objective of excellence in research, scholarship,
and education by publishing worldwide in

Oxford New York

Auckland Cape Town Dar es Salaam Hong Kong Karachi
Kuala Lumpur Madrid Melbourne Mexico City Nairobi
New Delhi Shanghai Taipei Toronto

With offices in

Argentina Austria Brazil Chile Czech Republic France Greece
Guatemala Hungary Italy Japan Poland Portugal Singapore
South Korea Switzerland Thailand Turkey Ukraine Vietnam

Oxford is a registered trade mark of Oxford University Press
in the UK and in certain other countries

Published in the United States
by Oxford University Press Inc., New York

British Library Cataloguing in Publication Data
Data available

Library of Congress Cataloging in Publication Data
Data available
ISBN 978-0-19-925570-2

10 9 8 7 6 5

Typeset by Newgen Imaging Systems (P) Ltd, Chennai, India
Printed on acid-free paper by
CPI Antony Rowe, Chippenham, Wiltshire

Modern Social Theory

■ ACKNOWLEDGEMENTS

This book is the product of fourteen chapter contributions by prominent international scholars and teachers of social theory, edited by Austin Harrington. The contributing authors are Austin Harrington (Introduction, Chapter 1, Conclusion), Antonino Palumbo and Alan Scott (Chapter 2), Gianfranco Poggi (Chapter 3), John Holmwood (Chapter 4), William Outhwaite (Chapter 5), Dennis Smith (Chapter 6), Douglas Kellner (Chapter 7), Anthony Elliott (Chapter 8), Samantha Ashenden (Chapter 9), Anthony King (Chapter 10), Lisa Adkins (Chapter 11), Barry Smart (Chapter 12), Gerard Delanty (Chapter 13), and Robert Holton (Chapter 14). With the agreement of the contributors, each chapter has been extensively adapted by Austin Harrington for the purposes of creating a unified textbook entity, consistent in structure, style, and form.

As coordinator of the project, I would like to thank the contributors for their assistance in some of the additional editorial features that went into the making of this book, including the Glossary and the short factual biographies of theorists. I also thank three anonymous reviewers for comments in the initial stages of the project, and especially John Scott of the University of Essex for valuable guidance in the final stages. I am grateful to my two commissioning editors at OUP, Patrick Brindle and Angela Adams, for their support and encouragement. Lastly I particularly thank Mark Davis, a doctoral candidate at the University of Leeds, for vital final assistance in the preparation of the bibliography, the guidance on website links, and the referencing system.

A. H.

OUTLINE CONTENTS

■ DETAILED CONTENTS

■ LIST OF BOXES

■ NOTES ON CONTRIBUTORS

Lisa Adkins is Reader in Sociology at the University of Manchester, UK. She is the author of *Gendered Work: Sexuality, Family and the Labour Market* (Open University Press, 1995) and *Revisions: Gender and Sexuality in Late Modernity* (Open University Press, 2002). She is co-editor of *Sex in Question: French Materialist Feminism* (Routledge, 1996), *Sex, Sensibility and the Gendered Body* (Macmillan, 1996), and *Sexualizing the Social: Power and the Organization of Sexuality* (Macmillan, 1996). She has published articles on gender, sexuality, and feminist social theory.

Samantha Ashenden is Senior Lecturer in Sociology at Birkbeck College, University of London, UK. She is the author of *Governing Child Sexual Abuse: Negotiating the Boundaries of Public and Private, Law and Science* (Routledge, 2004) and co-editor of *Foucault contra Habermas: Recasting the Dialogue between Genealogy and Critical Theory* (Sage, 1999). She has published articles on feminist theory, child sexual abuse, and the work of Jürgen Habermas.

Gerard Delanty is Professor of Sociology at the University of Liverpool, UK. His books include *Inventing Europe* (Macmillan, 1995), *Social Science beyond Constructivism and Realism* (Open University Press, 1997), *Social Theory in a Changing World* (Polity Press, 1998), *Modernity and Postmodernity* (Sage, 2000), *Citizenship in a Global Age* (Open University Press, 2000), *Challenging Knowledge: The University in the Knowledge Society* (Open University Press, 2001), *Community* (Routledge, 2003), and *Nationalism and Social Theory* (Sage, 2002) (with Patrick O'Mahony). He is the editor of the *European Journal of Social Theory* and co-editor of *The Sage Handbook of Historical Sociology* (Sage, 2003).

Anthony Elliott is Professor of Sociology at the University of Kent at Canterbury, UK. His books include *Social Theory and Psychoanalysis in Transition* (Blackwell, 1992), *Psychoanalytic Theory: An Introduction* (Blackwell, 1994), *The Mourning of John Lennon* (University of California Press, 1999), *Concepts of the Self* (Polity Press, 2001), *Critical Visions: New Directions in Social Theory* (Rowman & Littlefield, 2003), *Subject to Ourselves* (Polity Press, 1996), and *Social Theory since Freud* (Routledge, 2004). He is editor of *The Blackwell Reader in Contemporary Social Theory* (Blackwell, 1999).

Austin Harrington is Lecturer in Sociology at the University of Leeds, UK. He is the author of *Hermeneutic Dialogue and Social Science: A Critique of Gadamer and Habermas* (Routledge, 2001), *Art and Social Theory: Sociological Arguments in Aesthetics* (Polity Press, 2004), and *Concepts of Europe in Classical Sociology* (Routledge, 2006) (forthcoming). He is co-editor and translator of *The Protestant Ethic Debate: Max Weber's Replies to his Critics, 1907–1910* (Liverpool University Press, 2001) and co-editor of the *Routledge Encyclopedia of Social Theory* (Routledge, 2005) (forthcoming). He has published articles on hermeneutics, aesthetics, and German social thought.

John Holmwood is Professor of Sociology at the University of Sussex, UK. He is the author of *Founding Sociology? Talcott Parsons and the Idea of General Theory* (Longman, 1996) and co-author of *Explanation and Social Theory* (Macmillan, 1991) (with Alexander Stewart). He is editor of *Social Stratification* (Edward Elgar, 1996) (three volumes) and co-editor of *Constructing the New Consumer Society* (Macmillan, 1997). He has published articles on functionalism and evolutionary theory, theories of the welfare state, feminist epistemology, and gender and critical realism.

Robert Holton is Professor of Sociology at Trinity College Dublin, Ireland. He is the author of *The Transition from Feudalism to Capitalism* (Macmillan, 1985), *Cities, Capitalism and Civilisation* (Allen & Unwin, 1986), *Economy and Society* (Routledge, 1992), *Talcott Parsons on Economy and Society* (Routledge, 1986), and *Globalization and the Nation-State* (Macmillan, 1998), and co-author of *Max Weber on Economy and Society* (Routledge, 1989) (with Bryan Turner). He has published articles on migration, class, global networks, historical sociology, and rational choice theory. His research on globalization is funded by the Irish Research Council for the Humanities and Social Sciences.

Douglas Kellner is George F. Kneller Professor for the Philosophy of Education at the University of California, Los Angeles, USA. His books include *Herbert Marcuse and the Crisis of Marxism* (University of California Press, 1984), *Critical Theory, Marxism, and Modernity* (Johns Hopkins University Press, 1989), *Jean Baudrillard* (Stanford University Press, 1989), *Television and the Crisis of Democracy* (Westview Press, 1990), *The Persian Gulf TV War* (Westview Press, 1992), *Media Culture* (Routledge, 1995), *Grand Theft 2000: Media Spectacle and the Theft of an Election* (Rowman & Littlefield, 2001), *From 9/11 to Terror War: The Dangers of the Bush Legacy* (Rowman & Littlefield, 2003), *Media Spectacle* (Routledge, 2003), and co-author of *Postmodern Theory* (Macmillan, 1991) (with Steven Best).

Anthony King is Reader in Sociology at the University of Exeter, UK. He is the author of *The End of the Terraces: The Transformation of English Football in the 1990s* (Leicester University Press, 1998), *The European Ritual: Football in the New Europe* (Ashgate, 2003), and *The Structure of Social Theory* (Routledge, 2004). He has published articles on the work of Talcott Parsons, Pierre Bourdieu, and Anthony Giddens.

William Outhwaite is Professor of Sociology at the University of Sussex, UK. He is the author of *Understanding Social Life: The Method Called Verstehen* (Allen & Unwin, 1975), *Concept Formation in Social Science* (Routledge, 1983), *New Philosophies of Social Science: Realism, Hermeneutics and Critical Theory* (Macmillan, 1987), *Habermas* (Polity Press, 1994), and co-author of *Social Theory, Communism and Beyond* (Blackwell, 2005) (with Larry Ray). He is editor of *The Habermas Reader* (Polity Press, 1996) and co-editor of *The Blackwell Dictionary of Twentieth-Century Social Thought* (Blackwell, 1993).

Antonino Palumbo is Lecturer in Political Philosophy at the University of Palermo, Italy. He is the author of *Etica e governance* (Ila Palma-Athena, 2003). His publications also include 'Weber, Durkheim and the Sociology of the Modern State', in R. Bellamy and T. Ball (eds.), *The Cambridge History of Twentieth Century Political Thought* (Cambridge University Press, 2003) and 'Administration, Civil Service and Bureaucracy', in K. Nash and A. Scott (eds.), *The Blackwell Companion to Political Sociology* (Blackwell, 2001).

Gianfranco Poggi is Professor of Sociology at the University of Trento, Italy. He is the author of *Images of Society: Essays on the Sociological Theories of Tocqueville, Marx and Durkheim* (Stanford University Press, 1972), *Calvinism and the Capitalist Spirit: Max Weber's Protestant Ethic* (University of Massachusetts Press, 1983), *The State: Its Nature, Development and Prospects* (Polity Press, 1990), *Money and the Modern Mind: George Simmel's Philosophy of Money* (University of California Press, 1993), *Durkheim* (Oxford University Press, 2000), and *Forms of Power* (Polity Press, 2001).

Alan Scott is Professor of Sociology at the University of Innsbruck, Austria. He is the author of *Ideology and New Social Movements* (Unwin Hyman, 1990) and co-author of *The Uncertain Science: Criticism of Sociological Formalism* (Routledge, 1992). He is editor of *The Limits of Globalization* (Routledge, 1997), co-editor of *The Blackwell Companion to Political Sociology* (Blackwell, 2001), and co-editor and translator of *Georg Simmel on Rembrandt: An Essay in the Philosophy of Art* (Routledge, 2005). He has published articles on protest, labour contracts, trust, and the works of Max Weber, Émile Durkheim, and Karl Polanyi.

Barry Smart is Professor of Sociology at the University of Portsmouth, UK. His books include *Michel Foucault* (Tavistock, 1985), *Modern Conditions: Postmodern Controversies* (Routledge, 1992), *Postmodernity* (Routledge, 1993), *Facing Modernity* (Sage, 1999), *Economy, Culture and Society: A Sociological Critique of Neo-liberalism* (Open University Press, 2003), and *The Sports Star: A Cultural and Economic Analysis of Sporting Celebrity* (Sage, 2005). He is co-editor of the *Handbook of Social Theory* (Sage, 2001) and *Resisting McDonaldization* (Sage, 1999).

Dennis Smith is Professor of Sociology at the University of Loughborough, UK. He is the author of *Conflict and Compromise: Class Formation in English Society 1830–1914* (Routledge, 1982), *Barrington Moore* (Macmillan, 1983), *The Chicago School: A Liberal Critique of Capitalism* (Macmillan, 1988), *Capitalist Democracy on Trial: The Transatlantic Debate from Tocqueville to the Present* (Routledge, 1990), *The Rise of Historical Sociology* (Polity Press, 1991), *Zygmunt Bauman: Prophet of Postmodernity* (Polity Press, 1999), and *Norbert Elias and Modern Social Theory* (Sage, 2001). He is the editor of the journal *Current Sociology*.

■ A NOTE TO THE READER: THE SCOPE OF THIS BOOK

This book provides a comprehensive introduction to leading topics, theorists, and debates in modern social theory. It is suitable for undergraduate foundational courses in sociology and cultural studies and related disciplines of the social sciences and humanities, as well as for the general reader. The book is not primarily an introduction to social research methods or to empirical sociology. It has been designed as a guide to problems and traditions of analysis in modern social thought. It is appropriate for introductory courses in the principles of sociological enquiry, or for what is often called the 'sociological imagination'.

Topics and theorists have been chosen for their relevance to the most frequently discussed themes in contemporary social and cultural studies. While it is true that many of the most influential figures in modern social theory have been male European or North American authors, a particular consideration of the book has been to incorporate the many important challenges to mainstream social science that have arisen in recent decades from the sides of feminist, postcolonial, and multicultural criticism. Social theory is by definition a pluralistic discipline which must reflect the diversity of cultural, political, and methodological standpoints characterizing debate about society today.

The book begins with a short Introduction to the most important questions of methodology in social theory. Chapter 1 introduces the theme of modernity in social theory, together with eighteenth- and nineteenth-century currents of social thought. Chapters 2 and 3 expound the classical sociological legacies of Karl Marx, Émile Durkheim, Max Weber, and Georg Simmel. Chapters 4 to 14 trace the development of concepts, problems, debates, and research programmes in sociology and social theory from the early twentieth century to the present day. Separate chapters cover functionalism and its critics (Chapter 4), interpretive and interactionist theory (Chapter 5), historical social theory (Chapter 6), Western Marxism (Chapter 7), psychoanalytic social theory (Chapter 8), French structuralist and post-structuralist theory (Chapter 9), theories of structure and agency (Chapter 10), feminist social theory (Chapter 11), postmodernism and its critics (Chapters 12 and 13), and theories of globalization (Chapter 14). Much of the emphasis of the book falls on later twentieth- and twenty-first-century social theory as the more classical period of 1890–1920 is amply covered in numerous currently available guides. The book does, however, also include three key chapters on the foundational ideas of Marx, Durkheim, Weber, and Simmel and their eighteenth- and nineteenth-century intellectual forebears.

The reader should note that the book is dedicated to theoretical thinking about social life in its broadest sense. It is not only concerned with technical concepts and vocabularies in the discipline of sociology. Social theory is closely related to the discipline of sociology and is usually studied as a subsection of this discipline. Indeed social theory is often also thought of as synonymous with the term 'sociological theory'. However, a slight difference of nuance should be noted between these two terms. 'Sociological theory' generally refers to theories propounded solely within sociology as an established discipline. 'Social theory', in contrast, generally refers not only to theories propounded within sociology but also to more general contexts of social thought to be found in other disciplines. Social theory is thus a wider term of reference. It encompasses contexts of thought about society to be found in subjects such as history, politics, economics, anthropology, philosophy, and cultural and literary criticism, as well as in sociology in the strict disciplinary sense. It is this broader understanding of the scope of social thought that the present textbook is designed to convey.

Only two areas have received relatively marginal treatment in this book. The first is what is called the 'philosophy of social science'. The philosophy of social science encompasses debates about the status of knowledge in the social sciences compared with knowledge in the natural sciences. Substantive social theory, on the other hand, refers more broadly and concretely to theories of social trends and historical legacies in contemporary society. It overlaps significantly with the philosophy of social science but is not the same as the latter. Thus this book is mostly concerned with substantive theoretical topics in social science, rather than with more purely philosophical issues.

The second area of omission is political theory. This book is an introduction specifically to social theory, rather than to political theory. The relevant difference between 'social' and 'political' in this context can be understood roughly as the difference between theories of social behaviour on the one hand and theories of appropriate forms of government on the other. This distinction is by no means hard and fast. Social and political theory overlap with and depend on one another in important ways; but political theory is more directly concerned with what are often referred to as 'normative' questions about the meaning of ideas of justice, liberty, equality, and democracy. These more specifically political debates have important applications in sociology and social policy, but they are not conventionally the primary topics of the subject areas termed 'social theory' or 'sociological theory'.

Each chapter of this book has been written by specialists in the field. Each chapter ends with questions for discussion, guidance on further reading, and relevant website addresses. Some sections of the discussions have been arranged in boxed case study form for added focus on particular issues.

At the end of the book can be found a Glossary of the more unfamiliar technical terms used by authors of the chapters. This Glossary is by no means exhaustive, but it aims to provide a few points of clarification for occasional words and phrases. All terms in the Glossary are marked with an asterisk (*) on their first relevant appearance in each chapter of the book. The Glossary is followed by a comprehensive list of short factual biographies of the major theorists and historical personalities discussed in this book, containing brief reference information. Names of listed theorists and personalities are also marked with an asterisk on their first relevant appearance in each chapter.

Lastly the reader should note that all sources cited in this book are referenced according to their first historical dates of publication in the original languages in which they were written. The purpose of this is to reinforce a sense of the historical chronology of developments in modern social thought since the nineteenth century. However, the reader should note that all references to page numbers of cited texts are to the recent translated and/or reprinted editions in English. Full details of the translated and/or reprinted editions appear in the bibliography at the end of the book. For example, 'Marx and Engels 1848: 50' refers to page 50 of the 1967 Penguin English edition of *The Communist Manifesto*, first published in German in 1848.

Introduction. What is Social Theory?

Austin Harrington

Social theory can be defined as the study of scientific ways of thinking about social life. It encompasses ideas about how societies change and develop, about methods of explaining social behaviour, about power and social structure, class, gender and ethnicity, modernity and 'civilization', revolutions and utopias, and numerous other concepts and problems in social life. This Introduction addresses some of the leading questions that arise when we start to think about the very idea of a 'science of society'. We begin by discussing the meaning of the word 'theory' and its various implications for 'method' and 'methodology' in social research. We also consider questions about the relationship of social theory to 'common sense', about the role of 'facts', 'values', and 'objectivity' in social research, and about the relation of sociology to other disciplines of the social sciences and the humanities such as political theory, psychology, anthropology, history, and philosophy.

The meaning of 'theory'

As a term of art, 'social theory' is a distinctly recent invention. No such term exists in English or in any other language before the twentieth century, and even in the twentieth century it is not common before about the 1940s. Auguste *Comte coined the term *sociologie* in France in the 1840s, but 'sociology' too did not gain widespread currency as a term until after 1900. However, the two separate words 'social' and 'theory' are very ancient in origin. An initial look at their etymologies will give us some clues to their meaning as a conjoined pair.

Our words 'social' and 'society' derive from the Latin words *socius* and *societas*. For the Romans, a *socius* was a member of a trading partnership. A *socius* was a merchant cooperating with other merchants as a partner, fellow, or 'associate'. A partnership or 'association' between merchants was a *societas*, which is the origin of our modern English word 'company' or 'business firm', as well as our keyword *society*. The commercial meaning of *societas* is directly preserved in other modern European languages such as in the French and Italian *société* and *società* and the German *Gesellschaft*. In this sense we can say that sociology and social theory are concerned with relations of 'sociation' between 'members' or 'partners', including not only business partners but a great many other kinds and processes of 'sociation' and 'socialization' between individuals.

Our modern word 'theory' derives from the ancient Greek word *theōria*. *Theōria* for the Greeks meant 'contemplation'. In the writings of the philosopher Aristotle, *theōria* referred to contemplation of the cosmos. It contrasted with *praxis*, from which our word 'practice' derives. *Praxis* for the Greeks referred to human beings' way of acting and conducting their lives on this earth, in the immediate everyday world. Clearly, this ancient Greek understanding of *theōria* differs from most common uses of the word 'theory' today. The Greek word *theōria* had a different set of connotations from most modern linkages of theory with 'scientific construction'. Today we tend to think of 'a theory' as being a 'scientific construct' or a 'scientific model'. In contrast, *theōria* for the Greeks did not itself mean science. Rather, it meant *reflection* on science: reflection on the value of science, as one mode of contemplating the cosmos among others—alongside art, myth, religion, and the most general discipline of thinking that the Greeks called 'philosophy', or 'love of wisdom'.

The ancient Greek meaning of *theōria* might not seem particularly relevant to us in the present day. It might seem to reinforce the rather widespread view that theory lacks relevance to daily life. Yet this would be to fail to appreciate the significance of the idea. *Theōria* for the Greeks was an indispensable aid to making sense of their lives in the ordinary world of society, in the world of the 'city' or what they called the *polis*, from which our word 'politics' derives. They believed that people who did not pause to engage in contemplation and reflection had no points of orientation for conducting their lives in practice, in the political world of actions and interactions with other people. Thus *theōria* for the Greeks remained indispensable to everyone who sought wisdom, happiness, and the good life in the realm of *praxis*.

It can be said that a recurrent tendency of modern times has been for theory to be equated with scientific knowledge per se and to lose its original additional connotation of critical reflective questioning about the *value* and *meaning* of science—in the context of politics, in the context of other modes of understanding, and in the context of the finitude and mortality of human life. The neglect of *theōria* in modern times was a particularly important concern for the Jewish-German philosopher Edmund *Husserl, founder of the movement of philosophical thought known as *phenomenology*. Writing in the 1930s, Husserl argued that unless the sciences recollected their sources of origination and meaning for everyday life, in the *'lifeworld' as he called it, they would be doomed to extinction (Husserl 1936). Either the sciences would become wholly absorbed into the production of technologies of mastery over nature or they would dissolve in a wave of revolt against all rational thinking *tout court*. Unfortunately, the rise of fascism and militarism in Europe in the 1930s and 1940s confirmed Husserl's fears, and the only remaining role for science in European society in this period remained as an instrument in the production of machines of war and persecution.

In a similar spirit, the Jewish-German émigré philosopher Hannah *Arendt argued that theory in the modern age comes to be increasingly subordinated to the search for technological control over physical and social life (Arendt 1958). Writing in the 1950s, Arendt suggested that where the original *vita contemplativa* or 'contemplative life' of the ancient Greeks had been intimately bound up with what the Greeks saw as the *vita activa* or 'active life' of public political participation, the 'active life' of the modern age no longer has the sense of practice and deliberation informed by contemplative reflection. Instead, modern consciousness of the world becomes increasingly oriented to control and productivity, where science serves the development of technology and where theory and philosophy serve at most as 'handmaidens' to science. In contrast, Arendt wanted to see a world in which theory and philosophy not only assist science but also remind science of its moral and political responsibilities, in the face of the fragility of the earth's resources and the mortality of human life.

Science and social science

This ancient context of *theōria* suggests clues for ways of thinking about the relationship of social theory to science today. If social theory is the study of ways of thinking about society scientifically, we can also say that it is a way of thinking about how far it is *possible* to study society scientifically. We can say that social theory is a practice of thinking about what science and 'being scientific' mean with respect to the social world.

The word 'science' in English has close connections with the natural sciences and is often used synonymously with them. However, the natural sciences are not the only disciplines of human enquiry with a claim to the title of science. In a general sense, to think scientifically is to apply a method or methods to the study of something and to follow these methods consistently and transparently. Usually it involves an effort to distinguish systematically between things that exist independently of the person observing them—what we call 'data' or 'evidence'—and ideas that are supplied by the person observing them as a way of ordering what he or she observes. Defined in this general sense, it is clear that physics, chemistry, or biology are not the only subjects of enquiry with a claim to the title of being sciences. Other subjects of study, such as history, archaeology, or art criticism, can also be sciences. In

French, the subjects known in English as the 'humanities' are called *les sciences humaines*, while in German the humanities are known as the *Geisteswissenschaften*—'sciences of the mind', or 'sciences of the works of the human mind'.

The particular association between science and natural science in English reflects a series of developments in early modern European history in which a number of precedents were set by the emergence of physics and astronomy in the seventeenth century and the emergence of chemistry and biology in the eighteenth and nineteenth centuries. From around the late eighteenth century, a variety of attempts were made to emulate the achievements of these natural sciences with the establishment of disciplines devoted to the study of human social and historical affairs. These included economics, philology and linguistics, history and art history, and notably 'sociology'. For a long time, it was believed that the new disciplines were only sciences if they copied or imitated the methods of the natural sciences. According to Auguste *Comte, who is the originator both of our word 'sociology' and of the concept of *'positive science' or *positivism, only one fundamental principle of science existed, and all particular sciences had to be unified under this principle. This principle was set by the science of physics, which Comte believed to proceed by pure observation, undistorted by any prior conceptions of the observer.

Virtually all social theorists and philosophers reject this nineteenth-century positivist conception of science today. Almost all commentators accept today that human affairs cannot be studied by imitation of the natural sciences, and they also reject Comte's rather simplistic characterization of the natural sciences themselves. Sociology is not a science in the sense in which physics is a science. The 'human sciences'—the humanities and the social sciences—study meanings, values, intentions, beliefs, and ideas realized in human social behaviour and in socially created institutions, events, and symbolic objects such as texts and images. These embodied meanings, values, intentions, beliefs, and ideas are products of contexts of intentional *agency by human actors in definite cultural and historical situations. Therefore they cannot be subsumed under general principles of regular cause and effect relations in the way that physical elements are treated by natural scientists, through repeatable experiments. Although natural scientists also, up to a point, deal with symbolic constructs that require *interpretive skills of various kinds, a scientific way of proceeding in biochemistry remains significantly different from a scientific way of proceeding in a subject such as literary criticism or religious studies.

This question of differences between the human sciences and the natural sciences raises a more general question about the role of what is called 'method' and 'methodology' in social research. It is to this that we now turn.

Method and methodology in social research

To be 'methodical' is to be systematic in the pursuit of something. To apply a 'method' or 'methods' is to use some particular technique or techniques in the pursuit or study of something. In social science we speak of 'qualitative methods', such as a programme of interviews, and of 'quantitative methods', such as the use of statistics. To have a 'methodology' is to follow a rationale that justifies one's selection of these particular methods for a given topic of study. Methodology thus refers to a theoretical principle or principles governing the application of a set of methods. The '-ology' in 'methodology' refers to a *theory* of methodical practice.

The central issue for any group of researchers who want to think about the methodology of their research project concerns the relationship between the pieces of evidence or data at their disposal and the theories governing the way in which they apply methods in order to produce and analyse this evidence or data. Here the word 'theory' is used in its more modern and familiar sense of 'scientific model' or 'scientific construction'. Two very general and basic questions we can ask in this connection are the following. What would research be like if it consisted *only of acts of data collection and no theories*? And conversely, what would research be like if it consisted *only of theories and no data collection*?

Let us look at the second question first. If research consisted *only of theories*, it would lack reference to the real world. Researchers would have no reason to go out into the field and interview people or analyse sources. If research consisted only of constructions in the imaginations of researchers, it would be empty of content; and it would be incapable of being validated or tested in any way. Any piece of speculation would have to be deemed as good as another.

But now let us look at the first question. If research consisted *only of data collection*, it would lack all order and sense. If research consisted only of heaps of information, it would be no more than a chaotic bundle of statements, impossible to decipher or evaluate or to apply to any meaningful purpose. It would be useless and pointless.

We can conclude from this that theory is impossible without *empirical observation, and equally that empirical observation is impossible without theory. To paraphrase a famous statement in the thought of the eighteenth-century *Enlightenment philosopher Immanuel *Kant, we can say that *theories without data are empty; data without theories are blind* (Kant originally wrote: 'Concepts without perceptions are empty; perceptions without concepts are blind') (Kant 1781: edition B, para. 76).

In reality, it never happens that a researcher's theoretical reflections entirely lack empirical content or that a researcher's empirical observations entirely lack theoretical construction. In every actual instance of research, a researcher's theoretical reflections are guided towards finding out some piece of evidence about an object of experience, and a researcher's observations of this object are always structured by his or her theoretical reflections. We can say that theories ought not to *dictate* or dogmatically *constrain* a researcher's field of observations; but we have to accept that theoretical thinking of *some kind* always underlies the researcher's observations.

Theoretical thinking supplies criteria for selections and discriminations of things that deserve investigation, and it is the only way in which researchers can produce ordered accounts and evaluations of their data. Thus theoretical thought is always presupposed in research; there are no observations that are not 'theory-laden'. There is no such thing as pure observation or pure reception of data. At a most basic level, theoretical thought refers simply to any ordinary person's mental ordering of his or her sense-impressions in everyday life.

One key implication of this connection between theoretical thought and ordinary everyday thought is that social theory relates in an important way to what is called 'common sense'.

Social theory and 'common sense'

Social theory is trained reflection on ways of knowing social life. But it is not only this, and it never begins purely as trained reflection. Social theory arises first and foremost from everyday life, from an enormous variety of contexts of conversation, discussion, and interaction between ordinary people. These are the same contexts that lead to the formation of such things as social movements, political parties, trade unions, and organized mass actions such as strikes and revolutions. Social theory emerges from these contexts and is only a more reflective expression of the disputes and agendas that dominate ordinary communication about social and political issues. It is itself a social product with a multitude of everyday contexts of origination.

The Italian Marxist writer Antonio *Gramsci once wrote that every ordinary person is, in principle, a theorist. Writing under imprisonment by the Italian fascist regime in the 1920s and 1930s, Gramsci wrote that 'everyone is a philosopher' (Gramsci 1926–37: 323). Gramsci meant that social theory is not something reserved for experts. Social theory is, and ought to be, the organic extension of social debates in which every ordinary person has a say and a capacity to contribute—and in the cases where it ceases to be the organic extension of such debates, it loses touch with its roots and is not worthy of its name. Gramsci's remark has its origins in the ideas of the nineteenth-century German philosopher G. W. F. *Hegel, who exercised a major influence on the early Karl *Marx. Hegel held that all philosophy develops progressively out of ordinary everyday consciousness, by a process of reflection on lived experience. A further source of inspiration for Gramsci was the eighteenth-century Italian historical philosopher Giambattista *Vico, who argued that all human beings have a capacity for understanding history because human beings *make* history. Vico held that where God made nature, man alone makes history, and that it is man's *making* of history which gives him his power to *understand* history. In this sense we can say that it is our action and participation in the social world that is the source of our ability to gain knowledge of history and social processes.

It can be said that the only important difference between social theory and common sense is that social theory seeks to systematize and clarify debate about goals and problems of social life through well-defined concepts and techniques of analysis. Building on common sense, social theory tries to draw distinctions between different ways of reacting to social life. It tries to distinguish emotional and moral ways of reacting from impartial reactions. It tries to discern reliable observations in contrast to prejudices and stereotypes, and it tries to untangle attitudes of detachment from attitudes of partisanship and vested interest.

In this sense, a thesis in social theory tries to do more than the typical lead article or editorial of a tabloid newspaper. In the tabloid article, information, emotions, moral judgements, and prescriptions for change are very frequently mixed up together. Similarly, a thesis in social theory tries to distinguish itself from a party-political manifesto or a state ideology or a nationalist myth or an interest-group platform. Although its motives of inception are frequently overtly political, social theory differs from political activism in an important sense. While many schools of social theory retain close links to political protest, the activity of theorizing and researching problems such as labour exploitation, environmental destruction, or sexism or racism remains a different activity from the activity of campaigning for policies to abolish them. The two kinds of activity depend on each other in very real and practical ways; but they remain distinct from each other. Social theory is not activism and cannot be turned into activism; it depends on practice and is guided by practice but is not the same as practice. This is at once its strength and its limitation.

To appreciate these ways in which social theory entails both an attitude of *involvement* in social life and an attitude of *detachment* from social life, we need to turn now to a range of issues bound up with the role of 'facts', 'values,' and 'objectivity' in social science.

'Facts', 'values', and 'objectivity'

On one level, all social science is a search for facts, for 'social facts'. The Latin root of our word 'fact' means 'something made' or 'something done', from *factum*, the participle of the verb *facere*, 'to make'. In addition, our modern sense of the word 'fact' refers to any state of affairs that is *real*, *definite*, and *incontrovertible*.

In these two senses of the word 'fact', it is a *fact* that six million Jews died in the Holocaust; and it is also a *fact* that ten thousand Palestinians died in the founding of the state of Israel in 1948. What is important in these two historical facts is less the exact numerical statistic than the fact that something real, definite, and incontrovertible happened and was made to happen by human agency. The Shoah and the Nakba (the evacuation of Palestine) are not legends, myths, or fantasies; they are facts. They did not happen of their own accord or by the agency of supernatural forces or spirits; they were done and made by real human actors acting in definite social-historical conditions which can be documented, observed, analysed, and interpreted.

However, the problem of facts for social science is that facts only ever appear to us laden with *values*. The Shoah and the Nakba are significant to us from the standpoint of moral and political values: they stand out to us precisely because they are an affront to human values. They concern us because they are events involving sufferings and crimes which ought not to have occurred. Here the difference between facts and values can be understood as the difference between the world as it *is*, or was, and the world as we *would like it to be*, or not to be. How the world *is* is one thing; how the world *ought* to be, or how it might be made better, is another. One way of responding to the world is 'descriptive'; the other way of responding is 'prescriptive'.

But the problem for social science in the real world is that facts cannot be *separated* from values. If we had no values, if we had no interest in value in the world, we would not be interested in any particular facts. We would not be struck by any particular facts as calling out for attention and demanding investigation. Although we are generally able to distinguish statements that claim to 'describe' how the world is from statements that 'prescribe' how the world ought to be, we cannot extract facts from values in any pure way. We cannot put all our values to one side in order to observe the world purely as a set of facts, undistorted by our frames of perception and feeling about what is right and wrong with the world. Social facts are meaningful to us only insofar they are value-laden, and we only come to be engaged with these facts insofar as we have values about how the world ought to be or ought not to be.

This explains why researching social facts almost always produces a diversity of points of view, which compete and often conflict with one another. Different social parties have different and often conflicting values about how the world should be, and different parties struggle with one another for the most authoritative account of the events and issues of the day. In the case at hand, numerous accounts exist of the causes of the Holocaust, and a broad spectrum of contested views reign about the causes and consequences of the founding of the state of Israel. Social science therefore has to consider a diversity of accounts, which very frequently turn out to be backed up by different sets of reasons worthy of consideration in their own right. In consequence, it is often very difficult, if not impossible, to speak of any one 'right answer' in the study of social affairs.

This raises a profound problem. If all research is possible only from value-laden points of view, how can research be 'objective'? How can there be agreement about the accuracy, validity, or insight of any particular piece of research?

There are ways of answering this question which need not lead us to think that value conflict is fatal for the possibility of validity in research. If facts cannot be separated from values, it does not follow that evidence about social life cannot be collected, analysed, and interpreted in transparent and methodical ways. The events of the Holocaust and the Nakba are both capable of being submitted to transparent techniques of scrutiny—for example: techniques of analysing documents and statistics, interviewing of witnesses, and the like—and although many different accounts of these events still remain, and are still bound to remain, it does not follow that no valid knowledge can be established about them. Furthermore, the impossibility of separating facts from values does not mean that researchers cannot realistically aim to work out procedures by which disagreements can be hammered out and rationally debated. If I am able to show you how I arrive at my position, giving reasons for each step and explaining to you how I believe these reasons to account for the matter under consideration, and if you are able to do the same, we at least have a minimal basis for discussion, which we can develop further through continued critical communication. Value conflict need not therefore entail that any statement by a party to a discussion has to be deemed as good as another, or that no agreement or no mutual critical discussion of any kind is possible. And it certainly does not follow that someone who denies that the Holocaust or the Nakba took place maintains as valid a position as someone who demonstrates that they did, by adducing evidence and methodically examining and explaining this evidence.

Objectivity therefore remains a realistic and rationally desirable goal for research. But it is important to emphasize that objectivity need not be seen as the only or ultimate *goal* or *motive* of research. Different schools of social theory take differing views about the purpose and relative importance of objectivity. Some schools view it as an end in itself, while others tend to view it as a means towards other, more practical ends—such as social justice and *emancipation, or liberation from oppression. In general, schools that emphatically subordinate objectivity to the pursuit of moral and political ends of social life are usually described as having a *normative* orientation of thought. The word 'normative' here refers to attitudes that give priority to the 'ought' above the 'is', to determining how the world should be made better, rather than solely to observing how it is. We will encounter many examples of such attitudes in the course of this book. But it should be stressed that numerous midway positions exist between the attitude of normative engagement on the one hand and the attitude of objective detachment on the other hand. All schools of social theory in fact advocate combinations of involvement and detachment, of both practical moral-political dedication and scientific distance. Social theory remains distinct from political activism but it is not a purely disinterested affair of reflection. As the German theorist Norbert *Elias (1983) counsels, pure involvement without detachment would be dogmatic and moralistic; but pure detachment without involvement would be pointless and meaningless.

Social theory and other domains of theory

We have now discussed a range of issues with a broad general relevance to all disciplines of the humanities and social sciences. These issues are particularly prominent in sociology and social theory but they are not, in principle, ones that *only* social theorists and sociologists are concerned with. The remaining sections of this Introduction will therefore try to provide some further characterization of the specific subject matters that social theorists and sociologists are concerned with. We end by looking at three main areas of overlap and difference between social theory and other domains: first, social theory and *political theory*; second, the relation of social theory to *psychology*; and third, the relation of social theory to *humanities disciplines*, such as anthropology, history, literary and art criticism, philosophy, and theology.

Social theory and political theory

Probably the closest cousin of social theory is political theory. Political theory has a long-standing position in the history of Western thought, reaching back to the writings of the ancient Greek philosophers, as well as the Roman statesmen, the Christian medieval theologians, and the political philosophers of early modern Europe. Political theory is closely related to the equally long-standing discipline of *jurisprudence*, defined as the study of the just administration of law in civil affairs, or legal theory. And political theory is also the father of the discipline of *economics*, or 'political economy' as it was known in the eighteenth century.

Political theory tends to be concerned with questions of a more overtly normative character than those most often addressed in social theory. It is typically concerned with questions such as: which systems of government best sponsor freedom, justice, and equality in social life? Or: when is obedience to a ruling power justified, and when is obedience to a ruling power not justified? In contrast, social theory tends to be more interested in issues about how the kinds of people who ask such questions first come to be constituted as social groups. That is, it is more directly concerned with the social behaviour of such groups and their structures and dynamics of organization.

Some schools of social theory accord a more central place to political questions than others. Hannah Arendt is one writer who held that social thought has genuine value only when it places political questions at the forefront of its agenda. Arendt emphasized the significance of the ancient Greek view of man as a 'political animal' (Arendt 1958). The philosopher *Aristotle wrote: 'Man is by nature a political animal' (Aristotle, *The Politics*, *c*.335 BC, para. 1253a1–3). Arendt's writings demonstrate the continuing importance of the idea in Greek thought that human beings are not fully human unless and until they take part in the life of the *polis*, in the political space. People who are excluded from the political space by privation of civil rights are prevented from realizing their human capacities—and by the same token, people who voluntarily exempt themselves from the political space by taking no interest in politics diminish their own human qualities of existence, at their peril. (And we may also note the ancient Greek word for a private-minded citizen who takes no interest in public political affairs was *idiotes*—the origin of our modern word 'idiot'.) This insight remains a vital consideration for social theory, despite a general academic division of labour between the two domains. Social theory is nothing if it is not relevant to politics.

Social theory and psychology

A second discipline closely related to social theory is psychology. The history of social thought shows many examples of close cooperation between psychology and sociology. In addition, the sub-discipline of psychoanalysis founded by Sigmund *Freud has been a pervasive source of influences in all the humanities and social sciences, as is discussed in Chapter 8 of this book.

But we must note some important differences between sociology and psychology. Psychology is mostly concerned with the emotional and affective behaviour of individuals, treated as physiologically conditioned actors who respond to sensory stimuli from an environment. In contrast, social theorists and sociologists are mostly concerned with the structure of material and symbolic relations between individuals, treated as members of collective groups in definite cultural and historical contexts. Although an important sub-discipline of psychology is 'social psychology', concerned with individual behaviour in social situations, psychology is generally less well equipped to deal with collectivities of actors and with the meaningful self-definitions of these collectivities in specific cultures. A further key difference in this connection is that unlike sociology, psychology retains close links with the natural sciences. Up to a point, psychologists are capable of testing their hypotheses through repeatable experiments. This is not possible in sociology, except in a very limited way.

One of the strongest impulses of the French sociological thinker Émile *Durkheim was to demonstrate that society consists of a region of reality in its own right—a *sui generis* reality, as he called it—which could not be explained entirely by the methods of psychology (Durkheim 1895). In his famous study of suicide, Durkheim (1897) sought to show that the reasons for people taking their lives could not be referred purely to psychological states in individual persons, such as a person's feelings of depression or despair. Psychological states necessarily depend on sociological factors, to do with the extent to which social collectivities provide resources of *integration for their constituent members. Durkheim's vision of sociology is discussed at length in Chapter 2 of this book.

Social theory and the humanities

We have already mentioned several general commonalities between social theory and humanities disciplines. It is now worth looking at some more specific areas of interaction. A first important area is *anthropology*.

Anthropology means literally the 'study of man'. As a discipline today, anthropology usually encompasses the study of human cultures and societies variously described as 'primitive', 'tribal', 'agrarian', or 'non-Western' in origin. These adjectives are notoriously difficult to apply, not least because very few cultures still exist today that are not affected in some way by developed socio-economic forms, typically originating from the West. Nevertheless, the distinctive concern of anthropologists is usually with societies showing more or less direct forms of interaction with a natural environment or ecology, based on elementary practices of cultivation of natural resources. Social theorists and sociologists share these interests, but they mostly concern themselves with the social structures of more technologically developed urban societies, with more complex political and economic infrastructures. They are generally less concerned with relatively isolated agrarian communities. Later chapters of this book discuss links between social theory and anthropology in relation to *functionalist theory and its critics (Chapter 4), in relation to sociological *ethnography (Chapter 5), and in relation to French *structuralist theory (Chapter 9).

Interactions between *history* and social theory have always been central to sociology and were particularly important for classical social thinkers such as Karl Marx and Max *Weber. The key areas of difference and cooperation between history and sociology are discussed at length in this book in Chapter 6.

Interaction between social theory and the *arts* and *cultural criticism* has also been very prominent in modern Western intellectual culture. In recent decades, renewed investigation of the meanings of 'high culture' and 'popular culture' in the context of consumer practices and new media technologies has led to a flourishing of academic subdivisions such as cultural studies, film studies, and media and communications studies. Many of the informing theories of these studies are discussed in this book under the chapters for *Western Marxism (Chapter 7), *structuralism and *post-structuralism (Chapter 9), feminist social theory (Chapter 11), and *postmodernism and its critics (Chapters 12 and 13). For a detailed overview of debates about art and aesthetics in social theory, see Harrington (2004).

Another key conversation partner in social theory is *philosophy*. We have seen that social theorists share with philosophers a basic interest in critical thinking about the way things appear to be with the world. They share the same spirit of 'reflective wondering' that the Greek philosophers held to be the origin of all *theōria*. Reflection on the meanings of our lives as historical, social, and political beings is as important to social theorists as it has always been to philosophers. But social theory differs from the traditional central domains of philosophy, such as logic, *metaphysics, and *epistemology. Social theorists are more concerned with the contributions of empirical social research to our understanding of human ways of thinking, sensing, and behaving. They are not as centrally concerned as philosophers with the logical status and coherence of concepts, arguments, and belief systems.

Lastly, we should note some differences between social theory and *theology*. Theology is the study of the principles of belief in God. Sociologists certainly share with theologians an interest in religion in society. But sociologists are not centrally concerned with the internal propositions of religious belief systems or with the ways in which religious beliefs express contexts of scripture and sacred writing. Mostly they are concerned with the ways in which religious beliefs interact with social and political institutions and powers. Consequently, social theorists and sociologists are not as well equipped as theologians to deal with questions of the meaning of ideas of the absolute or transcendental or infinite in human experience. The question of whether God exists, or of how God exists, or of why evil exists, or why the universe exists, are not questions that can be adequately framed or pursued (let alone answered!) from the standpoint of social-scientific enquiry alone.

Conclusion

We have seen that social theory is the study of ways of thinking about society scientifically. Further, we have also seen that it is the discipline of thinking about how far it is *possible* for society to be studied scientifically. Social theory is at once a source of explanatory concepts in social science and a source of ways of evaluating the point or use or meaning of such concepts. To theorize about social life is not only to develop scientific models of observable social processes. It is also to think critically about the conditions of possibility of scientific constructs. If all social analysis were purely theoretical, it would be merely speculative. But if all social analysis were purely empirical, it would be forgetful of its relationship to questions of meaning and practical purpose in human social life. In the most basic and ancient of senses, we can say that theory is reflection on the place and function of science in human existence.

■ QUESTIONS FOR DISCUSSION

1   In what sense is there, or can there be, a 'science of society'?

2   How much does social science hold in common with natural science?

3   Are there any acts of social research that can be carried out without the aid of theories or theorizing?

4   If all facts relevant to social research are value-laden, what does it mean for social research to seek to be objective? Can there be any social research that does not seek to be objective?

5   How important are objectivity and detachment in relation to practical values of liberation and emancipation in social knowledge and social life?

■ GENERAL FURTHER READING IN SOCIAL THEORY

All chapters of this book contain guidance on further reading for specific topics. In addition, various general reading sources can be recommended. These can be grouped into the following categories.

Textbooks in empirical sociology and cultural studies

Among some of the most tried and tested textbooks in empirical sociology are James Fulcher and John Scott's *Sociology* (Oxford University Press, 1999), Anthony Giddens's *Sociology* (Polity Press, 4th edn. 2001), Tony Bilton's *Introductory Sociology* (Palgrave, 4th edn. 2002), Mike Haralambos and Martin Holborn's *Sociology: Themes and Perspectives* (Collins Educational, 6th edn. 2004), and Peter Kivisto's *Key Ideas in Sociology* (Pine Forge Press, 1998). Some useful textbooks concentrating on cultural studies are Chris Barker's *Cultural Studies: Theory and Practice* (Sage, 2000). Other useful textbooks combining sociology and cultural studies are the following four books in the 'Understanding Modern Societies' series of the Open University Press: Stuart Hall and Bram Gieben's *Formations of Modernity* (1992), John Allen, Peter Braham, and Paul Lewis's *Political and Economic Forms of Modernity* (1992), Robert Bocock and Kenneth Thompson's *Social and Cultural Forms of Modernity* (1992), and Stuart Hall, David Held, and Tony McGrew's *Modernity and its Futures* (1992). Books designed as introductions to empirical social research with accessible theoretical elements include Tim May's *Social Research* (Open University Press, 3rd edn. 2001), Zygmunt Bauman's *Thinking Sociologically* (Blackwell, 1990; 2nd edn. with Tim May 2001), Mark J. Smith's *Social Science in Question* (Sage, 1998), and David Goldblatt's *Knowledge and the Social Sciences* (Routledge, 2000).

Other guides to social theory

Other guides to social theory that overlap with the present book in various ways include George Ritzer's *Sociological Theory* (McGraw-Hill Education, 6th edn. 2003), *Classical Sociological Theory* (Higher Education, 4th edn. 2003), and *Modern Sociological Theory* (McGraw-Hill Education, 6th edn. 2003), Bryan Turner's *Companion to Social Theory* (Blackwell, 2000), George Ritzer's *Companion to Major Classical Social Theorists* (Blackwell, 2003) and his *Companion to Major Contemporary Social Theorists* (Blackwell, 2003), George Ritzer and Barry Smart's *Handbook of Social Theory* (Sage, 2001), Ian Craib's two volumes *Classical Social Theory* (Oxford University Press, 1997) and *Modern Social Theory* (Harvester Wheatsheaf, 2nd edn. 1992), John Hughes, Peter Martin, and Wes Sharrock's two volumes *Understanding Classical Sociology* (Sage, 1995) and *Understanding Modern Sociology* (Sage, 2003), Bert Adams and Rosalind Sydie's two volumes *Classical Sociological Theory* (Pine Forge, 2002) and *Contemporary Sociological Theory* (Pine Forge, 2002), Patrick Baert's *Social Theory in the Twentieth Century* (Polity Press, 1998), Alex Callinicos's *Social Theory: A Historical Introduction* (Polity Press, 1999), and Pip Jones's *Introducing Social Theory* (Polity Press, 2003). Edited collections of profiles of individual theorists include Anthony Elliott and Bryan Turner's *Profiles in Contemporary Social Theory* (Sage, 2001), Anthony Elliott and Larry Ray's *Key Contemporary Social Theorists* (Blackwell, 2003), and Rob Stone's *Key Sociological Thinkers* (Macmillan, 1998). Books concentrating solely on the classical social theories of Marx, Durkheim, Weber, and Simmel are Ken Morrison's *Marx, Durkheim, Weber* (Sage, 1995), Larry Ray's *Theorizing Classical Sociology* (Open University Press, 1999), and Anthony Giddens's *Capitalism and Modern Social Theory* (Cambridge University Press, 1971), as well as the already mentioned volumes by Craib (1997), Ritzer (2003), Hughes, Sharrock, and Martin (1995), and Adams and Sydie (2002).

Collections of readings

Some useful edited collections of extracts from the famous primary texts of major social theorists—known as 'readers'—include Anthony Elliott's *The Blackwell Reader in Contemporary Social Theory* (Blackwell, 1999), Charles Lemert's *Social Theory: The Multicultural and Classic Readings* (Westview Press, 1999), *The Polity Reader in Social Theory* (Polity Press, 1994), *The Polity Reader in Cultural Theory* (Polity Press, 1994), James Farganis's *Readings in Social Theory* (McGraw-Hill, 1993), Jeffrey Alexander's *Mainstream and Critical Social Theory* (Sage, 2001), Jeffrey Alexander and Steven Seidman's *The New Social Theory Reader* (Routledge, 2001), and Roberta Garner's *Social Theory: Continuity and Confrontation: A Reader* (Broadview Press, 2000).

Guides to the philosophy of social science

Some useful books treating epistemological and methodological issues not usually addressed at length in textbooks on social research methods are Mark J. Smith's *Social Science in Question* (Sage, 1998), Malcolm Williams and Tim May's *Introduction to the Philosophy of Social Research* (University College London Press, 1996), Norman Blaikie's *Approaches to Social Enquiry* (Polity Press, 1993), Gerard Delanty's *Social Science beyond Constructivism and Realism* (Open University Press, 1997), and William Outhwaite's *New Philosophies of Social Science* (Macmillan, 1987). A useful collection of readings in this area is Gerard Delanty and Piet Strydom's *Philosophies of Social Science: The Classic and Contemporary Readings* (Open University Press, 2003).

Guides to political theory

Some good introductions to the neighbouring field of political theory are Will Kymlicka's *Contemporary Political Philosophy* (Oxford University Press, 2002), Jean Hampton's *Political Philosophy* (Westview Press, 1997), Jonathan Wolff's *An Introduction to Political Philosophy* (Oxford University Press, 1996), Raymond Plant's *Modern Political Thought* (Blackwell, 1991), and Robert Goodin and Philip Pettit's edited *A Companion to Contemporary Political Philosophy* (Blackwell, 1993).

Reference sources in A–Z format

Useful reference sources in A–Z format include William Outhwaite (ed.), *The Blackwell Dictionary of Modern Social Thought* (Blackwell, 2002), David Jary and Julia Jary (eds.), *The Collins Dictionary of Sociology* (HarperCollins, 3rd edn. 2000), George Ritzer (ed.), *The Sage Encyclopedia of Social Theory* (Sage, 2004), Austin Harrington, Barbara Marshall, and Hans-Peter Müller (eds.), *The Routledge Encyclopedia of Social Theory* (Routledge, 2005), Edward Craig (ed.), *The Routledge Encyclopedia of Philosophy* (Routledge, 1999), and Neil Smelser et al. (eds.), *The International Encyclopaedia of the Social and Behavioural Sciences* (Elsevier, 2002), also accessible on-line by institutional subscription and free of charge in partial form at **www.iesbs.com**

■ SOURCES IN THE PUBLIC MEDIA

A few recommendations can be made about sources in the non-specialized public media. Academic books and journals are not the only relevant sources. In the English-language media, this author particularly recommends the *London Review of Books* (fortnightly), the *New York Review of Books* (fortnightly), *Le Monde diplomatique* (monthly) (available in English as well as French, and other languages), *Radical Philosophy* (bi-monthly), and *New Left Review* (bi-monthly). In Europe and North America, some of the more independent-minded newspapers and magazines which regularly publish interviews and articles by leading world intellectuals on social and political affairs are *Le Monde* (in France), *El Pais* (in Spain), *Die Zeit* (in Germany, weekly), *Die Frankfurter Allgemeine Zeitung* (in Germany), *La Repubblica* (in Italy), *The Guardian* (in Britain), and *The Nation* (in the USA, weekly). The British weekly magazine *The Economist* is also useful for information on world economic affairs. A further general piece of advice to the reader is that wherever you are able to read a publication that is *not* written in the English language, it is generally good to do so. The English language currently enjoys a global intellectual hegemony which it is often good to resist, wherever you are able to do so. There are thousands of excellent books, journals, magazines, newspapers, and websites which never find their way into English translation, partly as a consequence of the cultural domination of Anglo-Saxon business interests in the global publishing market.

▌ WEBSITES

The Social Science Information Gateway (SOSIG) at **www.sosig.ac.uk/** Provides links to a database of over 50,000 social-science web pages.

Sociology On-line Homepage at **http://cgi.sociologyonline.co.uk/News/news.html** Contains an on-line work package in sociology, aimed at students and teachers.

Wikipedia Free On-line Encyclopaedia at **www.wikipedia.org**
Offers links to the history of sociology, covering key topics, terms, methods, and theorists.

Dead Sociologists' Society at **www2.pfeiffer.edu/~lridener/DSS/DEADSOC.HTML** Provides useful accounts of key sociologists with biographical information and summaries of their work.

Sociological Research On-line at **www.socresonline.org.uk/** Displays an on-line journal in sociology, containing articles on current empirical and theoretical topics.

1 Classical Social Theory, I: Contexts and Beginnings

Austin Harrington

The emergence of social theory as a distinctive way of thinking about society is concurrent with the rise of modernity. The rise of a scientific way of studying society is itself a product of the particular kinds of social conditions called 'modern'. In consequence, to come to grips with the concepts of social theory, we need to have an understanding of modernity, and to gain an understanding of modernity we need to have a grasp of the concepts of social theory.

This chapter introduces some of the foundational contexts of social thought in eighteenth- and nineteenth-century Europe that led to the emergence of sociology as a discipline in the twentieth century. The chapter sets out the fundamental characteristics of modernity as a condition of social life and the ways in which this condition is interpreted by writers belonging to the earliest waves of recognizably theoretical social thought. First we consider some key meanings of the terms 'modern', 'modernity', 'tradition', and 'traditional'. Then we look at the chief historical dynamics of the development of recognizably modern social conditions and the various explanations given to these dynamics by eighteenth- and nineteenth-century social thinkers.

In the last part of the chapter we turn to two basic questions which will be of concern throughout this book. The first is the question of how far the specifically Western European experiences of modernity and modernization that interested the first generations of social theorists have relevance and validity for *all cultures of the world*. The second is the complex question of whether the rise of modern scientific structures of consciousness is in every sense *good* for social life, or whether there are darker, more destructive sides of science and reason which we must consider.

We begin with some leading meanings of the terms 'modern' and 'traditional'.

Modernity and tradition: what is 'modern'? what is 'traditional'?

Our word 'modern' derives from the Latin *modus*, from which we also derive our word 'mode'. In a most basic sense, modernity is the *mode of our time*: that which is 'here and now', rather than 'then' or 'past'.

It has been remarked that our word 'modern' has its roots in the late fifth century AD, after the fall of the Roman Empire, when the Latin word *modernus* came to be used to refer to a new present era of Christianity, in contrast to a pagan past under the tutelage of the Romans. However, the first known occurrence of the word 'modernity' as an abstract noun is to be found in much more recent times. It appears in an article by the French poet Charles Baudelaire for the newspaper *Le Figaro* in 1863. Baudelaire here wrote of the experience of modernity in modern art and literature and the modern city as the impression of 'the transitory, the fugitive, the contingent' (*le transitoire, le fugitif, le contingent*) (Baudelaire 1863: 12). Baudelaire imagined the modern artist as someone who experiences time as a line rushing inexorably forward into the future. As each moment of the present is cast into the past, the modern artist tries to save the present from its obsolescence as the present becomes immediately past and 'outmoded'.

Modernity in this sense evokes the idea of radically changing times. *Modern*ism usually refers to specific cultural and intellectual movements of modernity that dramatize this experience in various ways. Modern*ization* usually refers to the process of emergence of modernity.

Modernity is often thought of as a period, with a beginning at a certain point in time. For some, modernity begins in the late eighteenth century with the onset of the Industrial Revolution in European countries and the spread of the ideas of the French Revolution and the so-called Age of *Enlightenment. For others, modernity begins earlier, with the Renaissance in Italy in the fifteenth century, or with the Protestant Reformation of the sixteenth century, or with the revolutions in science and mathematics of the seventeenth century. For still others, modernity is a more diffuse term that cannot be located in any definite period and is not limited to European historical developments.

Disagreements about when exactly modernity might be thought of as beginning suggest that modernity is not always best thought of solely as a 'period'. It is also possible, and in many ways more desirable, to think of modernity in a more open sense as a distinctive kind of *attitude to time*. In this sense modernity refers to an attitude of critical reflection on the past and critical distance from the past. It encompasses an orientation toward active shaping of the future through forms of collectively determined, rationally intended action. According to the historical theorist Reinhardt Koselleck (1979), modernity is the attitude in which society comes to objectify its past as 'history'. Modernity is the time in which society reflects on its past as a definite sequence of events culminating in the present, not as a repetitious cycle. 'Our time' becomes 'new time'; and 'new time' becomes that which places the 'Middle Ages' in between 'our time' and 'antiquity'. Time thus becomes something that society seeks to master and to make its own 'project'. In the words of Koselleck, modernity sees itself as determining its own future, as continually expanding its 'space of experience' under more and more ambitious 'horizons of expectation'.

Modernity is frequently contrasted with what is called 'tradition' or 'traditional' ways of living, or 'traditionalism'. Our word tradition comes from the Latin verb *tradere*, 'to hand over' to 'to hand down'. It signifies the idea of accepted, taken-for-granted ways of thinking and acting. Appropriate ways of behaving tend to be set by precedent and example, by the way things have 'always been', by what the priest or the father says or by what the ancestors did.

One of the most influential ways of distinguishing between 'modern' and 'traditional' societies in social theory was established in the middle decades of the twentieth century by the American *functionalist theorist Talcott *Parsons. Parsons distinguished between traditional social structures based on what he called 'ascription' and modern social structures based on 'achievement'. By 'ascription', Parsons sought to refer to the way in which social advantages of wealth, power, and status in traditional settings are for the most part *ascribed* to individuals at birth, by inheritance and by upbringing in a particular *social class or social 'stratum', in which for the most part remain for the rest of their lives. In contrast, by 'achievement', Parsons sought to refer to the way in which social advantages of wealth, power, and status in modern settings are increasingly *achieved* by individuals, irrespective of the initial privileges or lack of privileges with which they begin at birth. In modern settings, the positions of individuals in the *stratified structures of advantages and disadvantages are by no means entirely determined by achievement: ascription through inheritance of a privileged or non-privileged class background still plays a major role. But the tendency in modern settings is increasingly towards greater *social mobility* as individuals gain or lose their positions in the distribution of advantages by intended planned action oriented to formal education and a professional career (see Parsons 1951).

Traditional societies are often vaguely thought of as being 'undeveloped' in various senses. A traditional society might be one with a simple subsistence-based economy, or one with no advanced uses of production technology, or one with no complex political institutions. Traditionalism is often associated with so-called 'primitive' or tribal social forms, or with medieval society, or with the societies of the 'dark ages'. Sometimes traditional ways of living are blandly and problematically associated with all 'non-Western' cultures. There are, however, at least two reasons for being careful with the word traditional in these instances.

First, it is not really the case that traditional societies show no particularly developed uses of production technology. It is quite possible for societies to possess developed systems of material production and transportation and still to remain traditional in most important respects. According to the influential view of Max *Weber, societies do not necessarily cease to be traditional when they start to produce large quantities of material goods or to create armies or develop technical inventions. Rather, according to Weber, societies only cease to be traditional when they acquire a particular ethos of *methodical conduct of life*, when they acquire a distinctly calculative, planning, and *rationalizing attitude* to ways of organizing and ethically justifying and codifying social life (Weber 1920a, 1920b). In this sense, Weber argued that the civilization of ancient China remained for the most part traditional in its ways of life, even though ancient Chinese civilization already possessed many of the technical inventions that the West only acquired over a thousand years later in the Middle Ages (notably gunpowder). In Weber's view, the distinctive feature of Western Europe in the fifteenth and sixteenth centuries was that it began to adopt a peculiarly rationalizing attitude to ways of defining moral and political values, even though it did not start to produce large quantities of goods or to invent machines of production until much later.

Secondly, it is important to note that societies can very often possess both traditional attitudes in some respects and modern or modernizing attitudes in other respects, at one and the same time. Societies and social forms can, for example, have both modern or modernizing attitudes toward legal, political, and economic organization and distinctly traditional attitudes toward interpersonal relations of authority and toward gender roles. We might think today of the mafia business family, operating by *patriarchal codes of honour and subordination and at the same time remaining entirely in touch with modern technology and the modern economy. Many contemporary nation-states also go to considerable lengths to preserve what they believe to be their 'cultural traditions', such as elements of their religious institutions—the Catholic Church in many countries—or their political institutions (the monarchy in Britain, for example) (compare Hobsbawm and Ranger 1983; Anderson 1983). We can also say that many contemporary Islamic societies are both modern in some respects and traditional in others; and we can say the same of American society in the 1950s, and of Japanese society in the nineteenth century, and so on.

It is difficult, therefore, to speak confidently of any definite period of time when all or most cultures of the world ceased to be 'traditional' and became, entirely and unequivocally, 'modern'. Both the word traditional and the word modern refer primarily to attitudes and habits of mind and behaviour, rather than simply, or solely, to clearly definable periods and regions of world history. The social transformations that took place in Europe after the fifteenth century give us an exemplary insight into the ways in which social relations can become modern. But they are not the only contexts in which modern and modernizing processes can be observed; and European developments are by no means in themselves unambiguous cases of what is called 'modernity'.

With these points in mind, we can turn now in detail to the exemplary case of European modernity from the fifteenth century onwards. It is this case that most preoccupied the founding figures in sociological analysis in the nineteenth and early twentieth centuries. It is possible to refer to this case as the prototype of *Western modernity* or *occidental modernity*.

Western modernity

It is helpful to approach the structure of Western modernity in terms of three more or less distinct dimensions of social change: first a *cultural* dimension, encompassing the rise of science and the decline of religion; secondly a *political* dimension, encompassing the rise of the state, civil law, and ideas of democracy; and thirdly a *socio-economic* dimension, encompassing the rise of an international capitalist economy, bound up with processes of industrialization and urbanization.

Cultural modernity: science and the decline of religion

The rise of the natural sciences and the rediscovery of mathematics in the seventeenth century are central events in the intellectual development of Western modernity. They find dramatic expression in such famous episodes as Galileo's confrontation with the papacy in 1616. Galileo sought to demonstrate the truth of the theory that the earth revolved around the sun and that the earth was not the centre of the universe. This helio-centric theory had first been mooted by the Polish astronomer Copernicus in the sixteenth century, but was at odds with the traditional teachings of the Church. Galileo invented the telescope in order to *prove* the theory. He sought to show that knowledge was genuine only if it had a basis in demonstrable *empirical observation. Similarly, Francis *Bacon in England asserted that true knowledge arose solely from the authority of *experience* and *experiment* and personal individual enquiry, not from traditions and precedents. In Bacon's famous phrase, knowledge had to be free of such 'idols of the mind' as myth, superstition, and church dogma.

The seventeenth-century philosophers and scientists rejected the long-standing teaching of medieval Christianity that all creatures and things on the earth had a innate purpose in nature preordained by God. They rejected the Church's *teleological* view of the universe and replaced it with a *mechanistic* one. Creatures and things were regarded as subject to laws of nature that could be scientifically discovered and rationally deduced. God was the guarantor of laws that man could discover for himself and put to his own use. In this sense, Isaac Newton set out to determine the laws of gravity and motion, which God had set down in nature, by 'pre-established harmony'—in the phrase of the rationalist philosopher Gottfried Wilhelm von Leibniz. Similarly René *Descartes set out to prove—purely by *deductive philosophical reasoning, without appeal to any external authority—that con-sciousness cannot be deceptive. My existence is real, Descartes argued, because I *think* my existence: 'I think, therefore I am'; *cogito ergo sum*. Methodical thinking alone provides a basis for knowledge of the world, not scripture or revelation. God must exist, not because the Church or the Bible says that he exists, but because God's non-existence is not logically conceivable. In this regard, the fundamental intellectual feature of Western modernity is that the rationally thinking 'I', the ego, or the *Subject, comes to occupy the centre of the universe. In the development of European philosophy after Descartes, the 'Subject' becomes the last instance of authority before God.

The fifteenth-century Italian Renaissance and the sixteenth-century Protestant Reformation in northern Europe are significant because they set in motion the rise of the idea of *autonomously thinking individuals*, who are personally responsible for their own destinies and their own salvation. Renaissance artists and scientists such as Michelangelo and Leonardo da Vinci, together with the Protestant religious teachers Martin *Luther and Jean *Calvin and humanist political writers such as Thomas *More, *Erasmus of Rotterdam, and Michel de *Montaigne, all played their part in the generation of a sequence of developments lasting over several centuries to which we today refer by the name of *secularization*.

Secularization denotes the diminishing power and influence of formal religious institutions over social and political life. From the sixteenth century onwards, a distinction gradually comes to be introduced in Western European society between precepts set down by the Church and precepts gained through independent reading of scripture by individuals or through science and philosophy. It is this gradual process of separation between different sources of cultural authority that leads to the slow retreat of religion from the realms of education, art, philosophy, politics, and public discourse during the seventeenth, eighteenth, and nineteenth centuries in Europe. In the nineteenth century, Charles *Darwin's *Origin of Species* of 1859 represents one of the most emblematic moments of this process of secularization.

Although religious beliefs today may not appear to have diminished in prominence in public life, religion in the Western world no longer possesses anything like the same legally and politically sanctioned sovereignty over social organization that it enjoyed five hundred years ago. In the Western world today, despite the reversion to Creationism in the teaching curricula of some US high schools, the intellectual authority of religion over definitions of the physical universe and of the social world has been replaced, definitively, by that of science.

Elements of cultural and intellectual modernity and the spread of secularization are closely bound up with aspects of *political modernity*. It is to these concurrent political dimensions of modernity in Europe that we now turn.

Political modernity: law, democracy, and the state

During the period of the sixteenth-century Protestant conversions in northern Europe, notably in England, Holland, parts of Germany, and parts of Switzerland, the Catholic Church centred in Rome became increasingly subordinate to a new political agency in European history. This new political agency is the *state*, and especially the *nation-state*.

The rise of the state was a leading consideration for numerous legal and political writers in the sixteenth and seventeenth centuries. These figures wrote in the wake of wars of religion and deep factional conflicts driven by parties claiming divine warrant for their actions—notably the Civil War in England and the Thirty Years War in Germany, as well as the Dutch Protestant revolt against the Spanish empire at the end of the sixteenth century. It was in reaction to these kinds of events that a conception of the highest sovereignty of the state in maintaining law and order came to be developed in the writings of political philosophers such as Niccolò *Machiavelli and Thomas *Hobbes. This conception is often known as the doctrine of 'reason of state'. A conception of toleration, or state protection for freedom of religious conscience, in return for obedience to the laws of the state, occurred later in the writings of John *Locke. In eighteenth-century France, Locke's influence joined with increasing calls in public life for constitutional reform and for limitation of the powers of both the monarchy and the Church. These calls eventually culminated in revolution in 1789, abolition of the monarchy, and an attempt by Napoleon to spread the revolution to the rest of Europe in the early years of the nineteenth century.

In the New World, the men who met in Philadelphia to draft the Constitution in 1787 appealed to these same principles of separation between Church and state, and between the powers of the legislature, the executive, and the judiciary. They invoked the principles of representative democracy, of popular sovereignty and 'rights of man'. A key political idea of Western modernity is here that the state receives its authority to rule not by divine sanction—descending through a monarch, an emperor or a pope—but solely from the collective will of the *people*, or the 'nation'. According to this world-view, the people are endowed with inalienable rights, and the people alone resolve to vest authority in a sovereign power. In this connection, the French revolutionary slogan 'liberty, equality, and fraternity' finds its counterpart in Thomas *Jefferson's 'life, liberty, and the pursuit of happiness'.

Ideas of representative democracy and popular sovereignty emerged from the 'Age of Reason' or 'Age of Enlightenment' in eighteenth-century Europe. The writers of the *Enlightenment saw themselves as standing for rational scrutiny, enquiry, and, above all, 'critique'. In Prussia in the 1780s, the philosopher Immanuel *Kant titled his three chief works of philosophy *The Critique of Pure Reason* (1781), *The Critique of Practical Reason* (1788), and *The Critique of Judgement* (1790). In an essay of 1784, 'An Answer to the Question: What is Enlightenment', Kant spoke of 'man's *emancipation from his self-incurred immaturity' (Kant 1784). By 'immaturity' Kant meant uncritical submission to authority, at the expense of individual reflection, responsibility, and autonomy. Man's immaturity was 'self-incurred' because man had not yet found the courage to use his own innate faculties of reason. Man had instead surrendered control of his life to powers of questionable legitimacy—to monarchs and priests.

The ideas of French Enlightenment philosophers such as *Voltaire, *Montesquieu, *Rousseau, and *Diderot included the precept that all people are equal before the law and are innocent until proved guilty. They also included the insistence that illness and misfortune are not symptoms of divine malediction but have natural and social causes, and that religious and *metaphysical ideas develop from definite historical customs, not from timeless essences. Throughout the eighteenth and nineteenth centuries, these ideas led to numerous projects of reform and rational administration of the institutions of social life, including the foundation of state schools, hospitals, prisons, and police forces.

We now turn to the last feature of processes of modernization in the West concerning changes in the *economic* structures of society.

Socio-economic modernity: capitalism, industry, and the rise of cities

The rise of science as an intellectual force in Western modernity would not have been possible without at least two further factors. These included, first, the emergence of a social methodical ethos oriented to technical applications of scientific knowledge, and, second the emergence of a capitalist economy that stood to profit from the kinds of controlled experimental thinking that science represented. In this connection, many cultural historians have pointed out that while both the ancient Greeks and the early medieval Arab philosophers possessed virtually all the science and mathematics that early modern Europe possessed, what the Greeks and the Arabs did *not* share was the early modern Europeans' drive to separate science and mathematics from myth and religion and to seek redemption for science solely through its *this-worldly* technical and economic applications.

The existence of a continuous this-worldly demand for science was crucial for Western Europe's massive political and economic expansion from the fifteenth century onwards. Growths in merchant shipping trade, voyages of exploration across land and sea, to the East and to the West, and the discovery and colonization of the two continents of North and South America, were all crucial socio-economic developments. The cultural and political dimensions of Western modernity are fundamentally bound up with the spread of an international capitalistic trading system that continually sought and gained new markets, new sources of raw materials, and notably new sources of labour in the case of the slave trade.

It has been argued that the growth of an international trading system emanating from medieval European seaports such as Genoa, Pisa, Venice, London, Lisbon, and Amsterdam arose from some key changes in the practices of individual merchants. Merchants came to operate less and less on an ad hoc basis and more and more as organized trading companies, or 'societies'. They began to separate assets deemed to belong to the *family household* from assets deemed to belong independently to the *business*. Merchants acquired salaried employees, made use of accounting systems, and increasingly forged deals through intermediary partners or middlemen. Another important factor in this process was the greatly increased ability of moneylenders to lend capital to merchants and to charge interest on loans without the constraint of the traditional teachings of the Catholic Church against interest as a manifestation of the sin of greed. Later, the emergence of a complex capitalist economy was consolidated by the foundation of national banks in the seventeenth and eighteenth centuries and by the development of private property laws designed to protect property against arbitrary taxation. National banks and property laws helped merchants and industrialists to make reliable estimates of prices, to calculate necessary quantities of supplies, and hence to make predictable long-term investments of capital.

In the eighteenth and nineteenth centuries, it is possible to single out five basic factors accounting for the emergence of an advanced industrial capitalist economy in Europe. These are:

1. Enclosure and conversion of portions of common land into *private estates*, making possible concentrated large-scale farming and industrial development.

2. *Industrialization*, marked by replacement of artisans' workshops by factories employing systematically organized labour forces and machine technologies involved in both energy extraction and the manufacturing process.

3. *Free-trade* policies, based on the removal of state tariffs on imported goods. These mark the definitive end of all barter trading and the universal use of *money* as an abstract bearer of exchange value. Wealth is seen as increasing not by hoarding within the confines of a nation-state (a doctrine known as 'mercantilism'), but by its continual *free circulation* as capital.

4. *Urbanization*, marked by large industrial cities linked to trading ports and tied into a global economy. The cities grew from influxes of migrants from the countryside unable to find work on the land after processes of enclosure.

5. *Population growth*, arising from the demand for large industrial labour forces. Low wage levels meant that nuclear family units needed to rear greater numbers of working children to ensure a family's survival.

Processes of industrialization and urbanization and ideas of democracy and enlightenment were all central considerations for eighteenth- and nineteenth-century social critics and thinkers. In the next section we turn to the ways in which these eighteenth- and nineteenth-century writers developed ideas that were to become key objects of attention for canonical figures in social thought such as Marx, Durkheim, and Weber and thus helped to lay some of the foundations for the discipline we know today as 'sociology'.

Social theory in the nineteenth century

Social thought in the eighteenth and nineteenth centuries is represented by a number of key movements and a number of influential thinkers. In the following, we consider the movements of *political economy* and *utilitarianism, liberalism, positivism, socialism*, and theories of *social elites*. These are represented by the names—among others—of Adam Smith, Jeremy Bentham, John Stuart Mill, Alexis de Tocqueville, Auguste Comte, Herbert Spencer, Karl Marx, Gaetano Mosca, Vilfredo Pareto, Robert Michels, and Ferdinand Tönnies. We begin by looking at political economy and utilitarianism.

Political economy and utilitarianism: Adam Smith and Jeremy Bentham

Political economy refers to a succession of writers active from the late eighteenth century onwards, mostly in England and Scotland. Of all the works of British political economy, Adam *Smith's *The Wealth of Nations* of 1776 is widely recognized as the founding text of modern economic analysis. Smith and his disciples saw themselves as discovering laws of social behaviour that had universal application. These laws famously included the theorem that prices rise when goods are in short supply and drop when goods are abundant; and rise when goods are in demand and drop when they are not in demand. The political economists saw market theory as a solution to the moral problems of society. They proposed that egoistic action by individuals in private in fact had beneficial consequences in public. If each individual specialized in a particular trade and sold the products of this trade while purchasing the products of another, all individuals would help each other to satisfy their own interests. Adam Smith famously spoke of a 'hidden hand' of the market that coordinates private individual action through a collective mechanism of wealth distribution.

A little later, mostly in the first decade of the nineteenth century, the movement known as *utilitarianism developed out of the ideas of the political economists and the French Enlightenment critics, gaining currency mostly in early nineteenth-century Britain. The utilitarians maintained that traditional forms of philosophy and theology rested on irrational and unscientific assumptions. They believed that if society was to make progress and find practical benefit in its intellectual pursuits, it had to replace philosophical speculation by the scientific study of *utility*. Utilitarianism is chiefly associated with the writings of the English philosopher Jeremy *Bentham, who contributed to the foundation of the University of London as England's first entirely secular university. Bentham famously stated that the purpose of government was to guarantee 'the greatest happiness of the greatest number' (Bentham 1789). A rational society was one that maximized the aggregate well-being of its members by dispensing with wasteful or luxury pursuits for the few (such as high art and classical learning) and using the proceeds of these savings to satisfy the material needs of the greatest mass in society. Bentham and the utilitarians also emphasized that the purpose of the treatment of criminals by the state should be not only to punish but also to *reform* them. Bentham designed a plan for the modern prison which he called the 'Panopticon', allowing all prisoners to be surveyed and supposedly cared for by prison guards from the same vantage point. In addition, the utilitarians placed particular importance in medicine and the scientific study of health and illness. They insisted that society had to rid itself of all association of disease, deformity, and insanity with religious and superstitious notions of punishment for sin or demonic possession.

Closely linked to political economy and utilitarianism was the spread of the movement throughout the nineteenth century known in very broad terms as *liberalism*.

Liberalism and civil society: John Stuart Mill and Alexis de Tocqueville

Liberalism in nineteenth-century Europe and North America encompassed the belief that progress lay in the development of parliamentary democracy and constitutional law. Also important to nineteenth-century liberalism was the separation of religious affiliation from affairs of state, and especially from the provision of education. All the essential principles of nineteenth-century liberalism are succinctly formulated in the writings of the English Victorian philosopher John Stuart *Mill, most notably in his *On Liberty* of 1859. As a 'dominant ideology', liberalism in the nineteenth century meant freedom to own property and to trade in property and commodities without excessive taxation and arbitrary interference by the state. The defence of liberty was construed in 'negative' terms as the protection of each person's freedom to do as he or she pleases without harm to the freedom of another person to do the same. Government had to be 'limited', and it had to be 'representative' of the interests of the society it served. The state was to be the faithful servant of *civil society*.

The term 'civil society' in social thought—a term first developed by the eighteenth-century English and Scottish political economists—has come to refer to institutions in society that mediate between the laws and actions of the state and the private self-interested actions of individuals and families. In the context of nineteenth-century liberal ideology, civil society essentially encompassed all those who owned property, all those who owned a stake in the wealth of the nation, and who therefore held an entitlement to the vote. Civil society thus referred predominantly to the social and political agency of the *middle classes*. The German term for civil society, *bürgerliche Gesellschaft*, expressed in its very semantic form this key social fact that civil society is the society of the *burghers* or the *bourgeoisie*, the people of the towns. The bourgeoisie referred to those people whose wealth derived not from long-standing rent on inherited land—as with the aristocracy—but from trade and industry. Civil society in this respect also included the Jews among the European middle classes, many of whom held banking interests and who gained various civil rights in the nineteenth century, but who had previously been excluded from political and legal representation.

Recent decades have seen several influential historical studies of the relationship between liberal political ideology in the eighteenth and nineteenth centuries and the growth of an international capitalist economy. Three important examples of these are the works of the historians Albert *Hirschman, Karl *Polanyi, and Eric *Hobsbawm. These historians' writings are discussed in Box 1.

BOX 1. MODERNITY AND THE CAPITALIST ECONOMY: ALBERT HIRSCHMAN, KARL POLANYI, AND ERIC HOBSBAWM

In *The Passions and the Interests* Albert *Hirschman (1977) describes how dominant political values began to change in the eighteenth century with the rise of an *individualistic market economy. Human nature was once thought to be vulnerable to uncontrollable 'passions'—chiefly greed, envy, and wrath—which disrupted the commonwealth and had to be repressed by a strong state. In the eighteenth century, a new *ideology arose that held that these passions could be harmonized with the social good when they were transformed into 'interests'. *Commerce* was thought to 'soften' and 'civilize' human nature, by transforming malevolent 'passions' into benevolent 'interests'.

In his book *The Great Transformation*, the Hungarian historian Karl *Polanyi (1944) investigated the system of free trade in the nineteenth century that allowed European nations to gain supremacy over the world economy. Trade provided an incentive for nation-states to avoid declaring war on one another. It largely accounts for the relatively long period of peace in the nineteenth century. However, the international free-trade system also increasingly eroded and 'disembedded' the social fabric of the European nations. According to Polanyi, it was this structural social *'disembedding' that eventually created the conditions of chronic social conflict that were to culminate in the rise of fascism in twentieth-century Europe.

The British Marxist historian Eric *Hobsbawm provides an illuminating periodization of modern social history in his four books *The Age of Revolution 1789–1848, The Age of Capital 1848–1875, The Age of Empire 1875–1914*, and *The Age of Extremes 1914–1991* (Hobsbawm 1962, 1975, 1987, 1994). First comes a period of highly charged political agitation between the first French Revolution of 1789 and the defeated European revolutions of 1848. Then comes a period of both capitalist expansion and colonial aggrandizement in which the European states increasingly turned toward colonial market places for the products of their industrial economies. This created the series of imperial rivalries which exploded in the outbreak of the First World War. Hobsbawm characterizes the period 1914 to 1991 as the 'short twentieth century', in contrast to the 'long nineteenth century'. In his synopsis, the twentieth century effectively came to a close with the fall of the communist regimes of the Eastern Bloc and the end of the Cold War.

Over the course of the nineteenth century, the right to vote was slowly extended to less wealthy sections of the population in various parts of Europe, based on a lower property franchise. We must, however, bear in mind that truly universal suffrage, including crucially the extension of the vote to women, did not arrive until the twentieth century. And we must not forget that in the nineteenth-century USA, where European immigrants enjoyed more rights than they had done in the Old World, black Americans remained slaves until the Civil War and did not gain full civil rights until the 1960s.

In France in the 1830s, in the period of the Restoration of the monarchy after the 1789 revolution and the defeat of Napoleon, one of the most influential political commentators on liberalism was Alexis de *Tocqueville. Tocqueville was a civil servant of the French state under the constitutional monarchy of Louis-Philippe. Today he is chiefly celebrated for his book *Democracy in America* of 1835, as well as for a later study *The Ancien Regime and the Causes of Revolution in France* of 1856. Tocqueville's main concern in his treatise on America was to evaluate the factors contributing to social stability in the New World compared with old Europe. Tocqueville reflected on calls for democracy and reform in eighteenth-century French society. These calls never found realization in France until the turbulent years of the 1790s when they soon degenerated into dictatorship under the terror of the despotic revolutionary Robespierre. Tocqueville contrasted this violent introduction of democracy in France with the more peaceful society of the United States. Because American society possessed no *stratified structure led by aristocratic elites with high status and no monarchy, it was less vulnerable to violent overthrow by mob rule. In Tocqueville's observation, *solidarity in American society arose from the presence of 'voluntary associations' based on small clusters of individuals able to trust and cooperate with one another for mutual interests. He saw these voluntary associations as having their roots in the Protestant sects of the original English settlers. They provided the basis for the spirit of *egalitarianism and personal self-reliance in nineteenth-century American life.

Tocqueville's writings have been influential for contemporary liberal thinking about pluralism and mutual cooperation in civil society (compare Putnam 2000). However, it is important to note that Tocqueville's view of American society was not uniformly positive. Tocqueville conjectured that as the American economy and population grew larger and more complex, Americans would forfeit the safeguards that had once protected them from problems of mass popular dictatorship based on a 'tyranny of the majority'. His fears have not been proved to be wholly misplaced in the more recent twentieth- and twenty-first-century history of the USA.

Alongside liberalism, a further predominant intellectual movement in nineteenth-century society was *positivism*. Positivism is particularly represented by the thought of Auguste *Comte and Herbert *Spencer.

Positivism: Auguste Comte and Herbert Spencer

Auguste Comte is not only the originator of the term 'sociology'. He is also the progenitor of the conception of science known as *positivism*. In his *Cours de philosophie positive* of 1830 and his *Système de politique positive* of 1851, Comte held that genuine knowledge arose purely from *empirical sense-observation, free of distorting *metaphysical preconceptions. In Comte's view, disciplines such as psychology, sociology, and history had to follow the same principles set down by the already established natural sciences. Comte believed that empirical positive science would serve definite social purposes. Once human beings had found scientific answers to the world, they would be able to apply these answers to the removal of suffering, violence, and conflict.

Comte claimed to show that all societies evolved over time by laws of progress. Societies evolved towards higher stages of *integration in which social arrangements were reached by peaceful and rational means. Comte spoke of a 'law of three stages'. First came a 'theological stage' in which human beings mistake the natural world for themselves. The theological stage is characterized by beliefs in spirits and supernatural forces, where human beings project onto the natural world their own habits of thought, like children who treat inanimate objects as though they are animate creatures. Second came a 'metaphysical stage' in which humanity overcomes superstitious habits and mystical images of its world by means of abstract concepts. Thirdly and finally came a 'scientific stage' in which humanity replaces abstract speculative concepts with empirical knowledge based on unbiased observation. In his late writings Comte spoke of the overcoming of traditional religions through a new 'religion of humanity'. This was to be a secular civil religion in which human beings would recognize themselves as the authors of their own existence. Human beings would find ethical communion with one another not in the Church but only in the *state* as the most authentic representation of their social belonging.

Herbert *Spencer in England developed similar ideas in the later nineteenth century. In his *The Principles of Sociology* of 1882–98, Spencer propounded a theory of social evolution influenced partly by the writings of Charles *Darwin. Spencer held that liberal democracy and limited government were the best adapted systems of resolving conflict in society and of distributing goods to its members. Tyrannies or oligarchies were vulnerable in relation to their social environments. Democracy, in contrast, was more stable in the long run. Democracy was better adapted and therefore more likely to survive, to be 'selected' through history.

Spencer's ideas did not directly reproduce Darwin's theory of the 'survival of the fittest'. Darwin had developed this theory strictly with reference to biological reproduction in the animal and plant kingdoms and had never thought to apply it to historical-social affairs. Nevertheless, Spencer's suppositions reflected many popular misconceptions and prejudices of the time about the social implications of Darwin's theory and the evolutionary superiority of European society. Both Spencer's and Comte's philosophies are in these respects shot through with chauvinistic prejudice. Their writings are read today mostly for historical interest and are no longer taken seriously as social theories. Nevertheless, their various concepts of 'evolution', 'adaptation', *'differentiation', and *'integration' later came to be developed by more sophisticated theorists in rigorous and non-chauvinistic ways. These notably included *Durkheim around the turn of the nineteenth century and Talcott *Parsons in the 1930s.

Theories of elites: Gaetano Mosca, Vilfredo Pareto, and Robert Michels

The most influential nineteenth-century social writers active before about the 1870s were all liberal in their basic political views. Liberalism remained for the most part the dominant ideology of all nineteenth-century social thought until the outbreak of the First World War.

However, over the course of the century, written defences of liberalism show increasing signs of response to the rising tide of *socialism* as a political current. Karl *Marx and Friedrich *Engels were later to emerge as the most dynamic spokesmen of this movement with a massive impact on politics and society in the twentieth century—even though Marx himself did not establish a hegemonic movement around himself in his own lifetime.

An increasingly vociferous claim of the period is that the purely formal concepts of liberty, citizenship, and rights upheld by liberalism had to be made *substantive*. Several socialist writers argued that political equality of persons before the law had to become real social and economic relations of equality, through abolition of exploitation of the poor and reform of a state that served only the interests of the rich. This critique was central to the socialist view of the French Revolution as a bourgeois revolution serving the interests of the middle classes. In the socialist view, civil society essentially meant the rule of the bourgeoisie. In France, the Comte de *Saint-Simon and Pierre-Joseph *Proudhon as well as the English Chartists took similar views in the 1830s and 1840s, and there were kindred voices in Russian social thought, notably in the writings of the anarchist writer Mikhail Bakunin.

Nineteenth-century social consciousness became increasingly marked by emergent class tensions and conflicts as a result of processes of industrialization and expanding international trade. Much nineteenth-century social thought can consequently be read in terms of an attempt to preserve the framework of liberal politics in response to rising fears of the breakdown of social order and the claims of socialism. Yet at the very end of the century, both liberalism *and* socialism began to receive a series of highly sceptical diagnoses in the works of three writers chiefly recognized today as theorists of *social elites*. These are the Italian-born writers Gaetano *Mosca, Vilfredo *Pareto, and Robert *Michels.

Mosca, Pareto, and Michels wrote at a time that saw many challenges to the nineteenth-century system of liberal political consensus. These include the emergence of workers' movements and trade union movements, as well as conservative religious movements. The three elite theorists questioned the ability of civil society to contain and resolve these movements' mutually conflicting claims. They also doubted the sincerity and integrity of the moral and political ideologies governing these movements' representatives. Taking their cue from *Machiavelli, they speculated that it was the drive for *power* that explained the repeated failure of workers' parties to maintain an egalitarian structure and constantly to relapse into hierarchical structures led by elites and oligarchies.

In his book *The Ruling Class*, published originally in 1896, Gaetano *Mosca analysed the ways in which members of certain narrow social strata manage to reproduce themselves as self-perpetuating ruling cliques, while at the same time passing themselves off as representatives of the 'people' and of popular interests. Mosca subjected Marx's principles of historical *materialist explanation based on 'class struggle' to an analysis of the behaviour of socialist groups and parties themselves. He concluded that social-democratic and popular movements such as socialism never achieve their objectives without the leadership of a certain elite class of intellectuals who speak on behalf of the mass but who at the same time stand estranged from the mass.

Robert *Michels, in his study *Political Parties* (1911), applied this analysis directly to the organization of trade unions and socialist parties. Michels spoke of an 'iron law of oligarchy' in which political organizations, through the internal necessities of discipline and administrative continuity, inevitably become closed self-perpetuating cliques.

Vilfredo Pareto, in his treatise *The Mind and Society* of 1916 (originally titled *Trattato di sociologia generale*), claimed to discern two basic propensities of human social group behaviour. The first propensity of social groups was to optimize their pursuit of material interests, even at the cost of conflict with other groups. The second propensity of social groups was always to be led by small dynamic elites, however egalitarian the groups may feel themselves to be in their initial aspirations. Pareto claimed that all human social behaviour is driven by certain basic dynamics that he called 'residues' and 'derivations'. These essentially stemmed from the pursuit of power and material interest, dressed up in the language of morality. Following Machiavelli, Pareto classified some social movements as 'foxes' and some as 'lions'. 'Foxes' were short-term opportunist movements skilled at combining diverse interests and seizing power through cunning strategies. 'Lions' were long-term movements based on a principle of persistent 'aggregation', either of a conservative religious kind or of a revolutionary socialist kind.

Pareto's theories are the arguments of a speculative cynic. They rest on a certain stubborn idea of the basic dynamics of 'human nature'. They lack sensitivity to different self-descriptions of human actors in changing cultural and historical contexts. They also bear a certain intellectual complicity with the rise of fascism in Italy after 1920. However, there are certain elements in his work, together with that of Mosca and Michels, which find more sophisticated expression in other early twentieth-century theorists. Max Weber in particular is close to their work and was himself a teacher of the young Michels. Despite their conservative and sceptical outlook, the elite theorists also left a mark on the thinking of the Italian Marxist theorist Antonio *Gramsci; and they have had a wide-ranging impact in contemporary political science, especially in *rational choice theory.

The last sociological thinker we must now consider in this overview is the German writer Ferdinand *Tönnies.

Community and society: Ferdinand Tönnies

A slightly older contemporary of Max Weber and Georg *Simmel, Ferdinand Tönnies is chiefly celebrated today for his treatise of 1887, *Gemeinschaft und Gesellschaft*, usually translated as *Community and Society*. In this work, Tönnies argued that what he called 'communal relations' (*Gemeinschaft*) had increasingly come to be replaced by what he called *'societal relations' (*Gesellschaft*), through processes of industrialization, urbanization, and the spread of a differentiated capitalist economy. Unlike Mill, Tocqueville, or Marx, Tönnies did not write explicitly from a position of political advocacy for a particular type of government or social order. He saw himself as a sociological commentator, rather than a political critic. But his famous book in fact makes clear a number of quite striking *normative assumptions about the cohesiveness of the past and the breakdown of social glue with the coming of modern industrialism.

By 'communal relations' Tönnies meant a type of relations between individuals found in economies mostly dependent on agriculture in rural contexts, where small population units are typically congregated in villages. Families would be extended and members of kin would reside in close proximity. Means of livelihood would tend to be by subsistence, by direct economy from the land or small-scale craftsmanship. Exchange would largely take place by payments in kind or services without extensive mediation by money. Relations of authority would be of a mostly personal kind in traditionally defined roles. Traditional beliefs and skills would be transmitted orally and by example. This created a sense of ongoing continuity over time and generations.

By 'societal relations', Tönnies meant a type of condition in which relations are characterized by commercial exchange of goods and services. Goods are not produced and immediately consumed from the land but are exchanged for money. Labour and services become formalized, through wage contracts. Social relations divide between public professional roles on the one hand and private personal spheres on the other. Relations between individuals are increasingly mediated by an intervening world of impersonal and anonymous objects, codes, and institutions. With the rise of money economies, communities become fused together as a 'mass' in the same places, in the cities, and consequently begin to lose their distinct identities. Different parties interact with one another primarily for definite purposes, without preserving a continuous personal acquaintance of one another over time. Social change thus moves faster and becomes more discontinuous.

Tönnies's account of the two types of relationship is somewhat simplistic and suffers from a certain implicit nostalgia for lost community life. Nevertheless, it resonates with many of the centrally accepted analytical categories of classical social theory. These categories came to be developed in more technical ways by Durkheim, Weber, and Simmel at the turn of the nineteenth century.

Challenges to Western modernity: reason and the claims of science

We have now explored two basic aspects of the theme of modernity in social theory. First, we have discussed some leading substantive dimensions of modernizing processes in Western society, grouped around the three analytical areas of 'cultural modernity', 'political modernity', and 'socio-economic modernity'. Second we have looked at some leading theories and discourses of modernity in nineteenth-century European social thought, represented by the movements of political economy, utilitarianism, liberalism, positivism, and socialism and by the names of Smith, Mill, Tocqueville, Comte, and others.

We now turn to the two complex questions signalled at the outset of this chapter. The *first* is the question of how far these Western aspects of modernity have applicability to all cultures and societies of the globe. Is there one general paradigm of modernity that can be applied to all societies, or are there many different ways in which societies can be modern? The *second* question concerns whether there are any darker sides to the claims of eighteenth- and nineteenth-century social thinkers about 'progress', 'science', 'reason', and 'enlightenment'. We have already referred to some notable ideologies and prejudices of nineteenth-century thought, and we must now look at these more closely. Put simply, can the application of rational and scientific principles to social life and social organization be regarded as in every respect a 'good thing'?

We take up these questions in turn, beginning with the issue of Western-centred bias.

Eurocentrism in social theory

To address the problem of *'Eurocentrism' and general Western-centredness in social theory, it is worth first noting some ways in which sociology came to be institutionalized as a scientific discipline in Western universities in the twentieth century. Some of the most influential figures in mid-century American sociology were European émigrés, and several were also Jewish exiles from Nazi Germany. As Europe descended into chaos in the 1930s and 1940s, sociology and social theory—like many other academic subjects—found a flourishing home in the USA. The relative prosperity and stability of American society in the 1940s and 1950s suggested that America's political and economic system represented a model for the global study of processes of social modernization. It was in the USA that many of the canonical concepts of scientific sociology came to be defined. These concepts had been mooted by nineteenth-century European writers, but not always in systematic ways. They included the concepts of social 'evolution' and 'organization', social *'differentiation', *'integration' and 'adaptation', 'structure', 'action' and *'interaction', as well as *'stratification', power, democratization, and the 'mass society'. These concepts received intense analytical discussions in the USA in academic journals such as the *American Journal of Sociology* and the *American Sociological Review*, as well as at conferences and subsection committees of the American Sociological Association (founded in 1905) and the International Sociological Association (founded in 1949).

All the leading figures of this generation wanted to discard what they perceived as the ideological dogmas of nineteenth-century European thought. Norbert *Elias, for example, who emigrated to Britain, devoted his life's work to showing how the concept of 'civilization', or the *'civilizing process', had validity as a technical sociological concept only when it was rigorously distinguished from notions of cultural superiority (Elias 1939).

It is, however, fair to say that not all mid-twentieth-century social theorists overcame the Eurocentric and Western-centred prejudices of earlier generations of social thought. Many tended to take it as a matter of course that 'modern society' found its clearest and most paradigmatic form in the specific course of industrial development undertaken by European and North American society. Other world regions were often assumed to be still traditional or not-yet-modern societies. Furthermore, it was believed that insofar as other regions of the world became modern, they would necessarily take on the same features as those manifested in the history of the West. In the influential words of Max Weber, penned in 1920 and first translated into English by Talcott Parsons in 1930:

A product of modern European civilization studying the problem of universal history is bound to ask himself, and rightly so, to what combination of circumstances the fact should be attributed that in Western civilization, and in Western civilization only, cultural phenomena have appeared which (as we like to think) lie on a line of development having *universal* significance and validity. (Weber 1920c: 13)

These words of Weber should be treated with some care. Weber himself did not believe that other regions of the world either should or would necessarily develop in the same way as the West. He was fascinated by the sociologically relative position of the West in world history, devoting a significant part of his work to comparing intrinsic differences between the West and other civilizations of the world, including notably the ancient civilizations of

India and China. But in his concern with non-Western civilizations, Weber was to some extent exceptional among the canonical sociological theorists of the early twentieth century. By the time of the emergence of American modernization theory in the 1950s in the *structural-functionalist school developed by Talcott Parsons, the possibility that other cultures beside the European-North American bloc might represent alternative instances of modernity and modernizing processes was not seriously considered.

The assumption that only one basic paradigm of modernity exists, that this paradigm is represented by Europe and North America, and that all other societies of the world can and must reproduce this paradigm insofar as they become modern at all, has been challenged in recent decades by new generations of scholars concerned with problems of *ethnocentrism* in social theory and research. Since the withdrawal of the European powers from their former colonies in the 1950s and 1960s and the rise of increasingly multicultural societies, new sensitivities have arisen toward the relevance of different sociological explanations for different regions of the world. Sociologists have shown how different cultures and civilizations can be modern in different ways, at different times, and in different combinations of the features invoked by classical social thought. It need not follow that largely agrarian societies—such as large parts of India, Asia, and Africa—fall squarely outside the framework of modernity, or that the only respect in which they might enter processes of modernization is by undergoing industrialization processes on the model of nineteenth- and twentieth-century Europe and North America. There are many ways in which societies become modern, and some of these may share features in common with Europe, while others may not. There are no fixed certainties in theories of social change, and there is no unilinear course through which all societies need pass in order to become modern. To borrow a phrase developed in recent years by the Israeli historical sociologist S. N. *Eisenstadt, there can be multiple trajectories of modernization, or 'multiple modernities' (Eisenstadt 2002).

From the side of *postcolonial, or anti-colonial, interventions in dominant Western discourses about modernity and rationality, two significant writers have been the Algerian writer Frantz *Fanon and the Palestinian writer Edward *Said. Their works are discussed in Box 2.

The darker sides of Enlightenment

We turn now finally to the second question about darker sides to the idea of *Enlightenment. This issue is also relevant to the question of the nature of Western modernity and Western rationalism. The men of the eighteenth-century European Enlightenment believed confidently not only that their theories were true but also that their theories would be beneficial for social life when put into practice. Many of them believed that enlightened exploration and exploitation of the laws of nature and of the laws of society would naturally increase the sum of human happiness. In their view, the application of reason and science to society necessarily meant progress.

Today, from the standpoint of the end of the most violent century in human history, it is possible to give only limited endorsement to such assumptions. On the one hand, there are certainly *some* principles we can and should endorse. We cannot turn our back on the philosophy of the Enlightenment when we think of developments in medicine and of some technical inventions that facilitate human purposes by reducing dependency on

---

BOX 2. POSTCOLONIAL CRITICISM AND 'ORIENTALISM': FRANTZ FANON AND EDWARD SAID

A new area of intellectual partisanship in recent decades has been what is loosely termed *'postcolonial studies'. Postcolonial criticism has influenced many aspects of contemporary historical, literary, social, and cultural studies. It has arisen partly as a consequence of ongoing ethnic diversification in both Western and non-Western societies after European decolonalization and increasing globalization in world affairs. Two influential postcolonial theorists have been Frantz *Fanon and Edward *Said.

Frantz Fanon was active in the 1950s as a black Algerian writer in the war of independence for his country against French occupation. In *Wretched of the Earth* (1961) Fanon wrote of the effects of colonization and racism on the material welfare and the psychological health and mental outlook of African people. In this work, Fanon demonstrates the oppressiveness of colonialism not only in terms of its control over territory but also in its hold over indigenous African contexts of self-expression. Fanon shows how Western societies have enjoyed *hegemony not only in respect of political and economic political power but also in respect of a monopoly on dominant theories, languages, and discourses of social thought. Fanon shows the importance of resistance to imperialism as much at the level of globally influential *theories* and *discourses* as at the level of the real institutions that come to be erected in the image of these theories and discourses.

The Palestinian writer Edward Said develops a similar position in his influential book *Orientalism* (1978), a study of the impact of Western ideas about the 'Orient', the 'non-West', and the 'Third World'. Said here analyses the carving up of the Middle East by British and French imperial authorities in the nineteenth and early twentieth centuries and the role of racist European theories about Arabian desert peoples. Drawing on elements of Michel *Foucault's analysis of discourse and power (Foucault 1975), Said shows how the West's intellectual cartography of the 'Orient' has shaped and constrained the ways of life of Arab and Muslim peoples in direct institutional ways. Said shows how *Orientalism is a Western theoretical construct that literally maps out the course of modern Arab and Muslim history with oppressive effect.

---

physically exhausting manual labour. We also cannot forget that our modern idea of a rationally organized state, guaranteeing universal education, health care, and social security for the elderly, the infirm, the young, and those in the process of seeking work, owes its inception to the ideas of the Enlightenment. A fundamental principle of modern criminal and civil justice systems is that the function of laws of state is not to wreak vengeance on guilty parties but to reprimand and reform them and to compensate the victims or injured parties. This too we owe to the social philosophers of the eighteenth century. Likewise, all modern ideas of 'civil rights' and 'human rights' derive entirely from the eighteenth-century Enlightenment. In all these respects, the idea of the value of applying enlightened scientific enquiry to political and socio-economic organization is not something we can lightly dismiss. It is the linchpin, the governing presupposition, of our modern civilization.

On the other hand, many sinister consequences of this confidence in reason and science have become evident to us over the past century. Today we realize that technological inventions are not *emancipatory for human beings in every respect or in any unequivocal sense. Western medicine has been beneficial for society in many respects but not in every respect. The commercial application of biochemical science to agriculture and industry has not alleviated hunger, malnutrition, and ill health in any unambiguously positive way. Neither the welfare state nor the 'free market' has been a beneficial agency of human well-being in all regards. Hospitals, clinics, prisons, and schools have not in every respect furthered security, health, education, and knowledge for society. In some respects these institutions have served functions of control, discipline, regimentation, and surveillance in modern societies. Projects to realize *utilitarian ideals of the 'greatest happiness of the greatest number' have frequently endangered rather than safeguarded values of freedom of thought, enquiry, belief, expression, and creativity in modern social history.

As will become clear in later chapters of this book, numerous modern social theorists have heavily criticized the more optimistic assumptions of eighteenth- and nineteenth-century social thought. Many writers point to ways in which ideas that appear rational can also be deeply irrational. Many emphasize that what is healthy and normal from one point of view can also be deeply pathological from another point of view. Many writers demonstrate that science does not *necessarily* contribute to the increase of human happiness and is not *necessarily* superior to myth or religion as a system of understanding.

One of the most horrific cases of the uncritical social acceptance of science and technology that has been of repeated interest to twentieth-century social theorists and philosophers is the invention and use of the nuclear bomb. Today the possibility of human genetic cloning may represent a new case of defective moral public restraint of the uses of science and technology. Both these cases represent deeply problematic instances of the application of natural-science knowledge to social and political life. But social theorists have also been interested in numerous misuses and misapplications specifically of *social*-science knowledge to social and political life. Critics have pointed to the ways in which governments and states pursuing policies derived directly from disciplines such as economics, psychology, management studies, and business studies can sometimes be responsible for dehumanizing or *technocratic* cultures of governance in society. When governments and states exploit social-science knowledge for policies oriented overwhelmingly to objectives of *efficiency, productivity, orderliness*, and *systematicity*—at the expense of open moral and political public debate—there is a danger that social members become treated as pure objects of administration. There is a danger that social citizens become treated like patients of a social-scientific experiment in 'social engineering', to be controlled in mass numbers. Later chapters of this book will discuss the development of such critiques of science, modernity, and governance in the work of Max Weber (Chapter 3), in *Western Marxism (Chapter 7), in the ideas of Sigmund *Freud (Chapter 8), in the work of Michel *Foucault (Chapter 9), in feminist social theory (Chapter 11), in *postmodernism (Chapters 12 and 13), and several other contexts.

For many social theorists, one of most dreadful instances of the unrestrained application of scientific rationalizing principles to social organization is the rise of *totalitarianism in Europe in the 1930s, and in particular in the Nazi Holocaust of the Jews. This case is discussed briefly in Box 3, with reference to the work of Hannah *Arendt and Zygmunt *Bauman.

BOX 3. HANNAH ARENDT AND ZYGMUNT BAUMAN ON TOTALITARIANISM AND THE HOLOCAUST

The Holocaust has preoccupied numerous social theorists not only for the Nazis' barbaric use of chemical technology—lethal gas as a method of mass extermination. It has also concerned social theorists for the Nazis' use of planned, calculated, and scientific methods of controlling and organizing social agents. For many critics, the Holocaust is a terrible case of the misuse of both natural science *and* social science—specifically of social science perverted into the science of *mastery over people*. Two notable theorists in this regard have been Hannah *Arendt and Zygmunt *Bauman.

In her report on the trial of Adolf Eichmann, secretary of the planning commission for the Final Solution, published as *Eichmann in Jerusalem* in 1963, and also in her larger book *The Origins of Totalitarianism* of 1951, Arendt argues that the Holocaust was more than a purely contingent historical crime perpetrated in Germany in the 1940s against the Jewish people. Without diminishing the enormity and historical specificity of the Jewish people's suffering, Arendt argues that the Holocaust demonstrates a universal tendency towards barbarism latent in all modern mass societies. Her thesis is that when science and technology and rational techniques of planning and calculation are used for the sole and overwhelming purpose of gaining political and commercial control over mass numbers of people, society descends into barbarism. In her view, the two cardinal types of totalitarian regime represented by Hitler's fascism and Stalin's Soviet communism are only the most virulent examples of a tendency toward totalizing technical control over human beings latent in all modernity—including our own allegedly 'free' societies oriented to liberal democracy and market capitalism. Arendt argued that when violence is routinized, sanitized, and taken for granted in any society, the possibility of the perpetration of evil acts becomes *banal*. To the extent that Eichmann routinely followed orders and fulfilled the duties of his office, he behaved in principle no differently from any ordinary functionary of the modern state or of the modern business corporation. According to Arendt, Eichmann's shared personal responsibility for the Holocaust gives us a lesson in the 'banality of evil'.

Zygmunt Bauman's *Modernity and the Holocaust* (1989) develops Arendt's thesis in notable ways. Bauman argues that 'civilization' and the *'civilizing process' do not mean the removal of violence. They mean only the control of violence, its concentration in the hands of a sovereign power. In this sense, it was the Nazis' highly 'civilized' use of rational bureaucratic principles of organizational efficiency—their use of statistics and logistics, their codification of state law, their sanitization of public language, and, above all, their evacuation of all personal moral responsibility from the actions of individual holders of public offices—which brought about the Holocaust. Bauman writes: 'the Holocaust did not just, mysteriously, avoid clash with the social norms and institutions of modernity. It was these norms and institutions that made the Holocaust feasible. Without modern civilization and its most central essential achievements, there would be no Holocaust' (Bauman 1989: 87).

Conclusion

Modernity can be characterized as a distinctive kind of social attitude to time. Modern attitudes to time tend to involve processes of critical reflection on the past with a view to projects of collective determination of the future. Traditional attitudes tend to be marked by forms of acceptance and preservation of the past, without a developed belief in rational social agency over the future.

Real historical contexts give us examples of many different combinations of modern and traditional attitudes across cultures and civilizations. The particular concentration of modern attitudes and modernizing processes in European society from around the fifteenth century onwards has been very influential in the development of modern social theory. Many nineteenth- and many early twentieth-century social theorists regarded the European and North American experience of modernity as paradigmatic for all societies. This Western-centred assumption of classical social theory is difficult to sustain today because it ignores many different possible trajectories of modernizing experiences in different regions of the world.

However, once we bear in mind this limitation, it is possible, and important, to underline a few key features of the Western experience of modernity. These features include the rise of an international capitalist economy, which is bound up with processes of industrialization and urbanization and the rise of the nation-state. Also important to the Western experience are ideas of democracy and representative government, together with the rise of science and technology. With the declining political power of religious institutions come processes of secularization and scepticism toward myth and traditional authority.

In the classical terms of Ferdinand Tönnies, modernizing processes tend to demonstrate a preponderance of 'societal relations' of impersonal instrumental exchange over 'communal relations' of personal localized interaction. Unlike most agrarian and tribal social forms, modernizing societies are typically extensively differentiated in their systems of political and economic organization.

Eighteenth- and nineteenth-century European social writers frequently saw these kinds of developments in an unambiguously positive light. Although some writers, such as Tocqueville, took a more sceptical and nuanced view, others, such as Comte and Spencer, equated reason and science unequivocally with progress. Today we are less inclined to be optimistic. Today we recognize that reason, science and enlightenment are all two-sided affairs. As constructs of the mind and constructs of society, science, and enlightenment are implicated in some of the worst excesses of the modern world, including fascism, totalitarianism, and capitalistic industrial exploitation of the earth. But we should also recognize that reason, science, and the pursuit of enlightenment remain indispensable to the conduct of our lives. To think critically and responsibly about reason and science is itself to think reasonably and scientifically. Therefore it is advisable not simply to think of the follies of modernity as consequences of the use of reason. It is more appropriate to think of them as consequences of the *neglect* of reason, as consequences of a certain forgetting of the *moral intelligence of reason*. As will become clear in the remaining chapters of this book, this is an insight of cardinal importance to many of the leading themes and debates of modern social theory.

■ QUESTIONS FOR CHAPTER 1

1 What is a 'modern' attitude to life? What is a 'traditional' attitude to life? Are there any 'modern' forms of life that can at the same time be described as 'traditional'?

2 What features of social-historical change best characterize the Western experience of modernity? In what sense is it appropriate to speak of 'the West'? Are there any experiences of modernity which are not Western?

3 How informative is Ferdinand Tönnies's characterization of modernity in terms of the replacement of 'communal relations' by 'societal relations'?

4 What are some of the strengths and weaknesses of eighteenth- and nineteenth-century European social thought for discussion today?

5 What is meant by 'the Enlightenment'? Is the Enlightenment a legacy for which we should be thankful?

6 Is it possible to speak of reason and progress in history? Is it possible *not* to speak of reason and progress in history?

■ FURTHER READING

For some good overviews of the makings of nineteenth-century and early twentieth-century European social thought, the following titles can be recommended: Stuart Hughes's *Consciousness and Society: The Re-orientation of European Social Thought* (Knopf, 1958), Geoffrey Hawthorn's *Enlightenment and Despair: The Making of Sociology* (Cambridge University Press, 1976), Donald Levine's *Visions of the Sociological Tradition* (University of Chicago Press, 1995), Wolf Lepenies's *Between Literature and Science: The Rise of Sociology* (Cambridge University Press, 1988), Johan Heilbron's *The Rise of Social Theory* (University of Minnesota Press, 1995), Steven Seidman's *Liberalism and the Origins of European Social Theory* (Blackwell, 1983), John Burrow's *The Crisis of Reason: European Thought 1848–1914* (Yale University Press, 2000), and Raymond Aron's *Main Currents in Sociological Thought* (Penguin, 1965; 1968) (in two volumes).

An accessible encyclopedic introduction to European history and civilization is Norman Davies's *Europe: A History* (Oxford University Press, 1996). For an introduction to the culture of the European Renaissance, try Peter Burke's *The European Renaissance: Centres and Peripheries* (Blackwell, 1998). For surveys of the eighteenth-century Enlightenment, a good reference source is Alan C. Kors's *Encyclopaedia of the Enlightenment* (Oxford University Press, 2002). For more in-depth discussion of debates about the rise of the West and the emergence of capitalism, industrialization, and the nation-state, see Chapter 6 of this book by Dennis Smith. See also the titles cited in the further reading for Chapter 6. For Max Weber's views on the rise of the West, see Chapter 3 of this book by Gianfranco Poggi, and also Wolfgang Schluchter's *The Rise of Occidental Rationalism* (University of California Press, 1981).

The further debates mentioned in this chapter about modernity, science, myth, civilization, technocracy, rationality, and irrationality are developed at length in this book in Chapter 7 by Douglas Kellner (on Western Marxism), in Chapter 8 by Anthony Elliott (on psychoanalysis), in Chapter 9 by Samantha Ashenden (on structuralism and post-structuralism), in Chapter 11 by Lisa Adkins (on feminist theory), in Chapter 12 by Barry Smart (on postmodernism), and in Chapter 13 by Gerard Delanty (on modernity after postmodernism).

For an introduction to the work of Hannah Arendt, see Phillip Hansen's *Hannah Arendt* (Polity Press, 1993). For a collection of extracts from Arendt's writings, try *The Portable Hannah Arendt*, ed. Peter Baehr (Penguin, 2000). For an introduction to postcolonial studies, see Robert J. C. Young's *Postcolonialism: An Historical Introduction* (Blackwell, 2001). See also Henry Schwartz and Sangeeta Ray (eds.), *A Companion to Postcolonial Studies* (Blackwell, 2000), and Henry Louis Gates and Kwame Anthony Appiah's *Dictionary of Global Culture* (Penguin, 1998).

■ **WEBSITES**

SocioSite at **www2.fmg.uva.nl/sociosite/index.html** Contains links to numerous sociology-related sites.

A Sociological Tour Through Cyberspace at **www.trinity.edu/~mkearl/index.html** Displays links to areas of sociology, with a section on theorists.

Virtual Library of Sociology, at **http://socserv2.mcmaster.ca/w3virtsoclib/** Provides a search engine with a useful theory section devoted to key thinkers.

Modernity at **http://en.wikipedia.org/wiki/Modernity** Offers a comprehensive overview of the concept of modernity with links to related terms and historical events.

The European Enlightenment at **www.wsu.edu/~dee/ENLIGHT** Displays useful accounts of the culture of the Enlightenment.

2 Classical Social Theory, II: Karl Marx and Émile Durkheim

Antonino Palumbo and Alan Scott

Karl *Marx and Émile *Durkheim differ profoundly in their views about society. Durkheim was 24 on Marx's death in 1883 and rarely refers explicitly to the earlier thinker. Marx, for his part, did not subscribe to Durkheim's later nineteenth-century vision of a liberal impartial study of society, and on the few occasions where he used August *Comte's term 'sociology', which had limited currency in the mid- to late nineteenth century, it was to pour scorn on the pretensions of a bourgeois science of society. Yet despite these profound differences of outlook, Marx and Durkheim were both centrally concerned with the emergence of modern capitalism, and in particular with the rise of the modern system of the *division of labour and the evolution of a market society. Both approach these developments by focusing on the effects that the spread of market relations had on *solidarity and on society's ability to reproduce itself. Both therefore had to engage with the causes and implications of key developments—the Industrial Revolution in particular—as well as key events such as the French Revolution. Both sought to revise the simplistic and apologetic accounts of capitalist society commonly found in nineteenth-century social thought. Where they differ most strikingly is in the conclusions—the lessons—they draw from their intellectual engagement with modernity.

This chapter provides an overview of the main intellectual projects of Marx and Durkheim, treating each thinker in turn. We consider how both Marx and Durkheim produce accounts of the nature of the modern division of labour and the nature of the state and *civil society that in some respects are comparable and in other respects radically divergent. We begin with Marx.

Karl Marx: historical materialism and the critique of idealist philosophy

Karl Marx was born in Trier in Germany into a middle-class Jewish family, his father having converted to Protestantism to protect his position as a lawyer. Marx studied law, philosophy, and history at the universities of Bonn and Berlin, where he became one of the 'Young Hegelians', a movement of left-leaning followers of the philosopher G. W. F. Hegel. His radicalism having barred him from an academic career, Marx turned to journalism in 1842 when he became editor of the liberal newspaper the *Rheinische Zeitung*. The Prussian authorities soon forced the paper to close, and in the following year Marx emigrated to Paris where he became involved in the radical politics of German émigrés and French socialists. There he met Friedrich *Engels, the son of a German industrialist with textile manufacturing interests in Manchester.

In 1844 Marx worked on his *Economics and Philosophical Manuscripts* which developed a philosophical critique of capitalism. In the same year he and Engels moved to Brussels on their expulsion from France. In this period Marx published *The German Ideology*, co-written with Engels. Marx and Engels's *The Communist Manifesto*, which announced the appearance of a 'spectre' of communism that would haunt Europe, appeared in 1848, the year of revolutions throughout continental Europe. In that year Marx was able to return to Germany in order to found the radical *Neue Rheinische Zeitung* in Cologne, but this too was suppressed, forcing Marx to emigrate to London where he was to spend the rest of his life.

In Britain, Marx and Engels continued to involve themselves in the politics of the Communist League with the aim of convincing the communist movement to adopt their scientific approach. It was in London that Marx devoted himself to historical and economic research, famously in the British Library. His mature works are marked by a shift away from the philosophical influences of his youth—of which he had already been critical—towards economic theories. His attention focused increasingly on Scottish and English political economy, notably the theories of Adam *Smith and David *Ricardo. It was his engagement with political economy that was to mark the highpoint of his thought and enable him to develop a general theory of capitalism. The 1850s and 1860s saw the publication of the key works of Marx's economic theory, including the much delayed publication of volume 1 of *Capital* (*Das Kapital*) in 1867. Marx's health declined in the 1870s and it was only after his death in 1883 that the second and third volumes of *Capital* appeared, edited by Engels.

The first important event in the development of Marx's thinking is his engagement with German idealist philosophy. It is with this that we begin.

Marx, Hegel, and Feuerbach

Marx's thinking developed at first in response to the *idealist philosophy of G. W. F. *Hegel, and especially the version subscribed to by the Young Hegelians. Hegel had viewed the course of history as a process in which the human species obtains ever-increasing knowledge of itself. Hegel had held that history developed through 'contradictions' between ideas of reason and given realities. These contradictions necessarily resolved themselves by a process of rational development which he called *dialectic*. This logical progression or dialectic had as its goal a condition of freedom and 'absolute knowledge', consisting in the reconciliation of mind and matter, or of 'spirit' and 'nature', or of 'subject' and 'object'. History moved logically from stages of 'thesis' to stages of 'antithesis' and then to stages of 'synthesis'. In his own time, Hegel saw the modern state as the highest expression of community, and he saw Christianity as the highest religion.

In contrast to Hegel, Marx adopted a stridently *materialist* view of history. Marx insisted that all mental or spiritual life is fundamentally dependent on, and reflective of, the search of the human species for material survival. In the later development of Marxist thinking, this came to be known as Marx's *historical materialism*. It was for this reason that Marx initially turned to the philosopher Ludwig *Feuerbach, who had also criticized Hegel in favour of a radical materialism. Feuerbach summed up his philosophy in a now famous, if rather facile, pun: '*Man ist, was er isst*': 'one is what one eats'. Feuerbach saw religion as a projection of human qualities onto the infinite. Religion was a symptom of man's alienated state. Man was not the creation of God; God was the creation of man. Traditional religion had presented the world upside down in an illusory, inverted image.

Thus armed, Marx was to mount scathing attacks on central Hegelian themes and other ideas in the history of philosophy. According to Marx, religion, the state, and bourgeois society were not to be seen as the embodiment of Hegel's idea of reason. Rather, they were to be seen as *ideological reflexes of society's material structure. History was not an account of the long march of reason in human affairs. It was a chronicle of the ongoing struggle of exploiters and exploited, of the ruling classes and the subjugated classes. In his *Economic and Philosophic Manuscripts* of 1844 Marx argued that capitalism destroys what Feuerbach had called the *'species-being' of humanity. Capitalism degrades the essentially *social* nature of human beings into a merely selfish, egoistic nature. From Hegel and Feuerbach, Marx quickly moved to a wholesale critique of philosophy as a potential instrument of social change and emancipation. In his 'Theses on Feuerbach' of 1845, he famously stated that 'philosophers have only *interpreted* the world in various ways; the point is to *change* it' (1845: 423).

Yet despite his antagonistic relation to Hegel, Marx was to remain deeply indebted to German idealist philosophy. From Hegel, Marx retained a *teleological conception of history in which historical facts are connected to each other in a scheme driven by an ultimate goal or 'telos'. Marx's thinking consistently embodied Hegel's conception of a dialectic in which social change is seen as the outcome of attempts to solve inherent contradictions between opposing historical forces. Similarly, Marx also incorporated important elements of the philosophy of Hegel's main intellectual predecessor, Immanuel *Kant. When Marx insisted that science is the work of *critique*, he borrowed the concept of 'critique' from Kant. 'Critique' for Kant had meant examination of the 'conditions of the possibility of experience'. In Marx's view these 'conditions of the possibility of experience' were not only logical or intellectual; they were also *material* and *social*.

We now consider how Marx elaborates these ideas in the context of economic theory and the critique of capitalism.

Political economy and the critique of capitalism

Marx's thinking about economics develops as an attempt to undermine the assumption that market society is the spontaneous outcome of natural human tendencies to produce and exchange. That assumption found a famous theoretical elaboration in the early pages of Adam Smith's *The Wealth of Nations* (1776). According to *Smith, the *division of labour is the unintended consequence of multiple individual actions, each of which is driven by self-seeking natural drives. It is the market's 'invisible hand' that ensures that the public good is secured at the same time that each individual pursues his or her own private interests. In the market society, public and private interests coincide with one another.

Marx's lifelong objective was to refute what he saw as this simplistic and apologetic narrative of capitalism. To this end, he advanced an account of social change that rejected what he saw as the naive *individualism underlying classical economic theory, or 'political economy'.

Marx saw himself as uncovering the scientific laws underpinning the capitalist bourgeois society of his time. Those laws were to be arrived at through the application of a general theory of social change, based on the idea of a sequence of transitions from different *modes of production* through history. The three most significant modes of production in Marx's theory of history were:

- *feudalism*, based on relations of bondage between owners of land and landless serfs or peasants;
- *capitalism*, based on relations of exploitation between owners of property and propertyless workers; and

- *communism*, based ultimately on a classless society marked by abolition of private property and a withering away of the state.

Marx described social change as a succession of 'stages of development' each of which is part of a well-defined sequence or pattern. Each of these modes of production consists in a configuration of *forces of production*, comprising technology, and raw materials, and *relations of production*, encompassing forms of social organization of labour based on laws of ownership. In a key passage in his 1859 'Preface to the Critique of Political Economy', Marx describes these forces and relations of production as making up the economic *'base' of society. On top of this 'base' arises a 'superstructure', consisting of political institutions encompassing the monarchy, Church, and state and cultural ideas based on received customs and values, including religion, art, and philosophy. In the later development of Marxist thought, especially among the more reductive and dogmatic popularizers of Marx, which also included Engels, this 'superstructure' is said to have the function of *ideologically *legitimizing* the existing economic 'base' of society. It is said to be little more than a reflection of the material interests of the dominant class in society (for further discussion, see Chapter 7 of this book, pp. 155–6). In Marx's original words:

In the social production of their life, men inevitably enter into definite relations that are indispensable and independent of their will, relations of production that correspond to a definite stage in the development of their material productive forces. The sum of these relations of production constitutes the economic structure of society, the real foundation, on which arises a legal and political superstructure and to which correspond definite forms of social consciousness. The mode of production of material life conditions the social, political and intellectual life process in general. It is not the consciousness of men that determines their being, but, on the contrary, their social being that determines their consciousness. (Marx 1859: 389)

Marx believed that the inherently exploitative nature of capitalism and its inevitable self-destruction could be demonstrated from within the standpoint of political economy itself. His refutation of political economy and his more general critique of received social thought were to crystallize around six key themes:

- the transition from *feudalism to capitalism;
- use value, exchange value, and the commodity form;
- labour, exploitation, and *commodity fetishism;
- capitalist expansion and self-destruction;
- the role of the state, *civil society, and religion;
- private property, reform, and revolution.

We look at these six key elements of Marx's analysis in turn.

Feudalism and capitalism

Marx maintains that the individual producer depicted by political economy is the product of a market society, not its starting point. All notion of the isolated individual in political economy is incoherent: 'the human being is . . . an animal which can individuate itself only in the midst of society. Production by an isolated individual outside society . . . is as much of an absurdity as is the development of language without individuals living together and talking to each other' (1858: 84). Marx's idea of the essentially social and historical nature of man leads him to connect individual action to the role it plays in given systems of production and the class division it engenders and reproduces. He takes similar steps in relation to the central categories of political economy: labour, production, exchange, market, money, and ownership.

Marx argues that the social nature of labour, production, and exchange means that individuals face historically given productive forces as an external objective reality. No change can occur in this objective reality except through the dissolution of the system of social relations that underpins a historically given mode of production. In this connection, Marx points out that the genesis of the capitalist system of production is to be found in the disintegration of *feudalism and of the system of social relations supporting it:

> The historical movement which changes the producers into wage-labourers, appears, on the one hand, as their emancipation from serfdom and from the fetters of the guilds . . . On the other hand, these new freemen became sellers of themselves only after they had been robbed of all their own means of production, and of all the guarantees of existence afforded by the old feudal arrangements. (1867: 875)

The developments that made the rise of capitalism possible were acts of confiscation of church land and property by the state, enclosure of common lands into private estates, dismantling of the medieval system of *guild occupations, and systematic destruction of traditional customs and relations of authority. These changes had the effect of creating a new system in which members of the exploited class in society are left with virtually no direct access to the means necessary to ensure their material well-being, or to what Marx called the 'means of production'. Where peasants in the feudal system had access to land by which to feed themselves, the new type of worker under capitalism possesses only a sum of money, a wage. *Exploitation based upon principles of personal subjugation and obligation has been replaced by the seeming objectivity of the labour contract and by the 'cash nexus'.

Marx thus sought to show that class relations are inherently conflictual and that the capitalist mode of production rested on the systemic exploitation of one class by another class—the proletariat by the bourgeoisie. This explanatory framework was then used to unmask the ideological nature of bourgeois social, legal, and political arrangements. Marx's hope was that theory would contribute to the development of a revolutionary political movement that would, eventually, abolish class divisions and *emancipate the individual.

Use value, exchange value, and the commodity form

Capitalism for Marx is that mode of production which uniquely combines private owner-ship of the means of production with commodity production and the profit principle in a competitive, dynamic, and expanding market. In this definition, Marx follows the English political economist David *Ricardo in distinguishing between an object's *use value* and its *exchange value*. Where the use value of an object or substance lies in its suitability for a particular practical purpose, the exchange value of an object lies in the value acquired by this object as an article of trade—which can be seen as the object's price (although Marx does not see exchange value as technically the same as price). *Commodities* are items that are produced with the sole purpose of being sold. They are produced exclusively for their exchange value, for the market, and for profit.

Marx argues that while commodity production existed in pre-capitalist societies, capitalism is unique because commodity production becomes the dominant organizing principle for all of society's productive activities. All production becomes production for the market. Under capitalism, commodity production becomes a circular process in which value is realized in the market as profit and reinvested into production. In this sense, capitalism must be sharply distinguished from hoarding and piracy. Under capitalism, the embodiment of equivalent values in the medium of *money* becomes crucial to this expanding cycle. The past and future development of capitalism for Marx is synonymous with the extension of the commodification of goods and services and the absorption of more and more productive activity into the money economy. Forms of production and exchange that exist outside the money economy such as barter are gradually displaced by market relations. Capitalism tends toward a condition in which all production becomes commodity production and money becomes the sole medium of transaction.

Labour, exploitation, and commodity fetishism

An important corollary of this account of commodity production is what Marx defines as the 'labour theory of value'. In marked opposition to Ricardo and classical political economy, Marx proposes that the fundamental source of all value is *human labour*. Human labour has the unique capacity to generate more value than it expends in reproducing itself. On the one hand, Marx speaks of the labour value that is expended in any act of production: this is the value that is necessary for labour power to reproduce itself—i.e. the quantity of energy that a worker expends each day which must be replaced through food and rest in order that the worker be able to work again on the next day. On the other hand, Marx speaks of 'surplus value': this is the value that is added by labour beyond that which is expended in the act of production—i.e. the extra value that inheres in the object the worker has produced. Marx points out that the profit that the capitalist realizes when the product is brought to market ultimately depends on the ratio of this 'surplus' to 'necessary' labour power. This ratio can be increased in a number of ways, either simply through suppressing or cutting wages or through substitution of machines for humans. Crucially, Marx argues that labour power under capitalism becomes itself a commodity like any other. Labour power under capitalism becomes something to be bought and sold on the market at a given price. Therefore, Marx characterizes capitalism as a system of exploitation in which surplus value is extracted from wage labour and in which the commodity form comes to dominate over the life of the worker. Workers are exploited for their capacity to produce commodities and to generate surplus value, and their labour power is itself turned into a commodity. Thus the commodity form comes to exercise an external compulsion over the human subject. In early works, Marx describes this process in terms of *alienation*. Marx's conception of alienation is discussed in Box 4.

Marx argues that under conditions of exploitation and alienation, social life is experienced as a world dominated by the exchange of *things* in the medium of money. Money in Marx's phrase is 'an objectified relation between persons' (1858: 160). Under the rule of money, 'the social character of activity . . . appears as something alien and objective, confronting the individuals, not as their relation to one another, but as their subordination to relations which subsist independently of them . . . The social connection between

---

BOX 4. KARL MARX'S CONCEPT OF ALIENATION

Marx describes 'alienation' (*Entfremdung* in German) as a social-psychological condition based on estrangement of individuals from their natural and social environments. The term is derived from Hegel, who employed it to describe a process of inwardness in the self. For both Hegel and Marx, individuals are alienated or estranged from their world when they experience this world as something that has become 'externalized' (*entäußert*) or 'objectified' (*vergegenständlicht*) or *'reified' (*verdinglicht*). Where Hegel thought that a certain process of externalization was necessary for the constitution of the self, as a dialectic of 'subject and object', Marx argued that under capitalism individuals cannot 'reappropriate' this externalized aspect of themselves. The essence of their sense of self, which consists in their sociability and communality, has been removed from them. In the *Economic and Philosophical Manuscripts of 1844* Marx writes that

estrangement appears not only in the fact that the means of *my* life belong to *another* and that *my* desire is the inaccessible possession of *another*, but also in the fact that all things are other than themselves, that my activity is *other* than itself, and that finally—and this goes for capitalists too—an inhuman power rules over everything. (1844*b*: 366)

In particular, Marx distinguishes four main types of alienation:

- alienation from the *product of labour*: 'The worker places his life in the object; but now it no longer belongs to him, but to the object' (1844*b*: 324);
- alienation from *labour*: 'His labour is . . . not voluntary, but forced; it is forced labour' (1844*b*: 326);
- alienation from *oneself*: 'Estranged labour . . . tears away from him [the worker] his species-life, his true species-objectivity' (1844*b*: 329); and
- alienation from *other people*: 'Each man . . . regards the other in accordance with the standard and the situation in which he as a worker finds himself' (1844*b*: 330).

  Marx's conception of alienation has exercised a profound influence in modern social theory. It has found many echoes in the neo-Hegelian thinking of figures such as György *Lukács and Ernst *Bloch and the *existentialist Marxism of Jean-Paul *Sartre. To a certain extent, it can also be compared with Max *Weber's and Georg *Simmel's writing on the 'iron cage' of modern capitalism, bureaucracy, industry, and technology.

---

persons is transformed into a social relation between things' (1858: 157). In volume 1 of *Capital*, Marx refers to this transformation of relations between persons into relations between things as *'commodity fetishism'. In a society that comes to fetishize the objects of its production as objects of consumption, the workings of human *agency are mystified and *'reified'. It is this pseudo-objectivity that gives capitalism its opaque quality and makes it seem incapable of abolition or transformation.

Capitalist expansion and self-destruction

Marx argues that the drive for efficiency in capitalism is reinforced by the fact that capitalism is a competitive system, which means that it has an inbuilt dynamism. Capitalism must constantly revolutionize the 'forces of production', and failure to modernize will be punished by the market's competitive mechanisms. The individual capitalist is faced with a simple alternative: either growth and change or bankruptcy. Capitalists must therefore look constantly for new markets and cheaper and more efficient sources of labour, and new means of reducing labour costs. 'Modern industry never views or treats the existing form of a production process as the definitive one,' Marx writes (1867: 617). Capitalism remains in a constant state of flux. Modern capitalist societies generate change, innovation, and development as their very mode of social reproduction. Once the energies of modern industrial capitalism have been unleashed, vigorous development of the means of production and destruction of the old and creation of the new all constantly transform bourgeois society. In *The Communist Manifesto* Marx and Engels declare:

Constant revolutionizing of production, uninterrupted disturbance of all social conditions, ever-lasting uncertainty and agitation distinguish the bourgeois epoch from all earlier ones. All fixed, fast-frozen relations, with their train of ancient and venerable prejudices and opinions, are swept away, all new-formed ones become antiquated before they can ossify. All that is solid melts into air, all that is holy is profaned, and man is at last compelled to face with sober senses his real conditions of life, and his relations with his kind. (1848: 83)

At the earliest stage of its development, capitalism is characterized by the workshop: it brings together workers in the factory where specialization of skills and tasks can then develop. Large-scale industry and the development of machine-led manufacturing are an the realization of an inner logic that has driven it from the start. But this internal dynamic, what Marx calls 'the immanent law of capitalistic production' (1867: 929), will also be responsible for a spiralling cycle of crises of overproduction, amidst the generalized pauperization of the working class. Due to constant devaluations in the wages paid by capitalists to their exploited workforces, the great mass of the population will no longer be able to afford the very products that they themselves have produced. By this point, capitalism will have created the conditions for its self-destruction and for the revolutionary advent of a classless communist society. Capitalism will have dug its own grave by a 'dialectical contradiction' internal to the very principles of its working.

The critique of political liberalism

We have now considered most of the essential components of Marx's contributions to economic theory and the idea of historical materialism as a philosophy of history. At this point, it is appropriate to move to the more specifically political aspects of Max's thought which concern his conception of the role of the state and *civil society under capitalism and their relationship to reform, revolution, and religion. These sides of Marx's thought are important because here we find a less *deterministic Marx. We find a thinker who emphasizes the role of class struggle and the interplay between objective and subjective dimensions of class consciousness.

The state, civil society, and religion

One of the most systematic statements of Marx's views on the state and civil society under capitalism is to be found in his early essay from 1843, *On the Jewish Question*. Here Marx considers the demand of the Jews for political emancipation, i.e. for full civil rights. Marx considers what civil political *emancipation might mean in practice in a capitalist society. He argues that the question of Jewish emancipation can only be resolved by being subsumed under the question of real human emancipation, which must be more than merely political emancipation, defined as acquisition of formal rights. He points out that political emancipation for the Jews—or for any other oppressed religious community—means practically not *their* emancipation at all but only the emancipation of the *state* from religion, only the separation of the state from the Church, involving a lifting of restrictions on qualification to positions of public office based on religion. This is not substantive emancipation, in the sense of liberation from structural economic causes of oppression and inequality. Political freedom here merely stands in for real human freedom as a weak substitute, serving to keep individuals in thrall to one of the instruments of their unfreedom.

Marx further argues that in the discourse of civil political emancipation, the state becomes a kind of secular church. He writes that

Where the political state has attained its full degree of development man leads a double life, a life in heaven and a life on earth, not only in his mind, in his consciousness, but in reality. He lives in the political community, where he regards himself as a communal being, and in civil society, where he is active as a private individual, regards other men as means and becomes the plaything of alien powers. (Marx 1843: 220)

In the bourgeois political state, individuals live out their desire for freedom and sociability, which in fact remain beyond earthly reach under the capitalist system. The secular state appears to be a sort of pathway to Heaven, but is just as illusory as the ideas of Heaven propagated by traditional religion.

Marx's more general thought about religion here epitomizes the militant side of enlightenment. Marx argues that by shedding light on the actual workings of *this* world, historical materialism will expose the illusion of a life beyond death. Marx maintains that since religion represents an 'ideological reflex' of actual economic relations, its critique represents the necessary precondition for the unmasking of all other ideological forms. In the short 'Contribution to the Critique of Hegel's Philosophy of Right', Marx famously refers to religion as the 'opium of the people' (1844a: 244). Like a misused drug, religion administers to true needs in false ways. Religion promises something that the system it serves has no ability ever to deliver. Religion is at once 'the expression of real suffering and a protest against real suffering'. It is 'the sigh of the oppressed creature, the heart of a heartless world, and the soul of soulless conditions':

The abolition of religion as the illusory happiness of the people is the demand for their real happiness. To call on them to give up their illusions about their condition is to call on them to give up a condition that requires illusions. The criticism of religion is therefore in embryo the criticism of that vale of tears of which religion is the halo. (1844a: 244)

Private property, reform, and revolution

Marx considers that the demand for political emancipation often takes the form of demand for the lifting of property qualifications on franchise. The state is expected to annul private property as a condition of political participation. Marx argues that this creates the illusion that the state is the opposite of private property, or that it is a means for the revocation of property in general. Political freedom here becomes merely freedom of private individuals from social constraints on their right 'to pursue their own interests in their own ways', in John Stuart *Mill's phrase. Political liberalism perpetuates a situation in which communal life is confined to an ideal political realm, while merely freeing private individuals to pursue their egotistic interests without thought of others as members of a community.

This leads Marx to a more general critique of the discourse of *rights*, of both civil rights and human rights. He comments that 'the so-called rights of man, as distinct from the rights of the citizen, are quite simply the rights of the members of civil society, i.e. of egotistic man, and man separated from other men and from the community' (1843: 229). Marx concludes that the 'practical application of the right of man to freedom is of man to private property' (1843: 229). In this picture, security or 'police' (*Polizei*) becomes 'the supreme concept of civil society', ensuring that 'society is only there to guarantee each of its members the conservation of his person, his right to property' (1843: 230). In *The Communist Manifesto* Marx goes so far as to describe the state as little more than a 'committee for managing the common affairs of the whole bourgeoisie' (Marx and Engels 1848: 82). In *The Eighteenth Brumaire of Louis Bonaparte* (1852) Marx observed the populist dictatorship of the French leader of the Second Empire, Napoleon III. He demonstrated how the imperial French state dedicated itself to the defence of the property interests of the French middle classes. Thus in Marx's view, the state remains intimately involved in the reproduction of property relations. It does not represent the general public interest but only the particular propertied interests of the ruling class. Marx argues that true human emancipation will occur only with the dissolution of the distinction between state and civil society and with it the rights of the private individual.

Marx also voices similar objections against all socialist movements whose goal is not the revolutionary overthrow of capitalism but merely its political reform. Marx sees revolutionary processes as having the function of making individuals aware of their condition as members of an exploited social class. This awareness entails a transition from what Marx calls the 'class-*in-itself*' to the 'class-*for-itself*', that is, to a class with a *consciousness* of itself as a class (Marx 1858: 177–8). This idea comes to the fore in *The German Ideology*, where he proclaims that,

Both for the production on a mass scale of this communist consciousness, and for the success of the cause itself, the alteration of men on a mass scale is necessary, an alteration which can only take place in a practical movement, a *revolution*; this revolution is necessary, therefore, not only because the ruling class cannot be overthrown in any other way, but also because the class overthrowing it can only in a revolution succeed in ridding itself of all the muck of ages and become fitted to found society anew. (Marx and Engels 1846: 94–5)

It is this revolutionary consciousness which assures the spontaneous harmony between individual and collective interest and makes the communist society 'an association in which the free development of each is the condition for the free development of all' (Marx and Engels 1848: 105).

We shall shortly return to some remarks about Marx's theory of society in comparison with the work of Émile Durkheim. It is to Durkheim's work that we now turn.

Émile Durkheim: sociology as an autonomous science

Émile *Durkheim was born in the Lorraine district of France to a Jewish family. In 1887 he acquired a post at the University of Bordeaux and became Professor of Education at the Sorbonne in Paris after 1902. His most important works are *The Division of Labour in Society* (1893), *The Rules of Sociological Method* (1895), *Suicide* (1897), and *The Elementary Forms of Religious Life* (1912), as well as *Moral Education* (1922) and *Professional Ethics and Civic Morals* (1950) published after his death. In 1898 he also founded the journal *L'Année sociologique*, which has played a major role in the development of French sociology. By the time of his death, Durkheim established a formidable reputation, not only for himself but also for the integrity of sociology as a discipline. He influenced a generation of French social thinkers from Marcel *Mauss to Maurice *Halbwachs, Claude *Lévi-Strauss, Georges *Bataille, and many others.

In the following account, we look first at Durkheim's methodological conception of sociology as an autonomous science devoted to the study of 'social facts'. We then turn to Durkheim's subtle analyses of the dynamics and problems of social integration in modern societies, his conception of *'anomie', morality, and *individualism, and his view of the state and the role of religion in social evolution, all of which stand in a distinctively critical relationship to the work of Marx.

Durkheim's *The Rules of Sociological Method*

Durkheim's work is driven by a concern to establish sociology as an autonomous scientific discipline. This entailed two major undertakings: first, identifying a peculiar set of phenomena calling for genuinely sociological investigation; and second, defining a methodology adequate to the investigation. Both these undertakings are succinctly spelled out in Durkheim's early methodological treatise *The Rules of Sociological Method* (1895).

Durkheim's text sought to place sociology on the same footing as biology, but with an object of investigation entirely its own. Durkheim defined this as the study of 'social facts'. *The Rules* starts with the claim that 'social facts are *things*' and must be studied as such. This claim entails two assertions. First Durkheim maintains that social phenomena are distinct from physical phenomena but no less real than physical phenomena. Second Durkheim contends that social facts are external to, and exercise coercive power over, the individual. Therefore, social facts cannot be reduced to purely psychological facts about the interior life of an individual person. Social facts consist of 'manners of acting and thinking . . . capable of exercising a coercive influence on the consciousness of individuals' (Durkheim 1895: 43). As such, 'the determining cause of a social fact must be sought among antecedent social facts and not among the states of individual consciousness' (Durkheim 1895: 134). The independent nature of social facts justifies the existence of sociology as an autonomous discipline and calls for a distinctive sociological method. This method can imitate the rigour of the natural sciences in its concentration on the study of causal relations between observable phenomena in the social world.

Durkheim saw sociology as providing impartial and universally valid knowledge of the social world. In this sense, he regarded sociology as a *'positive science' in the spirit of

Auguste *Comte, although he did not share Comte's implicit *metaphysical and *teleological assumptions about morally superior stages of civilization. In *The Rules*, Durkheim attempted to bridge the gap opened up within positivism between prescriptive and descriptive statements by suggesting a distinction between 'normal' and 'pathological' dimensions of social life. This distinction found a practical application in Durkheim's work on suicide, which can be seen as a showcase of Durkheim's principles of empirical method. It is discussed in Box 5.

In addition to methodology, a general concern of Durkheim's early work was to formulate a theory of social change capable of supplying sound scientific analyses of features of modern industrial societies and of suggesting adequate solutions to problems of social conflict and inequality. In this regard, he grew increasingly dissatisfied with the confident

---

BOX 5. ÉMILE DURKHEIM ON SUICIDE: A SOCIOLOGICAL CASE STUDY

Durkheim's monograph *Suicide* of 1897 combines a focus on problems of *solidarity in modern societies with the elaboration of a rigorous empirical sociological method. Durkheim distinguishes between four basic types of suicide: what he calls 'altruistic suicide', 'anomic suicide', 'egoistic suicide', and 'fatalistic suicide'. For each of these four types he seeks the social determinants that describe the causes of these apparently purely private acts of individuals. These determinants not only enable him to classify different types of suicide but also to specify certain related 'pathologies' or 'morbidities' in the social fabric. Examples of *altruistic suicide* include the captain who feels morally obliged to 'go down with his ship', or statesmen forced to 'fall on their swords' out of shame for failures of public duty. Durkheim states that altruistic suicide occurs when the bonds that tie individuals to membership of social groups are too strong—too intense or too claustrophobic. Examples of *anomic suicide* are those that occur when individuals feel isolated and cut off from the social group. Anomic suicide occurs when the bonds that tie individuals to membership of social groups are too weak or too distant.

Durkheim speaks of degrees of the presence or absence of social *integration* and degrees of the presence or absence of social *regulation*, where 'regulation' refers to the morally binding effect of social *norms. Altruistic suicide is the consequence of too *much* integration, while egoistic suicide is the consequence of too *little* integration. Fatalistic suicide is the outcome of too *much* regulation, while anomic suicide is the outcome of too *little* regulation.

Durkheim's aim is to explain not individual suicides but correlations between suicide *rates* and different forms and degrees of social *solidarity*. Thus he argues that the fact that Catholic countries generally have lower rates of suicide than Protestant ones is not so much a reflection of the fact that for Catholicism suicide is a cardinal sin. Rather, it is an index of the extent to which Protestantism encourages *individualism and self-reliance and thus tends to foster both greater personal egoism and greater personal anxiety in individuals. Durkheim also notes that rapid economic growth frequently correlates with relatively high suicide rates because periods of economic growth tend to produce structural social changes of a kind that can bring about 'anomic' conditions of social life. In this context we may think of the successful but emotionally isolated stockbroker or financial services executive in the big metropolis.

In his monograph on suicide Durkheim demonstrated the scientific uses of his injunction to 'treat social facts as things'. Using a wide range of statistical data, he demonstrated that even suicide, even this most individual and lonely of acts, lends itself to systematic sociological analysis.

*utilitarian agendas and methodologies of figures such as John Stuart *Mill and Herbert *Spencer. He sought to adhere to scientific principles of detachment in a way that might also yield moral advice for attempts at improving social life. 'Because what we propose to study is above all reality', he wrote, 'it does not follow that we should give up the idea of improving it' (Durkheim 1893: p. xxvi). This concern underpins his first major work of substantive sociology, *The Division of Labour in Society* (1893), to which we now turn.

Solidarity and social differentiation: Durkheim's *The Division of Labour in Society*

In the same spirit as Marx's distinction between feudal and capitalist modes of production and Ferdinand *Tönnies's distinction between 'communal' and 'societal' relations, Durkheim distinguishes between two basic forms of social life, or between two kinds of *solidarity in the evolution of societies: between what he terms *mechanical solidarity* and what he terms *organic solidarity*.

By mechanical solidarity Durkheim means a condition of social life characterized by a strong sense of commonality or 'collective consciousness' (*conscience collective*). It is typical of societies with a *segmentary* structure composed of groups lacking any significant degree of internal differentiation, notably in the case of 'primitive' societies made up of tribes or clans. It is a condition marked by the absence of any developed system of division of labour. Social members have a weak sense of personal identity or self, but a correspondingly strong sense of community. Durkheim comments that in the condition of mechanical solidarity 'Every consciousness beats as one' (1893: 106). Each component element or segment of the society is more or less identical to the others and is joined to the whole society not by a relation of mutual economic interdependence but only in an 'external' 'mechanical' way, by a strong assertion of collective identity and through a highly visible system of punishment for deviants or breakers of rules. In traditional pre-modern societies marked by mechanical solidarity, justice systems have a *retributive character in which the entire community takes revenge on individuals who violate its rules in order to reassert itself in the face of the violation.

By organic solidarity Durkheim means a condition of social life characterized by high degrees of economic interdependence between individuals, involving an advanced system of *division of labour and advanced processes of professional specialization. Social members have a stronger sense of individual uniqueness and a correspondingly weaker identification with the community. For Durkheim, organic solidarity is the authentic condition of modern societies. In the modern age, solidarity is, or ought to be, 'organic' in the sense that, like a complex living organism, societies consist of interdependent systems or 'organs', each of which performs certain distinct functions in cooperation with other organs or systems. The component parts of the society are not replications of each other but mutually differentiated links within a chain of mutually cooperating economic actors. Modern societies are more culturally diverse and internally differentiated, but have a proportionally lower sense of *conscience collective*. Justice systems in societies marked by organic solidarity evince a *restitutive character where disputes are resolved by impartial third authorities rather than in the form of vendetta by the injured party or in the form of visible public exposure and shaming. Modern societies seek to restore deviant members to a normal way of life, where normality refers to a functioning role in the division of labour.

Echoing Marx, Durkheim presents the modern division of labour as an epoch-making event. The passage from the old order to the new entails a process of liberation of the individual from tradition and the emergence of a new kind of consciousness affirming the primacy of individual personal identity. Like Marx, Durkheim argues that the modern division of labour was possible only because of the collapse of the previous social order. What pushed people to specialize was the increase in 'social density' caused by the disintegration of older segmentary forms of society and the struggle for survival that this higher density generated. Durkheim postulates that 'the progress of labour is in direct proportion to the moral or dynamic density of society' (1893: 201). The increase in social density is not due to simple demographic growth but to the fact that people belonging to separate social groups come to interact more frequently and on a more permanent basis—most notably in the city and in every larger urban spaces.

In disagreement with Marx, however, Durkheim maintains that the division of labour is not a vehicle of class exploitation. Rather, it is to be viewed as a source of solidarity that is better adapted to modern conditions. Durkheim sees class division and conflict only as a side effect of the pace of social change, as a pathological product of modern society, but not as a fundamental contradiction inherent in modernity. This leads Durkheim to advocate a different course of action from that of Marx's proletarian revolution.

In *The Division of Labour in Society* and throughout his later works, Durkheim suggests that while the old world is dying, if not dead, the new world has not yet been born. He sees Europe as still standing at the point of transition between the pre-modern and the modern worlds, and such times of transition are times of hazard. The speed of social change creates the danger that pre-modern mechanical solidarity might disappear before modern organic solidarity is fully in place. Durkheim wrote that 'over a very short space of time very profound changes have occurred in the structure of our societies. They have liberated themselves from the segmentary model with a speed and in proportions without precedent in history. Thus the morality corresponding to this type of society has lost influence, but without its successor developing quickly enough to occupy the space left vacant in our consciousness' (1893: 339). The major problems Durkheim sees in this shortfall of solidarity in modern societies lie in what he calls *anomie*, which is discussed here in Box 6.

Solutions to anomie: occupational groups and intermediary agencies

Durkheim's response to anomie is not to embrace nostalgia for a lost world. Durkheim insists that modern societies must face the danger of anomie and solve it in uniquely modern ways. He warns that 'the remedy for the ill is nevertheless not to seek to revive traditions and practices that no longer correspond to present-day social conditions . . . We need . . . to find ways of harmonious cooperation between those organs that still clash discordantly together. We need to introduce into their relationship a greater justice by diminishing those external inequalities that are the source of our ills' (1893: 340). Durkheim is less interested in social order per se than in the forms of social solidarity and integration best adapted to specifically modern conditions. He concludes that only organic solidarity based on an increased

---

BOX 6. ÉMILE DURKHEIM'S CONCEPT OF ANOMIE

Durkheim defines *anomie as a state of *normlessness arising from social fragmentation and lack of authoritative social institutions capable of regulating social interaction. He writes that anomie, 'this malady of infiniteness which we suffer in our day' (1922: 43), is to be distinguished from egoism. Where egoism 'agitates and exasperates', anomie 'disorients and disconcerts' (1897: 382). Egoism produces social conflict, whereas anomie consists in moral void and social fragmentation. Anomie represents a socio-psychological condition of normlessness due to the absence, or weakness, of institutions and rules regulating social intercourse. In *The Division of Labour*, Durkheim discusses anomie as a macrological problem affecting economic relations. In *Suicide* he focuses on anomie as a more micrological problem. In his posthumously published lectures *Moral Education* (1922) and *Professional Ethics and Civic Morals* (1950), he deals with problems of anomie affecting the modern nation-state and secular societies in general.

What Durkheim calls anomie derives from the fact that the division of labour can have negative effects not only for the working classes but also for *all* those involved in the productive process and for society in general. What he calls 'forced division of labour' is more specifically comparable to Marx's conception of alienated labour. Forced division of labour consists in 'the fact that the working classes do not really desire the status assigned to them and too often accept it only under constraint and force, not having any means of gaining any other status' (1893: 293). In large-scale industry this imposition goes together with two further constraints: the regimentation of workers and their physical separation from the social environment and the routinization of working practices that transforms the worker into 'a lifeless cog'.

---

awareness and appreciation of interdependence can solve the modern anomic crisis; and that only those rules and roles that are felt to be just and fair will provide the necessary restraints on individual passions and desires. He particularly stresses the role of *norms and moral discipline in structuring individual action and fostering healthy personalities.

Durkheim's proposed remedies for anomie consist in the creation of institutions capable of establishing common goals and identities by reinforcing channels of communication between individuals and coordinating social functions. Durkheim looks especially to the role of *occupational groups*, to the role of a *corporatist state*, and to the role of a *secular moral education system* as possible solutions. He sees two vital functions played by these intermediary agencies: that of mediating between the individual and the state or the collective body, and that of educating people into recognizing interests prior to and more general than their own selfish interests. By 'occupational groups' Durkheim means such things as trade unions and other professional associations. He argues that such groups must have a democratic internal structure allowing people direct participation in decision-making at the local level and a well-defined constitutional role assuring them direct influence in the public sphere. In contrast to the medieval *guilds or the fascist system of corporations, Durkheim views these occupationally based social arrangements as inherently democratic. They represent social spaces where people with common interests and concerns can gather together, establish direct lines of communication, and form collective identities. They are not markets in which agents meet with competing preferences.

Morality and civil society

Durkheim viewed the division of labour as a source of solidarity capable of attenuating the atomistic forces generated by an increasing individualistic and pluralistic society. He particularly found inspiration in the French mutualist tradition which Marx had dismissed as 'petty-bourgeois socialism'. His concern was to find ways of moderating the pathological side effects of market societies through moral and political regulation, seeing the aim of such regulation as being to inhibit the spread of rabid economic individualism. Here we need to consider Durkheim's interest in the question of what value system is best suited for an increasingly differentiated and pluralistic modern society. Durkheim particularly concentrated on the role of *contracts, trust,* and *moral *individualism,* as well as on the role of the state and secular education. We now look at these key elements of Durkheim's political sociology.

Trust, contracts, and moral individualism

In contrast to Ferdinand *Tönnies and Henry *Maine, Durkheim rejects the idea that modern society is solely founded on relations of contract. Durkheim argues that contracts generally rest upon conditions that are themselves moral; that is, on non-contractual relations. Contracts must be respected, but the clause that they must be respected cannot be written into the contract itself without an infinite logical regress. Contracts are underwritten solely by the *moral force of society*: by relations of trust and mutual respect. Durkheim's argument here is echoed in a number of themes in contemporary social theory: in debates about 'trust', about 'social capital' and about the socially 'embedded' nature of economic relations (compare Gambetta 1988; Portes 1998; Granovetter 1985). What all these themes have in common, and what they share with Durkheim, is the view that economic relations—like the contract—are not self-sufficient but presuppose a context of social relations, networks, ties, and trust in order to function properly. Durkheim feared that without this moral basis of trust in economic exchange, civil society would decay into the mutual antagonisms of self-seeking individuals. Here he differed from Marx in two vital respects: he rejected Marx's claim that civil society is necessarily asocial, and he looked not to abolition of the state but to the emergence of intermediate associations in civil society as a way of re-entrenching solidarity. Durkheim argues that the Marxian critique of liberalism confuses two different forms of individualism: *particularistic egoistic individualism* (associated with *utilitarian philosophy) and *morally universalizing individualism* (associated with the philosophy of *Kant). Durkheim argues that it is not the particularistic individualism of the egoist that is celebrated in the doctrine of the Rights of Man but rather the idea of the moral responsibility and *autonomy of the individual: the idea of the individual as the moral embodiment of universal humanity. He emphasizes that 'individualism thus understood is the glorification not of the self, but of the individual in general. Its motive force is not egoism but sympathy for all that is human, a wider pity for all suffering, for all human miseries, a more ardent desire to combat and alleviate them, a greater thirst for justice' (Durkheim 1898: 48).

Durkheim argues that moral individualism is capable of preserving social solidarity at a time in which conventional theistic religion no longer holds a grip on society. He asserts that 'not only is individualism not anarchical, but it henceforth is the only system of beliefs which can ensure the moral unity of the country' (1898: 50). As society becomes more differentiated, less bound to territory and to tradition, its values have to become more universal. People cannot hold on to local traditions in a context in which horizontal differentiation breaks down locality and *particularistic values. Durkheim writes that 'we make our way, little by little, towards a state, nearly achieved by now, where the members of a single social group will have nothing in common among themselves except their humanity' (1898: 51). If the universal is all that people have in common, they must treat this as the sacred source of social cohesion. In what are today called 'multicultural societies', people cannot hope to find common agreement on the basis of purely particularistic belief systems. But they may, according to Durkheim, hope to find agreement on matters that are the common property of all the component elements, even though these of necessity will be of an abstract and highly general nature. Durkheim is thus committed to a form of *cosmopolitan *universalism.

The state and secular education

It should be noted that Durkheim does not regard individualism and rights as fully sufficient for the rebuilding of civil society. In addition, he stipulates that solidarity requires a pluralistic social milieu in which people are addressed neither simply as bearers of universal humanity nor as self-interested egoists but also as bearers of particular *group identities*. This leads to the important role of the *state* in Durkheim's social and political thought.

Durkheim views the state as the highest expression of social life within a multi-levelled system of rules and roles. He maintains that regulation by the state is enabling rather than merely constraining. The word 'state' for him is short for the set of institutions that constitute a political society: 'we apply the term "state" more especially to the agents of the sovereign authority, and "political society" to the complex group of which the state is the highest organ' (Durkheim 1950: 48). In this respect Durkheim's conception of the state strikingly differs both from that of Marx and from that of classical economic theory. Durkheim holds that the state is inherently connected to a political society and cannot be abolished without undermining the political nature of society, and further that 'far from being in opposition to social groups . . . the state presupposes their existence' (1950: 45).

It is in this connection that mediating public institutions have their importance: they are the medium through which the state is anchored in civil society. In the absence of linking instances such as occupational groups, rational governance is difficult and an unbridgeable distance opens up between the state and the individual. Durkheim therefore envisages a form of 'subsidiarity' in which each level of association—the level of the individual, the level of the group, and the level of the state—is expressed through mutual education. Civil society for Durkheim is thus more than Marx's realm of private competition. It includes groups which gather the interests of individuals into a higher instance, and the plurality of these groupings feeds societal demands into the political process. Durkheim thus describes the state as an agent whose duty is to call the individual to a 'moral way of life' (1950: 75) and to set the 'particularism of each corporation' in relation to 'the sentiment of general utility and the need for organic equilibrium' (1897: 384). The state acts as 'a special organ whose responsibility it is to work out certain representations which hold good for the collectivity' (1950: 50). It depends on a civil society consisting of active citizens contributing to democratic pluralism. Only an educated public respecting the sacred nature of universalist individualism and negotiating their differences in a pluralistic political society can realize the principles of the French Revolution of 1789 (Durkheim 1890). Mediating associations and the state must address the tendency of a modern market-based division of labour to deteriorate into conditions of blind anomie.

Where in his earlier work Durkheim saw this danger as restricted to the economic sector, he became increasingly preoccupied with its pervasive and structural nature. He thus implicitly acknowledged Marx's view of conflict as endemic but did not draw Marx's revolutionary conclusions. He increasingly came to look for value systems and institutions capable of accomplishing what he called a 'refashioning of the moral constitution of society' (1897: 142). This interest is notably reflected in his late work on religion, to which we now turn.

Religion and social evolution: Durkheim's *The Elementary Forms of Religious Life*

In his last great work, *The Elementary Forms of Religious Life* of 1912, Durkheim criticizes those currents of thought typified by Marx which reduce religion to *ideology or to metaphysical nonsense. In this work, he states that 'it is unthinkable that systems of ideas like religions . . . could be mere fabrics of illusion' (1912: 66). Durkheim here sets himself the task of demonstrating not only that religious phenomena are partially independent of material relations but also—remarkably—that religious beliefs and rites are at the root of scientific thinking and practice. Durkheim argues for the view that religion is in an important sense *rational*, rather than irrational. He defines religion as 'a unified system of beliefs and practices relative to sacred things, that is to say, things set apart and forbidden—beliefs and practices which unite into one single and moral community called a Church all those who adhere to them' (1912: 44). Religious beliefs engender a 'bipartite division of the universe' (1912: 38) into the *sacred* and the *profane*. These two worlds are to be conceived of 'not only as separate but also as hostile and jealous rivals' (1912: 37).

Drawing on research on *totemist practices among the Australian aboriginal and native American peoples, Durkheim considers the role of the totem as 'first and foremost, a name . . . an emblem' (1912: 108). In aboriginal societies, small kinship groups are given the name of a totem—usually a plant or an animal—which is often transmitted down the maternal or paternal line. Larger communities have names that incorporate a number of totemic groups known as 'phratries'. In the same way as a person can today be both a French and an EU citizen, so an aborigine can have more than one totemic identity. In the contemporary world we may also see aspects of totemic identity in such phenomena as football fandom, where a team and its supporters all associate with a distinct colour of shirt and a distinct set of symbols and slogans. For Durkheim, latter-day totemism is in principle no less rational or more mysterious than the 'primitive' kind of totemism.

Durkheim states that the rationality of these 'primitive' religions lies in their function for society. As emblems or names, totems and phratries not only define the group; they are also its source of cohesion and solidarity, expressed through religious practices, rituals, and code of dress. We are aware of our supra-individuality only in exceptional circumstances; but it is precisely these collective occasions that shape our identity and lend meaning to our mundane existence. Durkheim writes that in religious festivals and collective gatherings 'the result of that heightened activity is a general stimulation of individual energies. People live differently and more intensely than in normal times . . . Man becomes something other than what he was' (1912: 213). Religious experiences and revolution are instances of such mobilizations of collective energies whose significance often outlives the event of their occasion. Heightened emotions become transferred to religious images and collective representations which continue 'calling forth those emotions even after the assembly is over' (1912: 222). Durkheim here describes nothing less than the birth and rebirth of society in ecstatic collective experiences. God is seen as the image of society. Religious symbols—such as saints, angels, and spirits—are the symbolic *collective representations* through which social groups picture to themselves their own inviolate moral identity.

Durkheim's text was to exercise a profound influence on anthropological research in the twentieth century, in the work of figures such as Marcel *Mauss, Maurice *Halbwachs, Claude *Lévi-Strauss, Mary *Douglas, and many others (for further discussion, see Chapter 5 of this book, pp. 121–2 and Chapter 9, pp. 200–2).

Conclusion

Although they share more in common than is often recognized—especially by those who falsely identify Durkheim with conservatism—we must be aware that Marx and Durkheim arrive ultimately at very different conclusions from one another. Marx's goal throughout his life's work was to expose the underlying logic of capitalism from its birth to what he saw as its inevitable self-destruction. Durkheim does not share this orientation. Durkheim's understanding of the relationship between science and politics remains wholly different. His liberal political views are illustrated by his stance in the *Dreyfus affair in France in the 1890s, where he aligned himself with the progressive liberals, as well as in his essays on socialism and his patriotic response to the First World War in which he lost his only son. If Marx is the representative figure of the social theorist as firebrand, Durkheim represents the social theorist as moral educator.

In the history of sociology, Durkheim's conception of society as a complex whole composed of interdependent social facts has led him sometimes to be aligned with *functionalism*; that is, with the doctrine that societies are more than the sum of their parts and that social integration is achieved through mutual dependencies characterizing a complex, differentiated social system (for full discussion of functionalism see Chapter 4 of this book).

In this general respect, Durkheim shares with Marx an interest in analysing society as a *totality of material forces vastly greater and more powerful than the beliefs that any given individual may entertain about his or her world. It should, however, be noted that when Marx's thought is compared to that of Durkheim—and even more so when it is compared to that of Max Weber—Marx tends to underestimate the significance of cultural and mental practices beyond the sphere of purely material economic relations. It can be said that Marx retained some of the prejudices of political economy concerning the primacy of economic determinants over social, cultural, and historical differences. In contrast, Durkheim's late work on religion in *The Elementary Forms* illustrates the importance of collective beliefs, representations, identities, and cultural practices in sociological explanation. Where Marx tends to bind social theory to economics, Durkheim draws it more in the direction of cultural anthropology.

Marx and Durkheim particularly differ in their view of the status and consequences of social differentiation and the division of labour in the rise of modern capitalism. Marx views the division of labour as the instrument of a subtle and pervasive system of class exploitation. Durkheim, in contrast, sees the division of labour as a novel and effective source of solidarity. Durkheim maintains that to seek to abolish the division of labour is to escape from reality into an idyllic past or into an impossible utopian future. While Durkheim appreciates the force of 'social currents' and 'collective representations', he does not share Marx's trust in the emancipatory powers of revolution. He certainly did not adopt Marx's view of the Paris Commune of 1870 as a foretaste of the future communist society. Where Marx considered capitalism's problems to be inherent in it and only capable of resolution in a post-capitalist order, Durkheim identified tendencies to both self-destruction and *self-regeneration* in modern capitalism. For Durkheim, Marx's conception of class conflict and revolutionary overcoming rested on a mystical epistemology. Yet Marx, on the other hand, if he had lived to read Durkheim's works, might well have seen Durkheim's appeal to morality as ignoring certain basic inequalities of power and resources under capitalism, together with the ubiquity of exploitation.

Both Marx's and Durkheim's social theories possess a special urgency today, in different respects and for different reasons. Certainly it would be foolish to deny that the collapse of twentieth-century communism raises serious questions about the validity of Marx's ideas today. But numerous contemporary developments relating to the ever-widening spread of *neo-liberal capitalistic expansion and ever-increasing global inequalities point to the continuing relevance and validity of at least some elements of Marx's analysis (for further discussion, see Chapters 7 and 14 of this book). At the same time, Durkheim's concern with the growing gap between the state and the individual, with the remoteness of decision-making from those affected, and with the hollowing out of communities under poorly regulated market systems has lost little of its relevance.

■ **QUESTIONS FOR CHAPTER 2**

1　How compatible are the accounts of the modern division of labour given by Marx and Durkheim? Where do they agree and where do they diverge?

2　How does Durkheim's concept of anomie differ from Marx's concept of alienation?

3　Marx and Durkheim both criticize individualist explanations of social phenomena. Where do their critiques differ?

4　Is religion anything more than the 'the opium of the people', in Marx's phrase?

5　Is civil society merely a sphere of competing self-seeking individuals (Marx), or is it a necessary component of a democratic and pluralistic society (Durkheim)?

6   Is the state a 'committee for managing the common affairs of the whole bourgeoisie' (Marx), or a regulative moral authority in which social interests can, and should, attain their highest expression (Durkheim)?

■ FURTHER READING

The best starting point for reading Marx is *The Communist Manifesto*, available in Penguin (1967), or in a new edition with an introduction by Eric Hobsbawm (Verso, 1998). There are excellent selections from Marx in David McLellan's *Karl Marx: Selected Writings* (Oxford University Press, 2nd edn. 2000) and Jon Elster's *Karl Marx: A Reader* (Cambridge University Press, 1986). The essential source for Marx's economic theories is volume 1 of *Capital* (available in Penguin, 1976), especially chapter 1 on 'The Commodity'. Also important is the chapter in Marx's *Grundrisse* (available in Penguin, 1973), titled 'Chapter on money'. (Note that Marx's German word *Grundrisse*, meaning 'foundations' or 'outlines', is usually left untranslated in references to this book.) The best insight into Marx's early philosophical ideas can be found in his *Economic and Philosophical Manuscripts of 1844*, which is available in Penguin under the title *Karl Marx: Early Writings* (1975). An excellent straightforward account of Marx is David McLellan's *Karl Marx: His Life and Thought* (Papermac, 1987). A more entertaining account is by the journalist Francis Wheen, *Karl Marx* (Fourth Estate, 1999). A good analytical discussion is Shlomo Avineri's *The Social and Political Thought of Karl Marx* (Cambridge University Press, 1968). For Marxian terminology, see Tom Bottomore et al. (eds.), *A Dictionary of Marxist Thought* (Blackwell, 1985). For a survey of recent academic thinking about Marx, see *Karl Marx's Social and Political Thought: Critical Assessments*, in four volumes, ed. Bob Jessop and Charlie Malcolm-Brown (Routledge, 1990).

Four influential studies in 'analytical Marxism' (discussed further in this book, Chapter 7, pp. 168) are G. A. Cohen's *Karl Marx's Theory of History: A Defense* (Oxford University Press, 1978), Jon Elster's *Making Sense of Marx* (Cambridge University Press, 1985), John Roemer's *Analytical Foundations of Marxian Economic Theory* (Cambridge University Press, 1981), and Alex Callinicos's edited *Marxist Theory* (Oxford University Press, 1989).

For an introduction to Hegel, try Raymond Plant's *Hegel: An Introduction* (Blackwell, 1983), or Charles Taylor's *Hegel and Modern Society* (Cambridge University Press, 1979) and Shlomo Avineri's *Hegel's Theory of the Modern State* (Cambridge University Press, 1972).

The four core works of Durkheim are *The Division of Labour*, *The Rules of Sociological Method*, *Suicide*, and *The Elementary Forms of Religious Life* (to be read roughly in this order). Try to use the newer and better translations by W. D. Halls of *Rules* (Macmillan 1982) and *Division of Labour* (Free Press, 1984), and Karen Fields's translation for *Elementary Forms* (Free Press, 1995). Some well-chosen collections of extracts from all four of these books with other notable texts by Durkheim are *Émile Durkheim: Selected Writings* (Cambridge University Press, 1972) and *Durkheim on Politics and the State* (Polity Press, 1986), both edited by Anthony Giddens, as well as *Émile Durkheim: Sociologist of Modernity*, ed. Mustafa Emirbayer (Blackwell, 2003). Durkheim's political concerns can be seen in his article 'Individualism and the Intellectuals', in *Émile Durkheim on Morality and Society*, ed. R. N. Bellah (University of Chicago Press, 1973).

The standard intellectual biography of Durkheim is Steven Lukes's *Émile Durkheim: His Life and Work* (Penguin, 1973). At a more basic level, try Kenneth Thompson's *Émile Durkheim* (Ellis Horwood, 1982), Anthony Giddens's *Durkheim* (Fontana, 1978), or R. A. Jones's *Émile Durkheim: An Introduction to Four Major Works* (Sage, 1986). Also useful are Gianfranco Poggi's *Durkheim* (Oxford University Press, 2000) and Stephen P. Turner (ed.), *Émile Durkheim: Sociologist and Moralist* (Routledge, 1993). See also *The Radical Sociology of Durkheim and Mauss*, ed. Mike Gane and Keith Tribe (Routledge, 1992). Durkheim's political sociology is discussed by Antonino Palumbo and Alan Scott in 'Weber, Durkheim and the Sociology of the Modern State', in *The Cambridge History of*

Twentieth-Century Political Thought (Cambridge University Press, 2003). For the French reception of Durkheim, see Philippe Besnard (ed.), *The Sociological Domain* (Cambridge University Press, 1983). For instructive applications of Durkheim's analyses in the field of anthropology, see Jeffrey Alexander's edited volume *Durkheimian Sociology* (Cambridge University Press, 1988). For comparisons of Marx and Durkheim at a high analytical level, see David Lockwood's *Solidarity and Schism* (Oxford University Press, 1992) and Albert Hirschman's article 'Rival Interpretations of Market Society' in the *Journal of Economic Literature*, 20/2 (1982).

■ WEBSITES

The Marxist Internet Archive (MIA) at **www.marxists.org** Display numerous excerpts from writings by Marx, with commentaries and accounts of debates.

Marxism Page at **www.anu.edu.au/polsci/marx/** Presents texts by Marx, Engels, Lenin, Trotsky, and others.

The Durkheim Pages at **www.relst.uiuc.edu/durkheim/** Contains a useful biography with summaries of Durkheim's key texts and a glossary of terms.

Émile Durkheim Page at **www.emiledurkheim.com** Provides a good biography, presenting parts of Durkheim's major works (in the original French), a few quotations (in English), and a bibliography.

The Émile Durkheim Archive at **http://durkheim.itgo.com/main.html** Contains sections on key Durkheimian concepts, with a glossary and links to similar sites.

3

Classical Social Theory, III: Max Weber and Georg Simmel

Gianfranco Poggi

Max *Weber and Georg *Simmel lived in Germany in the period of the rise of the Prussian empire under Kaiser Wilhelm II. Both experienced the tragedy of the Great War, and both knew and appreciated each other. Together they sought to establish in their country the discipline of sociology, though both had a somewhat aloof relationship to it. Weber, trained as a lawyer and an economic historian, was appointed early to a chair in economics and remained identified with this discipline to end of his life. However, he remained primarily interested in economic history and in the relationship between the economic sphere of society and other spheres, especially religion, politics, *stratification, and law. Weber suffered a nervous breakdown in 1897 and remained seriously ill until 1903, but was widely recognized throughout his life as an academic scholar of the first rank. He held a professorship at Heidelberg University and published in specialist journals a number of extensive, thoroughly researched essays, each focused on a problem of acknowledged significance.

Simmel, a philosopher, identified himself with sociology only during a phase of his life. He taught for most of his life in Berlin and gained a professorial chair only toward the end of his career. Born to Jewish parents, he suffered from the persistent anti-Semitism of Wilhelmine Germany. In his intellectual style, he was, as one of his students put it, 'a philosophical squirrel', publishing many of his lectures in periodicals addressed to the broad cultured public. His lectures were brilliantly written but often had no systematic relation to one another.

In their different domains of engagement and styles of analysis, Weber and Simmel have exerted a profound influence on the development of sociological thinking in the twentieth and twenty-first centuries. This chapter outlines the leading intellectual contributions of the two thinkers, treating each in turn. At the end of the chapter we also discuss a few parallels between Weber and Simmel and the philosophy of Friedrich *Nietzsche and the psychoanalytic thought of Sigmund *Freud. We turn first of all to the work of Weber.

Max Weber: the idea of interpretive sociology

In the early 1890s Weber devoted his first major writings to the study of Roman law, dealing with agricultural estates and commercial partnerships and companies in medieval Italy. His doctoral dissertation examined directly the meanings of the terms *socius* and *societas*— 'commercial partner' and 'commercial partnership', or 'company', or 'society'—in medieval trading law (Weber 1889). Subsequently, he entered the field of sociology proper (at first without naming it so) by analysing in depth the data yielded by empirical enquiries into the conditions of agricultural workers in the eastern parts of Germany.

After 1900, Weber entered the so-called *Methodenstreit*, or 'methodological dispute', a lively and protracted dispute among German scholars active in various 'sciences of culture'—chiefly history, theology, law, psychology, philosophy, and economics (Weber 1903, 1903–6). The dispute concerned the appropriate ways to conceive and practise those disciplines. The basic issue was whether, how, and to what extent such practice should model itself on that of the natural sciences. The central dispute was: Can human events and arrangements be the object of general laws? Can the scholars studying them produce objectively grounded results, given that as human beings they are unavoidably implicated in the subject matter of their researches? Three key ideas informed Weber's thinking on this question, which we explore in turn. The first concerned the concept of 'understanding' or *verstehen*; the second concerned the role of values in research; and the third concerned the role of what Weber was to term *'ideal types'.

'Explanation' and 'understanding': the meaning of *verstehen*

We may begin by considering Weber's conception of what makes human beings unique. Weber chiefly characterizes 'man' (as such arguments are generally phrased) as an *interpretive animal* (Weber 1922b). That is, human beings are so constituted that in order to survive they must make sense of the world by selecting some of the innumerable, contradictory aspects which reality presents to them, and attaching *meaning* to them. Only in this manner can human beings order reality and orient themselves toward it in a coherent and productive manner, both in their judgements and in their related practices.

Weber here aligns himself with an intellectual tendency known as *'hermeneutics' which deals expressly with interpretation and which had a significant tradition in Germany, culminating, a generation before Weber's, in the thought of Wilhelm *Dilthey. Following Dilthey, Weber conveys this approach to historical cultural phenomena with the expression *verstehen*, meaning 'to understand' or 'to comprehend'. It suggests that the practitioner of a science of culture must seek to capture the mental processes presiding over the courses of action taken by individuals, and particularly those processes in which individuals orient themselves to others' actions. This theme of individual action in Weber's thinking has been called 'methodological *individualism'. It implies that accounts of socio-historical affairs must as far as possible refer to the states of mind of individuals involved in producing social arrangements and accommodating to them.

Weber also stresses, however, that the fact that those cultivating the 'sciences of culture' must seek to capture the subjective processes of human actors does not imply that they surrender the goal of *explaining* those phenomena. It does not mean that they limit themselves merely to describing and narrating social phenomena. A proper scientific account of any phenomenon must involve an attempt to explain its *causes*—even though any such attempt is necessarily selective and partial, and can be countered by and compared with other attempts. Evoking the subjective processes of human actors is an aspect of such an attempt, not an alternative to it. In this sense Weber defined sociology as a 'science which attempts the *interpretive understanding* of human action in order thereby to arrive at a *causal explanation* of its course and consequences' (1922b: 4) (emphasis added).

The role of values and ideal types

Weber was also very concerned about a possible short-circuit between the scholar's subjective make-up and the constitution of the object of study. In particular he was concerned that the *value preferences* of scholars might interfere in certain ways with their reconstruction of the facts-on-the-ground (Weber 1903, 1915). Weber emphasized that all research—about natural or about human affairs—is itself a form of motivated action which is oriented by the researchers' values or 'value ideas', by their sense of what is worth studying. But he also insisted that this legitimate connectedness, or 'value relevance' (*Wertbeziehung*), between scholars' values and their activity of research, should stop there.

It should not lead to an interference between the scholar's value judgement (*Werturteil*) and the judgements of fact to be construed from the data of the matter at hand. These data must be established in such a manner that the relative judgements can also command the assent of other agents who do not share the researcher's value position.

If this distinction is observed (but its observance is always a matter of degree), then the results of the research can become a public reality and serve as background and inspiration for establishing further facts and attempting new interpretations of them. In this manner one can, on one hand, recognize that the 'sciences of culture' involve a particular, unavoidably value-laden relation between the scholar and the object of study, and on the other hand demand of them, as from the 'sciences of nature', a commitment to producing results which can be publicly recognized as valid.

Weber confronts in the same manner a related issue: to what extent does the practice of the sciences of culture involve the formation and employment of *general concepts*? Weber rejects the view that significant human phenomena are always and exclusively 'historical'; that is, that they gain their significance only from the precise where, when, and how of their one-off occurrence. Instead Weber argues that all scientific discourse employs more or less general concepts, such that individual cases can be examples of general recurrent phenomena. But as concerns the sciences of culture, he adds two significant qualifications. First, concepts used in the cultural sciences do not aim at the formulation of general *laws* of human conduct, much less of laws of historical development. Secondly, the concepts appropriate to the sciences of culture differ from those employed in the sciences of nature. Concepts in the cultural sciences are *ideal-typical* concepts. Weber states that ideal-typical concepts, or 'ideal types', make up possible bunches of concepts or *typologies*, which can be used by the scholar to analyse and categorize particular features of the subject matter under consideration. Ideal types in this sense are tools for ordering information and for drawing out comparisons and differences between observed phenomena. They are, however, merely tools of analysis: they do not express a judgement about what is 'ideal' in a phenomenon in the sense of intrinsically worthy and admirable. With respect to the typology of forms of social action, Weber employs an ideal type of 'traditional action' (action motivated by received customs and traditions), an ideal type of 'affective action' (action motivated by emotions and impulses), and an ideal type of 'purposive-rational action' or action motivated by conscious methodical calculation of available means for achieving desired ends.

The point of Weber's ideal types is to provide conceptual benchmarks for the analysis of individual situations, where components of contrasting types are often mixed. They convey what could be called the bounded variety of cultural phenomena, allowing scholars to 'compare and contrast' systematically whole ranges of diverse yet interrelated aspects of social experience.

Religion, capitalism, and modernity

We now turn to Weber's substantive contributions to social theory. These are laid out in a number of now classic works. They include his famous study *The Protestant Ethic and the Spirit of Capitalism*, first published in 1904–5 and in a second revised edition in 1920, as well as his last unfinished magnum opus *Economy and Society*, published posthumously in 1922, and several other key texts which will occupy us shortly. The discussion that follows concentrates first on Weber's writings on capitalism, religion, and modernity. Then we turn to his contributions to the theory of politics, power, *stratification, bureaucracy, and *rationalization.

The governing principle behind Weber's massive and creative work on the sociology of religion is the following. Until relatively recent history, one of the most powerful agencies of social bonding and social transformation has been *religion*. Generally, Weber says, religion has a 'stereotyping' effect. That is, it stabilizes social arrangements, sustains the identity of social groups, and maintains the structure of the contexts in which groups contend with one another. In this manner, different religions can play a role in constituting and preserving different cultures and civilizations, as well as in changing and transforming them.

One can connect this theme with Weber's argument about the necessarily 'interpretive' posture of the human being. Although interpretive processes necessarily take place in the minds of individuals, individuals are normally induced by social arrangements to accept as valid certain pre-existent schemes and understandings of the world and its patterns of activity. World-views and institutions align the practices of discrete individuals with those of one another. In this manner, a plurality of such individuals may turn into a collectivity, a social entity capable of joint action on behalf of shared interests of whatever kind. Weber's generic expression for such an entity is *Stand*, generally translated in English as *'status group'.

The concern of Weber's *Protestant Ethic* study is primarily with the role of a particular religious world-view in 'authorizing' major social change. In most of his other main essays on the sociology of religion, his concern is primarily with the role of religion in grounding long-run differences between civilizations. But it is important to note that in neither of these cases does Weber assume the role of religion to be the *only* decisive factor. On the contrary, he argues that religious factors always interact with other cultural and social factors, including the important material factors of military and political power, economic and technological change, and legal relations, as well as the physical environment.

Weber's *The Protestant Ethic and the Spirit of Capitalism*

The basic argument of *The Protestant Ethic and the Spirit of Capitalism* can be summarized in the following five key steps:

1. Weber argues that the advent of modern capitalism—a complex and protracted event the beginnings of which he places in the late seventeenth century—was assisted not only by material and institutional conditions of various kinds, such as those emphasized by Marx. It was also assisted by an ideological one: by the development of what he calls the *spirit* of capitalism. The capitalist 'spirit' is a historically peculiar way of disciplining and justifying an individual's pursuit of gain through commercial and productive operations conducted peaceably and legally on the market. It encourages individuals to seek such gain through a particular kind of psychological commitment. It enjoins individuals to devote to their project not only their available capital and technical knowledge and skills but also, crucially, their capacity for sustained work, their sense of

personal responsibility, their willingness to invest the results of early gainful operations in the conduct of later ones, and their openness to innovation in the way they organize the labour of hired collaborators, devise new products or new services, and seek new customers and new markets.

In this regard, Weber argues that the standard way of conceptualizing the motivations of the early capitalist entrepreneurs—through a notion of egoistic material advantage—is inadequate. The idea of the spirit of capitalism attributes to such individuals a more complex *subjectivity, not grounded on sheer unbounded greed. Instead, what is crucial is an individual's willingness to put his or her own moral standing to the test of economic success, as the result of a capacity for renunciation and self-discipline. This motif is signalled by the recurrence in Weber's work of the notion of *'asceticism' or disciplined abstention from worldly pleasures.

2. On the face of it, the spirit of capitalism would appear to be a totally areligious vision. It would appear to lend meaning to human qualities and worldly activities which Christianity (like other religions) has always regarded as at best morally dubious. Weber's response to this problem is the following. Insofar as in early modern Europe religious concerns were widely and intensely felt by all, the spirit of capitalism could morally empower the first generations of capitalist entrepreneurs *only* if it had an unprecedented religious warrant. This could be provided only by the new understandings of Christianity brought forward by the Protestant Reformation, first set in train by the rebellious German monk Martin *Luther in the first decades of the sixteenth century.

The connection between the new forms of Protestant religiosity and early capitalist development had long been seen by scholars. It was a commonplace in Weber's day that Protestantism had something to do with a 'work ethic'. But which new forms of religiosity played the crucial role, and in what precise ways, remained an unsettled question. Weber gave a new and controversial answer to this question, which he demonstrated in an extremely scholarly and rigorous manner. Among the various forms of reformed Christianity, only one, namely Calvinism, or Puritanism, provided the spirit of capitalism with the required religious warrant. Calvinism was the movement that took its name from the teaching of the Swiss Protestant theologian, John *Calvin.

3. The main distinctive trait of Calvinism was the theological doctrine of 'predestination'. That is: God has consigned each human soul, through an inscrutable and unchangeable decree, either to eternal damnation or to eternal salvation in the afterlife. Not even a faithful believer can either know or modify such a fate. Thus, the compelling sense of the supreme significance of predestination induces in the believer an acute sense of anxiety. This anxiety cannot be relieved through sacramental acts, through good deeds or donations to the Church, because Calvinism denies legitimacy to such acts. Calvinism sees such acts as akin to magical practices, and thus idolatrous. The anxiety can, however, find an outlet in a historically novel form of asceticism, where believers commit all of their energies to the rational, methodical practice of their worldly *vocation* as an expression of their devotion to the greater glory of God. The German expression for 'vocation'—*Beruf*—had been introduced into German by Luther in his translation of the Bible with the meaning of 'calling', in the sense of being called to a station in this life by God. However, Weber argued that Luther had lent this idea of *Beruf* an interpretation which preserved essentially traditional ways of conducting oneself. In contrast, he argued

that no trace of traditionalism remained in the Calvinist Puritan conception, where the elect could gain some sense of their election only by tinkering relentlessly with all existing arrangements, by pursuing mastery over themselves.

4. Calvinist doctrine had not expressly authorized and encouraged believers to translate this new asceticism into a 'spirit of capitalism'. But that translation, Weber argued, was inevitable. The dogma of predestination placed a religious premium on ways of acting in the world which conferred moral dignity on entrepreneurship. It turned entrepreneurship into a test of one's moral worth. It allowed the systematic pursuit of gain to be practised by the protagonists of early capitalist development, as Weber put it, with 'an amazing good conscience'. This ethos was epitomized, Weber argued, in the life and works of the eighteenth-century American statesman, inventor, and entrepreneur, Benjamin *Franklin.

5. Yet this unintended internal link, or 'elective affinity' (*Wahlverwandschaft*) as Weber called it, between Calvinist religiosity and capitalist entrepreneurship has had paradoxical consequences. Over the generations, capitalism began to change the world in irresistible ways, to loosen and discredit traditional constraints on business conduct, and eventually to *secularize Western culture. Thus the pursuit of gain through entrepreneurship began to dispense with its earlier religious warrant. It has become self-sustaining and self-justifying, cut free from its earlier religious meaning and content. In fact, the capitalist *spirit* itself became dispensable, once the capitalist *system* had won the day. Today, Weber argues, the system demands of individuals—and not just of entrepreneurs but also of workers—the same commitment which it had originally derived from its moral significance. Today, Weber writes, we find ourselves confronted with an 'iron cage' or 'steel-hard casing' (*stahlhartes Gehäuse*), marked by obligations to work and to fulfil our professional vocations, but no longer with any encompassing ethical or metaphysical *meaning*. Weber declares:

The Puritan *wanted* to be a person with a vocational calling; today we *are forced* to be. For to the extent that asceticism moved out of the monastic cell, was transferred to the life of work in a vocational calling, and then commenced to rule over this-worldly morality, it helped to construct the powerful cosmos of the modern economic order. Tied to the technical and economic conditions at the foundation of mechanical and machine production, this cosmos today determines the style of life of all individuals born into it—*not* only those directly engaged in earning a living. This pulsating mechanism does so with overwhelming force. Perhaps it will continue to do so until the last ton of fossil fuel has burnt to ashes. According to Baxter, the concern for material goods should lie upon the shoulders of his saints like 'a lightweight coat that could be thrown off at any time'. Yet fate allowed a steel-hard casing to be forged from this coat. To the extent that asceticism attempted to transform and influence the world, the world's material goods acquired an increasing and, in the end, inescapable power over people—as never before in history. (Weber 1920*b*: 123–4)

Looking back over the entirety of Weber's study, we can see that Weber's central question is: did religious factors contribute to the genesis of capitalism and thereby to the central economic component of the onset of modernity? Weber's answer is that Calvinism played a significant role in the formation of the spirit of capitalism, and that this 'spirit of capitalism' in turn played a significant role in the emergence of capitalism itself. Weber thus contradicted all previous interpretations of the rise of capitalism, beginning with Marx's, which had invoked *only* material factors and had treated the religious aspects of modernization as merely derivative and secondary.

World religions and socio-economic change

In his other comparative essays in the sociology of religion, concentrating on Confucianism, Taoism, Hinduism, Buddhism, and Judaism, Weber addresses similar general questions to those at stake in *The Protestant Ethic*. He shows the extent to which these religions prevented the civilizations of China, India, and ancient Israel from encouraging or allowing developments analogous to Western modernization, and particularly the sustained *rationalization of all manner of social affairs, beginning with the economic and political dimensions. These essays date from 1914–19, carrying the title 'The Economic Ethics of the World Religions'. They appeared originally in a series of three volumes on the sociology of religion, also containing the second revised edition of the *Protestant Ethic* of 1920.

The scope of the argument calls on a whole range of factors besides those of religion. For instance, Weber's discussion of imperial China underlines the so-called 'hydraulic' factor: the maintenance of agriculture, and thus of civilization, required a centralized system of political control over floods and irrigation. In turn, such a system hindered the development of autonomous status groups analogous to those which played a leading role in Western modernization.

Within this broad framework, the core argument of the essays engages with the social consequences of religious forms represented in imperial China, pre-Raj India, and ancient Israel. Weber's argument is the following. The religions in question played a significant *negative* role as concerns the formation of anything like the spirit of capitalism. They did not put a spiritual premium on individuals' efforts to prove their moral stature by achieving a dynamic mastery of their worldly vocation. They discouraged or even condemned any detachment from tradition and any sustained commitment to innovation in business practices. At most, they allowed or encouraged the members of privileged status groups to develop not a rationality of mastery over reality, but a rationality of *adaptation* to reality, a recognition of and homage to its intrinsic harmonies. Weber demonstrates this difference particularly in the case of the Mandarins of imperial China, trained in the classic texts of *Confucius and his followers and engaged in the empire's administration. In this account, Confucianism strongly enjoined respect for tradition, valuing above all the correctness of behaviour.

A similar argument applies to status groups associated with the other Oriental religions, in particular the Hindu Brahmins and the Buddhist monks. These two constituencies were also trained in bodies of religious doctrine, and their commitment to religious values imparted a rationalistic tone to their existence. But such rationality was applied in the pursuit of ritual purity and in the rejection of any serious engagement with the illusory realities of this world. Thus their doctrines too, in different ways, prohibited the emergence of something like the Puritans' worldly asceticism. They discouraged a commitment to take seriously the things of the material world and to transform these things in everyday practice.

Weber concedes that ancient Judaism encouraged a commitment to worldly affairs similar to that of the Puritans. But he points out that this commitment focused chiefly on the pursuit of military and political power in the contest with Gentile peoples. In this sense, Judaism had a strongly *particularistic* intent, based on advancement of the interests of the in-group ('us') over against the out-group ('them'), the non-Jews or Gentiles. Weber shows how this attitude found expression in the economic sphere. Typically, each Jew, in trading with and working for other Jews, was expected to respect ethical constraints in his dealings with other Jews but not in his economic relations to Gentiles. For this reason, the Jews, despite their pre-eminence in trade and banking, failed to exert anything like as pervasive an influence on the wider economic relations of society as that of the Protestant Calvinists of early modern Europe.

We may notice here that Weber's was not so much a sociology of religion as a sociology of religions, in the plural. Weber did not study religion in the abstract, as Durkheim did in *The Elementary Forms of Religious Life*. Rather, Weber studied specific historical religions. He took on board the doctrinal content of different religious traditions and the associated differences in organizational structures, emphasizing their differential impact on the way believers positioned themselves within the cosmos. He was interested in the way different religions answer crucial questions about life before and after death and conceive of the Deity.

Power, stratification, and domination

We now turn to the second key focus of Weber's thinking, concerning the domain of *politics*.

We have seen that Weber is acutely aware of the significance of religious doctrines and the role of the personnel—prophets, priests, monks—who articulate these doctrines and elaborate the related practices. This concentration should *not*, however, lead us to think that Weber attributes to religious factors a general priority over other, qualitatively different kinds of factors. At the end of *The Protestant Ethic* Weber emphasized that it was not his intention to set out 'a one-sided spiritualistic analysis of the causes of culture and history in place of an equally one-sided *"materialistic" analysis' (Weber 1920b: 125). On the contrary, Weber argues that individuals can attribute significance to their lives with reference to several very different kinds of value schemes—not only religious values but also economic, political, intellectual, aesthetic, and erotic values.

Weber points out that dominant *status groups can orient their mutual activities by advancing particular material interests and seeking to make these interests prevail over competing ones. In this regard, he emphasizes that both 'ideal interests' and 'material interests' play a part in shaping social action and social movements through history. In one revealing passage Weber expresses this point with the metaphor of 'switchmen' on a railway line. Material interests are like trains on railway lines whose movement is unstoppable but whose direction can be changed by ideas, like the officers who operate the switches at the points: 'Not ideas, but material and ideal interests, directly govern men's conduct. Yet very frequently the "world images" that have been created by "ideas" have, like switchmen, determined the tracks along which action has been pushed by the dynamic of interest' (Weber 1920d: 280).

Much of the essence of Weber's thinking in these regards appears in his last great work *Economy and Society*, published in two parts in 1920 and posthumously in 1922. Of key importance for Weber in this late work are at least three cardinal factors: the factor of *power*; the factor of *stratification* in social structure, according to membership classes and status groups; and the factor of types of *legitimate* *domination*. We look at these three factors in turn.

Power, class, status, and parties

Weber reiterates that *which* social group prevails over others in a given historical context does not depend on anything like an overriding law of human development, assuring the greatest fulfilment of the qualities of the species–such as Marx's law of the rise of the Proletariat. Nor does it demonstrate the intrinsic superiority of the values held by the group that prevails over those of the others. It depends instead on contingent circumstances, and particularly on the quantum of power which a given group can successfully mobilize with respect to others. Such power, understood by Weber as a group's ability to assert its own interests even over the opposition of others, can express itself in a political form, resting on a key resource—the means of violence—which allows a group to threaten the physical survival and well-being of opposing groups.

But Weber also refers to two other forms of power: *economic* power and what we may call *ideological* power (Weber leaves this form unlabelled). Economic power is based on resources necessary for the reproduction of material life. Ideological power is based on a group's ability to generate valid collective understandings of the meaning of reality and valid norms required for the maintenance of social order. All these forms of power—the political, the economic, and the ideological—come into play in Weber's analysis of stratification and domination, to which we now turn.

The distribution of the three power forms, based on possession of, or exclusion from, their respective resources, generates respectively the political, the economic, and the ideological dimensions of *social inequality*, or what is also commonly termed 'stratification'. Each dimension involves a different kind of unit of co-equals (Weber 1922c):

- parties—understood in a very broad sense, designating individuals who do or do not enjoy access to a society's political centre and influence over its policies;
- classes—designating individuals on the basis of opportunities they may or may not have for asserting their interests on the market; and
- estates or 'status groups'—designating the degree of social honour and prestige a plurality of individuals may or may not possess (where 'status group' has a narrower meaning in this context than in Weber's writings on religion).

In conceptualizing three kinds of stratification units, Weber dissents expressly from Marx, for whom *class is the only significant unit. On the one hand, he agrees with Marx that social inequality tends to generate conflict between units, and that in the modern world the third type of unit (estate) loses significance with respect to class. On the other hand, he insists that parties are also significant collective players in modern societies. In fact, in keeping with the place held by political concerns in his own life, Weber theorizes chiefly the *political* form of power. This emphasis is particularly apparent in his analysis of forms of domination.

Domination and legitimacy

Weber is in no doubt that political power has its source in violence (Weber 1919a). However, he also insists that political power becomes more significant when it clothes itself in *legitimacy*, and transforms itself from mere power (*Macht*) into *domination (*Herrschaft*, literally 'lordship') (1922*d*). Domination expresses itself through commands evoking obedience. Legitimacy exists when those to whom the commands are addressed obey them because obedience seems to them dutiful, because they sense that they *ought* to obey in some morally significant sense.

In one of his most famous essays, 'Politics as a Vocation', to which we turn in a moment, Weber comments that the state has a 'monopoly on the legitimate use of violence' (Weber 1919*a*: 78). In the period of the rise of modern mass industrial societies, it is the state, and the state alone—not bandits or breakaway factions, or 'terrorists'—that can claim the greatest legitimacy for its use of force to preserve order—through a police force, a judiciary, and the threat of punishment for criminals. The state can claim a normative *ground* for obedience, and it is this ground that makes its domination legitimate, unlike the brute coercion and intimidation of the highwayman, the pirate, or the mafia cartel.

In his work on power and politics, Weber suggests a novel way to address an age-old question in political thought: what are the major kinds of government? Weber responds by analysing the notion of legitimacy (Weber 1922*d*). If legitimacy exists when the commander offers grounds (implicit or explicit) on which obedience is due, and if the commanded accept such grounds (implicitly or explicitly) and act upon them, then one may ask *what are* the grounds offered and accepted. According to Weber, the answers, ideal-typically formulated, are the following three:

- Legitimacy is *traditional* if the ground offered and accepted for obedience is chiefly that what has happened in the past has every right to keep happening in the present and future. Whoever commands in the present is regarded as the lawful descendant of the people commanded in the past. Thus the commands given repeat and re-enact those given in the past. Traditional legitimacy is typically to be found in the case of medieval monarchies, where a monarch is regarded as the legitimate descendant of a blood line and is owed allegiance by a company of loyal followers or patrons drawn from the nobility, who administer the monarch's realm in its outlying provinces.

- Legitimacy is *charismatic* if, on the contrary, the commands issued break with tradition but do so because the person issuing them demonstrably embodies extraordinary compelling forces which are entitled to introduce innovation. Charismatic legitimacy is typically provided by the warrior hero or by the prophet or breakaway religious leader.

- Legitimacy is *legal-rational* if the commands issued find obedience by virtue of being instantiations of general norms, where these norms are valid in turn because they are enacted according to recognized principles and procedures. Such principles and procedures authorize the issuing of commands by individuals as *holders of offices*, not in their personal capacity. Legal-rational legitimacy describes the structure of modern bureaucratic states.

The creative aspect of Weber's theory of legitimate domination is its insight that other significant aspects of domination typically vary with the nature of the legitimacy at stake. Weber shows how a whole range of political practices will be associated with a given *polity's type of legitimacy, including its different ways of empowering the rulers and constraining the subordinates, of handing out justice, of producing norms, and raising and expending economic resources. Among the practices Weber considers most significant are those concerning a polity's *staff*; that is, the relatively large number of individuals who administer it, who interpret and implement its policies on a day-to-day basis and mediate between its summit and its social base, between its centre and its periphery.

The key questions Weber raises in his analysis of political personnel concern how such individuals are typically recruited, trained, assigned tasks, financed, controlled. His answers make up a masterful set of ideal-typical concepts, spelling out the ways in which staffs have been constituted throughout history. Traditional polities are typically administered either by a *patriarchal staff, involving personnel standing in a relationship of personal dependence to the ruler, or by a *patrimonial staff, that is, personnel who put to the ruler's service resources which they control, formally or informally, in their own right,

---

BOX 7. MAX WEBER ON BUREAUCRACY AND THE MODERN STATE

The administrative arrangements characteristic of the modern state represent the ideal type of *bureaucracy*, to which Weber devotes close attention (Weber 1922f). Weber's analysis of bureaucracy is one of the chief sources of contemporary sociology of organizations. His understanding of the term 'bureaucracy' differs from the popular view today, where often it denotes inefficient, wasteful, incompetent operations. Weber's own awareness of such problems is qualified by two considerations. First, such problems are considerably worse in the case of traditional and charismatic types of domination than in the legal-rational type. Second, they are largely due to the fact that all administrative units, though established to carry out the will of the political centre, tend to become autonomous of it, to devise policies of their own, instead of implementing the official ones.

In Weber's treatment, modern bureaucratic systems are designed coherently with the polity's legal-rational administration. They tend to depersonalize the process of rule, to make it consist in the application of codified norms, in an effort to minimize expenditure of resources in pursuit of stated goals. To this end, bureaucracies consist in purposefully coordinated offices, held by appointees on the basis of ascertained competence, who dutifully apply principles and directives to the optimal performance of tasks. Individual officials do not own the resources required for that performance; they do not own the means of administration. They cannot dispose of resources at their personal will. Their expenditure is financed from public funds and is controlled and audited. The entire system is built like a pyramid, where each office depends on a higher one which typically controls a number of lower ones by issuing directives and reviewing decisions. Thus, bureaucracy maximizes uniformity. It secures continuity, predictability, and accountability of operations. Its pyramidal structure also implies a career ladder. Under these arrangements the performance of administrative tasks becomes a professional vocation, a *Beruf*.

In all these respects, bureaucracy for Weber represents an instance of the impersonal and anonymous character of modern social relations in which available means of social organization are subjected to processes of systematic professionalization and formalization. Bureaucracy is the phenomenon in which the private, personal, and emotional lives of individual office workers are strictly separated from their professional duties as replaceable functionaries in the system. Together with the modern system of business vocations divested of religious and ethical meanings, modern bureaucracy for Weber is the other pre-eminent instance of an emerging 'iron cage' of material obligations in which members of the social body can come to feel themselves 'cogs in the machine'.

including especially military resources. Charismatic rulers do not attribute particular significance to the routine concerns of administrators, being themselves engaged in feats which transcend and challenge those concerns. Thus typically they entrust these tasks to devoted followers, chosen without attention to their competence, letting them operate without much guidance other than their commitment to carry out the ruler's personal will (Weber 1922e). A charismatic ruler might be a figure such as Julius Caesar or Moses, or a tribal chief, or possibly a modern dictatorial figure such as Hitler.

Weber's account of legal-rational legitimacy appears especially in his analysis of the phenomenon of bureaucracy and its role in the modern state, which is discussed here in Box 7.

At least three general considerations account for Weber's interest in bureaucracy. First, it is most manifest in the political sphere. Secondly, the bureaucratic model, brought to perfection in the modern state, has subsequently asserted itself in other collective units—in business firms, educational establishments, political parties, and hospitals. But thirdly and most importantly, bureaucracy represents the most significant embodiment of what Weber sees as the master trend of modern society: the advance of *rationalization.

Rationalization and the rise of 'occidental rationalism'

By 'rationalization' Weber means that in all manner of social pursuits actors rely increasingly on a deliberate search for the *most efficient means to achieve goals*, optimizing their achievement and making the costs and outcomes of pursuits as predictable as possible. Calculation of the most efficient means of achieving desired ends takes increasing precedence over reflection on the ultimate ethical meaning of these ends themselves. In the most general sense, Weber sees technical efficiency, capitalism, and administration as gradually usurping the place of religion, myth, and metaphysics in the emergence of the modern world. This process is a demonstration of the development he famously calls 'disenchantment of the world' (*Entzauberung der Welt*), brought about by the rise of modern systems of social organization. As discussed in Chapter 7 of this book, the members of the *Frankfurt School of social research were later to describe this process in terms of the rise of *'instrumental reason', drawing on Weber's concept of means-end rationality or 'purposive rationality' (*Zweckrationalität*).

Weber developed this thinking about rationalization in two essays known as the 'Intermediate Reflections' and the 'Preface' (or 'Author's Introduction') to his collected three volumes of writings on the sociology of religion (Weber 1920c, 1920e), as well as in two famous lectures given in Munich in the winter of 1918–19, 'Science as a Vocation' and 'Politics as a Vocation' (Weber 1919a, 1919b). In these texts, Weber is preoccupied with the systematic rationalization of diverse spheres of social life or what he calls 'value-spheres'. He concentrates particularly on the spheres of the economy, science, law, politics, morality, the arts, and erotic life. Each sphere comes to develop in an autonomous fashion, evolving its own independent logic of validity. Each sphere comes into sharp conflict with the claims of other spheres and cannot be reconciled with them. Science, politics, and the economy come into conflict with religion, while art and the erotic life also come into conflict with morality.

Weber sees these processes of rationalization and *differentiation between spheres as a distinctive aspect of the culture of the West. These processes have enabled the West to impose its dominance on other cultures, compelling them to adopt some of its features. However, he emphasizes that in the West itself this aspect does not constitute an abiding and commanding goal, but has emerged due to a contingent constellation of historical circumstances. Furthermore, he is aware of the human costs of rationalization. It suppresses alternative ways of conducting social affairs. It removes meaning and significance from human experience. It marginalizes the related values of other cultures, due not to the intrinsic superiority of Western ones—a superiority in which Weber himself did not believe—but due to the greater technical efficiency of the practices of the Western course of development.

Weber feared that with the advance of processes of *secularization, a new 'parcellization of the human soul' would emerge, eliminating spaces for the development of personal autonomy and responsibility. Weber became haunted by the image of social life as an immense bureaucratic machine, and it was this that induced him to reject socialism, machine which he saw as adding to modern capitalism's fateful destruction of individual entrepreneurial spirit through its collectivization of productive resources. The same preoccupation marks, and in a sense also mars, Weber's thinking on political affairs. He emphasizes dangerously the role of leaders, suggesting that all true leaders are in a sense charismatic leaders. He justifies democracy only insofar as it constitutes the best way to select such leaders under modern conditions. Leaders in his view must exercise wide-reaching powers, first to defeat alternative leaders in a competitive party system, then to assert, if necessary through deadly force, the interests of their nation in the power struggles of sovereign states.

We shall shortly consider some further elements of Weber's pessimism about modernity in connection with the thought of his intellectual near-contemporaries Friedrich Nietzsche and Sigmund Freud. But we move now to the other key thinker under discussion in this chapter: Georg *Simmel.

Georg Simmel: the 'sociology of forms'

Simmel's sociological texts date from the early 1890s when he began writing about theories of social differentiation and theories of historical knowledge. His early writing shows the influence of both English and French positivism, on the one hand, and, with increasing prominence, German 'life-philosophy' or *Lebensphilosophie*, on the other hand—a movement of thought associated with the teaching of Wilhelm *Dilthey, emphasizing the constant flux and historical relativity of human knowledge and experience. After 1910, until his death in 1918, Simmel ceased to write directly on sociological matters, retiring to a more introspective mode of writing concerned almost exclusively with philosophy, art, and humanistic culture. Simmel's two most important books from the middle period of his intellectual career are *The Philosophy of Money*, of 1900, and his *Soziologie*, of 1908. The latter work weaves a number of pre-existent essays into a comprehensive discourse, ranging over numerous themes.

The following account concentrates on Simmel's most distinctively sociological contributions from this middle period of his life. We begin with his key conception of 'forms of interaction' and the 'sociology of forms', outlined in his 1908 *Sociology* and other essays from the same decade.

Interaction and exchange: Simmel's *Sociology* of 1908

In his most expressly articulated view of the identity of the discipline, Simmel assigns to sociology the task of considering not so much the content of social events, or the nature of the interests with which individuals relate to one another, as the *forms* of their interaction (Simmel 1908*a*: 3–57). Simmel argues that such 'forms of interaction' are distinct from the motives for which actors interact, and should therefore deserve separate consideration. We know, for instance, that the same interest can be pursued through different arrangements: one can seek to make money on the market either as a self-standing businessman or as a member of a partnership. And we know that the same form can be adopted in the pursuit of different interests. For instance, Ignatius of Loyola, founder of the Catholic Jesuit order in the sixteenth century, was a military man, and when he devoted himself to saving souls he organized his followers along the same lines as units intended to fight battles.

But Simmel stresses that while the forms of interaction are distinct from the contents of interaction, they are not indifferent to them. The properties of forms of interaction affect the way in which interaction is carried out. In committing sociology to the study of these properties, Simmel suggests its analogy to geometry. Sociology should catalogue the different patterns of relationships people establish when they interact, with whatever intent. Even if sometimes people may choose a pattern to adopt, they cannot choose *not* to adopt a pattern. Sociology should therefore discern the specific tendencies and liabilities of each pattern, pointing out the possibilities it opens up to interaction and those it forecloses.

One of Simmel's most sustained accounts of the role of forms is his essay 'The Significance of Numbers in Social Life' (Simmel 1908*a*: 87–104). Here Simmel demonstrates the difference made when the numbers of individuals or groups involved in a context of interaction are either *two* or *three*. When two units of actors are involved, the secession or disappearance of one party dissolves the relationship. When three units are involved, the relationship is not dissolved but leaves open the possibility of its continuing between the two remaining units. In the three-unit relationship, each unit may establish a closer relationship to one other unit than to the remaining one. Even within a family, with two parents and one child, the child may occasionally ally itself with one parent in order to turn the other parent into an outvoted minority over a given issue. This opportunity is open to each unit, and generates a complex dynamic. A three-member relationship is typically liable to create 'two against one' coalitions, possibly shifting ones, with varying outcomes. But the third party's position is not necessarily a weak one; it can also develop strategies intended to erode the coalition and to form a new one which involves itself, and excludes another party. In case of conflict between two other parties, the third can also make itself useful as a mediator or arbitrator—although a mediating position may carry liabilities of its own. Simmel's reflections here have clear implications for political party formations and international alliances, among many other cases. More recent elaborations of such ideas can be found in *rational choice theory and game theory.

Sociability and social process

It can be seen that Simmel articulates a programmatic understanding of sociology as a discipline dealing systematically with what could be called the 'geometry' of social life. But Simmel also advances an understanding of sociology which we could describe as 'residualist' in character. His intention was to establish sociology as a discipline without challenging existent disciplines of longer lineage and greater standing. These other disciplines, he argued, deal with highly visible and lasting social formations—such as firms, churches, states, political parties, and so on—and do a most useful job of that. However, they neglect formations which also express the ability of people to engage in joint activity in a less visible, less public, and less durable manner. Such 'residual' social formations deserve the attention of scholars. They include lesser expressions of human sociability, such as maintaining a correspondence, giving or taking part in a soirée, establishing an acquaintance, flirting, addressing or refusing to address a stranger, expressing gratitude, or wearing jewellery. Simmel here shows how sociology can uncover ways in which unexpressed, informal conventions regulate social conduct and sanction deviant conduct, and in this sense *constitute* conduct. A soirée, for instance, ceases to be experienced and appreciated as one if it has more than so many participants, or if too many participants fail to behave as they are expected to behave.

In all these respects, Simmel's overwhelming fascination is with the phenomenon of *sociability* (*Geselligkeit*), with the spontaneous generation of social relationships for whatever purposes, whether leisure, entertainment, sport, and the arts, or eroticism, work, or politics. Two particular interests of his were the phenomenon of *fashion* and the concept of the *stranger*. These two cases are discussed here in Box 8.

BOX 8.   GEORG SIMMEL ON FASHION AND THE STRANGER

Some of Simmel's best essays analyse numerous apparently minor forms of sociability which the established sciences of culture do not normally address. In the case of the distinctively modern phenomenon of *fashion*, Simmel (1905) points out that fashion expresses two contrasting and complementary needs of the individual. On the one hand, individuals signal their intent to distinguish themselves, to emphasize their individuality, by keeping ahead of the crowd and exploring experiences not universally accepted. On the other hand, by virtue of appearing fashionable, individuals affiliate themselves with other individuals like themselves and express a need for bonding and social belonging.

With the same intent, Simmel also discusses such figures as the pauper and, most notably, the Stranger. Simmel shows how these figures are socially constituted, how they consist in relations between individuals patterned by consistent though not expressly communicated understandings. The essay on 'The Stranger' (1908*b*) conceptualizes perceptively the position of Jews in Western society as excluded outsiders, but it also makes some more general points. Simmel memorably describes the Stranger as the person who 'comes today and stays tomorrow'. The Stranger is distinguished from the traveller or the vagabond. The Stranger embodies two basic and contrasting relations of individuals to space, namely staying put and moving on. This holds not only in purely physical terms but in the typical relations between the Stranger and the locals or natives. The Stranger generally seeks only limited acceptance, maintains some degree of detachment and 'otherness'. In turn, this may awaken complex reactions in the locals: on the one hand, curiosity, a sense that they have something to learn or acquire from the stranger; and on the other hand, negative feelings, often extending to outright hostility.

Simmel's 'residualist' understanding of sociology also relates to its concern with 'molecular' qualities of social life. Simmel shows how 'molecular' social phenomena can occur in the cracks between the more imposing social formations, as well as *within* those formations. Social formations preserve their visibility and perform their function only insofar as they are sustained on a day-to-day basis by a multitude of minute, inconspicuous episodes of interaction.

In this connection, Simmel considers whether an army or a church or a firm exists, other than as the loci of an incessant social process between individuals. It seems clear that certain major social formations such as a state are more durable than others. But Simmel asks: what precisely makes them durable? In what sense is a currently existing social entity, say, 'the French state', the same as the French state of two or four centuries ago, when none of the individuals involved in the French state's operations *then* is alive *now*? One of Simmel's chapters in the 1908 *Sociology* examines the various conscious and unselfconscious social strategies securing 'the persistence of social groups', showing how these groups also operate in much less conspicuous formations than a state.

It can be seen that one of Simmel's favourite ways of doing sociology consists in identifying a phenomenon and exhibiting a number of not-obvious aspects of it, often with the curious effect of making them obvious. In this regard, one of his most creative essays concerns 'Conflict'. Here he states at the outset the paradox that a phenomenon generally seen as negative has in fact a number of positive effects (Simmel 1908*a*: 118–69, 1908*c*). But as the analysis progresses, one realizes that it elaborates a rather obvious proposition, namely that two conflicting parties may be brought together by their conflict with a third party. We may think of the old Arab proverb: 'me against my brother; my brother and myself against our cousin; my brother, my cousin, and myself against our neighbour'.

Ambivalence and reciprocity

We have seen that Simmel is more interested in the *how* of social life than in the *what* of social life. Here we can note a remarkable difference from Weber's effort to identify recurrent major types of phenomenon. A related theme of Simmel can also be formulated as that of *ambivalence*. In accounting for what propels the social process, Simmel speaks of a certain 'unsociable sociability' of the individual actor (Simmel 1908*a*: 69–72). Simmel suggests that individuals can enter into and adhere to any given relationship only with a *part* of themselves. As they obey forces that draw them together, they unavoidably experience other forces that draw them apart. They can only accommodate temporarily, partially, and conditionally to each other's presence and each other's demands. By the same token, their relations, no matter how stable and settled they may seem, are always subject to a process of negotiation, for they constitute a compromise between each party's needs for closeness and distance, a compromise between the search for and acceptance of dependence on the one hand, and the hankering for autonomy on the other.

This does not mean that all parties can negotiate their positions equally, for some relations are markedly asymmetric, being structured by power. Simmel speaks specifically of 'super-ordination and sub-ordination' in social life (1908*a*: 181–306). Yet here, too, Simmel considers a further aspect of ambivalence. He notes how superior parties typically expect subordinate parties to possess some degree of self-determination. The superior does not want the subordinate to be wholly subjected to the superior's will, for such a subjection would in the end induce inertia, and the superior needs the subordinate to be more than inert. In this sense the superior can rely on the subordinate only if the latter is not *entirely* at the mercy of the superior. This conception recalls the idea of a 'dialectic of the master and the slave', originally formulated by the philosopher G. W. F. *Hegel and also echoed by authors as different as Marx and some contemporary feminist and postcolonial critics. In this thinking, a slave is progressively empowered by the fact that he has learned more and more and can challenge a master who is disempowered by the fact that he depends on the slave's labour.

More generally, Simmel's argument is that all social relations involve *reciprocity* or reciprocal effect. Simmel's German expression *Wechselwirkung* is often translated simply as 'interaction'; but the German term *Wechsel* specifically means 'exchange'. It suggests that we consider all social relations, including those apparently most remote from market and commerce—such as intimate relations—as involving exchange and reciprocity. In the mid-twentieth century, Peter Blau's *Exchange and Power in Social Life* (1964) derived much of its general theory of the social process from Simmel's metaphor of exchange. In exchange, ambivalence is particularly marked, for it involves giving as little as possible of something to get as much as possible of something else. Some parallels can be discerned here between Simmel's thinking about reciprocity and the work of the early twentieth-century French anthropologist Marcel *Mauss on 'the gift' (Mauss 1924).

Money and modernity: Simmel's *The Philosophy of Money*

Simmel differed from many German thinkers of the period who decried modernization as an insidious and destructive process, threatening distinctive values of German history and culture. In contrast, Simmel felt at home in the modern Berlin metropolis of his time and thus in modern society, although he was acutely aware of the historical peculiarities of the modern urban complex and the particular colour it was imparting to social experience. We cannot cover all aspects of Simmel's penetrating account of the distinctive features of modern culture here; but we can assemble a few of its exemplary threads, especially as they appear in his first magnum opus of 1900 *The Philosophy of Money*, as well as in the 1908 *Soziologie*.

A key theme in Simmel's account of modernity is his conception of, *individuation* or *individualization*, discussed also in different ways by Marx, Durkheim, and *Tönnies. Simmel considers the allowance increasingly made in modern societies for the distinctiveness, autonomy, and responsibility of individuals. But he does not account for this by invoking a notion of the loosening of the social bond, or a distancing between the individual and the group, or an eclipse of group memberships. Rather, he states that in modern society the groups to which individuals belong are no longer arranged *concentrically*, as they are in pre-modern societies. In traditional or pre-modern settings, an individual's membership of the family determined his or her membership of a larger kinship group, in a neighbourhood, in a religious unit, or in an occupational grouping. In modern society, by contrast, the groups to which an individual belongs *overlap*. His or her membership of such groups is *elective*, expressing the deliberate, contingent choices of the individual. As a result, individuals are likely to associate with some partners in one group and with others in another group. They are shielded from the incessant monitoring of any single set of associates and can develop a sense of autonomy. Individuals can weave a 'web of group affiliations' of their own (Simmel 1908*d*). It is the idiosyncratic content of each web that grounds individuals' sense of personal distinctiveness, and this distinctiveness increases as individuals' memberships multiply and vary over time. This contrast between concentric and overlapping sets of groups is another example of Simmel's geometrical imagery of social life.

A second theme in Simmel's idea of modernity is its conception of a link between economic action and the concept of renunciation. Simmel considers how renunciation differentiates economic action from robbery and piracy and the like insofar as it involves exchange; that is, a giving up something for something else. Exchange raises for the participants a question that is both quantitative and qualitative: a giving up *how much* of *what* for *how much* of *what?* Both aspects of the question are best handled when exchange goes beyond barter and becomes *monetary*. For money is intrinsically quantitative, and it can be given and taken in exchange for anything. Nothing is intrinsically money; anything can be money. What functions as money is thus the critical question, which can be solved only institutionally, through publicly sanctioned arrangements. Yet these arrangements need to be backed by public confidence, by what is called 'trust'.

In the highly developed money systems of modern cities, social life evinces the prevalence of instrumental over against expressive relations. It displays abstractness, a heightened significance of quantity over quality, and at the same time an awareness that everything is related to everything else. The characteristics of the modern money system are anonymity of possessions and people and a tendency toward unceasing movement. All these properties powerfully shape modern society, imparting to it its relentless dynamism. In arguing this, Simmel to an extent agrees with Marx's views about the centrality of economic phenomena, but he also problematizes Marx's account. For Simmel, the attachment of value to goods is essentially grounded on subjective cultural processes of exchange, not on the amount of socially necessary labour power invested in producing such goods.

One of Simmel's most often cited essays which complements *The Philosophy of Money* is his essay of 1903 'The Metropolis and Mental Life'. This is discussed in Box 9.

The 'tragedy of culture'

Simmel's argument about the impact of money on modern society borders on one he was to develop in the last years of his life about 'the tragedy of culture' (Simmel 1911*a*). By culture Simmel means a process of *self-cultivation*, where the mind of the individual is enriched by an encounter with the intellectual and artistic legacies of the past. This process is possible because the two parties to the encounter—me and the text I am reading, or me and the painting I am regarding—are both expressions of the same reality, the human spirit, in its subjective expression at one end and its objective expression at the other. The subjective growth of the living individual aims at an assimilation of the best the past can offer, involving a recognition that the products of the past speak to us and can nourish and

---

BOX 9. GEORG SIMMEL'S ESSAY 'THE METROPOLIS AND MENTAL LIFE'

Simmel spent most of his life in the Prussian city of Berlin, which by the turn of the nineteenth century had become the most rapidly expanding city in Europe. By the 1880s Berlin was experiencing some extremely intense and accelerated processes of modernization. Simmel felt compelled to question the meaning of this process of massive urbanization and the significance of its continually changing product, modern society itself. His famous short essay 'The Metropolis and Mental Life' develops considerations applicable to modernity at large on the basis of a brief but conceptually sustained analysis of the modern urban complex (Simmel 1903). Simmel presents the metropolis as a vast assemblage of highly varied and changing objects and forms of activity of all kinds. As such, it expresses the potentiality of the human spirit more openly than any other social context, offering individuals vast novel opportunities of experience and thus of cultivations of their personality. But by the the same token, metropolitan life threatens individuals with restless stimulation and excitement. To protect themselves from nervous exhaustion, individuals must adopt practices such as holding others at a distance and attitudes of blasé indifference. In turn, these practices and attitudes, necessary as they are, deprive individuals of an opportunity to appreciate deeply the objects and people they encounter, to form authentic associations. The anonymity of life in the larger city protects individuals from the close monitoring and sanctions of other people, allowing them to develop their personalities; but at the same time it engenders loneliness and alienation. In the USA, Simmel's writings on the city exerted an important impact on the *Chicago School of Sociologists, as discussed in Chapter 5 of this book, pp. 115-6.

---

ennoble us. But this process does not often attain its goal. According to Simmel's late tragic vision, mastering the makings of the products of culture requires an effort which most individuals cannot bear to sustain. They baulk at the effort, contenting themselves with a vague acquaintance of the works of the past or displaying a shallow connoisseurship of them. If this happens, a true process of cultivation fails to take place. Simmel calls this the 'tragedy of culture', which is relentlessly intensified in modern times as the objective world of social-cultural institutions becomes an insuperable mass beyond any possibility of organic assimilation by a single individual. Above all in the metropolis, the sheer accumulation of the products of human agency—technological, economic, political, and artistic—multiplies the occasions for cultivation open to the individual, but at the same time overwhelms the individual with multiplicity, variety, and restless change.

In these last reflections, Simmel shares several attitudes in common with Weber concerning the fate of the 'old European' cultural world-view. In the final section of this chapter we turn to some commonalities between Weber and Simmel in relation to the near-contemporary thinking of Friedrich *Nietzsche and Sigmund *Freud.

The tragic consciousness in Weber and Simmel: links with Nietzsche and Freud

Nietzsche and Freud have sometimes been placed together with Marx in the history of social theory as three cardinal exponents of what Paul *Ricœur terms the 'hermeneutics of suspicion' (Ricœur 1981). Where Marx interprets human action in terms of concealed material interests disguised by ideology, Nietzsche interprets human action in terms of hidden motives disguised by forms of self-deception. Similarly, Freud interprets human action in terms of unconscious wishes and desires that have been repressed or sublimated by culture and the conscious mind (for full discussion of Freud's influence in social theory, see Chapter 8 of this book).

Such strategies of 'deep interpretation' continue in the work of Weber and Simmel, who both read and admired the writings of Nietzsche and both responded to the same kinds of questions of social psychology and pathology that concerned Freud, although they did not attend to Freud's writings so closely. Together with Nietzsche and Freud, Weber's and Simmel's thinking shares a certain 'tragic' ethos in the sense that both thinkers point to dynamic tendencies of modernity—the rise of science, rationalization, and industrialization—which equip human action with unprecedented power over natural resources and at the same time bring about a feeling of meaninglessness and moral emptiness, a condition of social illness, melancholy, and neurosis. In Weber's classic phrase, modernity results in the 'disenchantment of the world', or 'elimination of magic from the world' (*Entzauberung der Welt*) (Weber 1920*a*: 105, 1920*b*: 60). The very processes that remove magic and superstition from the world are the same processes that tend to destroy a sense of the meaning of the cosmos. Under conditions of advanced rationalization, society comes to be concerned only with the most efficient means of achieving ends, not with the ultimate meaning and value of these ends themselves.

In the spirit of Nietzsche's writings on the 'superman' or *Übermensch*, Simmel's 'tragedy of culture' suggests that only a few people, true 'aristocrats of the spirit', can continue to aspire to appreciate cultural goods. In Simmel's later work, the inexhaustible potentiality of *life* is contrasted with the inexorable necessity of *forms* in which life can find expression, but which at the same time constrain and repress its fullness. Life is compelled in turn not only to produce forms but also to transcend them. Simmel here seems to resonate both an elitism and a 'cultural pessimism' widespread in intellectual circles of his time. Similarly, the recurrent appearance of the theme of *'asceticism' in Weber's *Protestant Ethic* and his emphasis on 'discipline' bear a remarkable affinity to Nietzsche's analyses of practices of self-mastery. The theme finds a more general expression in Freud's argument that all civilization depends on individuals' ability to repress and sublimate the socially disruptive claims and promptings of their libido—the core of the unconscious—by subjecting them to the demands of the 'superego'. An abiding implication of all such views is the possibility of a 'return of the repressed'. The restraints imposed by social institutions and by individual reflection on pre-rational urges and needs have such costs that they are threatened by potential breakdowns, such as those represented by the kinds of social malaise that led to fascism in Europe in the 1920s and 1930s.

According to Weber, rationalization and modernization are strongly associated with *secularization and with what Nietzsche proclaimed to be the 'death of God' (Nietzsche 1882). From this 'death of God' arises a danger of moral *nihilism, where moral values are no longer thought to be underpinned by unifying schemes of shared belief and are henceforth thought to be solely matters of personal choice. In this context, Weber's rather problematic emphasis on the need for charismatic leaders reflects partly the impact of Nietzsche's exaltation of the ethically sovereign individual, the *Übermensch*. In other authors, this motif is associated with a fear and contempt of 'the masses'. In his description of the advance of rationalization, Weber associates himself with Nietzsche's scathing criticism of one aspect of the late nineteenth century: its complacency about progress, its shallow assurance about the solidity and superiority of the current era. On the other hand, Weber does not express any backward-looking lamentation about the ravages of modernity. His view is that society must embrace the present, in all its contradictions and paradoxes.

Conclusion

Weber and Simmel share an understanding of social reality which emphasizes its intrinsically historical nature. Both appreciate the necessity of approaching social reality 'hermeneutically'; that is, with an eye to the subjective processes orienting the conduct of individuals. They also agree that in those processes, a given individual's activity intersects with and accommodates the results of the activities of many other individuals, both present and past. In these respects, Weber and Simmel contrast with Marx and Durkheim. Where the latter think of society and social change above all in terms of *structures* and *systems*, involving objective forces and dynamics operating above the heads of individuals, Weber and Simmel underscore the importance of *meaning*, individual *action*, and *subjectivity*.

At the same time, the orientations of the two thinkers differ markedly. Weber is chiefly interested in the continuities and discontinuities of historical events and the different sensitivities, competences, and action orientations generated across the human species. Weber is concerned with the historical diversity of ways of experiencing and evaluating reality, of constructing institutions and motivating and justifying action. Accordingly, his sociological work aims to conceptualize sharply the different value constructs and diverse sets of institutions constraining human activities, ranging across such fields as law, religion, politics, science, the economy, and the arts. Simmel, in contrast, focuses attention on the ways in which individuals—especially modern individuals—negotiate their existence in any social context, according to the patterns of interaction they weave in encountering each other. It is, so to speak, not the *what* of the socio-historical process that attracts his attention but the *how* of that process. Simmel has as keen a sense for conflict, contradiction, and tragedy, as Weber does; but where Weber emphasizes contrasts between material and ideal interests and between values, Simmel explores the import of the 'unsociable sociability' of human beings and the dynamic tension between the self and the other person as mutually interrelated, mutually differentiated members of shifting social forms. Read together, these two authors suggest how diverse the sociological enterprise can be.

■ **QUESTIONS FOR CHAPTER 3**

1 What methodological precepts distinguish Weber's vision of social science from that of Marx and Durkheim? Why is 'value relevance' important to Weber?

2 Why does Weber attach importance to religion in his account of the rise of capitalism and the emergence of the modern world?

3   What does Weber mean by 'legitimate domination'? What is the significance of legal-rational domination for modern social organization?

4   What aspects of social life are illuminated by Simmel's conception of 'forms of interaction', 'reciprocity', and 'sociability'?

5   What does Simmel regard as the driving forces of modernity? How do Simmel's reflections on money compare and contrast with Marx's and Weber's theories about capitalism?

6   In what sense are Weber and Simmel 'pessimistic' writers'?

■ FURTHER READING

The best place to begin reading Weber is *The Protestant Ethic and the Spirit of Capitalism*, either in the classic translation of 1930 by Talcott Parsons (published by Routledge, with an introduction by Anthony Giddens) or in the more accurate translation of 2001 by Stephen Kalberg (published by Blackwell), which includes some useful notes explaining Weber's difficult historical vocabulary. Another translation is available by Peter Baehr and Gordon Wells, published by Penguin in 2002, though this translation is based on the first edition of 1904–5, not on the revised and expanded edition of 1920. Most of Weber's other key shorter texts and extracts are available in *From Max Weber: Essays in Sociology*, ed. H. H. Gerth and C. Wright Mills (Routledge, 1948), and in a more recent and more accurate collection *The Essential Weber*, ed. Sam Whimster (Routledge, 2003).

For Weber's conception of the relation between 'interests and ideas' or between 'material factors and ideal factors' in religion and culture, see (in Gerth and Mills) 'The Social Psychology of the World Religions', alias (in Whimster) 'Introduction to the Economic Ethics of the World Religions'. For Weber's conception of rationalization, see the 'Author's Introduction' to Talcott Parsons's translation of *The Protestant Ethic*, alias 'Prefatory Remarks to the Collected Essays in the Sociology of Religion', in Stephen Kalberg's translation; also (in Gerth and Mills) 'Religious Rejections of the World and their Directions', alias (in Whimster) 'Intermediate Reflections on the Economic Ethics of the World Religions'. For Weber's methodological views, read his essay 'The "Objectivity" of Knowledge in Social Science and Social Policy', in *The Essential Weber*, together with 'Basic Sociological Terms', in Weber's *Economy and Society*, chapter 1. But do not attempt to read the rest of *Economy and Society* without having first read Weber's shorter and more accessible pieces.

Weber's dense and erudite style of writing can be difficult to read on a first attempt. For some good secondary introductions, see Dirk Käsler's *Max Weber: An Introduction to his Life and Work* (Polity, 1988), Ralph Schroeder's *Max Weber and the Sociology of Culture* (Sage, 1992), Martin Albrow's *Max Weber's Construction of Social Theory* (Macmillan, 1990), and Reinhard Bendix's *Max Weber: An Intellectual Portrait* (Methuen, 1966). On the Protestant ethic, see Gianfranco Poggi's *Calvinism and the Capitalist Spirit: Max Weber's Protestant Ethic* (Macmillan, 1983), Gordon Marshall's *In Search of the Spirit of Capitalism* (Hutchinson 1982), Randall Collins's 'Weber's Last Theory of Capitalism', reprinted in Collins's *Weberian Sociological Theory* (Cambridge University Press, 1986), and also Weber's replies to early criticism of the text from 1907–10 in *The Protestant Ethic Debate: Max Weber's Replies to his Critics, 1907–1910* ed. David Chalcraft and Austin Harrington (Liverpool University Press, 2001). For Weber's ideas in relation to politics and power, see David Beetham's *Max Weber and the Theory of Modern Politics* (Allen & Unwin, 1974) and Wolfgang Mommsen's *The Age of Bureaucracy* (Blackwell, 1974) and *Max Weber and German Politics, 1890–1920* (Chicago University Press, 1984). For an overview of Weber's methodology, see Sven Eliaeson's *Max Weber's Methodologies* (Polity Press, 2002). For Weber's relation to Marx, see Karl Löwith's *Max Weber and Karl Marx* (Allen & Unwin, 1982). For Weber's relation to 'cultural pessimism', see Lawrence Scaff's *Fleeing the Iron Cage* (University of California Press, 1989), Arthur Mitzman's *The Iron Cage: An Historical Interpretation of Weber* (Knopf, 1970), and Roger Brubaker's *The Limits of Rationality* (Allen & Unwin, 1984).

Accessible collections of essays and extracts from Simmel in English are *Simmel on Culture*, ed. Mike Featherstone and David Frisby (Sage, 1997), *Conflict and the Web of Group Affiliations*, ed. Kurt Wolff and Reinhard Bendix (Free Press, 1955), and *Georg Simmel on Individuality and Social Forms*, ed. Donald Levine (Chicago University Press, 1971). It is worth beginning with Simmel's essay 'The Metropolis and Mental Life', in *Simmel on Culture*. In Simmel's *The Philosophy of Money* one of the most interesting chapters is the last, titled 'The Style of Life'. Simmel's 1908 *Soziologie* is available in abridged form in English as *The Sociology of Georg Simmel*, ed. Kurt Wolff (Free Press, 1950). Also important is Simmel's essay at the beginning of the 1908 *Soziologie*, titled 'How Is Society Possible?', available in English in *Georg Simmel, 1858–1918*, ed. Kurt Wolff (Ohio State University Press, 1959). For Simmel's writings on women, see Chapter 11 of this book, p. 236, as well as *Georg Simmel on Women, Sexuality and Love*, ed. Guy Oakes (Yale University Press, 1984).

Some good secondary studies of Simmel are David Frisby's short *Georg Simmel* (Routledge, rev. edn. 2002) and longer *Sociological Impressionism: A Reappraisal of Georg Simmel's Social Theory* (Routledge, 1981) and his *Fragments of Modernity* (Polity Press, 1985). Also good are Gianfranco Poggi's *Money and the Modern Mind* (University of California Press, 1993), Donald Levine's *Simmel and Parsons* (Arno Press, 1980), and Lewis Coser's *Georg Simmel* (Prentice-Hall, 1965). On Simmel on art, see 'Georg Simmel: Money, Style and Sociability', in Austin Harrington's *Art and Social Theory: Sociological Arguments in Aesthetics* (Polity Press, 2004), 150–4.

■ WEBSITES

Verstehen: Max Weber's Homepage at **www.faculty.rsu.edu/~felwell/Theorists/Weber/Whome.htm** Provides a good resource at a basic level, including summaries of concepts such as bureaucracy and rationalization.

SocioSite on Max Weber at **www2.fmg.uva.nl/sociosite/topics/weber.html** Contains links to summaries of Weber's key texts.

Max Weber Studies at **www.maxweberstudies.org** Displays the site of a journal devoted to new translations of Weber texts and the reception of Weber's work in different language communities.

Georg Simmel On-line at **http://socio.ch/sim/index_sim.htm** Includes a biography with links to works in translation.

Georg Simmel Page at **www.cf.ac.uk/socsi/undergraduate/introsoc/simmel.html** Presents links to Simmel's work, taken from the Dead Sociologists' Society.

4

Functionalism and its Critics

John Holmwood

This chapter discusses the legacy of *functionalism in modern social theory. Functionalist theorists argue that society should be understood as a system of interdependent parts. They believe that there are specific requirements—functional prerequisites—that must be met in all social systems and that these can provide the basis for the comparative analysis of social institutions. Functionalism came to prominence in North American sociology in the 1950s. This was a period of affluence, consolidation, and growth in Western capitalism. At the time, several commentators—including notably Daniel *Bell—believed that the prosperous post-war years marked an 'end of ideology' (Bell 1962). By this they meant that the once defining conflict of nineteenth-century capitalism—between a bourgeois ideology of radical 'individualism' and a socialist ideology of 'collectivism'—had lost its relevance. The North American functionalist theorists affirmed this view of the obsolescence of ideological struggles between classes and collective social movements. They were frequently liberal in their political outlook, and the ideas of Marxism, which continued to exert a significant impact on sociology in Europe, played little role in their work.

This was the context in which Talcott *Parsons and Robert *Merton came to prominence. Parsons and Merton sought to distinguish sociology from other disciplines, such as economics and psychology, and to celebrate its relevance to the new social problems of affluent capitalism. For Parsons (1949a), the 'end of ideology' heralded a 'new age of sociology'. Parsons's claim was far-reaching in its implications. He argued that sociology was entering a 'post-classical' phase (Parsons 1937). Functionalism could provide a framework that would integrate the insights of *Durkheim and *Weber but would otherwise draw a line under sociology's past in creating the foundations for future development.

In this chapter, we first consider the origins of functionalist thinking in anthropological research from the early decades of the twentieth century. Then we look in detail at the key contributions of Merton and Parsons. The final parts of the chapter discuss various criticisms of functionalism, associated with rational actor approaches and with what came to be called 'conflict theory'.

Functionalism in anthropology

Although functionalism mainly came to prominence as a school in the 1950s, its origins can be traced to an earlier generation of writers working in the field of anthropology. These included notably the British-based anthropologists Bronislaw *Malinowski and Alfred *Radcliffe-Brown. Elements of a functionalist way of thinking can also be traced to the work of Durkheim.

A central methodological precept of the early twentieth-century anthropologists was that social actions are not to be explained by the immediate meanings they have for individual actors. They are to be explained by the *function* they serve for wider social groups. On this view, meanings for individual actors cannot be understood independently of a wider system of collective practices and beliefs within which they are embedded. These collective practices are to be explained in turn by the functions they serve for the system of social life as a whole. Different elements of social life depend on each other and fulfil functions that contribute to the maintenance of social order and its reproduction over time.

We can illustrate this mode of analysis by looking at a typical piece of explanation in functionalist anthropology. For many years, anthropologists had observed how the Hopi tribe of North America engage in a complex series of rituals and dances prior to the planting of their crops. The Hopi were well known for their rain dances. For anthropologists, it seemed clear that the Hopi dances could not be understood as instrumental action intended directly to produce the rains. At the same time, it did not seem right to suggest that the Hopi were behaving irrationally. The claim that they were behaving irrationally looked suspiciously like a judgement from the perspective of modern Western beliefs in the superiority of scientific knowledge.

The functionalist response to this puzzle was to suggest that the Hopi rain dance was not a form of instrumental activity but rather a form of *expressive* activity. This expressive activity served to reinforce the bonds of *solidarity among the group. It had the *function* of generating group cohesion. Such cohesion was important because the Hopi lived in dispersed shelters, and so the dances brought them together. In their other activities, such as planting and harvesting their crops, the Hopi showed themselves to be competent at organizing instrumental activities too. The Hopi rain dances were thus explained by the function they fulfilled in the life of the tribe as a whole. The function in question was that of the *reinforcement of group solidarity*.

It is a small step from this to suggest that all social relations fulfil certain functions and that all social groups need to meet certain universal functional requirements—even if these requirements are handled differently in different societies (compare Malinowski 1944). Examples of such 'functional prerequisites' could include sexual reproduction, economic subsistence, social control, socialization and education of new generations, and the management of sickness and death, as well as 'group solidarity'.

We should note here that in a typical case of functionalist explanation, the existence of a phenomenon or the production of an action is not explained by its direct efficient causes but rather by its indirect *effects* in relation to an environment. Functionalism departs from the traditional logic of causal argument where a cause precedes its consequences. Functionalists instead reverse this sequence and assign causal powers to effects (see further Isajiw 1968). Durkheim captured this distinction when he stated that 'when . . . the explanation of a social phenomenon is undertaken, we must seek separately the efficient cause which produces it and the function it fulfills' (1895: 95). In this respect, the functionalist anthropologist who asks 'why do the Hope dance for rain?' looks for an answer not in factors that immediately cause the Hopi to dance on a particular occasion. Rather, the anthropologist considers the effects or consequences of the Hopi's dancing for all the other elements of the Hopi's way of life, noting that these effects have a positive function for those other elements. The functionalist concludes that if the rain dance did not have this positive function, the dance would not be reproduced. Therefore the dance is explained by its function, by its effects in an environment of diverse other elements of a social system.

One problem for functionalism is that explanations of phenomena by reference to effects in an environment can often degenerate into scientifically illegitimate kinds of *teleology, where that which is described as the 'function' of a phenomenon is tacitly assumed to be the 'purpose' or 'goal' of the phenomenon. The function is implicitly described as something necessarily good, or alternatively it is imagined as marking an end-state to which the phenomenon tends to develop over time. These were the kinds of *metaphysical problems that infected much nineteenth-century thinking about social evolution. Most notorious were the assumptions of writers influenced by Darwinist notions of 'natural selection' and the 'survival of the fittest', as applied to history and society.

For this reason, the British anthropologist Radcliffe-Brown sought to distinguish sharply between *'diachronic' and *'synchronic' analysis: between the analysis of change in a system and the analysis of interaction among parts of a system at any given moment in time. According to Radcliffe-Brown, the task of anthropology (and sociology) lay primarily in synchronic analysis. Anthropology and sociology were not to make any illicitly diachronic assumptions about the positive, beneficial, or progressive unfolding of functional systems over time. He wrote that 'any social system, to survive, must conform to certain conditions. If we can define adequately one of these universal conditions, i.e. one to which all human societies must conform, we have a sociological law . . . [An] institution may be said to have its general *raison d'être* (sociological origin) and its particular *raison d'être* (historical origin). The first is for the sociologist or social anthropologist to discover' (Radcliffe-Brown 1952: 43). Sociology and anthropology were to aim at impartial scientific analysis of the recurring properties of social systems. They were not, however, to speculate on the meaning of the historical development of social systems over time.

There are some problems with functionalist explanations among early twentieth-century anthropological writers. The division between 'synchronic' and 'diachronic' analysis is something that came to haunt functionalism. This and other problems were directly addressed by the American sociological theorists who came to prominence in the 1950s, including particularly Robert *Merton. It is to Merton's work that we turn first.

Robert Merton: manifest and latent functions

Although Merton is standardly treated by commentators in a secondary position after Talcott Parsons, this procedure is somewhat invidious. In the following account, we look first at Merton's path-breaking article of 1949, 'Manifest and Latent Functions', which not only pinpointed a number of difficult issues in anthropological functionalism but also anticipated much of Parsons's important work from the 1950s. The article appeared in Merton's major collection of studies titled *Social Theory and Social Structure*, first published in 1949, which sought to codify functional analysis. Merton republished *Social Theory and Social Structure* twice in 1957 and 1968 with new additions. In 1941 he became Assistant Professor at Columbia University in New York where he remained for the rest of his career.

In order to produce a satisfactory statement of functional analysis, Merton proposed a distinction between *manifest* and *latent functions*. The former refers to the *conscious intentions* of actors; the latter to the *objective consequences* of their actions, which were often *unintended*. According to Merton, most of the mistakes of existing functionalism were the result of a conflation of these two different categories. In particular, existing functionalism failed to see adequately that the historical origins of an item can be explained by reference to the conscious intentions of actors, while the selection of the item and its reproduction is to be explained by reference to latent functions.

Merton's methodological strategy was to separate the scientific substance of functionalism from its historical origins in anthropology. This was necessary if functionalism was to be a proper framework for empirical research. In his view, the tendency hitherto was for functionalist arguments to supplant research rather than to support it. He identified three problematic postulates in anthropological functionalism: the postulate of the *functional unity of society*; the postulate of *universal functionalism*; and the postulate of *indispensability*. We look at these three in turn.

Merton associated the postulate of the functional unity of society primarily with Radcliffe-Brown. He cited the British author's comment that 'the function of a particular social usage is the contribution it makes to the total social life as the functioning of the total social system' (Radcliffe-Brown 1935: 397). According to Merton, it may be that some non-literate societies show a high degree of integration, but it is illegitimate to assume this would pertain to all societies. Moreover, it is possible that what is functional for society, considered as a whole, does not prove functional for all individuals or for some subgroups within the society. Conversely, what is functional for an individual or group may not be functional for the wider society. Merton suggested that alongside the concept of function, it was necessary to propound a concept of *dysfunction*, where the objective consequences of an item are negative for some individuals or groups. For example, inequality may have the function of motivating individuals to perform at their different job tasks, but high degrees of inequality may give rise to the alienation of some individuals and groups.

The second postulate of universal functionalism refers to what was a rather old debate in anthropology concerning 'survivals'; that is, practices that have no present role but are understood in terms of the past history of a group. This was used by some anthropologists to construct highly speculative evolutionary histories. Merton argues that if we accept that there are degrees of integration, then practices can 'survive' if they are functional for *some* individuals or groups, most typically for those groups who are *dominant* in the social system. This identifies *power* and *coercion* as important issues. Merton writes: 'far more useful as a directive for research would seem the provisional assumption that persisting cultural forms have a *net balance of functional consequences* either for society considered as a unit or for subgroups sufficiently to retain these forms intact, by means of direct coercion or indirect persuasion,' (Merton 1949*b*: 86).

Merton's final postulate of indispensability was directed as a criticism of Malinowski's view that every item fulfils a vital function and represents an indispensable part within a working whole. Merton comments that such an assumption makes unclear whether it is the *function* that is indispensable or the particular *item* held to be fulfilling the function. Merton argued that once this is clarified, it is evident that it is necessary to distinguish between functional *prerequisites*—preconditions functionally necessary for a society—and the particular social forms that fulfil those prerequisites. In Merton's view, while the prerequisites are for the most part indispensable, the particular forms or items that meet those functions are *not* indispensable. There are always alternative ways of meeting any particular function. Thus Merton points out that 'just as the same item may have multiple functions, so may the same function be diversely fulfilled by alternative items' (Merton 1949*b*: 87–8).

Each of Merton's qualifications of anthropological functionalism is designed to transform the postulates into *variables that can be the objects of empirical research. Furthermore, by identifying the possibility of dysfunction and by suggesting that practices can have different consequences for individuals and groups, depending on how they are placed within a social structure, Merton explicitly made power and conflict central issues for research within a functionalist paradigm. This is in line with another of Merton's ideas about how sociological theory should be built. He reiterated that theory and research belong together and that topics should be carefully chosen for lying in what he called a *'middle range' between minor working hypotheses of routine research and all-inclusive *'grand theory' (Merton 1949*c*).

One problem with Merton's essay, however, was its terminology. Merton's reference to both 'latent functions' and 'manifest functions' was unfortunate since his actual concern was to distinguish only between latent functions and manifest *motives*. His terminology encouraged critics to think that sociological functionalism neglected agency, just when agency was being identified as a central concern in American sociology. At the same time, Merton's proposed codification of social enquiry in terms of an analytical distinction between 'subjective motive' and 'objective function' was also the solution that Parsons had proposed. The further elaboration of Merton's critique of anthropological functionalism led him directly onto terrain occupied by Parsons concerning the relationship between actors' intentions and the objective consequences of their actions. It was this that took functionalism in the direction of all-inclusive 'grand' or *'unified' theory and away from the 'middle range'. Thus what in fact came to be identified as functionalism in American sociology did not develop in the way proposed by Merton. Instead it developed as a single all-embracing theoretical system, as set out by Talcott *Parsons. It is to Parsons's general theory that we now turn.

Talcott Parsons: functionalism as unified general theory

In 1927 Parsons took up a position at Harvard University where he would remain for the rest of his career until his death in 1979. Commentators commonly identify three phases in the development of his work: an early, a middle and a late phase. In the early phase, beginning in the 1930s, Parsons sought to develop a rigorous theory of the nature and structure of social action. In the middle phase, from the 1940s and 1950s, he was concerned with the structure and functioning of social systems. In the later phase, he was more concerned to set out processes of structural differentiation and a typology of different stages of social development. However, the core assumptions of his approach remain throughout.

Almost from the outset, Parsons's intention was to produce a scheme of general categories that would form the necessary foundation for social-scientific enquiry. Identifying these categories was the objective of his first major work, *The Structure of Social Action* (1937), a work that came to define European social theory for subsequent generations of North American sociologists. In this book, Parsons described how the classical generation of European social theorists active in the years 1890–1920 had brought about a decisive break with the past. The most important thinkers he addressed were Weber and Durkheim, but he also wrote extensively on the English economist Alfred *Marshall and the Italian theorist Vilfredo *Pareto. He did not consider it necessary to treat Marx because he believed that Marx belonged to a redundant stage of social thought whose insights had essentially been recuperated in the best way possible by Weber. Parsons argued that while no single one of these theorists presented all the elements of an appropriate general scheme, taken together they provided an early intimation of the functionalist synthesis of sociological theory, which Parsons would present as the basis of professional sociology. Parsons continued to develop and refine the scheme in all his subsequent writings. He was, in the words of the Preface to his middle-period treatise *The Social System* (1951), 'an incurable theorist'.

We begin with the following account with Parsons's analysis of action in *The Structure of Social Action*, before turning to his later more elaborate conceptions of social structures, functions, and systems.

Parsons's 'voluntaristic theory of action'

Any general theoretical scheme, Parsons argues, must represent the diverse influences on social behaviour and must take as its point of reference human *action*. In European sociology, Parsons first noted a tradition of *positivism, which sought to explain behaviour in terms of certain putatively 'objective' influences upon it. At the same time, he identified a counter-tradition, that of *idealism, which emphasized the 'subjective' aspect represented by Weber and German historical thought. In Parsons's view, these two traditions had developed in mutually antithetical ways. He argued that it would not do 'merely to say that both the positivistic and the idealistic positions have certain justifications and that there is a sphere in which each should be recognised. It is necessary, rather, to go beyond such eclecticism, to attempt at least in outline, an account of the specific modes of interrelation between the two' (1937: 486). It was necessary to provide 'a bridge between the apparently irreconcilable differences of the two traditions, making it possible in a sense, to "make the best of both worlds" ' (1937: 486).

As a first step in setting out how objective and subjective elements can be combined in a single scheme, Parsons developed what he called a *'voluntaristic theory of action', emphasizing the *'action frame of reference'. Within this theoretical framework, he focused on what he called the *unit act* and its component elements. The unit act did not refer to any concretely existing phenomena or to the empirical acts of any specific individual person. Rather, Parsons sought, by a process of logical abstraction, to identify the most basic elements of a wider scheme. Any manifestation of action could only be addressed once that wider scheme had been fully elaborated. Its categories were not to refer directly to concrete entities, even though, ultimately, the scheme must be capable of direct empirical application. For Parsons, unit acts are not concrete empirical components of a theory, as they are in methodological-individualist approaches.

Parsons defines action as intentional behaviour oriented to the realization of an end. Action occurs in conditional circumstances that must be calculated and utilized by actors in pursuit of their *ends*. Actors must accommodate and calculate upon *conditions* if their actions are to be successful. Ends and conditions (including *means*) are here analytically distinct categories. In addition, action involves effort or agency to transform circumstances in conformity to *norms, which govern ends and the selection of their means of realization. Finally, action, to be rational, must be adequate in terms of the *knowledge* necessary for the realization of ends. Thus Parsons refers to the 'intrinsic rationality of the *means–end relation' and to the necessary role of 'valid knowledge as a guide to action' (1937: 600).

Social systems and the 'problem of order'

Parsons states that the concept of the unit act 'serves only to arrange the data in a certain order, not to subject them to the analysis necessary for their explanation' (1937: 48). 'Explanation' requires a further step in the analysis, from unit acts to their location within *systems* of action. This step 'consists in generalising the conceptual scheme so as to bring out the functional relations in the facts already descriptively arranged' (1937: 49). In Merton's terms, this represents a move from consideration of manifest functions to that of *latent functions*.

This further generalization of the scheme is linked to what Parsons sees as *emergent properties* of systems of action. These are properties that arise in the coordination of actions and are not reducible to analysis in terms of unit acts alone. Here Parsons espouses a key methodological position which marks his explicit attachment to methodological *holism, rather than to methodological individualism. He writes that 'action systems have properties that are emergent only on a certain level of complexity in the relations of unit acts to each other. These properties cannot be identified in any single unit act considered apart from its relation to others in the same system. They cannot be derived by a process of direct generalisation of the properties of the unit act' (1937: 739). The concept of emergent properties serves to identify the 'elements of structure of a generalised system of action' (1937: 718), and these elements of structure are to be further analysed in terms of their functional relations; that is, in terms of the logical relations established in the theoretical system. This is what underlies Parsons's use of the analogy of an organism: 'the very definition of an organic whole is one within which the relations determine the properties of its parts. The properties of the whole are not simply a resultant of the latter' (1937: 32). It can be seen here that Parsons was very much preoccupied with the idea of systems of action in his early work, no less than in his later work in which he comes to use the word 'system' more and more frequently.

The idea of emergent properties of systems of social action is at the heart of what Parsons refers to as the 'problem of order'. Parsons here refers to the thought of the seventeenth-century English political philosopher Thomas *Hobbes, author of *Leviathan* (1651), written in the context of the English Civil War of the 1640s–1650s. Hobbes had sought to answer the question of how it is possible that a society of self-interested individuals does not end up in a state of 'war of all against all', which Hobbes also described as the *'state of nature'. Hobbes's answer was to postulate an external authority—the sovereign—to whom the power to enforce agreement is voluntarily given. For Parsons, this answer was too bleak and too directly focused on coercive power. Hobbes's mechanistic idea of the human animal neglected the *normative regulation of social relationships through aspects of cultural communication. Parsons did not intend to make the opposite kind of mistake by neglecting power. He acknowledged that sometimes social relationships do indeed descend into a war of all against all. Just as the English Civil War impressed itself on Hobbes, so Parsons was concerned with the rise of fascism in Europe and its terrible consequences (1942*a*, 1942*b*). But in his approach to such cases of disorder, he wanted first to set out a few basic sociological principles within an all-embracing theory that could account adequately for the everyday routine phenomenon of social order, through what he called 'normative integration', or through what is more commonly known as 'civil', 'normal', 'acceptable' social behaviour.

Parsons's way of solving this problem was to point to various mechanisms capable of securing the coordination of action. Action occurs in systems and these systems have an orderly character. There are two aspects of order, identified by Parsons. These are what we can term *personal order* and *interpersonal order*. Personal order involves a recognition that any given act is, for the actor, one among a bunch of other chosen and possible actions with a variety of different ends and different requirements for their realization. Interpersonal order involves a recognition that actions occur in contexts that include, as Parsons put it, 'a plurality of actors' (1937: 51).

Where means are scarce relative to ends, any individual actor will maximize outcomes by the most efficient selection of means and by placing his or her ends in a personal hierarchy of preferences. The ends of actors are determined by their preferences and values, but actors' cognitive reflection on the means to their ends is also governed by what Parsons terms a 'normative standard', namely a 'norm of efficiency'. In this regard, one of the most significant emergent properties of personal order is 'economic rationality' (1937: 288 ff.). As Parsons put it, 'economic rationality is thus an emergent property of action which can be observed only when a plurality of unit acts is treated together as constituting an integrated system' (1937: 40).

Fundamental issues of social theory arise for Parsons when systems of social action involving multiple actors are the focus. These are the issues of interpersonal order. It is here that Parsons confronts, directly the Hobbesian problem of social order. Interpersonal order concerns the coordination of systems of action where these systems include the activities of a number of actors. The actions of any given actor form the conditions and means of other actors in the system. Just as there is an interdependence of acts within the means–end chains of an actor's system of personal order, so there is an interdependence of acts and means–end chains among the interactions of a plurality of actors.

Power, values, and norms

In all his works, Parsons stresses the role of a common culture, both as the source of the standards governing interaction and as internalized within the personality as the basis of dispositions to act. At the same time, he is far from arguing that the stability of systems of action depends *only* on the functioning of common value elements, as many of his critics came to maintain—especially the 'conflict theorists'. Parsons's conception of normative order is more subtle than is often granted, and he most certainly intended it to include a treatment of issues of power. Several considerations can be noted in this connection.

The first consideration concerns Parsons's weighting of the significance of coercion (force) in relation to economic rationality and to common values. He writes that where the behaviour of particular actors is at stake, 'coercion is a potential means to the desired control, which is not included in the economic concept as such. It also has a similar double aspect—the exercise of coercive power as a means and its acquisition as an immediate end' (1937: 239–40). In other words, coercive power does not define the social system in the sense of being the ground on which the system is based. Rather, coercive power is a relation *within* the system. Thus Parsons writes that coercion 'cannot be a property of the *total* action system involving a plurality of individuals; it can only apply to some individuals or groups within a system *relative* to others. Coercion is an exercise of power over others' (1937: 740). What Parsons is concerned to establish here is that the coercive aspects of power do not define its essential features. Power is not simply something that one person has at the expense of another; it is also something that is generated within social relationships as a mutual benefit or 'facility', as he terms it.

The final emergent property of the total action system is thus to the requirement that 'in order that there may be a stable system of action involving a plurality of individuals, there must be normative regulation of the power aspect of individuals within the system; in this sense, there must be a distributive order' (1937: 740). In other words, the distribution of resources within the system, and therefore the actions by which those resources are produced and reproduced, must be governed by some legitimizing principles or *norms*.

The fact that most people, generally, most of the time, do not freak out, commit murder or rape in the streets, cannot simply be attributed to the fact that if they were to do so, they would be punished with physical force by representatives of a system of state laws. Individuals internalize the threat of physical punishment for deeds they ought not do. Sanctions restrain individuals from carrying out such acts before they even contemplate them. But individuals are restrained from so acting not simply by sublimated fear of the consequences. Rather, they come to develop a sense of the intrinsic normative illegitimacy of such acts, based on an understanding that such acts are 'wrong' or 'evil', 'indecent' or 'distasteful', and so on, in an ethically significant sense. It is in this manner that Parsons—by a similar route to Durkheim—arrives at a sociological understanding of our ideas of morality and civilization. What is called 'moral', 'civil', or 'lawful' behaviour in ordinary laypeople's language is explained sociologically by reference to processes of socialization that involve a fusion between elements of *coercion* on the one hand and elements of *common value understandings* on the other.

As Parsons developed this theory—chiefly in *The Social System* (1951) and after—he went on to offer further distinctions between different *levels of analysis*. He distinguished between the level of the *personality*, the level of the *social system*, and the level of *culture* (later adding a fourth level of the 'biological organism'). These levels correspond to the analytical distinctions made in his earlier statement of the action frame of reference.

• The level of the *personality* corresponds to the individual actor viewed as a system. As well as conscious motivations, it includes unconscious motivations or what Parsons calls 'need dispositions'. The latter are important for understanding how *sanctions* operate. Actors respond not only to positive rewards, as economists suggest, but also to internalized feelings of guilt, anxiety, and the need for approval.

• The level of *culture* refers to symbols and meanings that are drawn upon by actors in pursuit of their personal projects and in their negotiation of social constraints and facilities. The three key features of the cultural system are 'that culture is *transmitted*, it constitutes a heritage or a social tradition; secondly, that it is *learned*, it is not a manifestation, in particular content, of man's genetic constitution; and thirdly, that it is *shared*. Culture, that is, is on the one hand the product of, on the other hand a determinant of, systems of human social interaction' (1951: 15).

• The level of the *social system* corresponds to the level of interaction among a plurality of actors which was Parsons's primary focus concerning the 'problem of order' in *The Structure of Social Action*. The social system is a structure of positions and roles organized by normed expectations and maintained by sanctions.

Parsons proposes that each of the three levels forms a system in its own right, where the characteristic of a system is logical coherence in the relations among its parts. At the same time, each system functions in relation to other systems and *'interpenetrates' with them. And in turn, this 'interpenetration', or interdependence, *also* constitutes a system. This is what Parsons had previously referred to as the 'total action system'. In his middle-period work, Parsons sees the total social system as having four basic functional prerequisites which are necessary to its constitution and operation. Parsons describes these in the following four-part scheme, which he terms the AGIL scheme:

- The first prerequisite is *adaptation* (A). This refers to the relationship of a system to its external environments and the utilization of resources in pursuit of goals.

- The second prerequisite is *goal attainment* (G). This refers to the directedness of systems toward collective goals.

- The third prerequisite is *integration* (I). This refers to the maintenance of coordinated relationships among the parts of the system.

- The fourth prerequisite is *pattern maintenance* or *latency* (L). This refers to a society's symbolic order as a generalized series of mutually reinforcing meanings and typifications.

Once again, Parsons does not argue here that actual, empirically existing social systems manifest integration and interdependence in the way described in the analytical theory. The functional imperatives only identify general tendencies generated by concrete systems, namely tendencies toward integration and interdependence—although these tendencies are never fully realized in actual empirical systems. The functional imperatives supply the axes of the two-by-two tables that proliferate throughout Parsons's later writings. Figure 4.1, taken from Parsons's late text titled *Social Systems and the Evolution of Action Theory* (1977a), presents his idea of the subdivisions of the social system, defined by priorities accorded to one or other of the functional prerequisites in its organization.

Structural differentiation

A final key element in Parsons's functionalist theory is his conception of 'structural differentiation', which is entailed by the fourfold AGIL scheme of functions. In this conception,

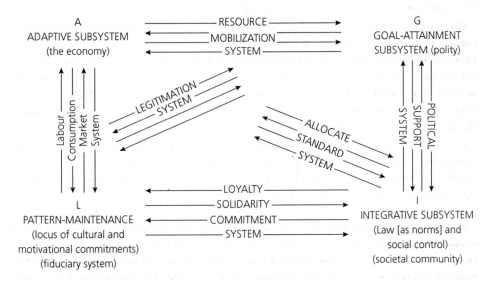

Figure 4.1 Format of the societal interchange system

Source: (Parsons 1977c: 366).

societies are classified according to the extent of institutional specialization around functions; for example, the extent to which political institutions are separated from economic institutions; or the extent to which economic institutions are separated from the household; or the extent to which the household specializes around functions of socialization. Societies can be characterized according to different patterns and degrees of structural differentiation.

In his books *Societies: Evolutionary and Comparative Perspectives* (1966) and *The System of Modern Societies* (1971a), Parsons sets out a developmental account of the emergence of modern societies. These are conceived in terms of evolutionary stages derived from the application of the four-function paradigm. One problem with this, however, was that his scheme of functional imperatives was supposed to apply to *all* societies in the *synchronic dimension*. It ought to have followed from this that societies with lesser degrees of specialization could be no less 'adequate' than those with greater degrees of specialization. The only way in which there could be an 'internal requirement' for greater structural differentiation would have been on the assumption of an overarching system goal of more effective performance. This would have carried some problematic *teleological implications. The idea of the superiority of higher over lower stages of developmental complexity carried the implication that better-adapted forms are realized out of the deficiencies of 'lesser' forms. The way in which structural differentiation occurs around the four functions, each with its characteristic subsystem, is suggestive of an overall 'end' to the process. In this scheme, modernity–or more specifically North American modernity, which Parsons (1966) called the new 'lead' society of modernity—is presented as the culminating stage of social development. It is in this respect that the Parsonian model of modernization can be criticized for its Western-centredness, as discussed in Chapters 1 and 13 of this book (pp. 31–3, 275).

In general, many sociologists have felt uneasy about the seemingly endless conceptual elaboration that makes up the bulk of Parsons's writings. Unlike Weber, whose reflections on sociological concepts derived from a more historical focus on definite empirical problems, Parsons was less engaged with empirical questions. This is not to say that Parsons took no interest in empirical matters at all. He frequently claimed that the ultimate purpose of his theoretical scheme was to facilitate practical sociological research. In addition, he wrote a number of important empirically oriented articles in fields such as the sociology of professions, deviance, youth, medicine, social *stratification, and the family. Parsons's analysis of the family in particular is discussed in Box 10.

But whatever Parsons's insights into empirical problems—and they are undoubtedly strong ones—there is always a sense in his work that it is the theory that drives the argument, rather than the findings or the data. Rather than providing a means for integrating theory and research, as he had intended, he seemed to have driven a wedge between them.

American sociologists in the 1960s increasingly found sympathy with the views of C. Wright *Mills (1959), one of Parsons's most outspoken critics. They increasingly took the view that Parsons's 'grand theory' was arid and pointless, and that the emperor of theory had no clothes. The presentation of North American modernity as the end-state of social development also seemed to represent an extreme form of functionalist teleology, revealing ideological biases inherent in a scheme that Parsons had wished to present as neither partial nor ideological but simply and innocently as an 'indispensable logical framework' (1937: 733). In the remaining sections of this chapter, we consider some key criticisms and some further critical extensions of functionalism that came to be propounded in Anglo-American sociology from the 1960s to the 1980s.

BOX 10. TALCOTT PARSONS ON THE NUCLEAR FAMILY:
A FUNCTIONALIST APPROACH

Parsons's account of structural *differentiation proposes that with increasing social complexity, institutions become more specialized around particular functions. Parsons illustrates this in the case of changing forms of kinship with the rise of modern industrial society. Where kinship had previously served a number of functions—for example, regulation of sexual activity, socialization of children, meeting of the basic needs of subsistence, and organization of political authority—these functions had become more dispersed across institutions. With the rise of processes of industrialization, economic needs were met by paid employment that took place outside the family household. Authority was mediated through political institutions where office holders were elected or chosen on merit. It seemed that the functions of the family were very much reduced to those of the regulation of sexuality and the socialization of children. In Western society since the nineteenth century, the form of the family was changing, becoming much more focused on the nuclear family—the nexus of father, mother, and their children—with fewer obligations to extended kin (Parsons 1949b, 1949c, 1956, 1977a).

When Parsons first turned his attention to the sociology of the family in the 1940s, there was something of a moral panic about the family in American society. Commentators had seized upon a rising divorce rate and a falling birth-rate to suggest that the family was in crisis, deriving in part from its loss of functions. Perhaps unsurprisingly, Parsons concluded that the problems had to do only with *transition*, and were not fundamental. The functions of the family were fewer but they were no less important. Divorce rates had increased but they were stabilizing, and rates of remarriage remained high, indicating that marriage continued to play a meaningful role at the centre of people's lives.

As Parsons developed his arguments about the nuclear family, he was concerned to demonstrate how its internal structure reflected its more restricted functions. He identified how male and female roles were concentrated respectively on instrumental and expressive aspects. The male role was concerned with the external linkage of the family to the world of occupations and paid work, while the female role was more associated with the rearing of children. Although housework was an instrumental task, its menial character was alleviated for women through the emotional significance with which it was invested.

According to Parsons, the family produced the human personality through child socialization. It was therefore important that the family remained an environment on which a child could fully depend and in which it could invest all of its emotional resources. But it was also important that the family did not become too isolated. The family was 'a differentiated subsystem of a society, not itself a "little society" or anything too closely approaching it' (1956: 19). Family members needed other roles outside the family. The most important one according to Parsons was the father's occupational role.

Alongside the socialization of children, the family also had a secondary function of stabilizing adult personalities. The marriage pair was more concentrated when compared with extended kin relationships. In both cases children were important to parents insofar as they allowed for an element of acceptable 'regression' in which parents could express 'childish' elements of their own personalities. In this regard Parsons accepted some of the insights of psychoanalysis and sought to incorporate them in his own theory.

Parsons's analysis of the family soon came to be criticized by feminist sociologists for its inadequate theorization of the position of women in families. These important critiques are discussed later in this chapter in Box 12.

Criticisms of functionalism: objections and alternatives

Parsons's theory is subtle and complex, but it is certainly not without problems. In some cases, criticisms of his work have rested on simple misunderstandings. In other cases, they have pointed to some genuine deficiencies. Here we must bear in mind that Parsons's critics did not always represent a unified position. Frequently they criss-crossed between different and mutually exclusive criticisms as their own positions unfolded. We now look at four main bodies of criticism from the late 1960s onwards. These are (1) conflict theory, (2) Marxist criticisms, (3) rational actor or rational choice approaches, and lastly (4) 'neo-functionalist' approaches. In Box 12 we also discuss some feminist responses to Parsons's analysis of the family. We begin with conflict theory.

Conflict theory

For C. Wright *Mills (1956), James *Lockwood (1956), Ralf *Dahrendorf (1958), John *Rex (1961), and Randall Collins (1975), the problem with Parsons's theory was straightforward: it was too one-sided. Parsons's language of systems gave far too much weight to interdependence and integration, neglecting independence and contradiction. It also seemed to give greater emphasis to values and norms than to power. These 'conflict theorists', as they came to be called, drew inspiration from Marx and Weber, to whom Parsons had indeed failed to give proper attention in *The Structure of Social Action*, especially Marx. It was true that Parsons had not merely excluded Marx from the founding sociological generation of 1890–1920 for reasons of chronology. More especially, he had believed that Marx's writings were tied to a moment in capitalism that had been superseded and that the German thinker's ideas had been too influenced by the ideological formations of early capitalism to be relevant to the mid-twentieth century (Parsons 1949*d*). Conflict theorists did not greatly disagree with Parsons's judgement on Marx and the superiority of Weber in this regard. Dahrendorf, Rex, and Wright Mills certainly tended to draw more inspiration from Weber than from Marx. But they felt that Weber owed more to Marx than Parsons had allowed for and that Parsons's attempt to synthesize Durkheim and Weber had meant that the more conflict-oriented aspects of Weber's writings had been lost. It was Durkheim's approach, with his emphasis on order and social *solidarity, that dominated Parsons's interpretation of the classics.

In his essay 'Out of Utopia' (1958), Dahrendorf disagreed with Merton's implied judgement that the problem with Parsons's scheme was that it was too generalized. The problem was rather that Parsons was insufficiently explicit about the values that informed his approach. For Dahrendorf, the 'consensus' model with its emphasis on synchronic analysis and on processes tending toward integration was part of a long-standing conservative tradition in social thought reaching back to *Plato. It was utopian in the sense that it rested on a model of society in which change and conflict are wholly absent. As Dahrendorf suggested, 'it may well be that society, in a philosophical sense, has two faces of equal reality: one of stability, harmony, and consensus, and one of change, conflict and constraint. Strictly speaking, it does not matter whether we select for investigation problems that can be understood only in terms of the equilibrium model or problems for which the conflict model is required.

There is no intrinsic criterion for preferring one to the other' (1958: 127). The problem, then, was that Parsons had placed consensus above conflict for no good reason. A similar argument was put forward by Rex, who argued that while 'perfect cooperation' and 'perfect conflict' are polar theoretical cases, 'all actual cases lie somewhere along the continuum between perfect cooperation and perfect conflict' (1961: 54). Like Dahrendorf, Rex argued that 'Durkheim and Parsons have unduly restricted the scope of sociology to the study of forms of perfect co-operation' (1961: 54). Dahrendorf, Rex, and Mills all recommended that sociological attention should be redirected toward conflict.

The criticisms of the conflict theorists struck a chord. Yet their own position was unstable for a number of reasons. Parsons had in fact sought to account for both power *and* consensus in his model. Therefore it was difficult to argue that the two models could be kept entirely apart and used separately for different purposes. In Parsons's actual thinking, the issues of conflict and cooperation, and power and legitimation, were very much intertwined. This was Parsons's argument when he set out to synthesize positivism and idealism in *The Structure of Social Action*. He repeated this in his response to the conflict theorists (1971*b*: 385) and especially in his opposition to C. Wright Mills's book *The Power Elite* (1956), which he saw as resting on an inadequate 'zero-sum' view of power, where a gain in power for one group is wrongly automatically equated with a loss in power for another group (Parsons 1967).

On the whole it can be said that the conflict theorists were more successful in pointing out the empirical significance of conflict *within* systems—in terms of the power of classes (Dahrendorf 1958) or the power of elites (Mills 1956)—than they were at finding a way of expressing this in the general language of analytical theory. In Box 11 we consider a more subtle extension of conflict theory in the work of David *Lockwood.

Marxist criticisms

To a large degree, the fate of conflict theory was overtaken by more radical approaches. By the late 1960s, the USA was embroiled in the Vietnam War and opposition to it was growing. Along with the anti-war movement, there was an increasingly radical movement of civil rights for black Americans, while the women's movement and feminism waited in the wings to emerge in the 1970s as a powerful force for change. The growth of universities and favourable employment opportunities for sociologists were conditions that encouraged disciplinary transformation (compare Turner and Turner 1990). A younger generation of sociologists influenced by the new social movements promoted radical sociologies in opposition to the functionalism of their seniors. They were on the side of dissent and change, not the side of the system and order (compare Becker 1967).

While their own sympathies lay with Weber rather than Marx, the conflict theorists had contributed to a re-evaluation of the relation between Marxism and academic sociology. In the changed social and political circumstances of the 1960s, many sociologists were now open to a more explicit appropriation of Marxism. By the early 1970s, conflict theory appeared insufficiently radical and its theoretical arguments less sophisticated than those of Marx. It was not just that the Durkheim–Parsons axis of theorizing was called into question but that the whole generation of 1890–1920, including Weber, was seen to represent a 'bourgeois reaction' to Marxism (Therborn 1976).

BOX 11. DAVID LOCKWOOD ON 'SOCIAL INTEGRATION' AND 'SYSTEM INTEGRATION'

David *Lockwood (1964) developed the argument of the conflict theorists on a different tack. He agreed with the conflict theorists that Parsons placed too much emphasis on mechanisms of *integration, but he argued that they were too much concerned with overt conflict between actors. Drawing on Marx's analysis of capitalism, Lockwood suggested that what was missing was a concept of system contradiction. Simply put, Parsons had no place for the idea that the parts of a social system may contain tendencies toward mal-integration—or contradiction. According to Lockwood, those tendencies may eventually come to the surface in the form of oppositional interests and conflicts among actors, and these conflicts may or may not be contained by the *normative order. Rather than proposing two separate models, then, Lockwood argued that it was necessary to consider the question of cooperation, conflict, and social change in terms of two distinct but interrelated sets of processes. One concerned normative processes of *social integration*; the other concerned material processes of *system integration*. The problem was that Parsons had conflated the two types of integration and had overemphasized the aspect of mutuality between the two corresponding sets of processes. The task for sociologists was to be more aware of contradictions within the system and of how they were managed at the level of social integration.

   Lockwood's argument can be seen as returning to and reinforcing Merton's statement of functionalism. Merton had argued for the importance of recognizing the role of 'dysfunctions', which is similar to what Lockwood meant by problems of 'system integration'. At the same time, while it is apparent that the idea of 'function' lends itself to general expression, it is not clear that the same is true of 'dysfunction' or contradiction. Dysfunctions and contradictions seem to be specific to particular cases, rather than to have a general form. If this is so, Lockwood's argument, properly understood, would reinforce Merton's turn away from general theory towards middle-range theory. Indeed, when he returned to the themes of his earlier article in a book-length discussion of Marx and Durkheim and the 'problem of disorder', Lockwood (1992) declared himself to be uncomfortable with the way in which such discussions tended to conclude with a new general framework of social theory, rather than with specific programmes of substantive research.

For North American sociologists, Alvin *Gouldner's *The Coming Crisis of Western Sociology* (1970) was the definitive statement of these criticisms. Gouldner was a one-time functionalist, turned its sternest critic. The book was part of a wider critique of conservative social theory, which, like Dahrendorf, he traced back to Plato (Gouldner 1965). But Gouldner also sought to extend the analysis to the relationship between academic sociology and other agents of advanced welfare capitalism. At best, professional sociology seemed irrelevant to the pressing social and political issues of the times. At worst, professional sociology was partisan, not only for implicitly supporting the status quo but also for being part of what Gouldner described as the modern 'military-industrial-welfare complex'. In Gouldner's view, this complex was in collusion with government agencies, including the military, on an increasingly large scale. Sociology had become absorbed into the management of the advanced state as part of the apparatus of social control. Parsons's theory, which seemed so abstracted from the world, was an expression of the dominant interests of welfare capitalism.

In place of professional claims to objectivity, Gouldner proposed that sociology should organize its activities in 'new theoretical communities' connected to the new social movements that were emerging to challenge welfare capitalism. In this way, he directly subverted the professional ambitions of Parsons and Merton and set an agenda for radical sociology. These were the kinds of attitudes that would evolve into postmodern criticisms of general theory in the 1980s.

A similarly radical body of criticisms came from the side of feminist sociologists, who took a highly sceptical view of Parsons's work on the family. These criticisms are discussed in Box 12.

BOX 12. FEMINIST CRITICISMS OF PARSONS

Parsons himself suspected that his functionalist analyses of women, work, and the family were oversimplified. For example, he was aware that many women were in paid employment, although he correctly observed that the tendency was for women to be found in jobs that mirrored their family roles and for competition for jobs between men and women to be restricted. 'In general,' he observed, 'the woman's job tends to be of a qualitatively different type and not of a status which seriously competes with that of her husband as the primary status-giver or income earner' (1956: 14). Nonetheless, he was rather insensitive to the asymmetry between men and women, where men were enjoyed a primarily public role and women were restricted to dependency in the domestic sphere.

In the period of the emergence of second-wave feminism in the 1960s, several feminist writers began to point to the changed fertility conditions that meant that a large part of women's lives would be spent without dependent children in the household. This would involve new social problems, including female poverty on divorce or in old age, given increasing female longevity (Myrdal and Klein 1956). Parsons had written that the fact that 'the normal married woman is debarred from testing or demonstrating her fundamental equality with her husband in competitive occupational achievement creates a demand for a *functional equivalent' (1949e: 193). Parsons had accepted that housework was a relatively menial task, suggesting that women might instead develop specialized interests in matters of taste relating to personal appearance, furnishing, and the like—although he acknowledged that these could frequently be expressed as neuroses. Once again, this was something that feminists also came to argue, but in a much more radical way, notably in the influential book by Betty *Friedan *The Feminine Mystique* (1963). Increasingly, feminists were to identify such 'dysfunctions' in a more systematic and rigorous way. Much like the conflict theorists, they would see functionalism as an obstacle rather than a means to a fruitful understanding of the family. They pointed out that dependency within the family was increasingly a reflection of power relationships, and that far from being a place that stabilized adult personalities, the family was frequently a site of violence and abuse. Women were tied to unsatisfactory relationships precisely because the gender segregation of employment and lower pay for women meant that they were economically dependent.

Some feminists have suggested that Parsons was correct in his description of the nature of the family-household and its relation to the occupational sphere (Johnson 1989). However, there is no doubt that he lacked a feminist sensibility and that the weight of his analysis was to emphasize the positive functions for society of the nuclear family, rather than its dysfunctions for women (see Barrett 1980). Yet it should be acknowledged that Parsons was one of the first male sociologists to write of the close interconnections between age, sex, family, and social *stratification. The more usual response by male sociologists— even those of a radical persuasion—was to concentrate on the class relationships of the occupational sphere and to regard the household and gender as secondary matters. For a more detailed overview of feminist interventions in social theory, see Chapter 11 of this book.

Rational actor approaches

For other critics, the problem with functionalism was its concentration on systems at the expense of individual actors. This problem was also seen as linked to functionalism's concern with elaborating a general conceptual framework, rather than specific testable propositions. One major criticism came from those who held that the social sciences could be unified only if sociologists based their research on the testable *individualistic concepts of economics or psychology. Representatives of this line of argument defended a conception of the individual as 'rational actor' or 'rational egoist', capable of 'rational choices'. This school of approach provided the foundation for what is commonly called *'rational choice theory', which has been especially prominent in economics. Here we look at the work of two among several champions of rational actor thinking. These are George *Homans and James *Coleman.

Homans maintained that functionalism was unscientific because it deviated from the proper hypothetico-deductive form of scientific explanation. Functionalists had fashioned a conceptual scheme, and however necessary a conceptual scheme may be, it is not the same as a *theory*. A theory involves testable propositions about the world and, according to Homans, these are conspicuously lacking in the functionalism of Parsons. Homans's idea of theory was avowedly positivist and firmly methodological-individualist.

For Homans, functionalists analyse social systems in terms of roles and their normative expectations but nowhere explain why and how norms exist. The answer, he suggested, is to be found only in direct examination of social interaction in terms of the attributes of real individuals, their dispositions, motives, and calculations. These attributes are derived from the studies of psychologists and economists and can be given a general form as the basis of sociological explanation. Homans (1961) proposed that the units from which sociological explanations should be fashioned were the real, concrete acts of individuals. Explanations of macro-phenomena had to be based on micro-foundations. Where Parsons had argued that 'the very definition of an organic whole is one within which the relations determine the properties of its parts', Homans argued that the 'whole' is nothing more than the resultant of the properties of its parts. Homans called his approach 'social *behaviourism', adapting the terminology of behavioural psychology.

Other critics of functionalism, including notably Peter Blau (1964), took inspiration from the *utlilitarian axioms of economics, arguing in a similar fashion to Homans that theory needed to be built from propositions about actors. Similarly, from a conflict theory perspective, Randall Collins (1975) accepted Homans's critique of functionalism and set out to produce a compilation of causal principles that would constitute 'conflict sociology' as an explanatory science.

One of the most ambitious of such enterprises was undertaken by James *Coleman. Coleman had been a student of Merton and was an early critic of Parsons (Coleman 1971). He continues to be influential in social theory. Towards the end of his career, he produced a major treatise in rational actor theory that sought to develop the explanatory theory proposed by Homans and to present it in a mathematical form (Coleman 1991). Coleman presented a further argument for the individualist approach. This is that the data collected by social scientists comprise evidence about individual behaviour, about individuals and their opinions. The social system *as a whole* cannot be observed. Social theory, Coleman wrote, 'continues to be about the functioning of social systems of behavior, but empirical research is often concerned with explaining individual behavior' (1991: 1). For this reason, while he accepted that concrete social systems are what sociologists want to explain, Coleman argued that it is rational actor thinking that offers the best building blocks with which to construct an explanatory theory that is directly supported by empirical evidence. For example, while trust may be important in maintaining stable social relationships, it is vulnerable to actors defaulting on it. Coleman therefore argued that rather than constructing an analytical theory that makes trust a central presupposition of social order, it would be better to examine the different empirical circumstances that serve to sustain or undermine trust. This will be facilitated by the use of models describing dilemmas faced by rational actors in behaving altruistically when confronted with the possibility that other actors may 'free-ride'; that is, fail to live up to an expectation or take self-interested advantage of the altruism of others.

Over the years, the debate between functionalists and rational choice theory has been continuous (see further Turk and Simpson 1971; Coleman and Fararo 1991). Although there are strong advocates of rational actor approaches, many sociologists find these approaches compromised by reductionism and by an excessively behaviouristic form of *objectivism. Rational choice theory tends to lack a sense of the expressive, creative, and self-interpretive character of action. It typically lacks a sufficiently strong or 'thick' concept of the *reflexivity of actors who monitor their own preferences. It has difficulties in accounting for meaningful social norms that are presupposed in action, in historically specific contexts of ethical belief, and that are not merely the products of intended action (Bohman 1991). These are arguments that have been developed in *interpretive or *hermeneutical traditions of social thought, and they have particularly been defended recently by writers such as Charles *Taylor (1989), Hans *Joas (1992), Margaret *Archer (Archer and Tritter 2000), and others (for detailed discussion of interpretive social theory, see Chapter 5 of this book). Here it is important to note that Parsons's emphasis on the subjective meaning of action was itself an attempt to draw on the insights of the interpretive tradition and to develop them as part of a systematic theory. In this regard at least, it can be argued that Parsons provided the definitive critique of the utilitarian concept of action, on which a large part of rational choice theory is based (see further Scott 1995; Lockwood 1992).

We now turn lastly to a revived strain of functionalist thinking prevalent in the 1980s known (somewhat artificially) as 'neo-functionalism'.

'Neo-functionalism'

Two of the strands of criticism directed at Parsons lead back to his starting place. Conflict theory set out a dualistic approach to sociological problems, where Parsons had sought to synthesize the dualism, mediating between positivism and idealism and between power and consensus. For its part, rational actor theory promoted the utilitarian scheme of action as the micrological foundation for a scientific sociology, which Parsons had already criticized in *The Structure of Social Action*. Yet many critics did not recognize this as Parsons's own starting point. They usually viewed sociological functionalism as a positivistic systems approach that neglected action. Anthony *Giddens's criticism is typical: 'there is no action in Parsons' "action frame of reference", only behaviour which is propelled by need dispositions, or role expectations. . . . Men do not appear in [Parsons's writings] as skilled and knowledgeable agents, as at least to some extent masters of their own fate' (1976: 16, 70).

A similar view of functionalism was taken by Jürgen *Habermas, whose work is discussed at length in Chapters 7 and 13 of this book (pp. 164–5, 279–83). In his *The Theory of Communicative Action*, Habermas (1981*b*) argued that social enquiry had been unhelpfully divided between two conceptual strategies, one taking the standpoint of 'systems', which 'ties the social scientific analysis to the external perspective of the observer', the other taking the standpoint of the *'lifeworld', which 'begins with members' intuitive knowledge' (1981*b*: 151). According to Habermas, 'the fundamental problem of social theory is how to connect in a satisfactory way the two conceptual strategies indicated by the respective notions of "system" and "lifeworld" ' (1981*b*: 151). Habermas offers his own theory as just such a generalized integration of categories.

Several contemporary theorists have proposed general theories as alternatives to Parsons, arguing that their schemes avoid his problems because they incorporate action from the start. However, it can be argued that what they propose is very similar in conceptual structure and intention to Parsons. This can be illustrated briefly with reference to the work of Giddens, whose contributions are discussed in greater detail in Chapters 10 and 13 of this book (pp. 217–20, 287–9). Although Giddens argues vigorously that his own theory of *'structuration' has no 'functionalist overtones at all' and has declared that it would be helpful to 'ban' the term altogether (1981: 16, 19), he proposes certain universal 'structural features' that are remarkably similar to those of Parsons. Giddens identifies four basic structural principles, with similar points of reference to Parsons's four functional imperatives. Giddens calls them 'signification', *'legitimation', 'authorisation', and 'allocation'. He argues further that two aspects of these principles can be identified as follows: 'one is how far a society contains distinct spheres of "specialism" in respect of institutional orders: differentiated forms of symbolic order (religion, science, etc); a differentiated "polity", "economy" and "legal/repressive apparatus". The second is how modes of institutional articulation are organised in terms of overall properties of societal reproduction: that is to say "structural principles" ' (1981: 47–8). This is very similar to Parsons's AGIL scheme.

A common pattern in contemporary discussion is that each critic of functionalism is careful to distance his or her position from that of Parsons, but has little difficulty in accusing others of converging with his scheme (see further Holmwood and Stewart 1991; Holmwood 1996). Thus Giddens (1982: 158–9) accuses Habermas of converging with Parsons, while Archer (1988: 87) offers the same criticism of Giddens. Jeffrey *Alexander (1988) takes these convergences as indications of a 'new theoretical movement' *back* to functionalism, which he calls 'neo-functionalism'. In the 1980s Alexander set himself the self-conscious task of reviving functionalism through the project of a four-volume rewriting of Parsons's *The Structure of Social Action*, each volume devoted respectively to nineteenth-century positivism, Marx and Durkheim, Weber, and Parsons (Alexander 1982*a*, 1982*b*, 1983, 1984). According to Alexander, Parsons's approach was deficient in its detail but correct in its fundamentals. Current social theory is converging on a reinvigorated functionalist paradigm that recognizes action alongside function (Alexander 1985, 1998; Colomy 1990; Munch 1987). Alexander argues that Merton's middle-range approach is insufficiently ambitious. What is required is a revised exercise in unified general theory.

Yet one may reasonably question whether neo-functionalism is anything more than a restatement of the standard approach which retains its problems. From Parsons's perspective, if empirical circumstances are less than fully integrated, this implies that there must be relevant factors that operate in addition to those represented within the general theoretical statement. For Habermas, Giddens, Alexander, and Margaret Archer, such factors are assigned to actors, thought of as acting concretely, while the structural-system point of view is bracketed or taken as a given. This is what is promoted by Alexander when he defends neo-functionalist analysis against the older functionalist paradigm's overextension of the concept of system. Alexander writes that functional analysis 'is concerned with integration as a possibility and with deviance and processes of social control as facts. Equilibrium is taken as a reference point for functional systems analysis, though not for participants in actual social systems as such' (1985: 9). Yet despite Alexander's claim for a fully integrated theoretical statement, it can be argued that his project rests on an unsatisfactory unreconciled dualism between grand theory construction on the one hand and empirical data input on the other hand.

Conclusion

There is some validity in Kingsley Davis's (1959) assertion that functionalism is integral to sociology. The concepts, issues, and problems of functionalism are not easily avoided. Simple oppositions between functionalist and action approaches are inadequate because the most elaborate and extended forms of functionalist argument are themselves based on a highly developed concept of action. In the case of Parsons, they incorporate the very action assumptions that are often taken to express an opposition to functionalism. This is why Parsons's writings have retained lasting significance, no matter how difficult they may be to read. Taken as a whole, they contain one of the most sophisticated statements of problems that have beset sociological enquiry since the earliest days.

While the project of general theory remains attractive to some sociologists, there can be no doubt that it has been increasingly singled out for criticism. For some *postmodernist commentators, it is an example of inappropriate 'grand narrative' (for further discussion of this theme, see Chapter 12 of this book). For some feminist writers, it is an expression of a masculine taste for abstraction. In light of this, other sociologists have been attracted by the promise of rational actor theory to provide a science of society capable of reuniting theory and research. Where conflict theorists argued that functionalism overemphasizes consensus and social order, neglecting conflict and power, rational actor theorists argue that functionalism overemphasizes systems and neglects individual actors. The rational actor theorists argue that there is no such thing as a social system, that only individual actors interact with each other, and that the motives and calculations of individuals can and should be taken as the building blocks of general social theory.

Yet the rational actor theorists' ambition to produce a deductive system of interlocking laws and propositions—after the fashion of Homans and Coleman—seems almost as unlikely to win general support as Parsons's original ambition in unified functionalist theory. In all of the approaches that have followed in the wake of functionalism, what seems to be missing is some evidence of direct integration between theory and empirical research. Parsons's own contribution was directed toward establishing sociology as a collective collaborative enterprise. Yet in retrospect, it seems that Parsons probably did more than anyone else to establish theory as an activity for autonomous 'grand theorists', separated from immediate empirical research programmes. This has certainly not helped to improve the poor public image of 'theory', in contrast to 'research' which tends to be seen as something more open to new findings. In the early 1960s, the arguments of Merton and Lockwood were seen as being insufficiently ambitious in their aspirations and too much preoccupied with discrete empirical issues. Today, however, it can be argued that the most likely context in which functionalism might flourish again is not as an all-embracing theoretical scheme but as an empirically grounded enterprise directed at specific explanatory problems.

QUESTIONS FOR CHAPTER 4

1 What are the advantages of explaining social life in terms of systems and functions?

2 Is Merton's 'middle-range theory' preferable to Parsons's 'unified theory'?

3 What is 'social order'? How satisfactory is the functionalist explanation of social order?

4 Does functionalism neglect power, conflict, and social change?

5 Does rational actor theory provide a better basis for sociological explanation than functionalism?

6 Is it possible to avoid functionalist explanations in sociology?

7 How convincing is the functionalist account of the nuclear family?

FURTHER READING

Talcott Parsons's writings are numerous. Particularly important to read are his first book *The Structure of Social Action* (McGraw-Hill, 1937) and his middle-period work *The Social System* (Free Press, 1951). But these will be difficult to approach without first reading some of the secondary guides. Useful introductions and studies are Peter Hamilton's short *Talcott Parsons* (Tavistock, 1983), Neil Smelser and A. J. Trevino's edited *Talcott Parsons Today: His Theory and Legacy in Contemporary Sociology* (Rowman & Littlefield, 2001), Uta Gerhardt's *Talcott Parsons* (Cambridge University Press, 2003), Guy Rocher's *Talcott Parsons and American Sociology* (Nelson, 1972), Jonathan H. Turner and Alexandra Maryanski's *Functionalism* (Benjamin Cummings, 1979), and John Holmwood's *Founding Sociology? Talcott Parsons and the Idea of General Theory* (Longman, 1996), which considers convergences between Parsons and the more recent work of Anthony Giddens, Jeffrey Alexander, and Jürgen Habermas from a critical perspective. A study of the politics of functionalism is W. F. Buxton's *Talcott Parsons and the Capitalist Nation State: Political Sociology as a Strategic Vocation* (University of Toronto Press, 1985). Other notable studies include Jeffrey Alexander's *Theoretical Logic in Sociology*, iv: *The Modern Reconstruction of Classical Thought: Talcott Parsons* (University of California Press, 1984), Donald Levine's *Simmel and Parsons* (Arno Press, 1980), Bernard Barber and Uta Gerhardt's *Agenda for Sociology: Classic Sources and Current Uses of Parsons's Work* (Nomos, 1999), Thomas Fararo's *Social Action Systems:*

Foundation and Synthesis in Sociological Theory (Praeger, 2001). For an evaluation of Parsons's approach to the family, see the broad study by Lynn Jamieson, *Intimacy: Personal Relationships in Modern Societies* (Polity Press, 1998).

A comparison between functionalism and exchange theory and rational actor approaches is M. K. Mulkay's *Functionalism, Exchange and Theoretical Strategy* (Schocken Books, 1971). One of the most comprehensive books on American sociological theory by a leading neo-functionalist is Jeffrey Alexander's *Twenty Lectures: Sociological Theory since World War II* (Columbia University Press, 1987), which also covers exchange theory and conflict theory. Also substantial as guides to technical sociological theory in the American scientific tradition are Randall Collins's two books *Four Sociological Traditions* (Oxford University Press, 1994) and *Theoretical Sociology* (Harcourt Brace, 1988). Two collections of readings in functionalism are Paul Colomy's *Functionalist Sociology* (Edward Elgar, 1990) and *Functionalist Sociology* (Edward Elgar, 1990). See also James Lockwood's 'Some Remarks on "The Social System" ', in the *British Journal of Sociology*, 7 (1956).

For a detailed introduction to Robert Merton, see Piotr Sztompka's *Robert K. Merton: An Intellectual Profile* (Cambridge University Press, 1986). In Merton's own writings, it is best to begin with the chapter 'Manifest and Latent Functions' in his main work *Social Theory and Social Structure* (Free Press, 1968). A key text for criticism of functionalism from the standpoint of conflict theory is John Rex's *Key Problems of Sociological Theory* (Routledge, 1961). An informative overview of evolutionary thinking in social theory is Jonathan H. Turner and Leonard Beeghley's *The Emergence of Sociological Theory* (Dorsey Press, 1981).

■ WEBSITES

Functionalism at **www.wikipedia.org/wiki/functionalism** Provides an overview of functionalism, with links to associated theorists.

Conflict Theory at **www.wikipedia.org/wiki/Conflict_theory** Contains a summary of conflict theory, with links to texts and associated theorists.

Rational Choice Theory at **www.wikipedia.org/wiki/Rational_Choice_Theory** Covers rational choice theory, with links to related terms.

Rational Choice Theory Essay **http://privatewww.essex.ac.uk/~scottj/socscot7.htm** Contains an essay by John Scott on rational choice theory.

Quotations from Talcott Parsons at **www.mdx.ac.uk/www/study/xpar.htm** Displays quotations, with links to key concepts.

<table>
<tr><td>**5**</td><td># Interpretivism and Interactionism</td></tr>
</table>

Interpretivism and Interactionism

William Outhwaite

'Interpretivism' is a label for approaches stressing the importance of subjective meanings carried by actions and institutions in the social world. It is particularly associated with the methodological ideas of Max Weber and Georg Simmel and their influence on subsequent generations of writers. Interpretive thinking is also seen as encompassing what is known as the *'phenomenological sociology' of Alfred *Schutz and the 'sociology of knowledge' approaches of writers such as Karl *Mannheim, Peter *Berger, and Thomas *Luckmann.

This chapter discusses interpretive approaches in social theory in conjunction with a second tradition of thought with entirely separate origins but with many theoretical similarities to interpretive work. The parallel tradition is *'interactionism', or 'symbolic interactionism', associated with the *Chicago School of sociologists represented by the names of George Herbert *Mead, Herbert *Blumer, and others, as well as more loosely with the work of Erving *Goffman and Harold *Garfinkel and their pupils from the 1960s. Where interpretive thinking is largely European in origin, interactionist research developed mostly in the United States from the 1930s onwards.

The two traditions of analysis are grouped together in this chapter around several interrelated themes bearing on the concepts of *interpretation, action, interaction, knowledge, meaning,* and *language.* First we discuss the idea of interpretation in early twentieth-century European thought, beginning with Max Weber's conception of *'interpretive sociology'. Then we cross the Atlantic to look at the work of G. H. Mead and the Chicago sociologists. Next we turn to the broad paradigm known loosely as the 'sociology of knowledge', encompassing the work of Karl Mannheim and more recent developments in the sociology of science and cognition. In a final step, the discussion turns to a body of ideas about the role of language and meaning in social life known broadly as *'hermeneutics'.

The idea of interpretation: understanding from the inside

Interpretive social theory is motivated by an interest in knowledge which is rather different from the more general scientific interest in explaining social processes. One way of putting this is to say that it is interested in what Robert *Merton called 'insider knowledge'—rather than, or as well as, 'outsider knowledge' (Merton 1949a). Interpretive theory is interested in knowledge of *what it is like* to be a social actor of a particular kind, and in how such people understand their social situation. Another way of expressing the same idea is to say that interpretivists are more interested in 'understanding' (from the inside) than in 'explaining' (from the outside).

Looking back at Chapters 2 and 3 of this book, we can see that Marx and Durkheim tended to emphasize social forces of which social actors are mostly unaware: exploitation through the wage contract, differential proneness to suicide resulting from marital status, religious affiliation, and so on. Durkheim, in one of his rare comments on Marxism, expressed approval of the idea of explaining social processes not by people's conscious actions but by 'the more profound causes which escape consciousness' (Durkheim 1895: 171). Weber and Simmel, by contrast, were more interested in exploring the inner meaning of action for the actors themselves. It was not enough for Weber to demonstrate that certain types of Protestant Christians in early modern Europe were exceptionally innovative in their economic behaviour; he wanted what he called a 'meaningfully adequate' explanation of this in terms of their situation and beliefs to supplement the demonstration of this causal association. Otherwise, he said, all we have is a fact to be explained.

In general, and quite roughly speaking, it can be said that whereas Marx and Durkheim were interested in matters of *structure,* in the large-scale macrological features and dynamics of social life, Weber and Simmel were concerned more with matters of subjective *meaning, action,* and individual *agency.* Similarly, it can be said that whereas the *functionalist theories of *Parsons and Merton were concerned with social systems and macrological structures, the writers to be discussed in this chapter are more interested in the micrological elements of meaning, action, and interaction.

Simmel and Weber drew on a nineteenth-century line of discussion which moved from a concern with the interpretation of literary texts to a rethinking of the foundations of history, economics, psychology, and the other human sciences. Wilhelm *Dilthey and other German historical philosophers developed what we would now call a research programme for history and the other human sciences based on the distinctiveness of human psychic expressions and the understanding of those expressions. In a move which was to become a definitional feature of later interpretive social theory, Dilthey emphasized the continuity between everyday understanding and more formal processes of interpretation. His distinction between the natural sciences and the human sciences was developed in large part in opposition to Auguste *Comte's *positivism. In a parallel formulation, two German *Neo-Kantian philosophers, Wilhelm *Windelband and Heinrich *Rickert, argued that the study of culture is essentially concerned with individual and unique or 'one-off' processes. The cultural sciences relate these processes to shared human values, whereas the natural sciences are concerned with general laws about objects which are essentially remote from questions of value. We are interested, for example, in the French Revolution not just as a member of a class of revolutions exhibiting certain common features—this would be, for Rickert, a natural-scientific mode of approaching it—but as a unique event, embodying, and perhaps also violating, certain crucial human values. Rickert in particular was a major influence on Max Weber.

At the time of Weber's death in 1920, the main intellectual elements of interpretive social thought and the styles of research corresponding to it were already in place. Simmel and Weber had taken theories of 'understanding'—still often referred to by the German word *verstehen—out of the philosophy of history, philology, and Biblical *hermeneutics and had put them at the centre of the relatively new discipline of sociology.

On the other side of the fence, in opposition to hermeneutical and idealist thinking, there was now a more aggressive variant of positivism. This was the logical *empiricism or 'logical *positivism' of the *Vienna Circle, in whose 'unified science' the statements of all sciences were seen as reducible to material-object language or to statements in physics. According to one member of the Vienna Circle, Otto *Neurath, *verstehen* was of no more importance than 'a good cup of coffee' which revives the flagging scientist (Neurath 1973).

The next sections of this chapter trace the main developments in interpretive thinking after 1920. We begin with the work of Alfred *Schutz.

Alfred Schutz and phenomenological sociology

The most direct response to Weber's attempt to bring together explanation and understanding came from the leading interpretive theorist of the mid-twentieth century, Alfred Schutz. Schutz initiated the tradition of sociological *phenomenology with a book first published in Vienna in 1932 with the title 'The Meaningful Constitution of the Social World' (translated in 1972 as *The Phenomenology of the Social World*). Schutz felt that the problem with Weber's *ideal types was not that they were insufficiently scientific but precisely the opposite: Weber was too quick to impose them on the phenomena he described, paying insufficient attention to their grounding in acts of typification performed by ordinary members of society. For Schutz, the social scientist merely constructs additional or second-order typifications based on those already carried out by ordinary people in every-day life:

The observational field of the social scientist—social reality—has a specific meaning and relevance structure for the human beings living, acting, and thinking within it. By a series of common-sense constructs they have pre-selected and pre-interpreted this world which they experience as the real-ity of their daily lives . . . The thought objects constructed by the social scientists, in order to grasp this social reality, have to be founded upon the thought objects constructed by the common-sense thinking of men [sic] living their daily life within their social world. Thus, the constructs used by the social scientist are, so to speak, constructs of the second degree, namely constructs of the constructs made by actors on the social scene, whose behaviour they scientist observes and tries to explain in accordance with the procedural rules of his science. (Schutz 1962a: 59)

Schutz refers to everyday life as the *'lifeworld'. This term, like many of Schutz's main concepts, is taken from Edmund *Husserl's phenomenological philosophy. Phenomenology in Husserl's original sense meant an approach to knowledge which focuses on our experience of things, bracketing out the issue of whether or not they really exist or are optical illusions, or of what they are made of. The lifeworld in this sense means the world of common-sense perception, before it is subjected to theoretical analysis by sci-entists. In Schutz's more informal use of phenomenological terminology, it refers to the so-cial world which we interpret and make meaningful through our 'typifications' (Schutz and Luckmann 1973). A person comes to the door in a police uniform; we assume he or she is a police officer and behave accordingly. We may of course be wrong in our assump-tion; the person may be a robber impersonating a police officer, or someone going to a fancy-dress party. But the point, for Schutz, is that we make sense of the world through what he calls our 'stock of knowledge' at hand which we do not normally problematize. One of Schutz's most famous essays, 'The Stranger' (1962b), is about persons finding their way around in unfamiliar surroundings and negotiating social situations in which they are not 'at home'. We inhabit multiple social realities, based on the nature of our knowledge of people, places, and so on. We can construct concentric circles of people we know intimately, people we recognize or whose names we know, people we have seen only on TV, and so on.

Schutz was not a full-time academic, and he wrote mostly essays. He was, however, very influential, and can now be seen as an important figure linking Simmel and Weber to more recent and radical developments in interpretive social theory. Some of the appeal of interpretive social theory after the 1960s derived from the radical forms of political protest in the student and 'alternative' movements. A focus on small-scale or micro-interactions in everyday situations may have wider implications for social structural analysis. Schutz believed that systematic theorists like Parsons could be criticized for neglecting or denying the need for social theory to be grounded in attention to the 'subjective point of view' (see Schutz and Parsons 1978). But Schutz himself was by no means radical in either a political or an intellectual sense. In a typically phenomenological gesture, he suggested that his work was complementary to more systematic types of theory such as functionalism or neoclassical economic theory and that it opened up an area linking everyday or common-sense social understanding with more systematic analysis.

When Schutz emigrated to the USA, his closest contacts were with other followers of Husserl, but he was also led into a more intense engagement with the North American philosophical tradition known as *pragmatism*. In the next section we cross the Atlantic to look at the development of pragmatism in the work of George Herbert *Mead and his impact on the Chicago School of sociologists.

George Herbert Mead and American pragmatism

The philosophical movement known as pragmatism developed in the late nineteenth century from the work of Charles Sanders *Peirce. Peirce stressed that questions of knowledge which had been central to Western philosophy since the time of *Descartes should no longer be abstracted out of the practical context in which they occurred: that of people's active engagement with the world and their attempts to make sense of it. Thus pragmatist thinkers are concerned with how we develop and test our knowledge and the concepts we form of things in the world. The popularity of this approach in North America is often explained rather simplistically by a cultural context in which settlers from Europe, escaping religious and other ideological conflicts, were more concerned with the practicalities of making a living in their new environment on the basis of hard facts and hard cash. But it is also worth noting some parallels between pragmatism and the related appeals to 'practice' in the work of Marx and Engels or to 'life' in that of Friedrich *Nietzsche.

By the end of the nineteenth century, the American philosopher William *James, brother of the novelist Henry James, had systematized pragmatism as a philosophical approach and developed it in relation to, notably, the psychology of religious experience. James was exceptionally influential in Europe, as well as in North America. Social theorists such as Weber and Durkheim were impressed by his work. Durkheim in particular took an interest in pragmatism as a philosophical approach which he saw as having affinities to his own variety of neo-Kantianism (Durkheim 1955: 28). In the twentieth century, pragmatism was developed further by John *Dewey. Dewey, like James, was concerned to work out the implications of pragmatism for other areas of knowledge and in particular for social and political philosophy and democratic theory. These social and political concerns were also an important aspect of the work of George Herbert Mead. Mead, though he published little systematic work himself, reached a wider public though the work of his student Herbert *Blumer and became one of the founders of social psychology. Mead's main book *Mind, Self and Society* was put together after his death by his students in 1934.

Unlike philosophers and social theorists who began from the individual and his or her action, Mead focused on situations of social *interaction*. In humans, this is symbolically mediated. We respond to others' gestures, rather than just to their behaviour, and we put ourselves imaginatively in their place, in what Mead called 'taking the role of the other'.

These expectations may be momentary, as when I interpret your gesture as meaning that you are waving me on in a traffic queue. Or they may be more systematic expectations. Mead distinguished between the 'I', the individual ego, and the socially structured 'me', made up of others' expectations of me. The 'me' refers to a self which is produced and constantly reshaped in social interaction and in the reciprocal exchange of perspectives (Mead 1934). An individual may have multiple and overlapping 'me's, arising from different situations and roles—professional, personal, and so forth. In his studies of the formation of the ego in a child's relationship to the mother and father and other members of kin, Mead was the first to speak of an emotionally immediate partner to interaction as a 'significant other'–in a today familiar phrase.

Mead's approach implied a novel conception of knowledge, language use, and socialization. Most fundamentally, it involved what has been called a conception of the 'creativity of action' (Joas 1980, 1992). Mead called his approach 'social behaviourism', but it is very different from that of J. B. *Watson or B. F. *Skinner. Whereas *behaviourists focus only on observable behaviour and avoid any speculation about the mental processes which accompany it, Mead's interactive conception necessarily involves conjectures about the ways in which humans interpret each other's behaviour in complex structures of intentional action and interaction—what Harré and Secord (1972) later called 'act-action structures'. More generally it involves what Harré and Secord ironically called the 'anthropomorphic model of man': 'treating people as if they were human beings'.

Symbolic interactionism and the Chicago School

The term 'symbolic interactionism' was introduced in 1937 by the Chicago sociologist Herbert Blumer. The Chicago sociology department, founded by Albion *Small in 1892, was not the first in the country, but it was the first to develop a collective conception of social research. This was oriented to the ethnic and other urban crises of early twentieth-century Chicago and to reformist impulses from Jane *Addams and others. The Chicago sociologists began conducting ethnographic studies of local social problems, permanently shaping the image of sociology as typically concerned with the observation of 'low life'.

An admirer of Simmel, Blumer saw his main achievement as bringing together Herbert Mead's pragmatic philosophy and social psychology with the sociology of W. I. *Thomas and others. W. I. Thomas is today remembered principally for his slogan: 'If men define things as real, they are real in their consequences' (Thomas and Thomas 1928). Blumer showed how this idea fitted well with C. H. *Cooley's idea of the 'looking-glass self', based on our idea of how we appear to others and Mead's distinction between the 'I' and the 'me' (Blumer 1969; Cooley 1902). In other words, we relate to people and things according to our interpretations of them; we respond to a threatening gesture before it becomes a real threat, or to a friendly approach indicated by a momentary smile.

This 'creative' model of action can be contrasted with that of Talcott Parsons in his book *The Structure of Social Action*, also published in 1937. Although Parsons described his conception of action as *'voluntaristic', Parsons in practice emphasized an orientation to prevalent shared norms, in an approach increasingly criticized as conservative. In contrast, the interactionist sociologist's account is continuous with social actors' own more or less conscious awareness of what they are doing. It does not offer a description or explanation of their actions at a radically different level. In this sense the symbolic interactionist approach is consonant with Schutz's model of typifications, in which those of the social scientist build on and reconstruct those produced by ordinary members of society.

Blumer's systematization of interactionism coincided with the eclipse of the Chicago School by other centres of US sociology, and it was particularly important because Mead himself did not present his work in a systematic way. Interactionism continued as an oppositional current to functionalism as sociology expanded in the USA and Britain after the Second World War. Among the main second-generation representatives of symbolic interactionism were Blumer's students Anselm *Strauss, Tamotsu Shibatani, Howard *Becker, and others. By the 1960s the functionalist idea that a theory should be precisely formulated, systematic, and of general application was giving way to a more pluralistic and informal conception of theories as sensitizing frameworks. In this sense, interactionists returned to some of the original pragmatist ideas that had inspired Chicago sociology. An influential text by Glaser and Strauss (1967) formalized a version of this approach in the idea of 'contexts of awareness'. Strauss in particular produced substantial work in the sociology of medicine.

One of the most influential and theoretically creative strands of interactionism in later years followed the original pragmatist model in stressing the informal and negotiated aspect of social roles and social interaction in general. This occurs notably in the ethnographic work of Erving *Goffman and Harold *Garfinkel, who are discussed in the following two sections of this chapter.

Erving Goffman and the 'presentation of self in everyday life'

Erving Goffman obtained his doctorate at Chicago with a thesis based on fieldwork in the Scottish Shetland Islands. He remains perhaps best known for his first book, *The Presentation of Self in Everyday Life* (1956). For Goffman, the notion of 'performing' social roles means just that: we are 'on stage' in our everyday lives, moving between 'front stage' and 'back stage', dressing to create an impression, even if only an understated one, and constantly monitoring the impression we create. We are constantly engaged in 'interaction rituals'. Sometimes, as in our homes, the stage metaphor is almost literal, as we admit visitors to some rooms or parts of rooms and not others. On the other hand, it serves in Goffman's presentation as a guide to a more fundamental issue. As he stresses at the end of the book,

The claim that all the world's a stage is sufficiently commonplace for readers to be familiar with its limitations and tolerant of its presentation, knowing . . . that it is not to be taken too seriously . . . This report . . . is concerned with the structure of social encounters—the structure of those entities in social life that come into being whenever persons enter one another's immediate physical presence. The key factor in this structure is the maintenance of a single definition of the situation, this definition having to be expressed, and this expression sustained in the face of a multitude of potential disruptions. (Goffman 1956: 246)

In a later book, *Frame Analysis* (1974), Goffman shows how situations can be shaped by a variety of alternative perspectives. We must use 'frame clues' and 'frame conventions' to know—or rather guess—whether someone is joking or serious, blinking or winking, polite or sarcastic, unaware of a social convention or deliberately flouting it. We are confronted with multiple realities in the form of a choice between alternative perspectives. And these interpretations may be self-fulfilling; to misidentify a look as rude or hostile and to act accordingly may land you in hospital.

Goffman is often criticized for portraying a rather sad social world without sincerity or spontaneity, where people are constantly monitoring their performances and calculating their effects. Are all cultures as obsessed with impression management as he suggests, or is he falsely universalizing particular features of advanced capitalist societies? The evidence of cross-cultural studies suggests that Goffman may have been right in his assumptions. Certainly the model of *'dramaturgical action', as he called it, should be put alongside that of norm-directed and economically rational action as part of the repertoire of social theory.

In his book *Asylums* (1961), Goffman coined the term 'total institution', placing prisons in one and the same category as hospitals, care homes, clinics, army barracks, boarding schools, ships, and monasteries. Goffman's preoccupation with the intensely self-contained character of 'total institutions' is movingly conveyed in the 1970s film *One Flew over the Cuckoo's Nest*, starring Jack Nicholson. In *Asylums* Goffman writes that

A total institution may be defined as a place of residence and work where a large number of like-situated individuals, cut off from the wider society for an appreciable period of time, together lead an enclosed, formally administered round of life. Prisons serve as a clear example, providing we appreciate that what is prison-like about prisons is found in institutions whose members have broken no laws. . . .

Every institution captures something of the time and interest of its members and provides something of a world for them; in brief, every institution has encompassing tendencies. When we review the different institutions in our Western society, we find some that are encompassing to a degree discontinuously greater than the ones next in line. Their encompassing or total character is symbolised by the barrier to social intercourse with the outside and to departure that is often built right into the physical plant, such as locked doors, high walls, barbed wire, cliffs, water, forests, or moors. (Goffman 1961: pp. xiii, 4–5)

Harold Garfinkel and ethnomethodology

The US sociologist Harold *Garfinkel was a contemporary of Goffman, and his work shows affinities with the latter's. Like Goffman, Garfinkel was interested in the 'dramaturgy' or 'dramatic structure' of situations of social interaction. One of Garfinkel's first studies, published in 1956, is titled 'Conditions of Successful Degradation Ceremonies'. It explores the ways in which the victim of an act of humiliation is defined as an outsider and the perpetrators are defined as acting in the public interest and according to universal values. Garfinkel later developed his analysis in three main directions. First, he looked more closely at the reasoning processes through which people come to define situations in certain ways. Secondly, having studied under Talcott Parsons, he reformulated Parsons's concern with the problem and maintenance of social order in terms of contexts of everyday interaction. But where Parsons had been concerned with the conditions of war and peace at the level of entire societies (following the seventeenth-century English philosopher Thomas *Hobbes), Garfinkel was interested in the maintenance of order in microcosmic interactions. Third, Garfinkel realized that the implicit rules that guide social interaction could be identified through studying situations where they are breached, and that he and his students could deliberately cause these rules to break down.

Garfinkel coined the term *'ethnomethodology' to describe the study of the reasoning processes routinely followed in everyday life. He documented these in studies of a trial jury and other sites of 'mundane reasoning'. He noted that conversational exchanges were marked by what linguists call 'indexicality': by the use of expressions like 'I', 'you', 'here', and 'now', which are given meaning solely by space-time *context*. Elliptical expressions like 'the next lecture will be in the other room' can be unpacked by listeners with the necessary background knowledge to mean: 'the next lecture in this series will be in the second of the two lecture theatres which we are using this semester'. Forcing people to spell out what they mean by shorthand references of this kind is perceived as irritating and rude. One of Garfinkel's experiments involved asking people what they meant when they asked 'How are you?', and offering an unexpectedly detailed response. In another experiment, which demonstrates how we try to produce order and meaning in puzzling situations, a researcher posing as a counsellor gave a random succession of 'yes' or 'no' responses to the victim's requests for advice, leading him or her into more and more contorted attempts to reconstruct the logic of the 'counsellor's' replies. Garfinkel draws the theoretical conclusion:

In accounting for the stable features of everyday activities, sociologists commonly select familiar settings such as familial households or workplaces and ask for the variables that contribute to their stable features. Just as commonly, one set of considerations are unexamined: the socially standardized and standardizing, 'seen but unnoticed', expected, background features of everyday scenes. The member of society uses background expectancies as a scheme of interpretation. With their use, actual appearances are for him recognizable and intelligible as the appearances-of-familiar-events. Demonstrably, he is responsive to this background, while at the same time he is at a loss to tell us specifically of what the expectancies consist. When we ask him about them he has little or nothing to say. (Garfinkel 1967: 36)

Like interactionism, ethnomethodology tended to become polarized between detailed sociolinguistic studies, in which its original anti-positivistic thrust disappeared, and more speculative and essayistic philosophical reflections. One very fruitful classic text of American sociology in the late 1950s which avoided these two extremes and became an intellectual bestseller was David *Riesman's *The Lonely Crowd* (1950). This is discussed in Box 13.

Both European interpretive thinking and American interactionist research share an emphasis on continuity between formal sociological reasoning and the informal pragmatic reasoning carried on by ordinary members of society. Both traditions of approaches converge on the idea that all people are to some extent sociologically knowledgeable and skilled. This idea has had a wide influence in social theory and has led to important explorations of the idea of *'reflexivity' in modern social life. The theme of the *knowledgeability* of social actors also brings us now to a further important component of the broad terrain of approaches concerned with meaning, action, and context. This is the 'sociology of knowledge'.

BOX 13. DAVID RIESMAN'S *THE LONELY CROWD*

Interpretive social theory is also represented in popular and theoretically unpretentious works such as David *Riesman and his colleagues' enormously influential book on American society, *The Lonely Crowd* (1950). Riesman had been a student of the critical social philosopher and psychologist Erich *Fromm. He applied his model of social character to the history and present condition of the USA in the 1940s and 1950s. Riesman traced the development of American character through three successive ideal types:

1. a pre-modern 'tradition-directed' orientation;
2. the robust and apparently self-sufficient 'inner-directed' character, respectful of parental and other authority figures from an older generation, who is characteristic of high modernity, as described in Max Weber's *Protestant Ethic and the Spirit of Capitalism*;
3. the more recently predominant 'other-directed' character, oriented to and seeking the approval of peer groups. Other-directed characters tend to conformism, but with the possibility of developing a more autonomous orientation.

By 'other-directed' Riesman did not mean 'altruistic'; and by 'inner-directed' he did not mean 'selfish'. The 'other-directed' character reflected a type of person from the affluent metropolitan suburbs, typically employed in the services professions, and typically surrounded by friends and colleagues as members of loose-knit networks of sociability. The 'other-directed' person is both more in touch with the feelings of other close associates and at the same time beset by a loneliness, by an anxiety to appear normal and to join with the crowd.

Although the authors conducted some interviews, they relied on more informal data sources. They declared that 'mainly … this book is based on our experiences of living in America—the people we have met, the jobs we have held, the movies we have seen' (1950: 5). *The Lonely Crowd* can be compared with *Tocqueville's classic observations of the USA in the 1830s and with more recent studies such as Robert Putnam's *Bowling Alone* (2000).

The sociology of knowledge

The broad field of enquiries known as the sociology of knowledge combines elements of thinking found in both interpretive and interactionist traditions of research. Philosophers have agued for centuries about the nature and grounds of our knowledge. In the early twentieth century, however, there was increasing interest in the idea of the *social* bases of knowledge. Wilhelm Jerusalem, who had overseen the publication in German of William James's book *Pragmatism* of 1907, introduced the concept of a 'sociology of cognition' (*Soziologie des Erkennens*) in 1909. What soon came to be called the 'sociology of knowledge' took several forms. Here we look at three main schools of approach: first, a phenomenological school inaugurated in Germany by Max *Scheler and Karl *Mannheim, and later resumed in the USA by Peter *Berger and Thomas *Luckmann; secondly, an anthropological tradition beginning with Durkheim and Marcel *Mauss; and third, a more recent school loosely referred to as *'social constructionism', arising out of sociological studies of the natural sciences.

Karl Mannheim's sociology of knowledge

The idea of a sociology of knowledge that developed in Germany in the 1920s had its roots in Marxist theories of class society. The phenomenological philosopher Max *Scheler and especially the Hungarian-born theorist Karl *Mannheim generalized the Marxist theory of ideology into a post-Marxist approach. This held that all knowledge outside mathematics and natural science could and should be understood in relation to the *social groups* which generated and sustained it. This, for Mannheim, did not entail *relativism* between the different perspectives of different classes, generations, and cultures. Rather, it entailed what he called *relationism*. It was an approach which aimed at objective knowledge through an awareness of the social and historical relativity of particular, partial perspectives on a given topic.

Mannheim criticized the principle drawn in German Neo-Kantian philosophy that held that the context of the *genesis* of a particular proposition or idea has no bearing on the - *validity* of the proposition or idea. For example, Mannheim showed how the context of emergence of the statement that we find in the Christian New Testament where Jesus proclaims that 'the first will be last and the last will be first' *does* have a bearing on its validity. This statement has to be considered in light of the position of the Christian slaves under the rule of the Romans. It expresses the yearning of a particular social group for emancipation in a definite context of social history. Therefore it is not a statement whose meaning can be isolated from its particular context of material social relations and held up abstractly as an article of unchanging validity, with an unequivocal or universally recognizable message.

Mannheim presented this conception of the sociology of knowledge in several texts. His first book was a study of nineteenth-century European conservative thought, titled *Conservatism* (1925). In this work he links the conservative critique of dogma and rationalism in political affairs, its approval of 'common sense' and 'sound judgement', to the world-view of an aristocracy threatened by modernity and democracy in the form of the French Revolution and its effects elsewhere in Europe. In his major treatise of 1929 *Ideology and Utopia*, Mannheim generalized an originally Marxist conception of the way in which political doctrines and, more broadly, views of the world, alternate between two functions. Either they serve to justify and 'stabilize' the status quo, or they serve to criticize and subvert it:

The concept 'ideology' reflects the . . . discovery . . . that ruling groups can in their thinking become so intensively interest-bound to a situation that they are simply no longer able to see certain facts which would undermine their sense of domination . . .

The concept of *utopian* thinking reflects the opposite discovery . . . that certain oppressed groups are intellectually so strongly interested in the destruction and transformation of a given condition of society that they unwittingly see only those elements in the situation which tend to negate it. (Mannheim 1929: 36)

Mannheim believed that intellectuals were well placed to accede to an objective knowledge of social relations based on relative detachment from particular roles and perspectives. This was due to their 'relatively free-floating' or unattached social position. Mannheim spoke of 'socially unattached intellectuals' (*freischwebende Intelligenz*).

Mannheim's work and other German approaches, including particularly the work of Schutz, reached English-speaking audiences in the 1960s and 1970s, through the impact of Peter Berger and Thomas Luckmann's influential book *The Social Construction of Reality* of 1966. This is discussed in Box 14.

Anthropological approaches to knowledge

A parallel tradition of approaches to social contexts of knowledge developed in France from a more anthropological source. In the early years of the century, Émile Durkheim, Marcel *Mauss, and others had suggested that systematic links obtained between different forms

---

BOX 14. PETER BERGER AND THOMAS LUCKMANN'S *THE SOCIAL CONSTRUCTION OF REALITY*

In the 1960s the two Austro-German-born authors Peter *Berger and Thomas *Luckmann argued that the sociology of knowledge in the early twentieth century had been too concerned with formal belief systems and political ideologies. Taking their point of departure from the phenomenological sociology of Alfred Schutz, they argued for a reorientation of the sociology of knowledge towards *everyday commonsense knowledge*, promoting the slogan of the 'social construction of reality'. Among many formulations, they expressed this difference between formal knowledge and everyday knowledge as the difference between the knowledge of the criminologist and the knowledge of the criminal. The one has a set of theoretical principles; the other has a practical know-how, born of experience, from life on the streets.

Berger and Luckmann were explicitly relativistic in their approach, arguing that the sociology of knowledge should be concerned with 'whatever passes for "knowledge" in a society' (Berger and Luckmann 1966: 15). Society in their view is both an objective and a subjective reality. As an objective reality, society results from subjective processes of definition and conceptualization. In this sense Berger and Luckmann reinvigorated the phenomenological tradition in sociology, linking it to more substantial conceptions of society derived from Durkheim. They saw sociological analysis as involving a task of harmonizing two basic propositions: on the one hand, the proposition that 'society exists only as individuals are conscious of it'; on the other hand, the proposition that 'individual consciousness is socially constructed'. (1966: 96). In their words:

Durkheim tells us: 'The first and most fundamental rule is: Consider social facts as things.' And Weber observes: 'Both for sociology in the present sense, and for history, the object of cognition is the subjective meaning-complex of action'. These two statements are not contradictory. Society does indeed possess objective facticity. And society is indeed built up by activity that expresses subjective meaning. And, incidentally, Durkheim knew the latter, just as Weber knew the former. It is precisely the dual character of society in terms of objective facticity and subjective meaning that makes its 'reality *sui generis*'. (Berger and Luckmann 1966: 30)

This approach provided a strikingly new analysis of the *legitimation of belief systems and the maintenance of 'symbolic universes'. Berger and Luckmann showed how the idea of *reification introduced by Marxist writers can be seen as involving a 'forgetting' of the socially constructed character of reality. They affirmed that 'if the integration of an institutional order can be understood only in terms of the "knowledge" that its members have of it, it follows that the analysis of such "knowledge" will be essential for an analysis of the institutional order in question, (1966: 82–3).

of social organization and different belief systems. In his *The Elementary Forms of Religious Life* of 1912, Durkheim had shown, for example, how Australian *totemic religion could be explained by the tribal and clan organization of aboriginal societies. Representations of the cosmos could be shown to reflect the spatial organization of settlements, which in turn reflected their social structure. All religion was 'about something'. Religion was too pervasive in human societies to be simply based on illusion. It was actually the form in which human societies celebrated themselves and their solidarity.

More fundamentally still, Durkheim suggested that sociology could resolve the long-standing dispute between *empiricists and rationalists over whether knowledge comes just from experience or also from categories of thought pre-loaded into the human mind. Durkheim maintained that Immanuel *Kant's conception of *a priori categories of thought supplied by the human mind was essentially correct. But Durkheim also maintained that these categories are themselves shaped *socially* and that they derive from *society* in a certain sense. A Durkheimian approach to knowledge and cognition was developed further by the French structural anthropologist Claude *Lévi-Strauss, who is discussed in Chapter 9 of this book.

In more recent times, the British anthropologist Mary *Douglas studied the way in which societies categorize the world in simple oppositions between, for example, 'clean' and 'dirty', where dirt means 'matter out of place' (Douglas 1966). Following the Durkheimian school, Douglas saw these as the key to our understanding of the most fundamental opposition in social life between the 'sacred' and the 'profane'. It is in this sense that creatures or substances that fall outside familiar categories or that fall in between categories can be at once dangerous, or poisonous, *and* special or sacred. Transsexuals, for example, may be suspect because they are 'neither one thing nor the other'. An unusual creature, or people born with deformities, may be objects of abomination or they may be objects of special veneration. It is in this connection that we can understand the literal meaning of the Hebrew word 'holy' as 'set apart'. Douglas and those working with her became increasingly interested in the political implications of this model, in relation to internal power struggles within cultures and in relation to public policy controversies. Her model is Durkheimian in its stress on the need for cultures to preserve themselves by rituals of *solidarity and punishment for deviants. It is neo-Durkheimian in the sense that cultures are also seen as divided and 'adversarial' (Douglas 2002).

In the USA in the 1970s, the anthropologist Clifford *Geertz developed a notion of 'thick description' as a programme for *ethnographic practice. By 'thick description' Geertz meant detailed immersion in the relationships and 'webs of significance' spun by actors in particular contexts of interaction. Geertz found inspiration in the work of the British philosopher Gilbert *Ryle who had been concerned with the sort of sensitive description that can differentiate between someone who intentionally *winks* and someone who unintentionally *blinks* or twitches. In a particular social context—such as a school classroom full of boys playing a prank on the teacher—the wink may function as a sign with a particular meaning, which it is the ethnographer's task to decipher. Thus 'thick description' for Geertz is a way of proceeding in social science which brings in the cultural context and makes sense of what is observed. It emphasizes that explanation in the social sciences is not often a labour of simplification—like, say, Einstein's simple elegant equation $E = mc^2$ but rather one of 'substituting complex pictures for simple ones while striving somehow to retain the persuasive clarity that went with the simple ones' (Geertz 1973: 33). In his book *The Interpretation of Cultures* (1973), Geertz writes:

In finished anthropological writings . . . [the] fact—that what we call our data are really our own constructions of other people's constructions of what they and their compatriots are up to—is obscured because most of what we need to comprehend a particular event, ritual, custom, idea, or whatever is insinuated as background information before the thing itself is directly examined. (Geertz 1973: 9)

Geertz in this sense illustrates the way in which ethnography can be pursued as a work of narration where social relations are read like a text.

Social studies of science: the rise of social constructionism

A third broad field of sociological studies of knowledge developed in the USA and Britain in the 1960s in relation to theories of valid knowledge in the natural sciences. The field emerged partly in response to the 'falsificationist' theory of science propounded by Karl *Popper (1935). Popper had proposed that good scientific theories cannot be pronounced 'true'; they can only be deemed to be 'not yet disproven', or not yet 'falsified'. Popper held that a good scientist should test theories to destruction, constantly looking for counter-evidence and giving only conditional credence to theories which have so far survived empirical testing.

Popper broke with many of the claims of *positivist philosophers about science. However, he still retained some of their assumptions and entertained a rather idealistic image of scientific progress. Moving beyond Popper and adopting a more radical position, the American historian and methodologist Thomas *Kuhn showed that scientists were very profoundly bound by shared assumptions and conventions or what he called *'paradigms'. In his influential book *The Structure of Scientific Revolutions* (1962), Kuhn showed how the development of natural science was shaped by social influences at every level, from small-scale research teams to larger scientific communities and ultimately whole societies. In Kuhn's picture, scientists are much more conservative and collectivistic than in Popper's idealistic image of science. They are relatively unwilling to question core assumptions of their paradigm, and they move *en masse* from one paradigm to another only when its inadequacies become overwhelming and an alternative is available. This is in part a matter of the internal 'thought style' of a scientific community, as Ludwig Fleck (1935) had earlier called it. And scientific change also interacts with, and depends closely upon, general meta-physical images of the world or 'world-views', and is related closely to contexts of institutional power and authority. Copernicus's heliocentric theory, for example, had to wait nearly a century before gaining acceptance. Galileo had to struggle bitterly with the papacy and the Catholic Church for institutional endorsement of his scientific discoveries.

Further extensions of the Kuhnian thesis occur in the work of the Austrian philosopher of science Paul *Feyerabend (1975). For Feyerabend, to be 'a good empiricist' is to consider seriously even the most unfashionable or apparently outlandish theories. In what he provocatively called an 'anarchistic' theory of knowledge, Feyerabend proclaimed that 'anything goes'.

Kuhn's idea of 'paradigms' can also be compared to what the French theorist Michel *Foucault termed 'epistemes' in his book *The Order of Things* of 1966, a brilliant study of forms of scientific thought in Europe in the eighteenth and nineteenth centuries (discussed at length in Chapter 9 of this book, pp. 206–8). In contrast to simple models of enlightenment in which dialogue and truth undermine illegitimate power, Foucault bound the two ideas of knowledge and domination together, stressing the involvement of disciplinary power in what he termed 'regimes of truth'. Along with the work of French historians such as Georges Canguilhem (1977) and Paul Veyne (1971), the ideas of Kuhn, Feyerabend, and Foucault challenge us with some fundamental questions about what counts as true in different cultures and different historical worlds.

Since the 1970s Kuhn's work has inspired a variety of projects in what has come to be known as 'social studies of science', also broadly understood as contributions to *'social constructionism'. These projects are united by a rejection of triumphalist or *Whiggish notions of the emergence of truth from error. They favour a more sensitive reconstruction of historical and social contexts of scientific discoveries in relation to the emergence of new disciplines. In this vein, the French anthropologist Bruno *Latour showed in his influential ethnographic study *Laboratory Life* (Latour and Woolgar 1979) how the chaotic mess on a scientist's desk, made up of research reports, photocopied articles, equations written on the back of old plane tickets, and so forth, is gradually shaped into the scientific paper. Together with Michel Callon, Latour subsequently developed an 'actor-network theory', in which scientific knowledge is socially constructed by a variety of 'actors', including its objects themselves, such as the molluscs of a Breton fishing port or the research objects and equipment in a laboratory. In this sense Latour's ethnographic approach to knowledge challenges long-standing *metaphysical distinctions in Western philosophy between conscious intentional human agents, supposedly belonging to a realm of 'culture', and non-conscious physical objects or forces, supposedly belonging to a realm of 'nature'. In Latour's work, the scientists' materials, instruments, and institutional spaces of research can be just as much 'actors' as the scientists themselves.

In Britain, the so-called Edinburgh school of the sociology of science pursued a similar programme in the 1970s. Barry Barnes (1974, 1977) emphasized the need for interpretive charity in relation to alternative conceptual schemes, while David Bloor (1976) stressed in a Durkheimian manner the social constraints exercised by scientific communities. The image of social construction was fed back into much of the sociology of natural scientific knowledge, with the idea that natural entities, since they are conceptualized in human languages in ways which vary over time and space, are basically social constructions. It was argued that the sociology of scientific knowledge should be methodologically relativistic and should not privilege whatever conceptions might happen to be favoured at the time of writing. This 'strong programme' of the sociology of science, as it came to be called, affirmed a position of neutrality between currently accepted scientific views and alternative or historically outmoded conceptions, regarding neither as in principle more valid than the other. Further variants of a social constructionist approach to science have been developed by Ian Hacking (1999).

A further broad element in the sociology of knowledge is the rise of *postmodernism in the 1980s, as proclaimed among others by the French theorist Jean-François *Lyotard. Lyotard's influential book *The Postmodern Condition: A Report on Knowledge* (1979) gave new impetus to social constructionism, foregrounding the idea of stubborn conflicts between different *cognitive ideas of the world or 'language games', in the phrase of the philosopher Ludwig *Wittgenstein. Lyotard's work is discussed at length in Chapter 12 of this book, pp. 260–2.

It should, however, be noted that some of the themes today packaged as 'postmodern sociology' were already present in developments in hermeneutics and the philosophy of language from earlier decades of the twentieth century. It is to this last main body of approaches that we turn now.

Language and hermeneutics

In general, it can be said that interpretive approaches in social theory get under way by reflecting on similarities between the understanding of human social processes and the understanding of texts. Understanding the rules and relations of conduct that underpin a particular social situation is like learning a language and reading a text. And if understanding a society is in this way *like* learning a language, it may also *require* us to learn a language or to use it in a specialized way. In the 1930s Austrian philosopher Ludwig Wittgenstein, who had begun with a simple conception of the way language maps onto the world, came to develop a more complex idea of 'language games' in which certain moves have meaning and make sense. In a religious language game, for example, words like 'prayer', 'sacred', 'holy', 'salvation', and so on, have a specific meaning which is given to them only *by* and *in* this context.

One important effect of Wittgenstein's philosophical legacy in social science was the introduction of the concept of *'speech-acts' and *'performatives'. This was developed in the 1960s by the analytical philosophers John *Austin (1962) and John *Searle (1969). They showed how, for example, when a priest says 'I pronounce you man and wife', or the rector of a university says 'I confer on you the title of Bachelor of Arts', the priest and the rector instantaneously *create* the social fact of marriage or graduation for the couple or student concerned. This way of analysing linguistic performances and competences has been taken up by a variety of theorists in recent years, from Jacques Derrida and Jürgen Habermas to feminist theorists such as Judith *Butler (for further discussion, see Chapters 9, 11, and 13 of this book, pp. 202–6, 243–5, 279–83).

We conclude our discussion here by looking at several writers influenced by Wittgenstein and by other ideas about language. Three of these are the British writer Peter *Winch and the German philosophers Hans-Georg *Gadamer and Jürgen *Habermas.

Peter Winch, Hans-Georg Gadamer, and the early Jürgen Habermas

In his book *The Idea of a Social Science and its Relation to Philosophy* (1958) Peter Winch developed Wittgenstein's ideas into a radically anti-positivist, linguistically based model of social science. Winch argued that to understand a society is to learn to use language in the way its members do. If the members of this other society talk about witches in ways which assume the reality of witchcraft, so must the social scientist. Winch, like Schutz, set up his argument partly in support of Max Weber and partly in opposition to him. He claimed that Weber had been wrong to suggest that understanding needed to be complemented by causal analysis. For Winch, knowing a society meant learning the way it is conceptualized by its members. He thus revived a central principle of nineteenth-century German *historicism, according to which every age must be understood in its own terms. Winch directly identified himself with the German idealist tradition by insisting that social relations are 'like' logical relations between sentences in language (1958: 126).

Winch's book and a subsequent article by him, titled 'Understanding a Primitive Society' (Winch 1970), sparked off a debate in Britain in the early 1960s about *relativism and anti-relativism in social science. The debate focused on Winch's discussion of the work of the British anthropologist Edward *Evans-Pritchard, who had studied the beliefs and practices of the north African tribespeople, the Azande and the Nuer (1937, 1940). At issue was essentially what we mean if we say that witchcraft is real to the Azande people. A relativist is likely to say that what counts is the Azande's *belief* in the reality of witchcraft, and that it is irrelevant to add that back home in Oxford or Paris most people no longer believe in witchcraft or do not consider it scientifically proven or provable. Anti-relativists—such as Ernest *Gellner (1985)—are prone to insist that there is a fact of the matter about whether witchcraft works, that in fact it does *not* work, and that the role of the social observer is to try to explain the reasons for the prevalence of such false beliefs.

In the same period, the German philosopher Hans-Georg *Gadamer introduced the concept of 'philosophical hermeneutics', which also found its way into social-science discussions. In his book *Truth and Method*, first published in 1960, Gadamer extended the traditional scope of hermeneutics, which had formerly been limited to the theory of interpretation of texts, including particularly the Bible. Gadamer insisted on a practical dimension of interpretation, conceived in the philosopher Martin *Heidegger's sense of an 'encounter' between the 'horizon' of the interpreter and the 'horizon' of the text itself. Gadamer's philosophical hermeneutics was conceived in opposition to the methodological emphasis of traditional hermeneutic theories that had been concerned predominantly with accuracy, technique, and impartiality. Gadamer's aim was to describe the underlying process, the existential encounter between two perspectives or 'horizons of expectation', which makes interpretation possible. Understanding is not only a matter of immersing oneself imaginatively in the world of the historical actor or text. It is an at once reflective and practical process which operates with an awareness of the temporal and conceptual distance between the text and the interpreter and of the ways in which the text has been and continues to be reinterpreted and to exercise an influence over us. For Gadamer, this 'effective history', as he called it (*Wirkungsgeschichte*), which traditional historicist hermeneutics had tended to see as an obstacle, is an essential element which links us to the past and to other cultures. Our 'pre-judgements' are what make understanding possible. Pre-judgements, or 'prejudices', do not necessarily limit understanding, though they may do so.

The conception of hermeneutics espoused by Gadamer became central to the early work of the German critical social theorist Jürgen *Habermas, whose work is discussed at length in later sections of this book (Chapter 7, pp. 164–5, and Chapter 13, pp. 279–83). In his early text *Logic of the Social Sciences* (1967), Habermas welcomed Gadamer's critique of historical objectivism, which he saw as the equivalent of positivism in natural science. However, Habermas also maintained that Gadamer's stress on the fundamental nature of language—expressed in his claim that 'Being that can be understood is language'—amounted to a form of 'linguistic idealism'. In Habermas's view, Gadamer's stress on the value and wisdom of past historical traditions and his rehabilitation of the category of 'prejudice' suggested a conservative approach. Habermas argued that this conception of interpretation failed to deal with the possibility of systematic distortions in relations of dialogue between subjects, due to the effects of power, *domination, and *ideology. Habermas and Gadamer debated these issues in the late 1960s and early 1970s. On the one side stood Gadamer's idea of tradition and openness to the worldviews of past cultures and ancient classical civilizations. On the other side stood Habermas's idea of *enlightenment, *emancipation, and ideology critique. More recent theorists have tended to stress compatibility between hermeneutics and Habermasian critical theory, rather than conflict between them. Several writers have espoused a conception of 'critical hermeneutics' (Thompson 1981; Outhwaite 1987; Hoy and McCarthy 1994; Harrington 2001).

Hermeneutics and critical theory can also be brought into relation with the school of *realist philosophy of science developed in Britain by Mary Hesse, Rom *Harré, Roy *Bhaskar, and others. For Hesse and Harré, science is an attempt to produce models of real entities and processes in the world, aiming particularly at causal relations. Where Harré (1993) combines this realism about natural science with a social-constructionist social psychology, Bhaskar (1979) is more sympathetic to theories such as Marxism, as well as to Anthony *Giddens's theory of *'structuration' (on Bhaskar's and Giddens's work, see, Chapter 10 of this book, pp. 217–20, 227–8). For both Harré and Bhaskar, meanings are real and have causal effects. Bhaskar has sought to overcome positivism in social science without at the same time acquiescing in cultural relativism or an idealizing overestimation of the significance of texts and linguistic constructs in social life.

All of these more critical responses to hermeneutics can be seen as attempts to reconcile the rival claims of causal 'explanation' with meaningful 'understanding' in social science—just as Weber had attempted to reconcile them at the beginning of the twentieth century. In general, hermeneutics in a broad sense continues to exist as a major research tradition in the humanities and social sciences; and social scientists who might not sign up to an explicitly hermeneutic programme mostly accept at least the importance of hermeneutic issues today.

Conclusion

The approaches discussed in this chapter all possess what Wittgenstein called a certain 'family resemblance' to one another. Although they have very diverse origins and trajectories of development, several common themes unite the broad fields discussed here under the brackets of phenomenological sociology, interactionism, sociology of knowledge, and philosophies of language and hermeneutics. We may not be able to identify a single proposition or set of propositions to which all these fields would subscribe, but they share a general orientation or style of theorizing. All the approaches focus in various ways on themes of meaning, understanding, action, interaction, language, context, and everyday knowledge. These themes point us to a shared general outlook which marks out these approaches in opposition to positivism.

A common general issue concerns the status of what Robert Merton called 'insider' and 'outsider' knowledge. The essential question is, to put it crudely: does one have to *be* an insider in order to *understand* an insider? A strong insider view would tend to cut the ground from under the feet of interpretive theory. It would suggest that the only culture we can really understand is our own culture. This would be a very relativistic way of thinking. On the other hand, the idea that only uninvolved disinterested outsiders can do proper, value-free social research, and that therefore researchers should be steered away from studying the social contexts they know best, has become less fashionable than it once was. It would seem that it is not necessary to be an insider in order to understand one; but it would also appear that there can be no purely disinterested position from which all social contexts can be observed in a reliable way. It would appear that all understanding and observation requires, and enables, at least some empathic engagement with the subjective perspectives of the insiders or the others to whom one does *not* belong. It is possible to suggest, as Gadamer and Habermas have done, that ethnographers, historians, or social scientists cannot suspend their own beliefs in any free-floating way; and therefore that an appropriate model of interpretation ought to be more one of a critical 'hermeneutic dialogue' between the standpoint of the people one is studying and the standpoint of one's own culture.

The relation between interpretive and other approaches has traditionally been framed in terms of a contrast between 'understanding' and 'explanation'. There is, however, something unsatisfactory about setting things up in this way. For as Winch and Geertz showed in different ways, some interpretive descriptions are also explanatory, at least in a preliminary sense. Often what we call explanation in the social sciences takes the form of showing a possible reason why some observed effect has occurred. Such explanations are inherently open-ended, since it is always open to others to suggest an alternative explanation or to argue that the effect has been misdescribed. Durkheim characteristically tended to knock down a small number of possible explanations and then suggest that his was the *only* possible one, but his critics saw through this ruse. Explanations accepted as successful can tend to be incorporated into the description of the entity or event, rather as the molecular structure or atomic weight of a chemical substance becomes a definitional property of it.

It is possible to combine the approaches discussed in this chapter in mutually critical ways. In particular, symbolic interactionism and phenomenological sociology can be enriched by a closer attention to language. Ethnomethodology, in the work of Garfinkel, *Cicourel, and others, is a major example of this enrichment. Similarly, Gadamer's notion of the 'fusion of horizons' forms a useful corrective to Winch's radical relativism. Likewise, it may be useful to complement interpretive approaches as a whole with more structural perspectives drawn from *critical theory, *structuration theory, *reflexive sociology, or *realism. Interactionism is valued by many social scientists as a 'sensitizing' perspective, even if they believe that it needs to be complemented by more system-based analyses. The reproduction of class and gender relations in everyday linguistic communication is clearly a crucial aspect of interaction, but structural material inequalities and systemic societal dynamics will also need to be taken into account. Finally, the sociology of knowledge can be seen as benefiting from a more sharply political edge. There are at least two aspects to this. First, certain uses of language and forms of knowledge may be denigrated in invidious ways, as 'common', vulgar, or 'native'. Secondly, a subordinate perspective, the 'view from below', may give a clearer understanding of unequal social relations. This has certainly been a central tenet for Marxism as well as for what has come to be called 'feminist standpoint epistemology', as developed by writers such as Dorothy *Smith and Sandra *Harding. Methodologically, these approaches entail taking the standpoint of the excluded, not purely as a piece of political partisanship or a gratuitous rejection of social-scientific value neutrality, but as the best way of understanding a context of inequality and marginalization.

It is true that some interpretive theorists have denied a need for cooperation with other methodologies in social science, just as some empiricists, functionalists, or rational choice theorists have not always recognized a need to attend to hermeneutic issues. Here we are back with familiar controversies over the place of sociology and other humanistic disciplines 'between science and literature', as the German writer Wolf Lepenies (1985) has put it. In some disciplines, such as history or anthropology, an interpretive approach may be accepted more or less automatically. In others, such as economics, it may seem exotic and eccentric. But what the debates have shown is that interpretation is not just an option in social theory; it is the way in which we obtain access to the social world. Hence precision of meaning has something like the same importance in social theory as precision of measurement has in many areas of natural science. It follows that researchers in the social sciences and humanities had better be explicit that this is what they are engaged in.

◼ QUESTIONS FOR CHAPTER 5

1   How far are all social actors amateur sociologists? What is the relation between this 'lay sociology' and more formal social theory?

2   What similarities and differences can be discerned between European and North American traditions of interpretive and interactionist sociology?

3   What it does it mean to have 'empathy' for the experiences of another person or people?

4   What does it mean to say that reality is 'socially constructed' or 'linguistically constructed'? What follows from these claims?

5   What does it mean to say that all knowledge is 'relative' to social contexts? Is there a problem of 'relativism' in the sociology of knowledge?

6   Must one be a member of the oppressed to be able to understand the oppressed? Is experience of suffering a necessary precondition for explaining suffering sociologically?

7   Are there any elements of social reality for which interpretive and interactionist thinking fails to account adequately?

◼ FURTHER READING

For a broad overview of interpretive approaches to social enquiry, see William Outhwaite's article 'The History of Hermeneutics', in the *International Encyclopaedia of the Social and Behavioral Sciences* (Elsevier, 2001) (**www.iesbs.com**). For a good overview of these and other issues in social theory, see Mark J. Smith's *Social Science in Question* (Sage, 1998). Some good collections of extracts by influential interpretive writers are Fred Dallmayr and Thomas McCarthy (eds.), *Understanding and Social Inquiry* (University of Notre Dame Press, 1977), Kurt Mueller-Vollmer (ed.), *The Hermeneutics Reader*

(Blackwell, 1986), and Josef Bleicher (ed.), *Contemporary Hermeneutics* (Routledge, 1980). Studies showing how interpretive perspectives can be combined with other approaches in social theory are Anthony Giddens's *New Rules of Sociological Method* (Polity Press, 2nd edn. 1995), John Thompson's *Critical Hermeneutics* (Cambridge University Press, 1981), William Outhwaite's *New Philosophies of Social Science* (Macmillan, 1987), and Gerard Delanty's *Social Science beyond Constructivism and Realism* (Open university Press, 1997). See also Zygmunt Bauman's *Hermeneutics and Social Science* (Hutchinson, 1978). An illuminating account of hermeneutics in relation to literary theory is David Hoy's *The Critical Circle: Literature, History and Philosophical Hermeneutics* (University of California Press, 1978). Peter Winch's short book *The Idea of a Social Science and its Relation to Philosophy* (Routledge, 2nd edn. 1990) can be recommended as an elegantly written classic. Gadamer's work is best approached through Georgia Warnke's guide *Gadamer* (Polity Press, 1987) and Kurt Mueller-Vollmer's *The Hermeneutics Reader* (Blackwell, 1986). For a critique of the theme of 'hermeneutic dialogue' in Gadamer, Habermas, and other German writers, see Austin Harrington's *Hermeneutic Dialogue and Social Science: A Critique of Gadamer and Habermas* (Routledge, 2001). See also Gary Schapiro and Alan Sica's edited *Hermeneutics: Questions and Prospects* (University of Massachusetts Press, 1984).

For a collection of writings in phenomenology and sociology, see Thomas Luckmann's edited *Phenomenology and Sociology: Selected Readings* (Penguin, 1978). A good place to begin reading Schutz is his essay 'Common Sense and Scientific Interpretation of Human 'Action', in *Alfred Schutz: Collected Papers, vol.* i (ed.) M. Natanson (Nijhoff, 1966). See also Nick Crossley's *Intersubjectivity: The Fabric of Social Becoming* (Sage, 1997), which deals with Schutz, Mead, Merleau-Ponty, and Foucault. For a comparison between Schutz and ethnomethodology, see Burke Thomason's *Making Sense of Reification: Alfred Schutz and Constructionist Theory* (Macmillan, 1982).

A good introduction to the Chicago School is Martin Bulmer's *The Chicago School* (University of Chicago Press, 1984). A useful textbook in symbolic interactionism is Robert Prus's *Symbolic Interaction and Ethnographic Research* (State University of New York Press, 1996). For an informative account of symbolic interactionism, see Hans Joas's article 'Symbolic Interactionism', in Anthony Giddens and Jonathan Turner (eds.), *Social Theory Today* (Polity Press, 1987), as well as Joas's longer study *G. H. Mead* (Polity Press, 1985). Two primary works in the area are Ken Plummer's edited collection of papers *Symbolic Interactionism* (in two volumes) (Edward Elgar, 1991) and Herbert Blumer's papers *Symbolic Interactionism* (Prentice-Hall, 1971).

Goffman is a very readable author. It is good to start with *The Presentation of Self in Everyday Life* (Penguin, 1971) or *Asylums* (Penguin, 1991). For secondary guides, see Tom Burns's *Erving Goffman* (Routledge, 1992) and Peter Manning's *Erving Goffman and Modern Sociology* (Polity Press, 1992). Garfinkel's use of technical jargon may seem off-putting at first, but his accounts of experiments make lively and entertaining reading. A good secondary guide is John Heritage's *Garfinkel and Ethnomethodology* (Polity, 1984). For a collection of readings, see Roy Turner's *Ethnomethodology: Selected Readings* (Penguin, 1974).

The field of the sociology of knowledge is helpfully tackled through Peter Berger and Thomas Luckmann's very clear and accessible *The Social Construction of Reality* (Penguin, 1966). Karl Mannheim's work can be approached through David Kettler, Volker Meja, and Nico Stehr's *Karl Mannheim* (Horwood, 1984) and Volker Meja and Nico Stehr's *Knowledge and Politics: The Sociology of Knowledge Dispute* (Routledge, 1990). Try also John Law (ed.), *Power, Action and Belief: A New Sociology of Knowledge* (Routledge, 1986), or more recently Doyle McCarthy's *Knowledge as Culture: The New Sociology of Knowledge* (Routledge, 1996). In the field of social studies of science, see Steve Fuller's *Science* (Open University Press, 1997) and Steve Woolgar's *Science: The Very Idea* (Horwood, 1988). See also Micheal Lynch's *Scientific Practice and Ordinary Action: Ethnomethodology and Social Studies of Science* (Cambridge University Press, 1993). For the idea of social constructionism, try Ian Parker (ed.), *Social Constructionism, Discourse and Realism* (Sage, 1998).

WEBSITES

Alfred Schutz at **http://plato.stanford.edu/entries/schutz/** Provides a discussion of Schutz and his influence, with a bibliography.

The Chicago School at **http://cepa.newschool.edu/het/schools/chicago.htm** Gives a good overview of the Chicago School with links to profiles of the main associates.

Erving Goffman at **www2.fmg.uva.nl/sociosite/topics/sociologists.html#GOFFMAN** Provides a biography, with discussions and excerpts from Goffman's texts.

The Sociology of Knowledge at **www.trinity.edu/~mkearl/knowledg.html** Displays an overview, with links to related theorists and texts.

Karl Mannheim at **www.radford.edu/~junnever/theory/mannheim.htm** Contains links to sites on Mannheim.

6 | Historical Social Theory

Dennis Smith

Historical social theory, or 'comparative historical sociology', as it is also known, focuses on long-term social processes and on differences and similarities between societies at different times in history. It tries to make sense of what we know, or believe we know, about the way many different types of society, past and present, have been held together and at the same time divided by different forms of government, economic organization, culture, religion, kinship, ethnicity, and class structure. When historical social theorists look at different societies and different historical periods, they want to identify and understand the underlying patterns in the way human beings act, think, and feel. They want to link these patterns to the overarching structures—such as the family, government, or the economy—that shape the way human beings enter into social relationships. They also want to see how the behaviour of people within those relationships affects those overarching structures, sometimes reinforcing them, sometimes weakening or transforming them. Above all, they want to know: why do societies change? Why do societies differ? What are the social processes driving historical change and creating similarities and differences?

This chapter looks at a number of key historical social theorists. We concentrate on the work of five main groups of twentieth-century writers active from around the 1940s onwards. The first group includes Neil *Smelser, Seymour Martin *Lipset, and Shmuel *Eisenstadt: these writers are associated with *functionalism* in historical sociology. The second group includes T. H. *Marshall, Joseph *Schumpeter, and Friedrich *Hayek: these writers address themes of *capitalism, citizenship,* and *democracy.* The third group includes Reinhardt *Bendix and Norbert *Elias, who address issues of *power* and *conflict.* The fourth group includes Barrington *Moore, Theda *Skocpol, and Charles *Tilly: these writers are notable for their writings on the role of the *state, violence,* and *revolution.* The last group includes Immanuel *Wallerstein, Michael *Mann, and Perry *Anderson, whose writings focus on the *dominance of the Western world.*

We begin by discussing the emergence of historical thinking in social thought from the eighteenth century to the present day, together with some of the central general questions of historical social theory.

Historical thinking in social theory

Historians, sociologists, and social theorists all use ideas and empirical evidence referring to two kinds of things. One is the way social structures change and social processes occur over time: for example, how styles of warfare or the organization of the family develop from one century to the next. The other is how specific instances or types of social structure and social process are similar to, or different from, each other: for example, the ways in which the organization of the military or relationships between husbands and wives are similar and different when comparing, say, eighteenth-century China and eighteenth-century Britain. Thus historical social theory has two basic dimensions: a *historical* dimension and a *comparative* dimension.

In general, statements about how things change over time and how things differ from or resemble each other are central to scientific and philosophical arguments, especially those that depend on demonstrating that a supposed 'cause' precedes in time a supposed 'consequence' or that argue that when causal conditions vary across cases, so do consequences. Here the interests and practices of historians and sociologists overlap to a great extent. It is true that the professional self-understanding of many historians emphasizes the importance of recording the details of particular circumstances, taking an *ideographic* approach, while the professional identity of many sociologists places more emphasis upon the discovery or attribution of regularities across cases, taking a *nomothetic* approach. Historians tend to be interested in individual cases for their own sake, whereas historical sociologists tend to be more interested in structural generalities or commonalities among cases.

However, in their actual work, historians and sociologists regularly combine both ideographic and nomothetic elements.

The major works of classical social theorists such as Marx, Weber, and Durkheim are deeply embedded in a historical understanding of society, oriented to explanations for similarities and differences between processes of macro-social change in different historical epochs and in civilizations, in the East as well as the West. What today is called 'historical sociology' only appears to be a sub-specialism of social theory because of the rise to prominence in the mid-twentieth century of a search for recurrent social universals discoverable at all times and places. This search was given a large boost by Talcott *Parsons's attempt to restructure sociology in terms of invariant propositions reminiscent of economics. Today this kind of project is reflected in the influence of *rational choice theory.

Historical social thought in the West began to take a recognizably modern form during the eighteenth century. As the power of organized religion gradually weakened, especially among the educated classes, scholars took up a task of providing 'rational' and 'scientific', explanations for the character and development of human societies, explanations that aimed to replace the narratives provided by the Bible. Although many scholars had fairly clear ideas about what kinds of social arrangement were 'good' and which were 'bad,' historical sociology borrowed an ideal taken from natural science. This ideal was to examine what 'is' in as clear-sighted a way as possible, without allowing perceptions to be distorted by value-laden assumptions about what 'ought to be'.

Thinkers such as David *Hume, Adam *Smith, Adam *Ferguson, *Montesquieu, and Alexis de *Tocqueville were linked by their commitment to a shared ideal. They sought to examine comparative data about social arrangements in the past and present in order to establish generalizations about human nature, social order, and change. The object of making these generalizations was to give men and women knowledge relevant to their attempts to make themselves and their societies better, within the discoverable limits of possibility. The agendas of historical social thinkers in the nineteenth and early twentieth centuries were dominated by themes such as:

- the origins of social solidarity and conflict;
- the nature of social hierarchy and interdependence, as illustrated, for example, by slavery and the market;
- the dynamics of social change; for example, the origin and nature of war and revolution;
- the nature of empires and civilizations and the causes of their rise and fall;
- the rise of rational bureaucracies, especially the state, and the different forms taken by the state, such as dictatorship and democracy;
- the development and spread of capitalism;
- the relationship between the West and the rest of the world.

The writings of historical social thinkers from Adam Ferguson in the late eighteenth century to Weber and Durkheim in the early twentieth century constitute a first 'long wave' of historical sociology. This wave came to a halt in the period between the two world wars of the twentieth century. It can be said that a consensus broke apart as political and social life in the West in this period came to be dominated by a bitter contest between three ideologies that were far more concerned with the future than with understanding the past. The three ideologies were *communism*, under the leadership of the Soviet Union, *fascism*, led by Hitler's Third Reich, and *capitalist democracy*, led by the Western European colonial powers of Britain and France as well as the USA. Over half a century later, we can observe that it was this third system of capitalist liberal democracy, spearheaded by the USA and Western Europe, which won the long war of attrition—the Cold War—against the Soviet Union, after the earlier defeat of fascism.

The Allied victory in 1945 generated an intellectual climate in which historical social thinking could flourish once more. Yet by this time, the agendas of social science were strongly influenced by the determination of the USA and the Western powers to show that capitalism and democracy could be combined to generate social and political arrangements superior to available alternatives. Capitalism and democracy thus climbed to the top of the agenda in the second long wave of historical sociology that began in the late 1940s. It is to this body of work that we now turn.

Mid-century American historical sociology: the influence of functionalism

In this section we look at six writers who rose to prominence in the first decades after the Second World War. They are Neil Smelser, Seymour Martin Lipset, S. N. Eisenstadt, T. H. Marshall, Joseph Schumpeter, and F. A. Hayek. What links them is their belief that the question of how societies should be organized had been settled definitively by the defeat of the Nazis and the rise to global power of the United States. In their view, modern societies would be capitalist and they would be democracies. Two questions remained to be worked out: how would societies that were not already capitalist democracies move in this direction? How were capitalism as an economic system and democracy as a political system to be combined and made to function together?

The Parsonian school: Neil Smelser and Shmuel Eisenstadt on long-term social processes

As we saw in Chapter 4 of this book, Talcott Parsons's approach to historical change was deeply influential in American sociology in the early post-war years. *Structural functionalism was sometimes accused of being 'static' and unable to cope with social change. It is true that Parsons himself declared that 'a general theory of the processes of change of social systems is not possible in the present state of knowledge' (Parsons 1951: 586). But Parsons did at least think that 'the process of rationalization', as described by Max Weber, was 'a general directional factor in the change of social systems' (Parsons 1951: 499). He also argued that change was often accompanied by 'strains' due to the resistance of vested interests and the fact that society's established expectations were challenged and disrupted (Parsons 1951: 513).

Neil *Smelser, a student of Parsons, developed the Parsonian idea that the key to understanding social change was structural *differentiation, meaning an increase in the number of subsystems in a society and a shift to a higher degree of complexity in the relationships between these subsystems. Smelser sought to inject a more explicit historical dimension into the Parsonian approach in ways that echoed some of the emphases of the conflict theorists on change and discontinuity, but without the conflict theorists' general hostility to Parsons's functionalist thinking (see Chapter 4 of this book, pp. 100–1). Smelser applied this approach in his book *Social Change in the Industrial Revolution* (1959). His subject was the Lancashire cotton industry between 1770 and 1840, the time of the English Industrial Revolution. Smelser argued that structural differentiation typically happened as a result of two conditions. First, key social agents became dissatisfied with what Parsons called the 'goal-achievements' of the social system, i.e. its capacity to deliver desired resources and commodities. Secondly, they saw the 'prospect of facilities . . . to correct this imbalance', i.e. the chance to change social arrangements. Subsequently, social control mechanisms through the family, religion, and the police ensured that disturbances were handled in such a way that resources such as money and human energy were mobilized. As a result, innovations were brought about that satisfied societal demands, and the new norms of action became routinized.

Smelser analysed several empirical examples of structural differentiation. Looking at the textile industry (Smelser 1959: 69–128), he argued that the spread of Methodism in the manufacturing districts strengthened values legitimizing manufacturers' complaints about bottlenecks in the existing industrial structure. Disturbances caused by industrial difficulties were handled and channelled through the lawcourts. Tolerance for new ideas was shown by the Patent Office, and there were innovations in the machinery of industrial production. Smelser also considered other aspects of social change in the textile districts, especially in family structures.

Structural-functionalist theory was able, Smelser wrote, 'to relate a multitude of complex social phenomena to a single set of analytical propositions without varying the logic of the propositions themselves' (1959: 384). One serious problem with Smelser's work, however, was that it did not test the assumptions of his theory against competing theories, other than that of structural functionalism. Instead of 'telling it like it is', according to a range of diverse empirical data, Smelser tended to present his subject 'like it had to be', according to a pre-established model.

In a similar manner to Smelser, the Israeli historical sociologist Shmuel *Eisenstadt examined the development of specialized political institutions and movements that resisted traditional values and practices. In his book *The Political Systems of Empires* (1963), Eisenstadt investigated large pre-industrial societies, especially what he called 'historical bureaucratic empires', including ancient Egypt, China, Rome, Byzantium, and the major European states during the period of *absolutist rule. He sought to define the conditions under which specialized political systems developed in these societies and how they were perpetuated, avoiding collapse or being overthrown. He argued that such political systems developed when rulers began to follow their own plans, rather than accepting traditional values and goals. Other factors included new types of social actors created by the growth of towns, by new religious movements, and by the spread of the market. These 'free-floating resources' became 'a reservoir of generalized power' (1963: 27).

The ruler and the bureaucracy were part of a three-way structure of conflict and compromise in these empires. Powerful traditional groups such as landowners competed with new urban, commercial, and religious interests, and both had a tense relationship with the central government. Rulers were often committed to traditional values at the same time as pursuing their own goals. On the other hand, the new social interests resisted attempts by the ruler and bureaucracy to restrict their independence and to tax them heavily. Meanwhile, government bureaucrats were liable to become corrupt, to line their own pockets, and build up their own power. These conflicts created constant pressure for change: sometimes marginal or 'accommodable', sometimes total, bringing about a fundamental alteration of society and government. One outcome of total change was the modern state, the result of an increase in structural differentiation. In modern states, government and society are very closely interwoven. Such states may be either despotic and *totalitarian or more democratic, allowing different groups to participate in the political process.

The strength of Eisenstadt's work is his analysis of structural tensions in societies that in various ways stand *in between* what we like to call 'tradition' and 'modernity'. Like Smelser, Eisenstadt sees a historical pattern of stability and disruption, followed by restored stability. But where Smelser stresses tendencies to restored stability, Eisenstadt stresses recurrent disruption. And unlike Smelser, Eisenstadt sees these conflicts as being society-wide, rather than contained within 'subsystems' such as the family. Where Smelser was concerned with specialized institutions and changes over decades, Eisenstadt examined changes in whole societies and over centuries. In *The Political Systems of Empires* he ends with the suggestion that historical bureaucratic empires stand at the crossroads between modern dictatorships and modern democracies. That thought connects Eisenstadt's work to the writings of another sociologist who applied structural-functionalist ideas to government and politics. This is the US writer Seymour Martin Lipset, whose work is discussed in Box 15.

In his later work, Eisenstadt ceased to write in a structural-functionalist mode. In the 1980s he completed a wide-ranging comparative study of ancient and modern civilizations influenced by Weber and by the ideas of the German philosopher Karl *Jaspers concerning 'axial age civilizations'. In his last work, Eisenstadt introduced the important theme of 'multiple modernities', as an alternative to Western-centred conceptions of modernity such as the rather US-centred Parsonian theory of modernization which dominated in the 1950s. The theme of multiple modernities represents a self-consciously globalized understanding of sociology which can be contrasted to *Eurocentric developmentalist thought in nineteenth-century evolutionary theory, such as that of Auguste *Comte and Herbert *Spencer (as discussed in Chapter 1 of this book, pp. 32–3).

BOX 15. SEYMOUR MARTIN LIPSET ON POLITICAL STABILITY AND INSTABILITY

In *Political Man* (1960), the American sociologist Seymour Martin *Lipset set out to determine historical preconditions for democracy. He classified societies according to whether they were 'stable democracies' or 'unstable democracies or dictatorships'. He tabulated various key indices such as urbanization, education, industrialization, and wealth. These enabled him to demonstrate that those societies with the highest scores were 'stable democracies' (see Lipset 1960: 31–8). In *The First New Nation* (Lipset 1963), Lipset applied this argument to the American case, discussing it from comparative and historical perspectives. The book was written at a time when the British, French, and other European empires were breaking up and American politicians were concerned that the ex-colonies in Africa and elsewhere might acquire communist-influenced governments.

Lipset's analysis placed emphasis on political institutions together with the strategies adopted by elites and especially values and national character. In his analysis, American history had produced a specific set of 'structured predispositions' for 'handling strains generated by social change' (Lipset 1963: 207). They included a stress on achievement and belief in equality. The tension between these two ideals was kept in check by a strong sense of nationhood. This was reinforced by a stable two-party system. This argument was presented cautiously, as a possible hypothesis. However, it was clearly playing to an American audience that was highly sympathetic to its main proposition. This was, to put it crudely, that America would remain strong as long as its citizens held fast to the principles of the Declaration of Independence. Like Neil Smelser, Lipset assumed that within industrial societies, especially if and when they became more like the United States, there was a natural tendency for the social system to solve all problems that it was set. Mainly, these problems turned out to be technical matters that needed pragmatic adjustments to fix them. This approach led to partial blindness with respect to endemic American problems such as the persistent discrimination against African-Americans. More recently Lipset revisited this analysis in his book *American Exceptionalism: A Double-Edged Sword* (1996).

Mid-century European historical sociology: the crisis in liberal democracy

On the other side of the Atlantic, the British sociologist T. H. *Marshall agreed with Parsons, Smelser, and Lipset that capitalist democracy was here to stay and would continue as the dominant type of society. However, he did not think that pragmatic adjustments were the only challenge. On the contrary, serious matters of fundamental principle remained unresolved. A similar view was taken, with some differences of emphasis, by two central European émigré writers: Joseph Schumpeter and Friedrich Hayek. Marshall's, Schumpeter's, and Hayek's contributions are discussed here in turn.

T. H. Marshall on social citizenship

Marshall's approach was both historical and structural. In his influential essay 'Citizenship and Social Class', Marshall (1949) described a long-run historical tendency for individuals in Western societies to achieve full membership of their national community and to acquire the same citizenship rights and duties as others, rich or poor. His main focus was the British case where the rise of citizenship, with its equalizing tendency, had coincided with the rise of capitalism, which tended to produce inequality. In Britain, civil rights, including the right to own property, to make contracts, and to speak freely, advanced strongly in the eighteenth century. Political rights, especially the right to vote, expanded in the nineteenth century. In the twentieth century, great progress was made with respect to social rights such as the right to welfare, health care, and education.

Marshall's problem, however, concerned the question of how the polarizing effects of the market were to be reconciled with the equalizing effects of citizenship. How could one tell when there was 'too much' inequality in the market place? To summarize the central problem: the rights and obligations created by contracts in the markets, including the right to get rich and make others work for low wages, were both *dependent* on principles of citizenship—including especially the right to protection for property—and *challenged* by citizenship principles, including especially *social* rights which implemented ideals of social justice and fairness. The tension between these two sets of principles was felt sharply in the education system, since by acquiring qualifications at school and in university, school-leavers and graduates felt a 'right' to a job of a certain income and status—and often the market denied their expectations.

Joseph Schumpeter on capitalism, socialism, and democracy

In his classic book *Capitalism, Socialism and Democracy* (Schumpeter 1941), Joseph *Schumpeter argued that capitalism had been very successful as a system for generating and distributing social goods but was likely to become increasingly socialistic in its political organization. Capitalism would be undermined by its very success. This success could be measured in terms of technological innovation and 'avalanches of consumer goods' (Schumpeter 1941: 68). It was due to two things. First, capitalism penalized failure and rewarded success. Secondly, it was driven by repeated examples of 'creative destruction' in the course of which new techniques, products, materials, and organizational methods destroyed old institutions and practices and put new ones in place (Schumpeter 1941: 83).

According to Schumpeter, this unsteady dynamism of the capitalist economy was increasingly the work of big business. Monopoly and oligopoly gave innovators protection, keeping rivals out of the market place. The organizations and work practices created by the bourgeoisie were systematic, rationalistic, and individualistic. Innovation became increasingly bureaucratized in the work of specialist teams. This array of characteristics enabled capitalism to generate great wealth and spread it through society. However, it also undermined the middle classes. In Schumpeter's narrative, the individual entrepreneur who had provided the dynamism and vision of the middle classes was becoming redundant as research teams took over. The entrepreneur's sense of personal ownership of the business declined as large corporations became limited companies with shareholders. Bourgeois family life weakened as opportunities to found family business dynasties diminished.

Schumpeter also considered the part played by intellectuals and enlightenment rationalism in undermining the prestige of the aristocracy. While the bourgeoisie was busy making money, the aristocracy had run government and provided the former with political protection. But now this balance was being eroded. The overall result was a drift towards socialism, defined as a system where control over production falls out of the hands of families and private investors and into the hands of a central public authority. Schumpeter could see certain advantages in this. Society would not have to support an idle leisure class. Wasteful competition would be abolished. Planning would avoid the need to manipulate interest rates. Irrational conflicts between the public and private spheres would be left behind. Socialism might even be democratic as long as politicians were not corrupt, if bureaucracies were strong and efficient, and if government resisted the temptation to try to run everything.

When Schumpeter surveyed long-run tendencies in the development of capitalism and democracy, he concluded that it was difficult to achieve advances in knowledge and rationality without the danger of a stifling of individual creativity in the business world and elsewhere. A rather similar view was taken by Friedrich *Hayek.

Friedrich Hayek on the free market

An émigré from Austria, Friedrich Hayek agreed with Schumpeter's central proposition that capitalist democracies were moving in the direction of socialism. However, his conclusions differed. In *The Road to Serfdom* (Hayek 1944), Hayek praised the laissez-faire free-market ethos of British capitalism in the nineteenth century. In his view, it brought prosperity and power to British society, a flowering of enterprise and science, and high expectations about the future. This era then came to an end with the great world recession of the 1930s, which Hayek recognized as giving socialism its chance. By socialism, Hayek meant bureaucratic planning in a similar sense to Schumpeter's use of the term. But in Hayek's view, the planners believed mistakenly that they could create rules and institutions that would take over from the market, or at least interfere with it on a large scale, producing wealth, investing this wealth rationally, and distributing it in a just way. In Hayek's diagnosis, such wholesale social engineering was a disaster. Socialistic planning could not work because there was no way to determine correct principles of social justice—planners were always bound to disagree. Furthermore, if the market was distorted or abolished, people would no longer receive the accurate and unbiased knowledge about supply and demand that was provided by the price system. It was far better to let individuals make their own economic and other decisions without being commanded by a central authority liable to make mistakes.

In the early 1940s, when Hayek wrote this book, it seemed likely that Britain would soon elect a Labour government, adopt wholesale planning, and lose the advantages it had inherited from its nineteenth-century industrial glory. In fact, one of the likely outcomes of socialist planning, Hayek believed, was resentment among the petty bourgeoisie and service classes, leading to increased support for fascist political movements. He even feared that Britain might go the way of Germany in the 1930s.

Hayek became fashionable among economists and politicians in the 1980s on both sides of the Atlantic when his arguments were invoked to justify the dismantling of many facets of public ownership, giving a freer hand to big business. He was particularly applauded by the Thatcher and Reagan administrations in Britain and the USA.

An influential counter-blast to Hayek came from the US economist J. K. *Galbraith. Galbraith had been influenced by Schumpeter's general approach, agreeing that big business had become dominant within capitalism. In his book *Economics and the Public Purpose* (1973), he envisaged the possibility of a thriving small business sector run by individual entrepreneurs who would provide non-standardized products and services in a creative way. But Galbraith strongly disagreed with Hayek, and with Hayek's close follower, Milton Friedman. In his books *The Affluent Society* (1958) and *The New Industrial State* (1967), Galbraith pictured consumers in a Hayekian world of private affluence and public squalor, imagining them going out for the day to 'picnic on exquisitely packaged food from a portable icebox by a polluted stream' and then going on to camp in 'a park which is a menace to public health and morals . . . on an air mattress, beneath a nylon tent, amid the stench of decaying refuse' (1958: 204). In other words, making the planners redundant meant making life in modern industrial society unbearable for most people.

The decades of the 1960s and 1970s were a watershed for much of the intellectual self-understanding of Western societies. While African-Americans protested at their lack of civil rights and the women's movement gathered strength, the United States suffered humiliation in Vietnam. The British empire in Africa crumbled, while oil producers in the Middle East asserted their independence. The assumptions and structures on which post-war capitalist democracy had been based were placed under threat. Historical sociologists responded by giving more prominence in their analyses to questions of power, class, and conflict, and they became more aware of the global context in which historical processes occurred. Two writers who stand at a point of transition between the earlier and later phases are the German émigré sociologists Reinhard *Bendix and Norbert *Elias. Bendix and Elias had a sense that there was a strong historical tide running in the direction of capitalism and democracy, but they were very sensitive to counter-currents to this trend and to the central significance of power and conflict. Bendix's work is discussed in Box 16. Elias's work is discussed in the following section.

Norbert Elias and the 'civilizing process'

Like Reinhard Bendix, Norbert *Elias came to prominence in the 1960s and 1970s, although he had been writing as early as the 1930s. Elias was keen on finding explanations for social processes not simply from a detached interest but from a deep involvement in the fate of humankind. Having lost his parents and other Jewish relatives to Auschwitz, Elias kept up a faith in wanting to improve humanity's capacity to shape the course of social processes, or at least to avert their worst consequences.

Elias offers a powerful and influential vision of how human beings and societies inter-connect and develop. At the centre of this vision are at least seven key ideas:

- The human capacity to exercise agency, to wield power, and to experience a sense of identity, self, and belonging is the result of being embedded in human social relationships. In this sense, power and identity are fundamentally relational.

- Social life takes place in complex networks of interdependence amongst people, groups, and institutions. Elias's term for these networks of interdependence is *figurations*. Figurations include patterns of kinship, class relationships, or structures of government.

- Figurations undergo change over time as a result of long-term, and largely unplanned, social processes which have a discoverable pattern or structure. The concept of 'process' is thus key to sociological analysis.

BOX 16. REINHARD BENDIX ON POWER AND CONFLICT

Reinhard *Bendix and Norbert Elias were German Jews in origin. Both emigrated from Germany as the Nazi party came to power, Elias to Britain and Bendix to the USA. Perhaps this background helps explain their sensitivity to issues of power and conflict within and between classes, states, and societies. From their separate perspectives, both were alert to these issues while their colleagues remained preoccupied with structural functionalism and the inner dynamics of democracy and capitalism as systems.

Like Max Weber, his main source of inspiration, Bendix examined nations and nation-states from the standpoint of internal and external power struggles. He did not see national cultures as clear and coherent but as complex mosaics of conflicting beliefs and tendencies. Every national culture was the result of past conflicts and of domination by successive elites, each replacing the previous one and leaving its mark. Bendix saw this complexity as an important resource for historical sociologists, whose task was to investigate a society's ideologies in association with its key social structures in order to find clues about how problems were managed in the past.

Comparison between societies showed that similar problems could be solved in different ways; it reduced the perception that the solutions adopted in one single society, such as the USA, were the necessary and inevitable ones. This approach can be seen in Bendix's *Nation-Building and Citizenship* (Bendix 1964; see also Bendix 1956, 1984). Here Bendix confronted at least indirectly the structural functionalism of Parsons, Eisenstadt, and Lipset, whose premises he did not accept. Bendix retrieved the moral concerns that Eisenstadt had pushed aside in the name of scientific objectivity. At the same time, he believed that Lipset had neglected the historical dimension, notably by assuming that other nations in the twentieth century could follow a road towards independence of the kind taken by the United States in the late eighteenth century under very different circumstances.

Bendix paid more attention than Lipset to the shape and dynamics of historical processes, especially the development of the central relationships between state and citizens in the course of nation-building. In *Nation-Building and Citizenship*, he pursued this strategy in the cases of Western Europe, Russia, Japan, and India. In the case of Western Europe, he traced the rise of patrimonial social order dominated by royal power, examining the way powerful monarchies of the early modern period defeated local resistance and established absolutist regimes. He investigated the rise of processes of bureaucratization and democratization in the nineteenth century, marked by the demands of mass popular movements to become part of the political process through extensions of voting rights, as well as the entrenchment of structural class differences between rich and poor. In contrast, Bendix showed how tsarist autocracy in Russia was much more dominant and suppressed any attempt at independent organization by pressure groups oriented to legitimizing their actions through a plebiscitarian franchise. In both Germany and Japan, aristocratic forces remained powerful throughout the nineteenth century and early twentieth century, and they had a decisive effect on the way industry developed and the nation-state took shape. Finally, in India the caste system organized local interests in such a way that the state had great difficulty in integrating the polity and establishing its own authority within it.

- Figurations and processes have powerful effects on the psychological make-up or *'habitus' of individuals and groups, especially on their capacity to exercise control over themselves, other people, and the natural world, such as through science. In this regard, there is such a thing as 'national habitus' or 'national character', which develops over centuries through complex interactions between elite groups and the whole of the society.

- One of the challenges of the human sciences is to foster people's capacity to exercise reasonable (non-repressive) control over themselves, by supplying knowledge about historical social processes and figurations that shape people's social existence.

- European social development in the past thousand years has been characterized by a long-run tendency—frequently interrupted and reversed—towards the development of increasingly dense and complex figurations in which relatively stable power monopolies appear and entrench high levels of self-control. These include the royal courts and central state bureaucracies.

- The processes by which men and women acquire increasing self-control and interdependence in relation to increasingly stable power monopolies make up an overall *civilizing process*. Civilizing processes can be detected across the course of history in diverse social-cultural contexts. But interruptions and reversals may also occur, leading to the onset of *decivilizing* tendencies that move toward decreasing control and increasing instability.

Elias sees sociology as a science of human figurations and long-term social processes. Its aim is to produce knowledge capable of eroding the fears and illusions endemic to relations between individuals, groups, and nations. It should be 'a destroyer of myths' (Elias 1970: 50). Elias's sociology is deeply rooted in his intuitive sense for the character and subtle qualities of social relations. He has a strong feeling for interconnectedness and growth, for processes of integration and expansion, and for the intertwining processes of disarticulation and fragmentation that always accompany them. At the same time, Elias can empathize with those who stand apart, feel sequestered, or look at life through a glass screen. He understands the appeal of an apparently well-defended and protected existence, such as in a royal court, in a bourgeois household, in a university college or an academic department, or within the self.

Elias's sociological understanding of the world revolves around a central tension: between merging and separation, between involvement and detachment, between inhibition and expression, between being 'part of' and being 'apart from'. Both these aspects of his vision come through in his most important work, *The Civilizing Process*, first published in 1939. By the 'civilizing process' Elias means a long-term development, with some reversals, characterized by increasing pacification and self-control. Elias draws his evidence from Europe between the Middle Ages and the early twentieth century. Through the civilizing process, human beings are drawn into ever-denser relations of mutual interdependence so that their fates become intertwined. Individuals gradually acquire a civilized 'habitus', or psychological make-up, which is expressed in inhibition, self-awareness, detachment, and a calculating manner. Civilized people keep their emotions under control. Such an orientation to civility, 'good manners', 'polish', 'discretion', and the like would not have been conceivable in the less regulated societies of early medieval Europe when aggression and fear primed people to engage in battle or flight at a moment's notice. External controls and self-control were both intermittent and unstable before the later Middle Ages.

In contrast, Elias describes how, in the early modern period, more stable and long-lasting forms of central power monopoly gradually came into being, especially through the formation of the royal courts. As kings pacified their territories, warlords were forced to attend court, to disavow violence, and to learn the skills of etiquette and political manipulation. It was the only way for the nobility to survive and advance. As pacification encouraged trade and industry, and as interdependence increased, the civilized habitus spread from the court to the counting house, and from the upper classes to the people at large. Elias traces these processes at the level of personal behaviour by showing how manners grew more precise and delicate over the centuries. Among many other details, he investigates the rise of table manners, including the proscription of belching and farting and other bodily indiscretions. This analysis is also developed in his book *The Court Society* (1969), a specific study of the seventeenth- and eighteenth-century absolute monarchy in France and its influence on French cultural manners and mores.

In addition to his master concept of the civilizing process, Elias argues that a typical and recurring pattern in social history is tension between *establishments*, able to define and defend standards of civilized behaviour, and *outsiders*, who are stigmatized for failing to meet those standards. Another key distinction is between an attitude of detachment, which allows one to observe and interpret events without being swayed by emotional responses, and an attitude of involvement, which both intensifies and distorts perception in the sense that events are felt and interpreted in an emotional way. A final concept Elias developed later in his career, especially in his last major study *The Germans* (1989), was that of 'decivilizing processes'. These entail a reversal of previous tendencies towards reasonable political centralization and pacification. In a society undergoing a decivilizing process, such as Germany under the rise of Hitler, violence increases as society fragments into warring groups acting with greatly reduced restraint. The desperate centralization of the Nazi state was a reaction to the breakdown of civil society in Germany.

One weakness of Elias's work is the other side of its strength. This is the very great, perhaps excessive, attention he pays to the aristocracy and court society acting as social pacemakers, as a vanguard for the civilizing process. Elias tends to downplay other causes of self-restraint in social change. One factor he should have paid more attention to in the emergence of distinctly controlled rationalized social conduct is the factor of *religion*, which Max Weber had examined in the case of the Protestant ethic. But together with Bendix, Elias made an important break with the structural-functionalist tradition, opening the way for a new phase in the development of historical social theory. The new phase came to place much more emphasis on power, coercion, and conflict, especially in relation to the state and revolution. It is to this new phase that we now turn.

The rise of nation-states: revolution and violence

By the 1970s there was a strong upsurge of historical social theory dealing with the topics of violence and revolution, exploitation and class, the rise of nation-states, and the rise of the West as a whole. These themes preoccupied writers such as Barrington Moore, Theda Skocpol, Charles Tilly, Perry Anderson, Immanuel Wallerstein, and Michael Mann. In the following section we look first at the work of Moore, Tilly, and Skocpol.

Barrington Moore: modernity and the agrarian power base

In his book *The Social Origins of Dictatorship and Democracy* (1966), the US sociologist Barrington *Moore presents the startling thesis that modern political systems have been fundamentally shaped by peasants and aristocrats in pre-industrial societies (see also Moore 1978). These political systems—democracy, fascism, and communism—differ from each other in the extent to which the central state penetrates the interests of the agents it seeks to serve. Moore argues that the functioning of the central state is deeply affected by the extension of the market into local communities in agrarian societies, especially the way in which agriculture comes to be commercialized. For example, in Prussia, serf labour was exploited to produce cash crops on large estates. In France, peasants were entrepreneurial but had to share their profits with aristocratic landlords demanding *feudal dues. In England, sheep farmers forced peasants off the land. These different strategies went hand in hand with different patterns of alliance and conflict between aristocracy, bourgeoisie, and the state. In England, the aristocracy and bourgeoisie acting together kept the Crown in check. In France, Crown and nobility stuck close together, producing *absolutism. In Japan and Germany, similar alliances kept the bourgeoisie politically weak, though it grew stronger economically. By contrast, in Russia and China, the bourgeoisie was weak economically as well as politically, and so the authoritarian alliance between ruler and aristocracy was unable to build up its strength by taxing rich traders. As a result, the bourgeoisie could not resist peasant revolutions when they came.

Moore explains major transforming events such as revolutions and civil wars in terms of particular inter-group conflicts, alliances, and changes in the integration and disintegration of social groups. A key variable is the type and degree of solidarity in the rural workforce. In England, the peasantry was thrown off the land and thus slowly destroyed. In India, the caste system divided local rural society. In Japan, inter-class solidarity remained strong. In Germany, repressive labour control kept the peasantry weak and divided. In general, democracy was the outcome when the peasantry was gradually eliminated as a political force and the bourgeoisie became dominant. This was the case in Britain, France, and the USA. Fascism, on the other hand, was aided by a history of agrarian repression, while communism flowed from peasant revolutions, which in Russia and China were followed by repressive action against the peasants themselves.

Moore makes convincing use of the comparative method to build up a set of broad-ranging causal explanations. However, this strength is rather undermined by some weaknesses. One weakness is his neglect of inter-societal relation in the sense of global interaction. Another is his rather uncritical acceptance of capitalist-democratic ideology. In particular, his treatment of nineteenth-century English history comes too close to accepting at face value the benign myth of steadily expanding citizenship rights (also largely accepted by Marshall).

Charles Tilly: capital and coercion in the rise of states

Charles *Tilly, one of Moore's best-known students, has built his reputation in three areas: as a theorist of historical sociology, as an analyst of social movements, social protest, and contentious behaviour, and as the author of broad overviews of European history, most notably his *Coercion, Capital and European States AD 900–1990* (1990), which is considered here (see also Tilly 1995).

Tilly shows how the demands of constant war-making led rulers to extract resources from unwilling populations. Constant struggles over how much tribute should be paid to the state and what the state might do in return shaped the central organizational structures of the European national societies. A key factor was the extent to which a territory was either *coercion*-intensive, that is, able to support strong government pressure over the population, or *capital*-intensive, that is, economically productive and prosperous. Capital-intensive territories such as Italy and Holland tended to be highly urban, with a thriving merchant class. Coercion-intensive territories such as Prussia and much of Habsburg Eastern Europe tended to be much more rural and dependent on repressive forms of agriculture, sometimes based on serfdom. Tilly shows how where capital was plentiful, systems of fragmented sovereignty developed. Government remained relatively decentralized and sometimes took the form of city-states. Where conditions favoured coercion, large tribute-based empires tended to develop. By the sixteenth century, nation-states had an advantage in times of war because they could support large standing armies drawn from the countryside, while at the same time having the advantage of being able to tax their cities. The most successful nation-states, such as France and Britain, combined coercion and capital in what Tilly calls 'capitalized coercion'.

Tilly points out that the success of the nation-state as a form of government only seems inevitable to us in retrospect. As late as 1650, empires such as the Habsburg Empire and federations of city-states such as the Dutch Republic maintained a notable grip on territorial power in Europe. But Tilly shows how nation-states eventually prevailed, drawing on his other research on contentious behaviour and social protest. He shows how several European states gradually yielded a variety of rights to their populations and accepted a widening variety of tasks. One problem not explored at length by Tilly, however, is the question of the extent to which his generalizations apply outside Europe, such as in the USA or Asia. We may ask whether there is something distinctive about nation-state formation in Europe, perhaps as a result of the specific pattern of interstate competition between Britain, France, Spain, the Dutch, and so on. How would the USA fit into Tilly's model? Perhaps it would be best described in terms of 'fragmented sovereignty' along the 'capital-coercive path'.

Theda Skocpol on social revolutions

Theda *Skocpol is also a student of Barrington Moore. In her book *States and Social Revolutions* (Skocpol 1979), Skocpol adopts what she calls a 'non-voluntarist, structural perspective' on the origins of revolutions (1979: 14). She argues that revolutions are not simply made by conspirators but rather emerge as the unintended outcome of multiple conflicts shaped by complex socio-economic and international conditions. She attaches great importance to the inter-societal and world-historical contexts in which social revolutions occur. Modern social revolutions tend to occur in societies located 'in disadvantageous positions within international arenas' (1979: 23). A key factor is the state, which is more than simply an arena in which other interests struggle with one another. Skocpol accepts that the state has its *own* interests, which it can enforce by wielding coercive power and collecting taxes.

By 'social revolutions' Skocpol means 'rapid, basic transformations of a society's state and class structures, accompanied and in part carried through by class-based revolts from below' (1979: 33). She concentrates on three cases: the French Revolution of 1789, the Russian Revolution of 1917, and the Chinese Revolution of 1949, completed after a long civil war. In all three cases, she shows how rulers and aristocracies jointly ran the old regimes. These agencies shared, and squabbled over, the surplus gained from tax and rent. In all three cases, the old regime faced a sudden challenge from foreign states with greater economic and military strength. Faced with this challenge, the ruling establishment, which was internally divided, did not manage to respond effectively. At the same, in all three cases there were widespread lower-class rebellions, especially among the peasantry. This led to 'mass-mobilizing political leaderships' which were able to 'consolidate revolutionary state power' (1979: 41). In each case, the outcome was a 'centralized, bureaucratic, and mass-incorporating nation-state with enhanced great-power potential in the international arena' (1979: 41). The influence of the aristocracy was abolished in rural society and central government. The new regimes brought the masses into the political system and created systems of government that were more rationalized and centralized than before.

Skocpol's strategy of comparison between France, Russia, and China is to show that despite much dissimilarity between the cases, especially in their different levels of technological development, they all experienced the same distinctive phenomenon of social revolution as a result of the same distinctive set of causal factors. Here we may note that Skocpol's central argument partly resembles the argument made by Shmuel Eisenstadt in *The Political System of Empires*. The two analyses share in common an emphasis on endemic structural conflicts between the ruling power and traditional interests (the aristocracy), as well as on disputes among powerful groups about control over 'free-floating resources' (such as tax and rents). Both writers examine the resolution of those conflicts in favour of the state after a major structural transformation, involving greater centralization, bureaucratization, and involvement of mass populations in the *polity. Both authors also deliberately bracket the values, intentions, and motives of the major participant groups through the use of a self-consciously scientific framework.

Explaining the rise of the West

A further unifying theme for number of theorists in the last quarter of the twentieth century is the need to make sense of the West and its place in the world. Perry *Anderson explored the differences between Eastern and Western Europe in relation to *feudalism and the rise of capitalism. Immanuel *Wallerstein developed a distinctive approach to what he called 'world systems' emanating from centres of power in Europe and later from the USA. Michael *Mann began a study of the sources of social power geared toward explaining the power and dominance of the West, without at the same time neglecting other regions. All three writers reflect a debt to Marxism, which is qualified in various ways. We look at each in turn. The work of Michael Mann is discussed in Box 17.

Perry Anderson: feudalism and the transition to capitalism in Europe

Why and how did the capitalist mode of production originate in Western Europe? This is Perry Anderson's question in his books *Passages from Antiquity to Feudalism* (Anderson 1974a; hereafter *Passages*) and *Lineages of the Absolutist State* (Anderson 1974b; hereafter

---

BOX 17. MICHAEL MANN ON THE SOURCES OF SOCIAL POWER

The British-born sociologist Michael *Mann is the author of a major series of studies titled *The Sources of Social Power* (Mann 1986, 1993a). Mann here sets out to trace the leading edge of social power from Mesopotamia before 5000 BC to the formation of international capitalism in north-western Europe between the seventeenth and twentieth centuries. He defines social power as consisting in 'the capacity to integrate peoples and spaces into dominant configurations' (1986: 31). This includes the capacity to make resources operate in a way that is useful to those who control them. Societies are 'organized power networks'. Mann analyses four principal sources of social power: (1) economic power, (2) ideological power, (3) political power, and (4) military power. None of these has ultimate primacy. Different combinations predominate according to the world-historical context. For example, Mann believes that during the nineteenth century the role of political power in the internal workings of national states declined with the disappearance of aristocratic classes. He proposes that ideological power also grew less important in that period, especially in comparison with the great influence of Christianity during the Middle Ages in Europe.

In Mann's view, two types of configuration have recurred throughout human history. One of them consists of *empires of domination*, which used concentrated military coercion to control large territories with a centralized state. The Roman Empire is a classic example. The other type consists of *multi-power-actor civilizations*, a notable example being the city-states of ancient Greece. In the latter case, economic and ideological forms of social power predominated. Empires of domination had a tendency to fragment and to become decentralized. By contrast, multi-power-actor civilizations tended to move towards greater centralization.

A third historical tendency noted by Mann is that there was a steady drift by the leading edge of social power away from the Mediterranean towards the North Sea and the Atlantic. For example, the Scandinavians began to open up the Baltic Sea in the north at about the time that the Roman Empire collapsed. There was nothing inevitable about this drift. It was the result of 'a gigantic series of accidents of nature linked to an equally monstrous series of historical coincidences' (1986: 540). By the eighteenth century, Europe was integrated by four closely connected institutions: the capitalist mode of production; industrialism; the national state; and 'a multistate, geopolitical, diplomatic civilization' (1986: 471). In other words, Europe had become a modern form of multi-power-actor civilization (see also Mann 1988).

Lineages). In *Passages*, he looked at the dynamics of four modes of production: the slave mode, found in the Roman Empire and among the Vikings; the primitive communal mode, found in Germany; the nomadic mode, involving wandering goat-, sheep-, or cattle-herders on arid steppe-land; and the feudal mode. Anderson's main concern in this book is with the origins of the feudal mode of production. He explains feudalism as a result of the merging of the declining Roman Empire's slave mode of production and the primitive communal mode of production of the Empire's main adversaries, the Germanic tribes. This synthesis was relatively balanced in France and England. By contrast, Italy and Spain were more influenced by the Roman inheritance in urban trading and canon law, while Germany had a stronger tradition of peasant village solidarity and warlike knights.

In *Lineages*, Anderson looks at the origins and nature of the absolutist state, a form of government in which rulers claim absolute sovereignty over all their subjects. Here

Anderson argues that the feudal aristocracy faced difficulties as European societies became more peaceful and more commercialized. In place of the old system in which the lower orders were expected to fight or pay feudal dues to their masters, the market was penetrating into the countryside and providing a new basis for exchanging goods and services. The aristocracy's hold over the peasantry was loosening. It found greater difficulty in obtaining goods and services from the peasantry. In these circumstances, the absolutist ruler protected the class interest of the feudal aristocracy by ensuring it continued to benefit from the surplus produced by the peasantry. The task of extracting such surplus, by force if necessary, was moved upward from the local manorial court run by the local feudal lord to the central state apparatus. The crown, so to speak, 'took the aristocracy under its wing'.

This pattern differed between Western Europe and Eastern Europe. In the West, by the fourteenth century, the strength of the towns and a shortage of agrarian labour made it possible for the peasantry to throw off their feudal bond of serfdom. By contrast, in the East the state in conjunction with the larger landowners responded to a labour shortage by imposing serfdom on the peasantry for the first time. One reason the landowners were able to do this was that the towns were much weaker in the East and could not support those peasants that tried to protest.

Immanuel Wallerstein's world systems theory

The US historical sociologist Immanuel Wallerstein is the progenitor of a theory of *'world systems', involving 'centres' and 'peripheries' (Wallerstein 1974, 1980, 1989a). This theory has attracted renewed attention in recent years in the wake of debates about globalization. According to Wallerstein, the capitalist world economy, which first took shape during the sixteenth century, stretches across several *polities. It is linked together by market relationships reinforced by the strength of the states that dominate the centre or 'core' of the system. One factor maintaining the stability of the world system is the fact that the exploited majority dominated by countries at the centre are themselves divided into two tiers, which Wallerstein labels the 'periphery' (the larger lower tier) and the 'semi-periphery' (the smaller middle tier).

The main players in the system are social classes and 'ethno-nations' (Wallerstein 1979: 24). The bourgeoisie pursues capital accumulation and it clings to an ideology of scientific rationalism. By contrast, the proletariat is divided and ranked in terms of ethnicity, which makes it easier to control. Economic actors in world systems are managed within global structures with a high degree of vertical integration such as chartered companies (for example, the East India Company, a British trading company very active in the eighteenth and nineteenth centuries), merchant houses, and, more recently, *transnational corporations, such as General Electric. However, governments and national bourgeoisies also compete with each other. This means that as the balance of advantage shifts, so does the particular pattern of relationships in the capitalist world economy.

By the late sixteenth century, the system's core included England, the Netherlands, and northern France. The semi-periphery was centred on the Mediterranean, including Italy, southern France, and Spain. The periphery included America and Eastern Europe. By the nineteenth century, the British state had eclipsed both the Dutch and the French and become dominant in the core. During the same period Sweden and Prussia (later unified with Germany as a whole) moved into the semi-periphery. The periphery expanded to include Russia, the Ottoman Empire, India, and West Africa. During the twentieth century, the USA asserted its leadership of the core. After the Second World War, the USA shared the core with the USSR, Japan, and the European Union. Communist regimes such as those of Poland and Hungary belonged to the semi-periphery. The periphery consisted mainly of the Third World.

Wallerstein believes that the widespread protest movements of 1968 signalled the beginning of a 'revolution in the world-system' directed against domination by the core (Wallerstein 1989*b*: 431). He saw this revolution as fuelled by six movements: the Western 'old Left'; new social movements in the West concerned with women, ecological questions, and ethnic minority rights; the traditional communist parties of the socialist bloc; new movements for human rights in the socialist bloc; traditional national liberation movements in the Third World; and anti-Western Third World movements, often of a religious nature. Wallerstein recognizes that there was considerable mutual suspicion between these different 'anti-system' movements, but he thought that by the mid-1980s this mutual suspicion had decreased in intensity. In the current climate of anti-globalization movements, or global movements directed against global capitalist penetration, it appears that at least some of these movements have been joining together under a common banner.

Conclusion

This survey of historical social theory has travelled from the 1940s through to the last decade of the twentieth century. Since the collapse of the Soviet Union, the end of the Cold War, and the apparent triumph of Western liberal capitalist democracy, the agenda of historical social theory has been somewhat in disarray. On the one hand, interest in writers from the first phase such as T. H. Marshall and Talcott Parsons has revived. On the other hand, globalization has emerged as a new focus of historical social theory as part of a much larger complex of changes.

Today it would appear that older Western ideologies of communism, fascism, *Keynesian welfarism, and trust in the problem-solving capacities of science are in decline. As voter turnout diminishes at successive elections, public political participation appears under threat, while social relations appear to be ever-increasingly regulated through the market. Relations between government, business, and civil society today are not the same as they were in the post-war period. Large multinational businesses have broken free from the constraints imposed by national planning, just as they have untied themselves from their once close involvement with colonial administrations based in Europe.

In this context, one theme deserves a high place on the agenda of historical sociology in the early twenty-first century. It is the fact that despite the hegemonic influence of global business discourse, the free-market version of capitalism rediscovered during the 1980s is suffering a process of de-legitimation. *Neo-liberal forms of marketization have become implicated in the widespread fragility and vulnerability of the economies of the global South. In a great many regions of the world, large business corporations have become less and less responsive to the social constraints once imposed by national governments. The relatively cohesive post-1945 political and economic system that preoccupied many of the writers discussed in this chapter is largely a thing of the past. The system of social democracy that developed in Western Europe after the Second World War, founded on a welfare state offering universal provision, went together with what have been called 'thirty glorious years' of economic growth (Fourastié, 1979). Since the mid-1970s, the Western world has seen the end of this period of stability and the emergence of a new era of deregulated, crisis-ridden, neo-liberal economic policy.

These developments present historically minded social scientists with an important challenge. The question is whether social scientists will find the courage and imagination to use their research on long-term social processes to provide independent and insightful analyses of the structural alternatives available to human societies in a context of increasing global uncertainty. Here the potential uses of historical sociology have not changed. They are to help us think through the causes and consequences of long-term social processes. They are to make us aware of the alternative trajectories of social development that existed in the past and those that may exist for us in the present. The ultimate value of historical sociology is that it can improve our knowledge of the ways in which human beings may intervene in these processes and give societies a push in the direction we believe to be right.

■ **QUESTIONS FOR CHAPTER 6**

1   Why is historical thinking important to social theory?

2   What considerations distinguish the interests of the historical sociologist from the interests of the historian?

3   According to the theorists discussed in this chapter, what advantages and disadvantages can be discerned in capitalism, socialism, and democracy as systems of social organization?

4   What factors account for the rise of the nation-state in modern Europe?

5   What factors account for the dominance of the West in world history?

6   What is a revolution?

7   What are we to understand by the concept of 'civilization'?

■ **FURTHER READING**

A useful introduction to historical social theory is Dennis Smith's *The Rise of Historical Sociology* (Polity Press, 1991). Two recent guides to diverse topics in historical social theory are Gerard Delanty and Engen Isin's edited *Handbook of Historical Sociology* (Sage, 2003) and James Mahoney and Dietrich Rueschemeyer's *Comparative Historical Analysis in the Social Sciences* (Cambridge University Press, 2003). See also Dennis Smith's shorter essay 'Historical Analysis', in Melissa Hardy's edited *Handbook of Data Analysis* (Sage, 2004) and Phillip Abrams's older but still important work *Historical Sociology* (Open Books, 1982). Theda Skocpol's *Vision and Method in Historical Sociology* (Cambridge University Press,

1984) has chapters on individual figures, including Wallerstein, Anderson, Moore, Eisenstadt, Bendix, and Tilly. For guides to mutual influences between historians and sociologists, see Peter Burke's two books *History and Social Theory* (Polity Press, 1992) and *Sociology and History* (Allen & Unwin, 1980), and Mary Fulbrook's *Historical Theory* (Routledge, 2002).

Commentaries on T. H. Marshall's conception of social citizenship can be found in Jack Barbalet's *Citizenship* (Open University Press, 1988) and Gerard Delanty's *Citizenship in a Global Age* (Open University Press, 2000). On Lipset, see Samuel Huntington's article 'After Twenty Years: The Future of the Third Wave', *Journal of Democracy*, 8 (1997), 4, 3–12. On Hayek, Schumpeter, and Moore, see Alan Ebenstein's *F. A. Hayek: A Biography* (University of Chicago Press, 2003), Richard Swedberg's *Joseph A. Schumpeter: His Life and Work* (Polity Press, 1991), Dennis Smith's *Capitalist Democracy on Trial* (Routledge, 1990), and Dennis Smith's *Barrington Moore* (Macmillan, 1983). On Elias, see Stephen Mennell's *Norbert Elias: An Introduction* (Blackwell, 1992), Dennis Smith's *Norbert Elias and Modern Social Theory* (Sage, 2001), and Jonathan Fletcher's *Violence and Civilisation: An Introduction to the Work of Norbert Elias* (Polity Press, 1997). For collections of readings by Elias, see Stephen Mennell and Johan Goudsblom's edited *The Norbert Elias Reader* (Blackwell, 1998) and *Norbert Elias on Civilisation, Power and Knowledge* (Chicago University Press, 1998).

For further studies of the rise of the West and the rise of the nation-state, see Gianfranco Poggi's *The Development of the Modern State* (Stanford University Press, 1978) and John A. Hall's *Powers and Liberties: The Causes and Consequences of the Rise of the West* (Penguin, 1986), and the same author's *Coercion and Consent: Studies of the Modern State* (Polity Press, 1994), as well as John A. Hall and John Ikenberry's shorter guide *The State* (Open University Press, 1989). Also informative in the field of historical social theory are Arpad Szakolczai's three books *Reflexive Historical Sociology* (Routledge, 1999), *Max Weber and Michel Foucault* (Routledge, 1998), and *The Genesis of Modernity* (Routledge, 2003), covering figures not discussed in this chapter, including notably the Austrian émigré theorist Eric *Voegelin. A further valuable resource is W. G. Runciman's *A Treatise on Social Theory*, 3 vols. (Cambridge University Press, 1983), which deals with a broad range of problems and topics in historical sociology. See also Runaman's essay 'Comparative Sociology or Narrative History?', in his book *Confessions of a Reluctant Theorist: Selected Essays* (Harvester, 1989).

One important writer on historical social theory not discussed in this chapter is the Czech-born theorist Ernest *Gellner. His works are stimulating and accessible. Particularly worth reading is his book *Plough, Sword and Book: The Structure of Human History* (Chicago University Press, 1988), which develops a theory of secularization and modernization from an anthropological perspective.

WEBSITES

Comparative and Historical Sociology Homepage at **www.comphistsoc.org/** Displays a site for the American Sociological Association with thematically organized guidance in the field.

Historical Sociology at **www2.fmg.uva.nl/sociosite/topics/history.html** Presents many links to relevant sites and on-line articles.

Joseph Schumpeter page at **http://cepa.newschool.edu/het/profiles/schump.htm** Contains a biography of Schumpeter, with a bibliography and links to other resources.

Nation States at **http://faculty.plattsburgh.edu/richard.robbins/legacy/nation_state_resources.htm** Provides a list of sites on the organization of nation-states and international conflict from a historical and contemporary perspective.

Norbert Elias Foundation at **www.norberteliasfoundation.nl/** Displays an authoritative overview of Elias's work and the school of 'figurational sociology' he set in motion.

7 Western Marxism

Douglas Kellner

In investigating the genesis of modern societies, Karl Marx and Friedrich Engels developed a new *materialist theory of history and society, introducing the concepts of forces and relations of production, division of labour, *ideology, and class struggle as keys to understanding society and history. They formulated a conception of history as a succession of modes of production, charting the emergence of modern bourgeois society and its future transition to a communist society. The Marxist vision of society and history first appeared in Marx and Engels's *The Communist Manifesto* of 1848 in dramatic narrative form, proclaiming the rise of capitalism and bourgeois society and its revolutionary overthrow by an industrial proletariat. *Capital* (1867) and other classic Marxian texts developed a critical theory of capitalism, a model of socialism, and a project of revolution combining political economy, social theory, philosophy, history, and politics that provoked both fervent adherence and passionate opposition.

This chapter explores the development of Marxist social thought in the twentieth century, concentrating on what is called 'Western Marxism'. The term 'Western Marxism' was first used by the Soviet communist regime to disparage the turn to more diverse forms of Marxism in Western Europe after the 1920s. Since then, however, the term has become widely accepted as a generic category used to distinguish more independent and critical forms of Marxism from the dogmas of the Soviet and Chinese regimes. In this chapter we trace the spread of Western Marxism in Europe after the Russian Revolution until the 1960s and the rise of new syntheses between Marxism and other theoretical approaches since the 1970s under the ambit of 'cultural studies'. Among the key theorists under discussion are György *Lukács, Antonio *Gramsci, Ernst *Bloch, Walter *Benjamin, Theodor *Adorno, Max *Horkheimer, Jean-Paul *Sartre, Herbert *Marcuse, Louis *Althusser, Raymond *Williams, Stuart *Hall, and others.

We begin with a résumé of the classical Marxist conception of ideology formulated by Marx and Engels.

Western Marxism and the critique of ideology

Cultural forms in Marxist analysis are seen as emerging in specific historical situations and as serving particular socio-economic interests and functions. For Marx and Engels, the cultural ideas of an epoch serve the interests of the ruling class, providing *ideologies that legitimize class domination. In *The German Ideology* Marx and Engels had asserted that 'the ideas of the ruling class are in every epoch the ruling ideas' (1846: 64). Ideology in this sense describes how dominant ideas of a ruling class promote the interests of that class and help mask oppression and injustices in a given society.

The economic *'base' of society for Marx and Engels consisted of the forces and relations of production. The 'superstructure' consisted of legal and political institutions, along with culture and ideology. The goal of Marx's science of society and history was to grasp the primacy of this economic base in its relation to culture and politics. Marx and Engels sought to show how ruling ideas serve to naturalize, idealize, and *legitimize the existing society and its institutions and values. They argued that during the *feudal period, ideas of piety, honour, valour, and military chivalry expressed the interests of the ruling aristocratic classes. During the capitalist era, values of *individualism, profit, competition, and the market became dominant, articulating the ideology of the new bourgeois class and consolidating its class power.

In this sense Marx and Engels showed how ideologies appear to represent common sense and are thus often invisible and elude criticism. In a competitive and atomistic capitalist society, it appears natural to assert that human beings are primarily self-interested and competitive. In fact, human beings and societies are extremely complex and contradictory, but ideology smoothes over contradictions and conflicts, idealizing traits like individuality and competition and elevating them into governing conceptions and values.

After Marx's death in 1883, many different versions of Marxism began to emerge. The first generation of Marxist theorists and activists tended to focus on the economy and politics. The second generation ranging from German Social Democrats and radicals to Russian Marxists focused even more narrowly on economics and politics. Marxism became the official doctrine of many European working-class movements and was thus tied to the requirements of the political struggles of the day. In contrast, later generations of intellectuals after the Russian Revolution developed Marxian theories of culture, the state, social institutions, and psychology. Where Marxism was generally associated by the beginning of the twentieth-century with economic, political, and historical doctrines, a new generation of Marxists began turning attention to cultural phenomena in the 1920s and 1930s onwards. Many twentieth-century Marxian theorists employed Marxian theory to analyse past and present cultural, political, economic, and social forms in relation to their production, their imbrications with the economy and history, and their functions in social life.

The term 'Western Marxism' had first been used by the Soviet communists as a label of derision, aimed at what they saw as defeatist and revisionist thinking. Yet the term swiftly became adopted by European intellectuals to describe a more independent form of thinking distinct from that of the party line represented in Moscow. For many intellectuals active in the 1920s and 1930s, the Marxist movements arising out of Bolshevism in Russia and the Social Democratic Party in Germany had rested on an overly dogmatic and *deterministic conception of society. These intellectuals sought to develop alternative agendas that led to tensions between 'scientific' and 'orthodox' Marxism on the one hand and 'critical' Marxism on the other hand. In a later contribution from the 1970s, the British Marxist historian Perry *Anderson (1976) interpreted the turn from economic and political analysis to cultural theory in the 1930s as a symptom of the crushing of the European revolutionary movements of the 1920s and the rise of fascism. In the 1950s, on the other hand, the French *phenomenological philosopher Maurice *Merleau-Ponty (1955) provided the term with more positive connotations, emphasizing the centrality of struggle over culture, art, philosophy, language, and ideas to material social transformation.

Among two of the earliest partisans of this non-dogmatic conception of Western Marxism were the Hungarian critic György *Lukács and the German theorist Karl *Korsch. It is to their work that we turn first.

György Lukács and Karl Korsch: reification and the standpoint of the proletariat

In the early years of the century, Lukács wrote important books influenced by *Hegel and German idealist philosophy, including *Soul and Form* (1910) and *Theory of the Novel* (1910). Relatively quickly, Lukács converted to Marxism and briefly participated in the Hungarian Revolution of 1918 (see further Arato and Breines 1977; Feenberg 1981). Adopting an orthodox communist position, Lukács held that working-class revolution and socialism constituted solutions to the problems of bourgeois society. He became a lifelong adherent to the communist movement.

The ultra-Marxist Lukács of the early 1920s focused intently on developing philosophical, sociological, and political dimensions of Marxism before returning to cultural analysis later in the 1920s. He then went to Russia where he withdrew internally from Stalinism while working on a series of literary texts that have significant but largely unappreciated importance for cultural criticism. Lukács's literary studies employed theories of the mode of production, class and class conflict to provide economic grounding for cultural analysis. He saw history as constructed by a mediation of economy and society, viewing cultural forms in their relation to socio-historical development within a mode of production. He also demonstrated that cultural and artistic forms themselves illuminate material historical circumstances, when properly interpreted.

In his most influential work *History and Class Consciousness* of 1923, Lukács argued that the Marxian vision of *totality and its focus on the primacy of commodity forms provided the best methodological tools with which to analyse capitalist society and to discover forces that would overthrow it. Lukács asserted that adopting the standpoint of the working class enabled one to see how capitalist society produced *reification*, involving the transformation of human beings into *things*, in all dimensions of society—from the labour process to cultural production and even sexual relations. Lukács saw all domains of society, culture, and even intimate relations as pervaded by economic imperatives. The proletariat, however, stood in a privileged position to grasp societal reification and to organize to overcome it. The proletariat became, in Lukács's typically Hegelian phrase, the *'subject-object' of history. Hegel's classic analysis of the relation between master and slave, in which the slave's practical mastery of the situation leads to an inversion of the hierarchical relation to the master, was taken up in Lukács's analysis of proletarian class consciousness. For Lukács, every class perspective is necessarily partial and limited, especially the perspectives of the aristocracy and the bourgeoisie. However, the exception to this rule is the perspective of the proletariat, because the proletariat cannot understand its own social position without at the same time understanding the society *as a whole*, as a 'totality'.

In Germany after the abortive revolution of 1918, the political activist and theorist Karl *Korsch also developed a Hegelian and critical version of Marxism. In *Marxism and Philosophy* (1923), Korsch argued that Marxism involved *dialectical thinking, providing the mental forces to transform bourgeois society through a union of theory and practice. In a later work, Korsch (1938) asserted the importance of historical specificity to Marxian theory, maintaining that Marxism provided a historically determinate critique of capitalist society and alternatives to it (on Korsch, see further Kellner 1977).

Two other early Western Marxist thinkers who were to become influential were the Italian writer and party activist Antonio Gramsci and the German theological philosopher and critic Ernst Bloch. In the next section, we turn to Gramsci's conception of 'hegemony' and the 'philosophy of praxis'. Ernst Bloch's work is discussed in Box 18.

Antonio Gramsci: the theory of hegemony

The Italian Marxist theorist Antonio *Gramsci became secretary of the Italian Communist Party in 1921, before being imprisoned by Mussolini's fascist regime in 1926 until his

---

BOX 18. ERNST BLOCH ON HOPE, IDEOLOGY, AND UTOPIA

The German theorist Ernst *Bloch also responded positively to the Russian Revolution and the European revolutionary movements of the 1920s, but he developed a more *messianic and utopian version of Marxism. Bloch's three-volume work *The Principle of Hope* (1952–9) provided a systematic examination of the ways in which fairy tales and myths, popular culture, literature, theatre, and all forms of art, political and social utopias, philosophy, and religion contain *emancipatory moments. He showed how these elements of culture project visions of a better life that question the organization and structure of life under capitalism—or state socialism. In this magnum opus, he analysed the ways in which hope for a better world exists in everything from daydreams to the great religions, pointing to anticipatory visions of what would later be systematized and disseminated as socialism. He concentrated on analysing popular literature, architecture, department store displays, sports, clothing, and other artefacts of everyday life. He shows how the critique of ideology aims not only at political texts and manifest political doctrines but also at film, radio and the mass media, and everyday life in general. For Bloch, ideology contains a utopian dimension, in which its discourses, images, and figures produce images of a better world and illuminate what is deficient and lacking in this world and what should be fought for to bring about a freer and happier future. Bloch thus provided a more 'hermeneutical' account of the ways in which cultural history and socio-economic development point forward to socialism as the realization of humanity's deepest dreams and hopes.

Bloch developed a type of cultural theory that is quite different from other Marxian models that present ideology critique as the demolition of bourgeois civilization. Unlike dogmatic Marxist writing, Bloch did not directly equate culture with ideology in a wholly negative sense. This dogmatic model—found in Lenin and most Marxist-Leninists—had interpreted ideology primarily as a process of mystification and error, as 'false consciousness'. It had viewed the function of ideology critique as being simply to demonstrate the illusions of ruling-class interests in cultural objects that are then discarded under the heavy hammer of the 'scientific' Marxist critic.

Although Leninist Marxism also developed a more positive concept of ideology that viewed socialist ideas as constructive forces for promoting revolutionary consciousness, Bloch remained wary of those who stressed the unambiguously progressive features of socialist ideology. Instead, he saw emancipatory content in all living ideologies – socialist or capitalist – *and* deceptive illusory qualities as well. For Bloch, ideology was 'Janus-faced', two-sided: it contained techniques of manipulation and domination but it also contained a residue or surplus that can be used for social critique to advance *enlightened politics. Bloch rejected what he saw as the denunciatory 'half-enlightenment' of dogmatic Marxism. Half-enlightenment wrongly dismissed as superstition and legend everything that did not measure up to its 'scientific' criteria. It deluded itself by thinking that truth can be obtained solely by eliminating error rather than also by offering some alternative vision. Bloch believed that part of the explanation for the defeat of the Left by the Right in Weimar Germany was that the Left tended to focus on negative denunciations of capitalism and the bourgeoisie, while fascism inculcated an apparently more positive and attractive vision for the masses who desperately sought for a better life.

---

death in 1937. According to Gramsci, the ruling intellectual and cultural forces of the era constitute a form of *hegemony*, or domination by ideas and cultural forms that induce consent to the rule of the leading groups in a society. Gramsci argued that the unity of prevailing groups is usually created through the state, such as in the American Revolution or in the unification of Italy in the nineteenth century. In addition, the institutions of *civil society* also play a role in establishing hegemony. Civil society involves institutions of the Church, schooling, the media, and forms of popular culture. It mediates between the private sphere of economic interests and the family on the one hand and the public authority of the state on the other.

In Gramsci's conception, societies maintain stability through a combination of *force* and *consent*, involving obeisance to 'intellectual and moral leadership'. On the one hand, social orders are founded and reproduced through the agency of institutions and groups that violently exert power and domination to maintain social boundaries and rules—for example, the police, the military, or vigilante groups. On the other hand, other institutions involved in religion, schooling, and the media induce consent to the dominant order establishing a distinctive type of social system, such as market capitalism or fascism or communism. Societies also establish hegemony through an institutionalizing of *patriarchy or male supremacy, as well as through the rule of a dominant racial or ethnic group over subordinate groups. In his *Prison Notebooks* (1926–37), published after his death in various edited selections, Gramsci's key example is Italian fascism. Gramsci showed how fascism supplanted the previous liberal bourgeois regime in Italy through its control of the state and through its frequently repressive influence over schooling, the media, and other cultural, social, and political institutions.

The theory of hegemony for Gramsci involved both analysis of the ways in which prevalent political forces achieve hegemonic authority *and* the delineation of *counter-hegemonic* forces, groups, and ideas capable of contesting and overthrowing the existing hegemony. One illustration of this Gramscian analysis in recent cultural studies has focused on the conservative regimes of Margaret Thatcher in Britain and Ronald Reagan in the United States in the early 1980s. Stuart *Hall (1980*a*) and others analysed the ways in which the Thatcher–Reagan regimes promoted a counter-hegemony to social-democratic politics in the 1970s. In winning power, they achieved a new hegemony of market individualism. In the 1980s, conservative groups gained dominance through control of the state and the media and through the arm of cultural institutions such as think tanks and fund-raising political action groups. They succeeded in presenting the market not only as the source of wealth but also as the solution to all social problems, while the state became pictured as a cause of excessive taxation, over-regulation, and bureaucratic inertia.

In this context Gramsci defined ideology as the 'social cement' that holds together the dominant social order. He described his own 'philosophy of *praxis' as a mode of thought opposed to ideology, contesting dominant institutions and social relations and attempting to generate a socialist counter-hegemony. In his essay 'Cultural Themes: Ideological Material' (repr. 1985), Gramsci notes that the press in the 1920s had become the dominant instrument of producing ideological legitimation for existing institutions, but that many other institutions such as the Church, schools, and socio-cultural associations and groups also played a role. He called for sustained critique of the hegemonic forces that legitimized these institutions and the creation of alternative ideas and movements capable of challenging the existing system.

Gramsci's critique of dominant modes of culture would be taken up by the Frankfurt School and later by British cultural studies, to which we turn shortly. It is to the work of the Frankfurt School that we turn now.

Critical theory of society: the Frankfurt School

The term 'Frankfurt School' refers to the work of members of the Institute for Social Research (Institut für Sozialforschung) established at Frankfurt in Germany in 1923. Under its first director, Carl Grünberg, the Institute's work in the 1920s tended to be empirical, historical, and oriented towards problems of the European working-class movement. It was the first Marxist-oriented research centre affiliated to a historic German university. Max *Horkheimer became director of the Institute in 1930, gathering around him many talented theorists, including Erich *Fromm, Franz *Neumann, Herbert *Marcuse, and Theodor W. *Adorno. Under Horkheimer's direction, the Institute sought to develop an interdisciplinary social theory serving as an instrument of social transformation. The work of this era was a synthesis of philosophy and social theory, combining sociology, psychology, cultural analysis, and political economy. Most members had Jewish backgrounds and were forced to flee Germany after Hitler's ascendancy to power. The majority emigrated to the USA where the Institute became affiliated to Columbia University from 1931 until 1949, when it returned to Frankfurt.

The Institute's first major project under Horkheimer's direction was a systematic study of authority, an investigation into individuals who submitted willingly but irrationally to authoritarian regimes. This culminated in a two-volume work, *Studien über Autorität und Familie* (1936), and a series of studies of fascism. From the 1930s onwards the Institute referred to its work as the 'critical theory of society'. The term *'critical theory' was elaborated by Horkheimer in a seminal essay of 1937, discussed here in Box 19. For many years, 'critical theory' stood as code for the Frankfurt School's distinctive brand of Marxism, distinguished by its concern to found a radical interdisciplinary social theory on Hegelian-Marxian dialectics. The critical theorists argued that Marx's theories of money, value, exchange, and *commodity fetishism pertain not only to the capitalist economy but also to all social relations under capitalism. All human relationships under capitalism, public and private, can be shown to be dominated by exchange values and commodity forms.

In a series of studies carried out in the 1930s, the Frankfurt theorists developed accounts of monopoly capitalism and the new industrial state, focusing on the roles of technology, giant corporations, and mass communications in the decline of democracy and the erosion of the moral responsibility of individuals. They were to become best known for theories of 'the totally administered society', analysing the increasing power of capitalism and bureaucracy over all aspects of social life and the development of new forms of social control. They propounded research programmes that influenced many aspects of European Social theory until the 1970s.

Theories of the 'culture industry'

The Frankfurt School coined the term *'culture industry' to signify the process of the industrialization of culture and the commercial imperatives of mass production and consumption that determine it. The critical theorists analysed all cultural artefacts in contexts of

---

BOX 19. MAX HORKHEIMER'S ESSAY 'CRITICAL AND TRADITIONAL THEORY'

In a key article titled 'Traditional and Critical Theory', of 1937, Max Horkheimer argued that modern philosophy and science since Descartes suffered from abstraction and *objectivism, cut off from social practice. In opposition to this 'traditional theory' and especially to *positivism, the new 'critical theory' would be grounded in social theory and Marxian political economy. It would mount a systematic critique of existing society, allying itself to efforts to produce alternatives to capitalism and the monstrosity of fascism. Horkheimer proclaimed that critical theory would expose the way in which 'the concepts that thoroughly dominate the economy' metamorphose 'into their opposites: fair exchange into a deepening of social injustice; a free economy into monopolistic domination; productive labour into the strengthening of relations which inhibit production; the maintenance of society's life into the impoverishment of the people's' (1937: 247). The goal of critical theory was to transform these social conditions and to provide a theory of 'the historical movement of the period which is now approaching its end' (1937: 247).

Critical theory would produce analyses of the transformation of competitive capitalism into monopoly capitalism and fascism. It aimed to be part of the historical process by which capitalism would be replaced by socialism. Horkheimer declared that: 'The categories which have arisen under its influence criticize the present. The Marxist categories of class, exploitation, surplus value, profit, impoverishment and collapse are moments of a conceptual whole whose meaning is to be sought, not in the reproduction of the present society, but in its transformation to a correct society' (1937: 218). Critical theory is thus motivated by an interest in emancipation. It is a philosophy of social practice engaged in 'struggle for the future'. Critical theory must remain loyal to the 'idea of a future society as the community of free human beings, in so far as such a society is possible, given the present technical means' (1937: 230).

---

industrial organization where mediated objects exhibit the same features as other products of mass production: *commodification, standardization, and massification. In their view, the culture industries had the specific function of providing ideological *legitimation for capitalist society and integrating individuals into its way of life. Mass culture and communications stood at the centre of leisure activity in an industrial society as agencies of socialization and mediators of political reality. They were therefore to be seen as major institutions of modern life with a variety of economic, political, and cultural effects. In particular, the critical theorists were among the first to examine the impact of a consumer society on the very classes who were supposed to be the instrument of revolution in classical Marxism. They analysed the ways in which consumption and the culture industries function to stabilize capitalism. Accordingly, they sought for new agencies and models of political emancipation that could serve as norms for social science.

The two theorists most closely linked with the concept of the culture industry are Walter *Benjamin and Theodor *Adorno. Although Benjamin was not formally a member of the Frankfurt School, he exerted a profound influence over it and has been closely associated with the spirit of its work. It is to his writing that we turn first.

Walter Benjamin: mass culture and the decline of 'aura'

Active in Berlin and Paris in the 1920s and 1930s, Benjamin discerned relatively socially *emancipatory aspects in new technologies of cultural production such as photography, film, and radio. Benjamin was one of the first radical critics to look carefully at mass media culture in appraising its complex nature and effects. In his famous essay of 1936 'The Work of Art in the Age of Mechanical Reproduction', Benjamin noted how new mass media were supplanting older forms of culture. The mass reproduction of photography, film, recordings, and publications replaced the aspect of original uniqueness or magical 'aura' of the work of art in an earlier era. Freed from the elite aura of high culture, Benjamin believed that mass communications within limits could cultivate more critical individuals able to judge and analyse their world, just as sports fans could dissect and evaluate athletic activities. In particular, he asserted that processing the rush of images of cinema helped to create subjectivities better able to parry the flux and turbulence of experience in industrialized, urbanized societies. At the same time, he remained very critical of the products and functions of the culture industry. But he took a less negative attitude to its realm of possibilities than some of the other associates of the Frankfurt School.

Collaborating with the prolific German dramatist Bertolt *Brecht, Benjamin worked on producing film screenplays and radio plays, seeking to utilize the media as organs of social progress. In the essay 'The Artist as Producer' (1934), Benjamin argued that radical cultural creators should 're-function' the apparatus of cultural production, transforming theatre and film into a forum for political enlightenment, beyond pure 'culinary' audience pleasure. Working in the same spirit as Benjamin, it can be said that Bertolt Brecht in his writings on radio theory anticipated the Internet in his call for reconstructing the apparatus of broadcasting from one-way transmission to a more interactive form of two-way, or multiple-channel, communication (compare Silberman 2000: 41 ff.).

Benjamin wished to promote a radical media politics oriented to oppositional cultures. Yet he recognized that media such as film could have conservative effects. While he considered it progressive that mass-produced objects forfeited the 'aura' of traditional works of art and high culture, he recognized that film could create a new kind of ideological magic based on a cult of celebrity, through techniques such as the close-up which fetishized certain stars and images.

Benjamin also developed a unique approach to cultural history. In a micrological history of Paris in the nineteenth century known as the *Arcades Project*, or the *Passagenwerk* in German, Benjamin analysed shop window dressings, street junctions, architectural façades, and bohemian subcultures to elucidate the more general contours of the imperial French metropolis. This uncompleted project illustrated his fascination with the minutiae of daily consumer life, taking his inspiration from dada art and the surrealist poets and painters (Benjamin 1925–39; see also Buck-Morss 1977, 1989).

Theodor Adorno and Max Horkheimer's *The Dialectic of Enlightenment*

Adorno and Horkheimer answered Benjamin's more hopeful picture of the mass media in their influential yet deeply pessimistic book *Dialectic of Enlightenment*, which first appeared in German in 1947 (based on an earlier manuscript of 1944). They argued that the system of cultural production dominated by film, radio broadcasting, newspapers, and magazines was controlled by advertising and commercial imperatives, functioning to instil subservience to consumer capitalism. They sketched out a vision of history from the Greeks to the present that argued reason and *enlightenment turned into their opposite, transforming what promised to be vehicles of truth and liberation into tools of domination. Under the pressure of societal systems, reason became *instrumental*, reducing human beings to objectified things and nature to numerical quantities. Such modes of abstraction enabled science and technology to develop apace, but at the same time produced a moral void that led to social psychosis, culminating in the concentration camps of the fascist and Soviet communist regimes. As science and technology created tools of extermination, culture degenerated into mass entertainment, while democracy collapsed into fascism based on mass popular support for charismatic leaders. This perverse 'dialectic of enlightenment' induced individuals to dominate over their own bodies and to renounce their innermost needs and desires by assimilating themselves to a system that turned them into passive agents of war and persecution.

Although many critics have seen Adorno and Horkheimer's approach as too focused on the idea of manipulation and mass deception, it provides an important corrective to more populist approaches to media culture that tend to downplay the ways in which media industries exert power over audiences and tend to induce conformist behaviour (see the discussions in Kellner 1989*a*, 1995). We should also note that in sharply criticizing enlightenment scientism and rationalism in relation to systems of this domination, Adorno and Horkheimer implicated Marxism to a certain extent in this 'dialectic of enlightenment'. For in their view Marxism, too, at least in its reductive and dogmatic forms, affirmed the primacy of labour and instrumental reason in its celebration of 'socialist production' and 'progress'.

After the Second World War, Adorno and Horkheimer returned to Frankfurt to re-establish the Institute for Social Research in Germany, while Herbert Marcuse and Leo *Löwenthal and others remained in the USA. In 1966 Adorno published a major work of philosophical method, *Negative Dialectics*, in which he sought to redeem Hegel's conception of dialectical contradictions and syntheses as the logical motor of historical change. Adorno gave qualified support to what Marx had demonstrated as Hegel's *idealist reification of the material bases of social life. Adorno saw himself as pursuing Hegel's principle of dialectical 'negativity' in a way in which Hegel himself had betrayed through support of the Prussian national state as the most authentic agency of social belonging. Negativity for Adorno meant a work of exposing the disparity between the manifest ideals of society—ideals of liberty, equality, fraternity—and the actual reality of social repression. It meant demonstrating the difference, the 'non-identity', as Adorno called it, between concepts and things, or between values and ideas on the one hand and the material status quo on the other. In his last major work, *Aesthetic Theory*, of 1970, Adorno applied this conception to an understanding of *modernist art as a possible vehicle of truth and enlightenment about the 'system of illusions' that was consumer capitalism. Adorno proposed that in the modernist work of art—which he saw exemplified in the work of experimental composers such as Arnold Schoenberg and Alban Berg and avant-garde writers and dramatists such as Samuel Beckett—it was possible to discern a mode of aesthetic experience which threw light on the way intrinsically sensuous experiences are reduced by capitalist consumerism to purely functional bodily gratification.

During this period the Frankfurt theorists engaged in frequent methodological and substantive debates with other social theories, most notably in *The Positivist Dispute in German Sociology*, edited by Adorno (1969). In this work they criticized more empirical and quantitative approaches to social theory, including notably Karl *Popper's conception of empiricism and 'value-free' science. Against Popper, they defended their own more speculative and politicized brand of social research.

Jürgen Habermas: emancipation and the public sphere

In the 1960s, Jürgen Habermas, a student of Adorno and Horkheimer, produced a rich body of work based on Hegelian-Marxist ideas. His early work is discussed in what follows. His *later* work from the *late* 1970s onwards, which gradually led away from Marxism, is discussed in Chapter 13 of this book, pp. 279–83. In addition, Habermas's writings on *hermeneutrics are discussed in Chapter 4, pp. 125–7.

In his path-breaking book *The Structural Transformation of the Public Sphere* (1962), Habermas historicized Adorno and Horkheimer's analysis of the culture industry. He showed how bourgeois society in the late eighteenth and nineteenth centuries was distinguished by the rise of a *'public sphere' that stood between civil society and the state, mediating between public and private interests. Members of the middle classes could shape public opinion, giving expression to their needs and interests while influencing political practice. The bourgeois public sphere enabled the formation of a realm of democratic discussion and opinion that opposed state power and the powerful interests coming to shape society. It found expression in the numerous literary salons and cafés, newspapers and publishing houses that flourished in eighteenth-century Europe.

In the later chapters of his book Habermas analysed the transition from an enlightened liberal public sphere that had helped bring about the American and French revolutions to a media-dominated sphere in the stage of what he calls 'welfare state capitalism and mass democracy'. Echoing Adorno and Horkheimer, he saw this process as demonstrating a takeover of the public sphere by giant corporations, transforming it from a site of rational debate into one of manipulative consumption and passivity. What was called 'public opinion' shifted from a *critical* consensus emerging from discussion and reflection to a *manufactured* consensus based on the intervention of media experts and opinion polls. Habermas saw individual participation in public debate as having become fractured and transmuted into political spectacle, where citizen-consumers passively ingest entertainment and information. Citizens become spectators of media presentations that reduce audiences to recipients of news and novelty.

Habermas's critics have argued that he tends to idealize the earlier eighteenth-century public sphere, ignoring its exclusion of particular voices and neglecting various plebeian and women's public spheres alongside that of the bourgeois class (see the studies in Calhoun 1992 and Kellner 2000). Nevertheless, Habermas is right to point out that in the age of the eighteenth-century revolutions, a public sphere did indeed emerge, allowing at least some members of civil society to participate in political discussion and to organize and struggle against unjust authority. Habermas's account points to the increasingly important role of the media in politics and to ways in which corporate commercial forces tend to colonize this sphere for their own interests.

Habermas's distinctive version of critical theory introduced elements of linguistic philosophy and empirical sociological theory that had been ignored by earlier members of the Frankfurt School. In his second major treatise, *Knowledge and Human Interests* (1968), Habermas distinguished between what he called three types of 'cognitive interest' in science: (1) a 'technical' interest in control and objective causal knowledge, operative in the natural sciences; (2) a 'practical' interest in hermeneutic historical understanding, operative in the humanities; and lastly (3) an *'emancipatory' interest at stake in collective sociological self-knowledge, operative in the critical social sciences. Habermas argued that the emancipatory interest of critical social science brings together the interest of the natural sciences in causal explanation with the interest of the humanities in historical and intercultural understanding. In Habermas's model, critical social science views the theoretical idea of true knowledge about social life as being internally linked to the practical pursuit of justice in political life. Habermas saw this conception of emancipatory sociological knowledge as exemplified both in Marx's conception of the critique of ideology and in Sigmund *Freud's conception of psychoanalysis as a work of overcoming repressive pathological forms of consciousness. Both Marxian ideology critique and Freudian psychoanalysis represented forms of cognitive liberation from coercive and illusory structures of communication.

In *later* work from the *late* 1970s onwards, however, Habermas withdrew from some central elements of this thesis. His most distinctive break with the earlier Frankfurt School occurred in his two-volume work *The Theory of Communicative Action* (1981*a*, 1981*b*), which is discussed at length in Chapter 13 of this book.

Western Marxism from the 1960s to the present

In surveying the field of critical theory, one observes a heterogeneity of projects loosely connected by commitment to interdisciplinary analysis and an interest in radical social critique. In the 1960s the field of critical theory came to be complemented both by more activist forms of Marxism and by more academic forms. Four particular strands stand out in this period. The first is the work of Herbert *Marcuse in the USA. The second is the proliferation of *existentialist and autonomist Marxism in France and Italy. The third is the emergence of *'structuralist' and 'analytical' Marxism in the 1970s. The fourth is the rise of 'Cultural Studies' in Britain and the USA since the late 1970s. We now look at these four strands in turn.

Herbert Marcuse's *One-Dimensional Man*

Herbert Marcuse, an early member of the Frankfurt School who emigrated to the USA in 1934, worked for US intelligence during the Second World War, and then in the State Department. After the war he remained in the USA to pursue an academic career and rapidly ascended to the role of a guru of the American New Left in the 1960s. A philosopher by training, his first book *Reason and Revolution* (1941) introduced English-speaking readers to the dialectical thinking of Hegel, thematizing the unity of theory and practice, or 'praxis' in the popular term of the 1960s. His next book *Eros and Civilization*, of 1955, combined Marxism with Freudian psychoanalytic ideas. In this text, Marcuse's emphasis on polymorphic sexual liberation, play, utopian desire, and cultivation of an aesthetic ethos anticipated the counter-culture of the 1960s.

In *One-Dimensional Man* of 1964 Marcuse theorized the decline of revolutionary potential in capitalist societies and the development of new forms of social control. Marcuse argued that what he called 'advanced industrial society' creates false needs that bind individuals into the existing system of production and consumption. In this argument, mass media culture, advertising, industrial management, and liberal discourse reproduce the existing system and attempt to eliminate critique and opposition. The result is a 'one-dimensional' universe of thought and behaviour in which aptitudes for critical thinking begin to wither away. Marcuse here questioned two of the fundamental premises of orthodox Marxism: the idea of the proletariat as a reliable source of revolutionary opposition and the idea of the inevitability of capitalist breakdown. Rather than locating forces of revolutionary change exclusively in the working class, Marcuse championed the non-integrated forces of minorities, outsiders, and the radical intelligentsia, hoping to nourish oppositional thought and behaviour through what he called 'the great refusal'. Where the old Left had embraced Soviet Marxism in a doctrinaire and puritanical way, the New Left under Marcuse's influence combined critical Marxism with ideas of participatory democracy and an openness to a range of pluralistic alliances, embracing social movements around issues of gender, race, sexuality, peace, and the environment. Marcuse tirelessly criticized 'advanced industrial society' with its concomitant militarism, racism, sexism, imperialism, and its violent colonial intervention in developing countries in the so-called 'Third World' (see also Marcuse 1968, 1969, 1998*a*, 1998*b*).

French and Italian Marxism

'Existentialist Marxism' developed in France in the 1950s and 1960s under the influence of Jean-Paul *Sartre, combining philosophy, politics, and literary theory (see further Poster 1975). Based on Sartre's concept of freedom, *existentialist Marxism focused on the sufferings and desires of concrete individuals, considered as vulnerable mortal beings. In his *Critique of Dialectical Reason* (1960), Sartre combined Hegelian-Marxist concepts of alienation and class consciousness with his own existentialist philosophy of the ethical freedom of the autonomous human subject. Socialism in this sense made possible a reintegration of the 'class-for-itself' with the 'class-in-itself', or 'spirit' and 'existence', in Hegel's language. In the same period, Sartre also championed Frantz *Fanon's doctrine of revolutionary violence by the oppressed peoples of Western colonialism in the Algerian war of independence against France. Sartre evoked tremendous controversy and was criticized by the French liberal social philosopher Raymond *Aron.

In May 1968, radical students took control of the universities in Paris and joined with workers in a general strike that shocked the complacency of the advanced capitalist societies, believing themselves immune to challenge and upheaval. The French activists of 1968 found inspiration in the neo-Marxist ideas of the *phenomenological theorist Henri *Lefebvre (1947, 1974), who, like Bloch, had developed a critique of everyday life. A further stimulus came in the work of Guy *Debord, author of *The Society of the Spectacle* (1967) and the central figure in the anarchist Situationist movement which militated for revolutionary alternatives to consumerist escapism and spectacular distraction from misery. In these years many younger French intellectuals turned to the new forms of Marxism, including Jean *Baudrillard and Jean-François *Lyotard, who would later become part of a *poststructuralist and *postmodernist movement that went beyond Marxism. Influenced by George *Bataille and other maverick thinkers, Baudrillard's early work developed neo-Marxian critiques of the consumer society, exploring diverse utopian alternatives (see further Kellner 1989*b*). In the 1970s, however, Baudrillard declared that the emergence of a new postmodernity required altogether different forms of theory and politics, thus breaking with Marxism (for further discussion of Baudrillard's work, see Chapter 12 of this book, pp. 263–5).

In Italy in the 1970s, a form of Marxism developed known as 'autonomist Marxism', notably around the work of Antonio *Negri (1976). Autonomist Marxism sought to develop revolutionary politics outside the official European communist parties as these were deemed to be compromised by reformist attitudes. Harry Cleaver (1979) criticized the Frankfurt School and other forms of Western Marxism for exaggerating the power of capitalist hegemony and underestimating the force of working-class opposition. This outlook continues in Michael Hardt and Antonio Negri's book *Empire* (2000), which presents contradictions in globalization in terms of an imperializing logic of 'Empire' and an assortment of struggles by the 'multitude'. Hardt and Negri present the emergence of 'Empire' in forms of sovereignty, economy, culture, and struggle that open the new millennium to an unforeseeable flow of political surprises and upheavals.

Structural and analytical Marxism

Reacting against existentialist Marxism, Louis *Althusser developed a school of 'structuralist *Marxism' influenced partly by French *structuralist theory (discussed in Chapter 9 of this book). A member of the French Communist Party, Althusser argued that Marxism provided 'scientific' perspectives on capitalism which made possible a revolutionary transition to socialism. In *For Marx* (1965) and *Reading Capital* (1970), Althusser analysed links between the structures of the economy, state, and ideology in relation to material conditions of production that were 'in the last instance' the determining force of all domains of social life. Like Lukács, Althusser presented Marxism as a theory of the *'totality' of capitalist society and history. But he insisted that Marx undertook a sharp 'epistemological break' with Hegel in his later writings on economics. Althusser himself excoriated all Hegelian and 'idealist' elements that had entered Western Marxism. Championing what he called 'theoretical practice', he argued for the relative autonomy of theory in relation to what he called 'ideological state apparatuses'. Among others, Althusser's brand of Marxism influenced the Slovenian theorist Slavoj *Žižek who has combined structuralist Marxism with *Lacanian psychoanalytic theory (see Chapter 8 of this book, pp. 184–5).

Althusser has been criticized for his highly abstract Marxism, notably by the British socialist historian E. P. *Thompson (1978). In the 1980s, however, another academic form of Marxism developed in the English-speaking world known as 'analytical Marxism.' Like Althusser's work, analytical Marxism defended science and empirical research against

Hegelian idealist philosophy. G. A. *Cohen's influential *Karl Marx's Theory of History: A Defense* (1978) defended a strict *functionalist reading of historical materialism. Jon *Elster's *Making Sense of Marx* (1985) argued that Marx's methodology could only be understood in terms of methodological individualism and *rational choice theory. Marxian concepts of class and capital also found analytical treatment in the work of Eric Olin Wright (1978) and John Roemer (1981). Central to Cohen's account was Marx's distinction in the 1859 'Preface to the Critique of Political Economy' between 'forces and relations of production' (quoted in this book, pp. 44). Cohen concentrated specifically on Marx's proposition that at certain stages in the development of modes of production, the forces of production become 'fettered' by the relations of production. According to Cohen's functionalist-economistic reading of Marx, revolutionary transitions to new modes of production occur when the existing relations of production are no longer functional for the full and continuous expansion of the forces of production. Capitalism in this sense breaks the fetters of the old feudal order. In turn, communism is destined, in principle, to break capitalism's own fettering of the further growth of productive forces.

Cultural studies in Britain and the USA: the influence of Marxism

The variety of approaches that have come to be known in the Anglophone world as 'cultural studies' first emerged in Britain in the 1960s at a time of widespread sympathy for socialism. The historical forms analysed by the earliest phase of British cultural studies in the 1950s articulated conditions in an era in which there were still significant tensions in much of Europe between an older working-class culture and newer commercial kinds of popular culture emanating from the American culture industries. The initial project of cultural studies developed by Richard *Hoggart, Raymond *Williams, and E. P. *Thompson attempted to preserve working-class culture against the onslaughts of commercial mass culture. Thompson's enquiries into the history of British working-class struggles and the defences of working-class culture by Hoggart and Williams were part of a socialist project that regarded the industrial proletariat as a force for egalitarian social change. Williams and Hoggart supported projects of working-class education, viewing cultural studies as an instrument of social progress.

The attacks of Thompson, Hoggart, and Williams on Americanism and commercialism in the late 1950s and early 1960s partly paralleled the earlier work of the Frankfurt School. Yet the British writers valorized a working class that the Frankfurt School had seen as defeated by fascism in Europe and as unlikely to recover itself as a united class force. Slightly later in Britain, a second wave of cultural studies emerged at the Centre for Contemporary Cultural Studies at Birmingham University, led by the Jamaican-British theorist Stuart *Hall (Hall et al. 1980). The Birmingham School was continuous with the Hoggart–Thompson–Williams 'culture and society' tradition, as well as with the Frankfurt School. But the Birmingham School eventually paved the way for a more populist of 'postmodern' in cultural studies.

The Birmingham scholars developed a variety of critical approaches for the analysis and interpretation of cultural artefacts (see further McGuigan 1992; Kellner 1995). They came to focus on the interplay of representations of class, gender, race, ethnicity, and nationality in cultural texts, including media culture. They were among the first to focus on how audiences actively interpreted media culture in varied ways and contexts, analysing the factors that guided their responses. Employing Gramsci's model of hegemony and counter-hegemony, they identified both elements of domination and elements of resistance, struggle, and creativity.

Like the Frankfurt School, British cultural studies concluded that mass culture played an important role in integrating the working class into existing capitalist societies and that mass consumerism represented a new mode of capitalist hegemony. Both traditions at the same time identified forces of resistance to capitalist society, and both the Frankfurt theorists and the earlier forerunners of British cultural studies, especially Raymond Williams, looked to high culture, including avant-garde art and literature, as critical vehicles of political consciousness raising. But unlike the Frankfurt School, the later British writers valorized elements of resistance in popular media culture and in audience uses of media artefacts. In contrast, the Frankfurt School tended, with some exceptions, to see mass culture as an undifferentiated, homogenized tissue of domination—a difference that would seriously divide the two traditions.

In addition to studies of working-class culture, the Birmingham School focused on the potential of youth subcultures for resistance to hegemonic forms of capitalist society. The British scholars considered how popular culture made possible distinct youth identities and certain potentially counter-hegemonic forms of group membership. They studied patterns of conformity to dominant political ideologies in dress and fashion codes carried by members of the upwardly mobile white middle classes, and they demonstrated how subcultural groups could resist these forms by creating their own styles and identities. They pointed, for example, to black nationalist subcultures, to the punk movement, and to Asian and Jamaican-British forms of ethnic contestation (compare Hall and Jefferson 1976; Hebdige 1979). In contrast, the only member of the earlier Frankfurt School to treat youth culture as a serious political force was Marcuse.

Yet one problem with cultural studies is that it has rarely engaged adequately with modernist and avant-garde aesthetic movements. In its concern to legitimize the study of popular media culture, it has tended to turn away from so-called 'high' culture and to ignore the equally potentially oppositional dynamics of more 'advanced' forms of art, music and literature. In so doing, it has run a risk of bifurcating the field of culture into 'elite' and 'popular' in way that only inverts the positive/negative connotations of the older distinction between 'high' and 'low'. We need to be aware that early twentieth-century avant-garde movements such as expressionism, dada, and surrealism sought to develop cultural forms that would revolutionize society, and that access to the avant-garde elements of modernist art has not always been simply a privilege of dominant social classes and groups (compare Bürger 1974; Huyssen 1986).

British cultural studies has had a complex relation to Marxism since its beginnings. Although Stuart Hall (1983) and Richard Johnson (1987) grounded cultural studies in a Marxian model of the circuits of capital (production–distribution–consumption–production), Hall and other figures in cultural studies have not always pursued economic analysis consistently. Many practitioners of British and North American cultural studies from the 1980s to the present have tended to pull away from political economy altogether. Although Hall claimed that with Gramsci he would never deny 'the decisive nucleus of economic activity' (1988: 156), one might argue that Hall does not adequately incorporate economic analysis in his work. For example, Hall has proposed that the emergence of a new 'global postmodern' involves a pluralizing of culture, suggesting openings to the margins, to difference, to voices excluded from the narratives of Western culture. However, one might reply, in the more militant vein of the Frankfurt School, that the global postmodern also represents an expansion of global capitalism on the terrain of new media technologies and that the explosion of information and entertainment industries represents powerful sources of capital realization and social control. Global social and economic exchange certainly suggest a great many possibilities of cultural communication and subversion of dominant structures of power. But we must also recognize that such exchange can be limited by transnational corporations that are becoming powerful political and cultural arbitrators, threatening to constrict the range of cultural expression rather than to expand it (compare Best and Kellner 2001; Kellner 2003). For further discussion of these issues, see Chapters 12, 13, and 14 of this book.

In the 1980s, the neo-liberal turn in the economic policies of most governments of the developed 'First World' posed a profound crisis for the Left. This anxiety reached a head with the collapse of communism in the regimes of the Soviet Eastern Bloc and the revolutions of 1989. The challenges for Marxism posed by these developments are discussed here in Box 20, as well as in Box 34 in Chapter 13 of this book.

Conclusion

Whereas the work of Marx and Engels was inspired and shaped by the revolutionary movements of 1848, the construction and spread of a tradition of Western Marxism in the twentieth century was promoted by the success of the Bolshevik revolution of 1917 and then later by the cultural movements of the 1960s. Students and young militants throughout the world sought a version of critical and revolutionary Marxism independent of the orthodoxies and compromises of political parties and regimes such as the Soviet Union. They rejected scientistic kinds of Marxism in favour of more open-ended and less dogmatic thinking. In recent decades, Western Marxism has been supplemented, and to some extent supplanted, by more diverse forms of theory such as post-structuralism, psychoanalytic theory, discourse analysis, feminist theory, multiculturalism, and postcolonial theory. Nevertheless, it continues to be a vital strand of contemporary theory and research. Writers such as Lukács, Gramsci, Bloch, Benjamin, Adorno, Marcuse, and others continue to be of interest. Although they no longer enjoy the same intellectual hegemony they once held in some circles of the Left, their writings remain an important component of the tools of contemporary social theory. Marxism continues to provide insights into multiple contemporary problems and crises—from globalization to ecology, terrorism, imperialism, power, technocracy, postmodernism, and the information society.

BOX 20. MARXISM IN THE 1980s: RESPONSES TO THE COLLAPSE
OF COMMUNISM

The 1970s saw many debates and developments in Western Marxism. We may note that in 1973 Habermas wrote a study of what he called the *'legitimation crisis' in 'late capitalism', arguing that the post-war social-democratic policies of wealth redistribution in Western European states could no longer expect to confer legitimacy on the fundamental tendencies of capitalist economics (Habermas 1973). By the 1980s, however, as the Western European economies seemed to recover from the industrial disputes of the 1970s and the incumbent governments made a turn toward neo-liberal free-market policies, this sense of a basic problem of 'legitimacy' in capitalism seemed to retreat from mainstream public opinion. Political passions were cooling and an era of conservativism was inaugurated. The collapse of communism in Eastern Europe and the Soviet Union in the late 1980s and early 1990s presaged a turn away from Marxism in academic social science toward newer forms of *postmodernist, *post-structuralist, and multicultural approaches, as well as a turn by many former leftists to liberal theory and politics.

One characteristic line of argument was taken by Aronson (1995) who maintained that Marxism's nineteenth-century roots made it difficult to adapt to the changed conditions of the late twentieth century. Aronson asserted that Marxism had never adequately addressed distinctively twentieth-century issues of gender, race, sexuality, and other forms of exclusion, focusing too narrowly on economic factors and questions of class. Classical Marxism's hopes for revolution had been grounded in the historical forces of its time. But when the political parties and social classes that been the foundation of its hopes were defeated and the original doctrines could no longer account for the complexities of reality, it was time, Aronson argued, to move beyond Marxism to new theories and politics.

Ernesto Laclau and Chantal Mouffe's *Hegemony and Socialist Strategy*, first published in 1985, helped shape an influential version of 'post-Marxism' that criticized orthodox models and developed a conception of 'radical democracy' based on 'new social movements'. A later dialogue between Laclau, Judith *Butler, and Slavoj *Žižek continued to reconstruct the Western Marxist project on post-structuralist and multiculturalist lines (Butler et al. 2000).

Several theorists have also sought to explain the collapse of communism from the standpoint of Marxist premises and to appraise the future of Marxism after the demise of the Soviet Union. Some writers have used Marxism to explain the flaws of orthodox Marxism and the reasons for the Soviet collapse. Thus Kagarlitsky (1990) argued that Soviet communism betrayed Marxist principles, that it oppressed and alienated the working class and thus produced its own opposition. Likewise, Callinicos (1991) argued that the Soviet Union never departed from Leninist and Stalinist orthodoxy and that it was necessary to return to more authentic modes of revolutionary Marxism represented by Trotsky. Others argued that the Soviet Union failed to keep up with technological development while images of a more affluent life in neighbouring capitalist countries created disillusion, opposition, and eventually upheaval (see Blackburn 1991; Magnus and Cullenberg 1995; Callari et al. 1995).

In general, it has been argued that the collapse of communism cannot be regarded in any simplistic sense as proof of the error, naivety or obsolescence of Marxist ideas. On the one hand, the long-lasting political repressions and eventual implosion of the Soviet experiment certainly raise serious questions about the capacity of the Marxist vision of society to inform morally valid institutional arrangements for the administration of justice and the sponsoring of well-being in society. It has been argued that Marxism never provided an adequate account of the moral bases of politics, in the sense of determining just institutional arrangements for the recognition and reward of individual virtue and individual

continues

BOX 20 continued

moral responsibility—largely because it has tended to regard existing moral problems in world culture as essentially relative to the capitalist mode of production and hence as a transient and ultimately redundant phase of history (compare Lukes 1985). On the other hand, it must be stressed that the actual historical regimes that invoked Marx's social philosophy would almost certainly *not* have been endorsed by Marx himself, had he lived to witness their existence. The Soviet Union is perhaps best described as a form of heavily restricted, state-dictated capitalism, rather than as a genuinely communist society, in the strict sense in which Marx thought of communism as an 'association of free producers' in which 'the free development of each is the condition for the free development of all' (Marx and Engels 1848: 105). For this reason, it can be argued that the collapse of the Soviet bloc represented the end of a brutal legacy of perversions of Marx's ideas about history and society, rather than any demonstration of their intrinsic irrelevance to the contemporary world.

QUESTIONS FOR CHAPTER 7

1   In what ways do the Western Marxists build on the doctrines of Marx? In what ways do they depart from them?

2   How should the concept of ideology be defined? Is all ideology 'false consciousness'? If not, why not?

3   In what respects does the Frankfurt School's idea of critical theory diverge from 'traditional theory' or positive science?

4   Is the Frankfurt School's critique of mass culture 'elitist'? How far do more recent writers provide a better understanding of cultural life?

5   In what sense has Marxism declined over the twentieth and twenty-first centuries?

6   Does the collapse of Soviet communism invalidate Marxism?

FURTHER READING

Some good overviews of Western Marxism are Perry Anderson's *Considerations on Western Marxism* (Verso, 1976), Stephen Bronner's *of Critical Theory and its Theorists* (Routledge, 2002), Russell Jacoby's *Dialectic of Defeat* (Cambridge University Press, 1981), Leszek Kolakowski's *Main Currents of Marxism*, 3 vols. (Oxford University Press, 1978), Kevin Anderson's *Lenin, Hegel and Western Marxism* (University of Illinois Press, 1995), and Moishe Postone's *Time, Labor and Social Domination: A Reinterpretation of Marx's Critical Theory* (Cambridge University Press, 1993).

The key source for Marx and Engels's classical conception of ideology is *The German Ideology* (Lawrence & Wishart, 1975). Among numerous discussions of this conception are Stuart Hall's article 'The Problem of Ideology: Marxism without Guarantees', in Betty Matthews (ed.), *Marx: A Hundred Years On* (Lawrence & Wishart, 1983), Abercrombie et al., *The Dominant Ideology Thesis* (Allen & Unwin, 1980), Douglas Kellner's article 'Ideology, Marxism, and Advanced Capitalism', *Socialist Review*, 42 (Nov.–Dec. 1978), 37–65, and the texts on Gramsci and the Birmingham School cited below. For an interesting analysis, see also Alvin Gouldner's *The Dialectic of Ideology and Technology* (Seabury Press, 1977) as well as Gouldner's *The Two Marxisms* (Macmillan, 1980).

On the work of Ernst Bloch, see Jamie Daniel and Tom Moylan's edited *Not Yet: Reconsidering Ernst Bloch* (Verso, 1997). For some uses of Bloch's dialectic of ideology and utopia in contemporary cultural studies, see Fredric Jameson's article 'Reification and Utopia in Mass Culture', *Social Text*, 1: 130–48, as well as Jameson's *Late Marxism: Adorno, Or the Persistence of the Dialectic* (Verso, 1990). On Gramsci, ideology, and hegemony, see Jorge Larrain's *The Concept of Ideology* (Hutchinson, 1979) and *Marxism and Ideology* (Macmillan, 1983), Chantal Mouffe's edited *Gramsci and Marxist Theory* (Routledge, 1979), and Carl Boggs's *The Two Revolutions. Antonio Eramsin and the Dilemmas of Western Marxism* (South End Press, 1984). The classic essays of Walter Benjamin, including 'The Work of Art in the Age of Mechanical Reproduction', are collected in Benjamin's *Illuminations*, ed. Hannah Arendt (Cape, 1970). For an introduction to Benjamin, try Graeme Gilloch's *Walter Benjamin: Critical Constellations* (Polity Press, 2002). For an equally pioneering mode of cultural critique similar to Bloch and Benjamin, see Siegfried Kracauer's *The Mass Ornament* (Harvard University Press, 1963), based on essays originally written in German in the 1920s and 1930s.

Some good overviews of the Frankfurt School are Martin Jay's *The Dialectical Imagination: A History of the Frankfurt School and the Institute of Social Research, 1923-1950* (Heinemann, 1973) and Seyla Benhabib's *Critique, Norm and Utopia: A Study of the Foundations of Critical Theory* (Columbia University Press, 1986), also Martin Jay's *Marxism and Totality* (Polity Press, 1984), Douglas Kellner's *Critical Theory, Marxism and Modernity* (Johns Hopkins University Press, 1989), David Held's *Introduction to Critical Theory* (Polity, 1990), and Rolf Wiggershaus's *The Frankfurt School: Its History, Theories, and Political Significance* (Polity Press, 1994). Some good collections of readings from the Frankfurt School are Andrew Arato and Eike Gebhardt's edited *The Frankfurt School Reader* (Continuum, 1976) and Stephen Bronner and Douglas Kellner's edited *Politics, Culture and Society: A Critical Theory Reader* (Routledge, 1989). The key collection of Adorno's writings on the culture industry is Adorno's *The Culture Industry*, ed. Jay Bernstein (Routledge, 1991). See also Brian O'Connor's edited *Adorno Reader* (Blackwell, 2000). Two good introductions to Adorno are Martin Jay's *Adorno* (Harvard University Press, 1984) and Simon Jarvis's *Adorno: A Critical Introduction* (Polity Press, 1998). For a concise account of the Frankfurt School in relation to art and aesthetics, see Austin Harrington's *Art and Social Theory: Sociological Arguments in Aesthetics* (Polity Press, 2004), chapter 6. Adorno himself is difficult to read. A good place to begin is his short book *Minima Moralia* (Verso, 1981).

The best introduction to the early work of Habermas is Thomas McCarthy's *The Critical Theory of Jürgen Habermas* (MIT Press, 1978). A good collection of essays on Habermas on the public sphere is Craig Calhoun's edited *Habermas and the Public Sphere* (MIT Press, 1992). See also Box 28 in Chapter 11 of the present book on Nancy Fraser's feminist perspective on the public sphere. See also Douglas Kellner's essay 'Habermas, the Public Sphere, and Democracy: A Critical Intervention', in Lewis Hahn's edited *Perspectives on Habermas* (Open Court, 2000). On Marcuse, see Douglas Kellner's *Herbert Marcuse and the Crisis of Marxism* (University of California Press, 1984) John Bokina and Timothy Lukes's edited *Marcuse: From the New Left to the Next Left* (University of Kansas Press, 1994).

For further sources on Marxism in British and American cultural studies, see Stuart Hall et al. (eds.), *Culture, Media, Language* (Hutchinson, 1980), and University of Birmingham Centre for Contemporary Cultural Studies (ed.), *On Ideology* (Hutchinson, 1978). See also Richard Johnson's article 'What is Cultural Studies Anyway?', in *Social Text*, 16 (1986/7), Jim McGuigan's *Cultural Populism* (Routledge, 1992), Douglas Kellner's *Media Culture: Cultural Studies, Identity and Politics between the Modern and the Postmodern* (Routledge, 1995), and Ioan Davies's *Cultural Studies and Beyond* (Routledge, 1995). A useful reader is Meenakshi Durham and Douglas Kellner (eds.), *Media and Cultural Studies: Key Works* (Blackwell, 2001). For some Marxist perspectives on postmodernism, see David Harvey's *The Condition of Postmodernity* (Blackwell, 1989), Fredric Jameson's *Postmodernism, or the Cultural Logic of Late Capitalism* (Verso, 1991), Alex Callinicos's *Against Postmodernism* (Polity Press, 1990), Steven Best and Douglas Kellner's *Postmodern Theory: Critical Interrogations* (Macmillan, 1991), and Steven Best and Douglas Kellner's *The Postmodern Adventure:*

Science Technology, and Cultural Studies at the Third Millennium (Routledge, 2001). See also the titles in the Further Reading guidance for Chapter 12 and 13 of this book.

▧ WEBSITES

Marxist Internet Archive at **www.marxists.org/archive/marx/** Provides a good resource with a search facility and links to texts of Marx.

György Lukács at **www.marxists.org/archive/lukacs/** Contains a comprehensive biography, with sections from his major works.

Antonio Gramsci at **www.marxists.org/archive/gramsci/** Provides an introduction to Gramsci's life and thought, with links to selections from key texts.

Illuminations at **www.gseis.ucla.edu/faculty/kellner/Illumina%20Folder/index.html** Displays links to essays, excerpts, and articles by contemporary writers on the Frankfurt School and its legacy.

Herbert Marcuse at **www.marcuse.org/herbert/** Shows a site maintained by one of Marcuse's grandchildren, with a biography, an archive of major works, and reports on his legacy.

8 Psychoanalytic Social Theory

Anthony Elliott

Psychoanalysis, as developed by Sigmund *Freud and his followers, has had a major impact on social theory and modern sociology. Freud's central discoveries—the unconscious, sexual repression, the Oedipus complex, and the like—have been deployed by sociologists to theorize the self and human *subjectivity, *gender and sexuality, the family and socialization, language and *ideology, as well as the formation of cultural identities and forms of political *domination. Throughout the twentieth and twenty-first centuries, social theorists have engaged with the psychoanalytic tradition in order to conceptualize the relation between the individual and society, including the complex, contradictory ways that human subjects acquire, reshape, and transform the ideas, values, symbols, beliefs, and emotional dispositions of the wider society. This has been particularly evident over recent decades as Freudian themes and psychoanalytic motifs have been used to analyse sexual politics, issues of identity and lifestyle, and the nature of modernity and postmodernity.

This chapter looks at some of the most important elements of Freud's legacy for sociological thinking today. We also discuss some influential post-Freudian psychoanalytic theorists who came to prominence in the 1940s and 1950s onwards. These include the French theorist Jacques Lacan and more recent figures active since the 1960s, including Gilles *Deleuze, Félix *Guattari, Slavoj *Žižek and the feminist theorists Julia *Kristeva, Nancy *Chodorow, and Jessica *Benjamin.

Sigmund Freud's legacy for sociology

Freudian psychoanalysis shares with sociology a primary preoccupation with the fate of the individual self in a context of social relationships and wider cultural processes. While Freud's own writings derive primarily from clinical work with patients, and to that degree are at variance with the core methodologies of mainstream social science, his characterization of the human personality has certain parallels with, among others, Thomas *Hobbes's theory of human nature or with Marx's account of the self-seeking individual in capitalist society. But whereas both Hobbes and Marx stressed the impact of social forms in the constitution of the self, Freud's methodological starting point is the individual *psyche*, principally the instinctual impulses and libidinal longings that shape the human imagination.

The self for Freud is radically fractured or divided, split between consciousness of identity and a repressed *unconscious*. The biographical trajectory of the self according to Freud is carried on against the backdrop of a radical otherness of the unconscious. Freud analyses the psyche into three agencies: the id, the ego, and the superego. The id, lying at the root of unconscious desire, is that which cannot be symbolized yet constantly strives for expression in our daily lives—manifesting itself in dreams, daydreams, slips of the tongue, and the like. The unconscious id is a hidden area of the self which knows no reality, logic, or contradiction, and is at the root of how people can simultaneously express both love and hate—whether of their parents, their siblings, their friends or colleagues, and so on. Unconscious desire, infiltrates all human intentions, ideals, and imperatives. Freud sees therefore the ego as interwoven with the force of the id, and the self as a product of the unconscious. The superego is Freud's term for moral conscience. The supergo is responsible for the self's sense of prohibition and restraint, and is founded both in the ego and the wayward drives of the id.

In the following account, we look primarily role of these concepts in Freud's theories about repression, civilization, and the Oedipus complex.

Repression, civilization, and the Oedipus complex

While Freud's writings on human personality and the constitution of the self have been of interest to sociologists, it is his account of the relations between self and society—primarily in his late writings on civilization—that has had greatest influence. In his late writings, Freud comes to see human beings as living under the destructive force of a terrifying *death drive*, based on strict cultural prohibitions on sexual desire and enjoyment. These themes are set out in his magisterial books *Beyond the Pleasure Principle* (1920) and *Civilization and its Discontents* (1930). Civilization, Freud proposes, is repressive. Society imposes psychic demands upon individuals to achieve cultural conformity, demands that can produce intense personal misery and neurotic suffering.

According to Freud, ambivalence is at the core of an individual's relation to itself and to others. Just as the ego seeks to establish order and control over the disruptive unconscious, so cultural ideas must incorporate the deeper emotional strivings of social members, pressing the 'pleasure principle' into the service of the 'reality principle'. This is necessary, Freud contends, for the very reproduction of social life. The development of civilization, of social bonds, and the injunction to labour, all depend upon self-control. Yet it is precisely at this point, where a disjunction emerges between individual desire and social necessity, that Freud locates cultural pathology. The fundamental problem for Freud is that culture tends to rob the individual subject of unfettered instinctual enjoyment, and places gigantic restrictions on sexuality. Listening to the anxieties of his bourgeois patients each day in Vienna at the turn of the nineteenth century, Freud discovered a deep connection between personal, inner desires and the repressive social forms that engender excessive self-control. The denial of feelings, the structuring of sexuality into narrow paths of monogamy and marital legitimacy, and the rigid (male) insistence on genital monosexuality: these are, Freud argues, the oppressive emotional wounds inflicted by culture. Imposing order on the free flow of unconscious desire is a key task of civilization; but the balance between desire and order is constantly changing and can easily become too great burden for individuals and collectivities. When the imposition of social control, order, and structure results in repressive *closure, cultural life is liable to self-annihilation.

In his early writings, Freud understands the way in which individuals come to confront social regulation in terms of the polar opposites of desire and control, pleasure and reality, sexuality and self-preservation. Central to this structuring process of prohibition and repression is the Oedipus complex, which Freud outlines in his classic early work *The Interpretation of Dreams*, of 1900. The intervention of the father into the child–mother dyad is of key importance for grasping the institutionalization of moral imperatives, primarily because the paternal role is symbolic and thus suggestive of social regulation. In the ancient Greek myth, the young boy Oedipus is fated to murder his father and sleep with his mother. In studying the significance of this myth, Freud traced the origins of collective moral prohibitions back in history to a mythical event. The theorem of an original parricide, of a murder of the father, led Freud in *Totem and Taboo* (1913) to speak of a collective Oedipal moral imperative. Freud paints a picture of a 'primal horde', a collectivity of brothers dominated by an all-powerful father who monopolizes women. In anger and frustration, the brothers eventually kill and eat the father. Due to ambivalence and guilt, however, the brothers come to feel remorse for the killing. This unconscious anguish induces the brothers to identify with the dead father as a *'totem', and to invent moral restraints against the free expression of sexual desire. Just as in the Oedipal fantasy itself, the terror of the father is now 'owned' on the 'inside'. The regulation of society is instituted through a renunciation of desire, registered in the taboo against incest.

Freud's most developed account of culture and morality as a work of socially organized 'sublimation' is developed in his late book *Civilization and its Discontents* (1930). This is discussed in Box 21.

BOX 21. SIGMUND FREUD'S *CIVILIZATION AND ITS DISCONTENTS*

In *Civilization and its Discontents* (1930), Freud develops a conception of the 'death drive' as both the object and means of a system of repression laying the foundations of culture. Freud's theory of the death drive entails a radical reinterpretation of the organization of modern culture. By the death drive Freud understands a will to make clean, to purify, to return to order. Human misery and oppression are no longer understood as the outcome of sexual repression alone. Instead, Freud comes to equate culture with a fundamental constraint on self-destructiveness. Civilization protects against certain essentially aggressive liabilities of the death drive. 'The main renunciation culture demands of the individual', writes Paul *Ricoeur (1965: 307) of Freud's metapsychology, 'is the renunciation not of desire as such but of aggressiveness'.

By incorporating this new dualism into his analysis of modern culture, Freud is able to rewrite the problem of self and society as a contest between love and hate, or between love and death. Love is the principle of civilized co-belonging. Hatred and the death drive are forces that threaten to tear this apart. The Freud of *Civilization and its Discontents* unfolds love and death, *eros* and *thanatos* (Greek words for 'love and 'death', respectively), in the following way:

[C]ivilization is a process in the service of Eros, whose purpose is to combine single human individuals, and after that families, then races, peoples and nations, into one great unity . . . These collections of men are libidinally bound to one another. Necessity alone, the advantages of work in common, will not hold them together. But man's natural aggressive instinct, the hostility of each against all and of all against each, opposes this programme of civilization. The aggressive instinct is the derivative and main representative of the death drive which we have found alongside Eros and which shares world-dominion with it. (1930: 122)

The pathological compulsions of cultural life are rooted in a repressive structuring of love and hatred. Freud remains faithful to his earlier view that the reproduction of society depends on sexual repression; but in his late sociological vision this sexual repression becomes integrated into a deathly self-preservation, organized as a destructive assault on the human body, on others, and on nature. Freud particularly had in mind the highly authoritarian European societies before the First World War that sent thousands of young men to their death in 1914. But he also became acutely aware of the pathologies of fascism, racism, and anti-Semitism in the 1920s and 1930s as a form of breakdown of civilization, resulting from a transformation or degeneration of sexual repression into a will to exterminate the alien and disorderly. Today we may also think of the phenomenon of 'ethnic cleansing', as well as homophobia and 'moral panics' about people perceived as deviant.

Freud's writings on the fate of the self in contemporary culture have strongly influenced debates in social theory, from Herbert *Marcuse (1955) to Michel *Foucault (1976) and many others. Too much repression, Freud says, leads to intense unconscious anguish, hostility, and rage. At such a point, the intensification of unconscious desire can release the mental dams of sexual repression in a far-reaching way. The issue of the subjective seeds of social and political transformation are thus at the heart of Freud's contribution to sociology and social theory.

Psychoanalysis after Freud: developments in social theory

For many philosophers, artists, and writers, Freud's ideas have been as fertile and challenging as they have been contentious and problem-ridden. We may note in brief that Freud's own speculations about civilization and social dynamics from the later years of his life tend not to live up to the scientific claims and credentials that he began by attaching to psychoanalysis as a clinical project in his early years. They suffer from tendencies to reductionism and physiological determinism where problems of mental and psychological illness in individuals are generalized to whole collectivities of social agents. In making these generalizations from the individual to the collectivity, Freud tends to neglect the mediating role of shared social forms of cultural expression and shared communication systems transmitted through language which give different meanings to biologically lived experiences in different cultures and at different times in history. It is possible to object that Freud's speculations about certain putative 'universal constants' of human nature betray a pretension in psychoanalysis to universal scientific knowledge about human behaviour that fails to acknowledge its own cultural and historical limits, as one discourse about human life among others. The revolutionary brilliance and ingenuity of Freud's arguments about 'repression', 'displacement', 'condensation' 'unconscious wishes' and 'drives' prevented him from acknowledging that the story of sexuality and its manifold disguises might not be the *only* story to be told about human nature with an ultimate claim to truth.

These problems notwithstanding, Freudian ideas have loomed large in sociological conceptualizations of human subjectivity and interpersonal relationships and the mix of reason and irrationality in politics and history. The remainder of this chapter will discuss a few highly fruitful ways in which subsequent psychoanalytic writers critically extended Freud's thinking in various directions by adopting certain elements of his work and discarding others. We look at three key developments in the emergence of a psychoanalytic strain of social thought in the twentieth century. These are: first, a French *'structuralist' school, founded in the 1950s through the work of Jacques Lacan; second, feminist psychoanalytic thinking since the 1960s; and lastly postmodernist psychoanalytic theorizing, represented by the work of Gilles Deleuze and Félix Guattari. In Box 22 we also consider the role of psychoanalytic ideas in Marxist and functionalist social theory from the middle decades of the century.

French structuralist psychoanalysis: Jacques Lacan and his school

For many years the integration of psychoanalysis with Marxist and *functionalist theory developed by members of the *Frankfurt School on the one hand and Talcott *Parsons on

BOX 22. PSYCHOANALYSIS IN MARXISM AND FUNCTIONALISM: SOCIALIZATION AND THE 'AUTHORITARIAN PERSONALITY'

In the 1950s–1960s the *Frankfurt theorists Herbert *Marcuse and Theodor *Adorno turned to Freud in order to reconceptualize the relation between self and society. As noted in Chapter 7 of this book, the political motivation prompting this turn to Freud had its roots in Marcuse's and Adorno's attempts to conceptualize the rise of fascism, Nazism, and the effects of bureaucratic capitalism on private life. Significant moves in this direction had already been taken in the 1930s by Erich *Fromm, an early associate of the Frankfurt School who was to champion Freudian analysis (against Freud's more pessimistic inclinations) as a tool in the struggle for social liberation and the pacification of violence.

From Freud's theory of the Oedipus complex, and particularly his theorem concerning repression of infantile sexuality, Marcuse and Adorno developed the notion of the 'authoritarian personality' (Adorno et al. 1950). Driven by a desire for conformity and clear rules, the authoritarian personality seemed to be a character type strongly prevalent in the German middle classes, a type that hungered for strong leadership, social order, and regulation. But they argued that this personality type was not only to be found in Nazi Germany. In the advanced liberal societies of the West in general, tendencies towards authoritarianism and conformism were also increasingly evident.

Marcuse's radical Freudianism won a wide audience in the 1960s—not only in academic circles but also among student activists, artists, and sexual liberationists. In *Eros and Civilization* (1955), the core of his analysis rested on a distinction he drew between 'basic' and 'surplus' repression. Basic repression is the minimum level of psychological renunciation demanded by the social structure and cultural order. Surplus repression refers to the intensification of self-restraint demanded by asymmetrical relations of power. Marcuse describes the 'monogamic-patriarchal' family, for example, as a site of surplus repression. But he also emphasized that the so-called sexual revolution of the 1960s did not necessarily threaten power structures of the established social order. He particularly sought to show how demands for freedom and rebellion against the family could be routinely rechannelled for commercial interests.

Nonetheless, while Marcuse saw increasingly signs of surplus repression in late capitalist society, he remained remarkably optimistic about the possibilities for change. He argued that the performance principle ironically opens a path for the undoing of sexual repression. The material affluence of the advanced capitalist societies was a possible starting point from which a reconciliation between culture and nature could be undertaken—the ushering in of a stage of social development he called 'libidinal rationality'. Although vague about this undoing of sexual repression, Marcuse saw the emergence of emotional communication and mature intimacy issuing from a reconciliation of happiness with reason. 'Imagination', he wrote, 'envisions the reconciliation of the individual with the whole, of desire with realization, of happiness with reason' (Marcuse 1955: 258).

From within the school of *functionalism, a different approach to the integration of psychoanalysis and sociology was fashioned (for further discussion of functionalism, see Chapter 4 of this book). The focus of this approach lay with social order, socialization, and the reproduction of the social system. Talcott *Parsons employed Freudian ideas to understand how basic symbols and values are internalized by human subjects throughout the socialization process. According to Parsons's functionalist appropriation of Freud, the structure of the human personality is the outcome of an internalization of desired objects, role relationships, and ethico-cultural values that make up the broader social network. In this approach, it is the linkage of personality structure, the social system, and the cultural system that is stressed (see Parsons, 1964).

continues

Box 22 continued

Unlike Marcuse's and Adorno's emphasis on social manipulation of the unconscious, Parsons found a kind of pre-established harmony between the individual and society. While Parsons's attempt to blend sociological theory with psychoanalysis has few followers today, some aspects of this work have continued to be influential. Another exponent of a fusion of Freudian ideas with socialization theory is the German sociologist Norbert *Elias (1939), whose work on 'civilization' and *'civilizing processes' is discussed in Chapter 6 of this book.

the other was commonly regarded as the most important work in this sub-field of modern sociology. However, from the late 1960s onwards, the impact of French theory, particularly *structuralist and *post-structuralist philosophy, became increasingly influential in understandings of the social dimensions of psychoanalysis.

The key figure in this connection was Freud's French interpreter Jacques *Lacan. Seeking to rework the core concepts of psychoanalysis in light of structural linguistics, Lacan argued that the unconscious exemplifies key *linguistic* features. Lacan famously stated that 'the unconscious is structured like a language' (1973: 48). The subject, or the 'I', according to Lacan, is not transparent to itself. Rather, it is located in a system of signification from which identity is fashioned. For Lacan, linguistic *intersubjectivity is at the centre of psychological functioning and its disturbances. Distortions and pathologies at the level of the self are, Lacan says, located in 'the discourse of the Other'. Among the most central components of Lacan's work are, first, his conception of the 'Mirror Stage' in the formation of the ego, secondly his triangular conception of 'the Imaginary', 'the Symbolic' and 'the Real', and thirdly his distinctive use of the structural linguistic theory of Ferdinand de Saussure. We look at these three components in turn.

One of Lacan's most influential texts is his essay from 1949, 'The Mirror Stage as Formative of the Function of the I' (1949). In this essay, Lacan conceptualizes the infant's initial recognition of itself in a mirror or a reflecting surface, and how this generates a sense of identity. Through the mirror, Lacan argues, the infant makes an *imaginary identification with its reflected image, an identification to which the infant reacts with a sense of jubilation and exhilaration. But the mirror image of the self is, in fact, a *distortion*: the mirror lies. The mirror stage is radically 'imaginary', since the consoling unified image of selfhood which it generates is diametrically opposed to the actual bodily fragmentation and lack of coordination of the child. According to Lacan, these imaginary traps and distortions are a universal and timeless feature of self-organization. Lacan sees such illusions as directly feeding into and shaping pathologies of the self in contemporary culture.

Lacan's thinking in psychoanalysis revolves around three basic concepts that stand in a triangular relation to one another: the concept of the *Imaginary*, the concept of the *Symbolic*, and the concept of the *Real*. By the 'Imaginary', Lacan means the mental images projected by a particular individual self, a subject, in order to make sense of the chaos of its impressions, sensations, and desires. By the 'Symbolic', Lacan means the public code of language, the public order of legitimate standards of sense and reference and expected norms of conduct. The Symbolic order pre-structures the Imaginary for any individual subject. A child is inducted into the Symbolic order by its parents, through the workings of the Oedipus complex. By the 'Real', Lacan means every experience which erupts into the Imaginary or the Symbolic from the *outside*, every experience of a brute intensity—such as pain, shock, horror, or the witnessing of death—which defies the subject's ability to make sense of it in an ordered structured way.

To illustrate Lacan's terminology with a recent and rather sensitive example, we might say that the crashing of the two hijacked aeroplanes into the World Trade Center in New York on 11 September 2001 constituted a traumatic irruption of the *Real* into the taken-for-granted routines of the *Symbolic* order for New Yorkers going about their daily business. On 11 September 2001 the roots of this Symbolic order in a certain *Imaginary* projection of the invincible freedom and security of the USA were suddenly thrown into question (compare Žižek 2002).

Lacan was as interested in the symbolic dimensions of culture as he was in the imaginary drafting of the self. Rewriting the unconscious and the Oedipus complex in terms of the symbolic dimensions of language, Lacan's central theoretical point of reference was the structural linguistics of Ferdinand de *Saussure. Saussure's linguistic theories and their influence on French structuralist thought are discussed at length in Chapter 9 of this book (pp. 197–200). The specific relevance of Saussure's thinking to Lacan can be briefly stated here as follows.

According to Saussurian linguistics, language is a system of internal differences. Signs are composed of a *'signifier' (a sound or image) and a *'signified' (the concept or meaning evoked). Saussure asserts that the relation between the signifier and the signified is *arbitrary*, not 'natural'. The meaning of a word arises only through its differences from other words: the word 'pencil', for example, is *not* the word 'pen'. A 'book' is not a 'pamphlet', not a 'magazine', not a 'newspaper', and so on. Words do not directly refer to their objects in the sense of 'copying' or 'resembling' them. Language creates meaning only through an internal play of differences between spoken or written elements. Roughly speaking, Lacan's Symbolic corresponds to Saussure's concept of *langue*, and Lacan's Imaginary corresponds to Saussure's concept of *parole*.

Lacan accepts the key ideas of Saussure's structural linguistics, but he radicalizes the relation between the signifier and the signified. Lacan does not follow Saussure's primary search for the 'signified', or concept or reference. Instead, Lacan inverts Saussure's interpretation of the sign, asserting that the signifier has primacy over the signified in the production of meaning. Lacan states that 'no signification can be sustained other than by reference to another signification . . . We will fail to pursue the question further as long as we cling to the illusion that the signifier answers to the function of representing the signified, or better, that the signifier has to answer for its existence in the name of any signification whatever . . . We are forced . . . to accept the notion of an incessant sliding of the signified under the signifier' (1957: 165, 166, 170).

Lacan goes on to propose that the signifier is itself coterminous with the unconscious. This means that language, as a system of differences, *constitutes* the subject's repressed desire through and through. The subject, once severed from the narcissistic fullness of the Imaginary, is inserted into linguistic and symbolic structures that both generate the unconscious and allow for its contents to traverse the intersubjective field of culture. At the same time, access to ourselves and others is complicated by the fact that desire is itself an 'effect of the signifier', an outcrop of the spacings or differences of linguistic structures.

From this angle, the unconscious is less a realm on the 'inside' of the individual, or 'underneath' language, than an intersubjective space *between* subjects—located in those gaps which separate word from word, meaning from meaning. Lacan comments that 'the exteriority of the symbolic in relation to man is the very notion of the unconscious' (1966: 469). It is in this sense that advertising and consumer culture in general can be read in terms of schemes of displaced desire, as systems of internal symbolic references that attempt to manufacture a sense of wholeness, health, happiness, and meaning for the subject that is in fact non-existent. These items of culture attempt to paper over conflict, fragmentation, dissent, pain, and deprivation, through fabrications of unity, consensus, satisfaction, and contentment.

Problems with Lacan

Lacan's rereading of Freud has powerfully influenced social theory. His emphasis on symbolic structures in the constitution of the subject and the disruption of these structures through the fracturing effects of the unconscious has been of core importance to debates about social identity (see, for example, Ragland-Sullivan and Brivic 1991; Leupin 1991). His stress on the interweaving of language and desire has served as a useful corrective to accounts that portray the self as site of rational functioning. His linguistic reconceptualization of the unconscious powerfully deconstructs theories of representation which presume that mind and world automatically fit together.

Yet there are limitations with the Lacanian account of *subjectivity and social relations. While it is undeniable that Freud viewed self-misrecognition as internally tied to ego formation, Lacan's interpretation raises some problems. The difficulty with his conception of the distorting mirror is that it fails to specify the psychic capacities which make any such misrecognition possible. Lacan denies the expressive agency of the subject to such an extent that it becomes difficult to see how he can coherently speak of *any* self at all. Related to this problem is Lacan's tendency to suppress the radical implications of Freud's discovery of the unconscious by structuralizing it, by reducing it to a chance play of signifiers. Lacan tends toward a *deterministic conception of the self as a being constructed by forces that radically elude all possibility of the self's *autonomous appropriation of them (see for example the criticisms by Ricœur 1965; Castoriadis 1975; Laplanche 1987; Elliot 1999). It can be argued that in presenting desire as entirely and linguistically pre-structured, Lacan effectively strips the subject of any capacity for autonomous self-transformation.

However, despite these problems, Lacan has been a fruitful source of inspiration for several social critics. One recent exponent has been the Slovenian theorist Slavoj *Žižek, who has eclectically combined psychoanalysis with the structuralist Marxism of Louis *Althusser and Hegelian *dialectics. It is to Žižek's work that we now turn.

Lacan, Althusser, and Slavoj Žižek

Lacan himself was not especially interested in political applications of psychoanalysis. It was one of his followers, the French Marxist philosopher Louis Althusser, who brought Lacanian theory to the centre of debates in sociology (Althusser's work is also discussed in Chapter 7 of this book, pp. 167–8). In his influential essay 'Ideology and Ideological State

Apparatuses' (1971), Althusser analysed ideology in terms of the process by which individuals come to relate to themselves in a manner which supports dominant class relations. According to Althusser, ideology provides an imaginary identity, an imagined map for locating oneself in the wider social network. Echoing Lacan, Althusser uses the notion of the mirror stage to deconstruct ideology. Althusser argues that there is a duplicate mirror structure at the heart of ideology, a structure that grants to the self a political mirror in which it can recognize itself and other people. Althusser calls this process 'interpellation', involving a capturing of the individual within a net of received social meanings. This Lacanian–Althusserian account of the ideological 'subjection' of the subject has deeply affected debates in social theory about *agency, structure, class, social fragmentation, and cultural order.

Drawing on this framework, Žižek considers the ambivalence of unconscious desire and specifically the impact of fantasy in contemporary life. For Žižek, as for Althusser, ideology is an imaginary domain that implies a collective relationship to socio-symbolic forms of class, race, nationality, and gender. In contrast to Althusser, however, Žižek contends that ideology always outstrips its own social and political forms; it is a realm 'beyond' interpellation or internalization. Ideology, he says, is not something which magically sets to work on individuals, assigning identities and roles in the act of producing itself. Rather, it is an overdetermined field of passionate assumptions and commitments. 'The function of ideology', Žižek writes, 'is not to offer us a point of escape from our reality but to offer us the social reality itself as an escape from some traumatic, real kernel' (1989: 45).

Žižek's writing, stranded somewhere between high modernism and postmodernist pastiche, can be viewed as an attempt to develop a psychosocial diagnosis of the self in its dealings with the global capitalist economy. From Žižek's Lacanian standpoint, the self is marked by *lack, gap, and antagonism. The subject is alienated through self-blockage or internal trauma, all knowledge of which is displaced at the level of society and history. According to Žižek, politics vainly tries to build on a melancholy loss or lack at the core of desire, at the core of passions that people find too painful to acknowledge. In this sense, ideological discourse operating through fantasy provides a lining or support to the lack or antagonism that marks the self. Ideologies of nationalism, racism, or sexism structure the fantastic coherence of cultural formations—with the result that unconscious forms of libidinal enjoyment periodically erupt as symptoms, such as in the violent waves of killing and 'ethnic cleansing' that followed the break-up of the former Yugoslavia. Žižek sees the eruptions of neo-nationalism and ethnic xenophobia across Europe in precisely these terms. Racism in his sense is an outer displacement of that which people cannot accept within. The projection of a 'surplus of enjoyment' onto denigrated others, the dumping of distressing and painful affects onto socially constituted objects of antagonism, lies at the heart of the psychic dimension of strategies of political exclusion. This eruption of excess enjoyment, directed at the Other, represents an unbearable kernel of desire. Such excess is alleviated solely through its translation into an ideological symptom. Thus the collapse of Soviet *totalitarianism in Eastern Europe unleashed a surplus of fantasy. It involved the projection of pain onto something perceived as strange and Other.

It is possible to criticize Žižek's radicalization of Lacan in certain respects. It can be argued that if loss, lack, and absence are ideological anchors for desire, their composition would seem to be more internally differentiated than Žižek recognizes. Žižek sees ideology as a fantasy scenario, the sole purpose of which is to fill in or cover over elements of lack. There is a problem with this view insofar as it tends to flatten out the complex, contradictory reception of ideological forms by individuals. Žižek sees no significant difference between whether one is in the grip of *identity politics or reading philosophy and classical literature or watching a TV talk-show host such as Oprah Winfrey. These are all equally to be seen as pieces of ideological fantasy, aimed at effacing the sour taste of lack, gap, and antagonism (see further Elliott 2002). In this respect, Žižek has a tendency to pass over the multiplex ways in which people come to challenge political ideologies, and to treat the very worst and most sinister ideological formations on the same level as other relatively 'progressive' or 'intelligent' formations.

These problems in Žižek can to some extent be traced back to Lacan's account of culture. Lacan's linkage of the subject of the unconscious to the idea of the arbitrary nature of the sign tends to give an inadequate account of how some ideological and political meanings predominate over others in the shaping of the personal sphere. Instead, in Lacan's writing, cultural domination is equated with all language as such. As Dews (1987) and other critics have argued, Lacan's rather indiscriminate equation of language with domination seriously downplays the *historically specific* status of power, ideology, and social institutions in the reproduction of cultural life.

Psychoanalysis in feminist social theory

Psychoanalysis has also exerted a profound impact on debates about gender, sexuality, and the family in social research. One amongst many influential approaches in this field in the early 1970s was Juliet Mitchell's *Psychoanalysis and Feminism* (1974). In this book *Mitchell deployed Freudian and Lacanian psychoanalytic ideas as a means of connecting a discussion of gender power with an Althusserian Marxist theory of late capitalist society. Against this theoretical backdrop, she asserted that definitions of masculinity and femininity are framed through linguistic and historical structures—with man as a self-determining, autonomous agent, and woman as a lacking 'Other'. Mitchell argued that such gender dualism was highly conducive to capitalist social regulation, involving a split between private and public and giving rise to pathologies in familial life. Though criticized in some feminist circles, Mitchell's ideas have been influential in feminist sociology.

In the USA since the 1980s, the feminist theories of Nancy *Chodorow and Jessica *Benjamin have also been effective in contemporary sociology. These authors draw from psychoanalysis, but rather than turning to Lacan and French psychoanalysis, their work selectively incorporates the insights of Freudian and post-Freudian theory, as well as the *'object-relations' theories of the British and Austrian-British psychoanalysts Donald Winnicott and Melanie Klein. In contemporary French feminism, one of the most influential analysts of gender has been Julia *Kristeva. In the following sections, we look at the work of Chodorow, Benjamin, and Kristeva in turn. Feminist social theory as a whole is discussed in Chapter 11 of this book.

Nancy Chodorow: the mother–child relationship and male domination

Instead of following Freud's concentration on the father–son relationship as the basis of the Oedipus complex, Nancy Chodorow examines the mother–daughter relationship. In her pioneering book *The Reproduction of Mothering* (1978), Chodorow argues that mothers experience their daughters as doubles of themselves, through a narcissistic projection of sameness. Because daughters are perceived as the selfsame of the mother, differentiation of the self of the daughter is beset with emotional difficulties. The female child finds it painfully difficult to disengage from the mother's love. Locked in maternal narcissism, the daughter is emotionally hindered in the task of establishing a sense of independence and individuality. From this perspective, Chodorow reinterprets Freud's concept of 'penis-envy' not as biologically pre-given, but as a sign of the daughter's desire for autonomy. The daughter turns to her father, through an awareness of the social privilege that the phallus symbolizes, in the hope of achieving a sense of independence from the mother. Yet because fathers are emotionally distant and absent—for reasons to be examined—daughters are unable to break with the power and authority of the mother.

According to Chodorow, the emotional sensitivity and intuitive concern often taken as a hallmark of womanhood is a direct outcrop of these socio-structural patterns embedded in the early mother–daughter bond. Daughters grow up with a powerful sense of emotional continuity with their mothers, a continuity which provides the basis for a strong relational connection in women's adult lives. However, this relational component of feminine identity is achieved only at a severe personal cost. Since mothers do not perceive daughters as separate, girls remain without adequate affirmation of their sense of personal identity and agency. This results in a confusion of ego boundaries, coupled with a wider estrangement from personal needs, aspirations, and desires. Feelings of inadequate separateness, lack of self-control, and a fear of merging with others arise as prime emotional problems for women. Related to this is the socially devalued category of the feminine. For Chodorow, women's 'core gender identity' involving weak ego boundaries and immersion in narcissism comes to mirror a culturally devalued social position. One common way out of these difficulties for women, Chodorow argues, is through a defensively constructed set of personal boundaries. Denying what is needed within, women focus on what is needed by others, particularly the needs of men.

In a similar fashion, Chodorow argues for the existence of a distinctly masculine form of personality structure. Reversing Freud, Chodorow argues that masculine identity is forged against the backdrop of a primary identification with the mother. Such love for the mother among boys makes the achievement of maleness much more difficult than Freud had originally presumed. For what boys must at all costs repudiate, in order to forge a masculine selfhood, is their emotional intimacy with the mother. Boys must deny their primary bond to female eroticism, repressing their own femininity permanently into the unconscious. The originating cue for this repression comes, somewhat paradoxically, from the mother. Chodorow argues that boys are assisted in the developmental task of making their maleness through the mother's perception of gender difference. From the start of life, mothers propel their sons towards differentiation and autonomy, prizing assertiveness. Chodorow calls this pre-Oedipal mother–son bond 'anaclitic object-attachment'. This is a kind of attachment by which mothers relate to their sons as different and other from themselves.

Mothers lead their sons to disengage emotionally from care and intimacy. This prepares boys for an instrumental and abstract attitude towards the world, an attitude which will be expected from them in the public sphere of work and politics.

This account of gender relations suggests that exclusive female mothering produces an ideology of male domination. The absence of a primary attachment to males in pre-Oedipal childhood leads to an idealization of men and a devaluation of women. The only way out of this self-reproducing gender system, Chodorow argues, is through shared parenting. The inclusion of men in early parenting activities should lead to a break-up of established gender polarity. Both parents would be available to establish a caring, nurturing connection with their children. In this context, children of both sexes would be able to forge emotional intimacy and autonomy through a primary relatedness to both mother and father.

Chodorow's work presents a powerful account of those psychosocial forces that distort gender relations. Her model has exercised great influence (see, for example, Balbus 1982; Connell 1987). Her claim for a stable gender identity for males and females has proved attractive to many seeking to understand the persistence of patriarchal domination, and her arguments about female psychology are illuminating. Of key importance is her assertion that women want to have children in order to recapture the primary bond of the mother–daughter relationship. The reasoning is that women's lives are emotionally drained because men are cut off from sexual intimacy and interpersonal communication. From this angle, the desire to have a child is rooted in distortions in the current gender system. Conversely, the abstract traits of male selfhood help to explain the anxieties that many men experience in relation to intimacy. Masculinity, according to Chodorow, has come to involve the adoption of intolerance, insensitivity, and emotional coerciveness. From this angle, male sexual dominance, often involving the use of violence towards women, has its roots in the damaged, fragile, and precarious nature of masculine identity.

Chodorow's theory is open to criticism in some respects. There is something too neat and comfortable in her claim that exclusive female mothering produces asymmetric gender roles. She presents a model of woman as primary caretaker, with maternal desire fixed into *either* narcissistic *or* 'anaclitic' modes of identification. But is the institution of mothering really so limited to these two psychic categories? What of mothers who encourage 'feminine' modes of expression in their sons? What of the increasing phenomenon of single-parent, mother-led families? A further problem for some critics is that Chodorow's concept of 'core gender identity' returns to a pre-Freudian view of subjectivity, one that brackets Freud's analysis of infant bisexuality and instead affirms the consoling unity of personal identity. Consequently, instead of exploring the problematic cultural construction of sexual difference and gender, Chodorow only describes how dominant sex-roles become interwoven with core masculine and feminine identities. As a whole, her model resembles a functionalist account of how sexual identities are generated to mirror gender power in patriarchal modern societies. According to Jacqueline Rose (1986), Chodorow in this respect fails to get beyond a basic notion of 'gender imprinting'.

A third possible criticism concerns Chodorow's suggestion that under conditions of shared parenting, men would develop the kind of relational qualities that women possess, while women would be free to develop personal autonomy. Given Chodorow's own thesis about gender identity being powerfully shaped in negative and polarizing forms, it is not so clear how women and men might actually liberate themselves from the destructive gender identities that currently preoccupy them.

Jessica Benjamin: gender and agency

In *The Bonds of Love* (1988), Benjamin focuses on women's lack of agency in the wider social context of power relations. Like Chodorow, Benjamin sees the contemporary gender system as locating the mother at the pole of biological regression on the one hand, with the father at the pole of progressive agency on the other. But unlike Chodorow, Benjamin refuses to view the psychic world of the developing child as simply mirroring gender asymmetry. Instead, Benjamin contends that it is necessary to tackle head-on 'the problem of desire': that is, the identifications and cross-identifications through which an infant establishes basic differences between itself and other people. With this aim, Benjamin develops a concept of 'identificatory love', by which she refers to a pre-Oedipal phase of rapprochement in which the child seeks to establish a sense of both attachment to *and* separation from parental figures. Through identification, the small child is able to separate out a sense of self while remaining emotionally connected to others.

According to Benjamin, pre-Oedipal identificatory love is routinely denied and displaced in modern society. Children of both sexes cannot maintain their identificatory love for the mother since she is devalued by current sexual ideology. While boys can identify with the father and his phallus to separate from the mother and establish autonomous individuality, the same path to psychic individuation is denied to girls. A girl's empathic relationship to the exciting father is usually refused, with the result that women's 'lack' of desire returns as masochism in idealizations of male power. This means that the tension between dependence and independence, which underpins healthy emotional relationships, break down in society at large. Worse, sexual relations between men and women may grow diseased and deformed into master–slave patterns.

In *Like Subjects, Love Objects* (1995) and *The Shadow of the Other* (1998), Benjamin explores in more detail the range of multiple identifications that women and men forge or discover through sexual object choice. Here Benjamin focuses on constructions in which the adult self accepts multiplicity and difference, displays complementary erotic fantasies or gender ideals, and tolerates oscillating identifications. She forcefully questions Freud's construction of gender identity along the lines of splitting and polarization—masculinity versus femininity, activity versus passivity, same versus other. Oedipal theory, she argues, divides the sexes too neatly around the notion of anatomical difference, foreclosing the myriad paths through which individuals identify with both masculine and feminine ideals of the self.

Against the thesis that love object and identification are polarized (the boy *loves* his mother but *identifies* with his father), Benjamin focuses instead on the murky, indistinct emotional identifications with both mother and father, stressing throughout that interpersonal relationships and fantasies always coexist. Benjamin stresses the bisexual or 'polymorphous' (multi-directional) identifications of the most primitive stage of psychosexual development, in the pre-Oedipal phase. In her view, pre-Oedipal bisexuality suggests that the defensive repudiation of opposite sex identifications in the Oedipal stage depends on a denial of bisexual identifications and on an adoption of mutually exclusive gender positions. In this way, polarity is substituted for paradox in masculinist culture. But Benjamin also emphasizes that the recuperation of the pre-Oedipal phase can be revisited throughout life. Cross-identifications of the pre-Oedipal stage with tolerance for difference and multiplicity inform what she terms the 'post-Oedipal' configuration, in which a more playful and creative approach is taken to identity, sexuality, and gender. According to Benjamin, the psychological task of replacing splitting and polarization with the sustaining of psychic tension and the ability to manage opposing emotional dispositions towards self and other results from fluid boundaries between Oedipal and post-Oedipal configurations. For the boy, inclusion of denied feelings or blocked identifications depend on regaining contact with multiple identifications of the pre-Oedipal period, especially with experience of the mother as a creative subject.

Benjamin accepts paternal identification as potentially playing a positive role in the achievement of autonomous female subjectivity. However, she emphasizes that any identification with the father is likely to prove counter-productive as long as the cultural devaluation of women remains in place. In her view, merely an alteration of parenting arrangements—as proposed by Chodorow—is insufficient to transform gender structures. Non-repressive gender relations depend rather on replacing the cultural split of progressive autonomous father against regressive mother with new sexual identifications that permit a less rigid set of sexual roles. This would involve a repudiation of defensive modes of separation. That is, the father's phallus would no longer be used as the dominant medium to beat back an engulfing mother. Instead, children might construct more fluid sexual identifications—expressing both masculine and feminine aspects of identity—in relation to a socially and sexually autonomous mother and a more empathic caring father. Two figures of love and idealization—both mother and father—are equally necessary for the creation of non-patriarchal patterns of socialization.

Julia Kristeva: subversion and the feminine semiotic

In a different manner from Chodorow and Benjamin, Julia *Kristeva's reference point for situating gender and sexuality is the reading of Freud proposed by Lacan. In her book *Revolution in Poetic Language* (1974), Kristeva contrasts Lacan's account of the symbolic order—the social and sexual system of the Law of the Father—with those multiple psychic forces which she terms *'semiotic'. According to Kristeva, the 'semiotic' is essentially *pre*-linguistic. Semiotic processes include libidinal energies and bodily rhythms experienced by the child during the pre-Oedipal relationship with the mother. For Kristeva, these pre-Oedipal forms undergo repression upon entry to the social and cultural processes of the symbolic order. That is, the flux of semiotic experience is channelled into the relatively stable domain of symbolization and language. However, Kristeva contends that the repression of the semiotic is by no means complete. The semiotic remains present in the unconscious and cannot be shut off from culture.

Against this psychoanalytic backdrop, Kristeva explicitly connects her analysis of femininity with the idea of the maternal. Semiotic longing for the pre-Oedipal mother is part and parcel of selfhood, making itself felt through tonal rhythms, slips, and silences in everyday speech. These semiotic forces are subversive of the symbolic order, since they are rooted in a pre-patriarchal connection with the mother's body. Hence the subversive or disruptive potential of the semiotic is closely interwoven with femininity. But Kristeva emphasizes that it would be a mistake to say that the semiotic belongs exclusively to women. On the contrary, the semiotic is a pre-Oedipal realm of experience that comes into being prior to sexual difference. If the semiotic is 'feminine', this is a femininity that is always potentially available to both women and men in their efforts to transform identity and gender power. As children of both sexes initially belong to women—that is, to a woman's body—all individuals are faced with the emotional task of establishing a relation to the feminine. Femininity cannot be discussed without confronting the impact of the maternal.

Kristeva sees artistic creation and literary expression as possible containers for unspoken experience, giving symbolic form to the semiotic. It is in the cultural products of the artist or the writer that the semiotic may impress itself in symbolic structures, threatening established meanings. She finds such a poetics of the semiotic in the writings of numerous avant-garde authors, principally the French poets Stéphane Mallarmé, Lautréamont, and Antonin Artaud, as well as James Joyce. Although these are all male authors, Kristeva dwells at length on the aesthetic structures of poetic language and especially on the shifting fields of semiotic forces that unlink obvious meanings in these writers. She stresses that the energy of the pre-Oedipal semiotic ushers in a 'feminine articulation of pleasure', a realm of secret desires which defies patriarchal culture and language.

In other writings, Kristeva seeks to lend further content to the idea of semiotic subversion through the empirical study of motherhood. She argues that in pregnancy, woman can recover a repressed relation to the semiotic maternal through the profound emotional experience of giving birth. Pregnancy involves a kind of pleasurable creative linking with otherness. In her essay 'Women's Time', she argues that pregnancy reproduces 'the radical ordeal of the splitting of the subject: redoubling of the body, separation, and coexistence of the self and of an other, of nature and consciousness, of physiology and speech' (1986: 206). This mode of relating involves a potential reconstruction of human social relationships, one in which a new relation to the semiotic body, its pleasures, and its dismantling of fixed oppositions can overturn existing masculinist culture.

More recently, Kristeva has pursued themes of depression, mourning, and melancholia in modern culture. In depression, she suggests, there is an emotional disinvestment from the symbolic power of language. The depressed person, overwhelmed by sadness—often as a result of lost love—suffers from a paralysis of symbolic activity. In effect, language fails to fill in or substitute for what has been lost at the level of the psyche. As the depressed person loses interest in the surrounding world, in language itself, psychic energy shifts to a more primitive mode of being, to a maternal, drive-related form of experience. Depression produces a trauma of symbolic identification, which may then unleash a power of semiotic energy. In the force field of the semiotic—in rhythms, changes in intonation, semantic shifts—Kristeva discerns a means to connect the unspoken experience of the depressed person to established meaning, thereby permitting a psychic reorganization of the self. It is against this background that she stresses the deeper political implications of psychoanalysis. In her rather contentious view, psychotherapeutical work with patients is more likely to produce lasting personal and political changes than is political activity on a more institutional level. In Kristeva's rendering, psychoanalysis *is* radical political activity.

Kristeva's idea of the feminine semiotic as a possible mode of restructuring gender power has been fiercely criticized. Critics have argued that in collapsing the feminine with unconscious experience, Kristeva argues for a political pluralism without feminist content (see Nye 1989). It has been argued that Kristeva displaces women's actual experiences of both oppression and active gender struggle in favour of an abstract male model of semiotic literary practice. Kristeva has also been accused of *essentialism and sexual separatism, reducing semiotic subversion to the biological conditions of motherhood and thereby erasing the capacity of men (and also of women who choose not to be mothers) to partake in radical gender struggle.

It should be noted that neither of these criticisms is entirely fair. It is important to see that Kristeva is not claiming the semiotic realm as an exclusive province of either women or men, even if there may be an essentialist slippage in her account of motherhood. Rather, she insists that insofar as human beings are split desiring subjects, all human beings have a pre-Oedipal feminine connection to the mother, a connection which is potentially subversive of patriarchal logic and thought. Nonetheless, a problem remains in Kristeva's assertion of the political implications of the semiotic. She assumes that semiotic displacements in language and culture are in some sense equivalent to overturning and transforming social and political relations. This is a hazardous conclusion at best. We should ask about how semiotic silences and displacements might practically be used to overcome repressive gender relations. How might semiotic subversions transform or eradicate sexual violence or pornography?

Postmodernism and psychoanalysis: Gilles Deleuze and Félix Guattari

Related to the intertwining of psychoanalysis and feminism, *postmodernist appropriations of psychoanalysis have also been influential in recent years. In the writings of Michel *Foucault, Jean-François *Lyotard, and Jacques *Derrida (who are discussed in Chapters 9 and 12 of this book), there has been much debate about the fate of the individual, or 'death of the subject', in postmodernist culture. In these discussions, psychoanalysis has provided sociology with conceptual tools for questioning and deconstructing Enlightenment discourses of rationality and progress. One notable elaboration of psychoanalysis in this mould has been Gilles *Deleuze and Félix *Guattari's treatise *Anti-Oedipus*, of 1972, presented by the authors as a contribution to the theory of 'capitalism and schizophrenia'.

Deleuze and Guatarri contend that the Lacanian theory of desire, insofar as it binds the subject to the social order, works in the service of repression. They maintain that psychoanalysis in the Freudian and Lacanian vein functions in the interests of capitalism, as a kind of vortex around which the unconscious becomes bent out of shape. In their view, classical psychoanalysis functions to personalize desire, referring all unconscious productions to the incestuous sexual realm of the nuclear family. They criticize Freud's and Lacan's reduction of Oedipal prohibitions merely to signifiers which chain desire to normative representations, at the point at which we come to desire what capitalism wants us to desire. Instead, in a more radical gesture, Deleuze and Guattari seek to uncover this psychoanalytic privileging of desire rooted in lack as a product of Law. They argue that desire in fact precedes representation and self-identity, so that there is nothing at all personal to the flows of libido, which continually burst out anew. They propose giving full throttle to flows of libidinous energy, affirming the absolute 'positivity' of unconcious productions and treating schizophrenia as a potentially emancipatory model.

Anti-Oedipus was a courageous poetic attempt to explode the *normative power of categories like 'Oedipus' and 'castration', using psychoanalytic concepts against the colonizing conceptual logic of psychoanalysis itself. Deleuze and Guattari trace the 'free lines' of schizophrenic desire as affirmative force, as a series of enabling rhythms, intensities and transforming possibilities. From this angle, the schizoid process is what enables libidinal pulsations to be uncoupled from systems, structures, or cultural objects, which may in turn transform the production of the political network, making politics no longer unfold according to the repressive functioning of Law. Rejecting the rigid and closed worlds of Oedipus and capitalism, Deleuze and Guattari claim to speak for schizophrenia over neurosis, for flows of desire over lack, for fragments over totalities, differences over uniformity. They write that 'schizophrenia is desiring production at the limit of social production' (Deleuze and Guattari 1972: 35). Against the Oedipalizing logic of capitalist discourse, where desire is channelled into prescribed pathways, Deleuze and Guattari argue that the impersonalized flows of schizoid desire can herald a radical transformation of society.

Similar theoretical directions were taken in the early writings of the French philosopher Jean-François *Lyotard, whose work is discussed at greater length in Chapter 12 of this book (pp. 260–2). Lyotard argues that political society is itself secretly libidinal. Whereas Deleuze and Guattari hold that desire is codified and repressed capitalist arrangements, Lyotard views contemporary society as an immense desiring system. In Lyotard's picture, the postmodern is a vast libidinal circuit of technologies, a culture swamped with seductive signs and images. Underscoring the indeterminancy of intensities, Lyotard here effects a shift in focus away from theories of representation and structures of the psyche toward bodily intensities and erotogenic surfaces. In his text *Libidinal Economy* (1974), Lyotard constructs the excitations of libido on the model of the Möbius strip, conceptualized as an endless series of rotations, twistings, and contortions. The upshot of this, in political terms, is a series of proposals about how best to extract libidinal pleasure and intensity from postmodern culture. 'What would be interesting', Lyotard writes, 'would be to stay where we are, but at the same time to grab all opportunities to function as good conductors of intensities' (1974: 311).

The postmodern psychoanalytic thought of Deleuze, Guattari, and Lyotard emphasizes experiences of fragmentation, dislocation, and polyvalency in contemporary society. It is pitted against the view that social transformation might be linked to the undoing of hidden meanings or discourses—as suggested by theorists such as Marcuse and the early *Habermas. Instead, truth in postmodern psychoanalysis is located in the immediacy of libidinal intensity itself. In the postmodern imagination, the unconscious cannot be tamed or organized. Desire needs no interpretation; it simply is. It is within the diffuse, perverse, and schizophrenic manifestations of desire that new forms of identity, otherness, and symbolism can be found.

The issues raised by postmodern psychoanalysis have an interest in light of contemporary social transformations such as globalization and new communications technology. However, it is not apparent that postmodern psychoanalytic theories generate genuinely sustainable criteria for the critical assessment of social practices, politics, and value positions. As Dews (1987), Frank (1983), and other critics have urged, the dissimulation of libidinal intensities enjoined in many currents of postmodern psychoanalysis is something that can be ideologically marshalled by both progressive and reactionary political forces alike. One may argue that the idea of desire as something *ipso facto* rebellious and subversive is premised on a naive naturalism, failing to examine realistically the specific institutional forms in which unconscious passion is embedded. Here there is little consideration of the potential harm, pain, and damage that psychical states of fragmentation and fluidity may comprise. There is a grave danger of romanticizing 'schizophrenia'.

Conclusion

Postmodern variants of psychoanalytic thinking need to be placed alongside the full gamut of schools and developments in psychoanalytic social theory discussed in this chapter. Postmodern interventions are not understandable other than as polemical side-shots across the foundational work of Freud and the subsequent contributions of figures such as Lacan, Marcuse, Fromm, Parsons, and the Frankfurt School, as well as the work of feminist theorists such as Chodorow, Benjamin, and Kristeva.

We have seen that in Chodorow's work, psychoanalysis is part of an attempt to understand the psychic components of female and male socialization, especially in terms of the unconscious forces that shape gender roles. In Jessica Benjamin's work, psychoanalysis is deployed to rethink the dynamics of domination and submission within the wider frame of gender, society, and history. In Kristeva's texts, we find primarily a set of observations about transformations of the psyche and about how identity splices with disruptions in cultural life. For Lacan and the various Marxist writers who draw on his work, including Althusser and Žižek, psychoanalysis is the study of the precarious fabrications of identity that make up our sense of self in a world shot through with displaced representations of desire encoded in everyday language and the mass media.

The individual writers discussed in this chapter by no means exhaust the scope of psychoanalytic social thought. There have been numerous contributors to psychoanalysis since Freud whose work we have not been able to discuss here. Among others, these include particularly the Austrian-British psychoanalyst Melanie Klein and the British psychoanalyst Donald Winnicott, who both exerted a major impact on the study of child psychology. Alongside these, mention should be made of the work of Freud's daughter Anna, as well as of the Swiss psychologist Carl G. Jung who applied psychoanalysis to the study of myth, folklore, and fairy tales, speaking of various 'archetypes' of the soul. All these developments attest to the continuing vitality of Freud's revolutionary work in contemporary thought, despite its various methodological limitations and problematic assumptions about the nature of the human animal.

■ **QUESTIONS FOR CHAPTER 8**

1   How far are Freud's analyses of psychological illnesses in individual persons applicable to the study of whole societies and civilizations?

2   What sense can be given to Jacques Lacan's statement that the 'unconscious is structured like a language'? What does this proposition help explain about social and cultural life?

3   To what extent is psychoanalytic thinking oriented to the goal of social and political emancipation? How effective are combinations of psychoanalysis and Marxism?

4   How useful is psychoanalysis in explaining male domination and the position of women in society?

5   How much of Freud's work from the early decades of the twentieth century is relevant to the study of social behaviour today, in a multicultural or 'postmodern' context? Is the Oedipus complex still a valid tool of analysis?

■ **FURTHER READING**

Some general overviews of psychoanalysis in relation to social theory are Anthony Elliott's four books *Psychoanalytic Theory: An Introduction* (Duke University Press, 2nd edn. 2002), *Social Theory since Freud: Traversing Social Imaginaries* (Routledge, 2004), *Social Theory and Psychoanalysis in Transition: Self and Society from Freud to Kristeva* (Blackwell, 2nd edn. 1999), and *Subject to Ourselves: Social Theory, Psychoanalysis and Postmodernity* (Blackwell, 1996). Also useful are Stephen Frosh's *The Politics of Psychoanalysis* (Macmillan, 2nd edn. 1999) and Ian Craib's two books *Psychoanalysis: A Critical Introduction* (Polity Press, 2001) and *Psychoanalysis and Social Theory* (Harvester, 1989). See also John Forrester's *Language and the Origins of Psychoanalysis* (Macmillan, 1980).

For some helpful introductions to Freud, try Anthony Storr's *Freud* (Oxford University Press, 1989), Richard Wollheim's *Freud* (Fontana, 2nd edn. 1991), and Peter Gay's more detailed historical study *Freud: A Life for our Time* (Dent, 1988). See also Paul Ricœur's hermeneutical study *Freud and Philosophy* (Yale University Press, 1970) and Philip Rieff's *Freud: The Mind of the Moralist* (Chicago University Press, 1979), as well as the essays in Anthony Elliott's edited *Freud 2000* (Polity Press, 1998). Two excellent one-volume collections of readings from Freud are Peter Gay's *The Freud Reader* (Vintage, 1995) and Anna Freud's *The Essentials of Psychoanalysis* (Penguin, 1986). Freud is probably best approached first through *The Interpretation of Dreams* (Oxford University Press, 1999) and *Civilization and its Discontents* (Dover, 1994).

Two good introductions to Lacan (with an emphasis on literary and cultural theory) are Malcolm Bowie's *Lacan* (Fontana, 1991) and David Macey's *Lacan in Contexts* (Verso, 1988). The authoritative intellectual biography is Elisabeth Roudinesco's *Jacques Lacan & Co: A History of Psychoanalysis in France, 1925–1985* (Free Association, 1990). The work of Žižek can be approached through Elizabeth and Edmund Wright's edited *Žižek Reader* (Blackwell, 1999) or through any of Žižek's own lively books, such as *Looking Awry: An Introduction to Popular Culture through Jacques Lacan* (MIT Press, 1991) or *Enjoy your Symptom* (Routledge, 1993).

Some good guides to feminism and psychoanalysis are Jane Flax's *Thinking Fragments: Psychoanalysis, Feminism and Postmodernism in the Contemporary West* (University of California Press, 1991), Nancy Chodorow's *Feminism and Psychoanalytic Theory* (Polity Press, 1989), and Rosalind Minsky's collection of edited readings with commentaries *Psychoanalysis and Gender* (Routledge, 1996). A useful collection of readings from Kristeva is Toril Moi, *The Kristeva Reader*, ed. Toril Moi (Blackwell, 1986). For an introduction to the work of Deleuze and Guattari (who do not write in a conventionally clear way), see Ronald Bogue's *Deleuze and Guattari* (Routledge, 1989) or Paul Patton's *Deleuze and the Political* (Routledge, 2000).

■ WEBSITES

International Psychoanalytic Association (IPA) at **www.ipa.org.uk/** Displays the home page of the IPA, with links to psychoanalysis as a professional practice.

American Psychoanalytic Association (APSAA) at **www.apsa.org** Displays the home page of the APSAA with links to relevant literature, affiliate societies, and the practice of psychoanalysis.

The Freud Museum London at **www.Freud.org.uk/** Contains links to several sites on the life, work, and influence of Freud.

Jacques Lacan at **www.mythosandlogos.com/Lacan.html** Provides a comprehensive list of links to sites on Lacan, including excerpts and review articles.

Feminist Theory at **http://bailiwick.lib.uiowa.edu/wstudies/theory.html** Contains links to texts on (mainly French) feminist theory and psychoanalysis.

9

Structuralism and Post-structuralism

Samantha Ashenden

The movements of thought that developed in France from the late 1950s to the 1970s known as *'structuralism' and *'post-structuralism' have had a major impact in twentieth-century social science, as well as in the humanities, in aesthetics, and in literary theory. French structuralist and post-structuralist thinking from the radical decade of the 1960s and the 'generation of 1968' today stands as a potent source of influences behind such intellectual developments as feminist theory, *postcolonial theory, *queer theory, film and media theory, *deconstructive literary criticism, and *postmodernist thinking in the broadest sense.

It should, however, be noted that structuralism is often used rather loosely as a term and that the term 'post-structuralism' was eschewed by most of the writers so labelled. Broadly defined, structuralism can be defined as an attempt to provide a unified method for the social sciences through the development of a methodology drawn from the structural linguistics of the early twentieth-century French linguist Ferdinand de *Saussure. Saussure envisaged a general science of signs, called 'semiology'—today known more commonly as *'semiotics'—which was to study both linguistic and non-linguistic ways of creating meaning. In the 1950s in France, other writers came to prominence in related disciplines, most notably the anthropologist Claude *Lévi-Strauss and the literary critic Roland *Barthes, both of whom developed structuralist modes of analysis to examine kinship systems, myths, rituals, and a wide range of cultural artefacts. In the same period Jacques *Lacan synthesized structural linguistics with psychoanalysis (discussed in Chapter 8 of this book), while Louis *Althusser applied structuralist analysis to Marxism (discussed in Chapters 7 and 8). The Swiss psychologist Jean *Piaget developed a theory of genetic structuralism based on studies of cognitive development in children. In the early 1970s, Pierre *Bourdieu imported elements of structuralism into empirical sociology (discussed in Chapter 10), while Julia *Kristeva developed feminist positions in literary theory and philosophy drawn from structuralist and post-structuralist thought (discussed in Chapter 8). In a more postmodernist direction, Gilles *Deleuze and Jean *Baudrillard developed theories of capitalist media culture drawn variously from Marxism, psychoanalysis, and post-structuralist semiotics (discussed in Chapters 8 and 12).

This chapter begins by outlining Saussure's structural approach to linguistics and its further elaboration in the anthropology of Lévi-Strauss. We then concentrate at length on the movement away from structuralism made in the 1960s by the two major figures of Jacques *Derrida and Michel *Foucault, who today stand out as the two most influential representatives of a post-structuralist vision in French thought, even though neither of these thinkers accepted this label.

Ferdinand de Saussure and structural linguistics

In opposition to nineteenth-century linguistics and historical philology, mostly in the German *historicist tradition, Ferdinand de Saussure developed an account of language as a system of signs, emphasizing the need to study language *synchronically, rather than in terms of disparate histories of uses of words over time. Writing in the early years of the twentieth century, Saussure also set himself against earlier seventeenth- and eighteenth-century theories of language in which words tended to be seen in terms of naturalistic representations or imitations of things in the world, like pictures. In opposition to both these two schools, Saussure argued that signs produce meaning only by virtue of their relation to other signs, not through any organic relationship to the things they are held to signify. Signs are to be seen as *arbitrary*, established purely by convention. Language is to be studied as a system of relations. Language does not reveal a set of natural concepts. Rather, it reveals the structuring operations of the mind through which things are made to signify or to have meaning. Meaning is to be seen as differential, produced through differences between terms within a system, not predicated on any intrinsic properties of the terms themselves.

Saussure presented this thesis in his *Course in General Linguistics*, a series of lectures collated and published posthumously by his students in 1916. This book provides the kernel of structuralism as a theory of language—although it should be noted that Saussure did not use the term 'structure'; he used the term 'system'. In his *Course*, Saussure defends five key propositions, which we discuss in turn:

1. The sign comprises a signifier and a signified.

2. Signs are arbitrary.

3. Difference creates meaning.

4. Language is to be studied synchronically, not diachronically.

5. The proper focus of linguistics is not speech by individual speakers (termed *parole*) but language as an independent objective system (termed *langue*).

By the *'signifier', Saussure means a sound or image. By the *'signified', he means a concept or mental image to which the signifier refers. Signifier and signified together make up the 'sign'. Between any given signifier and signified, however, there is no necessary relation. Saussure demonstrates the arbitrary character of signs by comparing words with similar meanings across languages, arguing that no particular word is more appropriate than any other in designating a particular idea. He points out that the concept ' "sister" is not linked by any inner relationship to the succession of sounds *s-ö-r* [*sœur*] which serves as its signifier in French' (Saussure 1916: 67). Similarly, 'the signified "ox" has as its signifier *b-ö-f* [*bœuf* in French] on one side of the border and *o-k-s* [*Ochs* in German] on the other' (Saussure 1916: 68). Different societies use words to carve up the world in different ways. For example, different language communities make different categorizations of the colour spectrum; Eskimos have many different words for snow, while Europeans only have one word. Although some words retain partially naturalistic features, such as onomatopoeic words (words which 'sound like' the things they name), these are exceptions; and while many Asian languages retain pictorial elements, the basis of the production of meaning in these languages is not pictorial but relational.

Saussure emphasizes that 'arbitrary' does not imply that individuals can choose any signifier they like. In order to communicate, individuals have to follow the order of signs established in the linguistic communities to which we belong. Speakers must know the rules of language. Saussure comments that 'the signifier, though to all appearances freely chosen with respect to the idea that it represents, is fixed, not free, with respect to the linguistic community that uses it' (Saussure 1916: 71).

The key proposition in Saussure's account is that difference creates meaning. Meaning is a product of internal differences between terms in a language as a system. Saussure states: 'In language there are only differences *without positive terms*' (Saussure 1916: 120). Considered separately, signifier and signified are nothing but negations of other signifiers and signifieds. Only their combination produces a positive fact in the institution of a particular language. Saussure here reserved the French word *langue* for the systematic dimension of language. He distinguished this from the word *parole*, which he reserved for written or spoken language-in-use by individual persons. Saussure maintained that whilst language use only exists in space and time, use of language depends on a set of unstated rules that make language possible. To focus on *langue* was to focus on language as a system of these unstated rules of composition.

Saussure proposes that the relations between linguistic terms form two distinct groups. When we hear someone speak, or when we read something, we have a sequence. This is the

BOX 23. ROLAND BARTHES ON MYTH AND THE 'DEATH OF THE AUTHOR'

The writings of Roland *Barthes provided important statements of structuralist method and played an important role in popularizing structuralist ideas. Barthes applied Saussure's structuralist analysis of language to all sign systems, including images, gestures, and sounds. His early writings show strong similarities with the work of Lévi-Strauss. In his book *Elements of Semiology* (1964), one of Barthes's analysis focuses on the social meanings of eating, treating eating habits and codes in terms of syntagmatic chains. He shows how the arrangement of dishes on a menu is organized along an associative paradigmatic dimension—through basic oppositions between 'savoury' and 'sweet', and so on—while the syntagmatic combination of dishes produces a meal, a linear chain (1964: 27–8).

Barthes was concerned to provide an explicitly critical analysis of bourgeois society. To this end, in his major work *Mythologies* (1957) his observations examine the manner in which advertising operates. Barthes observes how the marketing of detergents is conducted in the language of international conflict, while wine, steak, and fries are portrayed as the 'alimentary sign of Frenchness' (1957: 36–9, 62–4). Barthes here sees semiology as a science of forms that aims to denaturalize myths by exposing the conditions of their production. He writes that 'myth is depoliticized speech' (1957: 142–3). Myth turns historical contingencies into eternal and apparently naturally justified states. Barthes analyses the cover of an issue of the magazine *Paris-Match*, showing a young black man in French army uniform saluting the tricolour. He shows how the image states the fact of French imperialism while operating to convert history into nature (1957: 115, 143). Barthes's aim is to examine the political interests served by such processes of naturalization.

This concern with questioning the function of processes of naturalization and suggesting the possibility of alternative patterns of signification especially clearly in Barthes's essay 'The Death of the Author' (Barthes 1968). Barthes here argues that the author is a distinctly modern figure, one whose function in literary criticism is to provide an explanation and delimitation of the meaning of a text. He contends that 'linguistically, the author is never more than the instance of writing, just as *I* is nothing other than the instance of saying *I*' (1968: 145). Barthes attacks cultural institutions that maintain control over the meaning of literary texts through recourse to the author as explanation. In place of this, he looks for the possibility of new interpretations of texts that might be produced by overthrowing the myth of *origins* entailed by the idea of the author. Barthes proclaims that the 'birth of the reader must be at the cost of the death of the Author' (1968: 148).

We can see here how *subjectivity and authorial voice in structuralist and post-structuralist thinking are not regarded as given but as organized through the *totality of language. Subjectivity is predicated on differences in linguistic and semiotic structures. Speakers and agents gain access to themselves and their identities as persons only through the institutionalized totality of language. This is at the root of the characteristic anti-humanism of structuralist and post-structuralist theory, where 'anti-humanism' refers to an antipathy toward *phenomenological and *hermeneutical ideas of the meaning-conferring powers of individual human agents.

empirically observable form of language which Saussure calls its *syntagmatic* dimension, characteristic of *parole*. A syntagm is formed by two or more consecutive units supported by linearity, by a line of some kind. Phrases and sentences are examples of syntagms. Within syntagmatic chains, terms gain value through their linear relation to others that are present. Such chains are distinct from what Saussure calls the associative or *paradigmatic* dimension of language, characteristic of *langue*. Associative relations are not supported by linearity.

They develop outside the context of spoken utterances or written statements by an individual. Unlike the syntagmatic dimension present in *parole*, the associative dimension unites terms 'in absentia' (Saussure 1916: 123). This associative dimension of *langue* forms a background of meaning, making up the 'inner storehouse' of the language spoken by each speaker (Saussure 1916: 123).

Among the more general ideas bequeathed by Saussure to social and cultural theory is his conception of the primacy of the whole over the parts. His model of *langue* is that of an 'absent totality' which does not itself exist in space or time. The *totality is instantiated in speech and writing, yet is only discernible beyond any individual act of speaking or writing. This idea shares something in common with Émile Durkheim's conception of the social as a '*sui generis* reality' that is more than the sum of its parts. It was to prove important later to both structuralist and post-structuralist theorists, including notably to Derrida and Foucault, as we shall see shortly. A further influential element of Saussure's account is that it does not see language merely as a means of expression or *instrument* of a speaking subject. Rather, it conceives language as the structuring precondition of thought, which stands beyond the mental agency of any individual speaking subject. Language is not seen as something merely at the disposal of an individual person. On the contrary, the subject is seen as in a certain sense at the *disposal of language*. This idea later came to be associated with the theme of the 'decentring of the *subject' in French structuralist and post-structuralist thought. The theme is especially prominent in the thinking of Derrida and Foucault, but it is also present in the literary criticism of Roland Barthes, who famously spoke of the 'death of the author'. Barthes's contributions to the study of myth and popular culture from a structuralist perspective are discussed here in Box 23.

Saussure's work was exclusively in the field of linguistics, but it became central to structuralism in social and cultural theory through the work of writers such as Barthes and Lévi-Strauss. It is to Lévi-Strauss's work that we turn next.

Structuralism in anthropology: Claude Lévi-Strauss

Claude *Lévi-Strauss was the first author to disseminate the term 'structuralism' and to import Saussure's linguistic insights into social science. He made important contributions to the study of kinship rules, primitive classification systems, *totemism, myth, music, and art. In each of these fields, he applied the methods of structural linguistics to social systems, aiming to uncover the universal rules underpinning the apparent diversity of social and cultural life.

The initial formative influences on Lévi-Strauss were Durkheim and Durkheim's nephew Marcel *Mauss. In particular, Lévi-Strauss drew on Durkheim's precept that social order forms a coherent system comprising subsystems, and that social facts precede the individual and give structure to individuality. Lévi-Strauss also drew on Mauss's (1924) account of the role of gift exchange in archaic societies, where exchange establishes *reciprocity* (see Lévi-Strauss 1950). But it was the Russian linguist Roman Jakobson who introduced Lévi-Strauss to the work of Saussure in New York during the Second World War. Most of Lévi-Strauss's anthropological fieldwork is based on studies of the tribes of Amazonian

South America. His major works are *The Elementary Structures of Kinship* (1949), *Tristes Tropiques* (1955), *Structural Anthropology* (1958), *The Raw and the Cooked* (1964), and *The Savage Mind* (1966).

Lévi-Strauss described structural linguistics as effecting a 'Copernican revolution' in anthropology and the human sciences in general. He wrote that 'first, structural linguistics shifts from the study of *conscious* linguistic phenomena to the study of their *unconscious* infrastructure; second, it does not treat *terms* as independent entities, taking instead as its basis of analysis the *relations* between terms; third, it introduces the concept of *system* ... finally, structural linguistics aims at discovering *general laws*' (1958: 83, 33, emphasis in original). These methodological tenets were to become central to Lévi-Strauss's way of proceeding. We can illustrate them by looking at his work on kinship systems and at an example from his study of myth.

In *The Elementary Structures of Kinship* (1949) Lévi-Strauss analyses what he sees as certain fundamental laws of exchange underpinning systems of kinship. He observes that all societies have restrictions concerning appropriate sexual partners, but that these restrictions vary and that the ways in which they are enforced also vary. He then searches for the underlying structures governing marriage relations that divide members into two categories, prohibited partners and possible partners. He argues that this basic *binary opposition is a product of the universality of the incest taboo and the accompanying rule of exogamous (non-blood-related) marriage. In other words, marriage is misunderstood if it is thought of purely as an individualized relation between two persons. Marriage is rather a fundamental form of exchange, which grounds human sociality. This law of exogamy is 'omnipresent'; it is 'the archetype of all other manifestations based on reciprocity, and ... it provides the fundamental and immutable rule ensuring the existence of the group as a group' (1949: 481). This is because exogamy 'provides the means of binding men together'. It superimposes on natural links of kinship artificial links of 'alliance governed by rule' (1949: 480). Lévi-Strauss comments that 'the prohibition of incest is less a rule prohibiting marriage with the mother, sister or daughter, than a rule obliging the mother, sister or daughter to be given to others. It is the supreme rule of the gift, and it is clearly this aspect ... which allows its nature to be understood' (1949: 481).

Marriage rules concerning the exchange of women generate a system of alliances and interdependencies that enable the social group to reproduce itself. Marriage for Lévi-Strauss is thus a fundamental form of exchange that upholds institutionalized relations between groups. He compares kinship to a linguistic system: 'like a phoneme, a device having no meaning of its own but helping to form meanings, the incest taboo struck me as a link between two domains' (1983: 142). Lévi-Strauss means the domains of *nature* and *culture*. The incest prohibition and exogamy are necessary to lift human beings out of biological relations into social relations. Lévi-Strauss comments that the prohibition of incest is '*the* prohibition'. It is as universal as language (1949: 493). Lévi-Strauss seeks to determine the laws underlying different systems of marriage by examining relations between elements as part of a system. His aim is to examine the unconscious activity of the mind that consists in imposing 'form' on 'content', or shape on matter (1958: 21).

This structuralist aspect of Lévi-Strauss's analysis can be clarified further with an example from his work on myth. Lévi-Strauss observes that myths have a storyline, or syntagmatic dimension. But he argues that to understand a myth, we need to examine the structural oppositions that it embodies, such as between 'nature' and 'culture', or between time and space, or between the 'raw' and the 'cooked'– food found in the wilderness and food prepared by the hands of man. He suggests that we read a myth as we read a musical score, both *diachronically along one axis and *synchronically along another. Read in this manner, a musical score ceases to be a simple succession of notes; it forms a meaningful whole (1958: 212). Using this model, he argues that individual elements of a myth taken in isolation are meaningless. Their meaning is to be found in the ways in which they are brought into relation and ordered as a totality. In a similar manner to Saussure, Lévi-Strauss insists on examining myth through the totality of the system of oppositional relations that compose it (1958: 210). Indeed he argues not only that myth is structured 'like language' but that myth *is* language. Myth gives symbolic expression to unconscious aspirations. It express properties of the human mind, and studying these properties allows us to understand the structural oppositions that operate in the human unconscious.

In a similar manner to Jacques *Lacan's structuralist psychoanalysis, Lévi-Strauss analyses the ancient Greek myth of Oedipus: the story of the exiled young boy condemned by prophecy to murder his father and sleep with his mother. Lévi-Strauss proposes that the Oedipus myth is constructed through a series of recurring oppositions between the underrating and overrating of blood relations. These antitheses build a series of transformations as the story progresses, so that the whole story constitutes an attempt to mediate between 'nature' and 'culture'. It is an attempt to resolve the contradiction between the belief that man is autochthonous (born of one principle, born of the earth—represented by Oedipus on his own, in exile) and knowledge that humans are the result of union between man and woman (born of two different parents, one male, one female—represented by Oedipus in the family). The myth is a way of attempting to manage conflict about where humans come from, about the origins of man (1958: 213–16).

From this brief discussion we can see that Lévi-Strauss conceives of cultures and their myths as totalities ordered through differences between terms. Structural anthropology aims to dig beneath the variety of human experience in order to uncover certain putatively universal laws governing human sociality and unconscious life. Lévi-Strauss does not attempt to search for the earliest version of a particular myth, for its 'origin'. Rather, he regards a myth as consisting in all its manifold versions. The key concern lies not with the origin but with symbolic order, and with how symbolic order is structured. As with Saussure, Lévi-Strauss's concern is not with tracing the history of our concepts and categories in order to reveal the most 'primitive' or 'authentic' form. What Lévi-Strauss calls the 'savage mind' is not more primitive or originary than the Western mind. In his view, essentially the same basic logical structures can be found among all human groups. Thus, instead of searching for the most ancient or original or authentic, Lévi-Strauss and Saussure enjoin us to look for the logical totality through which any individual elements of culture gain their meaning and validity.

Difference and deconstruction: Jacques Derrida

Jacques *Derrida is regarded as the first French theorist to pioneer a turn away from structuralism in the classical sense toward what has come to be called 'post-structuralism', which can also be thought of as a kind of radicalization of structuralism. Derrida's numerous books from the 1960s to the present day include *Of Grammatology* (1967), *Writing and Difference* (1968*a*), *Margins of Philosophy* (1972), *Glas* (1974), *Acts of Literature* (1992), and a spate of books since the 1990s treating more ethical and political themes, notably including *Spectres of Marx* (1993) and *The Politics of Friendship* (1994). Here we concentrate on two of Derrida's earliest texts: first, his book *Of Grammatology* (1967), in which he expatiates on the work of Saussure and Lévi-Strauss; and second, his essay 'Structure, Sign, and Play in the Discourse of the Human Sciences', reprinted in *Writing and Difference*. In this essay Derrida analyses what he sees as structuralism's continued reliance on Western philosophical *metaphysics. It is in this essay and some other early pieces that Derrida introduces his influential concepts of 'difference', *'deconstruction', 'decentring', and *'logocentrism'.

Speech, writing, and logocentrism

In *Of Grammatology*, Derrida considers a chapter of Lévi-Strauss's book *Tristes Tropiques*, titled 'A Writing Lesson' (Lévi-Strauss 1955). Lévi-Strauss here describes an encounter with the Nambikwara tribe, who had watched the Frenchman writing notes and then began making lines on paper themselves. Lévi-Strauss reports that in addition to making marks on the paper, the chief of the tribe attempted to augment his authority by pretending to read back to his fellow tribesmen from his own script. Reflecting on this, Lévi-Strauss experiences guilt. Lévi-Strauss blames himself for destroying the innocence of the Nambikwara by introducing them to writing. He suggests that writing allies itself with falsehood, violence, and exploitation (Lévi-Strauss 1955: 298 ff.).

Derrida sees this feeling of guilt in Lévi-Strauss about introducing the Nambikwara to writing as revealing an inconsistency in Lévi-Strauss's own thesis about the meaningless-ness of 'origins'. Derrida treats this as a powerful example of the manner in which the West has treated writing as a *secondary* transcription of speech, as something that corrupts the innocence and non-violence of oral communication. Against Lévi-Strauss's Western image of writing, Derrida stresses that 'violence does not supervene from without upon an inno-cent language in order to supervise it' (1967: 106). Rather, Derrida points to the 'originary violence of a language which is already a writing', the violence of difference and of classifi-cation itself (1967: 106). That is, words and names *themselves* differentiate—not just writ-ing. Therefore the absence of writing is not equal to 'innocence'. Derrida detects in Lévi-Strauss an 'ethic of presence, an ethic of nostalgia for origins, an ethic of archaic and natural innocence, a purity of presence and self-presence in speech' (1968*b*: 264).

The focus of Derrida's comments in *Of Grammatology* is a phenomenon much larger than Lévi-Strauss's anthropology. Derrida in fact raises claims against the whole history of Western metaphysics for what he calls its 'logocentrism' and 'phonocentrism'. Derrida's term 'logocentrism' derives from the Greek word *logos*, meaning both 'reason' and 'speech'. According to Derrida, Western philosophy since Plato has been logocentric in the sense that it has thought of concepts as existing as 'pure intelligibility', prior to their means of expression in the 'outer' structures of language, or *langue*. Derrida argues that Western *metaphysics has viewed meaning as having essential priority over its form of communica-tion, such as through writing. *Parole*, in the sense of 'inner speech' or 'inner thought', has been seen as essentially preceding *langue*. Derrida's other term 'phonocentrism' refers to what he sees as Western philosophy's privileging of speech over writing (from the Greek word for 'voice' or 'sound', *phonē*). Speech in Western culture has been regarded as a capacity immediately available to a self-present subject, such that writing becomes derivative, a mere transcription of speech.

The importance of these concepts becomes clear when we consider that Derrida's concern is to deconstruct Western metaphysics from within. Against logocentrism and phonocentrism, Derrida develops what he calls 'deconstructive' writing. Deconstruction is a form of criticism that operates through close readings of texts in order to pull apart their internal logic and destabilize their self-presence. Its aim is to reveal that which is assumed but repressed by the dominant frame of a text. Thus in *Of Grammatology*, Derrida examines Saussure's work to disclose what it cannot describe—what has been excluded in order that the text be constituted as it is.

A key step in Derrida's proposal for deconstruction concerns what he sees as a rather problematic aspect of Saussure's distinction between 'signifier' and 'signified'. Derrida sees this as a metaphysical distinction: a distinction between something regarded as essentially sensuous or sensible (the signifier) and something regarded as essentially non-sensuous and ideal or intelligible (the signified). The sensible is said to be exterior to a principle of interior 'pure intelligibility'. The sensible constitutes merely an 'outside' in relation to an 'inside'. According to Derrida, Saussure's linguistics—and classical structuralism more generally—remains caught in metaphysics insofar as it relies on what Derrida calls a 'transcendental signifier', an idea of pure intelligibility, which is expected to function as the origin of all meaning. Derrida highlights the way in which Saussure treats writing as derivative from, and possibly corrupting of, speech. He quotes Saussure's comment that 'language and writing are two distinct systems of signs; the second exists for the sole purpose of representing the first' (Saussure in Derrida 1967: 30). Derrida comments that this attributes to writing 'the exteriority that one attributes to utensils' (1967: 34). Derrida argues that despite Saussure's conception of *langue* as an 'absent totality', Saussure views spoken language as achieving full self-presence. Derrida argues that in this conception the exteriority of writing threatens to contaminate language by producing an 'eruption of the *outside* within the *inside*' (1967: 34), breaching the apparent self-presence of speech. The intrusion of writing into the self-presence of speech threatens this self-presence by a logic of the 'supplement'. In Derrida's view, Saussure wishes to place writing in an 'intra-linguistic leper colony' to contain the deformations it may produce (1967: 42).

It is in this general sense that Derrida declares famously, and provocatively, that 'there is nothing outside the text', or 'no outside-text' (*il n'y a pas de hors-texte*) (1967: 158). Derrida implies that there can be neither a master speaking subject which precedes any act of writing, nor any pure or natural 'external world' which stands outside the structuring effects of writing as they are played out in texts. Ideas of 'pure mind' and 'pure world', the 'subjective' and the 'objective', the 'ideal' and the 'real', are metaphysical effects of the play of language and writing.

Difference, decentring, and the deconstruction of the subject

In 'Structure, Sign and Play in the Discourse of the Human Sciences' (1968*b*) Derrida points to a recent 'event' or 'rupture' in the history of the concept of structure. He asserts that 'the history of metaphysics ... is the determination of being as *presence* in all the senses of this word' (1968*b*: 249). He points out the impossibility of thinking the concept of structure without a *centre*. The centre refers to 'a point of presence, a fixed origin' that organizes and delimits the free play of the structure, and yet is 'paradoxically, *within* the structure and *outside* it' (1968*b*: 247–8). That is, the centre is simultaneously the thing within a structure that governs the structure's structurality *and* that which escapes structurality. 'The center is at the center of the totality, and yet, since the center does not belong to the totality (is not part of the totality), the totality *has its center elsewhere*' (1968*b*: 248).

Derrida's thinking about the centre can be illustrated in several ways. We might think of the centre as the self, as the ego which arranges the world around itself in its conscious thoughts. But from a psychoanalytic point of view, the centre is not the conscious self. The self finds itself 'decentred' in relation to the unconscious. The centre appears to lie elsewhere, other to the self; it is that on which the self is dependent, and therefore is not the self's 'own'. The centre turns out to be not 'I' but 'It': the unconscious life of desire, or what Sigmund *Freud called the id. In an often quoted phrase of the nineteenth-century French Symbolist poet Arthur Rimbaud, '*Je est un autre*'—'I is an other'. Or as Freud wrote, equally famously: '*Wo Es war, entsteht das Ich*'—'Where id was, there ego shall be' (Freud, 1933: 112). We may also think of the concept of decentring as it has developed in postcolonial theory, notably among writers such as Edward *Said (1978) and Gayatri *Spivak (1999). The West has historically regarded itself as the centre—of Culture, Civilization, Rationality—but in order to constitute itself as the centre, the West has required an 'Other' which is apparently not the centre. And to the extent that the West depends on this Other in order to be a centre, the West is *not* the centre but is 'decentred'. Both these examples attest to Derrida's wide-ranging influence in cultural theory and criticism.

A further step in Derrida's argument concerns his reading of the idea of 'difference'. The significance of writing for Derrida is that it is not a transparent means of representation but a material process governed by a logic of *différance*, a word he deliberately misspells in French with an 'a'. The concept of *différance* is drawn from the French verb *différer,* meaning both 'to differ' and 'to defer', which becomes *différant* in the French present participle. Derrida argues that Western philosophy's logocentrism depends on a repressed logic of *différance*. Against the assumption that signifier and signified form a transparent and self-sustaining unity, he stresses that meaning has no point of origin. Meaning is always already transitional, deferred through endless chains of signifiers. This focus on a never-ending process of *différance* unsettles the *binary logic of structuralism. It also shows that binary oppositions are typically hierarchical, that one element is typically dominant, but that this hierarchical opposition is necessarily unstable since the meaning of each of the terms depends on the 'trace' of the other. We may think of the binary pairs male–female, mind–body, conscious–unconscious, nature–culture, presence–absence, and so on.

These aspects of Derrida's thought illustrate his movement beyond classical structuralism. Where Saussure and Lévi-Strauss tend to conceive of language and myth as closed semiotic systems, Derrida refuses this. Against any idea of the self-sufficiency of signifier and signified, Derrida stresses *différance*, 'supplementarity', and the 'trace'. He not only asserts that difference creates meaning but also that this chain of signification extends 'ad infinitum' (1968*b*: 249), resulting in no closure. Furthermore, Derrida understands difference as both spatial and temporal, as extending in a temporal process of deferring, so that signification occurs only through 'traces', through moments of difference in an endless chain of signification. Derrida abandons structuralism's distinction between the diachronic and synchronic in favour of an argument that there can be no final reading of a text. Any reading always generates a supplementary one. In this sense, any remedy to a deficiency is always a supplement which generates a further deficiency. Therefore there can be neither beginning nor end, no centre or point of presence or 'fixed origin'.

Yet while Derrida believes structuralism to be problematically complicit with the history of Western metaphysics, he does not simply proclaim the bankruptcy or 'end' of metaphysics. He emphasizes that 'there is no sense in doing without the concepts of metaphysics in order to attack metaphysics. We have no language—no syntax and no lexicon—which is alien to this history' (1968b: 250). He stresses that deconstruction presupposes the tradition that it at the same time contests and unravels.

In general, Derrida's vision of deconstruction seeks critically to radicalize structuralism's questioning of the idea of the centred autonomous human *subject. Derrida declares that he does not 'destroy' the subject but that he 'situates' it (1968b: 271). Against the 'metaphysics of presence', he proposes a *'Nietzschean affirmation . . . of the freeplay of the world without truth, without origin, offered to an active interpretation' (1968b: 264). His philosophy 'affirms freeplay and tries to pass beyond man and *humanism, the name 'man' being the name of that being who, throughout the history of metaphysics or of onto-theology—in other words, through the history of all of his history—has dreamed of full presence, the reassuring foundation, the origin and the end of the game' (1968b: 264–5).

This concern to 'decentre' and to 'situate' the subject is also key to the work of Michel Foucault. It is to Foucault's work that we now turn.

Discourse, knowledge, and power: Michel Foucault

Michel Foucault first came to prominence in Parisian intellectual life in the early 1960s with a work titled *Madness and Civilization* (1961). This was a study of the rise of modern medical institutions and discourses oriented to the scientific categorization and incarceration of deviant individuals as clinically insane. In Foucault's thesis, this development signalled the breakdown of an earlier medieval world-view marked by the unregulated anarchic presence of fools in the community, as well as by religious languages of possession by the devil and spirits.

After *Madness and Civilization* Foucault's reflections turned to the role of power, knowledge, and discourse in Western civilization, including the role of criminology, psychology, prisons, surveillance, discipline, education, and the state and the role of scientific institutions in definitions of the human person, especially concerning. His major works are *The Order of Things* (1966), *The Archaeology of Knowledge* (1969a), *Discipline and Punish* (1975), and *The History of Sexuality* (1976, 1984a, 1984b) (in three volumes). His writings have had an enormous impact in contemporary cultural and social research—from philosophy, literature, and the history of ideas to criminology, education, political theory, psychoanalysis, *postcolonial studies, and feminist theory. A homosexual, Foucault died of AIDS in California in 1984.

Together with Derrida, Foucault always rejected the label 'structuralist' and 'post-structuralist' as a description of his work (1966: p. xiv). Like Derrida, Foucault tended to proclaim that structuralism is characteristic of a system of thought that is about to be overcome. Nonetheless, certain features of his thinking mark it out as 'structuralist' in orientation. In the following discussion we look first at what Foucault describes as the 'archaeological' approach of the two major works of his middle period, *The Order of Things* (1966) and *The Archaeology of Knowledge* (1969a). Then we look at what he describes as the more 'genealogical' orientation of his later work on sexuality and subjectivity.

'Epistemes', discursive practices, and the 'end of man'

In *The Archaeology of Knowledge* Foucault describes his work as an attempt to reveal 'a positive unconscious of knowledge: a level that eludes the consciousness of the scientist and yet is part of scientific discourse' (1969a: p. xi). His aim is to discover 'on the basis of what historical *a priori*' (1969a: p. xxii) forms of knowledge become possible. That is, Foucault aims to analyse the epistemological preconditions for systems of thought and classification from a radically historical point of view. He describes his book as an 'archaeology' whose focus is the 'episteme'.

By 'archaeology' Foucault means the study of the rules of formation of discourse in any given epoch. It is the attempt to discern the historical conditions of possibility of forms of knowledge. Foucault uses the term 'episteme' to signify such rules of formation. By 'episteme', he means 'the total set of relations that unite, at a given period, the *discursive practices that give rise to *epistemological figures, sciences, and possibly formalised systems . . ., the totality of relations that can be discovered, for a given period, between the sciences when one analyses them at the level of discursive regularities' (1969a: 191). Archaeological analysis is addressed 'to the general space of knowledge', to 'the mode of being of things that appear in it', to 'systems of simultaneity', and to 'mutations' that form the threshold of new systems and epochs (1969a: p. xxiii). Foucault argues that the present order, the episteme from within which we think today, 'does not have the same mode of being as that of the Classical thinkers' of the seventeenth and eighteenth centuries in Europe (1969a: p. xxii). This difference is not, for Foucault, the result of progress, but rather of the way in which conditions of possibility of knowledge have altered.

The Order of Things is concerned with mapping the history of systems of classification. Foucault proceeds by considering what was common to the organization of the disciplines of natural history, economics, and linguistics in three successive periods. He argues that Renaissance science was characterized by relations of *resemblance*. What he calls the 'Classical' period (the seventeenth and eighteenth centuries) was characterized by systems of *representation*. What he defines as the 'modern' period (from the nineteenth century onwards) has been characterized by the *'positivities' of life, work, and language. Foucault argues that within each of these periods, different fields of study use the same rules of formation to define their objects. The three successive epochs are characterized by different rules for the formation of concepts and theories (1966: p. xxii).

Referring to the history of linguistics, Foucault comments on the way in which, from the nineteenth century onwards, the idea of a fundamental link between schemes of representation and things of the world was eclipsed by a 'profound historicity' (1966: p. xxiii). In particular, Foucault notes that with the abandonment of systems of naturalistic representation at the end of the eighteenth century, the idea of the expressive *humanistic subject* entered the scene of Western history. Foucault declares that before the end of the eighteenth century '*man* did not exist' (1966: 308). That is, the idea of man as such, as an epistemological category, is an invention of the *Enlightenment. Foucault proclaims that today this idea of 'man' has grown old and is coming to an end. This 'rift in the order of things', the 'new wrinkle in our knowledge' (1966: p. xxiii)', has produced the double bind of philosophical humanism. That is, since the end of the eighteenth century, the quest to disclose the nature of man through the development of philosophical anthropology has produced a situation in which humans have been interpreted simultaneously as knowing subjects and as known objects of their own knowledge. Thus the category 'man' designates what Foucault calls a 'transcendental-empirical double', where 'man' is seen both as the prime agent within the world (an empirical *object*) and as the prime 'condition of possibility' for the existence of the world (a transcendental *subject*). According to Foucault, this doubling ties the development of social institutions to processes of objectification and to forms of disciplinary discursive power under the rule of the 'human sciences'.

Foucault considers that modernity needs to be wakened from 'anthropological slumber' (1966: 340). He looks for a method of historical analysis free from the assumptions of philosophical anthropology (1969*a*: 16). He rejects *phenomenology and *hermeneutics, claiming that instead of a theory of the knowing subject, what is necessary is a theory of *discursive practices* (1966: p. xiv). This leads Foucault to reverse traditional questions of *subjectivity and *agency. In his essay 'What is an Author?' (1969*b*) he asks: 'How, under what conditions, and in what forms can something like a subject appear in the order of discourse?' (1969*b*: 118). Foucault suggests re-examining the functions of the subject by 'depriving the subject (or its substitute) of its role as originator and analysing the subject as a variable and complex function of discourse' (1969*b*: 118).

While Foucault does not rely on Saussure's structural linguistics to make this case, his thinking in *The Order of Things* is guided by a typically structuralist commitment to the idea of the autonomy of discourse. What is striking is his conception of the structural determination of epochs by overarching *epistemic principles. Foucault argues that the systems of statements that are possible in an episteme form a totality, and he suggests that the shift from one episteme to another takes the form of an epistemological leap. This is comparable in certain ways to Thomas *Kuhn's conception of abrupt shifts between incommensurable *'paradigms' in the history of science (discussed in Chapter 5 of this book, pp. 123–4). It is in this sense that Foucault speaks of three successive 'epochs' in *The Order of Things*, each organized according to radically distinct epistemic criteria. Like Saussure's linguistics and Lévi-Strauss's anthropology, Foucault here operates with a purely differential and nominalist account of meaning. His mode of analysis deliberately brackets questions of propositional truth in order to analyse the internal ordering of systems of statements. Foucault searches for the rules that underpin formations of discourse in each of the three epochs he analyses, deliberately avoiding engaging with the questions of truth and meaning raised by them. The archaeologist tries to produce a pure description of an episteme.

Genealogy, subjectivity, and power-knowledge

After *The Order of Things* and *The Archaeology of Knowledge*, Foucault changed his mode of investigation. While still using the tools of 'archaeology', his later work turned to more specific accounts of the ways in which human beings become subjects of particular kinds of knowledge and practice. Foucault here moved away from the concept of episteme to the concept of 'apparatus' or 'dispositive' (*dispositif*).

Foucault saw a problem with the concept of the episteme in his earlier work. He had spoken of the episteme both as grounding configurations of discourse and as being grounded *by* configurations of discourse. It signified the totality of the discursive regularities of an epoch, and at the same time it signified the preconditions or *a priori rules of formation of knowledge in an epoch. The concept of the episteme was thus rather circular. It tended to be closed to the role of non-discursive material factors in the constitution of discourses. Recognition of this problem led Foucault to reconceptualize the relationship of discourse more explicitly to the role of material practices and social institutions. Foucault describes this shift in terms of a move from archaeology to *genealogy*, where the episteme is replaced by the concept of the 'apparatus' or 'dispositive'. Foucault now abandons his commitment to the autonomy of discourse. He notes that 'the episteme is a specifically discursive apparatus, whereas the apparatus (*dispositif*) in its general form is both discursive and non-discursive, its elements being much more heterogenous' (1980: 196–7).

The notion of dispositive involves a recognition that discourses and practices are multiple and varied, that no one overarching totality exists under which all discourse can be said to serve. Foucault thus explores ways in which discourses and practices articulate each other to form different 'regimes of knowledge' (Foucault in Dreyfus and Rabinow 1982: 212). The task of genealogy is to locate and uncover particular sets of relations in which specific aspects of modern subjectivity are constituted by mapping significant relations within these diverse practices. Foucault is directly interested in questions of power and in the relation of 'power-knowledge' (*pouvoir savoir*) to what he calls the 'politics of truth'. Foucault characterizes genealogy as providing an 'historical *ontology of ourselves' (1984*c*: 45), a 'history of the present' (1976: 31). This he contrasts with conventional historical writing. Where the latter claims to study that which is distant from us in the name of objectivity, genealogy examines what is closest, but in an 'abrupt dispossession, so as to seize it at a distance' (1984*d*: 89). Foucault's genealogies begin with the present, not in order to affirm the present or to deny the present but rather in order to interrogate how the present has come to be constituted as it is. The aim is to unseat the naturalness of dominant ways in which aspects of our lives are thought about and acted upon, to 're-problematize'. Foucault examines how specific aspects of experience become figured as objects of knowledge and as sites of practical intervention. He asks how our forms of knowledge and reasoning are tied to the exercise of institutional power, and questions the limits and costs that such institutions impose.

In his later work, Foucault pursues two basic concerns. The first relates to the significance of discipline, punishment, surveillance, and what Foucault calls 'biopower'. This is discussed in Box 24. The second relates to the history of human sexuality, to which we turn next.

BOX 24. MICHEL FOUCAULT ON SURVEILLANCE, BIOPOWER, AND THE
PANOPTICON

During the 1970s Foucault studied the formation of the human subject through a series of substantive enquiries into the relationship between power and the growth of mental and physical capacities. These are laid out chiefly in his books *Discipline and Punish* (1975) and *The History of Sexuality*, volume 1 (1976). Foucault argues that power and knowledge are mutually productive in the constitution of human beings as specific sorts of subjects. He considers the entwinement of power and knowledge in specific sites, especially in discourses of sexuality and in mechanisms of punishment.

Foucault suggests three major sets of practices that constitute subjects: (1) practices of division, (2) practices of scientific classification, and (3) practices of subjectification. In relation to 'dividing practices', Foucault investigates various historical examples of schemes of binary oppositions between people. For example, he examines the exclusion of lepers from medieval and ancient cities. He contrasts the marginalization of lepers, their separation and rejection into the wilderness, with the quarantining of plague victims. Unlike lepers, the plague victims were confined and subject to supervision, as part of a positive attempt to preserve the health of the community (1975: 198–9). In relation to scientific classification practices, Foucault considers the emergence of scientific categories and practices that assign and distribute individuals to definite positions within a population. In this way, all members of a population become subject to 'constant surveillance' each 'in an individual way', through institutional expertise (1975: 199). In relation to subjectification practices, Foucault discusses the ways in which individuals turn themselves into subjects. This concerns how individuals come to act on themselves through such practices as religious confession, psychoanalysis, or sex therapy.

Foucault sums up these three lines of approach in the idea of 'biopolitics'. 'Biopolitics' refers to the general form or rationality of modern power. 'Biopower' is 'power over life' (1976: 143). It is a secularization of the Christian concern with the pastoral relationship, a relationship in which certain individuals, by virtue of their special qualities—such as closeness to God or possession of scientific expertise—can lead others to salvation. Biopower combines two axes. One axis is centred on the individual body as a machine to be made useful through discipline. Foucault speaks of an 'anatomo-politics of the human body'. The other axis is focused on the supervision and regulation of the body of the species. Foucault speaks of a 'biopolitics of the population' (1976: 139). These two axes of power produce new possibilities of knowledge, involving close institutional examination of individual case histories and the development of statistics relating to demographic patterns. Foucault argues that such individualizing and totalizing forms of knowledge operate through confessional technologies as institutional sites for the emergence of new 'sciences of man'. What is distinctive about biopower is that it exhibits a concern with enhancing life. It is bound up with the development of the modern state in its attempt to manage and enhance its strength. The state has a definite interest in the health of the population, in the management of sexuality and human reproduction, and in the maintenance of 'normalcy' and the elimination of disease and 'disability'. Medicine and psychiatry, therapy and surgery, in all senses of these words, become key to the control and maintenance of a norm of societal well-being.

In *Discipline and Punish* Foucault elaborates these ideas in relation to Jeremy *Bentham's eighteenth-century *utilitarian conception of the 'Panopticon'. The Panopticon was Bentham's design for a new type of prison in which individual cells radiate out from a central tower. In Bentham's plan, each cell was to house one inmate who is permanently visible to the guard in the central tower. The intended effect was that each prisoner would not be able to tell whether he or she was being observed at any one moment. Each prisoner would therefore become *self-policing*. Foucault observes that abstract

_____ continues

BOX 24 continued

techniques of power here combine with techniques for the control, supervision, and correction of specific individuals. Power is linked to the formation of personal capacities and to the training of individuals. These techniques develop in localized institutions with specific concerns, such as in control of the factory workforce, punishment of prisoners, and disciplining of children in schools. Such institutions function as observatories of individual behaviour and performance, as laboratories determining the development of practices of correction and reform. Foucault suggests that such institutionalized techniques make possible a certain kind of knowledge of the individual based on norms and 'normality'. This knowledge is gained by techniques of examination. It is one of the peculiarly demonic features of modern societies that such techniques are organized simultaneously through scientific laws and through the operation of normalizing judgements (see also Foucault 1980). Foucault's conception of discipline and surveillance can be compared in some ways with Erving *Eoffman's work on stigma and 'total institutions' (discussed in Chapter 5 of this book, p. 117)

In his last series of works, his three-volume *The History of Sexuality* (1976–84), Foucault examines how a science of sexuality began to develop in Western culture from the late eighteenth century onwards. He shows how this science of sexuality sought to join the individual and social bodies together and thereby to provide a new vector of power over life. In volume 1, devoted to the modern era, Foucault attacks what he calls the 'repressive hypothesis' (Foucault 1976). With this phrase Foucault refers to an assumption that power necessarily acts on sexuality through a repression of 'natural instincts'. The assumption suggests that a 'Victorian' era of repression has gradually been replaced by a new era of 'sexual liberation'. Although he mentions no names, it is possible to see Foucault's target here as being at least partly in the attempts of *Frankfurt School theorists such as Herbert *Marcuse and Erich *Fromm to synthesize Freud with Marx in an idea of liberation from repressive control. In general, Foucault is sceptical of the idea that modern enlightened knowledge about sex necessarily emancipates human societies from the repressive superstitions of traditional religious teaching about the sins of the flesh. Instead Foucault suggests that modern 'sexual science' is no less bound up with forms of power than traditional religious ideas of the body. Foucault argues that power is exercised through the production of, and incitement to, discourse about sex and sexuality. Discourses on sexuality produce new mechanisms of power by constituting subjects who understand themselves in terms of the truth of their sex. A proliferation of discourses on sexuality pins us to telling the 'truth of ourselves', of our 'private' 'secret' nature. This, Foucault argues, constitutes not a freedom from subjection but rather the development of new forms of subjection. A new 'technology of sex', constituted through medicine, psychiatry, pedagogy, and psychoanalysis, has become a key element of modern institutional power (1976: 116). Through it, individuals come to think of themselves and their desires in relation to scientific notions of normality. A modern *scientia sexualis* replaces more ancient ideas of the *ars erotica* or 'art of love'.

Foucault's concern in this volume and in volumes 2 and 3 of *The History of Sexuality* (1984*a*, 1984*b*) is to denaturalize certain deep-seated assumptions of modern Western culture. His aim is to re-problematize a dominant problematization, to disturb its naturalness, to shake its hold over us and to open spaces for thinking and acting differently. In this project we can see that while one of his early aims was to overcome structuralism, his later arguments and methods still reflect some of its characteristic principles. In his middle-period writings, Foucault asserted that structuralism and *phenomenology share common ground, rather than being opposites to each other. He maintained that structuralist formalization and *hermeneutic interpretation represent 'two correlative techniques' of the modern human sciences, the one being to discover structural invariants, the other being to discover hidden meanings (1966*a*: 299). Foucault saw structuralism together with phenomenology as destined to reinstate the 'transcendental-empirical doubling' of modern *anthropocentric culture. But we can see that Foucault's own work in genealogy exhibits some notable theoretical continuities with structuralism and hermeneutical phenomenology. These especially concern his account of how the human subject is constituted as an object of knowledge. In his concern to contest fixity and to suggest the possibility of our becoming otherwise than we are, Foucault continued to share with Saussure, Lévi-Strauss, Lacan, and Derrida a refusal to search for 'origins' in order to concentrate on symbolic structures and regimes of discourse. In line with structuralist and post-structuralist thinking, Foucault continued to treat the human subject not as a given or as a repository of meaning, but as an effect of discourse. In his thesis, 'man' as such emerges only with the *Enlightenment. Modern 'humanity' brings with itself a specific predicament that Foucault sees as tying us ever more closely to the truth of ourselves as a relation of power.

Conclusion

French structuralist and post-structuralist theory has been as influential in the human sciences as it is controversial in its attribution to particular thinkers. This chapter has sought to avoid suggesting any straightforward chronological transition from structuralism to post-structuralism in French thought. Such academic labelling tends to place more investment in the packaging of thought than it does in examining the salience of ideas. Post-structuralism cannot be understood either as a simple negation of structuralism or as some form of repeat of it. If anything, it is perhaps best thought of as a qualified radicalization of structuralism.

In considering the work of Saussure and Lévi-Strauss, we have seen the importance of the idea that language should be studied as a totality, where meaning is seen as a product of difference. This logical and differential account of meaning provided Saussure with a methodological solution to the limits of existing historical analyses of language. According to Paul *Ricœur (1969), it supplied Lévi-Strauss with a *'Kantianism without a transcendental subject'. That is, it enabled Lévi-Strauss to analyse social life in terms of a universal scheme of socially objectified concepts, leading him to develop rigorous and encompassing categorizations of a wide range of anthropological material. For Saussure and Lévi-Strauss, the synchronic dimension was clearly marked out from and privileged over the diachronic. In contrast, Derrida and Foucault break with the synchronic–diachronic distinction and with the idea of totality. Instead, they focus on *différance* and on the historical ontology of specific problematizations of experience. Yet while both of these moves led away from structuralism in the classical sense, Derrida and Foucault maintained a typically structural view of meaning as imposed rather than disclosed, as generated by systems of formal differences between signs. In these respects, all four thinkers provide illuminating ways of accounting for the human subject in ways that do not presuppose a prior human essence or a primordial external reality called 'nature'. Rather, in all four writers, as well as in the work of Roland

Barthes, the subject is regarded as a product of differential functions of language under definite discursive modes of constitution.

This provocative way of thinking has been immensely influential in contemporary sociology and cultural studies. It has deeply affected debates about cultural identities, gender and sexuality, about myth, symbolism and popular culture, consumption and the mass media, ethnicity, nationalism, and race. The ideas of structuralism and post-structuralism have been taken up into variants of Marxism, feminism, psychoanalysis, postcolonial theory, and postmodernism and have provided a point of departure for numerous contemporary theorists, from Pierre *Bourdieu to Slavoj *Žižek, and from Judith *Butler to Ernesto Laclau and Chantal Mouffe, among others.

▓ QUESTIONS FOR CHAPTER 9

1 What does Saussure mean by the arbitrariness of the sign?

2 How illuminating is Lévi-Strauss's concern to explain myth and kinship relations in terms of universal structures of language?

3 What similarities can be discerned between French structuralist theory and functionalist thinking in the work of Durkheim or Parsons?

4 What does Derrida mean by 'deconstruction'? How illuminating is his conception of the privilege of *logos* in Western metaphysics and the 'priority of speech over writing'?

5 How do Foucault's methodological premises about discourse, knowledge, 'epistemes', and 'genealogy' guide his substantive analyses of the operation of power in modern societies?

6 What are some implications of the structuralist and post-structuralist 'decentring of the subject' for discussions of human agency in social theory?

7 Why are themes of 'identity' and 'difference' important to social and cultural theory?

▓ FURTHER READING

Some useful introductions to structuralism and post-structuralism are John Sturrock's *Structuralism* (Fontana, 2nd edn. 1993), Terrence Hawkes's *Structuralism and Semiotics* (Routledge, 1978), Catherine Belsey's *Poststructuralism: A Very Short Introduction* (Oxford University Press, 2002), and Sarup Madan's *An Introductory Guide to Post-structuralism and Postmodernism* (Harvester, 1993). Try also John Lechte's *Fifty Contemporary Thinkers: From Structuralism to Postmodernity* (Routledge, 1994). A good collection of readings in structuralism with commentaries is John Sturrock's *Structuralism and Since: From Lévi-Strauss to Derrida* (Oxford University Press, 1979). A useful general reference source in cultural theory is David Macey's *Dictionary of Critical Theory* (Penguin, 2001). More detailed studies are Richard Harland's *Superstructuralism: The Philosophy of Structuralism and Poststructuralism* (Routledge, 1991), J. G. Merquior's *From Prague to Paris: A Critique of Structuralism and Poststructuralism* (Verso, 1986), Edith Kurzweil's *The Age of Structuralism: Lévi-Strauss to Foucault* (Columbia University Press, 1980), and Howard Gardner's *The Quest for Mind: Piaget, Lévi-Strauss and the Structuralist Movement* (Knopf, 1973). For a good comparison between Lévi-Strauss, Durkheim, and American functionalism, see Patrick Baert's *Social Theory in the Twentieth Century* (Polity Press, 1998). For a cogent critique of post-structuralism from the standpoint of critical theory, see Peter Dews's *Logics of Disintegration: Post-structuralist Thought and the Claims of Critical Theory* (Verso, 1987).

A good short introduction to Saussure is Jonathan Culler's *Saussure* (Fontana, 1976). Equally good is Jonathan Culler's *Barthes* (Fontana, 1983) and the same author's broader study in literary and cultural theory *Structuralist Poetics* (Routledge, 1975). The recommended English translation of Saussure's *Course in General Linguistics* is by Wade Baskin (Peter Owen, 1960). For an introduction to Lévi-Strauss, try Edmond Leach's *Lévi-Strauss* (Fontana, 1974). Among Lévi-Strauss's most accessible works are his *Totemism* (Penguin, 1973), *Myth and Meaning* (Routledge, 1978), and *Tristes Tropiques* (Penguin, 1973). Roland Barthes's *Mythologies* (Vintage, 2000) is fun to read. See especially his essay 'The Death of the Author', in Barthes's *Image, Music, Text* (Fontana, 1977).

For an introduction to Derrida, try Christopher Norris's *Derrida* (Fontana, 1987). For an in-depth literary study, see Geoffrey Bennington's *Jacques Derrida* (University of Chicago Press, 1993). See also Roy Boyne's *Foucault and Derrida: The Other Side of Reason* (Unwin Hyman, 1990). For a small selection from Derrida's voluminous writings, try Peggy Kamuf's *A Derrida Reader* (Harvester, 1991). Some good places to begin reading Derrida are part I, chapter 2, and part II, chapter 1, in *Of Grammatology* on Saussure and Lévi-Strauss. See the essays 'Structure, Sign, and Play in the Discourse of the Human Sciences' and 'Cogito and the History of Madness' (on Foucault) in *Writing and Difference* (Routledge, 1978) and the essay 'Différance', in *Margins of Philosophy* (University of Chicago Press, 1982). Also useful is the collection of interviews with Derrida titled *Positions* (University of Chicago Press, 1982).

Some useful introductions to Foucault are J. G. Merquior's *Foucault* (Fontana, 1991), Lois McNay's *Foucault: A Critical Introduction* (Polity Press, 1994), and Barry Smart's *Foucault* (Tavistock, 1985), as well as the editorial introductions to the three volumes in the Penguin series *The Essential Works of Michel Foucault* (Penguin, 1997–2000). Two very good collections of essays and extracts from Foucault are Paul Rabinow's edited *The Foucault Reader* (Penguin, 1984) and Colin Gordon's edited *Michel Foucault: Power/Knowledge* (Harvester Wheatsheaf, 1980). A good place to begin reading Foucault is his *Discipline and Punish* (Allen Lane, 1977). An excellent commentary on Foucault is Hubert Dreyfus and Paul Rabinow's *Michel Foucault: Beyond Structuralism and Hermeneutics* (University of Chicago Press, 1982). This book also contains an illuminating afterword by Foucault, titled 'The Subject and Power'. See also Gary Gatting's edited *Cambridge Companion to Foucault* (Cambridge University Press, 1994). For a very readable intellectual biography of Foucault, see James Miller's *The Passion of Michel Foucault* (Simon & Schuster, 1993). For an influential development of Foucaultian ideas in the field of psychology in relation to the concept of 'governmentality', see Nikolas Rose's *Powers of Freedom* (Cambridge University Press, 1999). For feminist perspectives on Foucault, see Lois McNay's *Foucault and Feminism* (Polity Press, 1992). For Foucault's relationship to the work of Habermas, see Samantha Ashenden and David Owen's edited *Foucault contra Habermas: Recasting the Dialogue between Genealogy and Critical Theory* (Sage, 1999), as well as Michael Kelly's edited *Critique and Power: Recasting the Foucault/Habermas Debate* (MIT Press, 1994) and David Hoy and Thomas McCarthy's *Critical Theory* (Blackwell, 1992).

▨ WEBSITES

Semiotics at **http://carbon.cudenver.edu/~mryder/itc_data/semiotics.html** Provides numerous links to sites on semiotics, including key texts and a 'semiotics for beginners' section.

Saussure's Lectures at **www.marxists.org/reference/subject/philosophy/works/fr/saussure.htm** Contains an on-line copy of the first chapter in Saussure's *Course in General Linguistics*.

Claude Lévi-Strauss at **www.marxists.org/reference/subject/philosophy/works/fr/levistra.htm** Contains an on-line copy of chapter II from *Structural Anthropology*.

Lectures by Derrida **http://prelectur.stanford.edu/lecturers/derrida/index.html** Presents Derrida's Stanford presidential lectures, including a biography, excerpts from key works, and interviews.

Michel Foucault at **www.theory.org.uk/ctr-fouc.htm** Includes links to Foucault's biography, essays on his work, and his relationship to queer theory.

10 | Structure and Agency

Anthony King

Structure and agency are key concepts in social theory. Structure refers to regular, relatively fixed, objective, and generalized features of social life. Structure usually refers to social institutions or 'systems', 'forces', or 'currents'. *Agency, on the other hand, refers to *action*. Agency usually refers to the action of human individuals or groups of individuals. Social theorists generally argue that social structure is reproduced by the actions of individuals through the mediation of rules, roles, and other resources broadly referred to as 'culture'. In this sense, structure refers to social facts that are independent of the individual and are able to determine and constrain individual action. In contrast, agency refers to the observation that while constrained by the realities of their world, individuals are capable of choosing alternative courses of action. Individuals can choose what to do, even though their choices are restricted and shaped in various ways by structural realities.

This chapter discusses the strengths as well as some shortcomings of this general account of social life. We concentrate mainly on the work of two influential contemporary theorists: Anthony *Giddens and Pierre *Bourdieu. We also look more briefly at two other - writers associated with a *realist school in British social theory who also employ the concepts of structure and agency. These are Roy *Bhaskar and Margaret *Archer. The chapter focuses particularly on Giddens's theory of *'structuration' and on Bourdieu's influential concepts of 'practice', *'habitus', and 'cultural capital'.

What are 'structure' and 'agency'?

The image of society as a dual reality of structure and agency appears to accord with everyday experience. It seems self-evident that human individuals are confronted by institutional realities over which they have no absolute or overall control. And it also seems self-evident that human individuals retain a degree of freedom to act as they wish or intend. The briefest consideration of personal experience seems to confirm this picture. On the one hand, I am constrained and conditioned to some extent in my life by the type of family, class, income bracket, culture, religious group, or region of the world in which I was born and brought up. I am deeply influenced by the society to which I belong, by its culture and politics. I cannot change these facts about my life overnight, and I cannot change the way the world is overnight. On the other hand, within these constraints, I can to some extent choose to follow what I want to do. I can form particular intentions and plans of action. I can choose to follow one career rather than another or to study one subject rather than another. I can to some extent resist the way the world is, and I can influence people or reach agreements with them about things that need to be done or changed.

For many social theorists, structure and agency are the premises from which all investigation of society needs to proceed. For example, Derek Layder declares that 'an adequate account must come to terms with the fact that "society" and its constituent elements are preconstituted and objective structures which constrain interaction' (Layder 1981: 1). Similarly, Alex Callinicos affirms that society consists of structure and agents and that the purpose of social theory is to reconcile these two distinct elements, that 'the explanatory autonomy of social structures is not inconsistent with the orthodox conception of agents' (Callinicos 1987: 38). Likewise, John Thompson underlines a concern 'to situate action within an overall context of social institutions and structural conditions' (1981: 141; see also Mouzelis 1995). Structure and agency are often described as the 'objective' and 'subjective' sides of social reality. The 'objective' elements refer to those aspects of society that are not reducible to individual knowledge or activity, while the 'subjective' aspects refer precisely to individuals and their personal capabilities.

In many discussions of structure and agency, the role of *culture* is often invoked as an important connecting concept. Culture is seen as ensuring that different individuals act in ways consistent with the reproduction of social structure as a whole. Culture ensures that individual actions are coordinated in ways that produce and reproduce social structures. It is argued that without culture individuals would act randomly, producing not a structured way of life but only chaos.

Anthony Giddens and Pierre Bourdieu: differences and similarities

Anthony *Giddens and Pierre *Bourdieu are two prominent figures in social theory who draw extensively in different ways and with different emphases on these twin concepts of structure and agency. Giddens made his career in the early 1970s through work on class structure, stratification, and Durkheim, developing a theory of 'structuration' in the 1980s. *Bourdieu made his career initially as an anthropologist working on a study of the Kabyle tribe in Algeria in the 1960s. In the 1970s, his interests became more sociological, focusing especially on education, culture, and class in France.

Since his earliest writings, Bourdieu's leftist political orientation has been evident. After his anthropological work on the Kabyle, Bourdieu dedicated most of his research to the analysis and critique of French society. He has focused on the way in which the French class system is reproduced through institutional and cultural mechanisms. Although Bourdieu could not be described as Marxist, his interest in class reflects the concerns of *structuralist Marxist theorists such as Louis *Althusser, Ralph *Miliband, and Nicos *Poulantzas who were dominant in the early part of Bourdieu's career. Bourdieu has remained oriented to rigorously empirical research throughout his work, focusing on the details of everyday life in different class *fractions*.

Giddens's work differs from Bourdieu's in notable respects. Giddens's early theoretical work was not directly concerned with empirical data, and his more recent work has been criticized for resting on rather thin sociological evidence. For many critics, Giddens's recent work is characterized by an excessively optimistic and *individualistic account of contemporary society under conditions of *post-Fordist employment practices. This view was also taken by Bourdieu. In one of his last publications, Bourdieu described Giddens as one half of 'a bicephalous Trojan horse' (Bourdieu and Wacquant 2001). In Bourdieu's view, the British Prime Minister Tony Blair was the other half of this miscegenation. Bourdieu saw Giddens and Blair as contributing to an undermining of social democracy through the surreptitious introduction of free-market values. Bourdieu became particularly suspicious of Giddens's later writings on the *'Third Way', which he saw as merely legitimizing the current social order, instead of criticizing it. Giddens's later work on the 'Third Way' and *'reflexivity' is discussed in Chapter 13 of this book (pp. 287–9).

However, Bourdieu's political disagreements with Giddens should not blind us to some notable similarities in their theoretical approaches. Bourdieu and Giddens follow comparable strategies in the way they deal with ideas about structure and agency. Although they employ different terminology, both seek to explain the reproduction of social structures through the agency of individuals acting in conformity with cultural rules and resources. In the following we deal first of all with Giddens's theory of 'structuration'.

Giddens's structuration theory

Giddens has always sought to produce new insights through syntheses of existing ideas. His work on social class from the 1970s was an attempt to reconcile Marxist and Weberian approaches in a theory of *stratification adequate to contemporary conditions

(Giddens 1979). What Giddens came to call *'structuration' is another example of his synthetic approach. Giddens first developed the theory in the late 1970s in *New Rules of Sociological Method* (1976) and *Central Problems in Social Theory* (1979), and subsequently in its fully fledged form in *The Constitution of Society* (1984).

In part, structuration theory is a response to the shortcomings of Talcott *Parsons's conception of *structural functionalism (discussed in Chapter 4 of this book). In his middle period and later work, Parsons had proposed that the social system had certain functional requirements that were met insofar as individuals fulfilled certain roles. Parsons appeared to give the social system a determining power over individuals who merely internalized certain values allowing them to perform roles. For some critics, Parsons seemed to reduce individuals to mere 'cultural dupes' who were unwittingly determined by certain systemic needs. According to Giddens, the social system could only operate through the *knowledgeable activity* of individuals. Giddens wanted to produce a theory that avoided any 'derogation of the *lay actor', a theory that did not neglect the everyday competences and rational self-consciousness of individuals (Giddens 1979: 71). Giddens insisted that 'an adequate account of human agency must first be connected to a theory of the acting subject' (Giddens 1979: 2). In order to develop a theory of the acting subject, Giddens drew on the work of Erving *Goffman and Harold *Garfinkel (discussed in Chapter 5 of this book). Giddens emphasized the importance of individual agency while at the same time insisting that structuration theory amounted to 'a recovery of the subject without lapsing into *subjectivism' (Giddens 1979: 44).

Giddens was conscious that there are dimensions of society which cannot be reduced to the individual. While he was sympathetic to the emphasis on individual agency in interactionist sociology, he criticized Goffman and Garfinkel's work for not accounting adequately for institutional realities. He asserted that institutions are not reducible to individual subjects and that 'society is not the creation of individual subjects' (Giddens 1984: p. xxi). In this sense, structuration theory is ultimately a synthesis of *interactionist and *interpretive thinking on the one hand, with its emphasis on agency, understanding, and subjective meanings, and *functionalist and *structuralist thinking on the other hand, with its focus on the operation of social systems and the resilience of objective structures. Structuration theory is designed to explain the reproduction of institutional orders through the knowledgeable agency of individuals. It is a kind of fusion of the work of Durkheim and Parsons on the one hand and the work of Weber, *Schutz,* Mead, Goffman, and Garfinkel on the other.

Structure, system, and 'tacit knowledge'

Giddens developed an elaborate *ontology to explain this active reproduction of the social system. He began by distinguishing between three basic levels of experience in the life courses of individual actors: a level of the 'unconscious', a level of 'discursive consciousness', and a level of 'practical consciousness'. The unconscious refers to subconscious motives, described by Freud in terms of psychoanalysis. *Discursive consciousness refers to those aspects of knowledge that individuals can describe reflectively and self-consciously. In between the unconscious and discursive consciousness stands the level of 'practical consciousness', which is crucial to structuration theory (Giddens 1979: 2). Giddens describes what he calls practical consciousness or *'tacit knowledge' in terms of stocks of mutual understandings between individuals that are assumed in everyday interaction. These stocks of tacit knowledge are vital to social practice but are effectively invisible.

Giddens notes that the success of Garfinkel's *ethnomethodology and Goffman's interactionism lay in uncovering these shared understandings that are taken for granted in social encounters (Giddens 1979: 80–1). Goffman and Garfinkel illuminated the background rules that remain invisible because humans never experience an ordinary social interaction without having already taken these rules for granted. Individuals only note what is natural when someone misjudges appropriate conduct or when a stranger does not know about these mutual stocks of knowledge. The purpose of Garfinkel's breaching experiments was to demonstrate the importance of background understandings to social life. Giddens's concept of 'tacit knowledge' thus seeks to capture this routine, pre-given and unthematized character of everyday knowledge in ongoing interaction. It refers ultimately to shared meanings which coordinate individual action and allow individuals to interact in mutually acceptable and predictable ways.

While 'practical consciousness' and 'tacit knowledge' are important to structuration theory, Giddens also posits three other decisive elements of analysis: the element of 'system', the element of 'structure', and the element of 'structuration'. The system refers to a society's major institutions, to its state and legal and administrative systems, to its social and class structure, and to its economy. Structuration refers to the process by which individuals reproduce these systems through their activities. In this analysis, the most decisive concept is that of 'structure'. According to Giddens, it is 'structure' rather than tacit knowledge which finally ensures that individuals act in a way that reproduces the social system as a whole. For Giddens, structure refers to rules and resources which exist only when they are employed in social practice (Giddens 1984: 25).

Borrowing a phrase from the structural linguistics of Ferdinand de *Saussure (discussed in Chapter 9 of this book), Giddens describes structure as 'a virtual order of difference' (Giddens 1979: 46). Structure is 'marked by the absence of the subject' (Giddens 1984: 25). In his theory of structural linguistics, Saussure had argued that *langue*, or language, consisted of a system of arbitrary *signifiers—sounds or inscriptions on a surface. The meaning of each signifier arose from its difference from other signifiers in that language; the meaning of each element was created by its non-identity with the others. By a 'virtual order of difference', Giddens means that structure is a system of rules of conduct, each of which differ from one another and imply one another. Like Saussure's concept of *langue*, structure is essential to any social act but is not immediately known to the agent. As *langue* frames everything that is said, limiting speech to certain comprehensible forms, so Giddens states that virtual rules of conduct 'structure' individual actions. They ensure that actions take a recognizable and predictable form. Structure for this reason has the aspect of *duality*. It is, Giddens says, both the *medium* of social action and the *outcome* of social action. Giddens illustrates this *'duality of structure' with a linguistic example: 'the duality of structure relates the smallest item of day-to-day behaviour to attributes of far more inclusive social systems; when I utter a grammatical English sentence in casual conversation, I contribute to the reproduction of the English language as a whole' (Giddens 1979: 77). In other words, social agents reaffirm and reproduce the rules on which they draw in their actions. Just as individuals necessarily draw on pre-given linguistic structures when they speak and thereby contribute to reproducing the entire linguistic system, so individuals contribute to reproducing the whole system of social rules whenever they act. Structure underpins social practice to ensure that it takes a meaningful and relatively predictable form.

Giddens's conception of structuration has been applied by a number of sociologists to concrete problems in social research. One interesting context of applications has been international relations research. This is discussed here in Box 25.

We shall shortly return to some problems with Giddens's use of the concepts of structure and agency. But first we move to some comparable ideas in the work of Pierre Bourdieu.

BOX 25. ANTHONY GIDDENS AND INTERNATIONAL RELATIONS THEORY

One among several contexts of application of Giddens's idea of structuration has been international relations research. In the 1980s, several reasearchers appealed to the concept of structuration in an effort to overcome the so-called *'realist' paradigm that had been dominant in international relations research since the Second World War (see further Wendt 1987). In drawing on the concept of structuration, these researchers showed how Giddens's theory could be applied not only at the level of the actions of individual persons but also at the macrological level of the agency of whole nation-states in a structural arena of global diplomacy.

Realism in international relations research has followed a different order of priorities from the ideas signified technically by realism in sociological theory. During the Cold War, international relations researchers in the realist school argued that international order consisted of strategies by individual nation-states aimed at a maximizing interests in power and advantage. The international order was seen as having a particular structure, resting on a 'balance of power'. A nation-state's position in this structure was seen as determining the strategies it was most rational for it to pursue.

Towards the end of the Cold War, several international relations theorists became dissatisfied with this realist approach. They gave more emphasis to the cultural aspects and differences of the actions of nation-states. They argued that important internal national norms affected the way a state interacted with other states, and consequently that the international system did not have the rigid structure affirmed by the realists. They developed a less deterministic account of the international order, describing their approach as 'constructivist' rather that realist. They appealed to Giddens's theory of structuration insofar as it seemed to allow for elements of both individual agency and structural constraint. Structuration theory allowed individual states more agency than under a realist paradigm, while at the same time recognizing the existence of a constraining context to which nation-states themselves contributed through their actions. The international order was a 'medium' of state action and an 'outcome' of state action. Individual states could transform the international order in certain ways, while at the same time remaining bound by its relatively intransigent structure. Their own transformative actions had the consequence of consolidating the structure, even as the structure underwent change.

In adapting Giddens's theory in this way, the international relations researchers sought to steer a middle path between both the *functionalist idea of an all-encompassing, all-determining global system and the *rational choice conception of advantage-maximizing actions by discrete nation-states. They saw themselves as bringing together the two sides of the dichotomy in a more satisfactory manner, emphasizing the interdependence of structure and agency and an interlacing of elements of fixity with elements of transformation.

Bourdieu and the idea of reflexive sociology

Like Giddens, Bourdieu also sought a way of reconciling objectivist tendencies in social theory with subjectivist tendencies. The *objectivist emphasis on structure is embodied for Bourdieu in French *structuralist theory, especially in the work of *Lévi-Strauss (discussed in Chapter 9 of this book). The *subjectivist emphasis on agency is embodied for Bourdieu in *phenomenological and *hermeneutical philosophy, especially in the *existentialism of Jean-Paul *Sartre.

When Bourdieu began propounding his theories in the 1970s, he rejected Sartre's existentialism as untenably *voluntarist. Bourdieu emphasized that human social life could not always be viewed in terms of unique personal choices. But Lévi-Strauss's structuralism was equally problematic, because human culture could not be reduced to a product of universal *cognitive templates operating above the heads of individuals. Human agents had to be seen as capable of recognizing the significance of the cultural products they themselves create through their actions. Bourdieu therefore sought to develop a social theory that explained the institutional realities of modern society without either obliterating individual agency or relapsing into subjectivist individualism. Like Giddens's synthesis of functionalism and interactionism, Bourdieu wanted to rescue the positive aspects of the work of both Lévi-Strauss and Sartre, to find a critical middle way between structuralism and phenomenology.

We begin here by looking at Bourdieu's first systematic treatise from the early 1970s, his *Outline of a Theory of Practice* (1972). This grew out of his anthropological studies of the Kabyle tribespeople in the 1960s and provided a theoretical basis for all his subsequent research. We then turn to his influential concepts of the 'habitus', 'field', and 'cultural capital'.

Bourdieu's *Outline of a Theory of Practice*

Bourdieu considers that the social scientist's position as an ideally impartial observer who is an outsider to the social processes under observation creates a problem for sociology and anthropology. The 'objective' and external position of the social scientist can have the consequence that the social life under study is misrepresented. Insofar as researchers are outsiders to the social realities they are studying, they invariably construct maps, models, and rules by which they orient themselves around this strange cultural landscape. The observer 'compensates for lack of practical mastery, by creating a cultural map' (Bourdieu 1972: 2). In so doing, however, researchers run a risk of reducing cultural life to a wooden system of rules which imposes itself on the actors. They face a danger of imposing their own curious and contemplative relation to the culture in question onto the practices of the natives. They need to gain insight into the way ordinary actors engage in social relations with the skill of 'virtuosos', like accomplished musicians. Since the researchers, as visiting intellectuals, have to think of social life in terms of rules and principles (because they do not know it intimately), they assume that native agents share this curious intellectualizing position. Bourdieu consequently calls for a *'reflexive sociology' in which sociologists try to theorize rigorously their own position in relation to the practices of the participants of their studies (Bourdieu 1990; Bourdieu and Wacquant 1992). A key requirement for such a 'reflexive sociology' is a grasp of the agency of the participant actors under observation, and of the agency of the researchers who study them.

For Bourdieu, social agents are 'virtuosos' in the sense they are not dominated by abstract rules but rather know the script so well that they can elaborate and improvise on the themes it provides (1972: 79). Bourdieu describes social actors as having a 'sense of the game', referring to footballers and tennis players as examples of this virtuosic sense. These players do not apply a priori principles to their play—only beginners need to do that. Confronted with diverse situations, they have an automatic understanding of what is appropriate. They know, for instance, when they should run to the net (1980: 66–7, 81). This virtuosic 'sense of the game' is not individualistic. It arises in social relations and refers to the understanding that actors develop about what other group members regard as tolerable. Bourdieu's discussion of honour among the Kabyle highlights this intersubjective sense of the game:

> The driving of the whole mechanism is not some abstract principle (principle of isotimy, equality in honour), still less the set of rules which can be derived from it but the sense of honour, a disposition inculcated in earlier years of life and constantly reinforced by calls to order from the group. (Bourdieu 1972: 14–15)

Kabylian men's sense of honour is a shifting agreement established and transformed through negotiation. Individuals do not solipsistically consult *a priori rules which determine their actions mechanically. As members of groups, individuals act according to a sense of practice which is established and judged by the group. The final determination of correct action is not whether an individual rigorously follows a rule but rather whether an individual's actions are interpreted as appropriate by others. Other members of a group decide whether an action is acceptable or sanctionable given their shared sense of honour, and they call those individuals to order who have acted against this socially agreed sense of rightness. It is in this sense that agents act within a fluid context of structure, marked by group expectations, norms of acceptable practice, sanctions, and relations of power.

The habitus and the field

In the *Outline* and other works form the 1970s and 1980s, Bourdieu developed a concept of the *'habitus' to overcome the impasse between excessively objectivist and excessively subjectivist approaches in social research (Bourdieu 1979, 1980, 1984). This term 'habitus' had also been used earlier in the twentieth century by Max Weber and Norbert *Elias, with different meanings. In Bourdieu's use of the term, the habitus overcomes subject–object *dualism by endowing subjective bodily actions with objective social force, so that the most apparently subjective individual acts necessarily assume broader social significance. Individuals have agency, but the kind of agency they have is prescribed by the culture of which they are members. Following Lévi-Strauss, Bourdieu insists that culture cannot be understood in individualistic or voluntaristic ways. Culture has an objectivity which precedes individual knowledge and understandings. The habitus comprises perceptual structures and embodied dispositions which organize the way individuals see the world and act in it. Bourdieu comments that 'the cognitive structures which social agents implement in their practical knowledge of the social world are internalized, embodied social structures' (Bourdieu 1979: 468).

The habitus derives from the structural socio-economic positions in which individuals find themselves. Individuals routinely internalize objective social conditions such as their economic class, with the result that they acquire the appropriate tastes and perform the appropriate practices for their social position. According to Bourdieu, the habitus facilitates the reproduction of social structure by imposing certain dispositions on the individual. Confronted by an autonomous social reality, individuals assume various cultural predispositions appropriate to their situation. Borrowing a phrase from *Nietzsche, Bourdieu argues that individuals evince an 'amor fati' ('a love of destiny') in which they automatically fulfil the appropriate role for their objective situation (Bourdieu 1979: 244).

Individuals display certain cultural tastes that reflect their structural situation. The habitus inscribes tastes into the very bodies of individuals. Bourdieu describes the way in which tastes imposed by social class are not intellectual judgements but instinctive bodily reactions against those things that do not fit that class's habitus (Bourdieu 1979: 486, 478). Actors feel intense embarrassment and even nausea when confronted with social practices that do not fit their habitus. The habitus even moulds the human physique. For instance, Bourdieu describes the bowed deportment of Kabylian women, which physically denotes their subordination in the tribal society (Bourdieu 1977).

Bourdieu's emphasis on the body in his discussion of the habitus is important. Corporeal human conduct is central to social life. The human body is an important signifier in social interaction, expressing social status and power as much as communicative intention. A person's treatment by others is substantially determined by his or her bodily conduct. Above all, bodily conduct has to become second nature to be successful. If actors do not act 'naturally', their actions are likely to take on different meanings. They may be interpreted as untrustworthy or insincere and encounters may go awry. Bourdieu is right to emphasize the role of the body in social communication, interaction, and domination (see also the discussion of the body in Chapter 11 of this book on feminist social theory, pp. 236–7).

According to Bourdieu, the habitus operates in a wider institutional setting which Bourdieu calls the 'field'. The 'field' refers to the structure of social relations in which an individual is located. The structure of social relations is independent of the individuals who occupy a field. This structure pre-exists individuals and determines struggles between them. The habitus plays a crucial role because it effectively links individuals to their position in the field and ensures that they reproduce it by acting in appropriate ways. Bourdieu argues that 'to think in terms of a field is to think relationally' (Bourdieu and Wacquant 1992: 96). The field has an objective status, similar to Giddens's 'system'. Bourdieu stresses that

what exist in the social world are relations—not interactions between agents and *intersubjective ties between individuals but objective relations which exist 'independent of individual consciousness and will', as Marx says . . . In analytic terms a field may be defined as a network, or a configuration of objective relations between positions. (Bourdieu and Wacquant 1992: 97)

Bourdieu's concept of the field is intended to enrich the concept of the habitus. Bourdieu shows how, in a field, groups struggle for supremacy and social distinctiveness. In particular, he notes how, in contrast to the middle classes, the working class tend to value functional clothing and food, making a cultural virtue out of an economic necessity. The economic position of the working class conditions them to view the elaborate habits of the bourgeoisie with disdain. Indulgence in certain tastes may come to seem repellent to the working class.

Conversely, upper-class groups typically regard those beneath them in status as vulgar and uncultured. At the same time, while superior groups try to monopolize certain cultural practices, subordinate groups attempt to adopt these practices in order to subvert the status of superior groups. In adopting the practices of superior groups, subordinate groups undermine the distinctiveness of these groups. We may think, for example, of the ways in which expensive fashion accessories come to be acquired by middle-income groups in a desire to imitate the rich and famous, and thereby gradually lose their distinctiveness.

The struggle for social distinctiveness is an empirically verifiable process which Bourdieu usefully illuminates. One of his most revealing discussions appears in his influential book from 1979, *Distinction: A Social Critique of the Judgement of Taste*. This is discussed in Box 26.

Cultural capital

The habitus of an individual is a product of his or her position in the field. The field is substantially formed by objective economic factors. The distribution of economic resources in a society or more specifically the market determines the social hierarchy. In a parallel to the structuralist Marxism of *Althusser, *Poulantzas, and *Miliband, Bourdieu here maintains that an economic base finally determines the structural form that a society can take. Dominant groups are those that monopolize economic resources, and the *hegemonic position of these groups over subordinate groups is a product of their economic power.

However, in addition to this notion of economic determination, Bourdieu also develops a concept of *'cultural capital'. Through the habitus, individuals and groups adopt certain cultural practices. These practices reflect people's economic position, but the habitus and the culture it imparts do not passively transmit the prior economic position in which individuals find themselves. Through adopting certain kinds of cultural practices, individuals can earn cultural capital. They can attain a higher status in the social order than their purely economic position would allow by adopting and monopolizing cultural activities that are admired and envied. Individuals and groups can develop cultural knowledge which is arcane and which raises them above other groups, even above those more economically powerful than them.

Bourdieu argues that intellectuals and artists, while relatively poor, have a rich habitus that involves a commitment to difficult and time-consuming cultural forms. These groups may not have the wealth of private sector professionals but they have the time and leisure to be able to master respected cultural activities, to acquire 'refinement'. This is also true of the traditional aristocracy. In this way, at least in France—which may or may not be a special case—possession of cultural capital allows intellectuals and artists to achieve a social standing superior to their purely economic position.

In this sense Bourdieu's concept of the habitus suggests a formula for social *status. For Bourdieu, social *status, defined as an individual's position in the social hierarchy, is a product of an individual's economic and cultural capital taken together. While financiers, stockbrokers, and bankers all have substantial economic capital, they are not automatically dominant in the social field because they are low in cultural capital. In contrast, skilled professionals such as doctors and teachers, as well as state employees such as police officers and

BOX 26. PIERRE BOURDIEU'S *DISTINCTION: A SOCIAL CRITIQUE OF THE JUDGEMENT OF TASTE*

In his book *Distinction: A Social Critique of the Judgement of Taste* (1979) Bourdieu adopts a sociological perspective on questions of taste, aesthetic judgements, and preferences in cultural goods. He elucidates the social conditions that make people's different tastes in art and culture what they are. His approach can be described as a form of sociological *Kantianism in the sense that his conception of the habitus functions in an analogous manner to Immanuel Kant's eighteenth-century philosophical conception of basic organizing *cognitive categories of human intellection and action.

Writing in the 1780s, Kant had divided the realm of rational intellectual life into three domains: the domain of theoretical reason (involved in science), the domain of practical reason (involved in morality), and the domain of aesthetic sensibility (involved in tastes about art). In each domain, Kant had sought to identify certain transcendental principles which make each of these aspects of human existence what they are. Kant had proposed that various cognitive categories precede human perception and make meaningfully ordered experience possible. These organizing categories essentially make the world what it is for human beings. In *Distinction*, Bourdieu seeks to show how these cognitive categories arise from prior *socio-economic conditions*, and that it is the socio-economic features of these categories that make the world what it is for human actors. He concentrates particularly on bringing to light the sociological dimensions of the categories involved in aesthetic sensibilities and cultural tastes in a given society. In this sense, his book can be seen as a sociological response to the last of Kant's three philosophical treatises, *The Critique of Judgement*, of 1790.

Elaborating the habitus empirically, Bourdieu carried out extensive quantitative and qualitative research into the habits and tastes of social classes in France in the 1970s. He divided French society into four main social classes; the working class, the petty bourgeoisie (the lower middle class) and the professional classes (the upper middle class), which he subdivided into private and public sector *fractions*. He called the private sector professionals the 'right bank', and the public sector professionals the 'left bank'. This was in reference to the River Seine in Paris. The north 'right' bank of the Seine has historically been associated with finance and government (the side of the Champs-Élysées). The south 'left' bank has historically been associated with art and culture (the side of the Latin Quarter and the University). The right-bank elite consisted of bankers, businessmen, lawyers, and brokers, while the left-bank elite referred to teachers, academics, intellectuals, artists, and writers. Bourdieu accepted that class positions in Paris were decisively determined by economic capital. Consequently, the right-bank elite were dominant. Nevertheless, cultural capital also played an important role in a class's social status. The right-bank elite possessed extensive economic capital but had little cultural capital. Cultural capital was substantially monopolized by the left-bank elite. The right-bank elite engaged in 'hedonistic' activities which conspicuously demonstrated their economic capital. They indulged in expensive foods and elaborate holidays in exclusive locations. The left bank, by contrast, chose activities which did not require significant economic capital but which demonstrated cultural sophistication and, above all, the time required to acquire these arcane tastes. In this way, the left bank distinguished itself from other groups. The left bank favoured difficult modern music and engaged in inexpensive but personally demanding sports such as cross-country skiing, mountaineering, and hill-walking.

Although not without its problems, Bourdieu's analysis of the left- and right-bank professionals is suggestive because it recognizes growing divide between public and private sector professionals in a context of *post-Fordist employment cultures. By contrast, his account of the working class and the petty bourgeoisie is less convincing, and has not been seen as providing an accurate sociology of these groups. It has been argued that Bourdieu exaggerates the extent to which the lower classes' lack of the economic and educational advantages of elites predestines them to particular ways of life. Nevertheless, Bourdieu's book remains one of the most important sociological analyses of class culture.

government officers, and relatively impoverished intellectuals and artists are able to contest social dominance by the materially rich through their monopolization of cultural capital. The social hierarchy is thus a product of a struggle between groups on the basis of both economic capital and cultural capital. Cultural capital is conditioned by economic capital but is not predetermined by it. For example, a graduate of an elite university may have come from a wealthy family background, but if the graduate then makes a successful career in the business world, it is the graduate's cultural capital acquired at university which must be identified as the prime cause of the graduate's success, rather than the economic capital of the graduate's family. Another graduate from the same elite university but not from a wealthy family background might in principle have the same chance of success, on the strength of the university-acquired cultural capital alone.

Bourdieu's conception of cultural capital is very clearly illuminated both in his book *Distinction* and in his study of the sociology of education, titled *Homo Academicus* (1984). The latter text is discussed in Box 27.

BOX 27. PIERRE BOURDIEU AND THE SOCIOLOGY OF EDUCATION

In the field of education research, Bourdieu's concept of the habitus has been enduring. When the habitus refers not to static cultural templates arising automatically from a prior material reality but more dynamically to exclusive group culture, it is very illuminating. Employing the concept in this way, Bourdieu makes some interesting arguments about the reproduction of social inequality in schools and academies. In the postscript to *Homo Academicus* (1984), his study of the French educational system, Bourdieu contends that the examinations that students have to pass to receive their all-important diplomas are not judged purely on objective academic criteria but also to some extent on criteria of social fitness. In his provocative thesis, the French academy is founded on a system of cultural exclusion where the values of the middle classes are imposed in the examining procedure. The physical mannerisms and writing style of students become criteria for grading them, rather than purely impartial pedagogical judgements. In his analysis of marking schemes, Bourdieu notes that 'the most favourable epithets appear more and more frequently as the social origins of pupils rise' (Bourdieu 1984: 198). Consequently, the academy remains closed to the children of the working classes, while it is conveniently monopolized by the professional classes with the requisite cultural capital.

There are some problems with Bourdieu's argument insofar as he overemphasizes the closure of the academy to non-professional social groups. He allows for no flexibility in the process, just as his formal definition of the habitus similarly tends to rule out negotiation and transformation. His thesis about the social determination of educational aptitudes and attainments comes close to a form of reductionism. A statistical correlation between family income levels and student educational achievements cannot be taken to imply that students are graded simply on the basis of their social origins. Nevertheless, Bourdieu's concept of the habitus allows him to develop a genuinely critical sociology of education. Education is at least in part a process in which privileged social groups affirm their superiority in the social structure by monopolizing important cultural institutions and resources. Bourdieu here exposes assumptions that can be taken for granted in the examination process. The habitus is not simply a reflection of a prior economic base, but it reveals the shared common culture of particular groups who mobilize themselves and exclude others on the base of that culture. A dominant group's material position in society is substantially a product of the culture on the basis of which it mobilizes itself to monopolize opportunities.

Both Bourdieu's and Giddens's reflections on structure and agency suffer from various problems to which we must turn in a moment. But before doing so, we move now to a third and last set of contributions to be found in the work of the British *realist theorists Roy *Bhaskar and Margaret *Archer.

Realist social theory: Roy Bhaskar and Margaret Archer

After his seminal contributions to the philosophy of science in the early 1970s, Roy Bhaskar became a prominent figure in British social theory. In a similar fashion to Giddens and Bourdieu, Bhaskar understands society in terms of the reproduction of structure by individual agency through the mediation of culture. Bhaskar's realism claims that society consists of certain dimensions of reality which cannot be understood by reference to individual activity and belief alone. Social action has emergent properties which exceed consciousness of the individual. Although no institutions would exist without individuals to fulfil the roles that compose them, they have properties which transcend the individuals who create the institutions. For Bhaskar, society consists of irreducibly *real* social structures.

Bhaskar endorses Giddens's structuration theory and explicitly relates it to his own work (Bhaskar 1979: 45). He describes his own realist theory as the 'Transformational Model of Social Action', and regards this as compatible with structuration. The transformational model of social action claims that society consists of structure and agency. Structure precedes individual agency but structure can only be reproduced and transformed through individual agency. Individuals are confronted by a social structure which constrains them but which does not finally determine them. In their actions, individuals can manipulate the structure by reinterpreting their situation and thus developing new forms of agency. In this way, individuals are able to transform the social structure.

In her 'morphogenetic social theory', Margaret Archer advocates a position close to Bhaskar's (Archer 1995). By 'morphogenetic' Archer refers to the process by which patterns or 'shapes' are generated in repeated social action. Like Bhaskar, Archer sees society as consisting of real social structures irreducible to individuals. Archer berates those social theorists who fail to recognize the dual nature of social reality, who either collapse structure into individuals or assimilate individuals to structure. For her, society consists *both* of objective structures *and* of individual agents. Neither of these two dimensions can be derived or reconstructed from each other.

Archer maintains that Giddens collapses the objective institutional fact of society into the individual. Unlike Bhaskar, she sees Giddens's structuration theory as a one-dimensional form of methodological individualism (Archer 1982: 458 ff., 1988: 72). In her book *Culture and Agency* (1988), Archer argues that culture emerges out of individual activity but that once it has been created, especially when it is embodied in physical artefacts, it has an objectivity which transcends the individual. Architecture, artworks, books, and mathematical formulas all attain an existence which is autonomous of everyday social intercourse. According to Archer, the autonomy of culture is decisive in explaining social reproduction and transformation. Individuals in a society are confronted by a cultural system which is independent of them. Often individuals draw automatically on the most obvious elements of this culture to perform regular practices which reproduce the system.

However, Archer also argues that the autonomous status of culture facilitates change. Since the cultural system does not depend merely on what people here and now believe, it can be drawn upon in different ways, or forgotten elements within it can be emphasized. In this way, individuals can develop new forms of practice and thereby transform the patterns of socio-cultural integration in their society. They can change the institutional structures of a society by developing new relations to the cultural system. Particular individuals may note and then eventually act upon potential contradictions between the cultural system and everyday practice. Individuals can draw on autonomous cultural resources to direct their everyday practice, producing either change or stasis.

Archer's criticisms of Giddens are not without merit. However, it can be argued that her own 'morphogenetic social theory' in fact resembles Giddens's theory in certain respects and arguably shares some of its problems. Her lexicon differs from Giddens's but her description of the autonomy and function of the cultural system follows structuration theory quite closely. It can be argued that her idea of the 'cultural system' operates in the same way as Giddens's idea of 'structure'. Archer's 'cultural system' consists of diverse formulas, rules, and ideas which are autonomous of individuals but upon which individuals must draw if they are to act in a recognizable fashion. The cultural system mediates between the institutions of the social system and the individual. It channels individual practice so that structural reproduction can occur, but it also allows for the transformation of the social structure through the agency of individuals.

Some of the most general problems with this way of theorizing are brought together in the next section. These problems can be described in terms of a basic dilemma of *determinism* and *individualism* in debates about structure and agency.

Problems of determinism and individualism in structure–agency thinking

Writers on structure and agency such as Giddens, Bourdieu, Bhaskar, and Archer tend to face a rather difficult dilemma. This dilemma can be described as having the following two sides. On the one hand, there is a side of **determinism*. On the other hand, there is a side of excessive methodological **individualism*. Let us look first at the determinist side.

Giddens, Bourdieu, Bhaskar, and Archer argue that social life is to be explained by the postulate of rules which direct individual action. Bourdieu claims that the habitus imposes certain tastes on individuals so that they necessarily adopt social practices appropriate for their class position. In Giddens's picture, individuals seem to have a more active say in how they follow the rules of structure. But still, their practices are said necessarily to instantiate structure and thereby to reproduce the wider social system to which these rules are attached. In each of these writers, institutional forms are said to be reproduced in accordance with cultural rules. These rules—be they Bourdieu's 'habitus' or Giddens's 'structure'—are said to direct or to determine individual action.

The danger here is that if it is said that individuals are directed by rules which impose on them and of which they are not fully aware, human agency tends to be denied.

It seems that individuals no longer consciously choose what to do but are merely directed by these prior rules. This determinism is clear in Bourdieu's writing. His concept of the habitus has a tendency to emasculate human agency, to reduce dynamic and uncertain social interaction to the inevitable reproduction of institutional structures. The habitus imposes certain forms of conduct on the individual. Individual agents reproduce the institutional structure of the field because they are determined by these unavoidable cultural predispositions.

The problem is similar for Giddens. Because of Giddens's emphasis on the creativity of the individual, the determinist implications of his structuration theory are less immediately apparent. But in fact, Giddens is not free from this problem either. Giddens emphasizes that structure is inexorably attached to the social system and therefore that for the most part individuals automatically reproduce the system. The implication of Giddens's theory is that structure ensures that individuals always act in a way which is compatible with that system. Although he does not explain this relationship, individuals necessarily act in a way which is consistent with social order.

Now let us look at the individualist side of the dilemma. Giddens and Bourdieu are right to want to reject determinism. Giddens is at pains to emphasize that his theory allows for the fact that individuals can always choose alternative courses of action and that whatever structural imperatives obtain, 'the individual could have acted otherwise' (Giddens 1984: 75). Similarly, Bourdieu asserts that his theory allows for the persistence of individual agency in the face of the objectivity of the habitus. Bourdieu has been incredulous at those critics of his work who have interpreted the habitus in a deterministic fashion (see Bourdieu and Wacquant 1992: 134). Bourdieu sees the habitus as allowing room for slippage: individuals, he claims, are not completely determined by the habitus but can manipulate the cultural resources available to them to develop new social practices. He insists that individuals still have agency under the habitus.

Here the danger for Bourdieu and Giddens, however, is that if individuals are free at any moment to do otherwise, it is possible that structure or habitus *do not really constrain what they do*. It is possible that if individuals possess this freedom, structure or habitus are not really guaranteeing that individuals act in appropriate ways—because at any time, individuals could adopt new forms of action at random. And if individuals can do otherwise *some* of the time, they *could* do otherwise *all* of the time—so that neither structure nor habitus prevent them from acting randomly. Therefore the danger in Giddens's and Bourdieu's theory is that individuals only *choose* to follow structure or habitus. And if they only choose to follow structure or habitus, they could at any moment choose *not* to follow them. Regular social interaction here seems to be explained finally only by individual choice.

The dilemma is thus this. *Either* structure–agency thinking tends to emasculate individual agency, claiming that individuals are determined externally by structures or habitus. *Or* structure–agency thinking tends to overassert the agency of individuals, leaving the persistence and resilience of regular social institutions impossible to explain and endowing individuals always with the possibility of acting otherwise. In this sense, structure–agency thinking tends toward a danger of determinism on the one hand and a danger of randomness of choices on the other hand. (For further discussions of this dilemma, see Sewell 1992; Schatzki 1987, 1997; Taylor 1993; King 2000a, 2000b, 2004).

Resolving the dilemma

The dilemma presented here is a deliberately heightened formulation of some rather abstract theoretical difficulties that have repeatedly troubled contributors to social theory. It should be emphasized that these theoretical difficulties do not mean that the concepts of structure and agency are useless for sociologists in empirical research. The concept of structure is plainly retrievable for pragmatic purposes. In any sociological study, the specific practices under examination have to be situated in a wider social and historic context. This background can usefully be called 'structure', with the proviso that 'structure' amounts to dynamic relations between actors in different times and places. Structure should not be seen as referring to any *metaphysical entity which exists above and beyond all individuals and their relations. At their most sustainable, realist theorists such as Archer or Bhaskar use structure in a purely *heuristic (non-metaphysical) way.

Social theory can avoid many difficulties with the concepts of structure and agency when it makes an effort to regard social life less in terms of individual agency 'reproducing' structure in any mechanical sense and more in terms of ongoing dynamic interrelations between actors. Human beings do not 'reproduce' structure 'by means of' culture. Rather, together humans interact with each other by reference to shared understandings. Through these interminable interactions, the social relations which compose a society are sustained and transformed. Thus a society should not be seen as consisting *ontologically or metaphysically of two basic substances, one substance called 'structure' and one substance called 'agency'. Rather, it should be seen as consisting of social relations between individual actors, all of whom act under various constraints which we call 'institutions', 'forces', 'trends', 'power' or 'powers', and so on. In these webs of social relations, both the regularity and the creativity of individual action become more explicable. Together, individuals orient themselves towards shared goals, and together they are able to develop new forms of practice. The social reality of relations between human persons should not be reduced to a static and *dualistic image of individuals confronting objective structures. Individual actors do not 'consult' cultural rules in their relationship to structures. Rather, they come to mutual understandings of what constitutes appropriate action, and are able to bind each other to these appropriate forms of conduct.

Conclusion

Structure and agency have been key concepts in social theory. In general, it is commonplace to argue that social structure is reproduced by means of the agency of individuals, through the mediation of cultural rules and resources. There are certain problematic tendencies in this way of thinking which may lead to an impasse between overly objectivist or *determinist* accounts and overly subjectivist or *individualist* accounts of the dynamics of social life. Structure–agency thinking either runs a risk of emasculating individual agency in order to explain structural reproduction, or it runs a risk of overemphasizing individual freedom and thereby leaving structural reproduction mysterious.

Nevertheless, the concepts of structure and agency continue to hold pragmatic value for empirical social research. The theoretical analyses of Giddens, Bhaskar, Archer, and especially Bourdieu have been fertile for sociologists, and the value of their work particularly comes into view when structure and agency are not thought of as rigid or static ontological poles but rather in terms of dynamic contexts of social relations between interacting individuals and groups. Human groups are not determined by rules which impose upon them, nor do they follow rules in private isolation. Individuals are able to act relatively predictably and to create social order because they routinely accept certain common understandings of what is appropriate, and these understandings become binding and constraining. It is the task of sociologists to analyse the historical significance of social processes that emerge from these dynamic relations.

■ QUESTIONS FOR CHAPTER 10

1   How useful are the concepts of structure and agency for social analysis?

2   How similar and how different are the social theories of Giddens and Bourdieu?

3   What is meant by an objectivist standpoint on social life? What is meant by a subjectivist standpoint? How are the problems of the two standpoints to be avoided?

4   How illuminating is Bourdieu's assertion that cultural tastes and educational achievements are functions of 'cultural capital'?

5   What differences are to be noted between the concept of class and the concept of habitus?

6   In what sense is socio-economic inequality a cultural phenomenon?

■ FURTHER READING

For useful introductions to the work of Giddens, see Lars Bo Kaspersen's *Anthony Giddens: An Introduction to a Social Theorist* (Blackwell, 2000), Kenneth Tucker's *Anthony Giddens and Modern Social Theory* (Sage, 1998), Ira J. Cohen's *Structuration Theory* (Macmillan, 1989), and Ian Craib's *Anthony Giddens* (Routledge, 1992). For a good overall account of Giddens's theory of structuration, see John Parker's *Structuration* (Open University Press, 2000). The best collection of secondary work on structuration theory is David Held and John B. Thompson's edited *Social Theory of Modern Societies: Anthony Giddens and his Critics* (Cambridge University Press, 1989). See also Christopher Bryant and David Jary's edited *Giddens' Theory of Structuration* (Routledge, 1991) and J. Clark, C. Modgil, and S. Modgil's edited *Anthony Giddens: Consensus and Controversy* (Falmer Press, 1990). For a wide-ranging collection of essays, see Christopher Bryant and David Jary's edited four volumes *Anthony Giddens: Critical Assessments* (Routledge, 1996). The key texts for Giddens's theory of structuration are *The Constitution of Society* (Polity Press, 1984), *New Rules of Sociological Method* (Hutchinson, 1976), and *Central Problems in Social Theory* (Macmillan, 1979). For an incisive critique of Giddens, see Alex Callinicos's two articles 'Anthony Giddens: A Contemporary Critique', *Theory and Society*, 14 5 (1985), 133–66, and 'Social Theory Put to the Test of Practice: Pierre Bourdieu and Anthony Giddens', *New Left Review*, 236 (1999), 77–102.

Some good studies and guides to Bourdieu are Derek Robbins's two books *The Work of Pierre Bourdieu* (Open University Press, 1991) and *Bourdieu and Culture* (Sage, 2000), David Swartz's *Culture and Power: The Sociology of Pierre Bourdieu* (Chicago University Press, 1997), Richard Jenkins's *Bourdieu* (Routledge, 1993), Bridget Fowler's *Pierre Bourdieu and Cultural Theory* (Sage, 1997), and Jen Webb, Tony Schirato, and Geoff Danaher's *Understanding Bourdieu* (Sage, 2002). An excellent advanced collection of essays on Bourdieu is C. Calhoun, E. LiPuma, and M. Postone's edited *Bourdieu: Critical Perspectives* (Polity Press, 1993). In this collection, see especially the contribution by Charles Taylor, titled 'To Follow a Rule'. See also the discussion in Craig Calhoun's *Critical Social Theory* (Blackwell, 1995), as well as Richard Shusterman's edited *Bourdieu: A Critical Reader* (Blackwell, 1999) and Derek Robbins's edited four volumes *Pierre Bourdieu* (Sage, 2000). A useful selection from Bourdieu's works is John B. Thompson's edited *Language and Symbolic Power: Pierre Bourdieu* (Polity Press, 1991). A good place to begin reading Bourdieu is his book *Distinction: A Social Critique of the Judgement of Taste* (Routledge, 1984), as well as his co-written book with Loïc Wacquant *An Invitation to Reflexive Sociology* (Polity Press, 1992). For further developments in French and American sociology influenced by Bourdieu, see Michèle Lamont and Laurent Thévenot's edited *Rethinking Comparative Cultural Sociology* (Cambridge University Press, 2000).

For a guide to British realist theory, see Andrew Collier's *Critical Realism: An Introduction to Roy Bhaskar's Philosophy* (Verso, 1994). Margaret Archer's key works are *Culture and Agency* (Cambridge University Press, 1988) and *Realist Social Theory* (Cambridge University Press, 1995). See also José López and John Scott's useful guide *Social Structure* (Open University Press, 2000) and Charles Crothers's *Social Structure* (Routledge, 1996). For a comparative critical study of Giddens, Bourdieu, Archer, and realist theory, see Anthony King's *The Structure of Contemporary Social Theory* (Routledge, 2004).

▣ WEBSITES

Homepage of Anthony Giddens at **www.lse.ac.uk/Giddens/** Includes a bibliography of key works and links to various lectures by Giddens.

Structuration Theory at **www.clas.ufl.edu/users/gthursby/mod/gidcns.htm** Contains an excerpt from a key text by Giddens dealing with structuration.

Roy Bhaskar at **www.raggedclaws.com/criticalrealism/archive/rts/rts.html** Provides an on-line transcription of a text of Bhaskar on realist theory of science.

Pierre Bourdieu at **www.utu.fi/erill/RUSE/blink.html** Contains links to sites on Bourdieu, with bibliographies, review articles, and excerpts from key works.

Bourdieu in Perspective at **www.isj1text.ble.org.uk/pubs/isj87/wolfreys.htm** Presents a lengthy article on Bourdieu's contributions to sociology and French intellectual life generally.

11 Feminist Social Theory

Lisa Adkins

There are a number of ways in which the history of feminist social theory has been thought and told. One of the most often rehearsed is the idea that feminist social theory has moved away from the ideals of *Enlightenment thought, associated with *universalist values of rationality, reason, and equality. It has been claimed that feminist social theory has moved instead towards 'post-Enlightenment' values, associated with ideas of 'difference', 'specificity', and *'particularism'. In this sense it has been suggested that feminist social theory has contested the ideals that classical social theory both embodied and contributed towards—ideals exemplified in the work of figures such as Marx, Weber, Durkheim, and Simmel.

While this narrative is widely told and certainly sheds light on some important trajectories of feminist social theory, it is misleading to speak of any straightforward shift from

Enlightenment to 'post-Enlightenment', or to *'postmodern', thinking in contemporary feminist theory. This assumption overlooks a number of ways in which contemporary feminist theorists have rethought and are rethinking the social categories of gender in full recognition of the problems associated with the traditions of Enlightenment thought. To understand this ambivalent and multi-sided legacy, this chapter provides an overview of feminist social theory by setting out three key moments or phases in the history of feminist interventions in social analysis. The *first* moment or phase involves the observation that both classical and contemporary social theory tends to exclude women from the object-domain of social theory and that masculinity remains routinely privileged in accounts of sociality and modernity. The *second* moment or phase involves attempts to correct this exclusion by means of a thoroughgoing historicization and sociologization of the category of woman, notably by means of the concept of *'gender'. The *third* moment or phase involves qualified criticism of feminist projects which seek to historicize and socialize the category of woman. This has involved the observation that sometimes such projects may simply *add* women into pre-existing theoretical frameworks, leaving the assumptions of such frameworks untouched and ignoring their fundamentally gendered character.

We begin by looking at feminist analyses of the association of modernity with masculinity in classical social thought. We then discuss some of the most important themes in contemporary feminist social theory concerning labour, reproduction, sexuality, and gender and the relation of gender to class and ethnicity.

Women in classical social theory: the exclusion of women from the social

Classical social theory sought to come to grips with the changes associated with industrialization, capitalism, urbanization, *rationalization, and the condition of modernity in the broadest sense. In this project, early feminist interventions in classical sociology pointed overwhelmingly to a privileging of the masculine subject in descriptions of the modern condition and to an apparent exclusion of women from the experiences and sensations of modernity. Whether it was from the dizzying experiences of rapidly urbanizing cities, or the political consciousness of wage labour, or experiences of alienation or *anomie, feminists have argued that the classical tradition tended to associate these experiences more with masculinity than with femininity. Feminist commentators have observed out that this exclusion of women took place in a variety of ways, but crucially revolved around an association of women with sets of relations deemed to be outside the institutions and experiences of the modern. In many classical narratives, women were typically associated with irrationality, tradition, corporeality, and the private and domestic spheres. They were not seen as directly part of the worlds of rationality, capitalism, the urban, and industrialism, represented by the public realms of wage labour, bureaucracy, and politics. Women's relations were almost seen to be pre-industrial or non-capitalist. Thus it has been argued that classical social theory tended to locate women in an antithetical relationship to the modern, indeed as outside the very object of social theory—the social. This can be illustrated in various aspects of the work of Weber, Durkheim, and Simmel.

Feminist perspectives on Weber, Durkheim, and Simmel

An important focus of attention for feminist critics has been Max Weber's conception of the transition from personal traditional forms of power to impersonal, legal-rational forms of *domination. Weber postulated that traditional modes of power are characterized by *patriarchal domination, by the rule of the father and the husband. This was a direct mode of domination that found its ideal-typical form in household groups organized via kinship arrangements and legitimized via the sanctity of tradition. Under this mode of domination, Weber saw women and children as subject to the authority of the patriarch. However, while Weber understood the power of the patriarch to be social in origin, he understood the domination of women to take place through unchanging characteristics of the relations between men, women, and children. Weber wrote that 'the woman is dependent because of the normal superiority of the physical and intellectual energies of the male, and the child because of his [*sic*] objective helplessness' (Weber 1922*a*: 1007; see also Sydie 1987: 59). In short, Weber assigned the household domination of women (and of children) to *nature*, and men's power to *culture*.

While Weber understood this mode of domination to be limited in scope and historically specific, he saw it as forming the bedrock of subsequent forms of power relations and social formations. Thus he understood the emergence of bureaucratization and processes of rationalization as involving a transformation of patriarchal domination. Rationalization involved a transformation from direct, patriarchal rule to impersonal, public modes of domination. In his writings, modern rational-legal power is imagined as an indirect, impersonal form of male power.

It can be argued that Weber's theorization here relies explicitly on a gendered *dualism where masculinity is overwhelmingly associated with rationalization and femininity is associated with the irrational. The operation of this dualism works to position both women and femininity outside the experiences and social relations of modernity; that is, outside the culture of rationality. This is evident in the ways Weber imagines the Protestant ethic and its control and suppression of emotions and desires as a masculine ethic. Associating women with irrationality, Weber tended to position women as unable to achieve the rational lifestyle that he saw as characterizing the condition of modernity (compare Bologh 1990; Wolff 1990; Hekman 1999; Gerhard 2003).

In general, feminist critics have argued that classical social theory typically understands social action as a matter of the dominance of mind over body, as a task of transcending and transforming the constraints of corporeality. In this sense classical social theory tends to deny or ignore the role of the body for both human subjects and social action, constructing a disembodied, abstract, rational subject as the ideal subject of modernity. Feminist commentators have pointed to ways in which such mind–body dualism is distinctly gendered, associating the body overwhelmingly with women (compare Grosz 1990; Weiss 1999). In classical narratives women are often positioned as unable to transcend corporeality.

They are often presented as being unable to achieve the mental condition required for participation in modern forms of social action. In *Suicide* Durkheim writes that man is 'almost entirely the product of society', while woman is 'to a far greater extent the product of nature' (Durkheim 1897: 385; see also Sydie 1987: 32). Durkheim also asserts that man's 'tastes, aspirations and humour have in large part a collective origin, while his companion's are more directly influenced by her organism' (Durkheim 1897: 385; see also Sydie 1987: 32). This is held to be so even for those women who participate in public life. In *The Division of Labour in Society*, Durkheim writes of such women: 'Certain classes of women participate in artistic and literary life just as men . . . But, even in this sphere of action, woman carries out her own nature, and her role is very specialized, very different from that of man' (Durkheim 1893: 19–20).

In Simmel's two notable essays 'The Relative and the Absolute in the Problem of the Sexes' and 'Female Culture' (1911*b*, 1911*c*), women are similarly positioned as unable to achieve the capacities for participation in the social. Two aspects can be observed in these essays. On the one hand, Simmel is unique in classical sociology in his concern to criticize the equation of masculinity with modernity. For Simmel, women's experience of life operates as a challenge to the alienating, contradictory, and dizzying experiences of modernity. Women possess a 'non-differentiated wholeness'; they remain centred, or 'grounded', in themselves. In contrast, Simmel saw men as suffering the ill fortune of experiencing all the fragmenting, alienating, and differentiating forces of modernity. On the other hand, Simmel locates femininity and women outside the socio-historical time of modernity. They remain outside the socio-cultural arrangements and experiences his theory describes. This is the case for Simmel as the 'non-differentiated wholeness' of women ensures that women do not, and cannot, experience or achieve the detachment and critical reflection necessary for participation in the cultural and institutional forms of modernity. In Simmel's social theory, women cannot transcend their being—a being which Simmel defined primarily in terms of sexuality—in order to become social agents. Femininity and feminine culture occupy a zone of 'being', rather than a zone of 'becoming', one of immanence rather than of transcendence. As Marshall and Witz comment, in the early sociological imaginary of Durkheim and Simmel 'women are locked into and overwhelmed by their corporeality, whilst men rise above it and are defined, determined and distinguished by their sociality' (Marshall and Witz 2003: 28; see also Felski 1995; Witz 2001).

The body as an 'absent presence' in classical and contemporary theory

While it is important to point to an exclusion of women from classical visions of the social, it is also important to note some ongoing legacies of this tradition today. In this connection, several feminist commentators have detected a reinstatement of the privileged masculine *subject of the classical tradition in more contemporary forms of social theory—even though it is frequently claimed that women and men are being released from the constraints, rules, and norms of gender associated with classical or 'high' modernity. Lois McNay (1999, 2000), for example, argues that the emphasis in recent social theory on increased possibilities for the self-fashioning of identity in late modern cultures recuperates classical notions of a privileged masculine subject. McNay points particularly to Anthony Giddens's widely cited analysis of late modern identity in terms of *'reflexivity' (discussed in Chapter 13 of this book, pp. 287–9). This is the case, McNay argues, since the idea of a self-fashioned identity fails to take into account certain embodied, embedded, and habituated aspects of identity, especially those connected to gender and sexuality, which are not straightforwardly available to self-fashioning. McNay is not suggesting here that gender and sexual identities are fixed. Rather, following Bourdieu (1972), she argues that there are aspects of identity which are not accessible to self-conscious transformation. She suggests that sexual desire and maternal feelings are relatively entrenched and pre-reflexive aspects of identity which are not open to deliberate alteration. McNay suggests that in emphasizing increased capacities for the self-fashioning of identity and overlooking issues of habit and embodiment, recent social theory reinstates the idea of an abstract, disembodied, rational and masculine subject found so commonly in the classical tradition.

The influence of the classical tradition has been detected in branches of contemporary theory which at face value appear to break with this legacy. In particular, recent sociological writing on the body has drawn attention to problems of mind–body dualism in classical sociology, but has not always sufficiently recognized the *gendered* aspects of this dualism (see for example, Turner 1984; Williams and Bendelow 1998). Writers on the body have suggested that mind–body dualism can be countered by discovering embodied themes and subplots in the works of Marx, Weber, Durkheim, and Simmel. Thus Shilling (1993) notes an embodied subplot in Marx's writings on emerging modes of capitalist modes of regulation. Specifically, Shilling suggests that in Marx's writings, capitalist forms of regulation develop not simply through consciousness (the mind) but also through the body. Capitalist technology ties and subordinates both working minds and bodies to machinery. Such contemporary accounts suggest that rather than being entirely absent, the body is an 'absent presence' in the classical tradition. It is, however, important to emphasize that such mind–body dualism is also a gendered dualism (Witz 2000). Contemporary sociologists of the body have not always sufficiently registered the fact that the classical tradition tended to associate specifically *women* with the body. As a result, the forms of embodied sociality that social theory discovers and makes explicit are in danger of remaining predominantly masculine.

Women and socialization: labour, reproduction, and sexuality

The legacies of classical social theory have led to an overwhelming impulse among feminist sociologists to *socialize* women. That is, feminist writers have sought to demonstrate how, rather than being outside the social, women are full agents in the social field and participate in all of the key facets of life delineated by the classical tradition. This project has been multifaceted and has both theoretical and empirical dimensions.

In the 1970–1980s, feminist sociologists developed projects that sought to establish how women experience alienation at the workplace, no less than men (see Pollert 1981; Westwood 1984). Existing sociological class analyses were criticized for their exclusion of women, especially the assumption that the class position of women is determined by, and can be read off from, the class position of men—for example, from husbands or fathers.

New class schemes were developed to allocate social class positions to women and hence modern forms of political consciousness to women (see Crompton and Mann 1986). Existing sociological studies of work and industry were criticized for their focus on occupations that have been predominately associated with men, including particularly manufacturing work, and for their assumption that women's employment in some way deviates from a masculine norm (see Beechey 1988). Feminist sociologists have instead examined occupations that have tended to be associated predominately with women, including clerical, secretarial, and care-based occupations (see Crompton and Jones 1984; Pringle 1988).

This project of 'socializing' women has involved a reassessment of those areas of life that the classical tradition located outside the domain of the social. Considerable attention has been paid to establishing the social organization and regulation of those aspects of life hitherto coded variously as 'natural', 'corporeal', or 'private'. Thus feminist sociologists have examined the social organization and regulation of human reproduction, including especially the role of medical institutions and technology in producing distinct forms of the regulation of reproduction and hence of the regulation of women (see Stanworth 1987).

Numerous writers on gender have also examined the socio-historical construction of sexuality. Following a groundbreaking essay by Adrienne Rich (1983) on the institutional construction of heterosexuality, much early work in this area delineated the social and public organization of heterosexuality, showing how heterosexuality is imbued with relations of power and constitutes an occluded source of women's oppression. One strand of this work has interrogated the significance of visual media, especially representations of women in advertising, film, and television. Such studies have noted how the representation of women invariably takes place with reference to sexual codes that position women as objects of a sexualizing male gaze (compare Pollock 1988; Mulvey 1989). This work underscores how some of the key institutions and characteristics of modernity, including the culture industries and the mass media, typically frame women as passive objects and men as active sexual subjects.

A further element in the project of socializing women has involved interrogations of household and domestic arrangements. In one of the best known of these interventions, Ann Oakley argued that housework needs to be understood as *work*, as a job 'analogous to any other kind of work in modern society'—rather than as a naturalized extension of femininity (Oakley 1974*a*: 2; see also Oakley 1974*b*). This has been a central tenet of feminist engagements with Marxism in social theory, to which we now turn.

Feminism and Marxism

The decades of the 1960s and 1970s saw a particularly intense series of debates about the relationship between Marxism and feminism. A key focus of discussion concerned the relations between domestic labour and the reproduction of labour power (see Secombe 1974). At issue was an attempt to confer on domestic labour both exchange value and surplus value—and not simply use value. That is, at issue was an attempt to understand domestic labour as central to the workings of capitalism. This was significant as Marxist theory traditionally tended to exclude domestic labour from analyses of production, ignoring the preconditions that made wage labour possible. Given the tendency of traditional Marxist thought to view women almost exclusively in familial and domestic terms, notably as family dependants of the proletariat, the extension of the concepts of production and labour relations to include domestic production was significant. Feminist reworkings of Marxist social theory allowed women as domestic labourers—as servicers of wage labourers and as bearers and rearers of children—to be included in the very sets of exchanges and relationships which Marx saw as defining industrial capitalism. This modification endowed women with modern forms of social and political identity, instead of excluding them from the modes of *subjectivity and *agency associated with modernity. It allowed for the articulation of distinctly feminist modernist claims such as 'wages for housework'.

A further line of argument came in the form of a questioning of *ideology in the constitution of inequality and power relations between men and women. One of the earliest and fullest accounts of this kind was provided by Michèle *Barrett (1980; see also Barrett and Phillips 1992). Barrett made two central claims: first, that 'women's oppression is not a theoretical prerequisite of capitalism but is historically embedded in its social relations and thus material'; and second, that 'the role of ideology in this process should not be underestimated' (Hamilton and Barrett 1986: p. iv). Barrett underlined that moves to rethink ideology outside economistic frameworks—where ideology tended to be understood as a mechanical reflection of an economic base—opened up an important space for feminist social theorists concerned with gender divisions, gender identities, and capitalist social formation. As she put it, 'it has become possible, within a new form of Marxism, to accommodate the oppression of women as a relatively autonomous element of the social formation' (Barrett 1980: 31).

Barrett rejected the view that women's oppression can be accounted for purely with reference to the 'needs' of capitalism; that is, via a purely *functionalist account, in the vein of Talcott *Parsons's work on the family (discussed in Chapter 4 of this book, pp. 99, 103). Barrett argued that the role of domestic and familial ideology was also crucial. Writing against the background of *Gramscian and *Althusserian Marxism, she claimed that unequal gender divisions of labour between men and women in both the workforce and the domestic sphere are grounded in what she termed a heterosexual familial ideology, which defined both women and children as dependants upon on a male breadwinner's family wage. Barrett showed how state welfare provisions and capitalist systems of wage labour embodied this familialist model. She also noted how gender identity and family ideology are 'embedded in our subjectivity and our desires' (Barrett 1980: 226), claiming that 'it is only through an analysis of ideology and its role in the construction of gendered subjectivity that we can account for the desires of women as well as men to reproduce the very familial structures by which we are oppressed' (Barrett 1980: 251). Highlighting the operation of a specific ideology of gender—the duality of masculinity and femininity— Barrett challenged gender-neutral assumptions in Marxism and expanded Marxist concepts to include not only women but also power relations between men and women. In short, Barrett articulated some distinctively Marxist-feminist principles.

Modernity as a gendered construct

Marxist-feminist and other approaches in the theoretical socialization of women have contributed greatly to correcting the one-sided terms and propositions of mainstream, or 'malestream', social science. One general objection to such approaches, however, is that they tend to be concerned largely only with *filling in the gaps* of maintream research. They advert to various occluded elements of women's experience in appropriate ways, but without always questioning the fundamental organizing concepts and categories of mainstream thinking. In general, it is possible to qualify this work as 'correctionist' in character. It represents an attempt to modify an androcentric bias via a strategy of inserting women into already existing theoretical discourses and narratives. This strategy continues to be of great importance, but it often tends to leave the major assumptions of the canon untouched in unfortunate ways. As a consequence, it sometimes fails to grasp adequately a crucial characteristic of the very narratives and discourses it seeks to correct, namely, that these narratives are gendered in character.

In contrast, some of the most important feminist work in recent years has sought not simply to include women in modernity, but also to explore what can be called the *gendering of modernity. In the words of Janet Wolff, such work has raised not simply 'a question of discovering women's point of view, or making visible those obscured by a masculinist view of modernity, or of promoting the hidden features of a "feminine sensibility" in modern life'. Rather, it has involved a 'project of the critical analysis of the discourses of modernity, in order to confront directly their constructions of masculinity' (Wolff 2000: 37–8; see also Harding 1986; D. E. Smith 1987).

In confronting this gendering of modernity, more recent feminist work has moved beyond correctionist writing in two respects. First, it has registered that the project of socializing women has tended to rely on a rather problematic dualistic distinction between 'sex and gender'. Secondly, it has shown how the woman who was animated in the project of the socialization of women was too homogeneous and in particular too exclusively endowed with white European bourgeois and heterosexual characteristics.

The remaining sections of this chapter discuss three further elements of feminist social theory in this latter framework: first, the idea of modern culture and society as a gendered construct; secondly, debates around the meaning of gender and the sex–gender distinction; and thirdly, debates about the relationship of gender to other dimensions of inequality, including 'race', ethnicity, and sexual orientation.

Constructions of femininity and masculinity

We have seen that both classical and more contemporary forms of social theory have tended to operate by excluding women from the domain of the social in favour of a masculinist vision of modernity. However, it is not true to say that women do not figure *at all* in classical visions of the social. In the nineteenth century, women often did figure in such visions, particularly those produced by poets, artists, and essayists; but it tended to be only certain *categories* of women who were made visible (compare Wilson 1991; Felski 1995).

In this connection, Janet Wolff notes that in Charles Baudelaire's essays on the experiences of nineteenth-century European cities, urban spaces are not the exclusive domain of men. Women appear very often in Baudelaire's writings as 'the prostitute, the widow, the old lady, the lesbian, the murder victim, and the passing unknown woman' (Wolff 1990: 41). Wolff notes the ambivalence that Baudelaire displays towards such figures in his writings. For instance, the prostitute and the lesbian are simultaneously figures of admiration and figures of disgust. Wolff notes how it was commonly assumed that women participating in the nineteenth-century public sphere on terms similar to men were manifesting masculine traits. Thus widows, lesbians, and prostitutes are described in Baudelaire as possessing masculine characteristics and mannerisms. Indeed Baudelaire's 'mixed admiration for the lesbian has much to do with her supposed "mannishness"' (Wolff 1990: 42).

Yet while the prostitute and the lesbian may have occupied some of the same city spaces as men, nineteenth-century writings ascribed heterosexual bourgeois women to entirely different city spaces. These typically included the rapidly developing sites of bourgeois consumption, notably the department store (compare Reekie 1993). The department store was an ambiguous space, both in a public and a private sense. The purchases made there by middle-class women were not simply for themselves but for the bourgeois family and home. The development of such bourgeois sites of consumption stemmed from, and was in part constitutive of, the rapidly developing bourgeois private sphere. As Wilson (1991) points out, in such public spaces middle-class women looked and were looked at. What counted in such spaces was respectability. The spaces of consumption and its very process were central to the development of respectable middle-class femininity (see also McClintock 1995; Lury 1996; Davidoff and Hall 1987).

What is important in these observations of the place and categorization of women in the literature of modernity is that they make explicit what is often left hidden in canonical social theory. They reveal that the changes and upheavals which classical social theory sought to illuminate rested on an increasing separation of public and private spheres of activity. The rise of sociology itself in the nineteenth century was closely bound up with this separation. It is important to note that the emergence of forms of differentiation between public and private was both classed and gendered. The backdrop to much classical social theory was the emergence and legitimation of new bourgeois ideals regarding the place of men and women in the social, as well new ideals of masculinity and femininity. The latter concerned the elaboration of ideals of a competitive masculinity and a domestic nurturing femininity, ideals which were realized in the formation of separate spheres of public and private. As Felski (1995) points out, while these arrangements were feasible only for a minority of middle-class households, the model of a *binary opposition between the sexes crystallized in the notion of separate spheres, underscoring a host of institutional practices and conventions. The latter included the sexual division of labour and the sexual division of political rights.

Seen in this light, we may say that the ambivalence displayed towards women who participated in the public sphere in the nineteenth century, including their very identification and classification as non-respectable women—for instance as prostitutes, widows, or labouring women—was made possible by new ideals of respectable femininity. We can understand classical sociology's naturalization of women's place in the domestic sphere, its romanticization of women's role as nurturing mothers, and its positioning of women as unable to transcend their corporeality, indeed *as* corporeality, in terms of a binary opposition between 'femininity' and 'masculinity'. It is in this sense that classical sociology made sense of modernity via 'a deeply gendered analysis of social life'—even as it laid claim to impartial universal validity (Marshall 1994: 2). While basing itself on a series of binary distinctions—between public and private, economy and family, universal and particular—social theory has not often considered the gendered character of its guiding distinctions. Such distinctions have led to a misleading conflation of modernity with masculinity, a classification of non-bourgeois women as non-respectable or 'mannish', and an assignment of bourgeois women to domesticity.

BOX 28. NANCY FRASER ON HABERMAS AND THE PUBLIC SPHERE

The US feminist Nancy *Fraser has examined an interesting subplot about gender in Jürgen *Habermas's influential conception of the *'public sphere' (discussed also in Chapters 7 and 13 of this book, pp. 164–5, 279–83). Referring to Habermas's view of modernization as involving an uncoupling of 'system' and 'lifeworld', Fraser suggests that Habermas's conception rests on a gendered subtext which prioritizes masculine identity.

Habermas argues that modernization involves a colonization of the 'lifeworld' by the 'system'. Criticizing this process of colonization, Habermas argues that the systems of the state and the market ought to be embedded in, and constrained, by lifeworld institutions. Habermas argues that the private sphere becomes dominated by the economic system and that the public sphere—the site and space of political participation—becomes dominated by the state system. He argues that this domination of the private sphere takes place via a set of exchanges conducted in the medium of money. It provides the economy with labour power in exchange for wages and demand for goods and services (commodities). In Habermasian social theory, as Fraser puts it, 'exchanges between family and (official) economy . . . are channeled through the "roles" of worker and consumer' (Fraser 1989: 123).

Intervening in this theory, Fraser points out that these roles of worker and consumer in capitalist societies are also distinctly gendered. This gendering means that the relations between the private sphere and the economy must be understood to take place via the medium of modern gender identity—not only by the neutral medium of money. In capitalist societies, the role of the worker has been gendered as male, at least until relatively recently (compare Lovell 2000; Adkins 2002). Thus the role of the worker has been historically associated with masculinity, embodied in struggles for a family wage. These struggles assumed that a worker is a man with a dependent wife and children. Given this gendering of the worker as male, women in capitalist societies have typically not been employed on the same terms as men (compare Adkins 1995; Pateman 1988; Pringle 1988; Walby 1986). As Fraser puts it, there has been 'a conceptual dissonance between femininity and the work role in classical capitalism [which] confirms the masculine subtext of that role' (Fraser 1989: 125). Moreover, the role of the private sphere in consumer capitalism is far from neutral: it has historically been overwhelmingly associated with women. It is women who have been typically charged with the work of domestic consumption, including the work of domestic display and taste-making, or what Bourdieu (1979) terms social 'distinction' (see also Delphy and Leonard 1992; Game and Pringle 1984; Hollows 2000; Lury 1996). Fraser thus concludes that Habermas fails to appreciate that one of the most important media of exchange in capitalist societies is gender identity. Habermas only understands the categories of 'worker' and 'consumer' in gender-neutral language of monetary exchange.

We can see here how Fraser makes several important conceptual moves. First, she shows how the problem with mainstream social theory is not so much that women have been straightforwardly excluded from the social but rather that gender remains a hidden and taken-for-granted component of it. Secondly, in her rethinking of the categories of worker, consumer, and exchange and the relations between public and private spheres, she does not simply correct the bias of social theory by merely *adding* women into an already existing framework. Rather, she engages in a *reconceptualization* of modernity along gendered lines.

One revealing exposure of a hidden subplot about gender in contemporary social theory is the work of the US feminist theorist Nancy Fraser in relation to Jürgen Habermas's concept of the public sphere. This is discussed here in Box 28.

The sex–gender distinction

We turn now to a second object of contention in feminist writing aimed at revising purely 'correctionist' research. This is the distinction between 'sex' on the one hand and 'gender' on the other.

In her classic work *The Second Sex*, the French feminist philosopher Simone de *Beauvoir famously declared: 'One is not born a woman, one becomes one' (1949: 295). For feminist theorists and sociologists, de Beauvoir's leitmotif has been vital to the project of socializing women. De Beauvoir explained how the social position, identity, and consciousness of women are products of a form of interaction which systematically positions woman as Other to a universal subject, a subject who is unmarked as Man. From de Beauvoir's standpoint, the hierarchical and antagonistic positioning of men and women was to be seen as socially produced. It was this injunction that allowed for a modern feminist concept of gender, a concept which, as Donna *Haraway puts it, was 'developed to contest the naturalization of sexual difference in multiple arenas of struggle' (Haraway 1991*a*: 131). The concept of gender was developed as a foil to the view found in much classical social theory that women exist outside the socio-historical time of modernity, typically via an association with nature. It was through the concept of gender that feminist theorists placed women inside the contours of the social and allowed for an elaboration of the category of woman as both collective and historical. It allowed women to be written into history.

There is, however, a problem with the concept of gender when it is formulated in this way, insofar as it relies on a rather problematic distinction between 'sex and gender'. 'Sex' has been defined as anatomical, physical differences between men and women, while 'gender' has been understood as the social meanings given to such differences. Sex has been understood to be biological; gender has been thought to be cultural. Sex has been typically understood as a neutral inscriptive surface, onto which external social meaning is mapped.

It was in this sense that Michèle Barrett took issue with feminists in the 1970s whom she saw as invoking universalizing, ahistorical, and biologistic notions of male dominance. Barrett argued that such accounts failed to grasp 'the distinction between sex as a biological category and gender as a social one' (Barrett 1980: 13). In the 1970s, the social category of gender provided a powerful platform to contest women's association with corporeality and nature and women's exclusion from the social and historical.

In retrospect, however, it is clear that the sex–gender distinction suffers from certain problematic *metaphysical assumptions. Specifically, the sex–gender distinction relies on a philosophical dualism between mind and body, society and nature, and history and nature. It associates gender with the mind, consciousness, history, and society; and sex with the body and nature. What these linkages crucially ignore is the *historicity of the body*, the historicity of the categories of sex, and the significance of *materiality* in the making of

---

BOX 29. JUDITH BUTLER ON DISCOURSE AND THE SEX–GENDER DISTINCTION

Following Michel *Foucault (1976, 1984*a*), Judith *Butler argues that sex is not a simple fact or static condition. Sex is a regulatory ideal that produces the bodies it governs. Sex is a *discursive construct*, a construct of discourses about the body. It is a regulatory force that has productive power: 'the power to produce—demarcate, circulate, differentiate—the bodies it controls' (Butler 1993: 1). Thus, rather than being a given or passive surface upon which gender is imposed, sex is an ideal whose materialization is compelled through highly regulated practices. Butler invites us to ask the following questions:

Does sex have a history? Does each sex have a different history or histories? Is there a history of how the duality of sex was established, a genealogy that might expose the binary oppositions as a variable construction? Are the ostensibly natural facts of sex discursively produced by various scientific discourses in the service of other political and social interests? . . . [P]erhaps this construct called 'sex' is as culturally constructed as gender . . . with the consequence that the distinction between sex and gender turns out to be no distinction at all. . . . Gender ought not to be conceived merely as the cultural inscription of meaning on a pre-given sex . . . gender must also designate the very apparatus of production whereby the sexes themselves are established. (Butler 1998: 279)

Butler concludes that gender is not to culture as sex is to nature. Rather, gender is the cultural means by which a 'natural sex' is established as pre-discursive, as 'nature'. In challenging the sex–gender distinction, Butler highlights how the use of this distinction has a purely 'correctionist' character. That is, it leaves the conventional philosophical dualisms of society–nature and mind–body untouched.

   Repudiating any correctionist strategy, Butler does not simply seek to insert women into the social. She asks how it is that in Western thought sex is established as pre-discursive or pre-social. In so doing, she does not simply add women into pre-existing theoretical narratives. She challenges the conventional universalizing distinction of Western philosophy between 'culture', and 'nature', and in doing so she suggests an alternative conception of the relationship between 'sex' and 'gender'.

'gender' (compare Laqueur 1990; Martin 1994). One of the most influential critical voices in this regard has been the US theorist Judith Butler, whose work is discussed here in Box 29.

   This significance of the historicity of sex and the body and the materiality of gender has been underscored by several recent feminist writers. These authors examine historically changing relations between nature and culture, and in many cases they argue for a thoroughgoing dismantling of differences between the two. In one notable instance of this, Celia Lury (2002) examines the process by which a human social type becomes a consumer 'brand' with definite gendered as well as racialized characteristics. For example, the iconography of Benetton, the global fashion company, illustrates this process well. Lury notes how the culturalization of human categories of genre, kind, or type is central to Benetton's brand image and marketing strategy. Hence in Benetton, the iconography of ' "race" is presented not as a matter of skin colour, of physical characteristics, as the expression of biological or natural essence, but rather of *style*' (Lury 2002: 591). Differences previously coded as nature are here rewritten as culture, or as Lury puts it 'not . . . gender, race and class, but lifeforms ™ and lifestyles ™' (Lury 2002: 599).

   What is important about such constructions of boundaries and their various processes of breakdown is, as Donna *Haraway puts it, that they unsettle the dualisms that 'have been systematic to the logics and practices of domination of women, people of color, nature, workers, animals' (Haraway 1991*b*: 177). In her own 'Cyborg Manifesto', Haraway (1991*b*) draws attention to a range of boundary and dichotomy breakdowns, including those between human and animal, nature and culture, organism and machine. These breakdowns mean that we 'find ourselves to be *cyborgs, hybrids, mosaics, chimeras' (Haraway 1991*b*: 177; see also Haraway 1997). In documenting such boundary breakdowns, writers such as Haraway and Lury note how new forms of power relations can emerge in such contexts, showing how the categories of gender, race, and class come to be rewritten in some surprising ways.

Heterosexuality and homosexuality

Further problems for the sex–gender distinction in feminist theory have turned on the issue of sexuality and sexual orientation. In particular, the distinction has tended to imply that gender is organized in terms of masculinity and femininity, that 'the sexes' are organized as a binary and complementary pair—with sexuality as an extension of this gender order. In short, the distinction has assumed a certain pervasive heterosexuality.

Historians and sociologists of sexuality have made clear that the modern sexual identity of heterosexuality and the very idea that sexuality makes up part of a person's embodied subjectivity is as much a specific historical product as the emergence of class identities (compare Foucault 1976; Seidman 1997; Smith-Rosenberg 1975). The historian Jeffrey Weeks (1981) shows how our modern concepts of heterosexuality and homosexuality emerged in the struggles of the middle classes to differentiate themselves from the older aristocracy and the emerging labouring classes. These concepts especially emerged in attempts by members of the middle classes to position themselves as morally superior to existing and emerging social groups. In a similar vein, other historians have delineated the emergence of a modern conception of the lesbian, demonstrating that the naming and identification of the lesbian as a category of person was not widespread until the early to mid-twentieth-century (Faderman 1981).

While sociologists and historians have challenged the view that sexuality is part of a pre-discursive nature, other writers have also asked—in much the same register as Butler—how it is that social theory imagines sexuality. How is it that a thinker such as Durkheim could declare: 'Precisely because man and woman are different, they seek each other passionately'? (Durkheim 1893: 17). For Steven Seidman (1996, 1997), the answer lies in the pervasive operation of a distinctly modern hetero/homosexual binary in social theory which both normalizes and universalizes heterosexuality. This normalization and universalization can only take place through, indeed requires, a positioning of homosexuality as *other* to heterosexuality. That is, social theory, and much early sociology of sexuality, including that which focused on homosexuality, did not question 'the social functioning of the hetero/homosexual binary as the master category of a modern regime of sexuality' (Seidman 1997: 88). Seidman argues that confronting this binary necessarily leads to reconceptualization: it provides grounds for a critique of the organization of social theory's key concepts and premises around a normative heterosexuality and for a rewriting of the texts of classical social theory. In Seidman's words, such a reconceptualization should make clear that 'the making of hetero-and-homosexualized bodies, desires, identities and societies . . . [are] master themes analogous to the rise of capitalism, the bureaucratization of social worlds, or modernization as social differentiation' (Seidman 1997: 96; see also Fuss 1991; Sedgwick 1990; Weston 1998).

Gender and its relation to exclusion

Some contributors have examined certain exclusionary effects of the concept of gender itself. Several writers have pointed to ways in which the concept of gender sometimes embodies unexplored dimensions of class and racial privilege. They have argued that in some cases the concept enacts certain modern ideals of liberalism that have only been imaginable and desirable for particular women from particular class and racial backgrounds, most notably from white middle-class backgrounds.

One object of criticism has been the view that the social categories of men and women are constituted in capitalist societies by indirect patriarchal control of women's labour power in the paid labour market, expressed in the horizontal and vertical gender segregation of paid work—the phenomenon of 'men's job's and 'women's jobs'. This view, which contains elements of both Weberian and Marxist theory, found popularity in the 1980s, particularly through the work of Heidi Hartmann (1979, 1981). It was the view that the segregation of women in paid wage labour encourages women's material dependency on men and hence relative powerlessness and exploitation in the domestic sphere. The main criticism that can be made of this account is that it fails to address the situation of women who are arguably *not* positioned in these ways, either in regard to the labour market or the domestic sphere. This criticism has particularly been articulated by African-American feminist writers.

African-American feminists have underlined how the household cannot always be imagined simply as a site of patriarchal oppression for women. They have shown how the household has also served historically as a site of resistance and solidarity—a 'homeplace' to use bell *hooks's phrase (hooks 1990)—against pervasive institutional racism, including the racism of the labour market. From this point of view, foregrounding women's segregation in paid wage labour only captures the situation of a select number of women, those who are relatively free to sell their wage labour as a form of alienable property. Such an assumption overlooks the complex historical positioning of a range of women in relation to labour as a form of property. Patricia Hill-Collins (1990) shows how the assumption ignores the historical positioning of African-American women in the political economy, including the historical ghettoization of black women in domestic work who live with and care for white families. Similarly, Carby (1982) criticizes received concepts of the family, patriarchy, and reproduction in feminist theory, suggesting that the common assumption that domestic labour contributes to social reproduction fails to understand the complexity of the positioning of black women. Carby asks: 'what does the concept of reproduction mean in a situation where black women have done domestic labour outside of their own homes in the servicing of white families? In this example they lie outside of the industrial wage-labour relation but in a situation where they are providing for the reproduction of black labour in their own domestic sphere, simultaneously ensuring the reproduction of white labour power in the "white" household' (Carby 1982: 392).

Examples abound of how some uses of the concept of gender can be exclusionary. The early emphasis in feminist sociology on the social condition of the housewife has been taken to task for its concern only with the problems of white middle-class Western women—the women who came closest to living a domestic ideal of femininity. Thus hooks (1984) criticized Betty *Friedan's (1963) *The Feminine Mystique* for focusing on the 'plight of a select group of college-educated, middle and upper class, married white women—housewives bored with leisure, with the home, with children, with buying products, who wanted more out of life . . . careers' (hooks 1984: 1). hooks maintains that a focus on the condition of the housewife ignores huge numbers of women working in jobs that neither liberate them from dependency on men nor make them economically self-sufficient.

Similarly, while much basic endorsement has been given to claims that women should have liberal political rights over their bodies, for instance reproductive rights, including the 'right to choose' abortions, some critics have emphasized that such claims can sometimes rest on a rather problematic notion of *ownership* of the body—on a liberal notion that the body is a 'property' of the self. The histories of race and class show that many women have been prevented from acceding to such an ideal of 'self-ownership' (compare Haraway 1991*a*; Pateman 1988).

Feminism and postcolonial theory

A final key zone of feminist engagement has involved *postcolonial analyses of the situation of women in non-Western contexts. Objection has frequently been taken to the ways in which Western feminist theorists have represented women from non-Western contexts. Thus Mohanty (1988, 2002) criticizes the ways in which particular Western feminist texts construct a 'Third World woman' as homogeneous, tradition-bound, and lacking in modern political rights. In her view, such texts tend to present an idealized image of Western women as, in contrast, 'modern', 'educated', 'liberated', and in control of their lives. Mills (1998) suggests that this practice can be related historically to colonial processes, and especially to ways in which white women living in colonial territories (for example British women in Africa and India) campaigned for the rights of colonized women whom they considered to be more oppressed than themselves (see also Ware 1992). In this sense, the colonized women acted as a vehicle for white colonial women to obtain a modern political subjectivity for themselves—one from which they could view themselves as privileged, modern, and enlightened. In this case it can be argued that some feminist discourse runs a risk of performing another act of domination: a kind of 'discursive colonization' of the lives and struggles of 'Third World women' (Mohanty 2002: 501). Drawing on the writings of other postcolonial critics such as Edward *Said (1978), Mohanty argues that what frames such textual strategies is a discursive system of classification which underlies Western Enlightenment knowledge systems. Such knowledge systems are based on a binary logic which repeatedly confirms and legitimizes the centrality of the West. This logic defines the non-Western as Other to the West, a definition which allows the West to represent itself as the 'centre'.

The Indian-American theorist Gayatri *Spivak (1988*a*, 1988*b*, 1992) also draws attention to colonizing tendencies in Western feminist theory. Spivak argues that what is called 'feminism' must be recognized as part of the heritage of the European Enlightenment, suggesting that the colonial object is constructed through long-standing European theories. Commenting on debates in the USA, Spivak remarks that as long as feminism 'remains ignorant of its own [theory], the "Third World Woman" as its object of study will remain constituted by those hegemonic First World intellectual practices' (Spivak 1988*a*: 81–2). She argues that such hegemony can occur even as attempts are made to attribute historicity and agency to colonial subjects. In her essay 'Can the Subaltern Speak?', Spivak (1988*b*) criticizes aspects of colonial historiography for its tendency to focus on elite indigenous subjects in colonial contexts, especially those performing administrative functions for colonial authorities. This focus excludes *subaltern subjects, that is, non-elite subordinated groups, even though such groups have historically been often involved in insurrections against colonial authorities.

What the arguments of Spivak, Mohanty, and others demonstrate is that some of the key concepts of Western feminist thought can be exclusionary unless suitably revised. The postcolonial critics show how not all women have been able to inhabit the category 'woman', as imagined by Western feminists. Some commentators have seen these arguments as demonstrating that the only reliable forms of knowledge that can be produced about women must be situated, partial, and local ones. In this respect it has been argued that post-Enlightenment values of difference, specificity, and particularism must rule. From this perspective, the history of feminist social theory is understood as an unfolding history of *difference*, a process of the release of the particular from the universal. As Rita Felski (2000) observes, in many feminist quarters the idea of 'difference' has become a doxa (see also Ahmed 1998).

However, a more nuanced way of evaluating these arguments might be to say that *both* the particular *and* the universal need to be thought at one and the same time. It would be preferable to seek strategies of critically reconstructing Western Enlightenment values and ideals while at the same time subjecting these values and ideals to rigorous sociological scrutiny. Of particular importance must be a recognition that gender is structured by, and is structuring of, divisions of race, class, and sexuality, as well divisions of 'First world'/'Third World', 'Western'/'non-Western', and 'North'/'South'. This has been made visible not only by postcolonial feminist theorists such as Mohanty and Spivak but also by historical studies such as that of Anne McClintock (1995). McClintock's study is discussed here in Box 30.

Feminist research such as McClintock's and others neither jettisons universalizing Enlightenment values of justice, freedom, and equality nor upholds these values in any culturally one-sided, Western-centred way. It shows how the categories of gender are not stable or culturally invariant and how they are historically constituted by and constitutive of divisions of race and class that are at the root of social inequality and oppression. It indicates a feminist theory of gender can and must be, simultaneously, a theory of racial difference in specific historical conditions of production and consumption. It suggests how it is possible and why it is important to rethink gender outside culturally short-sighted frameworks, while at the same time holding on to far-reaching *emancipatory ideals. In the words of Donna Haraway, the explanatory power of the category of gender depends on 'historicizing the categories of sex, flesh, body, biology, race, and nature in such a way that . . . binary, universalizing oppositions . . . implode into articulated, differentiated, accountable, located, and consequential theories

---

BOX 30. ANNE McCLINTOCK ON FEMINISM AND 'COMMODITY RACISM'

In her study *Imperial Leather: Race, Gender and Sexuality in the Colonial Contest*, Anne McClintock (1995) examines the emergence of an ideal of white domestic femininity in nineteenth-century European consumer culture, especially in the branding of commercial domestic products aimed at a white colonial female audience. McClintock shows how soap and other domestic products such as tea and biscuits were often presented in commodity imageries as embodying a colonial mission. Advertisements routinely located such products in colonial landscapes. The usually black people represented in such images were presented not as subjects but as a frame for the exhibition and display of commodities. As Lury puts it, the black woman's or man's 'function was to act as cipher, enabling a white perspective on imperialism to be conveyed' (Lury 1996: 160). McClintock shows how these advertisements did not display the uses to which the commodities were to be put—notably for domestic cleaning and laundry. Nor did they thematize the people who would use them, namely women, both black and white. The advertising imagery related instead to emerging ideals of bourgeois femininity which figured the proper white middle-class woman as one who did not work—and especially not for profit—and defined housework as a labour of love. In this sense, the commercial imagery of the nineteenth century can be understood as contributing to a consolidation of raced, classed, and gendered divisions. Specifically, this imagery wrote the new cult of domesticity through the script of a colonial imaginary which positioned colonized peoples as objects for an emerging European consumer culture. The middle-class ideal of white domestic femininity was figured through a new form of racism, which McClintock terms 'commodity racism' (see also Ahmed 2000).

---

of embodiment. . . . *Phallogocentrism was the egg ovulated by the master subject, the brooding hen to the permanent chickens of history. But into the nest with that literal-minded egg has been placed the germ of a phoenix that will speak in all the tongues of a world turned upside down' (Haraway 1991*a*: 148).

Conclusion

This chapter has documented three key moments in the development of feminist social theory. The first involved examining a certain exclusion of women from modernity in the classical tradition, via an association of modernity with masculinity. The second encompassed diverse projects of historicizing and socializing women with the aid of the concept of gender. The third element has involved various attempts to move beyond purely 'correctionist' thinking in feminist research by foregrounding the idea of the 'gendering of modernity'. The idea of modern culture and society as a gendered construct has led to a need to interrogate the guiding philosophical assumptions underlying distinctions between 'sex' as physical on the one hand and 'gender' as social or cultural on the other hand. It has given rise to a problematizing of dualisms of mind and body, culture and nature; and it has led us to see how the concept of gender can itself perform certain exclusionary effects when it is not adequately theorized, especially in regard to issues of 'race', class, and sexual orientation.

We have considered the view that certain forms of Western feminist theorizing enact discursive structures of hegemony as a consequence of insufficiently reflective reliance on Western Enlightenment knowledge systems. For some writers, these problems give cause for mistrust in Enlightenment values and lend support to the view that feminist theorists should abandon any attempt at general explanatory theories and should instead concentrate on the particular over the universal, on difference over sameness, and on the local over the general. However, it is also important to consider the arguments of many feminist theorists who, rather than simply reversing the values of the Enlightenment, seek to rethink the conventions of Western political discourse in a rigorously self-critical manner. Such essays in reconstruction demonstrate a need for ongoing elaboration of the social categories of gender and lay the ground for the future of feminist social theory.

■ QUESTIONS FOR CHAPTER 11

1 Can classical social theory be described as masculinist?

2 In what ways do classical and contemporary social theories exclude women from the social field?

3 What is meant by the 'gendering' of modernity?

4 How illuminating is the distinction between 'sex', and 'gender'?

5 Is feminism only relevant to Western women? If not, why not?

6 Can the history of feminist social theory be described as involving a shift from Enlightenment to post-Enlightenment values?

■ FURTHER READING

A good general introduction to feminist social theory is Sara Delamont's *Feminist Sociology* (Sage, 2003). A classic statement in feminist methodology and epistemology is Dorothy Smith's *The Everyday World as Problematic: A Feminist Sociology* (Open University Press, 1987). Some other guides and studies are Rita Felski's *The Gender of Modernity* (Harvard University Press, 1995), Mary Evans's *Gender and Social Theory* (Open University Press, 2003), Lois McNay's *Gender and Agency* (Polity Press, 2000), Barbara Marshall's *Engendering Modernity* (Polity Press, 1994), and Barbara Marshall and Anne Witz's edited *Engendering the Social: Feminist Encounters with Sociological Theory* (Open University Press, 2004). For some analyses of gendered subplots in classical and contemporary social theory, see Lisa Adkins's *Revisions: Gender and Sexuality in Late Modernity* (Open University Press, 2002), Michèle Barrett and Anne Phillips's edited *Destabilizing Theory: Contemporary Feminist Debates* (Polity Press, 1992), Carol Pateman's *The Sexual Contract* (Polity Press, 1988), and Carol Pateman and Elisabeth Grosz's edited *Feminist Challenges: Social and Political Theory* (Northeastern University Press, 1987).

Two useful studies in feminist theorizations of patriarchy are Sylvia Walby's *Theorizing Patriarchy* (Blackwell, 1990) and Anne Witz's *Professions and Patriarchy* (Routledge, 1992). Among notable contributions to feminist positions in postmodernism are Sara Ahmed's *Differences that Matter: Feminist Theory and Postmodernism* (Cambridge University Press, 1998), Rita Felski's *Doing Time: Feminist Theory and Postmodern Culture* (New York University Press, 2000), Donna Haraway's

Modest_Witness@Second_Millennium.FemaleMan©_Meets_OncoMouse™: *Feminism and Technoscience* (Routledge, 1997), and E. Probyn's article 'Bodies and Anti-Bodies: Feminism and the Postmodern', *Cultural Studies*, 13 (1987), 349–60. Some influential examples of feminist contributions to theorizations of race and racism are Patricia Hill-Collins's *Black Feminist Thought: Knowledge, Consciousness and the Politics of Empowerment* (Routledge, 1990) and bell hooks's *Ain't I a Woman? Black Women and Feminism* (Pluto, 1982).

Some influential analyses of gender from a philosophical point of view have come recently from Judith Butler and Donna Haraway. See particularly Butler's *Gender Trouble: Feminism and the Subversion of Identity* (Routledge, 1990) and *Bodies That Matter: On the Discursive Limits of 'Sex'* (Routledge, 1993), as well as Haraway's 'Gender for a Marxist Dictionary: The Sexual Politics of a Word' in her book *Simians, Cyborgs and Women: The Reinvention of Nature* (Routledge, 1991). See also Moira Gatens's *Imaginary Bodies: Ethics, Power and Corporeality* (Routledge, 1995).

For debates in feminist social theory about recognition, identity, and social justice, see particularly Seyla *Benhabib's *Situating the Self* (Cambridge University Press, 1992) and Nancy Fraser's *Unruly Practices: Power, Discourse and Gender in Contemporary Social Theory* (Polity Press, 1989), as well as Fraser's co-written book with Axel *Honneth *Recognition or Redistribution? A Political-Philosophical Exchange* (Verso, 2003). See also Nancy Fraser's debate with Judith Butler about the cultural and the socio-economic dimensions of identity in *New Left Review*, 227 and 228 (1998).

WEBSITES

The Feminist Theory Website at **www.cddc.vt.edu/feminism/enin.html** Provides useful research materials and information about the women's movement.

In the Web of Feminist Theory at **www.womensstudies.umd.edu/wmstfac/kking/teaching/602/602web.html** Provides a wide range of links to sites on feminist theory and women's movements.

The Feminist Archive at **www.femarch.freeserve.co.uk/** Includes material predominantly on second-wave feminism, with newsletters, articles, and links to related sites.

The Genesis Project at **www.genesis.ac.uk** Displays a site devoted to women's history in Britain containing information on collections in libraries, archives, and museums.

Activist and Feminist Resources at **http://sobek.colorado.edu/POLSCI/RES/act.html** Provides links to resources in women's studies and global feminist debates.

12

Modernity and Postmodernity: Part I

Barry Smart

TOPICS DISCUSSED IN THIS CHAPTER

Since the closing decades of the twentieth century social theorists have been preoccupied with the possibility that processes of change taking place in key aspects of social, cultural, and economic life are symptomatic of a wider transformation in modernity itself. A number of theorists have sought to underline the historic significance of such transformations by referring to the emergence of a new relationship to modern forms of life. For some analysts the transformations are considered to signify the appearance of relatively novel social, cultural, and economic forms and the possibility that 'new times' might be emerging. In some instances the argument has been presented that a qualitatively new social configuration has been taking shape. This is the broad context in which conceptions of the postmodern—of *postmodernism* and postmodernity—have proliferated in debates about the character of our times.

This chapter introduces some central debates about *postmodernism and postmodernity and the ideas of the theorists most often associated with these terms. We begin by reviewing several precursors to ideas about a postmodern turn in twentieth-century culture and society and their relationship to French *post-structuralist thought from the 1960s. Then we look at the contributions of four well-known theorists of postmodernity. These are Jean-François *Lyotard, Jean *Baudrillard, Fredric *Jameson, and Zygmunt *Bauman.

Chapter 13, which follows immediately after this one, introduces a second set of contributions to the same terrain of debate from a slightly different set of theoretical traditions. Both this chapter and the following chapter should be read in conjunction.

Postmodernism and postmodernity as terms of debate

Postmodernism and postmodernity are contentious terms. There has been considerable debate over the meaning and value of these terms for understanding the contemporary world and there has also been discussion and disagreement about how, or whether or not, to identify particular well-known authors with postmodern conditions or styles of thought. It is to a broad consideration of those theorists whose works are frequently designated as 'postmodern' or 'postmodernist' that we turn first.

Which theorists are 'postmodernist'?

When reference is made to postmodern conditions, the works of French theorists are often invoked. The writings of Michel *Foucault, Jacques *Derrida, Jean-François *Lyotard, and Jean *Baudrillard are frequently regarded as important influences on what has been called a postmodern condition, or as contributing to the development of theories of postmodernity. In contemporary discussion, these authors are frequently identified as sharing a common post-structuralist orientation. This is an intellectual position whose claim to coherence derives from its critical relationship to another problematic unity known as *'structuralism' (discussed in Chapter 9 of this book). It is argued that these theorists draw attention to a 'crisis of representation' and an associated instability of meaning in our understanding of cultural forms. Their work has been seen as challenging received views about language as a transparent mediator of the thoughts of speaking subjects. They show that the 'representational character of language is problematic' (Poster 1990: 12). Such questioning of the relationship between words and things leads to language, discourses, and texts being accorded a prominent place in cultural commentary. A corollary of this theme in post-structuralist thought is the absence secure foundations for knowledge and the retreat of confidence in the *Enlightenment assumption of an *autonomous rational *subject. Such ideas of thought have been viewed either as preparing the ground for postmodern social analysis, or as being indistinguishable from postmodernism (compare Dews 1987; Boyne and Rattansi 1990; Lemert 1990, 1997).

Various attempts have been made to clarify the relationship between post-structuralism and postmodernism. Commentators have remarked on some affinities between 'postmodern currents' and 'post-structuralist theories of desire'. A notion of postmodernism has been employed to describe a range of approaches that include post-structuralist contributions to literary theory, history, and philosophy, as well as developments in *pragmatist philosophy and post-positivist philosophy of science, and a textual orientation in cultural anthropology (compare Lash 1990; Callinicos 1990; Bernstein 1991). However, such extensions of the term postmodernism have been acknowledged to be problematic. It should be emphasized that post-structuralism and postmodernism are not identical. According to Andreas Huyssen (1984: 37–8), post-structuralism is to be viewed as 'primarily a discourse of and about modernism'—not postmodernism. Huyssen comments that the works of the French post-structuralist theorists are more appropriately described as providing us 'primarily with an archaeology of modernity, a theory of modernism at the stage of its exhaustion' (Huyssen 1984: 39).

With the notable exception of Jean-François Lyotard, relatively few extended and explicit uses of the terms 'postmodernism' and 'postmodernity' can be found in the works of the French figures usually identified with these notions. For example, when invited to clarify the relationship between his work and contemporary social thought, Michel Foucault (1983) indicated that he did not understand what was meant by the term 'postmodern'. In his essay 'What is Enlightenment?', in which he responded to Immanuel *Kant's famous essay of the same title from 1784, Foucault was deliberately dismissive of the term. He stressed that 'rather than seeking to distinguish the "modern era" from the "pre-modern" or "postmodern", I think it would be more useful to try to find out how the attitude of modernity, ever since its formation, has found itself struggling with attitudes of counter-modernity' (Foucault 1984c: 39).

Similarly, while Jacques Derrida's work is concerned to develop an ethical-political critique of assumptions intrinsic to modern Western philosophy, it too is not adequately represented by notion of postmodernism. To associate Foucault's and Derrida's writings with postmodernism in any sweeping way would be to subject them to considerable misinterpretation (compare Smart 1992, 1993, 1996). In contrast, both Lyotard and Jean Baudrillard do articulate a notion of the postmodern, and their contributions will be discussed shortly. But before we turn to their works, it is necessary to consider some earlier precursors to ideas about a postmodern turn in Western culture—before the period in which these ideas rose to the centre of intellectual fashions in the 1980s.

Precursors to postmodernism

It has been argued that various ideas of the postmodern can be traced to currents of thought in European culture from the late nineteenth and early twentieth centuries. In particular, an idea of the postmodern has been associated with the critical stance towards Western metaphysics expressed by the German philosophers Friedrich *Nietzsche and Martin *Heidegger. Both these figures questioned certain foundational elements of modern Western thought—notably the assumption that history moves by progressive enlightenment on a universal stage, or the idea of 'universal history'. Nietzsche and

Heidegger are celebrated for their interrogations of ideas of ultimate guarantees and unimpeachable grounds for 'reason', 'knowledge', and 'truth'. A certain affinity exists between their challenges to Western philosophy and the more recent thinking of figures such as Foucault, Derrida, Baudrillard, and Lyotard (see also Vattimo 1985).

Other early traces have been identified in the works of Max Weber and Georg Simmel. Both these thinkers have been seen as suggesting examples of a postmodern way of thinking insofar as they look sceptically at the achievements of modernity as a rational project. Weber spoke critically of modernity's relentless prioritization of means to ends over ends themselves, and of processes of inexorable 'value fragmentation' and spiritual 'disenchantment'. It has been suggested that Weber's work challenges us to consider 'which kinds of charisma and *rationalization will shape the "postmodern" world?' (Roth 1987: 89). Similarly, Simmel has been described as 'the first sociologist of postmodernity' insofar as he offers analyses of the crisis of modern culture and the exhaustion of modern cultural forms (Stauth and Turner 1988: 17). The work of the German critical theorist Theodor *Adorno is also argued to have anticipated 'many postmodern motifs' in his preoccupation with the irrational dynamics of rationalization and the paradoxical consequences of Enlightenment *universalism (Best and Kellner 1991: 225).

Since the middle decades of the twentieth century, various references to a postmodern thematic can be found in disciplines such as literary criticism and architecture, as well as in sociology, history, and philosophy. A conception of postmodernism was used to describe developments in the poetry of Spanish and Latin American writers around the first decade of the century (Calinescu 1977). Writing in the 1940–1950s, the British speculative historian of civilizations Arnold *Toynbee drew a contrast between a 'modern' era of Western history, extending from the end of the fifteenth century to the beginning of the twentieth century, and a subsequent 'post-modern age'. The latter was seen as commencing with the First World War, which Toynbee described as 'the first post-modern general war' (1954: 422). Toynbee identified an unparalleled predicament facing Western civilization arising from lack of correspondence between powerful and rapid developments in technology and slower, more uneven changes in humanity's spiritual, moral, and political capacities. Technological innovation was seen as rapidly outstripping society's ability to adapt to change.

A comparable notion of the postmodern is evident in the work of the American sociologist C. Wright *Mills. Reflecting at the end of the 1950s on the changing characteristics of the era, Wright Mills commented that people's basic understandings of social and cultural life were being 'overtaken by new realities' (1959: 184). Liberalism and socialism had 'virtually collapsed as adequate explanations of the world'. The result was that with increasing rationalization of modern society, 'the ideas of reason and freedom have become moot' (1959: 184, 185–6). Insofar as events called into question values and assumptions rooted in the Enlightenment, especially the idea of an intrinsic relationship between reason and freedom, Wright Mills speculated on 'the ending of what is called the Modern Age' and the emergence of 'a post-modern period' (1959: 184).

These reflections suggest a degree of continuity between earlier currents of thought and the wave of interventions from the 1980s more familiarly assembled under the banner of postmodernism. It is to these more recent commentaries that we turn now.

Postmodernism since the 1980s

Since the 1980s a conception of the postmodern has been employed in at least two key respects. As postmodern*ism*, the term has been used to refer to aesthetic, literary, and architectural styles, as well as to styles of thought. It has particularly been employed to describe a reaction to the culture of aesthetic modernism. In architecture, the term was first used to refer to building aesthetics reflecting 'an eclectic collage of contrasting architectural styles pillaged from disparate periods of history' (Burgin 1986: 45). As postmodern*ity*, the term has been employed to designate a particular social condition, a new 'social configuration'.

In general, what is called into question in debates about postmodernism are the ideals, aspirations, and consequences of modernity. At issue are the consequences of courses of action predicated on the assumption that increases in rationality necessarily lead to increases in freedom. What is placed under suspicion is the rule of reason, including especially the rule of an increasingly *instrumental rationality which accords priority to the efficiency of technical means. Postmodern consciousness turns away from the rule of a calculus that permits no 'interference of ethical norms or moral inhibitions', in the words of the British-Polish theorist Zygmunt Bauman. Bauman comments that the development of increasingly efficient technical means unquestioned ends 'gave human cruelty its distinctively modern touch and made the Gulag, Auschwitz and Hiroshima possible' (Bauman 1989: 23, 219).

Postmodernity in this sense is a mood of radical doubt, following from an undermining of the idea that our narratives and world-views can be rationally grounded or secured. Fragmentation of basic values is associated with a discrediting of permanent ahistorical foundations for knowledge and mistrust of notions of universal truth, notably as explicated in the work of the contemporary American pragmatist philosopher Richard *Rorty (1980, 1989). In the postmodern condition, existence is experienced as contingent. There is an awareness of uncertainty as more than a temporary condition. Indeterminacy and ambiguity are recognized as being corollaries of modernity, as effects of the modern way of life. Such an appreciation of 'contingency as destiny' can be seen as exemplifying a 'postmodern awareness', a discomfiture associated with what Bauman has called our 'postmodern discontents' (Bauman 1991, 1997).

At a more material level, one of the most often cited elements of a postmodern social condition is what has been called the transition to a 'post-industrial' phase in the development of Western capitalism. In the 1970s this thesis was unfolded particularly by the American sociologist Daniel *Bell, whose work is discussed in Box 31.

The French theorist Jean-François Lyotard identifies three general themes in debates about postmodernity. First, there is the theme of declining confidence in the idea of progress, especially scientific progress, and an associated loss of faith in *emancipatory narratives. Secondly, there is the theme of postmodernist aesthetics, as a movement in the arts, literature, architecture, and in popular culture and media culture. Thirdly, there is the theme of structural societal change, associated with *post-industrialism, *post-Fordism, consumer capitalism, and neo-liberal economic policy (Lyotard 1982).

Commenting on the first of these themes, Lyotard remarks that the development of techno-sciences appears to be self-propelling and ceases to be responsive to demands coming from human need. The consequences appear to be a deterioration and destabilization

BOX 31. DANIEL BELL ON POST-INDUSTRIAL SOCIETY

In the 1970s, in a consideration of signs suggestive of a change in 'the social framework of Western society', the US sociologist Daniel *Bell identified a relative shift in economic activity from goods to service production. Bound up with this was an increase in professional and technical workers and the creation of what Bell called a new 'intellectual technology' (Bell 1973: 9, 14). Bell described non-manual knowledge skills as forming the axial principle of a new *'post-industrial society'. These changed conditions have also often been described as a 'knowledge society' or 'information society', with particular emphasis being placed on non-material mental capacities, 'post-material values', access to information, and access to information technology. In this post-industrial scenario, Bell particularly identified technological innovation as ordering 'human experience within a logic of efficient means and . . . and as becoming virtually self-propelling (Bell 1980: 20). Similar observations are made by the Spanish sociologist Manuel *Castells in relation to globalization and the role of networks and global flows of information, capital, labour and migration (discussed in Chapter 14 of this book, pp. 296–7).

These developments are to be seen in a context of decline in the traditional manufacturing bases of the European and North American economies, joined with competition from Asian countries—especially, for example, in the Japanese car industry. Key accompanying factors have included downsizing of labour forces, cost-cutting, computerization of tasks, increasingly casualized or 'flexibilized' or *post-Fordist employment practices, and recurrent redundancies in heavy industries such as coal mining, metallurgy, and shipbuilding. Such gaps have been filled by an expansion in the services sector, particularly in financial services, and in leisure and consumption outlets, typically involving widespread de-skilling for large elements of the traditional working class and the phenomenon of 'McJobs'. Equally important have been production strategies aimed at small niche markets, growth in small businesses, typically including 'dot.coms' linked to the 'new economy' since the 1990s, as well as increased use of franchising and outsourcing arrangements, and exponential growth in computer software companies such as Microsoft.

In a similar vein, writers in the 1980s such as *Hall and Jacques (1989) and Hebdige (1989) spoke of an ethos of 'New Times', marked by an ideological discrediting of socialism in public opinion and the mass media. These writers commented on the impact of the Thatcher and Reagan administrations in Britain and the USA and their relationship to a new services-led economy. They pointed to the emergence of 'yuppies' and other commercial elites, as well as to the rise of a politically powerful property-owning lower middle class increasingly influential in national elections dominated by populist policies. Since the 1990s a new brand of economically liberal and socially conservative politics catering to the self-employed and to the ex-industrial electorate has been evident in the phenomenon of Republican 'middle America' or in the rise of Silvio Berlusconi's Forza Italia party in Italy, among many other examples. Underpinning all these developments have been reductions in the provisions of the welfare state, deregulation of labour security laws, curtailment of employment rights, and a curbing of the powers of trade unions.

These transformations can be seen as describing a political and socio-economic context for perceptions of postmodernity in the sphere of culture and ideas (compare Harvey 1990; Smart 1992, 1993).

of social conditions. Humanity appears divided into those facing the problem of responding to the challenge of increasing complexity and the others who continue to face the 'terrible ancient task of survival' (Lyotard 1979). Lyotard here draws attention to the way familiar cultural objects, social roles, and traditions have been destabilized or 'derealized' through the continuing development of the capitalist economy. There is also confusion about 'taste'. The aesthetic hierarchy implied by distinctions between 'elite' and 'mass' appears to collapse into an orgy of eclecticism in which 'anything goes', creating a 'degree zero of contemporary general culture' (1982: 76).

We look in detail at Lyotard's work in a moment. But first it is necessary to clear up a few common misunderstandings in uses of the terms 'postmodern' and 'postmodernist'.

Helpful and unhelpful uses of the terms 'postmodern' and 'postmodernist'

The difficulty of writing about postmodernism and postmodernity is that these terms do not clearly designate unambiguous realities. There is wide disagreement among contributors about appropriate uses of these terms. A further problem is that significant nuances among writers associated with postmodernism have at times been neglected by critics who have rushed to judgement. Sometimes criticisms are based on a parody of the thinkers at issue.

Certainly there are some ideas and slogans associated with postmodernism that have limitations and warrant criticism. Neglect of structural social and economic conditions and an excessive preoccupation with texts, with symbolic literary figuration, metaphor, rhetoric, and aesthetic forms, have been an obstacle to politically responsible, problem-solving analysis and critique. Deeply problematic have been tendencies in some forms of postmodernist writing to draw exaggerated and gratuitously *nihilistic conclusions from observations about ambivalence and indeterminacy in uses of language, about radical 'incommensurable' clashes between *'paradigms' and 'language games' and about wide-ranging cultural differences between moral belief systems. It is one thing to assert that objects and events of people's experience are always *'socially constructed', always laden with different cultural structures of perception according to differences of historical time and cultural space. It is quite another to assert that no rationally sustainable statements can be made about the world as something existing independently of any particular people's representations of it, as an objective reality. Although we can no longer to think of indubitable *'foundations' for knowledge—guaranteed by God, or by the certainty of our organs of sense, or by the self-evidence of logical thought—it does not follow that different social groups cannot arrive at rationally debatable agreements and understandings with one another about the nature of the world and about the meaning of moral and political values. It does not follow that claims to knowledge and truth and to principles of justice and morality become impossible to sustain. An important danger in some forms of postmodernism in this regard is a self-defeating kind of scepticism and *relativism.

However, such dangers of scepticism and relativism are not appropriately represented as weaknesses common to *all* writers who deploy a notion of the postmodern. In particular, it is a mistake to associate these dangers with Jacques Derrida's deliberately provocative statement that 'there is nothing outside the text' or with Michel Foucault's conception of radical epistemic shifts in 'regimes of truths' through history (discussed in Chapter 9 of this book). Derrida's and Foucault's writings break decisively with naively empiricist and positivist assumptions about scientific progress and with complacent ideas about the advance of reason in human history. But in no sense do these thinkers turn their backs on the value and moral necessity of rational self-questioning and the idea of 'enlightenment'.

In this regard, one example of a rather unfair position on postmodernism and post-structuralism is that taken by the German theorist Jürgen *Habermas. For Habermas, post-modernism represents little more than a conservative reaction to shortcomings associated with the project of modernity. It constitutes a form of anti-modernism promoting an abandonment of the 'unfinished task' of Enlightenment (Habermas 1980, 1985). (For further discussion of Habermas's position, see Chapter 13 of this book). These views of Habermas do not do justice to the range and diversity of commentaries on the postmodern. Against Habermas, it can be argued that a concept of postmodernity can be upheld in fruitful ways, so long as it is understood as referring to aspects of critical reflection on the modern and to a *critical reworking* of our ideas of the modern. It is in this sense that Lyotard describes the postmodern as 'undoubtedly a part of the modern . . . Postmodernism thus understood is not modernism at its end but in the nascent state, and this state is constant' (1982: 79). Similarly, a conception of postmodernity can be legitimately deployed to designate a particular relationship to the moral ambivalence, uncertainty, and lack of secure foundation that is now an intrinsic feature of modern social life. It is in this sense that Bauman speaks of postmodernity as 'modernity without illusions' (1993: 32). Bauman refers to

the modern mind taking a long, attentive and sober look at itself, at its condition and its past works, not fully liking what it sees and sensing the urge to change. Postmodernity is modernity coming of age, looking at itself at a distance . . . making a full inventory of its gains and losses . . . coming to terms with its own impossibility; a self-monitoring modernity. (1991: 272)

In these instances, references to the postmodern do not signify that the modern is being left behind. Rather, they signify that our relation to modern forms of life has been transformed, that we now stand in a different relationship to things modern. Postmodernity does not represent the passing of modernity, for modernity has not come to an end. Any notion of a radical rupture between modernity and postmodernity should be rejected. Therefore it is important to emphasize that postmodern analyses do not so much represent alternatives to modern forms of life as attempts to establish critically how our experience of the modern project has changed. It is to this more sociologically sensitive meaning of the term 'postmodern' that attention is directed in this chapter. We move now to the work of Jean-François *Lyotard.

Jean-François Lyotard: legitimation and the 'end of grand narratives'

Lyotard's book *The Postmodern Condition: A Report on Knowledge* first appeared in French in 1979. Lyotard here introduces a notion of the postmodern to describe the status of knowledge in 'highly developed societies' (1979: p. xxiii). Yet Lyotard's use of the term in this text is somewhat tentative. There is an implication that the term was adopted because it was already common currency among writers in North America. Lyotard states that 'the status of knowledge is altered as societies enter what is known as the postindustrial age and cultures enter what is known as the postmodern age' (1979: 3). The focus of the book falls on the ways in which culture in general and knowledge in particular have been transformed since the end of the nineteenth century, concentrating changes in the way scientific knowledge is legitimized. Whereas scientific knowledge formerly achieved legitimacy through appeal to particular *'meta-narratives' or 'meta-discourses'—such as the progressive emancipation of reason, or the liberation of labour, or the enrichment of humanity—*legitimation today seems to be bound up with *performativity. By 'performativity' Lyotard means control over contexts of information, notably control over reality under the aegis of science and technology.

Lyotard traces the discrediting of legitimatory 'grand narratives' to a series of developments that gathered momentum after the Second World War. These have included the continuous dominance of techniques and technologies of social organization that have deflected public discussion about the ends of action toward an increased preoccupation with means and instruments. Concern about the intrinsic value of knowledge has diminished as interest in the use of knowledge for optimizing efficiency of performance has increased. Lyotard comments that 'the seeds of "delegitimation" . . . were inherent in the grand narratives of the nineteenth century' (1979: 38). Lyotard enumerates two main factors for this current 'scepticism toward meta-narratives'. The first concerns crises in the foundations of scientific knowledge. The second concerns processes of co-option of knowledge into forms of capitalist *technocracy. We look at these in turn.

Crises of scientific knowledge

Legitimation through performativity arises from a crisis of scientific knowledge. This crisis is synonymous in Lyotard's picture with increasing recognition of forms of instability, indeterminacy, and undecidability in scientific categories and structures of inference. Lyotard refers to disturbances of divisions and boundaries between existing disciplines, as well as to overlaps between sciences and the appearance of new analytic spaces and territories. These contribute to a collapse of any grand hierarchy of learning that might regard physics as a foundation for all the sciences or that might privilege philosophy as the queen or judge of all disciplines.

With this comes a parallel decomposition in grand narratives of social and political legitimation. The assumption that science can gain legitimation through service to social, economic, and political practice comes to appear problematic. A scientific statement describing a situation may be deemed 'true', but it does not follow that a 'prescription statement based upon it . . . will be just' (Lyotard 1979: 40). Science loses any automatic warrant for legislating over other 'language games' and supervising the arrangement of social affairs. Science ceases to be something believed always capable of delivering 'greater justice, greater well-being and greater freedom' (Lyotard 1986: 76). Lyotard describes this transformation as 'an important current of postmodernity' (Lyotard 1979: 40).

At the same time, Lyotard emphasizes that the normative principle of science is not to develop through a 'positivism of efficiency'. On the contrary, science proceeds, or ought to proceed, in terms of a questioning, a challenging of the known, and a delineation of 'the unknown' (1979: 54, 60). In this sense science is unpredictable. As a practice, its pursuit of greater precision or accuracy leads not to more control but to new forms of uncertainty. While he acknowledges that research 'under the aegis of a paradigm tends to stabilize', Lyotard adds that in respect of scientific pragmatics it is *dissension* rather than consensus that needs to be emphasized, for the prevailing order of reason is always disturbed (1979: 61).

Capitalism and technocracy

Lyotard argues that transformations in the structures of society have affected the acquisition, classification, availability, and exploitation of knowledge. With the complexity of capitalist organization and a concomitant rise in the deployment of information technology 'comes a certain logic, and therefore a certain set of prescriptions determining which statements are accepted as "knowledge" statements' (1979: 4). Increasingly, he proposes, if a statement is to count as knowledge, it will need to be translatable into a language of computerization. In this process, the relationship between producers and users of knowledge assumes more and more the form of a commodity relation. As knowledge production and use becomes subject to commodification, so knowledge ceases to be 'an end in itself' and becomes an informational commodity. Increasingly the question demanded—by the state and by other supervisory institutions and client groups—'is no longer "Is it true?" but "What use is it?" In the context of the mercantilization of knowledge, more often than not this question is equivalent to: "Is it saleable?" And in the context of power-growth: "Is it efficient?"' (Lyotard 1979: 51). Lyotard here draws attention to a development first identified by Marx, where knowledge comes to be closely articulated with production. Knowledge is, in Marx's phrase, reduced to a 'direct force of production' (Marx 1858: 706).

Lyotard states that when philosophical and political narratives of legitimation have become problematic, reliance on 'performativity' or 'control over context' rises more and more to the fore. Lyotard describes an increasingly close affinity between technology and wealth, science and capital, a world in which legitimation is bound up with performance improvement. As commercial imperatives orient scientific research 'first and foremost toward technological "applications"', so 'corporate norms of work management' gain more and more of a hold over the research environment (1979: 45–6). What counts under these conditions is the contribution of learning and research to the performance of the social system. The relationship between those generating and transmitting knowledge and those receiving it is transformed into a relationship of production and consumption, based on an exchange value. Knowledge fields unable to demonstrate a contribution to system improvement are 'abandoned by the flow of capital and doomed to senescence' (Lyotard 1979: 47).

What is crucial for Lyotard is the incompatibility between the internal norms of scientific enquiry and the criterion of performance favoured by *technocratic authorities. Lyotard contrasts the idea of science as an 'open system', as something potentially critical, reflexive, and counter-cultural in its practice, to an emergent rule of *technocracy. Reflecting on the growing prominence of managerial procedures, Lyotard remarks that individuals are persuaded to ' "want" what the system needs in order to perform well' (1979: 62–4). Refusal to cooperate comes at a substantial cost, including withdrawal of funding. The postmodern condition of knowledge is thus one of tension between 'the imaginative development of knowledge' and attempts to subjugate knowledge to criteria of utility and system performance (1979: 64).

In these respects it is clear for Lyotard that modern values of scientific enlightenment and democratic struggle remain valid, and that in this sense 'modernity has not come to an end' (1993: 25). Fully in line with his early involvement in 1960s French Marxist circles, the overriding problem of contemporary social life for Lyotard remains that of capitalism. Lyotard highlights 'the redeployment of advanced liberal capitalism after its retreat under the protection of *Keynesianism during the period 1930–60, a renewal that has eliminated the communist alternative and valorized the individual enjoyment of goods and services' (Lyotard 1979: 38). In this context he speaks particularly of capitalism's subjugation of 'the infinite desire for knowledge that animates the sciences' to 'the endless optimalization of the cost/benefit (input/output) ratio' (1993: 25). Capitalism penetrates into language, turning words into units of information, in tandem with the rise of a hegemonic system of information technology and an emergent 'computerization of society' (1993a: 27).

Similar reflections on the imbrication of capitalism, information, and technocracy occur in the work of the British sociologist Scott Lash, who is discussed in Box 32.

BOX 32 SCOTT LASH ON POSTMODERNIZATION AND THE INFORMATION SOCIETY

Processes of transformation associated with the advent of an 'information age' have been explored by several sociologists. One wide-ranging approach can be found in Scott Lash's analysis of the impact of global communication flows on social and cultural life (Lash 2002). Lash notes how modern social institutions have increasingly been subject to processes of displacement under the rule of a new order of information. In the transition from a 'national manufacturing society to a global informational culture', there is a shift from 'exploitation' to 'exclusion' as the predominant form through which power operates (2002: 26, 28). At issue is the way in which social structures become eroded and displaced by a process of 'postmodernization' through flows of 'information, communications, images, money, ideas and technology' (2002: 28). Lash comments that 'postmodernization involves the displacement of normatively regulated, more or less unwieldy societal institutions and organizations (. . .) by smaller, value-inscribed, intensively bonded, more flexible cultural forms of life' (2002: 28). A new order of flexible enterprise wears away at embedded institutions in the areas of education, health, legal aid, culture, and the arts. Implied in this analysis is a shift from manufacturing capitalism to a neo-liberal capitalism in which service sectors and informational sectors achieve dominance.

Similar analyses have been developed by Manuel *Castells in relation to the 'network society' (discussed in Chapter 14 of this book, pp. 296–7), as well as by Claus Offe in relation to the theme of 'disorganised capitalism' (Offe 1985), and more broadly by Peter Wagner in relation to a transition from 'organised modernity' to 'disorganised modernity'. See also Lash (1999), Lash and Urry (1987, 1994), Urry (2000, 2003), Poster (1990), and Stehr (1994, 2001).

Jean Baudrillard: the consumer society and cultural analysis

We turn now to the second French theorist most often associated with postmodernism, Jean *Baudrillard. Like Lyotard, Baudrillard began his early work under the influence of Marxism and the French 1968 movement. But in the 1970s Baudrillard came to discard many of the classical tenets of Marxism in favour of a new type of cultural analysis indebted to *semiotics and French structural anthropology.

Baudrillard is often viewed as the key analyst of postmodern consumer culture (compare Kroker et al. 1989; Kellner 1989; Best and Kellner 1991; Gane 1991, 1993). In his books *The System of Objects* (1968) and *The Consumer Society* (1970), Baudrillard sought to extend a Marxist critique of capitalism to aspects of social and cultural life 'beyond the scope of the theory of the mode of production' (Poster 1988: 3). In subsequent works, commencing with *The Mirror of Production* (1973), Baudrillard criticizes Marxism for mirroring the primacy of the economy, claiming that it did not break radically enough with the theoretical perspectives of capitalist industrial societies. Advocating a more cultural turn in critical enquiry, Baudrillard argues that categories and concepts drawn from political economy are no longer meaningful for understanding 'the passage from the form-commodity to the form-sign' (1973: 121). The important issue in his view is 'the symbolic destruction of all social relations not so much by the ownership of the means of production but by *the control of the code*. Here there is a revolution of the capitalist system equal in importance to the industrial revolution' (1973: 122). In the consumer society, individuals not only like to slot into roles and to slot objects into categories, to enjoy a 'system of objects'—of house furnishings, appliances, gadgets, fashion accessories, and the like. Consumers also like to consume *signs*, signs of fashion and distinction, such as the designer label. The important object of consumption is not the material substance but the *image*, sign, or symbol, which achieves distinction only by relations of semiotic difference to other signs—to other brands, other fashion labels, and so on—within a mediated system. In these connections Baudrillard notes how consumption, signification, knowledge, and the whole field of culture have been subject to social abstraction. The work ethic has been dislocated as consumption has become the 'strategic element' and people have been 'mobilized as consumers' (Baudrillard 1973: 140–4). At the same time, while consumption becomes the strategic element in capitalist survival, it is also 'placed under the constraint of an absolute finality which is that of production' (1973: 128).

Baudrillard can be seen as critically extending Marx's analysis of the articulation of production and consumption (compare Smart 2003). But whereas Marx sought to dissect the distinctive features of a developing industrial society in the nineteenth century, Baudrillard seeks to make sense of late twentieth- and twenty-first century consumer capitalism. He comments that whereas it was formerly necessary to socialize 'the masses as labour power', what is now increasingly required is to 'socialize them . . . as consumption power' (1970: 82). While industrial production still remains important, Baudrillard emphasizes how—just as Marx had in fact anticipated—the application of science and technology to production entails that wealth creation becomes less and less dependent on manual labour time or on pure quantities of labour. Whereas industrial capitalist society was fundamentally a society of production, contemporary capitalist society especially engages its members in their capacity as consumers.

Baudrillard is also preoccupied with problems arising from the way in which Western thought since the Enlightenment has presented itself as 'a culture in the universal' (1973: 88-9). Concepts developed to make sense of modern forms of life—in the case of Marxism, concepts predicated on the metaphysics of the market economy—have been transported to other societies in often misleading ways. In Baudrillard's work, the cultural turn away from political economy leads to a focus on sign structures, on multiple symbolic orders and diverse informational networks of communication (Baudrillard 1987a). It is in this context that a number of references to the postmodern emerge in his writing. He writes of a 'destruction of meaning' and a 'state of excess', leading people to live with 'fatal indifference' to past movements of liberation (Baudrillard 1989, 1992a). Here there are some similarities between Baudrillard's comments an banality and 'banal strategies' and Lyotard's statement that 'progress carries on, but the Idea of Progress has vanished . . . Such is the banal destiny of all great ideals in what could be called postmodernity' (Lyotard 1986: 236). Elsewhere, however, Baudrillard comments that it is not clear whether postmodernism or the postmodern have any meaning when used purely as labels (see Crane 1993: 22).

Simulation, simulacra, and the mass media

The conventional aim of social theory has been to account for reality, to represent the truth of the real. Baudrillard, however, contends that such a conception of theorizing can no longer be sustained, at least in a literal sense. In a provocative and rather contentious move, Baudrillard declares that a 'precession of *simulacra' has undermined the possibility of appeal to an independent external referent or objective reality. By simulacra (or 'simulacrum' in the singular) Baudrillard refers to mediated simulations of reality. He describes a world in which electronic media of communication pervade every aspect of daily life—from television and film to the Internet and mobile phones. It is a world in which 'reality' is not independent of media. Rather, reality is so saturated by media simulation that taken-for-granted distinctions between the real and the imaginary constantly break down. Baudrillard declares that 'the age of simulation . . . begins with a liquidation of all referentials' (Baudrillard 1981: 4). He introduces a notion of the 'hyperreal' to describe a new situation where there is no independent referent. With simulation there is a 'generation by models of a real without origin or reality: a hyperreal' (Baudrillard 1981: 2). Instead of the real, there are merely *signs* of the real. In consequence, distinctions between 'true' and 'false', 'real' and 'imaginary', become increasingly problematic. Baudrillard points to the work of the Canadian media theorist from the 1960s Marshall *McLuhan, who famously coined the slogan 'the medium is the message'. Baudrillard speaks of an implosion of message and meaning in the medium, indeed of an 'implosion' of the real in the medium. He asserts that the 'medium and the real are now in a single nebulous state whose truth is indecipherable' (Baudrillard 1982: 103). Baudrillard addresses a mediatized condition of life in which it is very hard, if not impossible, to imagine the world without television. The world is one in which the flickering screen makes everything appear virtually equivalent, a world experienced more and more 'as shown on TV', a world viewed through the screen and *as* a screen. Penetration of televisual media into social life contributes to and compounds attitudes of political indifference, apathy, numbness, and information overkill that are a consequence of the global diffusion of market exchange relations and the commodification of more and more areas of social life.

There are, however, some rather controversial aspects of Baudrillard's work. Baudrillard contends that in a universally mediated world of this kind, there can be no deep truths for social theory to claim to uncover. He proclaims that insofar as the social is being buried 'beneath a simulation of the social', the objectives of social theory become problematic (1982: 67). He proposes a substitution of 'fatal theory' for critical theory, where theory constitutes an 'event in and of itself' (1977: 127). What seems to be implied in this shift is a notion of theory as provocation, as forcing things to their extremity, theory as an event that constitutes a 'challenge to the real' (Gane 1993: 122). Baudrillard proclaims that the value of theory lies 'not in the past events it can illuminate, but in the shockwave of the events it prefigures' (1987b: 215). His 'fatal theory' is a style of thinking that sets out deliberately to place question marks around universalizing normative ideals, such as 'emancipation', 'class struggle', 'enlightenment' and other articles of faith of the traditional Left canon. One can, however, retort that such gestures have the air of the gratuitous about them. Baudrillard's analyses of media culture and the consumer society are illuminating, but his characteristically polemical remarks on the political illusions of social theory are less persuasive. In his book on the first Gulf War of 1991, titled *The Gulf War Did Not Take Place* (1991), Baudrillard draws some rather facile inferences from the way in which the US forces' use of high-tech laser-guided bombs effaced the brute reality of the deaths of thousands of Iraqi soldiers and civilians. While it is true that both this war and the second assault on Iraq of 2003 played themselves out through a frightening distance from reality, Baudrillard's assertion that the real has 'imploded in the medium' has to be treated with great care in this instance.

Fredric Jameson: postmodernism and 'the cultural logic of late capitalism'

The US theorist Fredric *Jameson has also been an influential commentator on postmodern cultural forms. In his influential book *Postmodernism, Or the Cultural Logic of Late Capitalism* (1991), Jameson develops the thesis that the place and status of culture has been radically transformed under conditions of late capitalist liberalization. For Jameson, postmodernism refers to an idiom of representation emerging from a process of material transformation of the cultural sphere. Contemporary culture bears a relationship to the late capitalist economy which is neither one of functional autonomy nor one of direct casual dependence. The new features of culture include an erasure of the boundary between 'high' and 'mass' or commercial culture, expansion of the *culture industries, and an associated proliferation of popular cultural forms. There is a 'new depthlessness' exemplified by a 'new culture of the image or the simulacrum', as well as a 'weakening of historicity' and a simultaneous emergence of new emotional intensities. These motifs are bound up with 'a whole new technology, which is itself a figure for a whole new economic world system' (1991: 6). Postmodernism arises from 'the bewildering new world space of late or multinational capitalism' (Jameson 1991: 6). Cultural forms no longer shock, surprise, or threaten. Where modernism came to be canonized and institutionalized, today 'aesthetic production . . . has become integrated into commodity production generally'. In this sense, postmodern cultural forms have become 'one with the official or public culture of Western society' (Jameson 1991: 4).

On the one hand, Jameson discerns a culture of aesthetic modernism dominant largely in the earlier decades of the twentieth century, which resisted the constitution of cultural forms as commodities for consumption and was largely hostile to the rhetoric and reality of the market. On the other hand, he finds a new postmodern affirmation of the market as a vehicle for the popular reception of cultural goods. Whereas modernist forms of artistic experimentation and avant-gardism frequently engaged in a critique of commodification, postmodernism is 'the consumption of sheer commodification as a process' (Jameson 1991: p. x). Jameson traces a connection between the relative displacement of modernism by postmodernism and the development of capitalist modes of production from an earlier monopoly form to what Jameson describes as a 'new multinational and high-tech mutation' (1991: 157). Culture and the arts have lost the autonomy and critical distance they might once have had, or at least strove to achieve.

Jameson here sees a retreat of utopian politics, a disappearing public consciousness of alternative forms of social life, leading to an endangering of the possibility of critique. The corollary of processes of commodification is that everything has, in a certain sense, become 'cultural' (Jameson 1991: 48). Essential differences between the 'purely cultural' value of an artistic, scientific, or intellectual object and the 'purely economic' value of a physical object or substance appear to break down. As the boundaries between art and money become blurred, everything seems to take on the form of 'culture'. The profit motive, long associated with the development of a culture industry producing entertainment commodities for a mass market, becomes more prominent in the arts and in public goods. Commodification and the market system give rise to a new commercial order entering into the heart of the cultural realm.

Zygmunt Bauman: ambivalence, contingency, and 'postmodern ethics'

The Polish-British writer Zygmunt *Bauman has been another prominent contributor to ideas about postmodernity. In his books *Legislators and Interpreters* (1987) and *Modernity and the Holocaust* (1989)—discussed in Chapter 1 of this book, Box 3—Bauman describes a crisis in Western modernity's understanding of itself as a civilization oriented to universal values.

In place of *'legislative' ideas of universal laws, typical of European Enlightenment thought, a condition of sceptical self-distance and cultural relativity has established itself. Bauman describes this shift as expressing a more 'interpretive' texture of reason, averse to order-designing and order-managing pretensions.

The meaning of the postmodern for Bauman is not that existence is no longer modern. Rather, postmodern is to be seen as a part of the modern, insofar as everything that is received has become questionable for us. Postmodernity is the condition of thinking and acting that has become subject to modernity and that has consequently given rise to reflection on modernity. It is the condition that exists after recognition of the consequences of modernity, constructive as much as destructive. It is the state we find ourselves in after attempts have been made, through more modernization, to remedy deficiencies and unwanted effects—only to find, yet again, that the pursuit of order and certainty through design begets yet more unexpected forms of disorder and uncertainty. Postmodernity thus signifies a realization that modernity has limits, and that even as further rounds of modernization attempt to overcome or resolve these limits, yet more obstacles and contradictions are generated. In short, what is figured by the postmodern is not modernity at its end but 'modernity without illusions' (Bauman 1993: 32).

Bauman reflects on the prospects for nurturing modern values of increasing both 'the volume of human autonomy' and 'the intensity of human solidarity' (Bauman 1992: 107). But here, like Jameson, Lyotard, Baudrillard, David Harvey (1989), and many other commentators, Bauman notes how a new consumer society has emerged from processes of capitalist restructuring. As science and technology become direct forces of production, so the dignity of labour in the process of capital accumulation diminishes. With the development of an information-driven reflexive capitalism in which economic life is increasingly aestheticized, the structural importance of consumption increases. In a welter of texts, including *Modernity and Ambivalence* (1991), *Postmodernity and its Discontents* (1997), and *Work, Consumerism and the New Poor* (1998a), Bauman analyses a shift of emphasis from a work ethic to an aesthetic of consumption as the predominant factor in the reproduction of forms of *subjectivity. This involves a shift from an ethic of deferred gratification—marked by *ascetic self-control, lifelong planning, and rationalized domination over desire, famously outlined by Max Weber in *The Protestant Ethic*—to a new condition immediate consumption and deferred payment. It is exemplified by the 'buy now, pay later' philosophy promoted by credit-card companies. With this shift, social integration comes to depend more on the persuasive powers of seduction wielded by cultural intermediaries and less on directly coercive forces. The formation of a neo-liberal market society is associated with the strapping-in of individuals into a services-led economy marked by skill destruction and the constitution of the consumer as a subject of seduction. It is the fragile confidence of consumers, rather than the planned diligence of producers as members of industrial collectives, which increasingly seems to hold the key to the fortunes of the global economy.

A further aspect of Bauman's writing on post-modernity relates to the role of morality and ethics in social life, where experiences of ambivalence and uncertainty increasingly seem to prevail. According to Bauman, modern moral thought and its legislative practice has been predicated on an assumption of universally secure foundations. But such 'modern ambitions' have not been realized. Today there is little widespread belief in the possibility of an absolutely firm moral code. Bauman therefore explores what he describes as *'postmodern ethics', taking his inspiration partly from the thought of the French *phenomenological philosopher Emmanuel *Levinas. Here Bauman seeks to expose the impossibility of a 'universal and unshakably founded ethical code' (1993: 10), promoting the idea of individual moral responsibility as 'the most personal and inalienable of human possessions' (1993: 250). Such a 're-personalizing morality' means giving recognition to our unique unconditional responsibility towards the other. In this Levinasia vision, every ethical situation is unique. There are no hard-and-fast rules on which we can rely for answers to our moral dilemmas. The individual must decide for him- or herself on the right course of action, in the face of the manifest needs and vulnerability of the Other—of the other person or people, of the friend or the anonymous stranger. Yet as Bauman Points outs, a constant problem under postmodernity is that this *ethical* freedom of the individual is in danger of collapsing into sheer *consumer* freedom. The absence of definite prescriptions about how to act may simply degenerate into egoism.

In later work, Bauman followed the German sociologist Ulrich *Beck in developing his own version of the thesis of 'second modernity' or 'reflexive modernity' (for full discussion of Beck's idea of *'reflexive modernity', see Chapter 13 of this book, pp. 286–7). Bauman describes the passage from one form of capitalism to another later form as a shift from a 'solid' to a 'liquid' modernity (Bauman 2000). This represents an acknowledgement of the continuing relevance of the analysis offered by Marx and Engels at an earlier stage in capitalist modernization, presaged in their famous dictum in *The Communist Manifesto* that 'all that is solid melts into air' (Marx and Engels 1848: 83). Marx and Engels described how the competitive character of the capitalist mode of production leads to continual innovation, bringing about perpetual transformations of 'the whole relations of society'. There is an 'uninterrupted disturbance of all social conditions' as established relations are 'swept away' (Marx and Engels 1848: 83). Prevailing forms of life become fluid and convertible, through constant processes of modernization. Although in a sense modernity has always been fluid, the process of modernization did not come to an end with the displacement of traditional forms by modern forms. Rather, modern institutions and forms of life have themselves become subject to continuing rounds of modernization.

One loose assortment of themes that brings together the ideas of Bauman, Jameson, and other commentators on postmodernism relates to the renewed rise in religious fundamentalism as a reaction to feelings of insecurity, fragmentation, alienation, and disaffection from the global order. These themes are discussed here in Box 33.

Conclusion

Turbulence is an intrinsic feature of the condition termed postmodernity. To a great extent, the current global unrest is a corollary of the development of a more flexible or 'disorganized' capitalism. For many critics, it is a consequence of the pursuit of a *neo-liberal

BOX 33. POSTMODERNITY, FRAGMENTATION, AND RELIGIOUS FUNDAMENTALISM

Several commentators have seen one manifestation of 'postmodern discontents' in the phenomenon of religious fundamentalism. This resurgence has been described as a reaction to increased insecurities and risks generated by a global society. The increased prominence of Islam in world politics has been seen as part of a series of what Bauman has called 'postmodern responses to postmodern fears' (Bauman 1997: 184). One way of understanding the resurgence of fundamentalism—not only in Islam, but also in Christianity, Judaism, and Hinduism—is to see it as the symptom of a global tide of destabilization and *'disembedding' in cultural communities, of a breakdown of trust and solidarity in economic relations, and of new and more extreme forms of social inequality.

The reprise of assertions of ethnicity and religious identity also presents a particular challenge to the modern nation-state. The Islamic writer Akbar Ahmed has commented on the imposition of the form of the modern nation-state in the Middle East in the twentieth century. Ahmed notably concentrates on the case of the construction of Iraq as a nation-state by British colonial authorities after the collapse of the Ottoman Empire in the First World War. Ahmed emphasizes the insensitivity of the European nation-state form to ethnic differences in respect of language, custom, culture, and kinship lineage. Ahmed remarks on the plight of the Kurds in the 1990s, 'split between half a dozen nations', and on the way in which ill-informed nation-building continues to devastate the Middle East (Ahmed 1992: 133). Differences in ethnicity and religion rarely coincide with nationality, and the tensions that result are clearly evident in the current climate of world politics. Reflecting on the impact of Western institutional forms and resistance to them with the global expansion of their influence, Ahmed refers to the 'postmodernist era' as a turbulent time marked by 'permanent strife', in which some elements of the Islamic world and some elements of the Western world enter on a needless and destructive 'collision course' (Ahmed 1992: 264).

Increased global interdependence has produced a simultaneous increase in global disorder. The events of 11 September 2001 made clear both the extent of global interdependence and the illusion of global security. Global space, as Bauman puts it, now assumes 'the character of a frontier-land' (2002: 90). The frontiers around which conflicts occur are continually ebbing and flowing, and alliances likewise are shifting and flexible. Uncertainty and insecurity are endemic in a world of space-time compression, a world that Manuel *Castells describes in terms of global high-speed 'flows of capital, flows of information, flows of technology, flows of organizational interaction, flows of images, sounds and symbols', and flows of migrant people (Castells 1996: 412). Today we witness the emergence of a disordered and increasingly dangerous world, a world in which the USA appears simultaneously all-powerful and vulnerable. In this scenario, Fredric Jameson suggests that 'postmodern culture is the internal and superstructural expression of a whole new wave of American, military and economic domination throughout the world', where 'the underside of culture is blood, torture, death, and terror' (1991: 5). It follows that, the global impact of free-market informational capitalism, the long shadows cast by two American-led Gulf Wars, and the declaration of a 'war on terrorism' must occupy centre stage in any analysis of the condition called 'postmodernity' or 'globalization' or the 'new world (dis)order'. For a variety of positions on the case of '9/11', see Baudrillard (2002), Virilio (2002), Chomsky (2001), Žižek (2002), and Borradori (2003). See also the concluding statement by the editor of this book pp. 313–6.

ideology in economic policies. The movement from an industrial, manufacturing, and organized capitalism to an informational or knowledge- based and deregulated capitalism has led to increasing insecurity in people's lives both at home and at work. As Pierre *Bourdieu remarks, 'insecurity, suffering and stress' are outcomes of a system that has undermined 'all the collective structures capable of obstructing the logic of the pure market' in pursuit of greater corporate flexibility and profitability (Bourdieu 1998: 96; see also Gorz 1999; Beck 2000a).

It can be argued that postmodernity accompanies to capitalism in its 'consumer phase', reproduced in part through the equation of individual freedom with consumer freedom. Equally, as the economic independence of nation-states becomes subject to a global market place, social existence becomes more precarious. Bound up with this contingency is the articulation of global flows with local cultural forms and the emergence of numerous hybrid forms of social identity. Postmodern conditions in this sense reveal juxtapositions and collisions of different histories and transformations of space. It is this unsettled quality of contemporary social life that critics have identified with the labels of 'late modern' or 'hyper-modern' or 'postmodern'.

What is important in this discussion is the precise nature of the changes that have occurred, not the seemingly endless debates over different terms with which to describe them. In any event, there is much more common ground between the various accounts of 'late', 'reflexive', and 'post' modernity than some critics have been ready to acknowledge. What is clear today is a heightened scepticism about modern assumptions, a loss of faith in the idea that modernization will inevitably produce progress, or an enhancement of human well-being, or a safer, more egalitarian and humane future. At the same time, growths in scientific knowledge have not often led to greater certainty in everyday life. The world in which we find ourselves is changing rapidly in the face of far-reaching economic and technological developments and the pace and direction of change are not easy to predict. In such a fast-moving world, social theorizing becomes more important than ever.

■ QUESTIONS FOR CHAPTER 12

1 What do the concepts of postmodernism and postmodernity reveal about our relationship to modern forms of life?

2 Have modern values been discredited by postmodern ideas?

3 What does the term 'postmodern' contribute to debates about the conditions in which knowledge is produced and consumed?

4 How far is postmodernity a condition in which consumption has become paramount?

5 To what extent are postmodern forms of social and cultural life a corollary of the neo-liberal restructuring of capitalism?

6 Should contemporary religious groups take account of postmodernism?

■ FURTHER READING

Some good overviews of debates about postmodernism and postmodernity are Barry Smart's three books *Postmodernity* (Routledge, 1993), *Modern Conditions, Postmodern Controversies* (Routledge, 1992), and *Facing Modernity* (Sage, 1999), as well as David Lyon's *Postmodernity* (Open University Press, 1994), Gerard Delanty's *Modernity and Postmodernity* (Sage, 2000), Jim McGuigan's *Modernity and Postmodern Culture* (Open University Press, 1999), and Christopher Butler's *Postmodernism: A Very Short Introduction* (Oxford University Press, 2002). Also useful is Victor Taylor and Charles Winquist's edited *Encyclopedia of Postmodernism* (Routledge, 2001) and the same authors' four edited volumes of collected essays *Postmodernism: Critical Concepts* (Routledge, 1998). Some useful collections of readings are Thomas Doherty's *Postmodernism: A Reader* (Harvester, 1993), Joseph Natoli and Linda Hutcheon's *A Postmodern Reader* (State University of New York Press, 1993), and Lawrence Cahoone's *From Modernism to Postmodernism* (Blackwell, 1996). Some valuable critical assessments are Richard Bernstein's *The New Constellation* (Polity, 1991), Steven Seidman's *Contested Knowledge: Social Theory in the Postmodern Era* (Blackwell, 1998), Pauline Rosenau's *Postmodernism and the Social Sciences* (Princeton University Press, 1992), and Steven Best and Douglas Kellner's two co-written books *Postmodern Theory: Critical Interrogations* (Macmillan, 1991) and *The Postmodern Turn* (Guilford Press, 1997). See also the Further Reading section to Chapter 13 of this book.

Informative studies of postmodernism in relation to cultural and religious pluralism are Akbar Ahmed's *Postmodernism and Islam* (Routledge, 1992), Couze Venn's *Occidentalism: Modernity and Subjectivity* (Sage, 2000), Bryan Turner's *Orientalism, Postmodernism and Globalism* (Routledge, 1994), and Scott Lash's *The Sociology of Postmodernism* (Routledge, 1990). Two notable studies of postmodern art and literature are Andreas Huyssen's *After the Great Divide* (Indiana University Press, 1986) and Hans Bertens's *The Idea of the Postmodern: A History* (Routledge, 1995). Two illuminating contributions have been David Harvey's *The Condition of Postmodernity* (Blackwell, 1989) and Fredric Jameson's *Postmodernism, Or the Cultural Logic of Late Capitalism* (Verso, 1991), as well as the shorter article version of this book published in *New Left Review*, 146, (July–Aug. 1984), 52–92. Further sources are Zygmunt Bauman's four books *Legislators and Interpreters* (Polity Press, 1987), *Intimations of Postmodernity* (Routledge, 1992), *Modernity and Ambivalence* (Polity Press, 1991), and *Postmodernity and its Discontents* (Polity Press, 1997), as well as Bauman's two books on questions of ethics, *Postmodern Ethics* (Blackwell, 1993) and *Life in Fragments* (Blackwell, 1995). See also Peter Beilharz's *A Bauman Reader* (Blackwell, 2001). Baudrillard's writings can be approached through Mark Poster's edited *Jean Baudrillard: Selected Writings* (Polity Press, 1988) or through Baudrillard's own *Simulacra and Simulation* (University of Michigan Press, 1994). In Lyotard's *The Postmodern Condition*, the reader should begin with the essay appended at the end, 'An Answer to the Question: What is Postmodernism?'

■ WEBSITES

Contemporary Philosophy, Critical Theory and Postmodern Thought at **http://carbon.cudenver.edu/~mryder/itc_data/postmodern.html** Provides a good resource with a range of links to writers associated with critical theory and postmodernism.

Postmodernism On-line at **www.postmodernity.connectfree.co.uk/periodicals.htm** Contains links to on-line periodicals addressing aspects of postmodern conditions.

Everything Postmodern at **www.ebbflux.com/postmodern** Displays a comprehensive eight-page site with links to numerous resources.

Baudrillard on the Web at www.uta.edu/english/apt/collab/baudweb.html Contains informative writings by Baudrillard and commentaries on his work.

Lectures by Jameson at http://prelectur.stanford.edu/lecturers/jameson/ Provides a resource from Jameson's Stanford presidential lectures, including a biography, excerpts, and interviews.

13 Modernity and Postmodernity: Part II

Gerard Delanty

This chapter completes the discussion of modernity and postmodernity begun in Chapter 12 of this book. The range of approaches to be discussed reflect a variety of concerns, but an underlying theme is the view that modernity entails dimensions that are not fully appreciated in more extreme forms of *postmodernist writing. The chapter concentrates particularly on the work of theorists who have sought explicitly to defend the project of modernity against unsustainable forms of postmodernism that have proclaimed the wholesale bankruptcy of modern values and *normative ideas. As discussed in the previous chapter of this book by Barry Smart, there has been a notable preference in recent social theory to view postmodernism as *part* of modernity. The idea of the 'end of modernity' is not to be taken literally. There is a consensus that the notion of a radical rupture between modernity and postmodernity should be rejected. In general, postmodernism can be best understood today as a revolt against just one tendency within modernity, rather than as a movement against modernity as a whole.

The theories discussed in this chapter build on some of the positive gains made by postmodernism and at the same time go beyond postmodernism. We look primarily at the work of six theorists: Cornelius *Castoridias, Agnes *Heller, Jürgen *Habermas, Niklas *Luhmann, Alain *Touraine, and Ulrich *Beck, as well as the later writings of Anthony *Giddens on *'reflexivity'. We begin with a brief summary of the main criticisms that can be made of postmodernism's more extreme formulations.

Three problems with postmodernism

Three broad evaluative points can be made about postmodernism from the standpoint of modernity as a normative project. The first is that modernity needs to be seen as an ongoing process with many dimensions. It is advisable to think of modernity as being 'on endless trial', as the Polish theorist Leszek Kolakowski (1990) puts it. This is a way of thinking evident in many of the major names of contemporary social theory. It is even evident in the work of Jean *Baudrillard who has addressed ideas about postmodernism not in terms of the 'end of the illusion' of modernity but rather in terms of the 'illusion of the end' of modernity (Baudrillard 1992*b*). In many ways it is helpful to see postmodernism as a critique of certain tendencies within modern thought, but not as the proclamation of an entirely new kind of society. This is certainly the way *Foucault and *Lyotard understood their projects, and it is especially evident in Foucault's emphasis on what he called 'the permanent reactivation of an attitude', on 'a permanent critique of our historical era', oriented to finding out 'how the attitude of modernity, ever since its formation, has found itself struggling with attitudes of "counter-modernity"' (Foucault 1984*c*: 39).

A second point is that certain tendencies in postmodernist writing in the 1980s–1990s suffered from an overemphasis on the idea of societies as *texts* capable of simple *deconstruction. Over-relying on literary theory, some kinds of postmodernism have not been fruitful for sociological thinking and have not dealt adequately with questions of power and material social structures, as problems that need to be analytically distinguished from questions about representations, signs, and symbolic images. While much postmodernist writing has opened social theory to new dimensions, it has not always provided adequate accounts of the distinctive nature of structural social processes. But it should also be noted that preoccupation with exclusively cultural and symbolic matters has been questioned even within some strands of avowedly postmodern thinking itself. Increasingly we find postmodernist thinkers writing about new conceptions of the social dimensions of affairs, as dimensions to be distinguished from the more narrowly cultural. One contribution to this redirection is the idea of 'social postmodernism' proposed by Nicholson and Seidman (1995).

A third criticism is that some postmodernist writers have not always offered plausible grounds for normative political engagement. In some cases, the idea of a rational foundation for collective struggles has been uncritically dismissed as an illusion generated by the European eighteenth-century *Enlightenment. In contrast, many recent feminist and *postcolonial theorists have demonstrated that while postmodernism offers a useful starting point for critique, not all of its diverse strands have been able to offer guidance for an *emancipatory political project. This is an observation made in the discussion of feminist theory in Chapter 11 of this book.

It is worth remembering that postmodernism as a term was primarily a theory of *cultural* developments, and that while it was compatible with developments in French *poststructuralist thought, it was never intended to be a social or political theory as such. Originally, postmodernism was a movement in architecture, literature, and the arts, expressing revolt against the rigid formalism of aesthetic *modernism, which it sought to revitalize through an emphasis on emancipating 'content' from the structured and ahistorical 'form' of the modernist aesthetic (compare Bürger 1974). In bringing art and life closer together, postmodernism brought the aesthetic imagination to the brink of radical politics, but it has not succeeded in demonstrating aesthetics to be a fully self-sufficient arena for social critique (compare Delanty 2000: 131–55; Harrington 2004: 177–206).

The renewed theorizations of modernity to which we turn in this chapter take account of various limitations in the notions of modernization espoused by some twentieth-century social scientists. The theorists under consideration proffer new readings of history in areas as diverse as historical sociology, *world systems theory, cultural history, international relations, and postcolonial studies. They are critical of conventional modernization theory from the 1950s in the work of Talcott *Parsons and others, which tended to reduce modernity to a Western-centred view of the world, neglecting the multidirectional and conflict-ridden character of modernity. It is in this respect that several recent commentators have come to speak of 'multiple modernities', most notably the Israeli historical sociologist Shmuel *Eisenstadt (whose earlier work is discussed in Chapter 6 of this book) (see Eisenstadt 2002). These accounts respond increasingly to the view that modernity is not exclusively defined by the European Enlightenment and that there are many routes into and through it (compare Therborn 1995). The implications of globalization in this context will be discussed in the next chapter, but for the present it can be noted that debates about globalization and related issues of multiculturalism and *cosmopolitanism provide an important context in which to approach the ideas of the theorists discussed in this chapter.

We begin by looking at the work of Cornelius *Castoriadis and Agnes *Heller.

Modernity and the radical imagination: Cornelius Castoriadis and Agnes Heller

Several commentators have remarked on the significance of *creativity* as a dimension of social action (Joas 1992). This idea can be related to a conception of modernity as a project of transformation driven by the capacity to imagine alternatives. It is a theme central to the two theorists under discussion here.

In his major work *The Imaginary Institution of Society*, published originally in French in 1975, the Greek-born theorist Cornelius Castoriadis shifted debate about modernity away from an exclusive concern with capitalism, as was typical of Marxist approaches, and also away from concerns with an all-inclusive power, such as in the work of Foucault (see also Castoriadis 1990, 1991). For Castoriadis, the defining feature of modernity is the struggle between the radical project of *autonomy and the institutional project of *mastery*. Modernity is defined by a struggle between these two forces, and cannot be reduced to either of them. To the extent that there is something underlying these contrary forces, it is the *imagination*. All societies possess an *imaginary dimension, since they must answer certain symbolic questions as to their basic identity, their goals and limits. Modernity has come to rest on two kinds of imaginary significations: the imaginary of rational technical control, on the one hand, and the radical imaginary of autonomy, on the other hand. The purpose of Castoriadis's social theory is to defend the latter against the former.

Castoriadis does not equate technical control and mastery with capitalism; he sees them as also including the disciplinary regimes of power associated with the modern bureaucratic state. He argues that the distinctive feature of the radical imagination is human autonomy, which resists both economic and political power and institutional systems of *domination. He stresses the dimension of self-confrontation and especially creativity, which can never be fully institutionalized. Modernity contains within it the vision of an autonomous society. It thereby indicates a condition of perpetual resistance to institutional frameworks which attempt to domesticate the radical imagination and strip it of its creative agency. The focus on creativity offers an alternative theorization of modernity echoing the idea of *homo faber* in Aristotle and Marx: the idea of society as an artefact created by human beings.

With this argument, Castoriadis established a route out of the narrower and more dogmatic forms of postmodernism on the one hand and Marxism on the other. Where Marxism in his view had a tendency to reduce radicalism to class *emancipation, postmodernism led to a retreat from autonomy and became obsessed with denouncing modernity (Castoriadis 1990). He emphasizes that radicalism involves openness to the future, but is not based on disavowal of the past—for the past can be a source of creative inspiration. Capitalism, as Marx demonstrated, created the conditions for some of the most creative struggles in human history. These struggles contine to define the modern condition and have spread into wider domains, in the arts and culture, in the self, in interpersonal relations, and politics. But capitalism and class conflict are no longer the sole terrain of struggles for autonomy. Some examples of this expansion in radical politics are the counter-cultural movements of the 1960s and the rise of 'new social movements' since the 1970s. In these movements we find an expression of the radical imaginary on the terrains of gender and sexuality, 'race', ethnicity, and environmental activism, as well as in the arena of class exploitation. In general Castoriadis's work has led to a new thinking of modernity in terms of a 'field of tensions' on diverse 'sites of resistance' (compare Arnason 1989, 1991; Wagner 1994; Delanty 1999).

The Hungarian-born theorist Agnes *Heller reiterates some of Castoriadis's key ideas. She especially endorses the idea of a central conflict at the heart of modernity which creates possibilities for freedom but also undermines it. Heller's social theory can be read as a response to the circumstances of central and Eastern Europe under communism and is especially pervaded by a sense of the helplessness of *civil society in the face of powerful institutions. Her early work sees the central conflict of modernity as lying between institutions and 'everyday life' (Heller 1984). The concept of everyday life entered modern social thought via the writing of *Heidegger and other *existentialist philosophers. Heller developed the concept to refer to the primary nature of society as *intersubjective*, which she sees as the basis of the transformative capacity of society. Modern ideas of universality, critique, and *reflexivity are anchored in the structures of everyday intersubjective communication and gain their political force in resisting power.

In *A Theory of History* (1982), Heller outlined a conception of modernity that stressed three logics of development. First, there is the *capitalist logic of development*, involving private property, inequality, and domination. This is then confronted, secondly, with *democracy*, based on ideas of equality, decentralization of power, and citizenship. These are the two central logics of civil society and are in tension. However, alongside them lies a third logic of development, that of *state-directed industrialism*. By this logic, the state tries to provide a solution to the problems presented by the conflict between capitalism and democracy. Socialism has been an expression of this logic in modernity, even though capitalism in the West has had the upper hand. It is this variable and fluid condition that constitutes what Heller sees as the basic 'dynamic of modernity' (see Heller 1990). It is a dynamic of perpetual change and an attitude of questioning that leads to constant negation of tradition.

In her book *A Theory of Modernity* (1999), Heller also stresses *technology* as a key logic of modernity. Technology is seen as facilitating certain emancipatory possibilities and as at the same time threatening them. Modernity in this picture is not a homogenized or totalized whole, but 'a fragmented world of some open but not unlimited possibilities' (Heller 1999: 65). There is no promise of total freedom, and autonomy in Castoriadis's sense is not concentrated solely in democracy; it can also be found to a certain extent in technology. But neither technology or industrialism, nor capitalism, nor democracy, offer unambiguously progressive forces of development. Heller has continued to believe that democracy is the key to the emancipatory promises of modernity, but increasingly she recognizes that perhaps all that is possible is a balancing of the three or four logics of development (Heller 1993; Heller and Feher 1988).

In sum, Castoriadis and Heller offer important contributions to social theory by characterizing modernity in terms of struggles between different agencies, rather than in terms of a single logic of transformation. Castoriadis's work thematizes conflict between the project of autonomy and the project of mastery. Heller's work emphasizes tension between the logics of industrialism, technology, capitalism, and democracy. Emerging from these theories is a *relational* view of modernity as a process of social transformation that unfolds through conflict between contrary forces.

One illuminating connection in which these ideas can be joined together with the work of Habermas, Touraine, Beck, and Giddens is the revolutions in Eastern Europe of 1989. This case example is discussed in Box 34.

BOX 34. SOCIAL THEORY AND THE REVOLUTIONS OF 1989

The democratic revolutions that occurred in Eastern Europe in 1989–90 offer an interesting application of the social theories discussed in this chapter. The revolutions would appear to refute postmodernist notions of the 'end of modernity'. What came to an end in 1989 was not modernity *tout court* but just one kind of modernity, namely a modernity oriented to the project of state socialism. While it is possible to see the revolutions as demonstrating the end of a certain 'grand narrative' in *Lyotard's sense, it is also possible to seem them as re-establishing modern democratic principles of political legitimacy. Where *Baudrillard (1992*b*) sees the revolutions as an expression of the 'deconstruction of history', another perspective suggests a reconstruction of modernity. The events appealed to a new application of classical *Enlightenment ideas about liberty and *civil society (compare Dahrendorf 1990). The ideals that inspired the revolutions were the modern ideas of democracy, liberty, and justice, which had been preserved in the civil society movements of the communist period and which reasserted themselves in 1989 when a general structural crisis occurred in the Soviet system.

*Castoriadis's approach suggests a view of the 1989 revolutions as an expression of the radical *imaginary and a continuation of the modern struggle between democratic *autonomy and state-imposed systemic mastery. For *Heller and other East European writers such as Václav Havel, they are an instance of the eventual triumph of organic social agency over systemic institutional control—a vindication of what Havel called the moral 'power of the powerless' (Havel 1990). *Habermas described them as 'catching-up' revolutions, involving delayed attempts to institutionalize modern liberties (see Habermas 1991). From Habermas's perspective, the revolutions were the result of social movements emanating from the *'lifeworld' and asserting themselves against the 'system'. In 1989, state power was challenged by civil society and given legitimation by intellectuals. In the language of Alain *Touraine's social theory, the revolutions can be seen as a renewal of the capacity of society to create itself, to establish itself by autonomous popular agency.

One notorious view of these events in the early 1990s was put forward by the American political commentator Francis Fukuyama, who declared that the revolutions represented the 'end of history' (Fukuyama 1992). In his thesis, they spelled the end of ideological strife between East and West and the worldwide triumph of liberal democracy and free-market capitalism. The illusions and political prejudices of this view have been borne out by the subsequent course of events. One outcome of the revolutions was a rise in nationalism, xenophobia, right-wing extremism, and anti-Semitism. This situation is far from the end of ideological strife that Fukuyama claimed to predict. The triple transition—to capitalism, to democracy, and in many cases to national autonomy—has not been smooth. It has had diverse consequences, ranging from descent into ethnic war in the former Yugoslavia to the peaceful break-up of the former Czechoslovakia, as well as to German unification and the recent enlargement of the European Union (see further Offe 1996). At the same time, new forms of inequality, poverty, and unemployment have arisen as a consequence of the introduction of free-market capitalism in the former Eastern Bloc, while intense ideological battles continue to be played out elsewhere in the world in the name of religious values and cultural identities, notably in the Middle East but also in the West.

These developments indicate that the categories and institutions of modernity are still with us, however much they have been reshaped and reworked. To speak in the language of Ulrich *Beck, modernity has become more *reflexive*. Modernity today is unable to escape the legacy of history and has constantly had to come to terms with problems created by earlier phases of modernity. The revolutions in Eastern Europe therefore cannot be reduced to conservative, or *technocratic or extreme postmodernist arguments about the obsolescence of projects of real social self-determination. They are pertinent examples of the incompleteness of the project of modernity.

Modernity and the growth of communicative reason: Jürgen Habermas

Jürgen *Habermas is a staunch critic of both anti-modernist and postmodernist currents in contemporary thought. Habermas rejects the postmodernist notion that modernity has reached its limits. In a controversial essay, he dismissed the French post-structuralist theorists—chiefly Derrida, Lyotard, and Foucault—as nihilists who preferred to give up on politics and critical thought (Habermas 1980, 1985). This was a gross simplification of their work, as the previous discussions in this book have shown (Chapter 9, Chapter 12, pp. 202–12, 258–62). In other, more subtle ways, however, Habermas has continued to adhere to the idea of modernity as a progressive emancipatory project. In his polemical rejection of postmodernism, he establishes the need for an immanent critique of modernity. This entails the view that modernity contains *normative promises that are yet to be fulfilled. It is in this sense that Habermas speaks of modernity as an 'unfinished project' (1980, 1985). There are many dimensions to modernity, but the ones that are most important are those that enable society to contest power and domination through self-transformation, critique, *reflexivity, and the struggle for *autonomy. We look at each of these aspects of Habermas's thought in turn.

Habermas's *Theory of Communicative Action*

Habermas's major work of 1981, *The Theory of Communicative Action* (published in two volumes), presents an elaborate theory of modernity that considerably refines his earlier writing from the period of his attachment to the *Frankfurt School (discussed in Chapter 7 of this book, pp. 164–5). This work can be seen as the central text in the second generation of critical theory, the first generation being represented by *Adorno, *Horkheimer, *Marcuse, and others. In this work Habermas responded to the changed political environment of the 1960s and 1970s when new social movements arose and took critical theory in a new direction. Against the idea of an all-pervasive capitalist bureaucratic system that Horkheimer and Adorno identified with modernity in their pessimistic work *The Dialectic of Enlightenment* (1947), Habermas argued for possibilities of democratic transformation through a notion of social action as *communicative*. The basic idea is not too far removed from Castoriadis's idea of modernity as a conflict between autonomy and mastery. Modernity in Habermas's mature approach is a struggle between two kinds of rationality: *communicative rationality* versus *instrumental rationality*.

Drawing on a wide range of approaches, from developmental psychology, social evolutionary theory, and the philosophy of language, Habermas argues that language is the key normative medium of social interaction. In this view, linguistic communication is constitutive of social relations; it is the basis of socialization and of legitimation processes and democratization. The structure of communication is not so much the sign or the text but *intersubjective dialogue oriented to problem-solving, to processes of critical agreement and to rational consensus formation. Communicative action involves 'validity claims', such as assumptions about truth, moral rightness, and sincerity in any given assertion, utterance, or exclamation by an individual speaker. While everyday communication does not always involve explicit validity claims, the very activity of communication presupposes the possibility that communication can be 'unconstrained'; that is, that it can arrive at unco-erced consensus, where social actions are initiated not by intimidation or manipulation but by valid reasons. Habermas stresses the capacity of human communication to foster a more reasonable society. It is a theory governed by the belief that through *deliberative argumen-tation and reflection, people can resolve differences and reach agreement.

In his philosophical writings, Habermas proposes a radical consensus theory of truth, based on the hypothesis of an 'ideal speech situation'. Habermas developed this theory partly through dialogue with the work of the German linguistic theorist Karl-Otto *Apel, who introduced the ideas of the American *pragmatist philosophers to German-speaking audiences in the 1970s. On this theory, truth is not what happens to be agreed upon by a given bunch of people. It is what *could* and *would* have to be agreed upon by everyone, were everyone to have a free and equal opportunity to participate in the conversation and exchange rationally debatable grounds for their views—without exclusion, manipulation, or coercion. In this way Habermas establishes a normative foundation for critical social the-ory, bringing it out of the impasse of the earlier Frankfurt School's more pessimistic *ideo-logy critique. The critique of ideology in his work now becomes the critique of 'systematically distorted communication'. The concept of *dialogical rationality replaces Adorno's concep-tion of 'negative *dialectics'. The critical enterprise is focused on those points where power is resisted by the force of communicative reason. So long as people are able to engage in social action that obeys openly available rules of communication, there is the possibility that social action can resist unjust uses of power. Habermas is not saying here that commu-nication is always a rational reflective process; but he *is* saying that it *can* be, and often *is* rational, especially in those critical moments when people challenge power.

According to Habermas, the history of modernity can be rewritten as the progressive extension of communicative forms of rationality. Habermas's social theory is an evolu-tionary one, albeit one divested of *teleological assumptions. Social evolution cannot be explained by recourse to historical or natural laws of any kind. Instead, Habermas's theory of modernity rests on a conception of societal *learning processes* (Habermas 1976). Synthesizing elements of the work of Durkheim, G. H.*Mead, and Talcott *Parsons, Habermas argues that learning occurs both at the collective level of whole societies and at the level of individuals. Learning happens simply because not-learning is not possible. In this approach, which is also influenced by the developmental psychology of Jean *Piaget and Laurence *Kohlberg, learning is based on the acquisition of communicative com-petences. It involves *cognitive processes that cannot be reduced to rote imitation or *behaviouristic responses to an external environment. Learning and language use are a 'generative' competence, in the sense in which Noam *Chomsky uses this term. Habermas argues that the evolution of societies can be theorized in terms of generative trans-formations in cognitive competences and moral consciousness. Modernity emerges when societies solve problems in post-traditional and post-conventional ways, investing reflexive universalizing principles in the formulation of social norms, organizational rules, political practice, and legal systems. The transition to modernity occurs with the institu-tionalization of deliberative processes in the constitution of positive laws, and in the idea of the autonomy of art, in the primacy of human rights, and in the *secularization of religion.

Colonization of the lifeworld by the system

In the second volume of *The Theory of Communicative Action* (1981*b*), Habermas introduces a distinction between what he calls the *'lifeworld' and the 'system', both of which involve different forms of *integration. Drawing on and modifying the work of David *Lockwood (discussed in Chapter 4 of this book, p. 102), Habermas sees the lifeworld as based on 'social integration'. In contrast, the system is based on 'system integration', organized through the economy and through juridical-administrative steering by the state. Whereas the lifeworld presupposes a rationality that is primarily communicative, the system is driven by instrumental rationality. The tension between these two rationalities gives modernity its basic animus.

In this conflict of rationalities between the lifeworld and the system, communicative reason is threatened by instrumental reason. Habermas speaks of a 'colonization of the lifeworld' by the system, involving *commodification, instrumentalization, and over-legalization of social relations. This danger of system colonization results in distortions of communication and social pathologies. However, Habermas also argues that communicative action in the lifeworld has the capacity to resist colonization by the system. Key agencies in this connection are the role of *social movements*. Social movements carry the normative consciousness of modernity and defend the lifeworld against the system. These include not only traditional class struggles but also new movements such as the ecological movement, the women's movement, and anti-imperialist movements.

An analogous theorization of social movements that illustrates Habermas's ideas in certain ways occurs in the work of Alain *Touraine, who is discussed in Box 35.

Discursive democracy and the rule of law

In his later book *Between Facts and Norms* (1992), Habermas pulls back from the very sharp contrast he drew in his work in the 1980s between the 'lifeworld' and the 'system'. In this book he emphasizes that *communicative logics also extend into the system. The basis of the new approach is a theory of *'discursive democracy'. Where the older approach stressed non-institutionalized emancipatory practices, Habermas became increasingly interested in democratization as a process extending into all parts of society, including the highly in-stitutionalized spheres of a society's legal system. Perhaps because of the rise of new na-tionalist and xenophobic movements from the lifeworld, communicative rationality in his later work is no longer confined exclusively to the lifeworld. Habermas's idea of discursive democracy entails a more positive view of the role of law, which is no longer seen simply as a medium of 'juridification', or over-legalization. Habermas argues that law is an essential dimension of democracy.

Although he has been criticized for abandoning the radical ambitions of critical social theory in its original Frankfurt vintage, it is important to see that Habermas's later work dif-fers from liberal political theory in at least one major respect. The version of deliberative democracy he proposes is not characterized by a concern with compromises over private interests, in ways typical of liberal theories of justice, such as that of John *Rawls. Habermas's conception of discursive and deliberative democracy does not take private interests as given, and then seek for a principle of just redistribution of resources and

BOX 35. ALAIN TOURAINE ON SOCIAL MOVEMENTS AND COLLECTIVE AGENCY

Like Castoriadis, Habermas, and other writers, the French sociologist Alain *Touraine argues that a *post-industrial society based on consumers, service workers, and information brings about new kinds of *social movements*, beyond that of the traditional working class (Touraine 1969).

In the 1970s, in opposition to both orthodox Marxism and *structural functionalism, Touraine (1973) developed a theory of social action around the concept of historical renewal through social transformation. He wrote that 'society is not just reproduction and adaptation; it is also creation, self-production' (Touraine 1973: 3). The concept of 'self-production' indicated here is very different from Niklas *Luhmann's use of the same term (discussed later in this chapter). For Touraine, self-production refers to the ability of social actors to transform society reflexively by acting upon it. He wrote that 'Society is not merely a system of norms or a system of domination: it is a system of social relations, of debates and conflicts, of political initiatives and claims, of ideologies and alienation' (Touraine 1973: 30). Touraine related this idea to social movements, which are the agents of historicity.

In his more recent book *Critique of Modernity* (Touraine 1992), Touraine argues that contemporary society reflects a field of tensions between two polar tendencies: the tendency of collective *agency, based on *normative communication, which he calls the tendency of the *'Subject', and the tendency of systemic *rationalization, which he calls the tendency of 'Reason' (equivalent to 'instrumental reason' in Habermas's lexicon). The challenge of modernity is to unify these tendencies. But the problem for modernity is that the chances of a principle of unity are slight. According to Touraine, four main forces have dominated modernity: sexuality, commodity consumption, the business corporation, and the nation. These correspond to the spheres of personality, culture, economics, and politics. The problem today, however, is that these domains have become so fragmented that there is no longer a principle of unity. For instance, the personal order has become divorced from the collective order, and production and consumption have lost any ability to bring the two orders together.

Touraine sees some truth in describing the current situation as 'postmodern' insofar as this reminds us that the twentieth century has been a century not of progress but of crisis and dissolution of any overarching collective agency. Touraine's thesis is that the only unity that currently exists is that provided by instrumental rationality. On the one hand, Touraine postulates the idea of the 'Subject', or subjectivation—the *communicative agency of individuals—as a counterforce to the rule of 'Reason' or systemic rationality. On the other hand, he is in insistent that the Subject cannot by itself unify the shattered fragments of modernity. He writes that 'Society can no longer be defined as a set of institutions, or as an effect of a sovereign will. It is the creation of neither history nor the Prince. It is a field of conflicts, negotiations and mediations between rationalization and subjectivation, and they are the complementary and contradictory faces of modernity' (Touraine 1992: 358).

Touraine rejects both postmodernism and paternalistic *communitarianism as solutions to these problems (Touraine 1994, 1997, 1999). He sees the only solution in forms of democracy rooted in active citizenship. While his notion of the 'Subject' is somewhat vague, the strength of his work is his argument that the creative impetus of social action represents a challenge to power. In this respect he demonstrates how economic globalization has not undermined the capacity for oppositional political action. Even the most marginalized groups in society are capable not only of resisting domination but also of articulating new conceptions of society with an orientation to equality and solidarity.

opportunities for individuals to maximize their interests. Rather, it argues for principles of collective democratic communication capable of determining the very formation of the interests that come to be claimed as 'private' and thereby shaping these interests in ways that can express social solidarity and trust. In this sense, discursive democracy for Habermas can exist in any part of society, not only in the institutionalized spheres of law and constitutional politics but also in the private sphere and interpersonal relations.

Habermas also stresses the importance of discursive democracy to the challenges of globalization, and more especially to European integration (Habermas 2001). Insofar as it is the site in society where power is contested, it is no longer confined to the state or to the bourgeois public sphere. The normative claims of democracy are now to be found everywhere, and have extended beyond the traditional confines of the nation-state (see Habermas 1996, 1998). It is also in this sense that Habermas speaks of a 'post-national constellation' in European politics.

Criticisms of Habermas

Habermas's work is the 1970s and 1980s brought critical social theory out of the impasse of the first generation. It established a new way of theorizing modernity, emancipation, and social action and provided a normative foundation for critique. But Habermas's confident shift away from Adorno and Horkheimer's bleak view of instrumental reason has not been without problems. Many critics have taken issue with Habermas's unsympathetic attitude to post-structuralism, with his staunchly *universalist mode of argumentation, with his attempt to generate a grand evolutionary theory of society free from *metaphysical assumptions, and with his insistence on rational linguistic communication as a realistic agency of progressive social transformation.

Among some writers, sometimes described as representing a 'third generation' of critical theory, there is a certain dissatisfaction with Habermas's over-rationalized conception of the social as grounded in formal structures of language (compare Wellmer 1986). Habermas's neglect of the dimension of values and cultural experience has led to an emphasis on new questions in the writings of Axel *Honneth, a student of Habermas. Central to these concerns is the question of *'recognition' (Honneth 1985, 1990, 1992). For Honneth, it is the 'struggle for recognition' rather than the struggle for agreement that is the most fundamental fact about social action. With this argument, Honneth shifted attention toward ethical issues around injured cultural identities, gender equality, and respect for diversity of value spheres. Honneth's work on multiculturalism and the 'politics of recognition' here shows affinities with the approaches of North American theorists such as Nancy *Fraser, Seyla *Benhabib, and Charles *Taylor.

Niklas Luhmann's systems theory of modernity

The concept of communication is also central to the leading German representative of *'systems theory', Niklas *Luhmann. However, for Luhmann, communication is not the foundation of critique and democratization, as it is for Habermas. According to Luhmann, communication is a condition entirely disconnected from language and social action. For Luhmann, it is *systems* that communicate, not social actors. Luhmann replaces the idea of society with systems of communication.

Luhmann was a contemporary of Habermas who began publishing in the 1960s, developing much of his work through a dialogue with Talcott Parsons's *functionalism, and also with *cybernetic theory. In his major work *Social Systems* (1984), Luhmann proposes that modern society comprises a functionally differentiated system whose subsystems have become autonomous of each other and of the social system as a whole (see also Luhmann 1970, 1992). This theory has its origins in Parsons's evolutionary functionalism but it differs from Parsons in several major respects. Luhmann denies the possibility of an overall systemic unity. He also rejects the idea of modernization as a unilinear evolutionary process, and he does not view the social in terms of symbolically constructed realities or 'lifeworlds' based on modernizing social integration. Against Habermas, Luhmann argues that system integration is a more useful concept than social integration, and against both Habermas and Parsons, he denies the idea that normative values provide the glue that holds society together. Luhmann shifts the emphasis from integration to *differentiation*. He proposes that every subsystem is self-reproducing, where subsystems are seen as *'autopoietic', or 'self-creating'. Each subsystem tends to reproduce itself, and it does this by distinguishing itself from its environment. Systems are ultimately flows of information. Luhmann describes them as 'operationally closed' in the sense that they do not require 'meaning' in order to function. For this reason 'society' as such does not exist. All that exists is communication between social systems.

The implications of this are significant for politics, which Luhmann sees as no longer occupying a functionally central position in society. Luhmann in fact argues that modern society is centreless, and that there is no one central subsystem, such as the state or civil society. Not too surprisingly, this led to a dispute in the 1970s with Habermas, who strongly opposed the suggestion that politics has no central role to play (Habermas 1976; Habermas and Luhmann 1971). According to Luhmann, contemporary societies are characterized by *complexity* as a result of functional differentiation. The consequence is that political communication has become just one mode of communication among others. Habermas saw this as a very *technocratic view of society, a view he also rejected with the simple empirical argument that politics has always been a prominent motor of historical change. In reply, Luhmann argued that Habermas's theory presupposed a simplistic conception of system integration being confronted by social integration. He insisted that the point of systems theory was to demonstrate that it is through differentiation, not integration, that society functions. It is through the creation of differences or functional distinctions that social changes occur.

The notion of 'distinction', involving systemic societal production of differences, is of central importance in Luhmann's social theory. The basic codes by which information is processed are binary ones, creating a distinction between 'inside' and 'outside'. Luhmann's argument is that distinctions can be made only from within a given system. There is no absolute independent point from which society can observe or represent itself (such as God or the State or the Emperor). It is no longer possible to represent society as a whole. All external positions from which observation might proceed have disappeared today. Instead, Luhmann argues that all observation must take the form of 'self-observations', or, as he also says, 'self-descriptions'. Subsystems must make self-observations in order for them to distinguish themselves from their environment, i.e. from other subsystems. In this respect, the subject as codifier and narrator—in the sense of old European philosophies of history, in *Hegel and Marx or *Comte—is replaced by a subject as observer.

Luhmann's idea of an increase in second-order observations can be seen in many areas of society. For instance, in politics since the nineteenth and twentieth centuries, public opinion has increasingly functioned like a mirror for different groups in society, making power contingent. In artistic production, second-order observations are replacing first-order observations insofar as art no longer represents something largely outside itself, such as the 'natural world': modern art has become predominantly *self-referential*. In science, questions of methodology have become all important, for scientific truth is not a matter of proclamations but of method. In law, recourse to second-order observations is evident in the salience of questions of procedure (Luhmann 1990).

Luhmann argues that the future in modernist thought was a means of extending the present beyond itself. Modernism saw the present as a work of self-projection. Today, instead, the future is experienced increasingly in the form of *risk* (Luhmann 1991, 1992). Risks concern possible but not determined events. Risks are improbabilities resulting from a decision. It is through risk that we cognitively construct the future, which has no redemptive solutions to offer us. At most, this suggests a conception of the future as a strategy for the reduction of complexities and contingencies, but not as a utopian dream.

Luhmann's social theory is close to postmodernism in the central importance it gives to 'difference'. It is, however, important to note that for Luhmann modernity is *already* characterized by difference, by differentiation, and by what he calls 'loss of reference'. Difference is not simply a condition of postmodernity. Luhmann's systematic and challenging theory of modernity rivals that of Habermas and others. Read in the light of interests in global complexity and indeterminacy, it represents an innovative way of thinking about contemporary society is able to address issues of *non-linearity in self-organizing systems. It work suggests a view of society that is no longer to be understood in the traditional terms of nation-state territory or key institutions, or 'collective values' or 'cultural representations'. Society is not something spatial that is integrated by particular actors or powers or institutions. It is rather to be conceived of as a system of differentiated processes of communication.

However, Luhmann's work suffers from various difficulties. Apart from the obscurity of much of writing style, the main problem is his neglect of *social action*. His theory of communication is based on a simplistic notion of his binary codes that leaves little room for other kinds of communication and interaction that cannot be reduced to this *cybernetic logic. Luhmann also overstates the capacity of social systems to reproduce themselves, and pays insufficient attention to issues of crisis, *legitimation, conflicts and opposition. Politics is very inadequately theorized as 'steering'. Lastly, while Luhmann does emphasize what Parsons called *'interpenetration', this idea still plays a limited role in his theory. The result is a failure to take into account mixed organizational forms and mixed cultural forms.

Reflexive modernization

We now turn to a final body of work which explores the ideas of Habermas, Luhmann, and others in a more empirical vein. This work can be brought together under the theme of 'reflexivity' and 'reflexive modernity'. It is particularly represented by the work of Ulrich *Beck and Anthony *Giddens.

The idea of *reflexivity is a topical issue in social theory. As mentioned in Chapter 10, Pierre *Bourdieu defended what he called a *'reflexive sociology' (Bourdieu and Wacquant 1992). Reflexivity here means the application of something to itself. In this case a reflexive sociology is one that applies to itself the critical attitude that it directs to its research object. Reflexivity suggests self-confrontation. In the methodology of social science it entails a questioning of the position of the researcher in relation to the research process. In Luhmann's social theory, reflexivity is the logic of *'self-reference' by which systems reproduce themselves under conditions of contingency. In the work of Alain Touraine, discussed earlier in Box 35, reflexivity is suggested by the idea of historicity and by the capacity of society to act upon itself. The notion of reflexivity is also central to Habermas's conception of a critical *dialogic rationality. In the following discussion, we look at ideas of 'reflexive modernity' and 'late modernity in the work of Beck and Giddens.

Ulrich Beck on reflexive modernity and the risk society

Beck proposes that modernity itself has become 'subject to modernization' (Beck 1986, 1997, 1998; Beck et al. 1994). Contemporary social life has become more fluid, more insecure and uncertain, as modern forms of life have been recast through continuing processes of modernization. In a similar manner to *Lyotard and *Bauman, Beck speaks of a process of transformation from an earlier industrial form of modernity to a later 'second' modernity; but Beck eschews the idea of a condition of *post*modernity in favour of a thesis of 'reflexive modernization'.

Beck argues that the current form of modernity is especially shaped by the social impact of risk. His book *The Risk Society* was first published in German just after the disaster of the nuclear reactor that exploded at Chernobyl in the then Soviet Union in 1986. Much of the interest of Beck's book and the significance it attaches to environmental risk can be explained by the tremendous impact of that event. Beck here writes that 'just as modernization dissolved the structure of *feudal society in the nineteenth century and produced the industrial society, modernization today is dissolving industrial society and another modernity is coming into being' (Beck 1986: 10). What the term 'risk society' draws attention to is less a logic of modernity than a catastrophe inherent in modernity generated by the resources and liabilities of technology. The primary function of the state in this 'second modernity' is to deal with the societal consequences of risk, which have been engendered by primary modernization.

Risk for Beck is not strictly the same as physical danger or natural hazard. It does not come from nature alone. It derives primarily from *society* and is essentially human-made. More specifically, risk derives from science and technology: 'Risk may be defined as a systematic way of dealing with hazards and insecurities induced and introduced by modernization itself' (Beck 1986: 21). The growing power of technology in modern society leads to a situation of gigantic risks, and the need to control these risks becomes more and more important. It is no longer a question of the pursuit of an ideal condition but rather of the prevention of the worst. The state in this sense ceases to be any kind of utopian agency oriented to planning and social engineering and instead take on the role of a pragmatic crisis-managing expedient.

Beck notes that one of the most distinctive features of risk is its abstract character. Risk is not immediately observable. Radioactivity, greenhouse gases, microbiological entities, and pollutants of various kinds are not visible in the way that natural hazards such as hurricanes, floods, or earthquakes are. Most risks are depersonalized; they are detached from particular social actors, and make the attribution of responsibility difficult. Moreover, risks are very often global. They are not always nationally specific and cannot easily be controlled by national governments. Given these characteristics, managing risk is not easy. The problem is that risk is primarily a matter of incalculable side effects, which means that it becomes a condition of perpetual crisis.

Yet Beck also comments that the risk society tends to encourage new forms of politics. Risk induces reflexivity because there are no certain answers to its problems. Central to the politics of the risk society is the collapse of the self-legitimation of expertise. In the risk society everyone is potentially an expert, since expertise can no longer hide behind the mantle of scientific authority. It is no longer merely a question of the availability of information but of the definition of risk. It is a question of how we judge risk, and of where the burden of proof lies, of how to judge compensation, and of whom to trust. The risk society in this sense is a 'discourse society' (Beck 1986: 128–9). By this Beck means the public contestation of scientific claims and the clash of lay and expert voices. Under 'primary modernity', science was an instrument to scientize nature. Under 'second modernity' science has scientized society to the point that science has become the primary ground on which conflict takes place. Public platforms such as pressure groups and *NGOs contest the claims of experts, but they also rely upon and make use of science in order to frame their contestation and do not simply turn their back on science. Reflexive modernity is thus a condition in which science is now applied to science, by public actors as well as by experts.

Anthony Giddens on reflexivity and individualization

There is a further theme in Beck's theory of politics in the risk society which is also central to the later work of Anthony *Giddens. This is the theme of 'individuation' or 'individualization'. According to Beck and Giddens, in the risk society, individuals are set free from the constraints of industrial society and tradition. Agency breaks free from previously constraining structures. Individuation gives rise to 'sub-politics', by which they mean the shaping of society from below.

Giddens's earlier contributions to the theory of *'structuration' are discussed in Chapter 10 of this book. In his later work, Giddens theorizes modernity as a process of 'de-traditionalization'. In his books *The Consequences of Modernity* (1990) and *Modernity and Self-Identity* (1991), Giddens describes the institutional orders of modernity as being (1) capitalism, (2) industrialism, (3) social control of information, and (4) military power. But he also states that modernity is driven by dynamics of 'time-space distantiation' which increasingly generate a global world. Central to this is the development of *'disembedding' mechanisms by which social relations are lifted out of local contexts, together with the emergence of 're-embedding' mechanisms that attach new and more abstract meanings to social life. Societies are viewed as reflexive in their capacity to adapt to change and as undergoing various processes of emancipation.

Giddens argues that in pre-modern societies reflexivity was subordinated to the interpretation of tradition, which was passed on without transformation. With modernity, the interpretation of tradition is replaced by reflexivity: 'The reflexivity of modern social life consists in the fact that social practices are constantly examined and reformed in the light of incoming information about those very practices, thus constitutively altering their character' (Giddens 1990: 38). Giddens see modern individuals as utilizing knowledge in order to shape their lives in ways that had previously been impossible due to the constraints of particular social structures and traditions (Giddens 1991). Similarly, Giddens sees contemporary institutions as no longer fixed and structured but as reflexive in organization. An example of this is trust. In modernity, trust plays an important role because of the need to deal with depersonalized and abstract systems which often concern technical apparatuses. But trust also exists in daily life, especially in personal relations. The self has become more reflexive in the sense that the identity of individuals is constituted increasingly in 'self-monitoring' and 'self-control'. The individual reflexively appropriates expert knowledge. Giddens writes that 'expert knowledge is open to reappropriation by anyone with the necessary time and resources to become trained; and the prevalence of institutional reflexivity means that there is a continuous filtering back of expert theories, concepts and findings to the lay population' (Giddens 1994: 91). In the sense the self has become considerably empowered. Giddens presents a view of the individual as someone who can shape his or her own life project.

Both Giddens's and Beck's ideas about reflexive modernity are open to criticism. Both writers give too much weight to the idea of modernity as a process of de-traditionalization leading to individual autonomy. Tradition is rather poorly theorized as something that declines with modernity and is replaced by a 'post-traditional' order based on individuation. This leaves no room for collective action, social movements, and community action, which arguably become more important in modernity than in pre-modern societies. In Giddens's theory in particular, we find a naive view of modernity as a process of individual empowerment. The background to Giddens's later work in the 1950s is the rise of what he called *'Third Way' politics, which claimed to be a new politics 'beyond Left and Right', in which elements of each are combined (Giddens 1998). A central tenet of this doctrine is that individuals take responsibility for themselves and do not depend on the state. Giddens seriously overlooked the susceptibility of such discourse to appropriation by apologists for the dismantling of social democracy and for the rule of neo-liberal economic policies, most notoriously by the British New Labour government of Tony Blair after 1997. Lacking the critical dimension of Beck's work but sharing Beck's individualistic approach to politics, Giddens tended to see only the positive dimensions of capitalist modernity. While his earlier work drew attention to violence in modernity (see Giddens 1985), his later work jettisoned critical engagement with the negative consequences of modernity. Very questionable was his proposition that societies are always capable of adapting to disembedding mechanisms. It can be argued that the line between Giddens's concept of reflexivity and business discourse of 'flexibility' is a thin one. It has been suggested that Giddens's idea of self-monitoring might better be regarded in terms of what Michel Foucault described as disciplinary technologies of power over the self.

Conclusion

This chapter has considered the work of some major social theorists writing in the 1980s and 1990s. All the approaches discussed offer interpretations of modernity from positions generally hostile to postmodernism in its extreme forms. In addition, with the exception of Luhmann, all the writers under discussion began their careers by taking part in debates in *Western Marxism, while subsequently coming to recognize inadequacies with Marxist thinking.

Three themes can be highlighted in the theories discussed in this chapter. The first concerns social movements and resistance to power. According to Heller, Castoriadis, and Touraine, modernity has been based on the revolutionary dream that society can create itself without a state. The dream has been shattered, but the impulse still lives on at both ends of the political spectrum. In Castoriadis's terms, there is a strong emphasis on modernity as the imagination of alternatives. A second theme is the idea of autonomy, relating to the capacity of social action to shape society in the image of moral and political ideals. This is represented in different ways in the social theories of Habermas, Touraine, and Giddens, as well as Heller and Castoriadis. A third theme concerns continuity in the project of modernity. The theorists are agreed that modernity entails an ongoing process of renewal and does not simply come to an end. It is in this sense that modernity involves a condition of constant social transformation. Habermas in particular speaks of the 'unfinished project of modernity'.

Drawing on the ideas of these theorists, we can characterize modernity as a condition of self-confrontation, incompleteness, and renewal in which the past is reshaped by a globalized present. Modernity expresses self-confidence in the transformative project of the present as liberation from the past. Modernity involves the belief in the possibility of a new beginning based on human autonomy. In sum, it refers to a promise that the world can be continuously reshaped by human agency in diverse social contexts.

▨ **QUESTIONS FOR CHAPTER 13**

1   In what ways do the theorists discussed in this chapter depart from ideas associated with postmodernism?

2   In what ways do theorists discussed in this chapter depart from Marxism?

3   What does it mean for actors in society to be, or to strive to be, collectively autonomous?

4   Is Habermas's theory of communicative rationality sociologically naive?

5   Is Luhmann's systems theory sociologically technocratic?

6   What does it mean for individuals to be 'reflexive'? What it does it mean for institutions to be 'reflexive'?

7   What features of contemporary life best describe the concept of the 'risk society'?

■ FURTHER READING

Some good general guides to themes covered in this chapter are Gerard Delanty's two books *Modernity and Postmodernity* (Sage, 2000) and *Social Theory in a Changing World* (Polity Press, 1999), Peter Wagner's two books *Sociology of Modernity* (Routledge, 1994) and *Theorising Modernity* (Sage, 2001), Nigel Dodd's *Social Theory and Modernity* (Polity Press, 1999), and Bryan S. Turner's edited *Theories of Modernity and Postmodernity* (Sage, 1990). An informative text is Jeffrey Alexander's essay 'Modern, Anti, Post, and Neo: How Intellectuals Have Coded, Narrated, and Explained the "New World of Our Time"', in his book *Fin de Siècle Social Theory* (Verso, 1995). See also Peter Wagner's *A History and Theory of the Social Sciences* (Sage, 2001). A good anthology of key readings in the area is Anthony Elliott's edited *Blackwell Reader in Contemporary Social Theory* (Blackwell, 1999). An informative collection of essays that distinguish an acceptably sociological conception of postmodernism from more free-wheeling textualist versions is Steven Seidman and Linda Nicholson's edited *Social Postmodernism: Beyond Identity Politics* (Cambridge University Press, 1995). One of the best critical assessments of postmodernism is Perry Anderson's *The Origins of Postmodernity* (Verso, 1998). Some polemical critiques of postmodernism are Alex Callinicos's *Against Postmodernism* (Polity Press, 1989), Christopher Norris's *The Truth about Postmodernism* (Blackwell, 1993), Terry Eagleton's *The Illusions of Postmodernism* (Blackwell, 1996), John O'Neill's *The Poverty of Postmodernism* (Routledge, 1995), and Timothy Bewes's *Cynicism and Postmodernity* (Verso, 1997). See also the interesting study by Robert Pippin, *Modernism as a Philosophical problem* (Blackwell, 1991).

Some useful introductions to Habermas's work since 1980 are Robert C. Holub's *Jürgen Habermas: Critic in the Public Sphere* (Routledge, 1991), Martin Matustik's *Jürgen Habermas: A Political-Philosophical Profile* (Rowman & Littlefield, 2001), William Outhwaite's *Habermas: A Critical Introduction* (Polity Press, 1994), and David Rasmussen's *Reading Habermas* (Blackwell, 1990). Also very informative, although limited to Habermas's earlier work is Thomas McCarthy's *The Critical Theory of Jürgen Habermas* (MIT Press, 1978). Some good studies of Habermas's relationship to the earlier Frankfurt School are Seyla Benhabib's *Critique, Norm and Utopia: A Study of the Foundations of Critical Theory* (Columbia University Press, 1986), Raymond Geuss's *The Idea of a Critical Theory* (Cambridge University Press, 1981), and Deborah Cook's *Adorno, Habermas and the Search for a Rational Society* (Routledge, 2004). Some good studies of Habermas's work on communication, democracy, law, and discourse ethics are Stephen K. White's *The Recent Work of Jürgen Habermas* (Cambridge University Press, 1987), the same author's edited *Cambridge Companion to Habermas* (Cambridge University Press, 1995), Erik Eriksen's *Understanding Habermas: Communication Action and Deliberative Democracy* (Continuum, 2004), René Schomberg and Kenneth Baynes's edited *Discourse and Democracy: Essays on Habermas' 'Between Facts and Norms'* (State University of New York Press, 2002) and Peter Dews's edited *Habermas: A Critical Reader* (Blackwell, 1999). A useful collection of readings from Habermas is William Outhwaite's edited *The Habermas Reader* (Polity Press, 1996). For Habermas's relationship to Foucault, see Michael Kelly's edited *Critique and Power: Recasting the Foucault/Habermas Debate* (MIT Press, 1994) and David Hoy and Thomas McCarthy's *Critical Theory* (Blackwell, 1992). For normative debates about civil society in the thought of Habermas, Arendt, Foucault, and Hegel, see Jean Cohen and Andrew Arato's *Civil Society and Political Theory* (MIT Press, 1992).

The best general introduction to the work of Luhmann in English is William Rasch's *Niklas Luhmann's Modernity: The Paradoxes of Differentiation* (Stanford University Press, 2000). Luhmann himself is rather difficult to read and has not been widely translated in English. His major work is *Social Systems* (Stanford University Press, 1995). A more accessible place to begin is his *Observations on Modernity* (Stanford University Press, 1998).

Anthony Giddens's ideas about reflexivity are laid out in his accessibly written *The Consequences of Modernity* (Polity Press, 1990) and *Modernity and Self-Identity* (Polity Press, 1991). One among many critical responses to Giddens's writings on the 'Third Way' is Christopher Bryant and David Jary's edited *The Contemporary Giddens: Social Theory in a Globalising Age* (Palgrave, 2001).

■ WEBSITES

Modernity Resources at **www.clas.ufl.edu/users/gthursby/mod/** Provides a good collection of links to sites on the relationship between modernity and postmodernity.

Postmodernity and its Critics at **www.as.ua.edu/ant/Faculty/murphy/436/pomo.htm** Contains critiques of postmodernism from a predominantly anthropological perspective, with definitions of terms, accounts of theorists, and links to related sites.

Cornelius Castoriadis at **www.agorainternational.org** Provides a useful resource with a bibliography of Castoriadis's works and links.

Who is Habermas? at **www.csudh.edu/dearhabermas/habermas.htm** Provides links to numerous commentaries on Habermas's thought.

Niklas Luhmann at **http://en.wikipedia.org/wiki/Niklas_Luhmann** Displays pages from a free on-line encyclopedia, summarizing Luhmann's ideas, with links to related terms.

14 | Globalization

Robert Holton

The term 'globalization' conjures up many images. We think of processes of free trade and the movement of capital and labour around the globe, or of institutions such as the World Bank and the International Monetary Fund and a host of multinational companies, or of new technologies such as the Internet, or of the actions of non-governmental organizations (*NGOs) such as Greenpeace and Amnesty International. For some commentators, the predominant image is one of progressive economic advance. Others will think of street protest against global injustice. Both sinners and saints, it seems, inhabit the global domain. The former are represented by exploiters of cheap third-world labour and abuse of the natural environment, the latter by the courage of humanitarian bodies such as the health professionals of *Médecins Sans Frontières* and the like.

What if anything do all these images and conjectures have in common? They seem to point to such a wide-ranging set of issues that it may be asked whether the word 'globalization' has any consistent meaning. The aims of this chapter are first to ask what globalization means and to arrive at a working definition. We then move to ask whether globalization is a *multiple set of changes* or a *purely economic* phenomenon, whether globalization is *new*, and why globalization *matters* to social theory. The chapter looks first at the economic elements of globalization, and their relationship to the idea of flows, networks, *'disembedding', and the sovereignty of nation-states. Then we look at the more legal, political, and cultural aspects of globalization. We conclude by setting out some broader historical contexts for ways of thinking about globalization.

What is globalization? Towards a working definition

The relationship between globalization and social change raises important questions about the nature and dynamics of modernity and about long-run trajectories of change across millennia. Modernity has been seen as taking increasingly decontextualized forms, as not only restructuring work, culture, space, and time but also creating new forms of *'transnational' and 'trans-local' connection. For classical social theory in the nineteenth century, some of the most important social changes were set by the interlocking impact of the French and Industrial Revolutions. For social theory since the last decade of the twentieth century, it is the question of globalization that has dominated attention.

For some, however, globalization is simply a hyped-up way of talking about contemporary life. On this view, rather than the discovery of new matters of sociological importance, all we really have here is a new word for older social trends and issues. Some writers have taken the view that if globalization simply means cross-border movements of goods, people, and ideas, it is not new: it has been going on for hundreds, possibly thousands of years.

From an analytical point of view, there is certainly confusion as to the kind of concept or theory that globalization amounts to. James Rosenau (1996: 249) poses the following challenging questions. He asks: 'Does globalization refer to a condition, an end-state, or to a process? Is it mostly a state of mind, or does it consist of objective circumstances? What are the arrangements from which globalization is a departure?' In short, would we perhaps be better off without a concept prone to the twin problems of rhetorical overload and analytical incoherence?

The main difficulty with the term globalization is not that it is meaningless but rather that it has become an umbrella term for many different social changes. And it is also a term loaded with a lot of moral and political baggage. This is not something for us to shy away from, but rather a puzzle we must try to unravel. The position taken in this chapter is that to abandon the concept would be, on balance, more problematic than retaining it. What is required is a critical review and refashioning of the terms. This is above all because debates around globalization engage with some very real social changes and theoretical challenges, some with long-run historical origins, others very recent.

As a first approximation, globalization may be thought of as a range of evolving *processes, relationships,* and *institutions* that are *not contained within the borders of nation-states* and have significant that transnational elements. While globalization has become part of the rhetoric of the contemporary liberal economic order, its meaning and usefulness is far broader. There are many important empirical and theoretical issues that make little sense without a term of this kind. The term 'international' is not satisfactory because it retains a notion of social life as conducted *between* nation-states rather than *beyond* them. The term 'transnational' attempts to capture this idea of processes and interactions *inside* particular nation-states which affect the way of life of other nation-states and *jump across* nation-state boundaries in many diverse, complicated, and largely unregulated, disorderly ways.

Theorists now debate whether globalization is a new type of social change creating new identities and new forms of social organization. To the extent that it *is* a new type of social change, questions have arisen as to whether globalizing trends represent a juggernaut of economic power, seemingly beyond human control, or a renewal of market- and technology-driven changes able to rescue the world from hunger and conflict. The moral challenge is whether globalization functions only to the advantage of the rich and powerful, or whether it represents an opportunity for new forms of *cosmopolitan virtue that somehow transcend the confines and discords of nations and ethnic groups. Political debates have centred on whether globalization can be managed in a stable manner, and how far political institutions can be created to establish global democracy. Such debates are clearly interdisciplinary in scope, implicating a wide range of disciplines. Contributions to the study of globalization are evident across the span of disciplines from political science, economics, and geography to law, anthropology, and cultural studies.

We begin by analysing more closely the meaning of the term 'transnational'.

Globalizing trends: the idea of the 'transnational'

Globalization has been identified with an assumption that nation-states have ceased to be a significant unit of analysis for the study of social life. This contrasts with what has been seen as the predominant 'methodological nationalism' of nineteenth-century social enquiry (compare A. D. Smith 1983: 26; Wimmer and Schiller 2002). For previous generations of social theorists, the nation-state was indeed the core unit of social organization. While they were very aware of international developments, classical social thinkers such as Marx, Weber, and Durkheim tended to identify 'society' with social processes that were politically centred upon nations and upon interstate relationships. Modern society tended to be seen as an amalgam of trends evident in British society plus French society plus German society, and so on. The idea of a global domain was, at most, associated with international activities such as trade, empire, and war. While bridges beyond the methodological nationalism of classical social theory are evident notably in the work of Marx, it is only in recent decades—after the work of comparative historical sociologists such as Immanuel *Wallerstein (1974, 1976, 1979) and others—that this framework has fully broken apart. (For further discussion of Wallerstein's work, see Chapter 6 of this book, pp. 149–50).

However, this is not to say that the nation-state focus has been abandoned in any wholesale fashion. It lives on notably in the various 'realist' schools of international relations research. *'Realist' writers in international relations studies take the nation-state and the practice of *Realpolitik* as the fundamental basis for world affairs. They point to the robustness of the nation-state as an institution, claiming that much of what is seen as 'transnational' effectively remains international in scope. Any working definition of globalization should therefore be carefully designed to encapsulate both the trends that have been associated with challenges to nation-focused thinking *and* the counter-responses of realist political science. Why *should* we think of the world as something more than a system of nation-states, inhabited by national governments and nationally situated businesses? The answer will have to do with the significance of certain key *globalizing trends*.

The key trends generally associated with globalization are at least one or more of the following:

- intensified movement of resources, ideas, and peoples across boundaries, and patterns of social organization and power within which such movements take place;
- greater interdependency between different parts of the globe, including regions, cities, and localities as much as national societies;
- growing consciousness of the world as a single place, a 'global consciousness'.

Beyond this point, some fundamental choices have to be made in taking this definition much further. Can we speak of a singular economic phenomenon, or should we speak of a multidimensional set of processes that may include economic, political, and cultural elements, all of them moving in different directions, rather than in any one unitary pattern?

The economic interpretation of globalization is certainly widespread and draws attention to some fundamental features of our contemporary world. These include the global distribution of commodities, capital, and labour markets; the power of multinational corporations; new communication and information technologies; global consumer consciousness; and ideologies of free trade and global deregulation. However, the problem with predominantly economic definitions of globalization is that they can be overextended. While goods, capital, and technology flow across boundaries, so do political, cultural, and religious institutions, processes, and forms of thinking. It would not seem that human rights, popular music, Islam, or Christianity are any less global in their transnational origins, mobility, and impact than markets or money. Similar global flows seem to extend across the arbitrary boundary separating the economy from the rest of society. Accordingly, an increasing trend in recent work has been to define globalization in broader ways, drawing attention to multiple features, rather than any singular characteristic (compare Holm and Sorensen 1995; Held 1995; Holton 1998). In addition to economic globalization, there are elements of a global *polity* and a global *culture*, and these latter elements do not all necessarily point in the same direction as economic developments.

In this sense globalization is a set of processes with 'autonomous logics', rather than a single master process (Beck 2000*b*: 11).

Processes of globalization

What, then, are the main processes of globalization, and what are the links between them? These questions direct us to relationships, institutions, and types of social actors. In the following, we look at the role of five factors: markets; time-space compression; networks, flows, and *'disembedding'; *governance and regulation; and the nation-state.

Globalized markets

A first obvious candidate for factors driving globalization is markets. Markets would appear to be easier to globalize than forms of government or cultural identity. Global markets for capital, money, labour, goods, and services are fundamental features in all major theories of globalization. They are characterized by high levels of mobility across boundaries and are typically evident in significant levels of convergence in commodity prices, share prices, interest rates, and forms of managerial best practice (compare Sklair 2001; O'Rourke and Williamson 1999). While nation-states find it difficult to regulate the least mobile factor of production, namely labour, they find it almost impossible to track the most mobile processes such as electronic transfers of money—let alone impose tax on such transfers.

However, markets are not entirely unstructured or unregulated. Markets do not reallocate all resources on a daily basis through the price mechanism (see Williamson 1975). They rely on continuities in management, in levels of accumulated knowledge, on a predictable and reasonably dependable set of property rights, and on significant levels of trust between market participants. This is especially true in cross-border activity conducted within a range of culturally and politically diverse settings, against tight time-lines and in highly competitive settings. For formal organizations such as multinational companies, regulatory bodies and legal systems help to structure markets alongside more informal interpersonal networks. The human actors involved are not only corporate executives and their workforces but also market-oriented professionals, public relations and media personnel, and regulators.

Time-space compression and global cities

The broader dimensions of economic globalization have been analysed by a range of political economists, economic sociologists, and geographers. Such analyses typically emphasize changes in the relationship between globalization and changes in the social organization of time and space. For writers as diverse as *Giddens (1998), Harvey (1996), *Bauman (1998*b*), Virilio (1998), and *Castells (1996, 1998, 2000), globalization in its most general sense involves time-space compression. Very rapid communication and human movement renders the constraints of space less salient. As space becomes compressed, the structuring of human activity becomes dominated by a single global time. The social organization of space becomes increasingly transnational. For Saskia Sassen (1994), the transnational structuring of global capitalism takes place in global cities rather than in nation-states. Cities such as New York, London, Frankfurt, and Tokyo represent key centres of economic power and are the location of the core producer services on which corporate activity depends. Spatial maps of global power have less and less to do with national boundaries and more to do with relations between global cities.

Networks, flows and 'disembedding'

For Manuel *Castells, economic globalization is best understood through the notion of the 'network society' (Castells 1996, 1998, 2000). While nation-states depend on the idea of sovereign power centres regulating a given territory, the emerging global order depends on multi-centred networks linking capital, information, and power. What matters is not so much physical proximity in a given territory but simultaneous processes that are increasingly separated in space and highly mobile. In what Castells refers to as the 'space of flows', several interconnected patterns are evident. These include circuits of electronic impulses—the technological vehicles of globalization—comprising nodes and hubs where flows are strategically directed, such as through global cities. They also involve the formation of a *cosmopolitan managerial elite, who are the key human actors in the process. In these respects, a transnational network society comes to replace national societies.

According to Carnoy and Castells (2001), state institutions redefine their boundaries both *outwardly* on an international or supranational basis through insertion into long chains of decision-making and governance, and *inwardly* through regional devolution. At the same time, those excluded from networks are left spatially immobile and knowledge-poor. This latter group inhabits the space of *place* rather than the space of *flows*. In this process, the positive normative associations of cosmopolitanism tend to be reversed. They change from a virtuous democratic ideal of transnational peace to the class consciousness of elite globalizers, operating the space of flows through networks of power and personal mobility. Meanwhile, the space of place tends to breed *'identity politics' as a defensive form of popular mobilization. From this perspective, the prospects for democratic global politics tend to look bleak. They seem to be reduced to defensive operations mounted from the spaces of place against the dynamic pace-setting spaces of flows. As *Bauman (1998c) puts it, 'globalization for some, localization for others'.

Economies are always connected with wider aspects of human society, and the types of connection that may be found range from high levels of economic autonomy at one end of the spectrum to high levels of what Karl *Polanyi called cultural-historical 'embeddedness' at the other (Polanyi 1944) (for further discussion of Polanyi's work, see Chapter 1 of this book, Box 1). Economic autonomy is associated with the erosion of this embeddedness, or with *'disembedding'. It is associated with ideas of deregulation of markets, free trade, and what is termed laissez-faire. The assumption is that economies can operate without constant and intensive intervention of a political or moral kind. For some commentators, this not only does happen but *should* happen, because it is believed to generate higher levels of efficiency and productivity and hence to increase human welfare. An embedded economy, by contrast, means that economic, political, and cultural life is tightly interconnected. For opponents of economic globalization, *dis*embedded economies are seen as elevating economic values above all others, leading to high levels of global inequality and injustice.

Governance and regulation

Between the two ends of this spectrum—tightly embedded economies on the one hand, openly disembedded economies on the other—a range of possibilities can be observed. One important way of connecting economy and society is through the concepts of global regulation and *'governance'. While government is typically based on an idea of state sovereignty, 'governance' includes the broader rules through which multiple sets of actors—both state and non-state actors—organize social transactions. Regulation through governance occupies a range of mid-points between market freedom and state control. It may be institutionalized in formal organizations or it may be conducted in more informal networks. Economic 'deregulation' in this context is something of a misnomer, because market economies rely on a range of regulatory arrangements, better captured through the notion of 'governance'.

Well-known institutions such as the International Monetary Fund or the World Trade Organization seek to regulate aspects of economic life such as global financial stability and multilateral trading rules. Alongside them, a host of less well-known bodies include the Codex Alimentarius Commission which is concerned with food standards and the International Labour Organization involved with labour standards. More informal networks include the elite groupings around bodies like the World Economic Forum which acts as a strategic discussion forum for economic global governance.

The extension of global economic analysis beyond markets to regulatory arrangements and governance networks represents the most recent form taken by older-established traditions of political economy. These have sought to examine the power relationships in which markets operate and their implications for economic development and social inequality. These approaches represent an important bridge towards a multidimensional understanding of globalization, by linking economies with power, political institutions, and public policy.

An unresolved issue in political economy approaches is the extent to which market-derived economic power dominates political and cultural life. One line of argument is that economic globalization is so dominant that it creates political, legal, and cultural forms of globalization in its own image. If this is so, we may have to conclude that there is only one master process of globalization, namely economic globalization. But if it is not so, we will have to speak of multiple forms of globalization, whose different characteristics may involve conflict and antagonism, rather than unilinear consistency or mutual reinforcement. The remaining sections of this chapter test out these two propositions. We turn next to the position of the nation-state and the question of whether it is being weakened under economic globalization.

Is the nation-state being weakened?

The idea of one master process of globalization involves a number of possible mechanisms. One rather simplistic proposition that has come under increasing criticism is that economic globalization undermines or hollows out the legislative and executive powers of existing nation-states (Ohmae 1990, 1996). This amounts to a theory of globalization as anarcho-capitalism. One of the main problems with this is that it ignores the robustness of nation-state administrations, and specifically their involvement in new regulatory functions. It is true that some regulatory functions of the nation-state have receded in prominence, particularly state enterprise and interventionist macro-economic planning. But many nation-states have taken on new regulatory functions in recent years; for example, social regulation of personal relations affecting children, women, divorce, and abortion (compare Mann 1993b: 118). In Europe, the supranational legislative agency of the EU has adopted a significant number of the regulatory functions previously exercised by national governments, and it has sought to promote liberalizing policies that enhance the global competitiveness of European businesses. But in general, EU legislation has complemented and added to the regulatiory capacities of member states more than it has taken away from them. In addition, contrary to widespread perception, national welfare state expenditure is *positively correlated* with economic openness (Rodrik 1996; Evans 1997; Therborn 1999). That is to say, states with liberal economic policies open to foreign investment are not, on the whole, states with reduced welfare expenditure for the national population. However, what does seem clear is that economic globalization requires states and cultural formations that are conducive to the protection of private property rights. It requires nation-states to provide physical infrastructure and human capital for market use, and, at the very least, it encourages a global consumer consciousness (Carnoy 1993; Sklair 2001). Global economic competition can lead state governments to step up their powers of protection over domestic industry, but it can also encourage them frequently to relax legislation and legislative powers perceived to limit the competitiveness of national businesses in the global market place.

The idea of a global consumer consciousness has been theorized by George *Ritzer under the catchword 'McDonaldization'. Ritzer's thesis is discussed in Box 36.

BOX 36. GEORGE RITZER ON 'McDONALDIZATION'

For some theorists of globalization, the linkage between economy and culture produces what has been referred to as the 'Coca-Colonization' or 'McDonaldization' of the world. According to George *Ritzer (1993), the *rationalization of production and service delivery methods harnessed to standardized global marketing creates globalized consumers. Global corporations, media conglomerates, and advertising agents organize mass markets around standardized and predictable production formats and consumption routines. These involve globally recognizable products subsumed within global brands, and controlled through local franchise agreements that tightly prescribe how products are delivered. According to this theory, economic globalization creates global cultural convergence around standardized and privatized consumerism. The public domains of democratic politics and political participation are seen to decline accordingly (compare Barber 1996).

Whether such arguments are completely convincing has been hotly debated. One problem is the assumption that consumers are cultural dopes, rather than knowledgeable agents capable of making choices. One question to be asked is whether producers can simply create the consumers they require, or whether the many failures in consumer marketing suggest that a conception of relatively less standardized marketing strategies aimed at consumer niches would represent a more plausible sociological account. Further aspects of the debate about whether economic globalization causes cultural 'homogenization' are explored later in this chapter, in Box 37.

Problems of economic determinism

Claims for a single master process of globalization driven by capitalist economic interests have a good deal of empirical credibility and are widely believed by many critics of globalization. But these claims are susceptible to problems of economic *determinism. The idea of a single prime mover of globalization rests on the assumption of a single overarching dimension to social life. This is commonly assumed to be linked to the operation of some kind of core social function. According to some commentators, the core function is the drive for material survival and the pursuit of material self-interest. According to others, it is the search to realize social creativity through cooperative labour. Roughly speaking, the one viewpoint is vigorously pro-capitalist, or pro-liberal, while the other viewpoint is vigorously anti-capitalist, or Marxist. But in each of these two viewpoints, the economic reductionism that sees globalization in fundamentally economic terms rests on some version of a prime mover argument. For some partisans of the global anti-capitalist viewpoint, globalization is seen as driven by the pursuit of self-interest among the economically powerful at the expense of everyone else, or by a conflict between individual self-interest and collective *emancipatory struggle. In these kinds of arguments, the multiple dimensions of globalization tend to be reduced to a single unitary logic. The overriding difficulty is that there are other social processes, which meet the definition of globalization given above, but which are hard, if not impossible, to see as simple outgrowths of globalized markets and economic power. It is in this connection that we must turn now to some important legal, political, and cultural aspects of globalization.

Legal, political, and cultural globalization

One way of thinking about global multidimensionality is suggested by the British political sociologist David *Held (1995). Held speaks of global challenges to nation-states and national sovereignty brought about not only by developments in the world economy but also by a range of other processes that include international or transnational developments in law, political decision-making, and culture. A considerable literature now exists on what have been called 'alternative globalizations' or 'different globalizations' (compare Therborn 1999; Geyer and Paulmann 2001; Hopkins 2001).

In the legal sphere, international law has increasingly recognized powers, rights, and duties that go beyond the sovereignty of nation-states (Held 1995: 101). Symbolized by the Nuremberg trials of Nazi leaders, a significant trend has been toward the recognition of irreducibly universal human rights for individuals. This emergent global norm stands above and beyond the idea of national citizenship rights secured at the level of nation-states. Parallel conceptions of a common heritage of humanity have been articulated in environmental debates. Such norms have become globalized very quickly. It must be admitted that such norms have tended to remain more at the level of declaration than implementation. But it is clear that agencies such as the UN, along with some national governments and numerous NGOs such as Amnesty International, animated by global social movements and activists, have struggled greatly to secure implementation of such norms. In this connection, many critics of global corporations cite instances of corporate indifference or violation of human rights and environmental standards. It is hard to attribute the dynamic behind these developments purely to economic globalization, either from the positive liberal viewpoint or from the negative Marxist viewpoint.

In the political sphere, decision-making involves both governments and 'governance'. National governments in Western countries typically retain greater control over some matters such as taxation or immigration policy than over other matters. In a governmental sense, aspects of national sovereignty have clearly been pooled upwards, toward regional or global institutions. In Europe, this is evident at the level of the EU. It is also evident in matters of trade rules and agreements, as set by the World Trade Organization. On the other hand, it is less evident in the case of the UN: here even where some sovereignty is pooled or diluted via global harmonization of rules and standards, nation-states retain formal juridical sovereignty. In this case, transnational arrangements still require the consent of nation-states. It is for this reason that Held here speaks of *inter*national rather than *trans*national political decision-making. But still, on the whole, having signed upto bodies that operate in some sense beyond national mechanisms, nation-states have increasingly become subject to processes and procedures administered by transnational bureaucracies and articulated by transnational bodies of expertise. By signing up to transnational systems of rules, they become susceptible to transnational moral pressures to honour and comply with what has previously been agreed. This is not to deny that such pressures may be ignored, especially by more powerful states, notably by the USA. But still, the *normative pressure to comply with supranational requirements remains an effective factor in contemporary political decision-making.

Is legal and political globalization driven by economic globalization?

At this point, in order to be fully clear about the significance of legal and political globalization, let us once again pose the question of economics. Could it be objected that the kinds of legal and political globalization described so far have arisen primarily only in response to the challenges of economic globalization—as consequences of the latter, or perhaps as ideological 'functions' of it?

The question would seem to apply in two basic senses. The first is where economic actors support institutions to strengthen or stabilize the functioning of global markets. The second is where the operation of such markets creates effects on the natural environment and broader patterns of social and cultural life that are deemed unacceptable on grounds of economic sustainability and social stability.

In the first sense, many of the stronger regulatory bodies such as the World Bank or the WTO are explicitly charged with economic policy functions and interpret their mission very much in support of economic globalization. Corporations are major players and lobbyists in transnational fora. The EU itself has developed at many key moments very much as a market bloc to rival American capitalism. In the second sense too, much of the social and environmental debate encapsulated in the phrase 'globalization and its discontents' is engaged with an agenda set by economic globalization (compare Sassen 1998; Stiglitz 2002).

However, these narratives still have their limitations. Broader global processes need to be seen at work, and a broader theoretical framework needs to be defined. As Ulrich *Beck puts it, 'the various autonomous logics of globalization—the logics of ecology, culture, economics, politics and civil society—exist side by side and cannot be reduced or collapsed into one another' (Beck 2000a: 11). Another way of making the same general point is to advert to the globalization of processes such as the search for personal and social security and the elaboration of a meaningful identity, together with movements for human rights, greater political and social justice, and greater fairness in the distribution of resources.

In the latter connections, two useful examples can be given as illustrations. The first concerns active debates in the public sphere about the advantages and disadvantages of a market-driven global economy. Economic globalization, insofar as it has exploited low-cost labour or generated adverse environmental effects, is indeed responsible for the processes that its critics find unacceptable. But the moral criteria that are applied by critics are not in any direct sense the product of economic globalization. They draw instead on a range of traditional and modern precepts and attitudes towards nature, community, democracy, and social justice. Ideas such as living in harmony with nature or rights to popular self-government did not have to wait until the intensified processes of contemporary economic globalization to emerge, even though the capacity to organize coalitions of critics has depended in large measure on low-cost communication, information, and transportation technology.

The second example concerns links between globalization and issues of human security, including both geopolitical and personal security. These questions have been rather neglected by sociologists. Thomas *Hobbes's seventeenth-century conception of the *'state of nature', which saw life as 'nasty, brutish and short', raised in acute form the question of how to achieve personal and collective security. The answer for Hobbes centred on the creation of a strong sovereign power. For sociologists, this issue has typically been pursued through an analysis of the internal workings of the nation-state and through an interest in the economic causes of insecurity. The fragility of social life was only brought into focus recently with the emergence of a 'sociology of risk' (discussed in Chapter 13 of this book, pp. 286–9). Meanwhile, the study of international security tended to be left to the discipline of international relations.

In this second example of insecurity, one may argue that public perception of global threats to quality of life have more to tell us about the construction of the UN and its agencies such as the World Health Organization than merely patterns of corporate economic power. War may certainly be fought over economic issues, but the fear of war cannot be reduced to an economic calculus. Personal insecurity in the face of global environmental risk may come to centre on the actions of corporate or state polluters, but the search for understanding and effective redress is a far broader matter that many people see as involving the globalization of moral and political rights and responsibilities. The NGO slogan 'Think globally, act locally' is symptomatic of the world-view of many critics of economic globalization, implying a complex relationship between global aspiration and local competence.

To sum up the answer to our question 'Is legal and political globalization driven by economic globalization?', we may say the following. Legal and political globalization is both normatively independent of economic globalization and functionally related to it, but not functionally *reducible* to it.

Two case examples: global business regulation and the development of the Internet

A more multidimensional framework for thinking about globalization can be illustrated with two case examples. These are global business regulation and the development of the Internet, which we discuss in turn.

In their study of global business regulation across thirteen policy areas, Braithwaite and Drahos (2000) lend empirical depth to the idea of global complexity, emphasizing the involvement of multiple actors in global decision-making and governance. These include corporations and states, but they also involve intellectual communities of scientists, experts, and professionals, NGOs, and social movements. On the one hand, Braithwaite and Drahos conclude that the most influential actor in securing the globalization of regulation is the US government, and they also conclude that the most regularly effective interests in enrolling the power of global regulatory institutions are US corporations. On the other hand, the authors *also* conclude that a range of other actors have varying amounts of influence. In the environmental policy sector, Braithwaite and Drahos list nine different types of players, presented in Table 14.1.

Regulatory outcomes arise from complex interactions, conflicts, and accommodations between players. States sometimes act as agents for national business and sometimes as agents of domestic environmental movements. Businesses may sometimes support a deregulatory 'race-to-the-bottom' scenario, but sometimes they may encourage states such as Germany to support environmental regulation of sectors in which corporations have a Green competitive advantage. In this analysis, we are a long way from the sharply polarized and heavily moralized portrayals of global environmental good and global corporate evil.

In general, globalization of regulation typically proceeds through contests over principles and mechanisms of control. Contests of principles include familiar debates over deregulation versus regulation, and national sovereignty versus universal transnational norms. But they also include matters of process such as transparency and accountability and conflicts

Table 14.1 Influential actors in global environmental regulation

Organizations of states	OECD, EU, G-7, World Bank
States	USA, Germany, Norway, the Netherlands
International business organizations	Business Council on Sustainable Development, Industry Council for Ozone Layer Protection
National business organizations	US Chemical Manufacturers Association, Japanese Whaling Association
Corporations	DuPont, ICI, Lloyd's Register of Shipping
International NGOs	Greenpeace, International Organization for Standardization, World Rainforest Network
National NGOs	Environmental Defense Fund (USA)
Mass publics	Emerge episodically around events such as Bhopal and *Torrey Canyon*
Individuals	Rachel Carson, author of *Silent Spring*

Source: adapted from Braithwaite and Drahos (2000: 466).

over coercive mechanisms such as the use of military power as a mechanism of global security, as well as the economic coercion entailed by conditionality requirements of the IMF. These contests indicate that global agendas are not entirely dominated by the powerful. The influence of the numerous protest events that followed in the wake of the Seattle meeting of the WTO in 1999, including the foundation of the World Social Forum at Porto Alegre in Brazil in 2001, also give ample indication of this.

A second case example worth considering in this connection is the Internet. Here we have a communications technology that emerged from two rather disparate sources. The first was the US state, and more especially the US military, which funded research into a multi-centred communication system able to withstand nuclear attack. The second source comprised disparate groups of information technologists in California and elsewhere who wished to explore the possibility of interpersonal communications networks accessible by individuals—by individuals from below as well as by organizations from above. In the initial stages, the driving forces were higly variegated and owed comparatively little to corporate economic influence. Although corporate influence rapidly grew to prominence after 1980, symbolized by Microsoft, the legacy of an accessible tool of communication has continued. Many influential software engineers continue to supply technical expertise to the public domain, even while corporations seek to defend their intellectual property. The Internet as an engine and medium of globalized communication has clearly developed from multiple sources, and continues to reflect multiple user perspectives.

Global culture and 'glocalization'

Global cultural life is also an arena in which multiple and often competing or contradictory trends are in play. It can be argued that the picture is more complex and paradoxical than simple theories of McDonaldization and cultural imperialism would suggest (compare Holton 2000). At least three intersecting developments are evident. The first includes processes of homogenization in which the rationalized standardization of companies like McDonald's, Nike, and Starbucks does indeed prevail. Here it is certainly the case that powerful economic interests seek to create and dominate global consumer markets. But a second trend is resistance to global culture in its standardized consumerist form. This has been associated with a strong tendency for individuals and groups to identify with particular places and cultural repertoires and with the robustness of national identities, but not only in a blatantly nationalist form. The third has been the development of inter-cultural fusions or hybrids in which cultural elements from different sources are combined, such as in 'world music' and in a host of *syncretic fashion styles.

The complexity of cultural trends requires considerable analytical attention. The foremost reason for this is that the relationship between global culture and other national or local cultural forms and institutions is by no means easy to define. While it is conventional to think in terms of sharp distinctions between global, national, and local levels of activity, it is not obvious that such 'levels' can be distinguished from one another in any decisive way. The reality seems to be rather one of *interpenetration across highly permeable boundaries.

One influential way of proceeding has been through the notion of *'glocalization', developed by the British sociologist Roland *Robertson (1992, 1995). Robertson orginally developed the idea of a fusion of the global and the local to understand the *syncretic character of Japanese religion. A characteristic of Japanese religiosity, according to Robertson, is the borrowing of elements from different religions, notably Buddhism, whose influence came to Japan from the Asian mainland, and Shinto, the Japanese state religion. Japanese people may appeal to both for different purposes, rather than viewing themselves as either Buddhist or Shinto in affiliation. Robertson's discussion of global-local fusions involves an ambitious theory of social life in terms of mediation between the universal and the particular. Social life is localized or particularized in time and space but it is equally implicated in globalized or universalized discourses about the nature of the cosmos and humanity, embracing fundamental questions of meaning. In this respect, Robertson's key concepts are ontological, in the sense that they pertain to human social being, to aspects of the human condition. 'Glocalization' is, so to speak, our human fate. While possessing certain local roots, different peoples cannot understand their existence without an engagement with the global, which necessarily leads people to relativize the perspectives of their received cultural, religious, and historical traditions.

One revealing instance of ambiguities between the global, the national, and the local in the arena of popular culture is the Eurovision Song Contest. This case is discussed in Box 37.

Universalism and particularism

Roland Robertson's analysis of glocalization is set in a broad conceptual framework. At its most general level, the 'global field' is constituted through interactions between four component elements, namely individual human agents, national societies, societal *world systems, and lastly 'humankind' in some general sense (Robertson 1992: 27). Such interactions indicate varieties of interpenetration of the universal and the particular. Robertson speaks of 'the universalization of *particularism, and the particularization of universalism' (1992: 100). The premise of this thesis is that in a globalizing epoch, there are no longer any individuals or societies immune from global influence, even though the particular ties of space and time still matter. The global and the local are mutually self-constituting.

The idea of a 'universalization of particularism' can be seen in the global diffusion of a particular social form such as the free-market system or the nation-state form, which once arose in a specific historical context, namely in early modern Europe. The idea of a 'particularization of universalism' can be seen in the adaptation or relativization of general institutions and precepts to particular contexts. An example of this is the adaptation of the universal norm of human rights to particular needs and the incorporation of universal ideas of rights into particular national systems of citizenship. In the West over the last 200 years, the women's movement has brought about a concrete particularization of the abstract universal idea of the 'rights of man'. In these examples, we can see ideas of universal values coming to transform particular arrangements in definite contexts; and conversely, we can observe a counter-movement in which particular contexts inform and alter people's understanding of the meaning of the universal.

BOX 37. THE EUROVISION SONG CONTEST: CULTURAL IMPERIALISM
OR LOCAL SYNCRETISM?

In the Eurovision Song Contest, contestants represent different countries, each of which organizes a national contest to determine the European representative. On the night of the Contest, votes for each song are organized through national systems of voting. One interesting observation is that voters in particular countries often appear to support contestants from countries that border on their own, or with which they have historic ties. Here we may ask whether the Contest gives an example of national resistances to globalization. What would seem to speak against this is that elements of folk music and national costume have been relatively limited in the show. The overall musical idiom is the pop song, fusing Afro-American with European elements without any particular national point of reference. The contestants themselves are also often recent immigrants, again providing a multicultural rather than national element to the picture.

Hannerz (1992), writing of Sweden's contribution to one of the Contests in the late 1980s, reports the confusions that have arisen concerning the national integrity of the process. In Sweden's national contest, organized to determine a 'Swedish' entrant for the wider Eurovision Contest, 'it was quite acceptable that the . . . first runner-up had been performed by a lady from Finland, and the second by an Afro-American lady . . . Both [migrants] were thought of as representing the new heterogeneity of Swedish society . . . What was controversial was the winning tune, the refrain of which was "Four Bugs [a brand of chewing gum] and a Coca-Cola" . . . Of the two, Coca-Cola was more controversial . . . as a central symbol of "cultural imperialism" . . . What drew far less attention was that the winning tune was a calypso' (Hannerz 1992: 217). The favourite song of the Swedish contest thus drew all at once on Finnish, American, Afro-American, and West Indian elements.

The challenge here lies in determining not simply whether this is more of a global phenomenon or more of a national phenomenon. There is the third possibility that it represents an interpenetration of the global and the national: some kind of *'glocal' fusion of the global and the local. If so, we may ask: how widespread is this global or 'glocal' *syncretism? And this question raises several others. What is this glocal syncretism driven by? If it is driven primarily by globalized capitalist entertainment industries, why does it take the complex cultural forms that it does? If the cultural imperialism argument has less purchase, may we speak of certain kinds of emergent national, regional, or trans-local identity? This raises the question of the extent of the independence of global audiences from processes of global mass media production. Lastly we can also ask how significant such events really are for an under-standing of globalization. Are they trivial events, or are they salient in a more subtle way, perhaps as banal forms of cultural syncretism, analogous to the taken-for-granted forms of national symbolism discussed by Michael Billig (1995) in terms of 'banal nationalism'?

Another line of approach to these issues has developed around ideas of *'cosmopolitan democracy'. These have been formulated by David Held and others in terms of normative ideals of 'global civil society' or 'cosmopolitics' (Held 1995; Archibugi and Held 1995; Kaldor 2003). Debates about cosmopolitan democracy invoke universal values of trans-parency, accountability, peace, and justice in world affairs, and try to show how these values can be reconciled with, and enriched by, the particularistic cultural traditions of different national societies. Many would also see the development of transnational social movements as emergent indicators of cosmopolitan democracy founded on dialogue between the global, national, and local. The World Social Forum indicates processes of convergence in global social understanding from very diverse standpoints, issues, and agendas.

Differentiation and integration in globalization theory

To speak of multiple dimensions of globalization is to draw on a core idea in social theory about *differentiation*. According to *functionalist theory, society becomes differentiated over time between different component systems, each performing distinct social functions or sets of activities. In one very simple model, the economy deals with production, distribution, and consumption, the polity with the allocation of public resources in a legitimate manner, while culture provides meaning and a repertoire of symbolic and practical resources for social actors. Such differentiation has been said to provide advantages of specialization, with distinct sets of institutions such as markets, governments, and religious organizations occupying relatively autonomous places in the overall social system. Functionalist theory was propounded chiefly by Talcott *Parsons and Robert *Merton, but the idea of 'multiple dimensions' and 'multiple autonomous logics of development' is also to invoke the continuing legacy of the ideas of Max Weber.

The major challenge accompanying the idea of differentiation relates to how far it is compatible with social *integration. Can differentiation become excessive, leading to instability? Or has the need for strong forms of social integration been exaggerated? These issues, posed originally in the context of nation-states, become much more acute when we consider the transnational domain. A number of integration problems have been identified by commentators. One of the most serious is that the global economy appears to be in some sense out of control. At the very least, it is insufficiently regulated by political mechanisms and by public collective agency. Markets are unstable and prone to significant levels of risk, while corporate power backed by regulatory bodies such as the IMF lacks responsibility and legitimacy. A profound 'global democratic deficit' is evident insofar as the economy has globalized more rapidly than political institutions have been able to keep step, preventing them from responding in fully effective and democratic ways.

A further integration problem is the robustness of local and national identities, and the rather limited actual development of cosmopolitan consciousness, creating a deficit of *solidarity between peoples and individuals. The difficulty is that processes of globalization have led to extensive differentiation between the economy, the polity, and culture, which has incited, and has been compounded by, the revival of particularistic cultural identifications and affiliations or what is often referred to as *'identity politics'. One way of interpreting globalization and its discontents in this connection is to refer to a conflict between tendencies to further differentiation on the one hand and tendencies to *de-differentiation* on the other, where 'de-differentiation' does not necessarily mean the same as 'reintegration'. Robertson's idea of the global field draws attention to processes of *attempted* integration of the general with the particular. The 'glocal' in this sense is an *ontological feature of the human condition, linking universal aspiration with particular context. Even here, however, it remains unclear whether sustainable forms of integration can be achieved by glocal means, or whether the glocal simply subsumes conflicts over the distribution of global goods. Even if states and social movements see themselves as glocal, this does not mean that populations will necessarily be reconciled to the world order as it currently stands—not least in the present condition of profound economic inequalities and injustices between the rich and the poor, the powerful and the weak.

How new is globalization? Some historical contexts

So far in this chapter we have been concerned with globalization from the standpoint of very recent socio-economic developments. We end our discussion now by standing back from the contemporary situation in order to consider some more historical contexts for an understanding of the term.

Movements of people, goods, and ideas across wide political and cultural borders have been taking place for centuries, if not millennia. Movements of population in search of food, land, and freedom or trade between tribes, city-states, and regions go back a long way in human history. The question we must ask, however, is whether, or how far, such historical movements constitute meaningful instances of the concept of globalization. The crucial indicators would appear to have to do not only with cross-border movement but also specifically with closer interdependence between spatially separate social groups, together with a sense of the world as some kind of single place. Globalization may not require that individuals feel themselves to be global or develop global identities and attachments; but it almost certainly means that individual and group activities must take account of global interdependencies, whether economic, technological, political, or cultural. The need to take account of global interdependencies may denote a quality of becoming globalized through external constraint, by default. It suggests that individuals become enmeshed in something above their heads or beyond their personal control. This is indeed how many anti-globalist critics interpret the world. Lack of choice or democratic consultation about patterns of globalization is certainly the source of much discontent. But there are two alternative ways in which we can think about how individuals relate to globalizing processes in a historical context.

The first involves individuals actively participating in cross-border processes and global culture. They may be merchants or pilgrims, explorers or migrants, multinational managers or world musicians, colonizers or environmental activists. Activity of this type involves some kind of enlarged cross-border orientation, whether as a 'citizen of the world' or as an imperialist, a Muslim or a Jew or a Christian, a free trader or a member of a world-wide diaspora. The second, less overtly global orientation involves all of those people who make use of material and symbolic resources and repertoires that have an origin beyond their country of origin, whether technology, foodstuffs, political institutions, religious practices, or art and literature. Involvement in these social patterns may require no especially global consciousness; but such ideas, institutions, and resources may, nevertheless, have a long pre-existing cross-border history, whether they are key concepts in mathematics or forms of economic organization or world religions (compare Curtin 1984).

Some of the most ambitious attempts to produce long-run historical accounts of interactions and interdependencies along these lines have been produced by André Gunder Frank and his associates (Frank and Gills 1993). One of Frank's most radical claims is that a world system has existed for around 5,000 years, rather than 500 years. This proposition rests on evidence such as long-distance trade, market exchange, and forms of capital accumulation. Frank's main aim is to demonstrate the existence of an expansive capitalist core in world history. This position is significant for two reasons. First, it revises the familiar thesis that global capitalism originated in the period from the fifteenth century onward, symbolized by Christopher Columbus's voyage to the Americas. Second, it emphasizes the non-Western origins of globalization.

Another significant contribution to historical ways of thinking about globalization is A. G. Hopkins's edited volume *Globalization in World History* (Hopkins 2002). This centres on a fourfold typology of globalization, portrayed in Table 14.2. The typology is not organized around variations in some single structural principle, such as Marx's 'mode of production' or Weber's 'form of legitimate domination'. Rather, the typology is based on changes in institutional patterns of social organization in time and space. The four types of globalization sketched by Hopkins and his associates are not intended to be a Procrustean bed on which complex bodies of historical evidence are stretched until they fit neatly into

Table 14.2 Four historical types of globalization

Archaic	Pre-dates industrialization and nation-state	Associated with empires, cities, and trading diaspora
	Present in Asia, Africa, and parts of Europe	Actors involved include kings, warriors, priests, and traders
Proto	Emerges between c. 1600 and 1800, with state reconfiguration and commercial expansion	Multi-centred sources of indigenous change, including improved management of sea-borne commerce
	Present in Europe, Asia, and parts of Africa	Actors include explorers, slave traders, merchants, and pilgrims
Modern	Conventional Western-centred phase, post-1800, associated with industrialization and the rise of the nation-state	Involves both free trade and imperial expansion, and improved manufacturing, military, and communications technology
	Increased involvement of non-Western nations in later phase	Domestication of earlier forms of cosmopolitanism
	Emergence of global civil society	Actors involved include imperial colonizers, manufacturers, scientists, activists from non-governmental organizations
Postcolonial	Post-1950 emergence of a decolonized world, with new types of supra-territorial organization and regional integration	Post-imperial Revival of cosmopolitanism
	Continuing non-European sources of globalization, including Islam, as well as syncretic intercultural fusions such as jazz and world music.	Actors involved include business and political elites, migrants and asylum seekers, global civil servants, radical social movement activists, virtual networks around the Internet.

Source: adapted from Hopkins (2002: *passim*).

an appropriate category. Rather, the aim is *heuristic: to provide a plausible framework in which further historical data can be usefully organized.

One specific area in Hopkins's scheme where further debate is warranted concerns the analytical coherence of the fourth 'post-imperial' phase. The intensification of a globally interventionist US foreign policy since the turn of the millennium throws some doubt on any 'end of empire' thesis. Writers such as Michael Hardt and Antonio *Negri (2000) and David Harvey (2003) argue for a return of the forces of empire. Global market integration, it seems, is insufficient to create global security in an epoch of continuing interstate conflict and global terrorism. What remains unclear is whether this signifies a return to imperial modes of attempted global integration through military force, likely to be doomed to failure like previous empires, or whether it signifies the beginnings of a phase of de-globalization around violent modes of national or regional *Realpolitik*. The latter questions are raised by Michael *Mann (2003) with reference to the US-led occupation of Iraq that began in 2003.

Conclusion

Globalization matters to social theory because it raises many of the core issues in social enquiry about the nature and direction of social change, mobility and settlement, power and inequality, conflict and order, solidarity and identity, and complexity in social organization. But globalization also matters because it provides important examples of what Robert *Merton (1949c) called *'middle-range' theorizing, as against more speculative forms of *'grand theory'. The will to grand theory reflects several aspirations, from the search for a unified theory of society to the more activist vocation of prophecy. In the prophetic mode, analysts have seen globalization both as a harbinger of global riches and equally as the enemy of social justice, democracy, and community. The emotional appeal of such views has been eroded in considerable bodies of empirical research by less grandiose and more complex explanatory approaches. Accounts of globalization are littered with failed general theories and prophecies, from the assumption of the end of the welfare state and the nation-state to the idea of cultural homogenization and universal wealth distribution.

In the study of globalization, methodological nationalism has been challenged by a new methodological globalism. In its most radical forms, methodological globalism sees the fluidity of people, images, and resources across space as a new axial principle (compare Urry 2000). At the same time, however, we should be clear that not everything is in flux. The robustness of resistances, residues, and attachments to the ideal of a stable sense of security built around particular places and contexts constitutes limits to globalization (compare Scott 1997). The same is true of the many 'glocal' fusions in which would-be globalism seeks an anchorage in specific regional contexts. This applies whether we are speaking of the search for new markets around particular niches, or the search for general cultural meanings among populations that differ in tradition and identity.

It should be emphasized that the case for regarding globalization as in some sense long-run does not mean that nothing is new. While flows and interdependencies stretch out over time and space and must essentially be understood in historical dimensions, the velocity and intensity of cross-border transactions has increased dramatically in recent years. This undoubtedly has to do with developments in communications and information technology associated with the Internet, with the digitalization of information and penetration of the mass media into popular culture. Yet the strong resonance of a sense of virtually instantaneous time should not blind us to the historical complexity of the phenomenon of globalization. Rather than a single global time, there exists a complex array of temporal dimensions. These include a continuing sense of 'glacial time' or what the French historian Fernand *Braudel called *longue durée*, associated with slower-moving changes in relationships between humankind and the natural environment (Braudel 1967). They also include forms of cyclical time in which patterns of global expansion and de-globalization occur, often in response to failed projects for global integration. In all of this, globalization has helped stimulate an upsurge of interest in sociological accounts of space and time and in the historical transformations of the structures of human civilization.

■ QUESTIONS FOR CHAPTER 14

1   Is globalization another name for economic imperialism?

2   Is there one globalizing logic or more than one?

3   What relationships can be discerned between economic aspects of globalization and political, legal, and cultural aspects?

4   How far does globalization undermine the sovereignty of nation-states?

5   How new is globalization?

6   Are there any limits to globalization?

7   Can there be such a thing as a 'global civil society'?

■ FURTHER READING

Some excellent general introductions to controversies about globalization are David Held and Anthony McGrew's two books *Globalization/Anti-Globalization* (Polity Press, 2002) and *Global Transformations: Politics, Economics and Culture* (Polity Press, 1999), as well as the same authors' useful collection of edited readings *The Global Transformations Reader: An Introduction to the Globalization Debate* (Polity Press, 2000), especially the introductory chapter titled 'The Great Globalization Debate'. Also good is Leslie Sklair's *Globalization: Capitalism and its Alternatives* (Oxford University Press, 3rd edn. 2002). Other useful guides are Jan Aart Scholte's *Globalization: A Critical Introduction* (Macmillan, 2000), Malcolm Water's *Globalization* (Routledge, 1995), and Robert Holton's *Globalization and the Nation State* (Macmillan, 1998). Some influential statements have been Ulrich Beck's *What is Globalization?* (Polity Press, 2000), Zygmunt Bauman's *Globalization: The Human Consequences* (Polity Press, 1998), Martin Albrow's *The Global Age* (Polity Press, 1997), Barrie Axford's *The Global System* (Macmillan, 1995), and Anthony Giddens's *Runaway World: How Globalization is Reshaping our Lives* (Routledge, 2000).

Roland Robertson's *Globalization: Social Theory and Global Culture* (Sage, 1992) was one of the first books to place globalization on the intellectual map. A major contribution is Manuel Castells's *The Information Age*, in a three-volume series *The Rise of the Network Society* (Blackwell, 1996), *The Power of Identity* (Blackwell, 1998), and *End of Millennium* (Blackwell, 2000). Some path-breaking empirical studies are John Braithwaite and Peter Drahos's *Global Business Regulation* (Cambridge University Press, 2000) and Leslie Sklair's *The Transnational Capitalist Class* (Blackwell, 2001). See also John Urry's two books *Sociology beyond Societies* (Routledge, 2000) and *Global Complexity* (Polity Press, 2003). The most sceptical view of globalization in relation to the fate of nation-states is Paul Hirst and Graham Thompson's *Globalization in Question* (Polity Press, 1996). Some important studies of global cities, finance and capital flows are Saskia Sassen's three books *Cities in a World Economy* (Sage, 2nd edn. 2000), *The Global City: New York, London, Tokyo* (Princeton University Press, 2001), and *Losing Control? The Decline of Sovereignty in an Age of Globalisation* (Columbia University Press, 1996).

For cultural aspects of globalization, see Arjun Appadurai's *Modernity at Large: Cultural Dimensions of Globalization* (University of Minnesota Press, 1996). For some examples of thinking about globalization by geographical theorists, see David Harvey's *Spaces of Capital: Toward a Critical Geography* (Routledge, 2001), Edward Soja's *Postmodern Geographies* (Verso, 1989), Mike Davis's *Ecology of Fear: Los Angeles and the Imagination of Disaster* (Vintage, 1999), and Nigel Thrift's *Spatial Formations* (Sage, 1996).

In the activist mode, an important piece of investigative journalism is Naomi Klein's *No Logo* (Flamingo, 2001). Left-leaning texts are Justin Rosenberg's *The Follies of Globalization Theory* (Verso, 2001), Alex Callinicos's *An Anti-Capitalist Manifesto* (Polity Press, 2003), and Michael Hardt and Antonio Negri's much-discussed *Empire* (Harvard University Press, 2000). Richard Sennett's *The Corrosion of Character* (Norton, 1998) is a very readable study of the 'flexible' entrepreneurial individual. Another major treatise on this phenomenon in France is Luc Boltanski and Ève Chiapello's *Le Nouvel esprit du capitalisme* (Gallimard, 2000). On the side of liberal defences of globalization, two important books are Joseph Stiglitz's *Globalization and its Discontents* (Penguin, 2002) and Jagdish Bhagwati's *In Defense of Globalization* (Oxford University Press, 2004). For conceptions of 'cosmopolitan democracy', see David Held's *Democracy and the Global Order* (Stanford University Press, 1995), Mary Kaldor's *Global Civil Society* (Polity Press, 2003), and James Bohman's article 'The Globalization of the Public Sphere', in *Philosophy and Social Criticism*, 24/2–3 (1998).

■ **WEBSITES**

Centre for the Study of Globalization and Regionalization (CSGR) at www.warwick.ac.uk/fac/soc/CSGR/ Provides links to discussion groups, activities, research areas, and publications.

Globalization Research Centre—Africa (GRCA) at www.globalization-africa.org/ Contains links to current projects, events, and research papers on globalization with a focus on Africa.

International Forum on Globalization (IFG) at www.ifg.org/ Provides information by an alliance of activists, scholars, economists, researchers, and writers on joint activity and public education about globalization.

The Global 500 at www.fortune.com/fortune/global500 Contains information on the top 500 global companies.

Amnesty International (AI) at www.amnesty.org Displays the homepage of Amnesty International, a worldwide NGO devoted to the recognition and realization of human rights.

Conclusion: Social Theory for the Twenty-First Century

Austin Harrington

Our time at the start of the new millennium appears to be one of considerable uncertainty. For many people, the most significant ending of the twentieth century was not the formal passing of the year 1999 but the fall of the communist regimes of Eastern Europe and the Soviet Union between 1989 and 1993. These events marked the end of the Cold War and the end of the bifurcation of the world into the two opposing ideologies of capitalism and communism. Bleak as it was, the bipolar system that dominated the second half of the twentieth century created a degree of predictability in international relations, economic forecasts, and general social expectations that has today mostly disappeared. Today the world strikes us as a highly volatile place, marked by ever-widening gaps between the world's richest and poorest nations, by increasing environmental destruction, and by a vast imbalance of power between political entities of the West such as the USA and the European Union and the world's diverse other regions, continents, societies, and cultures. At present, the world offers little evidence of any framework of global civil society capable of holding the world's most powerful economies and governments to account and ensuring a fairer distribution of resources. Certainly no current global legal system secures all peoples an equal chance to determine their own livelihoods in an autonomous and simultaneously peaceful way.

If the fall of the Berlin Wall in October 1989 marked the end of the twentieth century, the symbolic beginning of the twenty-first century for many people was the crashing of four hijacked aeroplanes by Islamist terrorists into the World Trade Center in New York and the Pentagon in Washington on 11 September 2001. This event brought home to many people the vulnerability, the volatility, and the complacency of our current global life in the most dramatic and traumatic way. It would appear that intolerant and intolerable acts such as these are consequences of renewed rises in religious fundamentalism, nationalism, ethnic hatred, racism, and xenophobia in our world today, as much in opposition to the West as *within* the West. Without doubt, they are symptoms of a certain degradation of global social solidarity, reflecting the absence of any system of shared social, economic, and political life capable of fostering a mutual concern with the collective welfare of the species. We should remember that the world that saw 3,000 people die on 11 September 2001 is the same world that sees 2.3 million Africans die each year from HIV, partly as a result of the shortage of cheaply available drugs.

Since 11 September 2001, world politics appears to have entered a new or 'second' phase of globalization with an increasingly imperialistic and militaristic face. In a context of a general shift of the axes of world conflict from the capitalist–communist divide of the second half of the twentieth century to the oil-rich territories of the Middle East and the Islamic peoples who inhabit these lands, the system of Western-led neo-liberal economic policies that drove the boom of the final years of the last century has become conscious of a profound crisis in its resources of moral and political legitimacy. At a time stamped indelibly by the US-led 'war of pre-emption' on Iraq of 2003 and the revelation of subsequent torturing of Iraqi prisoners of war, and by the seemingly endless failure of attempts to establish peace and justice for the people of Palestine under Israeli occupation—to name only two among countless sites of conflagration—the world's dominant economic system seems compelled to maintain itself by force in the name of a 'war on terrorism'. If the closing years of the twentieth century ushered in what the French writers Luc Boltanski and Ève Chiapello (2000) call a 'new spirit of capitalism' based on a new type of flexible individual open to all opportunities for career advantage, the opening years of the twenty-first century appear to be ushering in a new international *state of nature in which all efforts to develop genuinely impartial legal bodies with universal transnational jurisdiction are being systematically undermined by the concerns of the world's most powerful states for 'national security'.

It is this coexistence of complex and unjust global conditions that makes rigorous social analysis so important today. When so much of our political life seems to be clouded by distractions from reality, by insuperable quantities of information, by manipulative publicity campaigns, by 'spin' and 'hype', or by the cult of media celebrity, critical social analysis has never been more important. At a time when political representation seems to be increasingly fashioned in the image of cinema and becomes less and less able to distinguish between fact and fiction, social theory is a vital tool of response. Sometimes it is tempting in this climate to throw up our hands in despair at the problems of the world, or to withdraw into a life of purely private apolitical concerns, or to fixate on single objects of blame at the expense of complexity and contradiction. This kind of reaction is dangerous for several reasons.

Firstly there *are* facts to be discovered and stated about the causes of our malaise, through rigorous research. There *are* illusions, prejudices, and lies to be purged from the spaces of our public and private lives. But we also have to accept that the answers to our problems are not always unambiguous or clearly given. When the ancient Greek philosopher *Plato compared ignorance to the perception of shadows on the walls of a cave lit by a dim fire, he made an assumption of the ultimate separateness of truth and enlightenment from the daily contexts of life in which people ordinarily experience the world. Today this kind of assumption is not possible for us. Today our reality is intrinsically a reality of shadowy appearances and shifting forms, of mediated images and messy contradictions. Our reality is not Plato's pure bright light of day outside the cave. This implies that in banishing falsehood and prejudice from politics and society, we cannot assume our answers to be always the true ones. However intractable or deluded the world may appear to us, we have to try out our answers in the here and how. We have to engage with the world as it is and try to transform it from within, through reasoned deliberation and communication.

The various schools of social theory discussed in this book offer a few conceptual tools for dealing with such troublesome realities. They offer techniques of analysis with a variety of empirical applications in practical contexts. It should be stressed that no particular school has a monopoly on authority. Each should be treated critically, as one among possible others. This does not mean that all schools and theories can be mixed together in one great soup. Not all of the theories are mutually compatible. Tensions and contradictions remain between some of them. Nor is it the case that if we could mix them all together, we could cream off the best parts and discard the rest. But many kinds of productive synthesis and mutual criticism are certainly possible, and it is for this reason that all the schools discussed in this book deserve equal consideration. Social theory, as with all scientific debate, is a pluralistic engagement marked by unity and disunity, at once by continuity and by discontinuity.

In a most general sense, social theory is a way of thinking about social life that helps us to address two perennial questions of human existence: *Who are we? What should we do?* These questions take on a special importance for us in modern times. To think about who we are and about what we should do is essentially to ask what it means for us to be *modern*, and it is this distinctive question of modernity that lies at the centre of social theory. The very existence of social theory as a scientific project is itself a creation of modernity. For societies that we today call 'ancient' or 'traditional', social theory is not a possible structure of thought, at least not in the sense in which we understand the word 'theory' today. Only modernity could have thought of applying a scientific conception to the making and shaping of its own world. Although ancient societies present us with many answers to the question of who we are and what we should do, these answers are no longer *our* answers, and they are not the answers of social theory. Ancient people thought about their world and about what they should do in it, but they did not believe their world to be capable or needful of radical change, to change from its roots. They did not, fundamentally, believe their world capable of rational transformation through collectively organized human agency.

To think about who we are and what we should do is to think about our *time*, about our place in time and our relationship to time. The thought of the significance of time and of being-in-time has been a recurrent motif for many of the most influential philosophers of modernity, from G. W. F. *Hegel to Friedrich *Nietzsche and Martin *Heidegger, as well as for more directly social and political thinkers such as Karl *Löwith (1949), Alexandre *Kojève (1933–39), Hans *Blumenberg (1966), Eric *Voegelin (1952), Hannah *Arendt (1958, 1971), and many others. As these thinkers make clear, ancient people certainly also thought about their time; but ancient people believed their time to be for the most part *given* to them, not *made* by them. Ancient people believed their time to be given to them by some being or beings *beyond time*, by God or by gods or the spirits. In contrast, while beliefs in God or gods or the spirits still remain very much with us as intellectual and emotional forces, modernity contains the idea that we human beings alone are responsible for making our world and our time. We who live in this world are the agents of our own destinies. We alone are the agents of history and politics, not gods or spirits. Certainly we are reminded repeatedly that we are not immortal, and that human beings are only one species of nature to inhabit this earth. No matter how far we may be capable of extending our longevity through medicine and natural science, each and every one of us is destined to die. Death is the insuperable horizon of all our existence. But the distinctive idea of modernity is that human beings are less and less capable of thinking of death as the gateway to some unchanging realm or to the start of some new life beyond time—called Heaven or Eternity. In the time of modernity, we come to realize more and more that nothing exists beyond death except *time*. We realize that nothing exists other than being-in-time and non-being-in-time: endless coming-to-be and ceasing-to-be. To be true to our time is to be modern, and to be modern is to face up to this predicament and seek ways of comprehending it.

Social theory contributes a few ways of addressing this predicament—along with the ideas of philosophy and the experiences of art and poetry. Social theory gives us reasoned accounts and diagnoses of attempts by modernity—sometimes beneficial attempts, sometimes disastrous attempts—to take possession of time and to compensate for death in our immediate and only real world: our social world of material inequalities between people, of violence and injustice. When Karl Marx declared that philosophers have only ever interpreted the world but that the point is to change it, he expressed only a more fundamental maxim of all modernity and of all modern theorizing. This maxim is that *theōria*—'contemplation', as the ancient Greeks defined it—finds no genuine truth unless and until it is mediated with *praxis*, with practical engagement with the tasks of the here and now: the tasks of politics, the tasks of using society's shared constituted powers to make its conditions of life better: freer, fairer, and happier for everyone. It can be said that the maxim of modernity is that though we remain mortal, we possess the power and the responsibility to make the best of our existence, by creating a world that offers everyone an equal chance for a fulfilling social life. Insofar as we are modern and want to be modern, we want to improve our conditions of shared life, not by ignoring the past or forgetting the past and not by repeating the past. We cannot have a rational will to want a future that is always the same as the past. We can only have a rational will to want to change the world for the better, as best we can.

■ GLOSSARY OF TERMS

The purpose of this glossary is to provide additional explanation for common technical terms occurring usually on more than one occasion in this book. It is not, however, intended to be a comprehensive dictionary of sociological terminology. With the exception of a few key terms that have deserved repeated definition in succinct form, the glossary does not cover terms explained at length in the main chapters of this book under particular section or subsection titles. It omits explanations for terms which the reader will find adequately described at the relevant page references listed in the index to this book. It has been designed to fill in some of the gaps between names for major sociological topics and unfamiliar words defined in any ordinary dictionary of the English language.

absolutism historical term referring to the absolute power of the sovereign over all subjects, typically under the European absolute monarchies of the seventeenth century; for example under the rule of Louis XIV of France. See further pp. 148–9.

action frame of reference term in the work of Talcott Parsons denoting the conceptual framework to be presupposed in all social enquiry, focusing on the agency of actors in contexts of structure. See further pp. 93.

agency term meaning the ability of individuals to act in pursuit of goals, in a context of constraints, determinants, and influences on their actions. See further pp. 215–16.

anomie term in the work of Émile Durkheim, meaning a condition of 'normlessness' or moral vacuum, resulting from a weakness or absence of rules regulating social intercourse; negation of the Greek word for 'law', *nomos*. See further pp. 54–5.

anthropocentric term meaning any way of thinking that places human images of the world at the centre of the universe, naively over-affirming the sovereignty of human beings as makers and knowers of existence.

a priori Latin term in philosophy meaning logically true and necessary, independent of observation in experience.

asceticism term referring to self-denying abstention from comforts and pleasures for the sake of a higher goal or inner truth; used by Max Weber to describe the rise of a Protestant 'work ethic' in relation to capitalism in early modern Europe and North America. See further pp. 70.

autonomy term from the Greek words *auto* and *nomos*, meaning 'self-law', or the ability freely to determine one's own actions and to be responsible for oneself; not to be subject to indoctrination or inducement by manipulative influences; a term originating in the philosophy of Immanuel Kant, used particularly by critical theorists such as Jürgen Habermas.

autopoietic term from the Greek word for 'creation', *poiesis*; used by Niklas Luhmann with the meaning of 'self-generation'.

base–superstructure term referring to the simplest form of the Marxist theory of ideology in which culture and politics are said to be determined by an underlying base of economic forces. The expression occurs in Marx's *Preface to 'A Contribution to the Critique of Political Economy'* (1859: 389) but nowhere else in his writing in any explicit form. The term is usually used to describe the more reductive and deterministic forms of 'vulgar Marxism' prevalent in Soviet doctrine and rejected by most of the Western Marxists. See further pp. 155.

behaviourism term referring to an approach in psychology initiated by J. B. Watson and continued by B. F. Skinner, which ignores mental activity and focuses purely on observable behaviour.

binary term from the Latin for 'two', *binarius*; elaborated by Jacques Derrida and used in structuralist and post-structuralist theory and feminist theory; refers to examples of logical opposites or pairings between two ideas, where one idea is said to be meaningful only by dependence on the other idea. The two ideas are said to prop each other up, usually with the one enjoying implicit or explicit dominance over the other; e.g. mind/body, rational/irrational, culture/nature, masculine/feminine. See further pp. 201.

civil society term prevalent in political thought from the eighteenth century onwards, referring to social relations that mediate between the private economic interests of individuals and families on the one hand and the administrative-bureaucratic interests of the state on the other hand. Civil society is the site of the public interest or public sphere, embodied in political institutions and associations. Marx saw civil society as little more than a cover for the interests of the bourgeoisie. Other thinkers, from both liberal and Marxist backgrounds, have regarded the concept in a more sympathetic light. See further pp. 48–9, 53–4, 157–9.

civilizing process term used by Norbert Elias for increasingly dense and complex social forms based on relatively stable power monopolies, such as royal courts or central state bureaucracies, tending toward levels of pacification, self-control, and the rise of cultures of manners and civility. See further pp. 141–4.

class term referring to the position of individuals in social structures as members of categories of people defined by unequal economic advantages and disadvantages, which also condition the access of these categories of people to other horizons of life, including power, status, education, and cultural resources. The term is defined classically by Karl Marx and Max Weber. See further pp.168–72.

closure term referring to completion, resolution, wholeness, or finality. These ideas are increasingly thrown into question by modern experiences of ambivalence, contingency, and complexity.

cognitive term deriving from the Latin word for 'thought'; refers to the mental input of actors who not only act upon desires, feelings, instincts, or stimuli but also think about what they desire, forming systems of belief about the phenomena of their world.

collectivism term referring to the view that society is 'more than the sum of its parts' and that explanation should proceed not from the individual but from supra-individual phenomena; a view defended by Émile Durkheim and by functionalist theorists; the opposite of methodological individualism.

commodity fetishism, commodification term used by Marx, denoting the form in which commodities under capitalism exercise power over their producers and consumers, appearing as alien objective forces; real social relations between humans are said to appear as social relations between things. See further pp. 46–7.

communicative term in the work of Jürgen Habermas; denoting non-instrumental, non-strategic social relations oriented to forms of normative agreement and understanding through reasoned dialogue between actors; emphasizing the role of language and everyday linguistic competence in the shaping of social relations toward morally acceptable and rational ends. Habermas's 'communicative' or 'dialogical' formulation of critical theory is usually contrasted with the earlier Frankfurt School's more 'dialectical' formulation, anchored more closely in Hegelian Marxism. See further pp. 279–80.

communitarian term for strands of recent North American political philosophy emphasizing the idea of community and the moral priority of community over self-interest; associated with the work of Charles Taylor, Alisdair Macintyre, Michael Walzer, Michael Sandel, Amatai Etzioni, and others.

cosmopolitan term from the Greek words *cosmos* and *polis*, meaning literally 'universal city'; suggesting the ideal of a global political community based on awareness of the existence of multiple political forms beyond the horizons of one's own locality.

critical theory/critical social theory term referring either (1) specifically to the programme of the early Frankfurt School, as formulated in Max Horkheimer's essay 'Traditional and Critical Theory' (1937); or (2) more generically to recent generations of theorists loosely influenced by the Frankfurt School but not necessarily closely aligned with it. In literary theory, this term may simply mean the 'theory of criticism'. See further pp. 160–5.

cultural capital term used by Pierre Bourdieu to describe benefits of education, knowledge, status, and cultural distinction used by their bearers in an analogous manner to economic capital for purposes of long-term social advantage. Such benefits are typically based on possession of economic capital in indirect, though not always immediate, ways. See further pp. 224–7.

culture industry term coined by Theodor Adorno and Max Horkheimer to denote the production of a mass culture through processes of industrialization driven by commercial imperatives; supplying ideological legitimation for capitalist consumption and production through broadcasting, fashion, advertising, film, and other forms of the mass media. See further pp. 160–1.

cybernetics term from the Greek word for 'steering' or 'control', *kubernan*; refers to theories of self-regulating systems based on closed circuits of information feedback; coined by the mathematician Norbert Wiener in the 1940s; developed in electronics and computer science, originally in US military research technology of the 1950s; applied to comparative analysis of man-made and biological systems by the anthropological theorist Gregory Bateson; influenced Niklas Luhmann's systems theory of society. Cybernetics remains a fertile resource for contemporary theories of the media, the Internet, and of complex systems and organizations.

cyborg term coined by Donna Haraway, referring to hybrids of organisms and machines; emphasizing inseparability and ontological continuity between human beings, machines, and animals; criticizing dualistic conceptions of culture and nature and human distinctness; highlighting the role of intelligent non-human technological agencies in contemporary society. See further pp. 249.

deconstruction term coined by Jacques Derrida, referring to a practice of reading texts and other meaningful objects that results in a dismantling or laying bare of the often hidden organizing principles or metaphysical assumptions that confer an appearance of unity, naturalness, or self-evidence in the item under consideration. See further pp. 204–6.

deductive term referring to processes of reasoning from given premises or starting points to logically valid conclusions. 'Deductive' is the opposite of 'inductive', which refers to conclusions arrived at by observations from experience.

deliberative term in the later work of Jürgen Habermas, referring to open and inclusive political debate as a model for reasonable social communication in general.

determinism term referring to problems of excessive causal attribution of observed phenomena to particular conditions, most typically to economic, material, or physical conditions which are regarded as structures placing heavily constraining limits on human agency, freedom, and consciousness.

diachronic term used in functionalist and French structuralist theory, referring to the transformation of phenomena over time. 'Diachronic' is the opposite of 'synchronic', which refers to the states and interrelationships of phenomena at any given moment in time.

dialectic term in the philosophy of G. W. F. Hegel, denoting logical progression in history based on contradictions between two sides of an idea resolved in a movement of synthesis. 'Dialectical materialism' was the official Soviet interpretation of Marx's application of Hegel's dialectic to economic analysis and the critique of capitalism. See further pp. 42, 162–4.

dialogic term in hermeneutics used by Jürgen Habermas to refer to the argumentative dimensions of intersubjective communication; also used in different senses by the Russian literary theorist Mikhail Bakhtin and the religious philosopher Martin Buber.

differentiation concept originating in the work of Émile Durkheim and Talcott Parsons; referring to the process by which social practices, institutions, and systems become specialized around distinct functions, driven by the division of labour, also involved in Max Weber's conception of autonomously rationalized 'spheres' in modern social life. See further pp. 53–4, 97–9.

discursive adjectival form of 'discourse', denoting instances of structured regulated communication through spoken or written language and other systems of symbolic inscription or representation. In the work of Michel Foucault 'discursive practices' are said to be bound up with forms of social organization, power, and control. In the work of Jürgen Habermas, 'discursive' refers to deliberative reflective communication. See further pp. 207–12, 281–3.

disembedding term in the work of Karl Polanyi describing an aspect of the experience of processes of modernization where different dimensions of social life lose a sense of meaningful interconnectedness or 'embeddedness' in received ways of life. These processes crystallize around functionally autonomous systems, most notably in the form of a global capitalist market place. See further pp. 297–8.

division of labour term meaning specialization of the economy around functionally interdependent trades, as well as specialization and coordination of tasks within each trade; theorized originally by Adam Smith; regarded by Émile Durkheim as a source of cohesion in modern societies, when correctly regulated. See further pp. 45–7, 53–4.

domination term from the Latin word *dominus* meaning 'rule' or 'rulership'; used technically in sociology to refer to structures of organizational subordination, particularly in the work of Max Weber, who used the German term *Herrschaft*. See further pp. 72–5, 235, 246–7.

dramaturgical model of action term in the work of Erving Goffman and others, stressing the theatrical aspect of social life, self-presentation, and role performance. See further pp. 110, 116–17.

dualism term in philosophy, referring especially to the philosophy of René Descartes, denoting the doctrine of the division of reality into two substances, mind and matter. Cartesian dualism has been criticized in modern social thought for its inadequate understanding of the interrelationship and interdependence of mind and body, thought and existence, culture and nature. See further pp. 235.

duality of structure term in the work of Anthony Giddens, describing structure in social life as the framework in which agents act and as the product that results from agents' actions, i.e. as both 'medium' and 'outcome' of social action. See further pp. 217–20.

egalitarian term denoting principles of equality between human beings and the desirability of political, social, and economic equality.

emancipation term meaning liberation from subservience or servility, originally from the bondage of the slave or the serf. In eighteenth- and nineteenth-century Europe, emancipation meant possession of full civil rights (especially for the Jews). Since the twentieth century, the term has widened to include freedom from oppressive moral and political norms, or from illusory beliefs, or from social conservatism, or from social injustice.

empirical term referring to knowledge based on observation from experience, from data given to the senses.

empiricist term denoting the doctrine that all knowledge is based *only* on observation from experience, from data given to the senses; denying the validity of other possible sources, methods, or forms of knowledge involving the labour of the mind, the imagination, language, and cultural communication.

Enlightenment term referring to the eighteenth-century Age of Reason in Western culture (when spelled with a capital 'E'); also referring more generically to social consciousness guided by rational thought and by critical scrutiny of existing ideas and institutions, with an orientation to realizing universally just laws and norms (when spelled either with a lower-case 'e' or with a capital 'E'). See further pp. 17, 160–5.

epistemological, epistemic term from the Greek word for 'knowledge'; refers to the theory of knowledge, or to the modes and methods by which knowledge is obtained.

essentialism term referring to questionable notions of basic, fixed, and unchanging identities in particular things, ideas, persons, or cultures; for example, the notion that women are 'essentially passive', men 'essentially active'.

ethnocentric term referring to habits of thought that misunderstand the distictness of people who differ in their basic cultural values, beliefs, or ideas of the world from those people who claim to explain their behaviour.

ethnography term referring to the practice of researching in detail a whole small-scale society or other social structure or process, using qualitative methods, usually involving a lengthy period of participant observation; a standard practice in anthropology but increasingly favoured also in sociology and even political science.

ethnomethodology term referring to the work of Harold Garfinkel and his associates; stressing microscopic participatory study of the ways in which people produce meaning and social order through ongoing interpretations of each other's actions. See further pp. 117–19.

Eurocentrism term referring to ways of thinking that unjustifiably extend the validity of European historical and cultural experiences to all cultures and civilizations of the world. See further pp. 32–3.

existentialism term denoting a movement in twentieth-century European philosophy, stressing the fragility and finitude of human existence and the responsibility of the human person in the face of a social universe that is no longer able to believe in God or to follow conventional moral norms and that is sceptical of the social benefits of science and technology; associated with the writings of Jean-Paul Sartre, Martin Heidegger, and others.

exploitation term in Marxism referring to the extraction of surplus value from human labour power for the benefit of the ruling class, especially for the purpose of profit under capitalism; depriving workers of the time, resources, and freedom to lead fully humane lives. See further pp. 46–7.

feudalism term referring to socio-economic relations in the Middle Ages in which landowners ('lords') grant protection and maintenance to the labourers of the land ('vassals') in return for services in kind, especially service in war. In Marxism, feudalism is seen as a mode of production in which surplus value is extracted from labour power in the form of personal ties of obligation to paternalistic authority figures. With the rise of capitalism, these traditional ties are gradually replaced by the anonymity and impersonality of the wage contract. See further pp. 147–9.

foundational, foundationalist term referring to the idea of unshakeable grounds for knowledge, founded in self-evident logical truths or in the certainty of sense-data. These grounds are said to remain constant across history and across cultures. The idea is criticized in postmodern and anti-positivist thought, particularly in the work of Richard Rorty.

Frankfurt School term referring to the associates of the Institut für Sozialforschung (Institute for Social Research) founded at Frankfurt University in 1923 and to its influence on several German-born Marxist theorists active after the Second World War in Europe and the USA; including Max Horkheimer, Theodor Adorno, Herbert Marcuse, Leo Löwenthal, Herbert Marcuse, Jürgen Habermas, and others. See further pp. 160–1.

functional equivalent term used by Robert Merton, suggesting that some social functions may be necessary but need not be met always in the same way. For example, it might be said that sport is a functional equivalent for religion.

functionalism term referring mainly to the work of American sociological theorists active in the middle decades of the twentieth century, represented by Talcott Parsons, Robert Merton, and others; influenced by Émile Durkheim and by the scientific anthropology of Bronislaw Malinowski and Alfred Radcliffe-Brown; holding that a society is to be studied in terms of interdependent 'systems' and 'structures' that perform interrelated 'functions' for the society as a whole; also known as 'structural functionalism'. See further pp. 87–8.

Geisteswissenschaften term in German for the 'humanities' or 'human sciences', meaning 'sciences of the mind' or 'sciences of the works of the human mind'; a term central to German hermeneutic thought.

Gemeinschaft term in German for 'community', especially in the work of Ferdinand Tönnies, where it is contrasted with the term *Gesellschaft* ('society'). See further pp. 30–1, 37.

gender term referring to problems and assumptions involved in defining human agents in society as 'men' or 'women', insofar as men and women are not only biological organisms differentiated by two types of organs of sexual reproduction but also self-interpreting members of contingent historically changing cultures, characterized by definite social structures that distribute roles, functions, identities, advantages, and disadvantages to men and women in different and frequently unequal ways. See further pp. 243–5. *See also* gendering *and* sex-gender distinction.

gendering term used by feminist theorists to stress that gender is not fixed or given but constructed, changing, and processual in character, and that many central concepts in social theory often regarded as neutral with respect to gender are not neutral but intrinsically gender-relevant; for example, the concept of the 'public sphere', which implies a gender-relevant concept of the 'private sphere'. See further pp. 239–40.

Gesellschaft term in German for 'society', especially in the work of Ferdinand Tönnies, where it is contrasted with the term *Gemeinschaft* ('community'). See further, pp. 30–1, 37.

glocal term coined by Roland Robertson, referring to fusions and interactions between simultaneously global and local processes. See further pp. 304–5.

governance term denoting processes of social regulation distinct from traditional state-centred forms of government; applies to organizations as well as to broader national and global arenas, typically involving consensus, rule-setting, and decision-making among the organized interests party to it; often seen by critics as divorced from full public scrutiny. See further pp. 298.

grand theory term used by critics of Talcott Parsons to describe his project for 'general unified theory' in social science. See further pp. 92.

guilds term referring to professional associations among craftsmen and merchants of the Middle Ages formed for mutual aid and protection in specific trades; regarded by Émile Durkheim as pre-democratic precursors of the modern trade unions and other 'occupational groups' that mediate between the individual, the market, and the state.

habitus term used especially by Pierre Bourdieu for distinct sets of attitudes, accomplishments, and habits determining how particular classes, cultures, or social groups behave in the world and look upon the world; also used by Norbert Elias and Max Weber in related senses. See further pp. 222–4.

hegemony term from the Greek word for 'leader', *hegemon*; defined by Antonio Gramsci as 'intellectual and moral leadership', involving a combination of *force* and *consent*. Hegemony is a more sophisticated concept of domination than the classical Marxist concept of ideology insofar as it involves an element of willing submission to leadership, which is at the same time subtly coerced. But Gramsci also speaks in a more positive sense of a possible working-class hegemony, arguing that the task of the working class is to recover hegemony from the bourgeoisie. See further pp. 157–9.

hermeneutics term from the Greek word 'to interpret', *hermeneuein*; refers to theories of understanding and interpretation, emphasizing the importance of interpreting the meanings that motivate actors to act or speak as they do, or 'putting oneself in the other's shoes'; associated with the thought of Wilhelm Dilthey, Martin Heidegger, Hans-Georg Gadamer, and more loosely with Max Weber's interpretive sociology. See further pp. 65, 125–7.

heuristic term meaning a construction of thought or mental tool that assists in producing knowledge of something; not to be confused with 'hermeneutic'.

historical materialism term referring to Marx's theory of history, based on transitions from one mode of production to the next, driven by contradictions between relations of material production and the legal, political and cultural forms that arise out of these modes of production. In Marxism and in social theory and sociology generally the term 'materialism' is most often used in a technical value-neutral sense, not in the more commonly value-laden sense of 'acquisitive' or 'money-grubbing', as in the phrase 'so-and-so has a materialistic attitude to life'. A materialist in social theory is someone who emphasizes explaining social behaviour by reference to basic physical essentials of life (such as food, shelter, power, or freedom to act on one's needs and desires, including freedom from suffering, disease, violence, or slavery) in relation to the life chances of *all* people, rich or poor, whether 'money-grubbing' or not. In Max Weber's sociology, 'materialist' theories of social life are balanced critically with 'idealist' or 'interpretive' theories, which emphasize not only the physical essentials of life but also the ideas, values, languages, and spiritual beliefs of individual actors..

historicism term referring to theories emphasizing the historical specificity of social and cultural life and the significance of historical time in human experience; either in the form of a deterministic scheme of development (Hegel's philosophy of history) or in a non-deterministic framework emphasizing historical relativity and diversity (the writings of Wilhelm Dilthey and others).

holism term meaning the 'view of the whole', especially the view that the parts of something can only be understood in terms of their contribution to the whole and that the whole is more than a 'sum of the parts'; a term close in meaning to 'collectivism' as a methodological precept.

homo faber term in Latin meaning 'man the maker', indicating the idea that society is an artefact, something made by man, rather than given in nature.

humanism term referring particularly to modern ways of thinking that affirm the agency and dignity of human beings as makers of their own world in a context of scientific enlightenment and scepticism toward religion; regarded by the French post-structuralist theorists as a complacent form of self-understanding, compromising the philosophies of Hegel, Marx, phenomenology, and existentialism.

idealism term in philosophy referring to the view that the world is made by the mind or made of ideas, not given to the senses; refers in social theory to traditions of thought emphasizing the constitutive role of meanings and mental images in social life, especially in nineteenth-century German thought.

ideal type, ideal-typical term in the work of Max Weber, referring to conceptual constructs deliberately devised by the social scientist in order to categorize, analyse, and compare observed phenomena in the social world in a systematic way. An ideal type can be thought of as a notional benchmark, in relation to which any actual phenomenon may either approximate or deviate. See further pp. 65–6.

ideology term used either in a strongly value-laden sense or in a relatively neutral descriptive sense, or—more commonly-in various critical combinations of these two senses. In the value-laden sense, ideology means socially generalized false belief, illusion, or 'false consciousness', typically serving the interests of a dominant ruling group. In the more neutral sense, ideology refers to any system of ideas expressed in cultural self-images and shared beliefs of particular social groups.

identity politics term referring to forms of political mobilization around issues of cultural identity, leading to demands for resources for particular groups in a different way from traditional welfare-state models of uniform citizenship rights. Identity politics emphasizes special communities of interests organized around ethnicity, religion, gender, nationality, regionality or sexual orientation.

ideographic term coined by the Neo-Kantian philosopher Wilhelm Windelband, referring to the detailed interpretive study of individual cases; associated with the methods of the humanities, as against those of the natural sciences.

imaginary term used as a predicative noun by the psychoanalyst Jacques Lacan, referring to projections of sense by the individual self; more widely used in social theory to refer to ways in which societies or social collectives represent ideas of their own identity and goals for change, especially in the work of Cornelius Castoriadis. See further pp. 181–3, 275–6.

individualism term with at least three distinct contexts of use which should not be conflated: (1) *methodological* individualism, referring to the view that social phenomena are explicable only in terms of the actions of individuals and relations between them (not in terms of collective entities, as with methodological collectivism); (2) *economic* individualism, referring to the modern social phenomenon of independent business or career initiative by individuals concerned to maximize their interests without significant regard for the welfare of others; (3) *moral* individualism, referring to the view that the basis of morality is individual autonomy and responsibility, rather than passive deference to tradition or received custom. (Émile Durkheim defended individualism in the third of these senses, and only partly in the second sense, but not in the first.)

instrumental reason term coined by the Frankfurt School to denote modern capitalist practices of subordination of all dimensions of social life to the most efficient achievement of economic profit and administrative order; adapted from Max Weber's concept of 'purposive rationality' or 'means–ends rationality', denoting the most efficient use of available means to given ends, without deliberation on the value of the ends themselves.

integration term developed by functionalist theorists, indicating that social systems typically maintain an orderly character through coordinating mechanisms, even during times of conflict. For example, fascism provided a means of integration for European societies during the 1930s depression, albeit a very unstable one. Integration is often regarded as the functional counterpart to differentiation. See further pp. 53–4, 97, 102.

interactionism term developed originally in the work of Herbert Blumer and associated with the work of the Chicago School; also known as 'symbolic interactionism'; used in a broader sense for approaches stressing the dynamic and creative aspect of social life as sustained by individual human actors in ongoing exchanges and interpretations. See further pp. 127–9.

interpenetration term in functionalism, emphasizing the interconnectedness and mutual impact of disparate social systems upon each other.

interpretive, interpretivist term referring to approaches emphasizing the meaningful character of social life and the need for interpretation of this meaningfulness; in preference to, or in addition to, quantitative analysis, measurement, and behavioural observation; specifically used in English translation for Max Weber's term *verstehende Soziologie*, where the German word *verstehen* means 'understanding'. See further pp. 127–9.

intersubjective, intersubjectivity term originating in the later phenomenological philosophy of Edmund Husserl; also present in the work of Alfred Schutz, G. H. Mead, and Jacques Lacan; adopted in later twentieth-century social theory by Jürgen Habermas, Anthony Giddens and others, referring to communicative exchange between interacting human agents, emphasizing that identities of the self are formed through social interaction and communication and that reference to the world as an objective reality is achieved only through shared understandings between actors.

Kantianism *see* Kant (in Biographies of Theorists)

Keynesian *see* Keynes (in Biographies of Theorists)

lack term in the psychoanalysis of Jacques Lacan, suggesting that culture, morality, and identity represent forms of compensation for more basic experiences of privation, denied pleasure, or bodily disorientation in sensory life.

lay actor term meaning any ordinary person who is not a social scientist; or more precisely, any ordinary person except in the case when this person acts as a social scientist. Professor X is a lay actor whenever he or she is out shopping or catching a train, but not when he or she is doing scientific fieldwork.

legislative term referring to prescriptive modes of thought preoccupied with universal moral laws, especially in the Enlightenment philosophy of Immanuel Kant; used by commentators on postmodernism, such as Zygmunt Bauman; not to be confused with the standard sense of the lawmaking power of government.

legitimation term meaning the rendering of something as legitimate in the eyes of certain people; referring to uses of symbolic resources that result in a given state of affairs appearing morally and legally sanctioned for particular social agents, disregarding the question of whether the state of affairs in question really *is*, intrinsically, legitimate.

lifeworld term originating in the phenomenological philosophy of Edmund Husserl; also used by Alfred Schutz and by Jürgen Habermas, referring to the everyday world as meaningfully experienced by ordinary actors in a pre-reflexive, non-scientific manner, distinguished by Habermas from the 'system', based on economic and administrative organization. See further pp. 113, 281.

logocentrism term coined by Jacques Derrida to refer to the highest authority awarded in Western philosophy to logically ordered thought, above play, semblance, ambiguity, and metaphor, especially in the philosophy of Plato; derived from the Greek word *logos*, meaning 'reason' or 'speech'. See further pp. 203–4.

materialism *see* historical materialism.

means–end relation term referring to the difference between what I want (my *end*) and my ability to get or produce what I want (my *means*). See further pp. 75–6, 93.

messianic term used to describe Jewish theological themes in the Marxist writing of Walter Benjamin, Ernst Bloch, and others, referring to the idea that a future communist society can be affirmed but not 'imagined' or 'represented', because it marks an unforeseeable and incalculable break with existing historical structures of thought and behaviour, like the coming of the Messiah to the earthly world.

meta-narrative term used by Jean-François Lyotard, denoting generalizing accounts of history or science that subsume disparate contexts of experience under a single overarching frame of reference. See further pp. 256–8.

metaphysics term in philosophy referring to systematic conceptions of the fundamental structures of reality, regarded by some twentieth-century philosophers as responsible for generating confusions in ordinary language.

middle-range theory term coined by Robert Merton recommending that theory be grounded in specific empirical problems for explanation, in preference to 'grand', abstract, or speculative theory. See further pp. 90–2, 102, 310 .

modernism term denoting cultural, intellectual, and artistic movements that express, interrogate, or celebrate ideas of modernity; a term with a relatively precise temporal reference, usually thought of as the period between about 1880 and 1970 in the arts and intellectual culture; to be distinguished from the term 'moder*nity*', which refers to generalizable modern social conditions and experiences with no definite chronological reference. Moder*nism* refers specifically to ways of expressing and articulating these conditions and experiences in late nineteenth- and twentieth-century culture, especially in the West.

naturalism term in the philosophy of science, denoting the view that social science shares essential characteristics in common with the natural sciences; a view criticized by interpretive hermeneutic traditions of thought. The most familiar form of naturalism has been 'positivism'. However, in the last third of the twentieth century, proponents of 'realism' or 'critical realism' have developed non-positivist versions of naturalism, which allow for some distinctiveness in the social sciences.

Neo-Kantian term referring to the revival of elements of Immanuel Kant's philosophy by German philosophers in the late nineteenth and early twentieth centuries, influencing debates about the methodology of the social sciences; notably in the thought of Heinrich Rickert and Wilhelm Windelband. These philosophers held that human knowledge divides into two complementary domains of competence each governed by distinctive scientific principles, namely the 'sciences of nature' and the 'sciences of culture'.

neo-liberalism term referring to economic policy prevalent since the 1980s, involving a return to classical eighteenth- and nineteenth-century economic principles of non-interference by governments in the workings of a free market; a central term in contemporary debates about globalization and the demise of socialism and social democracy.

NGOs term used as an abbreviation for 'non-governmental organizations'; referring to non-profit organizations that are neither attached to the state nor constituted as private businesses and are established for political or altruistic purposes, typically with charity status; for example, Oxfam, Amnesty International, Greenpeace.

nihilism term deriving from the Latin word for 'nothing', *nihil*; refers to forms of extreme scepticism about the possibility of cross-cultural agreement over values, especially about truth, goodness, justice, and morality; often associated with the philosophy of Friedrich Nietzsche and postmodernism.

nomothetic term from the Greek word for 'law', *nomos*; coined by the Neo-Kantian philosopher Wilhem Windelband; referring to the study of law-like regularities and generalities rather than historically specific cases and

contexts; associated with the methods of the natural sciences, as against those of the humanities.

non-linear term used by Niklas Luhmann, referring to developments over time in many different directions, not in a single direction.

norm term meaning an established standard of behaviour shared by members of a social group to which each member is expected to conform. According to Émile Durkheim, norms counteract tendencies towards egoistic actions that disregard the public good, especially during the rise of modern market societies. In the absence of norms, societies are susceptible to anomie.

normative term referring to discourse about how the social world *ought* to be (or not to be), in contrast to discourse that claims solely to describe and explain how the social world *is*, as a matter of fact, without explicit judgement of right or wrong. In the work of Talcott Parsons, 'normative' refers particularly to the function of moral norms in generating social integration. See further pp. 7–9, 54–5, 95–7, 324.

normlessness term in the work of Émile Durkheim, explicating the concept of anomie; referring to an absence of norms, or to a state in which the regulating authority of norms over the conduct of individuals is very weak. See further pp. 54–5.

object relations term in psychology, especially in the writings of the psychoanalysts Melanie Klein and Donald Winnicott; refers to the emergence of a sense of self in the child by differentiation from a surrounding world. The child experiences a sense of limitation caused by objects which are not part of the child and cannot be changed by the child (such as the breast of the mother).

objectivist term referring to approaches to social enquiry that overemphasize the relative importance of structural or systemic constraints on the actions of individuals, and underestimate the relative importance of individual agency in relation to structures and systems; usually involves an excessively narrow and strict definition of objectivity, sometimes with an appeal to the natural sciences as a model for social research; typically involves neglect of the expressive, 'subjectively meaningful' character of socio-cultural life.

ontological term deriving from the Greek participle of the verb 'to be'; refers to enquiry about what exists, or does not exist, in the world; or about what kinds of entities are believed by people to exist; for example, spirits, ghosts and witches or—alternatively—atoms, neurones, H_2O, electricity, DNA. The term can also be used to refer to enquiry about what social life consists of; for example, about whether social life consists of real structures or only of bundles of individuals.

Orientalism term referring to Western discourse about the East, the Orient. Edward Said (1978) defines 'Orientalism' as the West's essentializing construction of that which is 'Other' to itself. See further pp. 34.

paradigm term meaning a scientific framework or theoretical construct. In the work of Thomas Kuhn, science is said to proceed by discontinuous leaps and bounds from one paradigm to another, rather than by ever-closer steps to an independently existing objective reality. See further pp. 123.

particularism term referring to cultural beliefs, values, identities, or traditions said to possess local or limited significance rather than general universal significance; a term with contested uses. According to some writers, 'particularistic' describes something lacking general relevance, such as a 'single-issue agenda'. According to others—especially feminist and postcolonial writers—this negative way of using the term is problematic, indicative of prejudice against voices constructed as being in the 'minority', such as the voices of women or non-white people. See further pp. 305–7.

patriarchal term meaning rule by men or male domination, especially (but not only) in traditional or non-democratic societies; a term either with a relatively narrow meaning, referring to male domination in the organization of families; or with a broader meaning, referring to more generalized, indirect, institutional forms of male cultural and political hegemony. See further pp. 235.

patrimonial term referring to inheritance of positions of power and especially property by younger men from older male authority figures, originally by sons from the father of the family.

performative term coined by the philosopher J. L. Austin, referring to linguistic utterances which create the state of affairs to which they refer in the act being uttered; for example, the utterance of the priest at a wedding, 'I hereby pronounce thee man and wife'.

performativity term referring to the idea that speech and language involve not only description of the world but also action and performance in the world, typically involving the transmission of relations of power. Alternatively the term may simply mean 'efficiency of operation'.

phallogocentrism term in feminist theory, coined by Julia Kristeva and Hélène Cixous, combining the term 'logocentrism' (coined by Jacques Derrida) with the word 'phallus'; used to refer to a masculine privileging of

ordered logical thought in Western philosophy above play, semblance, ambiguity, and the like. See further pp. 249.

phenomenology term deriving from the Greek word for 'appearance' or 'appearing'; referring in philosophy to the method and school of thought founded by Edmund Husserl, involving description of things in the world insofar as they appear to consciousness as objects of experience for subjects who are conscious of them. Phenomenological analysis proceeds by bracketing questions about the causation or purpose of objects of experience in order to concentrate on describing the manner in which such objects appear to subjects *as* objects with particular meanings. For example, the phenomenologist concentrates on describing the meaning of someone's raising his or her arm as a sign or indication *to* or *for* someone, rather than trying to identify the physical stimuli that may have caused the person to raise his or her arm. Phenomenological philosophy influenced interpretive sociological writers such as Alfred Schutz. See further pp. 3, 112–14.

polity term referring generically to any unit of politically organized power, such as modern nation-states (e.g. France, the UK) or empires (e.g. the USSR, the Roman Empire) or ancient or medieval city-states (e.g. ancient Athens, Renaissance Florence) or, most recently, new governmental entities emerging above the level of the nation-state, such as the European Union.

positive science term meaning empirical science, claiming to be free from metaphysical speculation; 'positive' in the sense of observing what is given or 'posited' in experience, though not necessarily in the sense of 'optimistic' (although this sense is often implied).

positivism term coined in the nineteenth century by Auguste Comte, referring to the strongest form of empiricism which holds that experimental observation is the only valid source of knowledge and rejects all other sources of understanding—such as theology, metaphysics, or poetry—as incapable of rigorous validation. Positivism found many adherents in the early twentieth century, including notably the members of the Vienna Circle, also known as the 'logical positivists'. See further pp. 27–8, 203–4.

positivity term referring to social experience insofar as it is felt to be given or 'posited', as if it were a thing of nature, impervious to change or negation by criticism.

postcolonialism term meaning the study and theory of cultures, societies, and history in the light of Western colonial conquest. See further pp. 34, 166, 205, 247–9.

post-Fordism term meaning the observation or thesis that modern industrial production has moved away from mass production in large factories—as pioneered in the 1920s by the American automobile manufacturer Henry Ford—towards specialized markets based on small flexible units of production and flexible labour forces. See further pp. 257–8.

post-industrial term referring to the declining position of manufacturing industry in Western economies since the 1970s and the dramatic expansion of sectors of the economy devoted to services, finance, leisure, and consumption. See further pp. 257–8.

postmodernism term referring to 'the contemporary movement of thought which rejects totalities, universal values, grand historical narratives, solid foundations to human existence and the possibility of objective knowledge. Postmodernism is sceptical of truth, unity and progress, opposes what it sees as elitism in culture, tends towards cultural relativism, and celebrates pluralism, discontinuity and heterogeneity'. This succinct definition has been quoted from Eagleton (2003: 13).

post-structuralism term referring to a style of theorizing influenced by the first wave of French structuralist writers that radicalizes or critically transforms their ideas in various ways, emphasizing instability in textual meanings as functions of unbounded systems of differences between signifying elements; often associated with the thinking of Jacques Derrida and Michel Foucault, although not accepted by them as a label for their work. See further pp. 212–13.

pragmatism term with a technical meaning in philosophy in the USA after the nineteenth-century philosopher C. S. Peirce; refers to the view that the content and validity of concepts and ideas consists in their practical applicability, effectiveness, or usefulness for life; associated with the thought of William James, George Herbert Mead, and John Dewey; a major influence on early twentieth-century American sociology and social psychology. See further pp. 114–15.

praxis term in Greek, meaning 'practice', also spelled with an 'x' in German; a key term in Western Marxism, especially among those strands with an orientation to phenomenological and anthropological thinking, such as in the work of Antonio Gramsci, Jean-Paul Sartre, and György Lukács.

public sphere term first coined in the 1960s by Jürgen Habermas (translating the German word *Öffentlichkeit*), denoting the set of institutions, fora, and agencies in civil society that mediate between private economic interests on the one hand and state administrative interests in order and control on the other hand. The public sphere is the site of public opinion formation, most notably in the media. In Habermas's normative definition, the public

sphere ought to consist in what the eighteenth-century philosopher Immanuel Kant defined as the 'free use of public reason', unmanipulated and undistorted by state propaganda or by commercial interests that corrupt the transparency, veracity, and maturity of the media and the political arena. See further pp. 164–5, 242, 281–3.

queer theory term referring to theories of the construction of sexual orientations under definite social and historical conditions, concentrating on homosexuality but also examining heterosexual relations. See further pp. 245–6.

rational choice term denoting a school of thought influenced by economic theory and by utilitarianism, holding that social life is best analysed in terms of decisions and calculations by individual actors aimed at maximizing advantages through strategies of cooperation and non-cooperation with other actors; preceded in 1960s sociology by the contributions to exchange theory developed by George Homans and Peter Blau; associated more recently with the work of the economist Gary Becker, as well as James Coleman, Jon Elster, and others. See further pp. 104–5.

rationalization term in the work of Max Weber and all theorists influenced by him; refers to the penetration of spheres of modern social life by rational principles of organization, oriented especially to bureaucratic efficiency and procedural systematicity. Weber proposed that under processes of rationalization, modern social life divides into discrete spheres of autonomous validity, each sphere following an independent logic of development. These include the market, the state, and the judiciary, as well as science, religion, art, morality, and erotic life. Following Weber, sociologists do not normally use this term in a *normative* sense; that is, in the sense of something necessarily good (or bad). 'Rationalization' is thus to be distinguished from more value-laden phrases such as 'the growth of reason' or 'the progress of reason'. See further pp. 75–6, 254–5.

realism term in the philosophy of science, referring to commitment to belief in the independent existence of natural and social reality and its irreducibility exclusively to discourses, representations, or mental constructions by individual human agents; holding that scientific theories are potentially true statements about reality, rather than merely convenient fictions useful for action in the world; associated in Britain with the work of Roy Bhaskar, Rom Harré, Margaret Archer, Andrew Collier, and others. In international relations theory, realism has a distinct meaning, referring to the view that relations between states are best understood in terms of struggles for power and self-preservation, disregarding all differences of political ideology. See further pp. 227–9, 264–5, 295.

Realpolitik term in German, deriving originally from the leadership of the nineteenth-century Prussian chancellor Otto von Bismarck, involving ruthlessly realistic and opportunistic foreign policy; today used in the context of international relations to refer to state interaction and conflict involving hard-headed diplomacy or aggressive defence policy or warfare without a specific or explicit ideology.

recognition term originating in the philosophy of G. W. F. Hegel, associated more recently with the work of Charles Taylor and Axel Honneth; refers to the striving of social groups and individuals for respect as particular groups or individuals with particular identities, rights, and entitlements before the law and in civil society.

redemptive term originating in Judaeo-Christian theology but not necessarily to be used in a religious sense; refers to the rescuing, compensating, or making good of something in history that has suffered violence, derision, or oblivion in the present, by everyday habit or by a majority consensus.

reflexive sociology term in the work of Pierre Bourdieu, meaning any practice of sociological enquiry capable of considering *itself* as a possible object of sociological analysis and explanation.

reflexivity term meaning 'reference to oneself', 'application to oneself', or 'reflection on oneself'. The subject of an action is simultaneously the object of the action (for example in the French reflexive verb *s'habiller*, 'to get dressed' or 'to dress oneself'). The term implies self-awareness, self- monitoring, and usually, though not necessarily, self-criticism. Reflexivity can pertain to individual persons or to institutions. See further pp. 221–2.

reification term deriving from the Latin word for 'thing', *res*; used in Marxism with the meaning 'reduction to a thing', i.e. the reduction of persons, ideas, sensory qualities, or expressive agencies to commodities or to pure objects of consumption, administration, or quantitative categorization.

relativism term with a variety of contested definitions. In the narrowest and least sustainable definition, relativism is the view that any one person's point of view is as good as another's, or that 'anything goes'. More broadly, it is the view that truth (or other ultimate values such as goodness or beauty) is not universal or absolute in its meaning or content but is best understood as what is 'accepted as true', or as 'what counts as true', for people in particular cultures, societies, and periods of history. In social theory and philosophy, relativism is often used as a term of criticism, emphasizing that while values and beliefs have meaning only in definite social-historical contexts and are

in this sense 'relative' to the latter, it is *not* the case that such values and beliefs are wholly incapable of being rationally argued about and agreed upon by different participants from different cultural standpoints. See further pp. 120.

restitutive term used by Émile Durkheim to refer to modern legal systems in which disputes between parties are mediated by an impartial third authority (the lawcourt), which compensates the victim and protects the perpetrator from reprisal by the victim.

retributive term used by Émile Durkheim to refer to pre-modern or tribal justice systems in which offenders are punished directly in public by their victims or in the name of their victims.

secularization term deriving from the Latin word *saeculum*, meaning the 'temporal age', in the sense of 'the order of time', not eternity; refers to the thesis that members of modern societies both gradually cease to believe in God and gradually cease to sustain structures of organization in which religious faith determines the constitution of public, legal, and political institutions, including especially the relation of the state to the Church. See further pp. 21, 57–8, 75, 266–9.

self-reference term with a technical meaning in the work of Niklas Luhmann, denoting the manner in which an entity refers to itself in the act of referring to anything which is *not* itself, as having an identity only insofar as it is not something else. Luhmann's use of this term can be compared to structuralist and post-structuralist theories of meaning in terms of relations of difference between signifiers.

semiotics term deriving from the Greek word *semeion*, meaning 'sign'; refers to theories of the generation of meaning in texts and other symbolic objects through differential relationships between signs. See further pp. 198–200.

sex and gender terms conveying a distinction between sex as an anatomical condition and gender as a cultural condition. Sex is said to be given, while gender is said to be non-given, changing, and constructed. The distinction has been useful to feminist theorists in overturning essentializing definitions of woman and femininity, but has been criticized by more recent feminists for overlooking the degree to which anatomical categories of sex and the body are *also* historically changing and discursively constructed. See further pp. 236–7, 243–5.

signifier and signified terms in semiotics and structural linguistics, where 'signi*fier*' refers to a sign which denotes or connotes some meaning, and where 'signi*fied*' refers to meanings signified by this sign. For example, in the US national flag, the Stars and Stripes functions as the signi*fier* and the USA functions as the signi*fied*.

simulacrum term in postmodernist theory, used principally by Jean Baudrillard, Gilles Deleuze, and Pierre Klossowski, denoting copies that cannot be distinguished from the original things that they copy, thus collapsing all distinction between originals and non-originals, or between the 'real' and the 'fake'. In medieval theology, *simulacrum* in Latin meant a false image of God. Beyond these technical uses, 'simulacrum' usually means a superficial (but untrue) likeness. See further pp. 264–6.

social constructionism term referring broadly to any theories that regard reality as socially 'constructed' or 'constituted' by individuals in contexts of interaction, as an outcome of interpretive 'definitions of the situation'. More narrowly, the term refers to positions in the sociology of science that regard scientific concepts not in terms of references to independently existing natural phenomena but in terms of aspects of social interaction and communication between scientists and their laboratory environments; especially as used in the work of Bruno Latour, Steve Woolgar, David Bloor, and others. See further pp. 123–5, 203–6.

societal term sometimes used in preference to 'social', denoting the more structural-systemic properties of social life.

solidarity term developed originally in the work of Émile Durkheim, meaning the 'cement of society'; technically referring to the nature and degree of integration between constituent members of social collectives, irrespective of class differences and other inequalities. For Marxism, solidarity can obtain only within classes, in a consciousness of common class interests. See further pp. 53–4, 89, 97.

species-being term in the early writings of Marx, translating the German word *Gattungswesen*; taken from the philosopher Ludwig Feuerbach; used to mean the true social nature of human beings, which is said to be distorted and degraded under conditions of capitalist alienation and market individualism.

speech-act theory term referring to the work of the linguistic philosophers John Austin and John Searle, defining speech as involving action and performance in the world and as depending for its logical validity on the extent to which utterances by particular speakers can be meaningfully responded to by other speakers in practical situations of interaction. See further pp. 125.

state of nature term originating in the political thought of Thomas Hobbes and other seventeenth-century philosophers; used today in international relations contexts and globalization theory to refer to conflict between sovereign nation-states unregulated by any higher legal or moral authority, like beasts of nature fighting for survival in the absence of common norms. A 'global state of nature' would be the opposite of the concept of a 'global civil society'.

status group term used by Talcott Parsons to translate Max Weber's 'Stand' which has the meaning of 'status' and also the older meaning of 'estate'. Typically used in historical contexts, the term refers to groups in society possessing cultural advantages or positions of power that may be conditioned by economic factors and may lead to economic advantage but that are not themselves economic in nature; for example, priests, intellectuals, lawyers, knights, or other members of the aristocracy. See further pp. 72, 328.

stratification term referring to hierarchical divisions in social structures, based on layered bands or 'strata' of types of individuals possessing different advantages and disadvantages according to different degrees of wealth, power, status, and education; a more technical term for 'social inequality'.

structural functionalism term synonymous with the term 'functionalism', emphasizing the concern of functionalist sociologists with social structures and systems.

structuralism term referring to the work of French intellectuals in the middle decades of the twentieth century influenced by the 'structural linguistics' of Ferdinand de Saussure, as applied to diverse domains of the humanities and social sciences; referring to the work of Claude Lévi-Strauss, Roland Barthes, Jacques Lacan, Louis Althusser, and others. See further pp. 196–7.

structuration term in the work of Anthony Giddens, synthesizing the concepts of structure and agency; referring to the process by which a social system is reproduced by individual actors through the mediation of social structures. See further pp. 217–20.

subaltern term originally in the work of Antonio Gramsci, referring to the exclusion of working-class voices from bourgeois culture; more recently used in postcolonial theory, especially by Gayatri Spivak (1998a) and in Indian cultural studies, referring to dominated or oppressed groups who are excluded from hegemonic discourses and are unable to find a hearing for their cause, in contrast to other dominated or oppressed groups who *do* have a hearing within hegemonic discourses and who attempt to advance their cause in terms of these discourses.

subject term in philosophy referring to any being that is capable of consciousness, which can speak, think about itself, refer to itself and refer to objects, and be responsible to itself or for itself. The subject is the ego, the 'I'. Many uses of this term in social theory imply an idea of the type of human personality that is exemplary for an entire epoch of history, or for the present. It can be said that the subject of Western modernity is the rationally self-determining autonomous individual.

subjectivist term with the opposite meaning to 'objectivist', referring to approaches that overemphasize the relative importance of the subjective attitudes and agency of individual participants in a research project, in contrast to the social scientist's observations about general social facts beyond the immediate awareness of any given participant or group. The term can also refer to approaches that allow the subjective attitudes of social scientists themselves to have too much influence on the content of a piece of research.

subjectivity term referring to the self-consciousness of the subject or the ego, implying inner life, self-reflection, and autonomy, but also emotions, feelings, embodiment, desire, vulnerability, and finitude.

subject–object term in Western Marxism, taken from the philosophy of G. W. F. Hegel, particularly from the 'dialectic of master and slave', defining the proletariat as the initially passive object of capitalist exploitation which gains insight into the production process and thereby becomes the active subject of history, seizing power in a revolution; used especially in the idealistic writings of György Lukács. See further pp. 156–7.

synchronic term in functionalism and French structuralism, referring to the states and interrelationships of phenomena at any given moment in time, in contrast to 'diachronic', referring to the transformation of phenomena over time.

syncretism term referring to practices of creating cultural compounds or 'hybrids' from disparate elements with multiple origins in different languages and societies.

systems theory term referring to the work of Niklas Luhmann and other theorists; regarding society as consisting not of individuals or institutions but of systems and subsystems related to one another in complex modes and processes of communication; see also Buckley (1967). See further pp. 283–5.

tacit knowledge term in the work of Anthony Giddens, originally coined by the philosopher Michael Polanyi (brother of Karl Polanyi); also developed by linguistic philosophers, referring to taken-for-granted background understandings between ordinary people in everyday life that enable conversation and interaction but are not usually made an object of attention.

technocracy term meaning technological domination, either by the ubiquitous employment of machines and technical instruments or by systems of management and administration that prioritize technically efficient solutions to perceived problems, neglecting values of social and political dialogue and respect for human dignity and uniqueness. See further pp. 35.

teleological term with two basic contexts of use: (1) from the Greek word for 'goal', *telos*, referring to action oriented to *goals*; or (2) referring to belief systems that regard the universe or nature or history as having an ultimate goal, purpose, or end-state. One example of a teleological belief system is the medieval Christian world-view of God's design in nature, viewing each living creature as having a natural allotted purpose in the order of things. More modern examples of teleological ways of thinking have been ideas of the onward march of history toward liberal democracy (for example, Victorian liberalism) or toward communism (for example, Soviet state doctrine).

theôria term in Greek meaning 'contemplation', origin of our modern word 'theory'. See further pp. 1–3.

'Third Way' term used in the later work of Anthony Giddens, denoting the idea of an alternative to state-directed social democracy and free-market economics, based on a liberalized form of social democracy appropriate for a global age. See further pp. 217.

totalitarian term referring to the one-party state regimes of Nazi Germany under Hitler and the Soviet empire under Stalin and his successors; more abstractly referring to any social and political regime based on total integration of the individual into a system of uniform expectations reinforced by the threat of violent sanction; for example, the 'Big Brother' society of George Orwell's *Nineteen Eighty-Four*.

totality term common in Western Marxism and French post-structuralist thought, suggesting the idea of a fully integrated, self-contained whole, tolerating nothing that cannot be incorporated into a system, whether this be a system of thought (such as the idealist philosophy of Hegel) or a system of political control (such as the totalitarian state). Alternatively, the term may be used simply to denote anything that is a composite whole.

totem term meaning an object, species of animal or plant, or natural phenomenon symbolizing a clan, family, or tribe, usually with ritual associations, especially in the aboriginal societies of Australia and the Americas; regarded by Émile Durkheim as the most elementary symbol of the moral solidarity of the social group and the most primitive image of the sacred. See further pp. 58, 200.

transnational term to be distinguished from 'international', referring not to relatively well-regulated relationships between nation-states or between institutions more or less directly answerable to their home nation-states but to emergent, often *un*regulated relationships, exchanges, and flows of mobile capital, people, commodities, information, and ideas across nation-state boundaries. See further pp. 294–6.

unified theory term referring primarily to the work of Talcott Parsons, involving pursuit of a scheme of mutually consistent concepts with a systematic structure. See further pp. 92.

universalism term meaning true for all, or relevant to all, affecting all, or valid in all situations, not limited or local in significance, not context-bound but context-transcendent, relevant to humankind as a whole; a term often associated with the claims of the European Enlightenment but one with a normative logical content that need not be reduced to this historical context. (In social policy the term has a more specific meaning, denoting the principle that welfare services should be available to all by right and according to need, not restricted by individual abilities to pay.)

utilitarian term associated with the writings of Jeremy Bentham, referring to the doctrine in nineteenth-century English thought holding that the greatest good of society consists in the maximization of utility by, and for, individuals. See further pp. 24–5.

variables term denoting any element in a theory that can have different empirical states; any element that is not logically constant in the structure of the theory but is open to empirical variation.

verstehen term in German meaning 'understanding', in the sense of empathy or 'imagining oneself in the other's shoes'; used by Max Weber to describe the aims of his own 'interpretive sociology' (*verstehende Soziologie*). See further pp. 65, 111–12.

Vienna Circle term referring to the group of positivist philosophers and scientists active in Vienna in the 1920s–1930s who defended the unity of science on the model of the natural sciences, regarding social science as reducible to more basic sciences such as biology, chemistry, and physics; included Moritz Schlick, Rudolf Carnap, Otto Neurath, and more loosely the young Ludwig Wittgenstein.

voluntaristic term in the work of Talcott Parsons, denoting the idea that while human action is constrained by social structures and systems, it is voluntary, based on free will; not predetermined like the parts of a piece of machinery. See further pp. 93.

Western Marxism term denoting Marxism as it developed in the twentieth century in Europe and North America after the Russian Revolution, but not in the Soviet Union and not in Eastern Europe after 1945. See further pp. 154–5.

Whiggish term referring to belief in steady linear progress in science and politics, especially towards liberal democracy, deriving from the supporters of the Liberal Party in eighteenth- and nineteenth-century Britain, known as the Whigs.

world systems theory term in the work of Immanuel Wallerstein, referring to analyses of global historical social change in terms of exploitative relationships between economically dominant regional 'centres' and relatively undeveloped or disadvantaged regional 'peripheries' or 'semi-peripheries'. See further pp. 149–50.

■ BIOGRAPHIES OF THEORISTS

The following list of biographical entries provides brief reference information for prominent theorists discussed in this book, as well as for some relevant historical personalities. Entries include references to a small selection of the major works of named figures.

Addams, Jane (1860–1935). US feminist social reformer and pacifist, influenced the work of the Chicago School of sociology.

Adorno, Theodor W. (1903–69). Marxist theorist, member of the Frankfurt School, influenced by Hegel and German idealist philosophy, theorist of modernism in avant-garde art and music, hostile critic of mass culture and the 'culture industry'. Author of *Negative Dialectics* (1966) and *Aesthetic Theory* (1970); co-author of *Dialectic of Enlightenment* (1947), with Max Horkheimer. See further pp. 162–4, 180–1.

Alexander, Jeffrey (b. 1947). US theorist, advocate of neo-functionalist theory and the rehabilitation of the work of Talcott Parsons. Author of *Theoretical Logic in Sociology* (1982–4) (in 4 vols.). See further pp. 106–7.

Althusser, Louis (1918–90). French structuralist Marxist theorist, influential in the 1970s, committed to a mental hospital after killing his wife. Author of *For Marx* (1965) and *Reading Capital* (1970). See further pp. 167–8, 184–5.

Anderson, Perry (b. 1938). British Marxist historian of the rise of capitalism and the breakdown of feudal monarchies; leading editorial figure in the *New Left Review*. Author of *Lineages of the Absolutist State* (1974) and *Passages from Antiquity to Feudalism* (1974). See further pp. 147–9.

Apel, Karl-Otto (b. 1922). German philosopher of language and social science; demonstrated convergences between analytical philosophy of language, pragmatism, and German hermeneutics; a close associate of Jürgen Habermas. Author of *Towards a transformation of Philosophy* (1973).

Archer, Margaret S. (b. 1943). British theorist of structure and agency, sociologist of education and culture, advocate of realism in social theory. Author of *Culture and Agency* (1988) and *Realist Social Theory: The Morphogenetic Approach* (1995). See further pp. 227–9.

Arendt, Hannah (1906–75). German liberal political philosopher, Jewish émigré to the USA; influenced by ancient Greek thought; critic of social engineering and champion of political enlightenment. Author of *The Origins of Totalitarianism* (1951), *The Human Condition* (1958), *Eichmann in Jerusalem: A Report on the Banality of Evil* (1963), and *On Revolution* (1963). See further pp. 3, 9–10, 36.

Aristotle (384–322 BC). Greek philosopher, student of Plato and tutor of Alexander the Great; the most influential philosopher of the ancient world in Christian and Muslim philosophy of the Middle Ages. Author of works on logic, ethics, politics, poetics, rhetoric, zoology, and metaphysics.

Aron, Raymond (1905–83). French liberal social theorist in the tradition of Alexis de Tocqueville, influenced by Max Weber and German sociology, critic of Marxist thought, antagonist of Jean-Paul Sartre, supporter of post-war Western European social democracy. Author of *Opium of the Intellectuals* (1955) and *Main Currents in Sociological Thought* (1965).

Austin, John (1911–60). British philosopher of language influenced by Wittgenstein, originator of speech-act theory with John Searle, inventor of the concept of 'performatives' influencing Habermas, Derrida, and others. Author of *How to Do Things with Words* (1962).

Bacon, Francis (1561–1626). English seventeenth-century philosopher of empiricism and free individual enquiry; not to be confused with the Irish twentieth-century modernist painter Francis Bacon (1909–92). Author of *Novum Organon* (1620) and *Essays* (1625).

Barrett, Michèle (b. 1949). British feminist theorist of material culture, influenced by Marxism. Author of *Women's Oppression Today* (1980). See further pp. 239, 243.

Barthes, Roland (1915–80). French literary theorist and critic pioneer of structuralist semiotics in literary and cultural criticism, a founding influence in contemporary cultural studies. Author of *Mythologies* (1957), *Elements of Semiology* (1964), *S/Z* (1970), and *The Pleasure of the Text* (1973). See further pp. 199.

Bataille, Georges (1897–1962). French writer and anthropologist, influenced by Durkheim, Nietzsche, Marxism, and the surrealist poets; wrote about eroticism, community, exchange, transgression, the sacred, and the 'interior life'. Author of *Story of the Eye* (1928), *Inner Experience* (1943), and *Eroticism* (1962).

Baudrillard, Jean (b. 1929). French postmodern theorist of the media and consumer culture; influenced by semiotics, Marxism, and Marshall McLuhan; theorist of media simulation and the 'disappearance of the real'. Author of *The Consumer Society* (1970), *The Mirror of Production* (1973), *Symbolic Exchange and Death* (1976), and *Simulacra and Simulation* (1981). See further pp. 167, 253, 263–5.

Bauman, Zygmunt (b. 1925). Polish-British theorist of postmodernity and 'postmodern ethics'; influenced by Marxism, existentialism, and Norbert Elias. Author of *Legislators and Interpreters* (1987), *Modernity and the Holocaust* (1989), *Intimations of Postmodernity* (1992), *Postmodern Ethics* (1993), and *Liquid Modernity* (2000). See further pp. 266–9, 296–7.

Beauvoir, Simone de (1908–86). French feminist existentialist philosopher and novelist, influenced by Marxism; key figure in second-wave feminism; elaborated the idea of women as 'Other' to a universal subject who is unmarked as man; wife of Jean-Paul Sartre. Author of *The Second Sex* (1949) and *Adieux: A Farewell to Sartre* (1984). See further pp. 243.

Beck, Ulrich (b. 1944). German sociologist, theorist of risk, 'reflexive modernization', and globalization. Author of *The Risk Society* (1986); co-author of *The Normal Chaos of Love* (1990) with Elisabeth Beck-Gernsheim. See further pp. 286–7, 302.

Becker, Howard (b. 1928). US sociologist influenced by symbolic interactionism and the Chicago School, best known for work on deviance, medicine, and cultural institutions from an ethnographic perspective. Author of *Boys in White* (1961), *Outsiders* (1963), and *Art Worlds* (1982). See further pp. 116.

Bell, Daniel (b. 1919). US theorist of post-industrial society and consumer capitalism. Author of *The End of Ideology* (1962), *The Coming of Post-Industrial Society* (1973), and *The Cultural Contradictions of Capitalism* (1976). See further pp. 257–8.

Bendix, Reinhard (1916–91). German-American historical sociologist, influenced by Max Weber. Author of *Work and Authority in Industry* (1956), *Max Weber: An Intellectual Portrait* (1960), and *Nation-Building and Citizenship* (1964). See further pp. 142.

Benhabib, Seyla (b. 1950). Turkish-born US feminist theorist, influenced by Habermas and the Frankfurt School. Author of *Critique, Norm and Utopia* (1986) and *Situating the Self* (1992).

Benjamin, Jessica. US feminist psychoanalytic theorist, influenced by the 'object relations' theories of the psychoanalysts Melanie Klein and Donald Winnicott. Author of *The Bonds of Love* (1988) and *Like Subjects, Love Objects* (1995). See further pp. 188–9.

Benjamin, Walter (1892–1939). German Jewish Marxist theorist of culture, literature, and the mass media; loosely associated with the Frankfurt School; a close correspondent of Theodor Adorno; committed suicide in 1939 while trying to cross the French–Spanish border to escape pursuit by Nazi officers. Author of *The Origin of German Tragic Drama* (1928), *The Work of Art in the Age of Mechanical Reproduction* (1936), *Theses on the Philosophy of History* (1939), and *The Arcades Project* (1925–39). See further pp. 162, 188–9.

Bentham, Jeremy (1748–1832). British eighteenth- and nineteenth-century moral philosopher, founder of utilitarianism. Author of *A Fragment on Government* (1776) and *Introduction to the Principles of Morals and Legislation* (1789). See further pp. 24–5.

Berger, Peter L. (b. 1929). Austrian-born sociologist based in the USA, influenced by Alfred Schutz and phenomenology; theorist of the sociology of religion, knowledge, and culture. Author of *The Sacred Canopy* (1963), *The Homeless Mind* (1973), and *Desecularization of the World* (1999); co-author of *The Social Construction of Reality: A Treatise in the Sociology of Knowledge* (1966) with Thomas Luckmann. See further pp. 121.

Bhaskar, Roy (b. 1944). British philosopher of social science, influenced by Marxism, originator of 'critical realism'. Author of *A Realist Theory of Science* (1975), *The Possibility of Naturalism* (1979), and *Scientific Realism and Human Emancipation* (1986). See further pp. 127, 227–9.

Bloch, Ernst (1885–1977). German Marxist theorist, close to the Frankfurt School, influenced by Hegel and German theology. Author of *The Principle of Hope* (1952–59). See further pp. 158, 167.

Blumenberg, Hans (1920–96). German historical theorist of literature, metaphor, and scientific change; influenced by phenomenology, hermeneutics, and theological thought; recognized for studies of myth, symbolism, and secularization; notably defended the idea of the 'legitimacy of the modern age' against Karl Löwith's conception of secularization as a process of ontological 'decline' and 'desolation'. Author of *The Legitimacy of the Modern Age* (1996), *Work on Myth* (1979), and *Genesis of the Copernican World* (1975).

Blumer, Herbert (1900–87). US sociologist based at Chicago, inventor of the term symbolic interactionism in 1937; synthesized George Herbert Mead's pragmatist philosophy and social psychology with the sociology of W. I. Thomas and others. Author of *Symbolic Interactionism: Perspective and Method* (1969). See further pp. 110, 115–16.

Bourdieu, Pierre (1931–2002). French sociologist, influenced by Max Weber, Marxism, and structuralism; theorist of domination and the cultural reproduction of social inequality. Author of *Outline of a Theory of Practice* (1972), *Distinction: A Social Critique of the Judgment of Taste* (1979), *The Logic of Practice* (1980), and *The Weight of the World* (1993). See further pp. 221–9.

Braudel, Fernand (1902–85). French historian of the *Annales* school; studied global historical processes from the perspective of *la longue durée* ('the long term'). Author of *Capitalism and Material Life* (1967).

Brecht, Bertolt (1898–1956). German Marxist theorist, poet, and playwright; sought to use theatre and the mass media as organs of political consciousness-raising, involving the audience as active participants. Author of *The Three Penny Opera* (1929) and *The Rise and Fall of the City of Mahagonny* (1930) (in collaboration with the composer Kurt Weill), and numerous theatrical works.

Butler, Judith (b. 1956). US feminist theorist, influenced by Foucault and post-structuralism. Author of *Gender Trouble: Feminism and the Subversion of Identity* (1990) and *Bodies That Matter: On the Discursive Limits of Sex* (1993). See further pp. 243–5.

Calvin, John (1509–64). Swiss-French theologian, the second most influential figure in the Protestant Reformation of early modern Europe after Martin Luther; a central focus of Max Weber's *The Protestant Ethic and the Spirit of Capitalism*. Author of *Institutes of the Christian Religion* (1536). See further pp. 68–9.

Castells, Manuel (b. 1942). Spanish-American theorist of globalization, cities, information technology, and the network society. Author of *The Information Age: Economy, Society and Culture* (1996–2000) (in 3 vols.). See further pp. 296–7.

Castoriadis, Cornelius (1922–97). Greek-French theorist of social agency and the radical imagination; influenced by

Marxism, semiotics, and hermeneutics. Author of *The Imaginary Institution of Society* (1975). See further pp. 275–6.

Chodorow, Nancy (b. 1944). US feminist psychoanalytic theorist, critically adapted Freud's theory of the Oedipus complex from a feminist standpoint. Author of *The Reproduction of Mothering* (1978). See further pp. 186–8.

Chomsky, Noam (b. 1928). US theorist of linguistics and critic of behaviourism; inventor of the concept of 'linguistic competence' based on a theory of 'generative grammar'; also an outspoken critic of US imperialism and champion of anti-capitalism. Author of *Aspects of the Theory of Syntax* (1965), *Language and Mind* (1968), *American Power and the New Mandarins* (1969), and *Manufacturing Consent* (1979).

Cicourel, Aaron (b. 1928). US sociologist, co-founder of ethnomethodology with Harold Garfinkel; theorist of conversation analysis, medical communication, decision-making, and child socialization. Author of *Method and Measurement in Sociology* (1964).

Cohen, G. A. (b. 1941). Canadian-born political philosopher of egalitarianism, pioneer of 'analytical Marxism', applied functionalist principles to Marx's conception of historical materialism. Author of *Karl Marx's Theory of History: A Defense* (1978). See further pp. 186.

Coleman, James (1927–95). US sociologist of education and theorist of rational choice, influenced by economic theory, advocate of methodological individualism, critic of Parsons. Author of *Mathematical Sociology* (1964) and *Foundations of Social Theory* (1991). See further pp. 104–5.

Comte, Auguste (1798–1857). French nineteenth-century social thinker, founder of the terms 'positivism' and 'sociology', upheld a theory of evolutionary social progress. Author of *Cours de philosophie positive* (1830) and *Système de politique positive* (1851). See further pp. 2, 4, 27–8, 112.

Confucius (K'ung Fu-tse) (551–479 BC). Ancient Chinese philosopher who emphasized moral order, tradition, virtue, and gentlemanly education among the Chinese mandarins or officers of state. Author of *The Analects of Confucius* (compiled posthumously).

Cooley, Charles H. (1864–1929). US sociologist, influenced the Chicago School, best known for his idea of the 'looking-glass self'. Author of *Human Nature and Social Order* (1902). See further pp. 115.

Dahrendorf, Ralf (b. 1929). German-born liberal sociologist based in Britain, influenced by Max Weber, critic of functionalism, advocate of conflict theory, theorist of social class in a non-Marxist framework. Author of *Class and Class Conflict* (1959). See further pp. 100.

Darwin, Charles (1809–82). English nineteenth-century scientist, founder of the theory of evolution by natural selection. Author of *The Origin of Species* (1859) and *The Descent of Man* (1872).

Debord, Guy (1931–94). French Marxist theorist of consumerism and anti-capitalism; central figure in the Situationist International, a group of radicals prominent in the French 1968 movement. Author of *The Society of the Spectacle* (1967).

Deleuze, Gilles (1925–95). French theorist, influenced by Marxism, Nietzsche, structuralism, and psychoanalysis; theorist of technology, cinema, the body, and physical life; critic of phenomenology and of liberal humanistic thought. Author of *Difference and Repetition* (1968) and *Logic of Sense* (1969); co-author with Felix Guattari of *Anti-Oedipus* (1972) and *A Thousand Plateaus* (1980). See further pp. 191–3.

Derrida, Jacques (1930–2004). French theorist of deconstruction, associated with post-structuralism; influenced by Nietzsche, Heidegger, Saussure, and structural linguistics; leading theorist of textual ambiguity, 'différance', and 'logocentrism'. Author of *Of Grammatology* (1967), *Writing and Difference* (1968), *Margins of Philosophy* (1972), *Speech and Phenomena* (1973), and *Spectres of Marx* (1992). See further pp. 202–6, 253–4.

Descartes, René (1596–1650). French seventeenth-century rationalist philosopher, regarded as the founder of modern philosophy and modern geometry; proponent of a dualistic theory of mind and body (also known as 'Cartesian dualism') which has been the object of criticism in twentieth-century social thought. Author of *Discourse on Method* (1637) and *Meditations on First Philosophy* (1641). See further pp. 20.

Dewey, John (1859–1952). American pragmatist philosopher of education, democracy, religion, art, and civic well-being; defined all values with reference to 'experience' conducive to reasonable conduct and effective practice. Author of *Democracy and Education* (1916), *Human Nature and Conduct* (1922), *The Quest for Certainty* (1929), and *A Common Faith* (1934).

Diderot, Denis (1713–84). French Enlightenment philosopher; a sharp critic of European cultural beliefs, customs, and social conventions. Director of the French *Encyclopédie* (1745–72).

Dilthey, Wilhelm (1833–1911). German hermeneutic philosopher, influential in early twentieth-century German sociology; critic of positivism and progenitor of historicism as a methodology for the human sciences. Author of *Introduction to the Human Sciences* (1883). See further pp. 112.

Douglas, Mary (b. 1921). British anthropologist, theorist of cultural classification systems, symbolic boundaries, and risk. Author of *Purity and Danger* (1966), *Natural Symbols* (1970), *Risk and Culture* (1982), and *How Institutions Think* (1986). See further pp. 122.

Dreyfus, Alfred (1895–1935). French Jewish army officer, innocently accused of treason and imprisoned in 1893; released in 1899 after a pardon overturning a retrial which returned a second false verdict of guilt. The case divided France between anti-Semitic Catholic forces and liberal progressive forces. In 1898, the novelist Émile Zola wrote a famous letter—'J'accuse'—defending Dreyfus and accusing his accusers. Durkheim identified with the defenders of Dreyfus, the 'Dreyfusards'. Durkheim's essay 'Individualism and the Intellectuals' addressed the implications of the case for French democracy.

Durkheim, Émile (1858–1917). French founder of the discipline of sociology and founder of the journal *L'Année sociologique*; uncle of Marcel Mauss. Author of *The Division of Labour* (1893), *The Rules of Sociological Method* (1895), *Suicide* (1897), and *The Elementary Forms of Religions Life* (1912). See further pp. 51–60.

Eisenstadt, Shmuel (b. 1923). Israeli comparative historical sociologist of civilizations; influenced in early work by functionalism; later work advocating a conception of 'multiple modernities' influenced by Karl Jaspers's thesis of the 'axial age civilizations'. Author of *The Political Systems of Empires* (1963); editor of *The Origins and Diversity of the Axial Age Civilisations* (1986). See further pp. 136–7.

Elias, Norbert (1893–1990). German Jewish sociologist, émigré to Britain and the Netherlands; theorist of conflict, socialization, and the 'civilizing process'. Author of *The Civilizing Process* (1939), *The Court Society* (1969), and *The Germans* (1989). See further pp. 141–4, 222.

Elster, Jon (b. 1940). Norwegian-born theorist of rational choice; applied methodological individualist principles to the study of Marx and the philosophy of social science in general. Author of *Ulysses and the Sirens* (1979), *Making Sense of Marx* (1985), and *The Cement of Society* (1989).

Engels, Friedrich (1820–95). German-born inheritor of industrial interests in Manchester; lifelong intellectual and financial supporter of Karl Marx; disseminated Marx's ideas after his death. Author of *Anti-Dühring* (1878), *The*

Origin of the Family, Private Property and the State (1884), and *The Condition of the Working-Class in England in 1844* (1887); co-author of *The German Ideology* (1846) and *The Communist Manifesto* (1848) with Karl Marx; also editor of vols. 2 and 3 of *Capital* by Marx.

Erasmus of Rotterdam (1466–1536). Dutch Renaissance social critic; leading humanist scholar of classical antiquity in northern Europe during the Protestant Reformation, friend of Thomas More; published the first Greek edition of the New Testament in 1516. Author of *In Praise of Folly* (1509).

Evans-Pritchard, E. E. (1902–73). British anthropologist; studied African tribes in southern Sudan, including witchcraft beliefs among the Azande tribe; influenced debates about rationality and relativism in anthropology and the philosophy of social science, especially in the work of Peter Winch. Author of *Witchcraft, Oracles and Magic among the Azande* (1937) and *The Nuer* (1940). See further pp. 126.

Fanon, Frantz (1925–61). Algerian anti-colonial activist, theorist of racism and imperialism; influenced by Sartre's existentialist Marxism; prominent in the Algerian war of independence against France in the 1950s. Author of *Black Skin, White Masks* (1952) and *Wretched of the Earth* (1961). See further pp. 34, 167.

Ferguson, Adam (1723–1815). Scottish Enlightenment historical writer and philosopher, wrote on conflict and the division of labour in society. Author of *An Essay on Civil Society* (1767).

Feuerbach, Ludwig (1804–72). German nineteenth-century philosopher; follower and critic of Hegel; argued that God is the projection of man and an expression of human alienation, influencing Karl Marx's materialist critique of religion and idealist metaphysics. Author of *The Essence of Christianity* (1841) and *Basic Propositions of the Philosophy of the Future* (1843).

Feyerabend, Paul (1924–94). Austrian philosopher of science, émigré to the USA; early advocate of positivism, later advocate of strong relativism or 'epistemological anarchism'; famous for the provocative slogan that in science 'anything goes'. Author of *Against Method* (1975). See further pp. 123.

Foucault, Michel (1926–84). French theorist of power, knowledge, science, history, discourse, subjectivity, and sexuality, influenced by structuralism and Nietzsche. Author of *Madness and Civilization* (1961), *The Order of Things* (1966), *Discipline and Punish* (1975), and *The History of Sexuality* (1976–84) (in 3 vols.). See further pp. 201–12.

Franklin, Benjamin (1706–90). American statesman, scientist, and inventor; ambassador to France; involved in the drafting of the Declaration of Independence of 1776; Puritan moralist famous for the slogan 'time is money'; a key case figure in Max Weber's *The Protestant Ethic and the Spirit of Capitalism*.

Fraser, Nancy. US feminist theorist of social recognition and the politics of identity, influenced by critical theory. Author of *Unruly Practices* (1989) and *Justice Interruptus* (1997); co-author of *Redistribution or Recognition?* (2003) with Axel Honneth. See further pp. 242.

Freud, Sigmund (1856–1939). Austrian Jewish psychiatrist and founder of psychoanalysis, reviled by the Nazis. Author of *The Interpretation of Dreams* (1902), *Beyond the Pleasure Principle* (1920), *The Future of an Illusion* (1927), and *Civilization and its Discontents* (1930). See further pp. 175–9.

Friedan, Betty (b. 1921). US feminist and social reformer; regarded as the most influential figure in the early years of the post-war American movement for women's rights; founder of the National Organization for Women in 1966. Author of *The Feminine Mystique* (1963). See further pp. 103, 247.

Fromm, Erich (1900–80). German social psychologist, émigré to the USA, early brief associate of the Frankfurt School; combined Freudian psychoanalysis with social critique. Author of *The Art of Loving* (1956) and *To Have and To Be* (1976). See further pp. 160, 180.

Gadamer, Hans-Georg (1900–2002). German hermeneutic philosopher, influenced by Martin Heidegger; defined hermeneutics as a practice of the interpretation of existence, history, and tradition founded in dialogue between the past and the present; an early influence on Jürgen Habermas. Author of *Truth and Method* (1960). See further pp. 125–7.

Galbraith, John Kenneth (b. 1908). US economist, concerned with the fate of the public interest in capitalist economies. Author of *The Affluent Society* (1958) and *Economics and the Public Purpose* (1973). See further pp. 140–1.

Garfinkel, Harold (b. 1917). US sociologist, founder of ethnomethodology, theorist of tacit rules in social communication and interaction. Author of *Studies in Ethnomethodology* (1967). See further pp.110, 117–19.

Geertz, Clifford (b. 1923). US anthropologist, associated with a 'cultural turn' in social science modelled on the reading of texts, best known for his concept of 'thick description'. Author of *The Interpretation of Cultures* (1973) and *Local Knowledge* (1983). See further pp. 122.

Gellner, Ernest (1925–95). Czech-born anthropologist and philosopher of history based in Britain until 1993; commentator on Islam, nationalism, civil society, relativism, linguistics, and psychoanalysis. Author of *Relativism and the Social Sciences* (1985), *Plough, Sword and Book* (1988), *Reason and Culture* (1992), and *Postmodernism, Reason and Religion* (1992).

Giddens, Anthony (b. 1939). British theorist, influenced by Durkheim and Max Weber; exponent of 'structuration theory' based on synthesis of the concepts of structure and agency; advocate in later work of a 'Third Way' between state-directed social democracy and free-market economics. Author of *The Class Structure of the Advanced Societies* (1973), *The Constitution of Society* (1984), *The Consequences of Modernity* (1990), *Modernity and Self-Identity* (1991), and *The Third Way* (1998). See further pp. 217–20.

Goffman, Erving (1922–82). US sociologist, influenced by symbolic interactionism; exponent of a 'dramaturgical' perspective in social analysis and theorist of 'outsiders' and 'total institutions'. Author of *The Presentation of Self in Everyday Life* (1956), *Asylums* (1961), and *Stigma* (1963). See further pp. 110, 116–17.

Gouldner, Alvin (1920–80). US sociologist, influenced by functionalism in early work; later a stern critic of functionalism as politically conservative. Author of *The Coming Crisis of Western Sociology* (1970) and *For Sociology* (1973). See further pp. 102.

Gramsci, Antonio (1891–1937). Italian Marxist theorist, co-founder of the Italian Communist Party; imprisoned by the fascist regime under Mussolini from 1926 until his death. Author of *Selections from the Prison Notebooks* (1926–37). See further pp. 6–7, 157–9.

Guattari, Felix (1930–92). French Marxist theorist, influenced by psychoanalysis and structuralism. Co-author with Gilles Deleuze of *Anti-Oedipus* (1972) and *A Thousand Plateaus* (1980). See further pp. 192.

Habermas, Jürgen (b. 1929). German theorist of communication, democracy, universal political values, and the public sphere; second-generation associate of the Frankfurt School in the 1960s; early work influenced by Hegelian Marxism; later work from the late 1970s onwards moved closer to liberal political philosophy, pragmatism, and linguistic theory. Author of *Structural Transformation of the Public Sphere* (1962), *Knowledge and Human Interests* (1968), *The Theory of Communicative Action* (1981), and *Between Facts and Norms* (1992). See further pp. 125–7, 164–5, 279–83.

Halbwachs, Maurice (1877–1945). French sociologist, influenced by Durkheim and the philosopher Henri Bergson; theorist of collective memory and material culture. Author of *Population and Society* (1938), *The Causes of Suicide* (1930), *Collective Memory* (1950), and *The Psychology of Social Class* (1955).

Hall, Stuart (b. 1932). Jamaican-British theorist of ethnicity, difference, and cultural marginality, influenced by Marxism and post-structuralism; founder of the Birmingham school of cultural studies; pioneer of postcolonial theory and criticism. Author of *Hard Road to Renewal: Thatcherism and the Crisis of the Left* (1988); editor of *Culture, Media, Language: Working Papers in Cultural Studies, 1972–79* (1980) and *New Times* (1989) with Martin Jacques. See further pp. 168–70.

Haraway, Donna (b. 1944). US feminist theorist of technoscience; formulated a 'Cyborg Manifesto' questioning traditional distinctions between culture and nature, humans and animals, and 'man' and 'machine'. Author of *Primate Visions* (1989), *Simians, Cyborgs and Women* (1991), and *The Companion Species* (2003). See further pp. 249.

Harding, Sandra (b. 1935). US feminist philosopher of science, exponent of feminist standpoint epistemology. Author of *The Science Question in Feminism* (1986) and *Whose Science, Whose Knowledge?* (1991).

Harré, Rom (b. 1927). New Zealand-born philosopher of science and social psychologist based in Britain and the USA; theorist of realism in science, favouring an interactionist approach in preference to naturalistic and structuralist variants of realism. Author of *Social Being* (1980); co-author with Paul Secord of *The Explanation of Social Behaviour* (1972). See further pp. 126.

Hayek, Friedrich (1899–1992). Austrian-born economist, critic of socialism, advocate of free-market principles. Author of *The Road to Serfdom* (1944) and *The Constitution of Liberty* (1960). See further pp. 140–1.

Hegel, Georg W. F. (1770–1831). German nineteenth-century philosopher; the most systematic representative of German idealist philosophy in the early nineteenth century after Immanuel Kant; an early influence on Marx and influential in twentieth-century Western Marxism; celebrated (among other reasons) for his conception of the 'dialectic of master and slave' in which the slave is said to triumph over the master insofar as the master depends on the slave for vital needs, a thesis notably developed in the writing of the French phenomenological philosopher Alexandre Kojève. Author of *The Phenomenology of Spirit* (1807) and *The Philosophy of Right* (1821). See further pp. 6.

Heidegger, Martin (1889–1976). German existentialist philosopher; developed Husserl's phenomenological philosophy into a comprehensive analysis of Being and human existence; influenced post-war European philosophy; regarded modern science and metaphysics as a derivative mode of understanding in relation to the fundamental problems of existence; compromised by support for Hitler in the 1930s. Author of *Being and Time* (1927). See further pp. 126.

Held, David (b. 1951). British theorist of globalization, especially of the idea of 'global civil society' and 'cosmopolitan democracy' as normative possibilities. Author of *Democracy and the Global Order* (1995). See further pp. 306.

Heller, Agnes (b. 1929). Hungarian-born theorist based in the USA, influenced by György Lukács, Marxism, and phenomenology. Author of *A Theory of History* (1982) and *Theory of Modernity* (1999). See further pp. 276–8.

Hirschman, Albert O. (b. 1915). US economist and historian, theorist of industrial relations, social trust, and economic development. Author of *Exit, Voice and Loyalty* (1970) and *The Passions and the Interests* (1977). See further pp. 26.

Hobbes, Thomas (1588–1679). English seventeenth-century political philosopher; defender of the absolute sovereignty of the monarch; celebrated chiefly for his book *Leviathan* (1651), which argued that subjects must obey the sovereign to the extent that the sovereign protects them from violent death at the hands of enemies. Insofar as individuals agree to obey a sovereign, they depart from what Hobbes called the 'state of nature', marked by a 'war of all against all' where all individuals pursue conflicting egoistic desires. Hobbes wrote in the context of the English Civil War of 1640–60.

Hobsbawm, Eric (b. 1917). British Marxist historian of modern Europe since the French Revolution. Author of *The Age of Revolution* (1962), *The Age of Capital* (1975), *The Age of Empire* (1987), and *The Age of Extremes* (1994). See further pp. 26.

Hoggart, Richard (b. 1918). British historian of working-class culture, writer on education, influential in the first wave of British cultural studies. Author of *The Uses of Literacy* (1957). See further pp.168–9.

Homans, George (1910–89). US sociologist, proponent of social behaviourism based on methodological individualism; critic of Talcott Parsons; exponent of exchange theory, with Peter Blau. Author of *The Human Group* (1951) and *Social Behaviour* (1961). See further pp. 104.

Honneth, Axel (b. 1949). German critical theorist influenced by Habermas and the Frankfurt School;

exponent of a communicative theory of social justice based on recognition for injured and excluded social parties. Author of *The Struggle for Recognition* (1992).

hooks, bell (b. 1952) (née Gloria Watkins). US feminist theorist of race, racism, emancipation, and education, influenced by the pedagogical theorist Paulo Friere. Author of *Ain't I a Woman? Black Women and Feminism* (1981), *Talking Back: Thinking Feminist, Thinking Black* (1989), *Yearning: Race, Gender and Cultural Politics* (1990). See further pp. 246.

Horkheimer, Max (1895–1973). German critical theorist; became director of the Institute for Social Research at Frankfurt in 1930; central founding figure of the Frankfurt School; returned to Frankfurt in 1949 after emigration to the USA. Author of *Traditional and Critical Theory* (1937); co-author of *Dialectic of Enlightenment* (1947) with Theodor Adorno. See further pp. 160–1, 163–4.

Hume, David (1711–76). Scottish Enlightenment philosopher, sceptic, and empiricist; examined the nature of induction, causation, and personal identity. Author of *A Treatise of Human Nature* (1740).

Husserl, Edmund (1859–1938). German Jewish philosopher, founder of phenomenological philosophy; influential in interpretive approaches to social enquiry, especially in the work of Alfred Schutz and Maurice Merleau-Ponty; progenitor of the concepts of 'intersubjectivity', the 'lifeworld', and 'phenomenological reduction'. Author of *Logical Investigations* (1901), *Cartesian Meditations* (1929), and *The Crisis of the European Sciences and Transcendental Phenomenology* (1936). See further pp. 3, 113.

James, William (1842–1910). American pragmatist philosopher and psychologist; influenced early twentieth-century European thinkers; brother of the novelist Henry James. Author of *The Principles of Psychology* (1890), *Varieties of Religious Experience* (1902), and *Pragmatism* (1907).

Jameson, Fredric (b. 1934). US Marxist cultural theorist; influenced by the Frankfurt School and French literary theory. Author of *Postmodernism, Or the Cultural Logic of Late Capitalism* (1991). See further pp. 265–6.

Jaspers, Karl (1883–1969). German existentialist philosopher, influenced by Max Weber; propounded a thesis of the 'axial age civilizations' of ancient Greece, Israel, Persia, China, and India between 800 and 200 BC, seen as key determining episodes in the course of world history. Author of *The Origin and Goal of History* (1949).

Jefferson, Thomas (1743–1826). Third president of the USA (1801–9), chief architect of the Declaration of

Independence of 1776, and chief opponent of the centralizing policies of the Federalists led by James Hamilton during the formation of the American Constitution.

Kant, Immanuel (1724–1804). Prussian Enlightenment philosopher; the most influential figure in modern philosophy after Descartes; argued in opposition to eighteenth-century British empiricist philosophy that the possibility of knowledge of the world depends upon certain 'transcendental' a priori concepts and categories that are supplied by the human mind and are not given in experience. Author of *The Critique of Pure Reason* (1781), *The Critique of Practical Reason* (1788), and *The Critique of Judgment* (1790). See further pp. 22, 43, 112.

Keynes, John Maynard (1883–1946). British economist; advocate of active government fiscal policy to achieve high levels of employment; influential in the foundation of welfare states after 1945. Author of *The General Theory of Employment, Interest and Money* (1936).

Kohlberg, Lawrence (1927–87). US psychologist, influenced by Jean Piaget; theorist of cognitive development and moral reasoning from a psychological perspective; influenced Habermas's theory of communicative action. Author of *Essays on Moral Development* (1981).

Kojève, Alexandre (1902–68). French phenomenological philosopher; humanistic interpreter of Hegel's 'dialectic of master and slave'; later criticized by the French post-structuralist theorists. Author of *Introduction to the Reading of Hegel* (1947).

Korsch, Karl (1889–1961). German Marxist theorist, influenced by Hegelian dialectical thought. Author of *Marxism and Philosophy* (1923) and *Karl Marx* (1938). See further pp. 157.

Kracauer, Siegfried (1889–1966). German cultural theorist, émigré to the USA; theorist of film and photography, popular culture and the metropolis; influenced by Simmel and Marxism; close friend of Walter Benjamin and Theodor Adorno. Author of *The Mass Ornament* (1931), *From Caligari to Hitler: A Psychological History of the German Film* (1947), and *Theory of Film* (1960).

Kristeva, Julia (b. 1941). French-Bulgarian feminist psychoanalytic theorist and literary critic, influenced by semiotics. Author of *Revolution in Poetic Language* (1974) and *Tales of Love* (1983). See further pp. 189–91.

Kuhn, Thomas (1922–96). US historian and philosopher of science; theorized the history of science in terms of discontinuous 'paradigm shifts', casting doubt on linear progress in science; regarded as preparing the ground for

relativistic and anti-realist conceptions of science. Author of *The Structure of Scientific Revolutions* (1962). See further pp. 123–4.

Lacan, Jacques (1901–81). French psychoanalyst; interpreted the work of Sigmund Freud in terms of structural linguistics; best known for his statement that 'the unconscious is structured like a language'. Author of *Écrits* (1966). See further pp. 181–3, 189–91.

Latour, Bruno (b. 1947). French anthropologist and philosopher of science; theorist of scientific practice and legal reasoning in ethnographic terms, including non-human agency in relation to physical artefacts and instruments; associated with social constructionism; pioneer of actor-network theory (with Michel Callon). Author of *The Pasteurization of France* (1988), *We Have Never Been Modern* (1991), and *Pandora's Hope* (1999); co-author of *Laboratory Life* (1979) with Steve Woolgar. See further pp. 124.

Lefebvre, Henri (1901–91). French Marxist phenomenological theorist; pioneer of spatial analysis in relation to social deprivation and inequality, especially in urban research. Author of *The Critique of Everyday Life* (1947) and *The Production of Space* (1974).

Lévinas, Emmanuel (1906–95). French philosopher, influenced by phenomenology, existentialism, and Jewish theology; developed a moral philosophy emphasizing the dialogical relationship of the self to the 'face of the Other' as a primordial fact of existence; influencing themes in debates about postmodernism that focus on unique non-generalizable ethical situations, such as in the work of Zygmunt Bauman and others. Author of *Totality and Infinity* (1961) and *Otherwise Than Being or Beyond Essence* (1974).

Lévi-Strauss, Claude (b. 1908). French anthropologist, pioneer of structuralism in anthropology, following Ferdinand de Saussure's structural linguistics. Author of *The Elementary Structures of Kinship* (1949), *Tristes Tropiques* (1955), *Structural Anthropology* (1958), *The Savage Mind* (1966), and *Mythologies* (1964–71). See further pp. 200–202.

Lipset, Seymour Martin (b. 1922). US sociologist; studied democracy and democratization in comparative historical perspective. Author of *Political Man* (1960) and *The First New Nation* (1963). See further pp. 138.

Locke, John (1632–1704). English seventeenth-century philosopher of empiricism; theorist of liberal democracy and the origins of private property; supporter of religious toleration and separation of Church and state; influential in eighteenth-century France and North America. Author of *An Essay Concerning*

Human Understanding (1690) and *Two Treatises on Government* (1690).

Lockwood, David (b. 1929). British sociologist, theorist of social inequality and critic of functionalism; distinguished between 'social integration' and 'system integration'. Author of *Blackcoated Worker* (1958) and *Solidarity and Schism* (1992). See further pp. 102.

Löwenthal, Leo (1900–93). German Marxist theorist, member of the Frankfurt School, émigré to the USA; compiled studies of fascism, consumption, and the mass media, including film and the sociology of literature, as well as anti-communist hysteria in the USA in the 1950s. Author of *Literature and the Image of Man* (1957), *Literature, Popular Culture and Society* (1961), and *False Prophets: Studies on Authoritarianism* (repr. 1987).

Löwith, Karl (1897–1973) German-born philosopher of history, émigré to the USA; influenced by German philosophy and theology, especially by Martin Heidegger; viewed the rise of the modern world in terms of a process of secularization and ontological subjectivization in which individuals lose a sense of connectedness to a transcendent realm; notably criticized by Hans Blumenberg in relation to the question of the 'legitimacy of the modern age'. Author of *From Hegel to Nietzsche* (1941), *Meaning in History* (1949), and *Max Weber and Karl Marx* (repr. 1982).

Luckmann, Thomas (b. 1927). Austrian sociologist, influenced by Alfred Schutz and phenomenological philosophy; edited Schutz's later unfinished writings on 'structures of the lifeworld'. Co-author of *The Social Construction of Reality* (1966) with Peter Berger. See further pp. 121.

Luhmann, Niklas (1927–98). German theorist of social systems, influenced by Talcott Parsons and cybernetic theory; critic of Habermas. Author of *The Differentiation of Society* (1970) and *Social Systems* (1984). See further pp. 283–5.

Lukács, György (Georg) (1885–1971). Hungarian Marxist theorist influenced by Hegel, German philosophy, Weber, and Simmel; became in later work a rather dogmatic adherent of Soviet communism. Author of *Theory of the Novel* (1910), *History and Class Consciousness* (1923), and *The Destruction of Reason* (1955). See further pp. 156–7.

Luther, Martin (1483–1546). German sixteenth-century religious thinker; leader of the Protestant Reformation in northern Germany; believed that salvation was to be sought 'by faith alone', not by tribute to the Church or by outward deeds; translated the Bible into German in 1521–46.

Lyotard, Jean-François (1924–98). French theorist of postmodernism; influenced by Marxism, psychoanalysis, and post-structuralism; defined postmodernity in terms of the 'end of grand narratives' or 'scepticism toward meta-narratives'. Author of *The Postmodern Condition* (1979) and *The Differend* (1983). See further pp. 253–4, 256–8.

Machiavelli, Niccolò (1469–1527). Italian Renaissance political philosopher; adviser to the ruling Medici family of Florence; separated moral considerations from political expediency; associated with the view that in politics 'the end justifies the means'. Author of *The Prince* (1512).

McLuhan, Marshall (1911–80). Canadian theorist of the mass media, originator of the slogan 'the medium is the message'; influential in postmodern media theory. Author of *Understanding Media* (1964).

Maine, Henry (1822–88). English Victorian lawyer and historian; described the passage from ancient to modern society as a transition from *status* to *contract*; influential in late nineteenth-century English and French sociology. Author of *Ancient Law* (1861).

Malinowski, Bronislaw (1884–1942). Polish-born anthropologist based in Britain; pioneer of anthropological fieldwork in a functionalist framework; famously studied gift exchange systems among inhabitants of the Trobriand Islands in north-western Melanesia. Author of *Argonauts of the Western Pacific* (1922), *The Sexual Life of Savages* (1932), and *A Scientific Theory of Culture* (1944). See further pp. 88.

Mann, Michael (b. 1942). British-born historical sociologist; recognized for work on the history of social power. Author of *The Sources of Social Power* (1986, vol. i; 1993, vol. ii). See further pp. 148.

Mannheim, Karl (1893–1947). Hungarian-born theorist based in Germany until 1933 before emigrating to Britain; influenced by phenomenology and German historicism; founding theorist and methodologist of the sociology of knowledge and the sociology of culture. Author of *Conservatism* (1925), *Ideology and Utopia* (1929), *Essays on the Sociology of Knowledge* (1952), and *Essays on the Sociology of Culture* (1956). See further pp. 120–1.

Marcuse, Herbert (1898–1979). German-born Marxist theorist, émigré to the USA; member of the Frankfurt School; influential in the American 1968 peace movement. Author of *Reason and Revolution* (1941), *Eros and Civilization* (1955), and *One-Dimensional Man* (1964). See further pp. 166, 180–1.

Marshall, Alfred (1842–1924). English economist; synthesized classical political economy with the theory of 'marginal utility'. Author of *The Principles of Economics* (1890).

Marshall, T. H. (Thomas Humphrey) (1883–1981). British theorist of social policy, welfare, and social citizenship. Author of *Citizenship and Social Class* (1949) and *The Right To Welfare* (1981). See further pp. 138–9.

Marx, Karl (1818–83). German philosopher, resident in Britain for most of his life; influenced principally by German idealist philosophy, British economic theory, and French Enlightenment political thought. Author of *Grundrisse* (1858) and *Capital,* vol. i (1867); co-author of *The German Ideology* (1846) and *The Communist Manifesto* (1848) with Friedrich Engels. See further pp. 41–9, 59–60.

Mauss, Marcel (1872–1950). French anthropologist and sociologist, nephew of Émile Durkheim; editor of the journal *L'Année sociologique*; studied practices of gift exchange in primitive societies in terms of relations of power, obligation, and reciprocity; influenced structuralist anthropology, including the work of Claude Lévi-Strauss. Author of *The Gift* (1925); co-author of *Primitive Classification* (1903) with Émile Durkheim.

Mead, George Herbert (1863–1931). American pragmatist philosopher and social psychologist; theorist of the self, socialization, communication, language, and personal agency; a major influence on the symbolic interactionists. Author of *Mind, Self and Society* (1934) and *Philosophy of the Act* (1938). See further pp. 110, 114–15.

Merleau-Ponty, Maurice (1908–61). French phenomenological philosopher, influenced by Edmund Husserl and Martin Heidegger; defined human subjectivity from the standpoint of the 'lived body' of the self as a sensory-motor agency of feelings, sensations, desires, and intentions that pre-structure the conscious life of the mind, criticizing Cartesian dualism, emphasizing human finitude, praxis, and everyday life; defended a humanistic form of Marxism, with some similarities to the existentialist Marxism of Jean-Paul Sartre. Author of *The Phenomenology of Perception* (1945), *Humanism and Terror* (1947), and *Adventures of the Dialectic* (1955).

Merton, Robert (1910–2003). US theorist; examined the sociology of deviance, organizations, knowledge, and science in a functionalist framework; espoused theories of the 'middle range' (mediating between grand theory and non-theory). Author of *Social Theory and Social Structure* (1949; 2nd edn. 1968). See further pp. 90–2.

Michels, Robert (1876–1936). Swiss-Italian theorist of oligarchies, elites, and political parties; student of Max Weber, close to the work of Mosca and Pareto. Author of *Political Parties* (1911). See further pp. 28–30.

Miliband, Ralph (1924–94). Belgian-born Marxist theorist based in Britain; theorist of stratification and state power.

Author of *The State in Capitalist Society* (1969) and *Class Power and State Power* (1983).

Mill, John Stuart (1806–73). English Victorian empiricist philosopher; classical theorist of liberalism in politics. Author of *A System of Logic* (1843) and *On Liberty* (1859). See further pp. 27–7.

Mills, C. Wright (1916–62). US theorist of conflict, power, class, stratification, and elites; critic of Talcott Parsons. Author of *White Collar* (1951), *The Power Elite* (1956), and *The Sociological Imagination* (1959). See further pp. 100.

Mitchell, Juliet (b. 1940). British socialist feminist, influenced by psychoanalysis. Author of *Psychoanalysis and Feminism* (1974). See further pp. 185.

Montaigne, Michel de (1533–92). French Renaissance historical thinker and moral sceptic; critic of European prejudices. Author of *Essays* (c. 1571–92).

Montesquieu, Baron de (1689–1755). French Enlightenment political philosopher; influential in the French and American revolutions; argued for separation between the powers of the legislature, the executive, and the judiciary. Author of *The Spirit of the Laws* (1748).

Moore, Barrington (b. 1913). US comparative historical sociologist; examined the power bases of modern states. Author of *Social Origins of Dictatorship and Democracy* (1966). See further pp. 340.

More, Thomas (1478–1535). English Renaissance social critic and statesman under Henry VIII, friend of Erasmus of Rotterdam. Author of *Utopia* (1516).

Mosca, Gaetano (1858–1941). Italian theorist of oligarchies and elites; close to the work of Pareto and Michels. Author of *The Ruling Class* (1896). See further pp. 28–30.

Negri, Antonio (b. 1933). Italian Marxist theorist of Left autonomy; theorist of globalization and anti-capitalism; exiled from Italy by the Italian government until 1998 on grounds of suspected involvement in Left terrorism in the 1970s. Co-author of *Empire* (2000) with Michael Hardt. See further pp. 167.

Neumann, Franz (1900–54). German legal theorist, early associate of the Frankfurt School; émigré to the USA; defended democracy and the rule of impartial formal law within a socialist framework, criticizing Carl Schmitt's conservative attack on parliamentary democracy and the rise of fascism in Germany in the 1920s and 1930s. Author of *Behemoth: The Structure and Practice of National Socialism* (1942).

Neurath, Otto (1882–1945). Austrian philosopher and theorist of logical positivism; member of the Vienna Circle, developed a system for the visual display of quantitative information known as the Vienna Method or Isotype. Author of *Foundations of the Social Sciences* (1944).

Nietzsche, Friedrich (1844–1900). German nineteenth-century philosopher; forerunner of existentialism and philosopher of nihilism; celebrated for his conception of the 'superman' (*Übermensch*) based on 'sovereign personality', and for his doctrine of the 'death of God'. Author of *The Birth of Tragedy* (1872), *The Gay Science* (1882), *Thus Spoke Zarathustra* (1885), and *Beyond Good and Evil* (1886). See further pp. 254–5.

Pareto, Vilfredo (1848–1923). Italian theorist of power, elites, and economic advantage; forerunner of rational choice theory; close to the work of Mosca and Michels. Author of *The Mind and Society* (1916). See further pp. 28–30.

Parsons, Talcott (1902–79). US theorist; the most systematic theorist of functionalism (also known as 'structural functionalism'); influenced by Durkheim, Weber and evolutionary thought; introduced European social theory to the USA in the 1930s. Author of *The Structure of Social Action* (1937), *The Social System* (1951), *The System of Modern Societies* (1971), *The Evolution of Societies* (1977), and *Action Theory and the Human Condition* (1978); co-author of *Toward a General Theory of Action* (1951) with Edward Shils; and *Economy and Society* (1956) with Neil Smelser. See further pp. 92–9.

Peirce, Charles, S. (1839–1914). American nineteenth-century philosopher, mathematician, and logician; founder of pragmatism as a philosophical movement; also propounded a theory of semiotics. Author of *Collected Papers* (in 8 vols.) (1865–1914).

Piaget, Jean (1896–1980). Swiss-French psychologist; studied cognitive development in children; developed a theory of 'genetic structuralism'; influenced Habermas's theory of communicative action. Author of *The Child's Conception of Physical Causality* (1930), *The Moral Judgement of the Child* (1932), and *Genetic Epistemology* (1968).

Plato (c. 427–347 BC). Ancient Greek philosopher, disciple of the dissident sage Socrates (c. 470–399 BC); the single most influential intellectual figure of Western antiquity; notable for his conception of truth and justice as absolute values in themselves, knowable only by transcendence of everyday subjective opinion. Author of *The Republic* (c. 360 BC).

Polanyi, Karl (1886–1964). Austrian-born economic historian, emigrated to Britain and the USA; analysed the rise of international capitalism in relation to processes of 'disembedding' of historical cultural traditions. Author of *The Great Transformation* (1944). See further pp. 000–0.

Popper, Karl (1902–94). Austrian liberal philosopher of science based in Britain; linked to the Vienna Circle in early work, later became a critic of logical positivism, propounding a theory of 'falsification' based on acceptance of scientific theories until shown to be false; also a proponent of the concept of the 'open society' based on liberal critique of Hegelian-Marxist philosophy of history. Author of *Logic of Scientific Discovery* (1935), *The Open Society and its Enemies* (1945), and *Conjectures and Refutations* (1963).

Poulantzas, Nicos (1936–79). Greek-born Marxist theorist based in France, influenced by Louis Althusser; theorist of the state, social class, and stratification. Author of *Political Power and Social Classes* (1968) and *Classes in Contemporary Capitalism* (1974).

Proudhon, Pierre Joseph (1809–65). Nineteenth-century French utopian socialist writer, famous for the slogan 'property is theft'. Author of *What is Property?* (1840).

Radcliffe-Brown, Arthur (1881–1955). British anthropologist, pioneer of functionalism in anthropology. Author of *Andaman Islanders* (1922) and *Structure and Function in Primitive Society* (1952). See further pp. 88.

Rawls, John (1921–2002). US liberal political philosopher, the most influential American political philosopher of the twentieth century; originator of a Kantian theory of justice evaluating the relative priority of liberty of individuals over equality of individuals. Author of *A Theory of Justice* (1971), *Political Liberalism* (1993), and *The Law of Peoples* (1999).

Rex, John (b. 1925). South African-born sociologist based in Britain, critic of functionalism, proponent of conflict theory. Author of *Key Problems of Sociological Theory* (1961), *Race Relations in Sociological Theory* (1970), and *Social Conflict* (1981). See further pp. 100.

Ricardo, David (1772–1823). English eighteenth- and nineteenth-century economist; a wealthy stockbroker, friend of Jeremy Bentham and James Mill (father of John Stuart Mill); criticized at length by Marx; analysed distributions of goods between landowners, workers, and owners of capital, formulating an 'Iron Law of Wages' which stated that all attempts to improve the real income of workers are futile and that wages necessarily tend toward near-subsistence level. Author of *Principles of Political Economy and Taxation* (1817).

Rickert, Heinrich (1863–1936). German Neo-Kantian philosopher; influenced Max Weber's views on the methodology of the social sciences. Author of *The Limits of Concept Formation in the Natural Sciences* (1902).

Ricœur, Paul (b. 1913). French historical and literary theorist; influenced by hermeneutics, phenomenology, semiotics, and psychoanalysis. Author of *Freud and Philosophy* (1970), *The Conflict of Interpretations* (1974), and *Time and Narrative* (1983–90) (in 3 vols.).

Riesman, David (1909–2002). US sociologist, influenced by Weber; studied character, alienation, and personality in relation to social structures in the USA. Author of *The Lonely Crowd* (1950). See further pp. 119.

Ritzer, George (b. 1940). US theorist of globalization, influenced by Weber's theory of rationalization. Author of *The McDonaldization of Society* (1993). See further pp. 299.

Robertson, Roland (b. 1942) British sociologist; regarded as one of the first writers to define 'globalization' as a sociological concept; also inventor of the term 'glocalization'. Author of *Globalization, Social Theory and Social Culture* (1992) and *Globalization and Modernity* (2002). See further pp. 304–5.

Rorty, Richard (b. 1931). US pragmatist philosopher, critic of Anglo-American analytical philosophy; associated with postmodernism; sophisticated defender of relativism in cultural values, sceptical of universal claims to truth and of indubitable foundations for knowledge; advocate of 'post-foundationalism'. Author of *Philosophy and the Mirror of Nature* (1979) and *Contingency, Irony and Solidarity* (1989).

Rousseau, Jean-Jacques (1712–78). Swiss-French Enlightenment philosopher; influential in the French Revolution; champion of republicanism and direct democracy; believer in the natural goodness of man; critic of social and political corruption. Author of *The Social Contract* (1762), *Émile* (1762), and *Confessions* (1782).

Ryle, Gilbert (1900–76). British analytical philosopher of language, influenced by Ludwig Wittgenstein; criticized Descartes's dualism of mind and body as suggesting a notion of 'the ghost in the machine'; distinguished influentially between practical knowledge ('knowing-how') and theoretical knowledge ('knowing-that'). Author of *The Concept of Mind* (1949).

Said, Edward (1935–2003). Palestinian-American cultural theorist and literary critic, influenced by Marxism, psychoanalysis, and Michel Foucault; pioneer of postcolonial theory. Author of *Beginnings* (1975) and *Orientalism* (1978). See further pp. 34.

Saint-Simon, Claude Henri de Rouvroy, Comte de (1760–1825). Nineteenth-century French utopian socialist

philosopher; believer in progress through industry and science. Co-author of *The Reorganisation of European Society* (1814) with Augustin Thierry.

Sartre, Jean-Paul (1950–80). French existentialist writer and philosopher, influenced by Hegel, Marx, Edmund Husserl, and phenomenological philosophy; outspoken public intellectual of post-war France, famously spoke of man as 'condemned to freedom'. Author of *Nausea* (1938), *Being and Nothingness* (1943), and *The Critique of Dialectical Reason* (1960). See further pp. 166–7.

Saussure, Ferdinand de (1857–1913). Swiss-French linguist, pioneer of structural linguistics; defined linguistic meaning in terms of differential relations between signs. Author of *Course in General Linguistics* (1916). See further pp. 197–200.

Scheler, Max (1874–1928). German theorist, influenced by phenomenology, Nietzsche, and German historicism; influenced Karl Mannheim, Alfred Schutz, and others in the development of the 'sociology of knowledge' as a field of investigation; elaborated a conception of 'philosophical anthropology' emphasizing the importance of feeling, emotion, desire, will, and compassion in human action and thought. Author of *The Nature of Sympathy* (1912), *Problems of a Sociology of Knowledge* (1926), and *Man's Place in Nature* (1928).

Schmitt, Carl (1888–1985). German conservative legal and political theorist, influential in international relations theory; student of Max Weber; critic of democracy and bureaucracy, theorist of *Realpolitik* and of 'friend–enemy relations'; argued that the essence of political sovereignty lay in the ability to 'decide in the emergency case' and to prevail over disorder; compromised by support for the Nazis. Author of *The Concept of the Political* (1932) and *Political Theology* (1934).

Schumpeter, Joseph (1883–1950). Moravian-born economist, émigré to the USA; influenced by Weber; critic of both Marxism and classical economics. Author of *Capitalism, Socialism and Democracy* (1942) and *History of Economic Analysis* (1963). See further pp. 139–40.

Schutz, Alfred (1899–1959). Austrian phenomenological philosopher, émigré to the USA; influenced by Weber, Edmund Husserl, and Henri Bergson; founder of phenomenological sociology. Author *The Phenomenology of the Social World* (1932), *Collected Papers* (1962–66) (in 3 vols.); co-author of *Structures of the Lifeworld* with Thomas Luckmann (1973). See further pp. 112–14, 121.

Searle, John (b. 1932). US philosopher, pioneer of speech-act theory (with John Austin). Author of *Speech Acts* (1971) and *The Construction of Social Reality* (1995).

Simmel, Georg (1858–1918). German philosopher; the second most influential founding figure in German sociology after Max Weber; examined relations of interaction and exchange in terms of social 'forms'. Author of *The Philosophy of Money* (1900) and *Sociology* (1908). See further pp. 77–82.

Skinner, B. F. (1904–90). US psychologist; leading twentieth-century exponent of behaviourism as a scientific methodology. Author of *Walden Two* (1948) and *Beyond Freedom and Dignity* (1971).

Skocpol, Theda. US historical sociologist; examined the social causes of revolutions. Author of *States and Social Revolutions* (1979). See further pp. 146–7.

Small, Albion (1854–1926). US sociologist based at Chicago; influenced by Georg Simmel; influential in urban sociology. Author of *Introduction to the Study of Society* (1894).

Smelser, Neil (b. 1930). US theorist, influenced by Talcott Parsons; exponent of functionalism applied to historical sociology. Author of *Social Change and the Industrial Revolution* (1959); co-author of *Economy and Society* (1956) with Talcott Parsons. See further pp. 135–6.

Smith, Adam (1723–90). Scottish Enlightenment philosopher and economist; regarded as the founder of modern economics; advocate of free trade and private enterprise as solutions to political conflict. Author of *The Wealth of Nations* (1776). See further pp. 24–5.

Smith, Dorothy (b. 1926). Canadian feminist theorist, originator of feminist standpoint epistemology. Author of *The Everyday World as Problematic: A Feminist Sociology* (1987) and *The Conceptual Practices of Power: A Feminist Sociology of Knowledge* (1990).

Spencer, Herbert (1820–1903). English Victorian social philosopher, influenced by Charles Darwin, Auguste Comte, and evolutionary thought. Author of *The Principles of Sociology* (1882–98) (in 3 vols.). See further pp. 28.

Spivak, Gayatri Chakravorty (b. 1942). Indian-American feminist theorist, influenced by deconstruction; pioneer of postcolonial criticism; translator of Jacques Derrida's *Of Grammatology* (1967). Author of *In Other Worlds: Essays in Cultural Politics* (1988), *Outside in the Teaching Machine* (1993), and *A Critique of Post-Colonial Reason* (1999). See further pp. 248.

Strauss, Anselm (1916–96). US interactionist theorist, methodologist of qualitative research and medical sociologist; developed a method of 'grounded theory'. Co-author of *The Discovery of Grounded Theory* (1967) with Barney Glaser. See further pp. 116.

Taylor, Charles (b. 1931). Canadian political philosopher , influenced by Hegel, Gadamer, and hermeneutics thought; theorist of ethical value, communitarianism, and the expressive self, emphasizing the historical situatedness of moral and political beliefs; critic of positivism, utilitarianism, ethnocentrism, and abstract universalizing forms of liberal political philosophy such as those of Kant, J. S. Mill, or John Rawls. Author of *Hegel* (1975), *Human Agency and Language* (1985), *Philosophy and the Human Sciences* (1985), *Sources of the Self* (1989), *Multiculturalism and the 'Politics of Recognition'* (1992), and *Modern Social Imaginaries* (2004).

Thomas, W. I. (1863–1947). US sociologist, member of the Chicago School; recognized for his conception of the lay actor's 'definition of the situation'. Co-author of *The Polish Peasant in Europe and America* (1918) with Florian Znaniecki. See further pp. 115.

Thompson, E. P. (1924–93). British Marxist historian, influential in British cultural studies, critic of Althusser. Author of *The Making of the English Working Class* (1963) and *The Poverty of Theory* (1978). See further pp. 168–9.

Tilly, Charles (b. 1929). US historical sociologist; examined the rise of nation-states in Europe. Author of *Coercion, Capital and European States, AD 900–1990* (1990) and *Popular Contention in Great Britain, 1758–1834* (1995). See further pp. 145–6.

Tocqueville, Alexis de (1805–59). French nineteenth-century liberal political thinker and commentator; celebrated for his conception of 'voluntary associations' as sources of democratic solidarity. Author of *Democracy in America* (1835) and *The Old Regime and the Revolution* (1856). See further pp. 25–7, 134.

Tönnies, Ferdinand (1855–1936). German founding figure in sociology, a contemporary of Weber and Simmel; famously distinguished between a disappearing condition of *Gemeinschaft* ('community') and an emerging condition of *Gesellschaft* ('society'). Author of *Community and Society* (1887). See further pp. 30–1, 37.

Touraine, Alain (b. 1925) French theorist of social action and collective agency; influential in contemporary social movements research. Author of *The Self-Production of Society* (1973), *Post-Industrial Society* (1974), and *Critique of Modernity* (1992). See further pp. 282.

Toynbee, Arnold (1889–1975). British historian, speculative theorist of the rise and fall of civilizations. Author of *A Study of History* (1934–61) (in 10 vols.).

Vico, Giambattista (1668–1744). Italian Enlightenment philosopher of history; postulated that civilizations rise and fall in evolutionary cycles and that all civilizations begin from a state of myth; and that history is the work of human agency, not divine providence. Author of *The New Science* (1721).

Voegelin, Eric (1901–85). Austrian-born theorist, émigré to the USA; influenced by phenomenology, hermeneutics, existentialism, and theological thought; recognized for philosophical studies of religious ideas and metaphysical belief systems in a historical sociological framework; especially concerned with the link between political ideas of legitimate sovereignty and theological images of the cosmos among ancient civilizations and their relationship to the modern world. Author of *The New Science of Politics* (1952) and *Order and History* (1956–2000) (in 5 vols).

Voltaire (1694–1778). French Enlightenment philosopher, outspoken atheist and critic of the Church; famous for his essay *Candide* (1759), a satire on traditional doctrines of theodicy (involving explanation for the existence of evil), especially as formulated in the writings of the seventeenth-century philosopher Gottfried Wilhelm von Leibniz, who held that the real world is 'the best of all possible worlds'.

Wallerstein, Immanuel (b. 1930). US historical sociologist; exponent of world systems theory based on relations between 'centres' and 'peripheries'. Author of *The Modern World-System* (1974–89) (in 3 vols.). See further pp. 149–50.

Watson, J. B. (1878–1958). US psychologist, founder of behaviourism as a methodological principle in 1913. Author of *Behaviourism* (1930).

Weber, Max (1865–1920). German theorist, the founding figure in German sociology; pioneer of 'interpretive sociology' based on *verstehen* ('understanding'). Author of *The Protestant Ethic and the Spirit of Capitalism* (1904–5),

Politics as a Vocation (1919), *Science as a Vocation* (1919), and *Economy and Society* (1920–2). See further pp. 000–0.

Williams, Raymond (1921–88). British socialist theorist, cultural historian, and literary critic; the founding figure in British cultural studies. Author of *Culture and Society* (1958) and *The Long Revolution* (1961). See further pp. 168–9.

Winch, Peter (1926–97). British philosopher, influenced by Ludwig Wittgenstein; stressed the distinctness of the social sciences from the natural sciences. Author of *The Idea of a Social Science and its Relation to Philosophy* (1958). See further pp. 125–7.

Windelband, Wilhelm (1848–1915). German Neo-Kantian philosopher; influenced early twentieth-century German sociology; originator of a distinction between 'nomothetic' law-based science operative in the natural sciences and 'ideographic' interpretive science operative in the humanities.

Wittgenstein, Ludwig (1889–1951). Austrian philosopher of language resident in England; one of the most significant philosophers of the twentieth century; associated in early work with the Vienna Circle; moved from a defence of logical positivism to a more complex account in which 'language games' are seen as constructing 'forms of life', influencing many developments in post-war interpretive social analysis. Author of *Tractatus Logico-Philosophicus* (1921) and *Philosophical Investigations* (1953). See further pp. 125.

Žižek, Slavoj (b. 1949). Slovenian Marxist psychoanalytic theorist, influenced by Jacques Lacan; theorist of consumption, popular culture, xenophobia, film, and the mass media. Author of *The Sublime Object of Ideology* (1989), *Tarrying with the Negative* (1993), *The Ticklish Subject* (1999), *The Fragile Absolute* (2000), and *Welcome to the Desert of the Real* (2003). See further pp. 184–5.

■ REFERENCES

This bibliography provides details for texts cited in author-date form in the main chapter discussions of this book. It omits details for texts cited in the Further Reading sections at the end of each chapter. Texts cited in author-date form are referenced by their first historical dates of publication in the original languages in which they were written. However, all references to page numbers are to recent translated and/or reprinted editions in English. Full details of the translated and/or reprinted editions appear in the listing below. For example, references in Chapter 2 to 'Marx and Engels 1848: 50' refer to page 50 of the 1967 Penguin English edition of *The Communist Manifesto*, first published in German in 1848.

Adkins, L. (1995), *Gendered Work: Sexuality, Family and the Labour Market*. Buckingham: Open University Press.

—— (2002), *Revisions: Gender and Sexuality in Late Modernity*. Buckingham: Open University Press.

Adorno, T. W. (1966), *Negative Dialectics*, repr. London: Routledge, 1973 (originally in German).

—— (ed.) (1969), *The Positivist Dispute in German Sociology*, repr. London: Heinemann, 1976 (originally in German).

—— (1970), *Aesthetic Theory*, repr. Minneapolis: University of Minnesota Press, 1997 (originally in German).

—— et al. (1950), *The Authoritarian Personality*. New York: Harper Row.

Ahmed, A. (1992), *Postmodernism and Islam: Predicament and Promise*. London: Routledge.

Ahmed, S. (1998), *Differences that Matter: Feminist Theory and Postmodernism*. Cambridge: Cambridge University Press.

—— (2000), *Strange Encounters: Embodied Others in Post-Coloniality*. London: Routledge.

Alexander, J. C. (1982a), *Theoretical Logic in Sociology*, i: *Positivism, Presuppositions and Current Controversies*. Berkeley: University of California Press.

—— (1982b), *Theoretical Logic in Sociology*, ii: *The Antinomies of Classical Thought: Marx and Durkheim*. Berkeley: University of California Press.

—— (1983), *Theoretical Logic in Sociology*, iii: *The Classical Attempt at Theoretical Synthesis: Max Weber*. Berkeley: University of California Press.

—— (1984), *Theoretical Logic in Sociology*, iv: *The Modern Reconstruction of Classical Thought: Talcott Parsons*. Berkeley: University of California Press.

—— (1985), 'Introduction', in J. C. Alexander (ed.), *Neo-Functionalism*. London: Sage.

—— (1988), 'The New Theoretical Movement', in N. J. Smelser (ed.), *Handbook of Sociology*. London: Sage.

—— (1998), *Neofunctionalism and After*. Oxford: Blackwell.

Althusser, L. (1965), *For Marx*, repr. London: Allen Lane, 1969 (originally in French).

—— (1970), *Reading Capital*, repr. London: Verso, 1997 (originally in French).

—— (1971), 'Ideology and Ideological State Apparatuses', repr. in *Essays on Ideology*. London: Verso, 1984 (originally in French).

Anderson, B. (1983), *Imagined Communities: Reflections on the Origin and Spread of Nationalism*. London: Verso.

Anderson, P. (1974a), *Passages from Antiquity to Feudalism*. London: Verso.

—— (1974b), *Lineages of the Absolutist State*. London: Verso.

—— (1976), *Considerations on Western Marxism*. London: New Left Books.

—— (1998), *The Origins of Postmodernity*. London: Verso.

Archer, M. (1982), 'Morphogenesis versus Structuration: On Combining Structure and Action', *British Journal of Sociology*, 33/4: 456–83.

—— (1988), *Culture and Agency: The Place of Culture in Social Theory*. Cambridge: Cambridge University Press.

—— (1995), *Realist Social Theory: The Morphogenetic Approach*. Cambridge: Cambridge University Press.

—— and Tritter, J. (2000), *Rational Choice Theory: Resisting Colonization*. London: Routledge.

Archibugi, D., and Held, D. (eds.) (1995), *Cosmopolitan Democracy: An Agenda for a New World Order*. Cambridge: Polity Press.

Arendt, H. (1951), *The Origins of Totalitarianism*. New York: Harcourt Brace.

—— (1958), *The Human Condition*. Chicago: University of Chicago Press.

—— (1963), *Eichmann in Jerusalem: A Report on the Banality of Evil*. London: Penguin.

—— (1971), *The Life of the Mind*. New York: Harcourt Brace.

Arnason, J. (1989), 'The Imaginary Constitution of Modernity', *Revue européenne des sciences sociales*, 20: 323–37.

—— (1991), 'Modernity as a Project and as a Field of Tension', in A. Honneth and H. Joas (eds.), *Communicative Action: Essays on Jürgen Habermas' 'The Theory of Communicative Action'*. Cambridge, Mass.: MIT Press.

Aronson, R. (1995), *After Marxism*. New York: Guilford Press.

Austin, J. (1962), *How to Do Things with Words*. Oxford: Oxford University Press.

Balbus, I. D. (1982), *Marxism and Domination: A Neo-Hegelian, Feminist, Psychoanalytic Theory of Sexual, Political and Technological Liberation*. Princeton: Princeton University Press.

Barber, B. (1996), *Jihad versus McWorld*. New York: Ballantyne Books.

Barnes, B. (1974), *Scientific Knowledge and Sociological Theory*. London: Routledge.

—— (1977), *Interests and the Growth of Knowledge*. London: Routledge.

Barrett, M. (1980), *Women's Oppression Today: Problems of Marxist-Feminist Analysis*. London: New Left Books.

—— and Phillips, A. (eds.) (1992), *Destabilizing Theory: Contemporary Feminist Debates*. Cambridge: Polity Press.

Barthes, R. (1957), *Mythologies*, repr. London: Vintage, 2000 (originally in French).

—— (1964), *Elements of Semiology*, repr. London: Cape, 1967 (originally in French).

—— (1968), 'The Death of the Author', in *Image, Music, Text*, repr. London: Fontana, 1977 (originally in French).

Baudelaire, C. (1863), *The Painter of Modern Life and Other Essays*, repr. London: Phaidon, 1995 (originally in French).

Baudrillard, J. (1968), *The System of Objects*, repr. London: Verso, 1996 (originally in French).

—— (1970), *The Consumer Society: Myths and Structures*, repr. London: Sage, 1998 (originally in French).

—— (1973), *The Mirror of Production*, repr. St Louis: Telos Press, 1975 (originally in French).

—— (1977), *Forget Foucault*, repr. New York: Semiotext(e), 1987 (originally in French).

—— (1981), *Simulations*, repr. New York: Semiotext(e), 1983 (originally in French).

—— (1982), *In the Shadow of the Silent Majorities*, repr. New York: Semiotext(e), 1983 (originally in French).

—— (1987*a*), *The Ecstasy of Communication*, repr. New York: Semiotext(e), 1988 (originally in French).

—— (1987*b*), *Cool Memories*, repr. London: Verso Books, 1990 (originally in French).

—— (1989), 'The Anorexic Ruins', in D. Kamper and C. Wulf (eds.), *Looking Back on the End of the World*. New York: Semiotext(e) (originally in French).

—— (1991), *The Gulf War Did Not Take Place*, repr. Bloomington: Indiana University Press, 1995 (originally in French).

—— (1992*a*), 'Revolution and the End of Utopia', in W. Staerns and W. Chaloupka (eds.), *Jean Baudrillard: The Disappearance of Art and Politics*. London: Macmillan (originally in French).

—— (1992*b*), 'The Thawing of the East', in id., *The Illusion of the End*, repr. Cambridge: Polity Press, 1994 (originally in French).

—— (2002), *The Spirit of Terrorism*. London: Verso.

Bauman, Z. (1987), *Legislators and Interpreters: On Modernity, Post-Modernity and Intellectuals*. Cambridge: Polity Press.

—— (1989), *Modernity and the Holocaust*. Cambridge: Polity Press.

—— (1991), *Modernity and Ambivalence*. Cambridge: Polity Press.

—— (1992), *Intimations of Postmodernity*. London: Routledge.

—— (1993), *Postmodern Ethics*. Oxford: Blackwell.

—— (1997), *Postmodernity and its Discontents*. New York: New York University Press.

—— (1998a), *Work, Consumerism and the New Poor*. Buckingham: Open University Press.

—— (1998b), *Globalization: The Human Consequences*. Cambridge: Polity Press.

—— (1998c), 'On Glocalization: Or Globalization for Some, Localization for Others', *Thesis Eleven*, 54: 37–49.

—— (2000), *Liquid Modernity*. Cambridge: Polity Press.

—— (2002), *Society under Siege*. Cambridge: Polity Press.

Beauvoir, S. de (1949), *The Second Sex*, repr. London: Penguin, 1983 (originally in French).

Beck, U. (1986), *Risk Society: Towards a New Modernity*, repr. London: Sage, 1992 (originally in German).

—— (1997), *The Reinvention of Politics: Rethinking Modernity in the Global Social Order*. Cambridge: Polity Press.

—— (1998), *Democracy without Enemies*. Cambridge: Polity Press.

—— (2000a), *The Brave New World of Work*. Cambridge: Polity Press.

—— (2000b), *What is Globalization?* Cambridge: Polity Press.

—— Giddens, A., and Lash, S. (1994), *Reflexive Modernization: Politics, Tradition and Aesthetics in the Modern Social Order*. Cambridge: Polity Press.

Becker, H. (1967), 'Whose side are we on?', *Social Problems*, 14: 239–47.

Beechey, V. (1988), 'Rethinking the Definition of Work', in J. Jenson, E. Hagen, and C. Reddy (eds.), *Feminization of the Labour Force: Paradoxes and Promises*. Cambridge: Polity Press.

Bell, D. (1962), *The End of Ideology: On the Exhaustion of Political Ideas in the Fifties*. New York: Free Press.

—— (1973), *The Coming of Post-industrial Society: A Venture in Social Forecasting*. New York: Basic Books.

—— (1980), *Sociological Journeys: Essays 1960–1980*. London: Heinemann.

Bendix, R. (1956), *Work and Authority in Industry*, repr. Berkeley: University of California Press, 1974.

—— (1964), *Nation-Building and Citizenship: Studies of our Changing Social Order*. New York: Wiley.

—— (1984), *Force, Fate and Freedom: On Historical Sociology*. Berkeley: University of California Press.

Benjamin, J. (1988), *The Bonds of Love*. New York: Pantheon Books.

—— (1995), *Like Subjects, Love Objects*. New Haven: Yale University Press.

—— (1998), *The Shadow of the Other*. London: Routledge.

Benjamin, W. (1925–39), *The Arcades Project*, repr. Cambridge, Mass.: Harvard University Press, 2000 (originally in German).

—— (1934), 'The Artist as Producer', repr. in *Collected Writings*, vol. ii. Cambridge, Mass.: Harvard University Press, 1999 (originally in German).

—— (1936), 'The Work of Art in the Age of Mechanical Reproduction', in id, *Illuminations*, repr. New York: Shocken, 1969 (originally in German).

Bentham, J. (1789), *Introduction to the Principles of Morals and Legislation*, repr. Oxford: Oxford University Press, 1996.

Berger, P., and Luckmann, T. (1966), *The Social Construction of Reality*. London: Penguin.

Bernstein, R. J. (1991), *The New Constellation: The Ethical-Political Horizons of Modernity/Postmodernity*. Cambridge: Polity Press.

Best, S., and Kellner, D. (1991), *Postmodern Theory: Critical Interrogations*. London: Macmillan.

—— (2001), *The Postmodern Adventure: Science, Technology, and Cultural Studies at the Third Millennium*. London: Routledge.

Bhaskar, R. (1979), *The Possibility of Naturalism*. Brighton: Harvester.

Billig, M. (1995), *Banal Nationalism*. London: Sage.

Blackburn, R. (ed.) (1991), *After the Fall: The Failure of Communism and the Future of Socialism*. London: Verso.

Blau, P. (1964), *Exchange and Power in Social Life*. New York: Wiley.

Bloch, E. (1952–9), *The Principle of Hope*, 3 vols., repr. Cambridge, Mass.: MIT Press, 1986 (originally in German).

Bloor, D. (1976), *Knowledge and Social Imagery*. London: Routledge.

Blumenberg, H. (1966), *The Legitimacy of the Modern Age*. Cambridge, Mass.: MIT Press, 1983 (originally in German).

Blumer, H. (1969), *Symbolic Interactionism: Perspective and Method*. Englewood Cliffs, NJ: Prentice Hall.

Bohman, J. (1991), 'The Limits of Rational Choice Explanation', in J. S. Coleman and T. J. Fararo (eds.), *Rational Choice Theory: Advocacy and Critique*. London: Sage.

Bologh, R. (1990), *Love or Greatness: Max Weber and Masculine Thinking—a Feminist Inquiry*. London: Unwin Hyman.

Boltanski, L., and Chiapello, E. (2000), *Le Nouvel Esprit du capitalisme*. Paris: Gallimard.

Borradori, G. (2003), *Philosophy in a Time of Terror: Dialogues with Jürgen Habermas and Jacques Derrida*. Chicago: University of Chicago Press.

Bourdieu, P. (1972), *Outline of a Theory of Practice*, repr. Cambridge: Cambridge University Press, 1977 (originally in French).

—— (1977), *Algeria 1960*, repr. Cambridge: Cambridge University Press, 1979 (originally in French).

—— (1979), *Distinction: A Social Critique of the Judgement of Taste*, repr. London: Routledge, 1984 (originally in French).

—— (1980), *The Logic of Practice*, repr. Cambridge: Polity Press, 1990 (originally in French).

—— (1984), *Homo Academicus*, repr. Cambridge: Polity Press, 1996 (originally in French).

—— (1990), *In Other Words: Essays towards a Reflexive Sociology*. Cambridge: Polity Press (originally in French).

—— (1998), *Acts of Resistance: Against the New Myths of our Time*. Cambridge: Polity Press (originally in French).

—— and Wacquant, L. (1992), *An Invitation to Reflexive Sociology*. Cambridge: Polity Press (originally in French).

—— (2001), 'New Liberal Speak: Notes on the New Planetary Vulgate', *Radical Philosophy*, 105: 6–7 (originally in French).

Boyne, R. and Rattansi, A. (eds.) (1990), *Postmodernism and Society*. London: Macmillan.

Braithwaite, J., and Drahos, P. (2000), *Global Business Regulation*. Cambridge: Cambridge University Press.

Braudel, F. (1967), *Capitalism and Material Life, 1400–1800*, repr. London: Weidenfeld & Nicolson, 1973 (originally in French).

Buck-Morss, S. (1977), *The Origins of Negative Dialectics*. New York: Free Press.

—— (1989), *The Dialectics of Seeing*. Cambridge, Mass.: MIT Press.

Buckley, W. (1967), *Sociology and Modern Systems Theory*. Englewood Cliffs, NJ: Prentice Hall.

Bürger, P. (1974), *Theory of the Avant-Garde*, repr. Minneapolis: University of Minnesota Press, 1984 (originally in German).

Burgin, V. (1986), *The End of Art Theory: Criticism and Postmodernity*. London: Macmillan.

Butler, J. (1993), *Bodies That Matter: On the Discursive Limits of 'Sex'*. London: Routledge.

—— (1998), 'Subjects of Sex/Gender/Desire', in A. Phillips (ed.), *Feminism and Politics*. Oxford: Oxford University Press.

—— Laclau, E., and Žižek, S. (2000), *Contingency, Hegemony, Universality: Contemporary Dialogues on the Left*. London: Verso.

Calhoun, C. (ed.) (1992), *Habermas and the Public Sphere*. Cambridge: MIT Press.

Calinescu, M. (1977), *Five Faces of Modernity*. Bloomington: Indiana University Press.

Callari, A., Cullenberg, S., and Biewener, C. (1995), *Marxism in the Postmodern Age*. New York: Guilford Press.

Callinicos, A. (1987), *Making History: Agency, Structure and Social Change*. Cambridge: Polity Press.

—— (1990), 'Reactionary Postmodernism?', in R. Boyne and A. Rattansi (eds.), *Postmodernism and Society*. London: Macmillan.

—— (1991), *The Revenge of History: Marxism and the East European Revolutions*. Oxford: Polity Press.

Canguilhem, G. (1977), *Ideology and Rationality in the History of the Life Sciences*, repr. Cambridge, Mass.: MIT Press, 1988 (originally in French).

Carby, H. (1982), 'White Woman Listen! Black Feminism and the Boundaries of Sisterhood', repr. in L. Back and J. Solomos (eds.), *Theories of Race and Racism*, London: Routledge, 2000.

Carnoy, M. (1993), 'Multinationals in a Changing World Economy', in M. Carnoy et al., *The New Global Economy in the Information Age*. University Park, PA.: Pennsylvania University Press.

—— and Castells, M. (2001), 'Globalization, the Knowledge Society and the Network State', *Global Networks*, 1/1: 1–18.

Castells, M. (1996), *The Information Age: Economy, Society and Culture*, i: *The Rise of the Network Society*. Oxford: Blackwell.

—— (1998), *The Information Age: Economy, Society and Culture*, ii: *The Power of Identity*. Oxford: Blackwell.

—— (2000), *The Information Age: Economy, Society and Culture*, iii: *End of Millennium*. Oxford: Blackwell.

Castoriadis, C. (1975), *The Imaginary Institution of Society*, repr. Cambridge: Polity Press, 1987 (originally in French).

—— (1990), *World in Fragments: Writings on Politics, Society, Psychoanalysis and the Imagination*, repr. Stanford: Stanford University Press, 1997 (originally in French).

—— (1991), *Philosophy, Politics, Autonomy: Essays in Political Philosophy*. Oxford: Oxford University Press (originally in French).

Chodorow, N. (1978), *The Reproduction of Mothering: Psychoanalysis and the Sociology of Gender*. Berkeley: University of California Press.

Chomsky, N. (2001), *9/11*. New York: Seven Stories Press.

Cleaver, H. (1979), *Reading 'Capital' Politically*. Austin: University of Texas Press.

Cohen, G. A. (1978), *Karl Marx's Theory of History: A Defense*. Oxford: Oxford University Press.

—— (1996) 'Self-Ownership, History and Socialism: an Interview with G. A. Cohen', *Imprints* 1, 1.

Coleman, J. (1971), 'Collective Decisions', in H. Turk and R. L. Simpson (eds.), *Institutions and Exchange: The Sociologies of Talcott Parsons and George Caspar Homans*. New York: Bobbs-Merrill.

—— (1991), *Foundations of Social Theory*. Cambridge, Mass.: Harvard University Press.

—— and Fararo, T. (1991), *Rational Choice Theory: Advocacy and Critique*. London: Sage.

Collins, R. (1975), *Conflict Sociology: Toward an Explanatory Science*. New York: Academic Press.

Colomy, P. (ed.) (1990), *Neofunctionalist Sociology: Contemporary Statements*. Cheltenham: Edward Elgar.

Comte, A. (1830), *Cours de philosophie positive*, repr. New York: AMS Press, 1974 (translated as *The Positive Philosophy*) (originally in French).

—— (1851), *Système de politique positive*, repr. New York: Franklin, 1968 (translated as *The System of Positive Polity*) (originally in French).

Connell, R. W. (1987), *Gender and Power: Society, the Person and Sexual Politics*. Cambridge: Polity Press.

Cooley, C. (1902), *Human Nature and the Social Order*. New York: Scribner's.

Crompton, R., and Jones, G. (1984), *White-Collar Proletariat: Deskilling and Gender in Clerical Work*. London: Macmillan.

—— and Mann, M. (1986), *Gender and Stratification*. Cambridge: Polity Press.

Curtin, P. (1984), *Cross-cultural Trade in World History*. Cambridge: Cambridge University Press.

Dahrendorf, R. (1958), 'Out of Utopia: Toward a Re-orientation of Sociological Theory', *American Journal of Sociology*, 64: 115–27.

—— (1990), *Reflections on the Revolution in Europe: In a Letter Intended to Have Been Sent to a Gentleman in Warsaw*. London: Chatto & Windus.

Davidoff, L., and Hall, C. (1987), *Family Fortunes: Men and Women of the English Middle Class 1780–1850*. London: Hutchinson.

Davies, I. (1995) *Cultural Studies and After*. London: Routledge.

Davis, K. (1959), 'The Myth of Functionalism as a Special Method in Sociology and Anthropology', *American Sociological Review*, 24: 757–72.

Debord, G. (1967), *The Society of the Spectacle*, repr. New York: Zone Books, 1994 (originally in French).

Delanty, G. (1999), *Social Theory in a Changing World: Conceptions of Modernity*. Cambridge: Polity Press.

—— (2000), *Modernity and Postmodernity: Knowledge, Power and the Self*. London: Sage.

Deleuze, G., and Guattari, F. (1972), *Anti-Oedipus: Capitalism and Schizophrenia*, repr. New York: Viking, 1977 (originally in French).

Delphy, C., and Leonard, D. (1992), *Familiar Exploitation: A New Analysis of Marriage in Contemporary Western Societies*. Cambridge: Polity Press.

Derrida, J. (1967), *Of Grammatology*, repr. Baltimore: Johns Hopkins University Press, 1976 (originally in French).

—— (1968*a*), *Writing and Difference*, repr. London: Routledge, 1978 (originally in French).

—— (1968*b*), 'Structure, Sign, and Play in the Discourse of the Human Sciences', in *Writing and Difference*, repr. London: Routledge, 1978 (originally in French).

—— (1972), *Margins of Philosophy*, repr. Chicago: University of Chicago Press, 1982 (originally in French).

—— (1974), *Glas*, repr. Lincoln: University of Nebraska Press, 1986 (originally in French).

—— (1992), *Acts of Literature*, repr. London: Routledge (originally in French).

—— (1993), *Spectres of Marx*, repr. London: Routledge, 1994 (originally in French).

—— (1994), *The Politics of Friendship*, repr. London: Verso, 1997 (originally in French).

Dews, P. (1987), *Logics of Disintegration: Post-Structuralist Thought and the Claims of Critical Theory*. London: Verso.

Douglas, M. (1966), *Purity and Danger*, repr. London: Routledge, 2002.

—— (2002), 'Culture as Explanation: Cultural Concerns', in *International Encyclopedia of the Social and Behavioral Sciences*. Amsterdam: Elsevier.

Dreyfus, H. L., and Rabinow, P. (1982), *Michel Foucault: Beyond Structuralism and Hermeneutics*. Chicago: University of Chicago Press.

Durkheim, E. (1890), 'The Principles of 1789 and Sociology', in R. N. Bellah (ed.), *On Morality and Society: Selected Writings*. Chicago: University of Chicago Press, 1973 (originally in French).

—— (1893), *The Division of Labour in Society*, repr. London: Macmillan, 1984 (originally in French).

—— (1895), *The Rules of Sociological Method*, repr. London: Macmillan, 1982 (originally in French).

—— (1897), *Suicide: A Study in Sociology*, repr. London: Routledge, 1952 (originally in French).

—— (1898), 'Individualism and the Intellectuals', in R. N. Bellah, *On Morality and Society: Selected Writings*. Chicago: University of Chicago Press, 1973 (originally in French).

—— (1912), *The Elementary Forms of Religious Life*, repr. New York: Free Press, 1995 (originally in French).

—— (1922), *Moral Education: A Study in the Theory and Application of the Sociology of Education*, repr. New York: Free Press, 1961 (originally in French).

—— (1950), *Professional Ethics and Civic Morals*, repr. London: Routledge, 1957 (originally in French).

—— (1955), *Pragmatism and Sociology*, repr. Cambridge: Cambridge University Press, 1983 (originally in French).

Eagleton, T. (2003), *After Theory*. New York: Basic Books.

Ebenstein, A. (2001) *F. A. Hayek: A Biography*. London and New York: Palgrave.

Eisenstadt, S. N. (1963), *The Political Systems of Empires*. New York: Free Press.

—— (ed.) (2002), *Multiple Modernities*. New Brunswick, NJ: Transaction Publishers.

Elias, N. (1939), *The Civilizing Process*, repr. Oxford: Blackwell, 1994 (originally in German).

—— (1969), *The Court Society*. Oxford: Blackwell, 1983 (originally in German).

—— (1970), *What is Sociology?* repr. London: Hutchinson, 1978 (originally in German).

—— (1983), *Involvement and Detachment*, repr. Oxford: Blackwell, 1987 (originally in German).

—— (1989), *The Germans: Power Struggles and the Development of Habitus in the Nineteenth and Twentieth Centuries*, repr. Cambridge: Polity Press, 1996 (originally in German).

Elliott, A. (1999), *Social Theory and Psychoanalysis in Transition: Self and Society from Freud to Kristeva*. London: Free Association Books.

—— (2002), *Psychoanalytic Theory: An Introduction*, 2nd edn. Durham, NC: Duke University Press.

Elster, J. (1985), *Making Sense of Marx*. Cambridge: Cambridge University Press.

Evans, P. (1997), 'The Eclipse of the State? Reflections on Stateness in an Epoch of Globalization', *World Politics*, 50/1: 62–87.

Evans-Pritchard, E. E. (1937), *Witchcraft, Oracles and Magic among the Azande*, repr. Oxford: Oxford University Press, 1976.

—— (1940), *The Nuer*. Oxford: Oxford University Press.

Faderman, L. (1981), *Surpassing the Love of Men: Romantic Friendship and Love between Women from the Renaissance to the Present*. New York: Morrow.

Fanon, F. (1961), *The Wretched of the Earth*, repr. London: Penguin, 1967 (originally in French).

Feenberg, A. (1981), *Lukács, Marx and the Sources of Critical Theory*. Totowa, NJ: Rowman & Littlefield.

Felski, R. (1995), *The Gender of Modernity*. Cambridge, Mass.: Harvard University Press.

—— (2000), *Doing Time: Feminist Theory and Postmodern Culture*. New York: New York University Press.

Feyerabend, P. (1975), *Against Method*. London: New Left Books.

Fleck, L. (1935), *Genesis and Development of a Scientific Fact*, repr. Chicago: Chicago University Press, 1979 (originally in German).

Foucault, M. (1961), *Madness and Civilization*, repr. London: Tavistock, 1967 (originally in French).

—— (1966), *The Order of Things*, repr. London: Tavistock, 1970 (originally in French).

—— (1969a), *The Archaeology of Knowledge*, repr. London: Tavistock, 1972 (originally in French).

—— (1969b), 'What is an Author?', in P. Rabinow (ed.), *The Foucault Reader*. London: Penguin, 1984 (originally in French).

—— (1975), *Discipline and Punish: The Birth of the Prison*, repr. London: Allen Lane, 1977 (originally in French).

—— (1976), *The History of Sexuality*, i: *An Introduction*, repr. London: Allen Lane, 1979 (originally in French).

—— (1980), *Michel Foucault Power/Knowledge: Selected Interviews and Other Writings, 1972–1977*, ed. C. Gordon, London: Harvester Wheatsheaf (originally in French).

—— (1983), 'Structuralism and Post-structuralism', in, id., *Aesthetics, Method, and Epistemology: the Essential Works of Michel Foucault 1954–1984*, vol. ii. J. London: Allen Lane, 1998 (originally in French).

—— (1984a), *The History of Sexuality*, ii: *The Use of Pleasure*, repr. New York: Pantheon Books, 1985 (originally in French).

—— (1984b), *The History of Sexuality*, iii: *The Care of the Self*, repr. New York: Pantheon Books, 1986 (originally in French).

—— (1984c), 'What is Enlightenment?', repr. in *The Foucault Reader*, ed. P. Rabinow. London: Penguin, 1984 (originally in French).

—— (1984d), 'Nietzsche, Genealogy, History', repr. in *The Foucault Reader*, ed P. Rabinow. London: Penguin, 1984 (originally in French).

Fourastié, J. (1979), *Les trente glorieuses: ou, La Revdution invisible de 1946 à 1975*. Paris: Fayard.

Frank, A. G., and Gills, B. (1993), *The World System: Five Hundred Years or Five Thousand?* London: Routledge.

Frank, M. (1983), *What is Neo-structuralism?* repr. Minneapolis: University of Minnesota Press, 1989 (originally in German).

Fraser, N. (1989), *Unruly Practices: Power, Discourse and Gender in Contemporary Social Theory*. Cambridge: Polity Press.

Freud, S. (1900), *The Interpretation of Dreams*, repr. New York: Basic Books, 1955 (originally in German).

—— (1913), *Totem and Taboo*, repr. in *The Origins of Religion: 'Totem and Taboo' and 'Moses and Monotheism'*. London: Penguin, 1985 (originally in German).

—— (1920), *Beyond the Pleasure Principle*, repr. London: Penguin, 2002 (originally in German).

—— (1930), *Civilization and its Discontents*, repr. London: Penguin, 2002 (originally in German).

—— (1933), *New Introductory Lectures on Psychoanalysis*, repr. London: Penguin, 1973 (originally in German).

Friedan, B. (1963), *The Feminine Mystique*. New York: Norton.

Fukuyama, F. (1992), *The End of History and the Last Man*. New York: Free Press.

Fuss, D. (ed.) (1991), *Inside/Out: Lesbian Theories/Gay Theories*. London: Routledge.

Gadamer, H. G. (1960), *Truth and Method*, repr. London: Sheed & Ward, 1975 (originally in German).

Galbraith, J. K. (1958), *The Affluent Society*, repr. London: Penguin, 1979.

—— (1967), *The New Industrial State*, repr. London: Penguin, 1974.

—— (1973), *Economics and the Public Purpose*. repr. London: André Deutsch, 1974.

Gambetta, D. (1989), *Trust: The Making and Breaking of Cooperative Relations*. Oxford: Blackwell.

Game, A., and Pringle, R. (1984), *Gender at Work*. London: Pluto Press.

Gane, M. (1991), *Baudrillard: Critical and Fatal Theory*. London: Routledge.

—— (ed.) (1993), *Baudrillard Live: Selected Interviews*. London: Routledge.

Garfinkel, H. (1956), 'Conditions of Successful Degradation Ceremonies', *American Journal of Sociology*, 61: 420–4.

—— (1967), *Studies in Ethnomethodology*. Englewood Cliffs, NJ: Prentice Hall.

Geertz, C. (1973), *The Interpretation of Cultures*. New York: Basic Books.

Gellner, E. (1985), *Relativism and the Social Sciences*. Cambridge: Cambridge University Press.

Gerhard, U. (2003), ' "Illegitimate Daughters": The Relationship between Feminism and Sociology', in B. Marshall and A. Witz (eds.), *Engendering the Social: Feminist Encounters with Sociological Theory*. Buckingham: Open University Press.

Geyer, M. H., and Paulmann, J. (2001), 'Introduction: The Mechanics of Internationalism', in M. H. Geyer and J. Paulmann (eds.), *The Mechanics of Internationalism: Culture, Society, and Politics from the 1840's to the First World War*. Oxford: Oxford University Press.

Giddens, A. (1976), *New Rules of Sociological Method: A Positive Critique of Interpretive Sociologies*. London: Hutchinson.

—— (1979), *Central Problems in Social Theory: Action, Structure and Contradiction in Social Analysis*. London: Macmillan.

—— (1981), *A Contemporary Critique of Historical Materialism*. London: Macmillan.

—— (1982), *Profiles and Critiques in Social Theory*. London: Macmillan.

—— (1984), *The Constitution of Society: Outline of the Theory of Structuration*. Cambridge: Polity Press.

—— (1985), *The Nation-State and Violence*. Cambridge: Polity Press.

—— (1990), *The Consequences of Modernity*. Cambridge: Polity Press.

—— (1991), *Modernity and Self-Identity: Self and Society in the Late Modern Age*. Cambridge: Polity Press.

—— (1994), 'Living in a Post-Traditional Society', in U. Beck, A. Giddens, and S. Lash, *Reflexive Modernization: Politics, Tradition and Aesthetics in the Modern Social Order*. Cambridge: Polity Press.

—— (1998), *The Third Way: The Renewal of Social Democracy*. Cambridge: Polity Press.

Glaser, B., and Strauss, A. (1967), *The Discovery of Grounded Theory*. New York: de Gruyter.

Goffman, E. (1956), *The Presentation of Self in Everyday Life*, repr. London: Penguin, 1971.

—— (1961), *Asylums*. New York: Anchor Books.

—— (1974), *Frame Analysis*. New York: Harper Row.

Gorz, A. (1999), *Reclaiming Work: Beyond the Wage-Based Society*. Cambridge: Polity Press.

Gouldner, A. W. (1965), *Enter Plato: Classical Greece and the Origins of Social Theory*. London: Routledge.

—— (1970), *The Coming Crisis of Western Sociology*. London: Heinemann.

Gramsci, A. (1926–37), *Selections from the Prison Notebooks*, repr. London: Lawrence & Wishart, 1971 (originally in Italian).

—— (1985), 'Cultural Themes: Ideological Material', in *Selections from Cultural Writings*. repr. London: Lawrence & Wishart (originally in Italian).

Granovetter, M. (1985), 'Economic Action and Social Structure: The Problem of Embeddedness', *American Journal of Sociology*, 91/ 3: 418–501.

Grosz, E. (1990), 'Inscriptions and Body-Maps: Representations and the Corporeal', repr. in T. Threadgold and A. Cranny-Francis (eds.), *Feminine/Masculine/Representation*. St Leonards: Allen & Unwin.

Habermas, J. (1962), *The Structural Transformation of the Public Sphere*, repr. Cambridge, Mass.: MIT Press, 1989 (originally in German).

—— (1963), *Theory and Practice*, repr. Cambridge: Polity Press, 1988 (originally in German).

—— (1967), *Logic of the Social Sciences*, repr. Cambridge, Mass.: MIT Press, 1988 (originally in German).

—— (1968), *Knowledge and Human Interests*, repr. Boston: Beacon Press, 1971 (originally in German).

—— (1973), *Legitimation Crisis*, repr. London: Heinemann, 1976 (originally in German).

—— (1976), *Communication and the Evolution of Society*, repr. London: Heinemann, 1979 (originally in German).

—— (1980), 'The Unfinished Project of Modernity', repr. in M. Passerin d'Entrèves (ed.), *Habermas and the Unfinished Project of Modernity*. Cambridge: Polity Press.

—— (1981*a*), *The Theory of Communicative Action*, i: *Reason and the Rationalization of Society*, repr. Cambridge: Polity Press, 1984 (originally in German).

—— (1981*b*), *The Theory of Communicative Action*, ii: *Lifeworld and System*, repr. Cambridge: Polity Press, 1987 (originally in German).

—— (1985), *The Philosophical Discourse of Modernity: Twelve Lectures*, repr. Cambridge: Polity Press, 1987 (originally in German).

—— (1991), 'What does Socialism Mean Today? The Revolutions of Recuperation and the Need for New Thinking', in R. Blackburn (ed.), *After the Fall: The Failure of Communism and the Future of Socialism*. London: Verso.

—— (1992), *Between Facts and Norms: Contributions to a Discourse Theory of Law and Democracy*, repr. Cambridge, Mass.: MIT Press, 1996 (originally in German).

—— (1996), *The Inclusion of the Other: Studies in Political Theory*, repr. Cambridge, Mass.: MIT Press, 1998 (originally in German).

—— (1998), *The Postnational Constellation: Political Essays*, repr. Cambridge: Polity Press, 2001 (originally in German).

—— (2001), 'A Constitution for Europe?', *New Left Review*, 11: 5–26.

—— and Luhmann, N. (1971), *Theorie der Gesellschaft oder Sozialtechnologie*. Frankfurt am Main: Suhrkamp.

Hacking, I. (1999), *The Social Construction of What?* Cambridge, Mass.: Harvard University Press.

Hall, S. (1983), 'The Problem of Ideology: Marxism without Guarantees', in B. Matthews (ed.), *Marx: A Hundred Years On*. London: Lawrence & Wishart.

—— (1988), *The Hard Road to Renewal: Thatcherism and the Crisis of the Left*. London: Verso.

—— and Jacques, M. (eds.) (1989), *New Times: The Changing Face of Politics in the 1990s*. London: Lawrence & Wishart.

—— and Jefferson, T. (eds.) (1976), *Resistance through Rituals: Youth Subcultures in Post-War Britain*. London: Hutchinson.

—— et al. (eds.) (1980), *Culture, Media, Language: Working Papers in Cultural Studies, 1972–79*. London: Hutchinson.

Hamilton, R., and Barrett M. (1986), *The Politics of Diversity: Feminism, Marxism and Nationalism*. London: Verso.

Hannerz, U. (1992), *Cultural Complexity: Studies in the Social Organization of Meaning*. New York: Columbia University Press.

Haraway, D. (1991*a*), ' "Gender" for a Marxist Dictionary: The Sexual Politics of a Word', in id., *Simians, Cyborgs and Women: The Reinvention of Nature*. London: Free Association Books.

—— (1991*b*), 'A Cyborg Manifesto: Science, Technology and Socialist-Feminism in the Late Twentieth Century', in id., *Simians, Cyborgs and Women: The Reinvention of Nature*. London: Free Association Books.

—— (1997), *Modest_Witness @Second_Millennium: FemaleMan©_Meets_OncoMouse™: Feminism and Technoscience*. London: Routledge.

Harding, S. (1986), *The Science Question in Feminism*. Milton Keynes: Open University Press.

Hardt, M., and Negri, A. (2000), *Empire*. Cambridge, Mass.: Harvard University Press.

Harré, R. (1993), *Social Being*, 2nd edn. Oxford: Blackwell.

—— and Secord, P. F. (1972), *The Explanation of Social Behaviour*. Oxford: Blackwell.

Harrington, A. (2001), *Hermeneutic Dialogue and Social Science: A Critique of Gadamer and Habermas*. London: Routledge.

—— (2004), *Art and Social Theory: Sociological Arguments in Aesthetics*. Cambridge: Polity Press.

Hartmann, H. I. (1979), 'Capitalism, Patriarchy and Job Segregation by Sex', in Z. R. Eisenstein (ed.), *Capitalist Patriarchy and the Case for Socialist Feminism*. New York: Monthly Review Press.

—— (1981), 'The Unhappy Marriage of Marxism and Feminism: Towards a More Progressive Union', in L. Sargent (ed.), *The Unhappy Marriage of Marxism and Feminism: A Debate on Class and Patriarchy*. London: Pluto.

Harvey, D. (1989), *The Condition of Postmodernity: An Enquiry into the Origins of Cultural Change*. Oxford: Blackwell.

—— (1996), *Justice, Nature and the Geography of Difference*. Oxford: Blackwell.

—— (2003), *The New Imperialism*. Oxford: Oxford University Press.

Havel, V. (1990), 'The Power of the Powerless', in id., *Living in Truth*. London: Faber & Faber.

Hayek, F. A. (1944), *The Road to Serfdom*, repr. London: Routledge, 1976.

Hebdige, D. (1979), *Subculture: The Meaning of Style*. London: Methuen.

—— (1989), 'New Times: After the Masses', in S. Hall and M. Jacques, (eds.), *New Times: The Changing Face of Politics in the 1990s*. London: Lawrence & Wishart.

Hekman, S. J. (1999), *The Future of Differences: Truth and Method in Feminist Theory*. Cambridge: Polity Press.

Held, D. (1995), *Democracy and the Global Order*. Cambridge: Polity Press.

Heller, A. (1982), *A Theory of History*. London: Routledge.

—— (1984), *Everyday Life*. London: Routledge.

—— (1990), *Can Modernity Survive?* Cambridge: Polity Press.

—— (1993), *A Philosophy of History in Fragments*. Oxford: Blackwell.

—— (1999), *A Theory of Modernity*. Oxford: Blackwell.

—— and Feher, F. (1988), *The Postmodern Political Condition*. Cambridge: Polity Press.

Hill-Collins, P. (1990), *Black Feminist Thought: Knowledge, Consciousness and the Politics of Empowerment*. London: Routledge.

Hirschman, A. O. (1977), *The Passions and the Interests: Political Arguments for Capitalism before its Triumph*. Princeton: Princeton University Press.

Hobsbawn, E. J. (1962), *The Age of Revolution 1789–1848*. London: Weidenfeld & Nicolson.

—— (1975), *The Age of Capital 1848–1875*. London: Weidenfeld & Nicolson.

—— (1987), *The Age of Empire 1875–1914*. London: Weidenfeld & Nicolson.

—— (1994), *The Age of Extremes: the short twentieth century, 1914–1991*. London: Michael Joseph.

—— and Ranger, T. (eds.) (1983), *The Invention of Tradition*. Cambridge: Cambridge University Press.

Hollows, J. (2000), *Feminism, Femininity and Popular Culture*. Manchester: Manchester University Press.

Holm, H.-H., and Sorensen, G. (1995), *Whose World Order?* Boulder, Col.: Westview Press.

Holmwood, J. (1996), *Founding Sociology? Talcott Parsons and the Idea of General Theory*. London: Longman.

—— and Stewart, A. (1991), *Explanation and Social Theory*. London: Macmillan.

Holton, R. J. (1998), *Globalization and the Nation-State*. Basingstoke: Macmillan.

—— (2000), 'Globalization's Cultural Consequences', *Annals of the American Academy of Political and Social Science*, 570 (July): 140–52.

Homans, G. C. (1961), *Social Behaviour: Its Elementary Forms*. London: Routledge.

—— (1964), 'Bringing Men Back In', *American Sociological Review*, 29: 809–18.

Honneth, A. (1985), *The Critique of Power: Reflective Stages in a Critical Theory of Society*, repr. Cambridge, Mass.: MIT Press, 1993 (originally in German).

—— (1990), *The Fragmented World of the Social*, repr. New York: SUNY Press, 1995 (originally in German).

—— (1992), *The Struggle for Recognition: The Moral Grammar of Social Conflicts*, repr. Cambridge: Polity Press, 1995 (originally in German).

hooks, bell (1984), *Feminist Theory from Margin to Center*. Boston: South End Press.

—— (1990), *Yearning: Race, Gender and Cultural Politics*. Boston: South End Press.

Hopkins, A. G. (ed.) (2001), 'Different Globalizations', *Policy, Organisation and Society*, 20/2 (entire journal issue).

—— (ed.) (2002), *Globalization in World History*. London: Pimlico.

Horkheimer, M. (1937), *Critical Theory*, repr. New York: Herder & Herder, 1972 (originally in German).

—— and Adorno, T. W. (1947), *The Dialectic of Enlightenment*, repr. New York: Herder & Herder, 1972 (originally in German).

Hoy, D., and McCarthy, T. (1994), *Critical Theory*. Oxford: Blackwell.

Husserl, E. (1936), *The Crisis of the European Sciences and Transcendental Phenomenology*, repr. Evanston, Ill.: Northwestern University Press, 1970 (originally in German).

Huyssen, A. (1984), 'Mapping the Postmodern', *New German Critique*, 33: 5–52.

—— (1986), *After the Great Divide: Modernism, Mass Culture, Postmodernism*. Bloomington: Indiana University Press.

Isajiw, W. W. (1968), *Causation and Functionalism in Sociology*. London: Routledge.

Jameson, F. (1991), *Postmodernism, Or the Cultural Logic of Late Capitalism*. London: Verso.

Joas, H. (1980), *G. H. Mead: A Contemporary Re-examination of his Thought*. Cambridge: Polity Press, 1985 (originally in German).

—— (1992), *The Creativity of Action*, repr. Cambridge: Polity Press, 1996 (originally in German).

Johnson, M. (1989), 'Feminism and the Theories of Talcott Parsons', in R. A. Wallace (ed.), *Feminism and Sociological Theory*. Newbury Park, Cal.: Sage.

Johnson, R. (1987), 'What is Cultural Studies Anyway?', *Social Text*, 16: 38–80.

Kagarlitsky, B. (1990), *The Dialectic of Change*. London: Verso.

Kaldor, M. (2003), *Global Civil Society: An Answer to War*. Cambridge: Polity Press.

Kant, I. (1781), *The Critique of Pure Reason*, repr. Cambridge: Cambridge University Press, 1998 (originally in German).

—— (1784) 'An Answer to the Question: What is Enlightenment?', repr. in *Kant's Political Writings*, Cambridge: Cambridge University Press, 1970 (originally in German).

Kellner, D. (1977), *Karl Korsch: Revolutionary Theory*. Austin: University of Texas Press.

—— (1989*a*), *Critical Theory, Marxism and Modernity*. Baltimore: Johns Hopkins University Press.

—— (1989*b*), *Jean Baudrillard: From Marxism to Postmodernism and Beyond*. Cambridge: Polity Press.

—— (1995), *Media Culture: Cultural Studies, Identity and Politics between the Modern and the Postmodern*. London: Routledge.

—— (2000), 'Habermas, the Public Sphere, and Democracy: A Critical Intervention', in L. Hahn (ed.), *Perspectives on Habermas*. Chicago: Open Court Press.

—— (2003), *Media Spectacle*. London: Routledge.

King, A. (2000*a*), 'The Accidental Derogation of the Lay Actor: A Critique of Giddens' Concept of Structure', *Philosophy of the Social Sciences*, 30/3: 362–83.

—— (2000*b*), 'Thinking with Bourdieu against Bourdieu: A "Practical" Critique of the Habitus', *Sociological Theory*, 18/3: 417–33.

—— (2004), *The Structure of Social Theory*. London: Routledge.

Kojève, A. (1933–9), *Introduction to the Reading of Hegel*, repr. Ithaca, NY: Cornell University Press, 1980 (originally in French).

Kolakowski, L. (1990), *Modernity on Endless Trial*. Chicago: Chicago University Press.

Korsch, K. (1923), *Marxism and Philosophy*, repr. London: New Left Books, 1970 (originally in German).

—— (1938), *Karl Marx*. London: Chapman & Hall.

Koselleck, R. (1979), *Futures Past: On the Semantics of Historical Time*, repr. Cambridge, Mass.: MIT Press, 1985 (originally in German).

Kristeva, J. (1974), *Revolution in Poetic Language*, repr. New York: Columbia University Press, 1984 (originally in French).

—— (1986), 'Women's Time', in *The Kristeva Reader*, ed. T. Moi. Oxford: Blackwell (originally in French).

Kroker, A., Kroker, M., and Cook, D. (1989), *Panic Encyclopedia: The Definitive Guide to the Postmodern Scene*. London: Macmillan.

Kuhn, T. (1962), *The Structure of Scientific Revolutions*. Chicago: University of Chicago Press.

Lacan, J. (1949), 'The Mirror Stage as Formative of the Function of the I', repr. in *Écrits: A Selection*. London: Routledge, 1977 (originally in French).

—— (1957), 'The Agency of the Letter in the Unconscious, or Reason since Freud', repr. in *Écrits: A Selection*. London: Routledge (originally in French).

—— (1966), *Écrits*. Paris: Seuil (text in French original).

—— (1973), *On Feminine Sexuality: The Limits of Love and Knowledge (The Seminar, Book 20, Encore)*, repr. New York: Norton, 1998 (originally in French).

Laclau, E., and Mouffe, C. (1985), *Hegemony and Socialist Strategy*, repr. London: Verso.

Laplanche, J. (1987), *New Foundations for Psychoanalysis*, repr. Oxford: Blackwell, 1989 (originally in French).

Laqueur, T. (1990), *Making Sex: Body and Gender from the Greeks to Freud*. Cambridge, Mass.: Harvard University Press.

Lash, S. (1990), *Sociology of Postmodernism*. London: Routledge.

—— (1999), *Another Modernity: A Different Rationality*. Oxford: Blackwell.

—— (2002), *Critique of Information*. London: Sage.

—— and Urry, J. (1987), *The End of Organized Capitalism*. Cambridge: Polity Press.

—— (1994), *Economies of Signs and Space*. London: Sage.

Latour, B., and Woolgar, S. (1979), *Laboratory Life: The Social Construction of Scientific Facts*. London: Sage.

Layder, D. (1981), *Structure, Interaction and Social Theory*. London: Routledge.

Lefebvre, H. (1947), *The Critique of Everyday Life*, repr. London: Verso, 1991 (originally in French).

—— (1974), *The Production of Space*, repr. Oxford: Blackwell, 1991 (originally in French).

Lemert, C. (1990), 'The Uses of French Structuralism in Sociology', in G. Ritzer (ed.), *Frontiers of Social Theory: The New Synthesis*. New York: Columbia University Press.

—— (1997), *Postmodernism Is Not What You Think*. Oxford: Blackwell.

Lepenies, W. (1985), *Between Literature and Science: The Rise of Sociology*, repr. Cambridge: Cambridge University Press, 1988 (originally in German).

Leupin, A. (1991), *Lacan and the Human Sciences*. Lincoln: University of Nebraska Press.

Lévi-Strauss, C. (1949), *The Elementary Structures of Kinship*, repr. Boston: Beacon Press, 1969 (originally in French).

—— (1950), *Introduction to the Work of Marcel Mauss*, repr. London: Routledge, 1987 (originally in French).

—— (1955), *Tristes Tropiques*, repr. London: Jonathan Cape, 1973 (originally in French).

—— (1958), *Structural Anthropology*, repr. New York: Basic Books, 1963 (originally in French).

—— (1964), *The Raw and the Cooked: Introduction to a Science of Mythology*, repr. London: Jonathan Cape, 1970 (originally in French).

—— (1966), *The Savage Mind*. Chicago: Chicago University Press (originally in French).

Lipset, S. M. (1960), *Political Man: The Social Bases of Politics*, repr. Baltimore: Johns Hopkins University Press, 1981.

—— (1963), *The First New Nation: The United States in Comparative and Historical Perspective*, repr. London: Heinemann, 1964.

—— (1996), *American Exceptionalism: A Double-Edged Sword*. New York: Norton.

Lockwood, D. (1956), 'Some Remarks on "The Social System"', *British Journal of Sociology*, 7: 134–46.

—— (1964), 'System Integration and Social Integration', in G. Zollschan and W. Hirsch (eds.), *Explorations in Social Change*. London: Routledge.

—— (1992), *Solidarity and Schism: The Problem of Disorder in Marxist and Durkheimian Sociology*. Oxford: Oxford University Press.

Lovell, T. (2000), 'Thinking Feminism with and against Bourdieu', *Feminist Theory*, 1/1: 11–32.

Löwith, K. (1949), *Meaning in History: The Theological Implications of the Philosophy of History*. Chicago: University of Chicago Press.

Luhmann, N. (1970), *The Differentiation of Society*, repr. New York: Columbia University Press, 1982 (originally in German).

—— (1984), *Social Systems*, repr. Stanford: Stanford University Press, 1995 (originally in German).

—— (1990), *Essays on Self-Reference*. New York: Columbia University Press (originally in German).

—— (1991), *Risk: A Sociological Theory*, repr. New York: De Gruyter, 1993 (originally in German).

—— (1992), *Observations on Modernity*, repr. Stanford: Stanford University Press, 1998 (originally in German).

Lukács, G. (1910), *Soul and Form*, repr. London: Merlin Press, 1974 (originally in Hungarian).

—— (1915), *The Theory of the Novel*, repr. London: Merlin Press, 1971 (originally in German).

—— (1923), *History and Class Consciousness: Studies in Marxist Dialectics*, repr. London: Merlin Press, 1971 (originally in German).

Lukes, S. (1985), *Marxism and Morality*. Oxford: Oxford University Press.

Lury, C. (1996), *Consumer Culture*. Cambridge: Polity Press.

—— (2002), 'From Diversity to Heterogeneity: A Feminist Analysis of the Making of Kinds', *Economy and Society*, 31/4: 588–605.

Lyotard, J.-F. (1974), *Libidinal Economy*, repr. Bloomington: Indiana University Press, 1993 (originally in French).

—— (1979), *The Postmodern Condition: A Report on Knowledge*, repr. Manchester: Manchester University Press, 1986 (originally in French).

—— (1982), 'An Answer to the Question: What is Postmodernism?', in id., *The Postmodern Condition: A Report on Knowledge*, repr. Manchester: Manchester University Press, 1986 (originally in French).

—— (1986), *The Postmodern Explained: Correspondence, 1982–1985*, repr. Minneapolis: University of Minnesota Press, 1993 (originally in French).

—— (1993), *Political Writings*. Minneapolis: University of Minnesota Press.

McClintock, A. (1995), *Imperial Leather: Race, Gender and Sexuality in the Colonial Contest*. London: Routledge.

McGuigan, J. (1992), *Cultural Populism*. London: Routledge.

McNay, L. (1999), 'Gender, Habitus and the Field: Pierre Bourdieu and the Limits of Reflexivity', *Theory, Culture and Society*, 16/1: 95–117.

—— (2000), *Gender and Agency: Reconfiguring the Subject in Feminist and Social Theory*. Cambridge: Polity Press.

Magnus, B., and Cullenberg, S. (1995), *Whither Marxism? Global Crises in International Perspective* London: Routledge.

Malinowski, B. (1944), *A Scientific Theory of Culture and Other Essays*. Chapel Hill: University of North Carolina Press.

Mann, M. (1986), *The Sources of Social Power*, i: *A History of Power from the Beginning to AD 1760*. Cambridge: Cambridge University Press.

—— (1988), *States, War and Capitalism: Studies in Political Sociology*. Oxford: Blackwell.

—— (1993a), *The Sources of Social Power*, ii: *The Rise of Classes and Nation-States, 1760–1914*. Cambridge: Cambridge University Press.

—— (1993b), 'Nation-states in Europe and Other Continents: Diversifying, Developing, not Dying', *Daedulus*, Summer: 115–40.

—— (2003), *Incoherent Empire*. London: Verso.

Mannheim, K. (1925), *Conservatism*, repr. London: Routledge, 1986 (originally in German).

—— (1929), *Ideology and Utopia*, repr. London: Routledge, 1936 (originally in German).

Marcuse, H. (1941), *Reason and Revolution: Hegel and the Rise of Social Theory*, repr. Boston: Beacon Press, 1960.

—— (1955), *Eros and Civilization: A Philosophical Inquiry into Freud*. Boston: Beacon Press.

—— (1964), *One-Dimensional Man: Studies in the Ideology of Advanced Industrial Society*. Boston: Beacon Press.

—— (1968), *Negations: Essays in Critical Theory*. Boston: Beacon Press.

—— (1969), *An Essay on Liberation*. Boston: Beacon Press.

—— (1998a) *Towards a Critical Theory of Society*, repr. London: Routledge, 1998.

—— (1998b) *Technology, War and Fascism*. London: Routledge.

Marshall, B. (1994), *Engendering Modernity: Feminism, Social Theory and Social Change*. Cambridge: Polity Press.

—— and Witz, A. (2003), 'The Masculinity of the Social: Towards a Politics of Interrogation', in B. Marshall and A. Witz (eds.), *Engendering the Social: Feminist Encounters with Sociological Theory*. Buckingham: Open University Press.

Marshall, T. H. (1949), 'Citizenship and Social Class', in id., *Sociology at the Crossroads, and Other Essays*, repr. London: Heinemann, 1963.

Martin, E. (1994), *Flexible Bodies: Tracking Immunity in American Culture: From the Days of Polio to the Age of AIDS*. Boston: Beacon Press.

Marx, K. (1843), 'On the Jewish Question', in: *Early Writings*, trans. R. Livingstone and G. Benton, repr. London: Penguin, 1975 (originally in German).

—— (1844a), 'A Contribution to the Critique of Hegel's Philosophy of Right, Introduction', in: *Early Writings*, trans. R. Livingstone and G. Benton, repr. London: Penguin, 1975 (originally in German).

—— (1844b), 'Economic and Philosophical Manuscripts of 1844', in: *Early Writings*, trans. R. Livingstone and G. Benton, repr. London: Penguin, 1975 (originally in German).

—— (1845), 'Theses on Feuerbach', in: *Early Writings*, trans. R. Livingstone and G. Benton, repr. London: Penguin, 1975 (originally in German).

—— (1852), *The Eighteenth Brumaire of Louis Bonaparte*, repr. New York: International Publishers, 1972 (originally in German).

—— (1858), *Grundrisse*, repr. London: Penguin, 1973 (originally in German).

—— (1859), 'Preface to *A Contribution to the Critique of Political Economy*', in: *Early Writings*, trans. R. Livingstone and G. Benton, repr. London: Penguin, 1975 (originally in German).

—— (1867), *Capital: A Critique of Political Economy*, vol. i, repr. London: Penguin, 1976 (originally in German).

—— and Engels, F. (1846), *The German Ideology*, repr. London: Lawrence & Wishart, 1964 (originally in German).

—— (1848), *The Communist Manifesto*, repr. London: Penguin, 1967 (originally in German).

Mauss, M. (1924), *The Gift*, repr. London: Cohen & West, 1954 (originally in French).

Mead, G. H. (1934), *Mind, Self and Society*. Chicago: University of Chicago Press.

Merleau-Ponty, M. (1955), *Adventures of the Dialectic*, repr. Evanston, Ill.: Northwestern University Press, 1973 (originally in French).

Merton, R. K. (1949*a*), *Social Theory and Social Structure*, repr. New York: Free Press, 1968.

—— (1949*b*), 'Manifest and Latent Functions', in id., *Social Theory and Social Structure*, repr. New York: Free Press, 1968.

—— (1949*c*), 'On Sociological Theories of the Middle Range', in id., *Social Theory and Social Structure*, repr. New York: Free Press, 1968.

Michels, R. (1911), *Political Parties: A Sociological Study of the Oligarchical Tendencies of Modern Democracy*, repr. New York: Free Press, 1949 (originally in German).

Mill, J. S. (1859), *On Liberty*, repr. London: Penguin, 1982.

Mills, C. W. (1956), *The Power Elite*. Oxford: Oxford University Press.

—— (1959), *The Sociological Imagination*. Oxford: Oxford University Press.

Mills, S. (1998), 'Post-colonial Feminist Theory', in S. Jackson and J. Jones (eds.), *Contemporary Feminist Theories*. Edinburgh: Edinburgh University Press.

Mitchell, J. (1974), *Psychoanalysis and Feminism*. London: Allen Unwin.

Mohanty, C. T. (1988), 'Under Western Eyes: Feminist Scholarship and Colonial Discourses', *Feminist Review*, 30: 61–89.

—— (2002) ' "Under Western Eyes" Revisited: Feminist Solidarity through Anticapitalist Struggles', *Signs*, 28/21: 499–535.

Moore, B. (1966), *The Social Origins of Dictatorship and Democracy: Lord and Peasant in the Making of the Modern World*, repr. London: Penguin, 1969.

—— (1978), *Injustice: The Social Bases of Obedience and Revolt*. London: Macmillan.

Mosca, G. (1896), *The Ruling Class*, repr. New York: McGraw-Hill, 1939 (originally in Italian).

Mouzelis, N. (1995), *Sociological Theory: What Went Wrong? Diagnosis and Remedies*. London: Routledge.

Mulvey, L. (1989), *Visual and Other Pleasures*. London: Macmillan.

Munch, R. (1987), *Theory of Action: Toward a New Synthesis Going beyond Parsons*. London: Routledge.

Myrdal, A., and Klein, V. (1956), *Women's Two Roles: Home and Work*. London: Routledge.

Negri, A. (1976), *Communists Like Us: New Spaces of Liberty, New Lines of Alliance*, repr. New York: Semiotext(e), 1989 (originally in Italian).

Neurath, O. (1973), 'The Scientific Conception of the World: The Vienna Circle', in id., *Empiricism and Sociology*. Dordrecht: Reidel.

Nicholson, L., and Seidman, S. (eds.) (1995), *Social Postmodernism: Beyond Identity Politics*. Cambridge: Cambridge University Press.

Nietzsche, F. (1882), *The Gay Science*, repr. New York: Random House, 1974 (originally in German).

Nye, A. (1989), *Feminist Theory and the Philosophies of Man*. London: Routledge.

O'Rourke, K., and Williamson, J. (1999), *Globalization and History*. Cambridge, Mass.: MIT Press.

Oakley, A. (1974*a*), *The Sociology of Housework*. London: Martin Robertson.

—— (1974*b*), *Housewife*. London: Allen Lane.

Offe, C. (1985), *Disorganized Capitalism: Contemporary Transformations of Work and Politics*. Cambridge, Mass.: MIT Press (originally in German).

—— (1996), *Varieties of Transition: The East European and East German Experience*. Cambridge, Mass.: MIT Press (originally in German).

Ohmae, K. (1990), *The Borderless World*. London: Collins.

—— (1996), *The End of the Nation State: The Rise of Regional Economies*. London: HarperCollins.

Outhwaite, W. (1987), *New Philosophies of Social Science: Realism, Hermeneutics and Critical Theory*. London: Macmillan.

Pareto, V. (1916), *The Mind and Society: A Treatise on General Sociology*, repr. New York: Dover, 1963 (originally in Italian).

Parsons, T. (1937), *The Structure of Social Action: A Study in Social Theory with Special Reference to a Group of Recent European Writers*. New York: McGraw-Hill.

—— (1942*a*), 'Democracy and the Social Structure in Pre-Nazi Germany', *Journal of Legal and Political Sociology*, 1: 96–114.

—— (1942*b*), 'Some Sociological Aspects of the Fascist Movements', *Social Forces*, 21: 138–47.

—— (1949*a*), 'The Professions and Social Structure', repr. in id., *Essays in Sociological Theory: Pure and Applied*. New York: Free Press 1954.

—— (1949b), 'Age and Sex in the Social Structure of the United States', repr. in id., *Essays in Sociological Theory: Pure and Applied*. New York: Free Press, 1954.

—— (1949c), 'The Kinship System of the Contemporary United States', repr. in. id., *Essays in Sociological Theory: Pure and Applied*. New York: Free Press, 1954.

—— (1949d), 'Social Classes and Class Conflict in the Light of Recent Sociological Theory', repr. in. id., *Essays in Sociological Theory: Pure and Applied*. New York: Free Press, 1954.

—— (1951), *The Social System*. New York: Free Press.

—— (1956), 'The American Family', in id., R. F. Bales, et al. (eds.), *Family, Socialization and Interaction Process*. New York: Free Press.

—— (1964), 'Social Structure and the Development of Personality: Freud's Contribution to the Integration of Psychology and Sociology', in id., *Social Structure and Personality*. New York: Free Press.

—— (1966), *Societies: Evolutionary and Comparative Perspectives*. Englewood Cliffs, NJ: Prentice Hall.

—— (1967), 'On the Concept of Political Power', in id., *Sociological Theory and Modern Society*. New York: Free Press.

—— (1971a), *The System of Modern Societies*. Englewood Cliffs, NJ: Prentice Hall.

—— (1971b), 'Commentary', in H. Turk and R. L. Simpson (eds.), *Institutions and Exchange: The Sociologies of Talcott Parsons and George Caspar Homans*. New York: Bobbs-Merrill.

—— (1977a), *Social Systems and the Evolution of Action Theory*. New York: Free Press.

—— (1977b), 'Equality and Inequality in Modern Society, or Social Stratification Revisited', in id., *Social Systems and the Evolution of Action Theory*. New York: Free Press.

Pateman, C. (1988), *The Sexual Contract*. Cambridge: Polity Press.

Polanyi, K. (1944), *The Great Transformation*, repr. Boston: Beacon Press, 1957.

Pollert, A. (1981), *Girls, Wives, Factory Lives*. London: Macmillan.

Pollock, G. (1988), *Vision and Difference: Femininity, Feminism and the Histories of Art*. London: Routledge.

Popper, K. (1935), *The Logic of Scientific Discovery*, repr. New York: Basic Books, 1959 (originally in German).

Portes, A. (1998), 'Social Capital: Its Origins and Applications in Modern Sociology', *Annual Review of Sociology*, 24: 1–24.

Poster, M. (1975), *Existential Marxism in Postwar France: From Sartre to Althusser*. Princeton: Princeton University Press.

—— (ed.) (1988), *Jean Baudrillard: Selected Writings*. Stanford: Stanford University Press.

—— (1990), *The Mode of Information: Poststructuralism and Social Context*. Cambridge: Polity Press.

Pringle, R. (1988), *Secretaries Talk: Sexuality, Power and Work*. London: Verso.

Putnam, R. D. (2000), *Bowling Alone: The Collapse and Revival of American Community*. New York: Simon & Schuster.

Radcliffe-Brown, A. R. (1935), 'On the Concept of Function in Social Science', *American Anthropologist*, 37: 395–6.

—— (1952), *Structure and Function in Primitive Society: Essays and Addresses*. London: Cohen & West.

Ragland-Sullivan, E., and Brivic, S. (eds.) (1991), *Joyce between Genders: Lacanian Views*. Tulsa, Okla.: University of Tulsa Press.

Reekie, G. (1993), *Temptations: Sex, Selling and the Department Store*. St Leonards: Allen Unwin.

Rex, J. (1961), *Key Problems of Sociological Theory*. London: Routledge.

Rich, A. (1983), 'Compulsory Heterosexuality and Lesbian Existence', in A. Snitow, C. Stansell, and S. Thompson (eds.), *Powers of Desire: The Politics of Sexuality*. New York: Monthly Review Press.

Ricœur, P. (1965), *Freud and Philosophy*, repr. New Haven: Yale University Press, 1970 (originally in French).

—— (1969), *The Conflict of Interpretations*, repr. Evanston, Ill.: Northwestern University Press, 1974 (originally in French).

—— (1983–5) *Time and Narrative*, 3 vols., repr. Chicago: University of Chicago Press, 1984–8 (originally in French).

Riesman, D. (1950), *The Lonely Crowd*. New Haven: Yale University Press.

Ritzer, G. (1993), *The McDonaldization of Society: An Investigation into the Changing Character of Contemporary Social Life*. Newbury Park, Cal.: Pine Forge Press.

Robertson, R. (1992), *Globalization: Social Theory and Global Culture*. London: Sage.

—— (1995), 'Glocalization, Time-Space and Homogeneity-Homogeneity', in M. Featherstone, S. Lash, and R. Robertson (eds.), *Global Modernities*. London: Sage.

Rodrik, D. (1996), 'Why do More Open Economies have Bigger Governments?', *National Bureau of Economic Research Working Paper no.* 5537, Apr.

Roemer, J. E. (1981), *Analytical Foundations of Marxian Economic Theory*. Cambridge: Cambridge University Press.

Rorty, R. (1980), *Philosophy and the Mirror of Nature*. Princeton: Princeton University Press.

—— (1989), *Contingency, Irony and Solidarity*. Cambridge: Cambridge University Press.

Rose, J. (1986), *Sexuality in the Field of Vision*. London: Verso.

Rosenau, J. (1996), 'The Dynamics of Globalization: Toward an Operational Formulation', *Security Dialogue*, 27/3: 247–62.

Roth, G. (1987), 'Rationalization in Max Weber's Developmental History', in S. Whimster and S. Lash (eds.), *Max Weber, Rationality and Modernity*. London: Allen & Unwin.

Said, E. (1978), *Orientalism*, repr. London: Routledge, 1980.

Sartre, J. P. (1960), *Critique of Dialectical Reason: Theory of Practical Ensembles*, repr. London: Verso, 1976 (originally in French).

Sassen, S. (1994), *Cities in a World Economy*. Thousand Oaks, Calif.: Pine Forge Press.

—— (1998), *Globalization and its Discontents*. New York: New Press.

Saussure, F. de (1916), *Course in General Linguistics*, repr. London: Peter Owen, 1960 (originally in French).

Schatzki, T. (1987), 'Overdue Analysis of Bourdieu's Theory of Practice', *Inquiry: An interdisciplinary Journal of Philosophy*, 30/1–2: 113–35.

—— (1997), 'Practices and Actions: A Wittgensteinian Critique of Bourdieu and Giddens', *Philosophy of the Social Sciences*, 27/3: 283–308.

Schumpeter, J. A. (1941), *Capitalism, Socialism and Democracy*, repr. London: Allen & Unwin, 1981.

Schutz, A. (1932), *The Phenomenology of the Social World*, repr. London: Heinemann, 1972 (originally in German).

—— (1962a), 'Common Sense and Scientific Interpretation of Human Action', in *id., Collected Papers*, vol. i, ed. M. Natanson. The Hague: Nijhoff.

—— (1962b), 'The Stranger', in *id., Collected Papers*, vol. i, ed. M. Natanson. The Hague: Nijhoff.

—— and Luckmann, T. (1973), *The Structures of the Life-World*. Evanston, Ill.: Northwestern University Press.

—— and Parsons, T. (1978), *The Theory of Social Action: The Correspondence of Alfred Schutz and Talcott Parsons*. Bloomington: Indiana University Press.

Scott, A. (ed.) (1997), *The Limits of Globalization: Cases and Arguments*. London: Routledge.

Scott, J. A. (1995), *Sociological Theory: Contemporary Debates*. Cheltenham: Edward Elgar.

Searle, J. R. (1969), *Speech Acts: An Essay in the Philosophy of Language*. Cambridge: Cambridge University Press.

Secombe, W. (1974), 'The Housewife and her Labour under Capitalism', *New Left Review*, 83: 3–26.

Sedgwick, E. (1990), *Epistemology of the Closet*. Berkeley: University of California Press.

Seidman, S. (ed.) (1996), *Queer Theory/Sociology*. Oxford: Blackwell.

—— (1997), *Difference Troubles: Queering Social Theory and Sexual Politics*. Cambridge: Cambridge University Press.

Sewell, W. H. (1992), 'A Theory of Structure: Duality, Agency, and Transformation', *American Journal of Sociology*, 98/1: 1–29.

Shilling, C. (1993), *The Body and Social Theory*. London: Sage.

Silberman, M. (2000), 'Introduction', in *Bertolt Brecht on Film and Radio*. London: Methuen.

Simmel, G. (1900), *The Philosophy of Money*, repr. London: Routledge, 1978 (originally in German).

—— (1903), 'The Metropolis and Mental Life', repr. in *Simmel on Culture*, ed. M. Featherstone and D. Frisby. London: Sage, 1997 (originally in German).

—— (1905), 'The Philosophy of Fashion', repr. in *Simmel on Culture*. ed. M. Featherstone and D. Frisby. London: Sage, 1997 (originally in German).

—— (1908a), *Soziologie*, repr. as *The Sociology of Georg Simmel*, ed. K. H. Wolff. New York: Free Press, 1950 (originally in German).

—— (1908b), 'The Stranger', repr. in *The Sociology of Georg Simmel*, ed. K. H. Wolff. New York: Free Press, 1950 (originally in German).

—— (1908c), 'Conflict', repr. in *Conflict and the Web of Group Affiliations*, ed. K. H. Wolff. New York: Free Press, 1955 (originally in German).

—— (1908d), 'The Web of Group Affiliations', repr. in *Conflict and the Web of Group Affiliations*, ed.

K. H. Wolff. New York: Free Press, 1955 (originally in German).

—— (1911*a*), 'The Concept and Tragedy of Culture', repr. in *Simmel on Culture*, ed. M. Featherstone and D. Frisby. London: Sage, 1997 (originally in German).

—— (1911*b*), 'The Relative and the Absolute in the Problem of the Sexes', repr. in *Georg Simmel, on Women, Sexuality, and Love*, ed. G. Oakes. New Haven: Yale University Press, 1984 (originally in German).

—— (1911*c*), 'Female Culture', repr. in *Georg Simmel, on Women, Sexuality, and Love*, ed. G. Oakes. New Haven: Yale University Press, 1984 (originally in German).

Sklair, L. (2001), *The Transnational Capitalist Class*. Oxford: Blackwell.

Skocpol, T. (1979), *States and Social Revolutions: A Comparative Analysis of France, Russia, and China*. Cambridge: Cambridge University Press.

Smart, B. (1992), *Modern Conditions, Postmodern Controversies*. London: Routledge.

—— (1993), *Postmodernity*. London: Routledge.

—— (1996), 'Postmodern Social Theory', in B. S. Turner (ed.), *The Blackwell Companion to Social Theory*. Oxford: Blackwell.

—— (2001), 'Sociology, Morality and Ethics: On Being with Others', in G. Ritzer and B. Smart (eds.), *Handbook of Social Theory*. London: Sage.

—— (2003), *Economy, Culture and Society: A Sociological Critique of Neo-liberalism*. Buckingham: Open University Press.

Smelser, N. (1959), *Social Change in the Industrial Revolution: An Application of Theory to the Lancashire Cotton Industry, 1770–1840*. London: Routledge.

Smith, A. (1776), *The Wealth of Nations*, repr. London: Penguin, 1970.

Smith, A. D. (1983), 'Nationalism and Social Theory', *British Journal of Sociology*, 34: 19–38.

Smith, D. E. (1987), *The Everyday World as Problematic: A Feminist Sociology*. Milton Keynes: Open University Press.

Smith-Rosenberg, C. (1975), 'The Female World of Love and Ritual: Relations between Women in Nineteenth-Century America', *Signs*, 9: 1–29.

Spencer, H. (1882–98), *The Principles of Sociology*, 3 vols., repr. London: Macmillan, 1969.

Spivak, G. (1988*a*), *In Other Worlds: Essays in Cultural Politics*. London: Routledge.

—— (1988*b*), 'Can the Subaltern Speak?', in C. Nelson and L. Grossberg (eds.), *Marxism and the Interpretation of Culture*. Urbana, Ill.: University of Illinois Press.

—— (1992), 'French Feminism Revisited: Ethics and Politics', in J. Butler and J. W. Scott (eds.), *Feminists Theorize the Political*. London: Routledge.

—— (1999), *A Critique of Postcolonial Reason: Toward a History of the Vanishing Present*. Cambridge, Mass.: Harvard University Press.

Stanworth, M. (ed.) (1987), *Reproductive Technologies: Gender, Motherhood and Medicine*. Oxford: Blackwell.

Stauth, G., and Turner, B. S. (1988), *Nietzsche's Dance: Resentment, Reciprocity and Resistance in Social Life*. Oxford: Blackwell.

Stehr, N. (1994), *Knowledge Societies*. London: Sage.

—— (2001), *The Fragility of Modern Societies: Knowledge and Risk in the Information Age*. London: Sage.

Stiglitz, G. (2002), *Globalization and its Discontents*. New York: Norton.

Sydie, R. A. (1987), *Natural Women, Cultured Men: A Feminist Perspective on Sociological Theory*. Milton Keynes: Open University Press.

Taylor, C. (1989), *Sources of the Self*. Cambridge: Cambridge University Press.

—— (1993), 'To Follow a Rule', in C. Calhoun, E. LiPuma, and M. Postone (eds.), *Bourdieu: Critical Perspectives*. Cambridge: Polity Press.

Therborn, G. (1976), *Science, Class and Society: On the Formation of Sociology and Historical Materialism*. London: New Left Books.

—— (1995), 'Routes to/through Modernity', in M. Featherstone, S. Lash, and R. Robertson (eds.), *Global Modernities*. London: Sage.

—— (1999), 'Introduction: The Atlantic Diagonal in the Labyrinths of Modernities and Globalizations', in G. Therborn and L.-L. Wallenius (eds.), *Globalizations and Modernities: Experiences and Perspectives of Europe and Latin America*. Stockholm: Swedish Council for Planning and Co-ordination of Research.

Thomas, W. I., and Thomas, D. S. (1928), *The Child in America: Behavior Problems and Programs*. New York: Alfred A. Knopf.

Thompson, E. P. (1978), *The Poverty of Theory*, repr. London: Merlin Press, 1995.

Thompson, J. B. (1981), *Critical Hermeneutics: A Study in the Thought of Paul Ricœur and Jürgen Habermas*. Cambridge: Cambridge University Press.

Tilly, C. (1990), *Coercion, Capital and European States, AD 900–1990*. Oxford: Blackwell.

—— (1995), *Popular Contention in Great Britain 1758–1834*. Cambridge, Mass.: Harvard University Press.

Tocqueville, A. de (1835), *Democracy in America*, repr. New York: Doubleday, 1969 (originally in French).

—— (1856), *The Ancien Regime and the Causes of Revolution in France*, repr. London: Dent, 1988 (originally in French).

Tönnies, F. (1887), *Community and Society*, repr. New York: Dover, 2002 (originally in German).

Touraine, A. (1969), *The Post-Industrial Society: Tomorrow's Social History: Classes, Conflicts and Culture in the Programmed Society*, repr. New York: Random House, 1971 (originally in French).

—— (1973), *The Self-Production of Society*, repr. Chicago: University of Chicago Press, 1977 (originally in French).

—— (1992), *Critique of Modernity*, repr. Oxford: Blackwell, 1995 (originally in French).

—— (1994), *What is Democracy?*, repr. Boulder, Co.: Westview Press, 1997 (originally in French).

—— (1997), *Can We Live Together? Equal and Different*, repr. Cambridge: Polity Press, 2000 (originally in French).

—— (1999), *Beyond Neoliberalism*, repr. Cambridge: Polity Press, 2001 (originally in French).

Toynbee, A. (1954), *A Study of History*, vol. ix. Oxford: Oxford University Press.

Turk, H., and Simpson, R. L. (eds.) (1971), *Institutions and Exchange: The Sociologies of Talcott Parsons and George Caspar Homans*. New York: Bobbs-Merrill.

Turner, B. S. (1984), *The Body and Society: Explorations in Social Theory*. Oxford: Blackwell.

—— (ed.) (1990), *Theories of Modernity and Postmodernity*. London: Sage.

Turner, J. H. and Turner, S. P. (1990), *The Impossible Science: An Institutional Analysis of American Sociology*. London: Sage.

Urry, J. (2000), *Sociology beyond Societies: Mobilities for the Twenty-First Century*. London: Routledge.

—— (2003), *Global Complexity*. Cambridge: Polity Press.

Vattimo, G. (1985), *The End of Modernity: Nihilism and Hermeneutics in Post-modern Culture*, repr.

Cambridge: Polity Press, 1988 (originally in Italian).

Veyne, P. (1971), *Writing History: Essay on Epistemology*, repr. Middletown, Conn.: Wesleyan University Press, 1984 (originally in French).

Virilio, P. (1998), *The Virilio Reader*, ed. J. Der Derian, repr. Oxford: Blackwell (originally in French).

—— (2002), *Ground Zero*. London: Verso (originally in French).

Voegelin, E. (1952), *The New Science of Politics: An Introduction*. Chicago: University of Chicago Press.

Wagner, P. (1994), *A Sociology of Modernity: Liberty and Discipline*. London: Routledge.

Walby, S. (1986), *Patriarchy at Work: Patriarchal and Capitalist Relations in Employment*. Cambridge: Polity Press.

Wallerstein, I. (1974), *The Modern World-System*, i: *Capitalist Agriculture and the Origins of the European World-Economy in the Sixteenth Century*. New York: Academic Press.

—— (1976), 'A World System Perspective on the Social Sciences', *British Journal of Sociology*, 27/2: 343–52.

—— (1979), *The Capitalist World-Economy: Essays*. Cambridge: Cambridge University Press.

—— (1980), *The Modern World-System*, ii: *Mercantilism and the Consolidation of the European World-Economy*. New York: Academic Press.

—— (1989a), *The Modern World-System*, iii: *The Second Era of Great Expansion of the Capitalist World-Economy*. New York: Academic Press.

—— (1989b), 'Revolution in the World-System', *Theory and Society*, 18/4: 431–49.

Ware, V. (1992), *Beyond the Pale: White Women, Racism and History*. London: Verso.

Weber, M. (1889), *The History of Commercial Partnerships in the Middle Ages*, repr. Lanham, Md.: Rowman & Littlefield, 2003 (originally in German).

—— (1903), 'The "Objectivity" of Knowledge in Social Science and Social Policy', repr. in *The Essential Weber: A Reader*, ed. S. Whimster. London: Routledge, 2003 (originally in German).

—— (1903–6), *Roscher and Knies: The Logical Problems of Historical Economics*, repr. New York: Free Press, 1975 (originally in German).

—— (1915), 'The Meaning of Ethical Neutrality in Sociology and Economics', repr. in *Max Weber on the Methodology of the Social Sciences*, ed. E. Shils and H. Finch. New York: Free Press, 1949 (originally in German).

—— (1919*a*), 'Politics as a Vocation', repr. in *From Max Weber: Essays in Sociology*, ed. H. Gerth and C. W. Mills. London: Routledge, 1948 (originally in German).

—— (1919*b*), 'Science as a Vocation', repr. in *From Max Weber: Essays in Sociology*, ed. H. Gerth and C. W. Mills. London: Routledge, 1948 (originally in German).

—— (1920*a*), *The Protestant Ethic and the Spirit of Capitalism*, trans. T. Parsons, repr. London: Routledge, 1958 (originally in German).

—— (1920*b*), *The Protestant Ethic and the Spirit of Capitalism*, trans. S. Kalberg. Oxford: Blackwell, 2002 (originally in German).

—— (1920*c*), 'Author's Introduction' ('Vorbemerkung'), repr. in *The Protestant Ethic and the Spirit of Capitalism*, trans. Talcott Parsons. London: Routledge, 1958 (originally in German).

—— (1920*d*), 'The Social Psychology of the World Religions', repr. in *From Max Weber: Essays in Sociology*, ed. H. Gerth and C. W. Mills. London: Routledge, 1948 (originally in German).

—— (1920*e*), 'Intermediate Reflections', repr. in *The Essential Weber: A Reader*, ed. S. Whimster. London: Routledge, 2003 (originally in German).

—— (1922*a*), *Economy and Society*, 3 vols. Berkeley: University of California Press, 1978 (originally in German).

—— (1922*b*), 'Basic Sociological Terms', in *Economy and Society*, repr. Berkeley: University of California Press, 1978 (originally in German).

—— (1922*c*), 'Class, Status, Party', repr. in *From Max Weber: Essays in Sociology*, ed. H. Gerth and C. W. Mills. London: Routledge, 1948 (originally in German).

—— (1922*d*), 'The Types of Legitimate Domination', in *Economy and Society*, repr. Berkeley: University of California Press, 1978 (originally in German).

—— (1922*e*), 'The Sociology of Charismatic Authority', repr. in *From Max Weber: Essays in Sociology*, ed. H. Gerth and C. W. Mills.

London: Routledge, 1948 (originally in German).

—— (1922*f*), 'Bureaucracy', repr. in *From Max Weber: Essays in Sociology*, ed. H. Gerth and C. W. Mills. London: Routledge, 1948 (originally in German).

Weeks, J. (1981), *Sex, Politics and Society*. London: Longman.

Weiss, G. (1999), *Body Images: Embodiment as Incorporeality*. London: Routledge.

Wellmer, A. (1986), *The Persistence of Modernity: Essays on Aesthetics, Ethics and Postmodernism*, repr. Cambridge: Polity Press, 1991 (originally in German).

Wendt, A. (1987), 'The Agent–Structure Problem in International Relations Theory', *International Organization*, 41/3: 335–70.

Weston, K. (1998), *Long Slow Born: Sexuality and Social Science*. London: Routledge.

Westwood, S. (1984), *All Day Every Day: Factory and Family in the Making of Women's Lives*. London: Pluto.

Williams, S., and Bendelow, G. (1998), *The Lived Body: Sociological Themes, Embodied Issues*. London: Routledge.

Williamson, O. E. (1975), *Markets and Hierarchies— Analysis and Antitrust Implications: A Study in the Economics of Internal Organization*. New York: Free Press.

Wilson, E. (1991), *The Sphinx in the City: Urban Life, the Control of Disorder, and Women*, London: Virago.

Wimmer, A., and Schiller, N. G. (2002), 'Methodological Nationalism and Beyond', *Global Networks*, 2/4: 301–34.

Winch, P. (1958), *The Idea of a Social Science and its Relation to Philosophy*, repr. London: Routledge, 1990.

—— (1970), 'Understanding a Primitive Society', repr. in T. McCarthy and F. Dallmayr (eds.), *Understanding and Social Inquiry*. Notre Dame: Notre Dame University Press.

Witz, A. (2000), 'Whose Body Matters? Feminist Sociology and the Corporeal Turn in Sociology and Feminism', *Body and Society*, 6/2: 1–24.

—— (2001),'Georg Simmel and the Masculinity of Modernity', *Journal of Classical Sociology*, 1/3: 353–70.

Wolff, J. (1990), 'The Invisible Flaneuse: Women and the Literature of Modernity', in id., *Feminine Sentences: Essays on Women and Culture*. Berkeley and Los Angeles: University of California Press.

—— (2000), 'The Feminine in Modern Art: Benjamin, Simmel and the Gender of Modernity', *Theory, Culture and Society*, 17/6: 33–53.

Wright, E. O. (1978), *Class, Crisis and the State*. London: Verso.

Žižek, S. (1989), *The Sublime Object of Ideology*. London: Verso.

—— (2002), *Welcome to the Desert of the Real! Five Essays on 11 September and Related Dates*. London: Verso.

■ INDEX